Taxation of Securities, Commodities, and Options

Taxation of Securities, Commodities, and Options

ANDREA S. KRAMER

A Ronald Press Publication

JOHN WILEY & SONS

New York · Chichester · Brisbane · Toronto · Singapore

Library of Congress Cataloging in Publication Data:

Kramer, Andrea S.
  Taxation of securities, commodities, and options.

  "A Ronald Press publication."
  Includes index.
  1. Taxation of bonds, securities, etc.—United States.
2. Commodity exchanges—Taxation—Law and legislation—
United States. 3. Put and call transactions—Taxation—
Law and legislation—United States.   4. Investments—
Taxation—Law and legislation—United States.   I. Title.

KF6415.K73   1986   343.7305'246   86-10971
ISBN 0-471-81260-9   347.3035246

Printed in the United States of America
10 9 8 7 6 5 4 3 2 1

Preface

S ecurities, commodities, and options are closely related, occasionally
fungible, investment vehicles. They are generally sold by the same
firms, bought for similar profit producing and risk shifting purposes,
and subject to similar, often overlapping, regulatory schemes. Yet, despite the interrelationships among these negotiable investment instruments, no single work has previously been available that discusses their
taxation with anywhere near the completeness or sophistication needed
by tax professionals and market participants. This book is intended to
fill that gap. It presents and analyzes in detail the policies, rules, and
interpretations—old, new, and frequently revolutionary—that govern
the federal tax treatment of securities of all types, commodities bought
and sold through cash, futures, and forward contracts, and options on
securities and commodities.

No area of federal tax law has changed as dramatically over the past
five years as that of negotiable investment instruments. In 1981, the
Economic Recovery Tax Act radically transformed the tax scheme for
commodities, most types of nonstock options, and government securities. It created a new category of taxable instruments (so-called section
1256 contracts), established the concept of "offsetting positions" in personal property, and closed a number of "loopholes" that permitted the
transfer of income from one tax year to the next. The Technical Corrections Act of 1982 and the Deficit Reduction Act of 1984 extended the
new tax scheme to stock options and certain stock positions.

The new scheme (layered as it is over older, more established principles) is technically and conceptually complex. This book is intended
as a guide through the complexity. I analyze the operation of the new
tax concepts—offsetting positions, straddles, mark-to-market treatment, 60/40 treatment, capitalization of interest and carrying charges
on straddle positions, and the modified wash sales and short sales rules.
I also explain the interrelationships between the new and old concepts—

for example, how the modified wash sales rule squares with the wash sales rule. The end result, I sincerely hope, is a guide for both the practitioner and the perplexed: a single source that can be used to understand the principles governing the taxation of securities, commodities, and options, to plan transactions in these instruments with confidence in the tax consequences, and to defend challenged tax positions.

An underlying issue throughout this book—after sorting and testing the nuts and bolts in this area of tax law—is the Constitutional and public policy implications of the new tax principles for negotiable investment instruments. The conventional wisdom among tax lawyers has been that the federal government has no power to tax unrealized increases in property value. The origin of this view is the Supreme Court's decision in *Eisner v. Macomber*,[1] decided six years after the Sixteenth Amendment authorized the Congress to establish an income tax. In *Eisner* the Supreme Court held that despite the Sixteenth Amendment the federal government has no authority to tax "gains derived from property" unless those gains are "severed" from the property. From that day to this, no court has challenged that view. But the Congress has thrown the gauntlet down to the *Eisner* decision by enacting the Economic Recovery Tax Act (and extending its principles in the Technical Corrections Act of 1982 and the Deficit Reduction Act of 1984). The notion that income must be "severed" from property is now irrelevant for large numbers of transactions in securities, commodities, and options. After 1981, the Code includes in taxable income appreciation in the value of a taxpayer's "positions" in these instruments regardless of whether that appreciation is realized or unrealized. The meaning of this attack on the *Eisner* principle for our tax system is explored throughout this book.

Finally, having provided a detailed guide to this area of tax law for the professional and the perplexed and a point of provocative departure for the student of federal tax policy, I hope I have also provided a readily and easily accessed reference work for anyone who has a question about how securities, commodities, and options are taxed. I have divided the book so that the table of contents provides a detailed road map through it. Further, I have spent considerable time constructing the index in an effort to assure that it will be of help not only to the specialist who has a specific, well-formulated question, but also to the taxpayer, IRS officer, student, and concerned market participant who wants to get into the text through the transactions, principles, and decisions he understands.

This book is divided into eleven parts. Each part is divided into chap-

[1]252 U.S. 189 (1920).

ters and the chapters are divided into sections and subsections. In general, I have tried to organize the material so that each major tax concept is self-contained within a part of the book. It may be helpful, however, to give at this point a brief overview of the scope of the various sections, the approach I have taken in each to the subject matter, and what I view as unique or new about the material and analyses presented.

Part One provides a description of the operation and regulation of the markets for corporate securities, government securities, municipal securities, commodities, and options. Beginning a tax treatise with an extended discussion of our nation's trading markets may appear at first as unusual, but I hope it will prove to be one of this book's great strengths. Many of the tax rules for securities, commodities, and options simply are not comprehensible without an understanding of how these investment instruments are traded, paid for (i.e., settled), and regulated. There is, however, no single source, or even a small number of sources, which provides this information. Accordingly, I have tried to discuss the relevant markets in sufficient detail to give a meaningful context to the tax scheme for negotiable investment instruments and to make sense out of particular tax rules. In addition, I have made extensive references to secondary sources to assist those readers who would like to conduct more detailed research into the operation and regulation of the securities, commodities, and options markets.

Part Two identifies the various types of participants in these markets. The categories of taxpayers, from investors to dealers to arbitrageurs, are discussed and the key issues with respect to each are analyzed. I have been particularly concerned here with the principles for and consequences of characterizing taxpayers as dealers, traders, or investors. Many of the issues discussed are the subjects of pending IRS audits and judicial proceedings.

Part Three covers capital transactions. The topics addressed include the computation of gain or loss for both corporate and noncorporate taxpayers, tax basis, holding periods, short sales, wash sales, and the various methods used to identify capital assets. Capital transactions are especially important for investors and traders. I have provided a detailed discussion of the identification of capital assets, which can be crucial for tax planning.

Part Four covers ordinary income transactions. In addition to analyzing the general tax principles, I discuss hedging transactions and the methods used to identify ordinary income property (including accounting methods and inventory methods). I explain how transactions qualify for the statutory hedging exemption from the so-called Straddle Rules and section 1256 treatment.

Part Five addresses dividends, interest, and security loans. I discuss the basic rules for the taxation of dividends as well as the timing and reporting of dividend income. I also discuss the difficult and unresolved issues concerning the deduction for intercorporate dividends. In addition, I discuss the tax consequences of loaning and borrowing securities and analyze tax-free and taxable lending transactions. Finally, I address the special problems associated with the receipt of dividends from personal holding companies, public utilities, regulated investment companies, and real estate investment trusts. The subjects of dividends, interest, and security loans have been modified by recent legislation, and I analyze the new rules in detail.

Part Six covers stock, other equity interests (i.e., publicly traded partnerships and trusts), and options on stock. First, I discuss the various types of stock interests, including most of the new and esoteric stock products, and analyze the tax rules that apply to them. I give special attention to the tax rules for so-called section 1244 stock, stock interests in federal agencies, and small business investment companies. The taxation of warrants and options on stock is thoroughly explored. Because of the unique and troublesome interplay between the taxation of stock and options on stock, I have been particularly concerned in Part Six to identify which tax rules apply when. Much of the material presented in Part Six is directly relevant to many unresolved tax questions at issue in pending IRS audits and judicial proceedings.

Part Seven covers debt securities and options on debt securities. I discuss the general principles for the taxation of debt securities, including original issue discount, market discount bonds, bond premiums, zero coupon securities, stripped bonds, and repurchase and reverse repurchase transactions. I address registration requirements, exchanges of debt securities, and tax issues with respect to retirements, redemptions, and dispositions. I discuss the taxation of specific types of debt securities: Treasury securities (including Treasury bills, United States savings bonds, and so-called flower bonds), municipal securities (including the tax consequences of popular credit-enhancing techniques), convertible debt securities, and mortgage-backed securities (including the various types of existing and proposed trading vehicles used to package mortgages). Finally, I address the unique questions associated with options on debt securities. Part Seven is long and detailed. I have attempted to analyze in one place all of the issues and tax rules that apply to traditional and new types of debt security products.

Part Eight covers commodities. I address the tax treatment of the principal trading instruments—cash, forward and futures contracts, and options on cash and futures contracts. I also address a variety of special types of commodity transactions, including cash and carry transactions, leverage transactions, and exchanges of futures for physicals (so-called EFP transactions). The entire area of commodity taxation was basically rewritten in 1981. Many questions are still open and many anomalies persist. In covering this area I have been particularly concerned to identify those questions and anomalies and to relate the new tax principles to the old rules.

Part Nine covers the taxation of "section 1256 contracts." I discuss the statutory definitions of regulated futures contracts, foreign currency contracts, nonequity options, and dealer equity options. I also discuss the unique tax rules applicable to section 1256 contracts, including the Mark-to-Market Rule, the 60/40 Rule, loss carry-back rules, and exceptions to section 1256 treatment. This is an area of great complexity and confusion. I have attempted to lay out these new tax rules so that they can be worked with effectively by both the tax specialist and the generalist.

Part Ten covers offsetting positions in personal property. I discuss the new concept of a "straddle transaction" and analyze the many unanswered questions about its application. I also provide readers with a general guide through this tax thicket, offering both detailed analyses and examples. In doing so, I explain the so-called Straddle Rules: the loss deferral rule, the modified wash sales and short sales rules, and the requirement to capitalize straddle interest and carrying charges. I also discuss so-called mixed straddles and the various elections available for their taxation. In addition, I discuss in detail the exceptions to the Straddle Rules. Finally, I discuss the attribution rules, disclosure requirements, and penalties. This section is designed to pull together in one place an array of complex and unique tax rules, including the temporary regulations issued by the Treasury in January 1985 and January 1986.

Part Eleven covers the tax treatment of gain or loss on terminations of certain contract rights and obligations. Many of the issues I discuss are the subjects of pending IRS audits and judicial proceedings. I analyze both the prior law and current statutory provisions in detail.

April 1, 1986

Note on Style and References

I refer to a taxpayer in this book as "he." I do not intend by my use of the masculine gender to make a point, sexist, benign, or otherwise. I use masculine pronouns rather than a barbarism such as "he or she" for brevity, simplicity, and familiarity.

In addition, I use a large number of abbreviations in this book, many of which may not be familiar to all readers. To provide easy translation and quick reference, I have listed all abbreviated words, phrases and proper names on the abbreviation list following the detailed contents.

When available, I use the official source for all tax citations. For legislative reports, I give parallel citations to both the official report and the permanent edition of the *United States Code Congressional and Administrative News*. Rules and regulations of security, commodity, and option exchanges are cited to the loose-leaf service that reprints the materials.

I have also prepared a chart to provide a quick overview of the tax treatment for actively traded negotiable investment instruments. The chart is the Appendix located at the back of this book. It provides, in summary fashion, a quick overview of current and prior law. Because it is impossible to indicate in chart format all of the nuances and considerations for the tax treatment of negotiable investment instruments, the chart should not be referred to without consulting the text.

There are four reference tables included at the back of this book. The tables provide handy lists of all cases, Internal Revenue Code sections, Treasury pronouncements, and legislative history that are referred to in this book. They identify where each listed item appears in the text.

Acknowledgments

Preparation of this book has been an enormous undertaking that would not have been possible without the help of many people. First, I want to thank Alton B. Harris. His encouragement, unselfish assistance, and hard work contributed greatly to this book. His understanding of the operation and regulation of the markets for securities, commodities, and options was invaluable. The strengths to be found in the chapters on the overview of these markets are all his; any mistakes or omissions are mine. I also want to thank Sara Beazley, Denise Berdelle, David Cubeta, Candace P. Davis, John D. English, Patsy Felch, Howard Gantz, Russell Hirai, Janet Goeltz Hoffman, Wendell Kapustiak, Theodore J. Kletnick, Daniel A. Lukas, J. Craig Long, Michael E. McElroy, Francisco J. Pereiro, Joseph B. Plauche, Jr., William A. Rogers, Vincent Samar, George T. Simon, Keith E. Smith, Rick E. Smith, Steven M. Surdell, Harriet Trop, James M. Ward, Larry Weinger, Robert Willens, and Deborah Yalowitz. They have contributed in many different and very special ways. Their comments, suggestions, guidance, and assistance contributed enormously to this book's organization, insights, and precision.

In addition, I want to thank Rosie Greer, Jennifer Leib, Arlene Mangrum, Louise Mulderink, Debra Niemann, Judyth Seiler, Jean Smith, Christy Tavitas, Ann Tolar, Wilma Troope, and B.J. Yates. Without their skills, commitment, and unflagging good spirits this book could not have been put together.

Finally, I want to thank my partners for their support, and my clients for their patience and understanding.

Contents

Appendix—Tax Treatment of Actively Traded Securities,
Commodities, and Options

Table of Cases

Table of Internal Revenue Code Sections

Table of Treasury Pronouncements

Treasury Regulations
Temporary Treasury Regulations
Proposed Treasury Regulations
Revenue Rulings
Revenue Procedures
General Counsel's Memoranda
Income Tax Unit Rulings
Internal Revenue News Releases
Treasury Decisions
Private Letter Rulings
Technical Advice Memoranda

Legislative History Table

Internal Revenue Bill of 1921
Revenue Act of 1950
Internal Revenue Code of 1954
Tax Reform Act of 1969
Tax Reform Act of 1976
Revenue Act of 1978
Economic Recovery Tax Act of 1981
Tax Equity and Fiscal Responsibility Act of 1982
Technical Corrections Act of 1982
Deficit Reduction Act of 1984
Technical Corrections Act of 1985
Tax Reform Act of 1985
Regulation of Government Securities
Special Reports and Studies

Index

Detailed Contents

PART FOUR TAXATION OF ORDINARY INCOME TRANSACTIONS

PART SIX TAXATION OF STOCK, OTHER EQUITY INTERESTS,
AND OPTIONS ON SECURITIES

PART ELEVEN TREATMENT OF GAIN OR LOSS ON TERMINATIONS OF CERTAIN CONTRACT RIGHTS AND OBLIGATIONS

Abbreviations

Many abbreviations are used in this book. The most common abbreviations include the following:

ACC .... AMEX Commodities Corporation
ACRNs .... adjustable rate convertible notes
AMEX .... American Stock Exchange
ARP ....adjustable rate preferred stock
CAPS .... convertible adjustable preferred stock
CATS ....Certificate of Accrual on Treasury Securities
CBOE...................................Chicago Board Options Exchange
CBT.. Chicago Board of Trade
CBTCC .... Board of Trade Clearing Corporation
CEA...Commodity Exchange Act
CFTC .... Commodity Futures Trading Commission
CME .... Chicago Mercantile Exchange
CMO................................... collateralized mortgage obligation
CMS .... collateralized mortgage security
CODE .... Internal Revenue Code
COMEX .... Commodity Exchange, Inc.
CSC.................................Coffee, Sugar & Cocoa Exchange, Inc.
DRA ....Deficit Reduction Act of 1984
EFP ....exchange for physicals
ERTA.............................. Economic Recovery Tax Act of 1981
FCC .... Federal Communications Commission
FCM ....futures commission merchant
FDIC............................Federal Deposit Insurance Corporation
FHLB............................... Federal Home Loan Bank System
FHLMC.....................Federal Home Loan Mortgage Corporation
FIFO ....first-in, first-out
FNMA ....Federal National Mortgage Association

FRB.. Federal Reserve Board
FRCNs .... flexible rate convertible notes
FSLIC ....Federal Savings and Loan Insurance Corporation
G.C.M...................................... General Counsel's Memoranda
GNMA...................... Government National Mortgage Association
GPM .... graduated payment mortgage pass-through certificate
HUD......................................Housing and Urban Development
IDB ....industrial development bond
INTEX ....International Futures Exchange (Bermuda) Limited
I.R.C. .... Internal Revenue Code
I.R...................................Internal Revenue News Releases
IRS .... Internal Revenue Service
I.T.. Income Tax Unit Ruling
KCBT.. Kansas City Board of Trade
LIFO...last-in, first-out
LTM .... leverage transaction merchants
LTR.. Private Letter Ruling
MBS ....mortgage-backed security
MBSCC.......................................MBS Clearing Corporation
MGE... Minnesota Grain Exchange
MidAm ....MidAmerica Commodity Exchange
MSE..Midwest Stock Exchange
Munis .... municipal securities
NASD .... National Association of Securities Dealers
NASDAQ..................... National Association of Securities Dealers
                                                Automated Quotation System
NFA...National Futures Association
NYCE .... New York Cotton Exchange
NYFE... New York Futures Exchange
NYME...................................New York Mercantile Exchange
NYSE ....New York Stock Exchange
OCC....................................The Options Clearing Corporation
OID ....original issue discount
OTC...over-the-counter
PBOT ....Philadelphia Board of Trade
PC................................... mortgage participation certificate
PHLX...Philadelphia Stock Exchange
Prop. Treas. Reg. .... Proposed Treasury Regulations
PSE..Pacific Stock Exchange
REIT .... Real Estate Investment Trust
Rev. Rul... Revenue Ruling

Part One

Overview of the Markets

One

Overview of the Corporate Securities Markets

Corporations issue securities of essentially three types: equity or rights to acquire equity (in the form of stock or warrants), debt (in the form of notes and bonds), and convertible securities (e.g., convertible bonds). Corporations issue such securities to raise money or to have paper that can function as an alternative to money. The issuance is either by means of a public offering, in which case secondary trading markets for the securities are likely to develop, or through private placements, in which case trading is restricted and can legally occur only in accordance with state and federal requirements.

Regulation of the issuance and trading of securities is vested at the federal level in the SEC and the various exchanges, and the NASD under its oversight. Regulation of the issuance and trading of securities at the state level is vested with the various state securities or "Blue Sky" commissioners. State securities regulations are not addressed in this book.[1] With respect to federal securities regulation, our basic concerns will be the types of transactions that are permitted or required and those market participants that are required to register with the SEC as broker-dealers.

---

[1] *See generally* individual states' annotated statutes for specific securities laws; BLUE SKY L. REP. (CCH); J. LONG, 1985 BLUE SKY LAW HANDBOOK: DEVELOPMENTS IN STATE SECURITIES REGULATION (Clark Boardman, Securities Law Series, 1984).

§ 1.1 TYPES OF SECURITIES

(a) CORPORATE STOCKS

Stocks, both common and preferred, evidence ownership of a corporation. The terms of issuance and rights attendant to ownership are prescribed by state corporate law, the corporation's charter and by-laws, stock exchange rules if the stock is listed, and NASD rules if the stock is publicly traded but not listed.[2] To evidence ownership, the stockholder receives a notice or an instrument, typically a stock certificate.[3]

(b) CORPORATE BONDS, DEBENTURES, NOTES, AND COMMERCIAL PAPER

Corporate bonds, debentures, notes, and commercial paper are all forms of corporate debt. The terms of the debt (e.g., interest rates or discount, principal repayment schedule including sinking fund provisions, and whether the debt is secured or unsecured) are specified in the corporation's charter, by-laws, or director's resolutions. The terms "bonds," "debentures," "notes," and "commercial paper" are not precisely defined and are often used interchangeably. For our purposes, "bond" is a generic term covering all corporate indebtedness evidenced by securities other than commercial paper. Commercial paper is short-term (270 days or less) unsecured notes issued at a discount and redeemed at face value.

Bonds can be issued in registered or bearer form. If the bonds are in bearer form they will be coupon bonds, that is, they will have detachable coupons, which must be presented to the corporation or its agent before interest payments will be made. Bearer bonds are transferred by delivery without registration on the records of the corporation. Registered bonds are of two types. One type has the principal but not interest registered with the corporation, and the bond has detachable coupons in bearer form. The other type has the principal and interest registered in the owner's name; there are no coupons, and all interest payments are made to the registered owner.[4]

---

[2] *See generally* M. TOROSIAN, MODERN STOCK MARKET HANDBOOK, 14–15 (1978).

[3] *Id.* at 15.

[4] For a discussion of corporate bonds generally, see Sauvain, *Corporate Bonds*, in HANDBOOK OF FINANCIAL MARKETS, SECURITIES, OPTIONS, FUTURES 245–68 (F. Fabozzi & F. Zarb eds. 1981) [hereinafter referred to as "HANDBOOK OF FINANCIAL MARKETS"]; *see also* TOROSIAN, *supra* note 2, at 56–57.

(c) CONVERTIBLE SECURITIES

Convertible securities can be converted or exchanged for a fixed number of shares of another class of securities (generally common stock) of the same corporate issuer. Typically, convertible securities are bonds or preferred stock with the added feature of an option to convert the security into a fixed number of shares of common stock.[5]

Securities that are convertible into common stock can be attractive investments because the holder enjoys the upside potential of price increases in the common stock while maintaining the greater downside protection available to bondholders or, to a lesser degree, to preferred stockholders.[6] At favorable market prices, holders of convertible securities may exchange the bonds or preferred stock for common stock, thereby converting a creditor or limited equity relationship into a full ownership interest. Declines in the value of common stock below the conversion price are typically not matched by declines in the value of the convertible securities because of interest or dividend requirements.[7]

(d) WARRANTS

Warrants give the holder the right to buy a fixed number of shares of stock at a specified price. In general, warrants must be exercised within an established time period, although it is possible for warrants to be issued for a perpetual exercise period or to provide that they must be exercised, if at all, at a specified time.[8] Warrants are similar to call options in that they provide a right to acquire shares, but warrants are issued by the corporation itself rather than by an independent third party option writer.[9] Warrants often are used as sweeteners, that is, they are issued in a package with other securities to lower the interest or dividend costs to the corporation.[10] Warrants issued with other securities are typically detachable, that is, they can be separated from the primary securities and traded in their own right.[11] Secondary trading markets for warrants are common.

---

[5]*See generally* Reilly, *Corporate Stocks*, in HANDBOOK OF FINANCIAL MARKETS, *supra* note 4, at 270–71.

[6]*Id.* at 271.

[7]*Id.*

[8]Francis, *The Different Types of Options*, in HANDBOOK OF FINANCIAL MARKETS, *supra* note 4, at 557–58.

[9]*Id.* at 556.

[10]*Id.* at 556–57.

[11]*Id.* at 557.

(e) "SECURITIZED" CORPORATE ASSETS

In recent years, corporations have significantly expanded their use of asset-based securities. The basic pattern is straightforward: a corporation sells identified assets (typically financial assets with an associated cash flow stream) to an affiliated or controlled entity (a trust or corporation) with no other assets or existing liabilities. This special purpose entity then issues securities backed (in one way or another) by these assets.[12] These "securitized assets" can be classified into three broad groups: traditional asset-backed securities, pass-through securities, and pay-through securities. Asset-backed and pay-through securities represent varying forms of secured debt—albeit ones that are likely to have unique wrinkles. Pass-through securities represent fractional interests in a pool of identified property. Asset-backed and pay-through securities result in a debt obligation of the issuer. Pass-through securities normally create no continuing liability for the issuer because they involve the sale of assets to the security holders. These three types of securitized assets will be discussed in turn.

(1) ASSET-COLLATERALIZED SECURITIES

The classic asset-backed security is best illustrated by a mortgage bond issued by a public utility company. By mortgaging specific property to collateralize the bond obligation, the utility creates the publicly traded equivalent of a secured loan. Two essential changes to this traditional approach have allowed for the development of contemporary asset-based securities. First, new special purpose entities (rather than the principal business organization) are used as the issuers. For example, so-called mortgage-backed bonds or MBBs are simply bonds issued by bank and thrift affiliates that have as their sole assets mortgages (not on the issuer's property) with an aggregate market value exceeding, typically by a substantial margin, the face amount of the issued bonds. Second, the assets that are used to back the securities certainly do not have to be limited to mortgages, whether on the issuer's or any one else's real property. Asset-backed securities can and have been issued based on receivables and there is no tax or other legal reason that assets of a wide variety of sorts could not be used.

---

[12]*See generally* Shapiro, *The Securitization of Practically Everything*, INSTITUTIONAL INVESTOR, May 1985, at 197.

(2) PASS-THROUGH SECURITIES

A pass-through security is created when someone, generally called the originator, puts assets into a "pool"—typically a grantor trust—and then sells obligations secured by a pledge of an undivided interest in the assets in the underlying pool. Cash flow from the assets, that is, principal and interest less servicing fees, is distributed or "passed-through" to the security holders pro rata without taxation at the pool or trust level. Shortfalls or deficiencies in the scheduled cash flow from (i.e., debt service payments on) the pooled assets are reflected in reduced payments on the security; unless these payments are in some manner guaranteed. The originator of the pool does not generally retain an ownership interest in the pooled assets. The pooled assets are treated for tax purposes as having been sold by the originator to the participation certificate holders. The certificates or securities, therefore, do not constitute debt of the originator or issuer but rather that of the borrowers (i.e., the debtors providing the cash flow on the assets).[13]

The basic structure outlined in the preceding paragraph applies to all pass-through securities; what varies is the nature of the pooled assets, the method for determining and distributing payments to security holders, and the presence and characteristics of guarantees. The archetypal pass-through security is the GNMA/MBS.[14] Commercial banks, savings and loan associations, and mortgage bankers assemble and pool mortgages; interests in the pool are issued; and GNMA guarantees timely payment of principal and interest. GNMA's guarantee makes these securities government pass-throughs. Beginning in 1977, private financial institutions began issuing essentially similar pass-through securities without a government guarantee or sponsorship.[15] Private pass-throughs may or may not carry a credit enhancement, that is, the backing of a bank in the form of a letter of credit or of an insurance company in the form of a bond.

Private mortgage-backed pass-throughs are generally available in types that parallel those issued or guaranteed by the federal housing agencies. For example, private pass-throughs have been issued using adjustable

---

[13]*See generally* K. LORE, MORTGAGE-BACKED SECURITIES, DEVELOPMENTS AND TRENDS IN THE SECONDARY MORTGAGE MARKET ch. 3, 5–8 (Clark Boardman, Securities Law Series 1985).

[14]For a discussion of GNMA and other federal agency pass-through mortgage-backed securities, see generally section 2.1(b). For a discussion of MBSs, see generally section 28.4.

[15]*See generally* F. FABOZZI, HANDBOOK OF MORTGAGE-BACKED SECURITIES ch. 6 (1985).

rate mortgages (ARMs) in the underlying pool and pools which now contain mortgages collected from multiple originators. The most interesting private mortgage-backed pass-through security to be proposed in the last several years is the TIM.[16] Basically, TIMs would be multiclass pass-through securities, that is, issuers would create several maturity schedules out of a single mortgage pool.[17] Because legislation is needed before TIMs can be used economically,[18] their prospects are unclear at this time.[19]

To date, mortgages have been the principal assets underlying private pass-through securities, but the pass-through concept is certainly not limited to mortgages. Recently, for example, private pass-through securities backed by auto loans have been issued; these securities are called certificates of automobile receivables or CARs. Obviously, the specific features of a particular security are critical to its evaluation as an investment, but from a tax perspective, the nature of the assets in the pass-through pool is largely irrelevant.

(3) PAY-THROUGH SECURITIES

In the early 1980s, the two drawbacks of MBBs—insufficient use of collateral and mismatch in cash flow patterns between the bonds and the mortgages—led to the design of the pay-through (or cash flow) bond.[20] Pay-through bonds share characteristics of both MBBs and pass-throughs. On the one hand, the security is a debt obligation of the issuing entity; there is no sale of the underlying assets to the security holders and hence no recognition of gain or loss by the issuer upon the sale of the securities. On the other hand, the source of the cash flow to pay the bond holders is the collateral itself; the cash flow from the mortgages (with a cushion or safety factor) services and supports the bonds, rather than having the bonds backed by an overcollateralization of mortgages based on market values.

The pay-through bond concept has spawned a number of innovative securities. Following FHLMC's introduction of CMOs in 1983,[21] CMOs—

---

[16]*See generally* K. LORE, *supra* note 13, ch. 6, 10–28.

[17]TIMs would be the pass-through equivalent of CMOs. *See generally* section 2.1(b)(4); *see also* section 28.4.

[18]Prop. Treas. Reg. § 301.7701-4(c)(2) (1984) treats a fixed investment trust with more than one class of ownership as an association.

[19]*See* section 28.4(b)(4).

[20]F. FABOZZI, *supra* note 15, at 149–200.

[21]For a discussion of CMOs, see generally section 2.1(b)(4), section 28.4(b)(2), and section 28.4(d).

both government and private—have become the most popular new mortgage-backed bonds by a wide margin.[22] In a CMO, the cash flow of the underlying mortgage pool is apportioned to different classes of bondholders, thereby creating short, intermediate, and long-term securities. Principal payments from the underlying mortgages are first applied exclusively to the short maturity bonds until paid off, then to the intermediate maturity bonds, and finally to the long maturity bonds. Multiclass pay-through bonds offer issuers two advantages: the ability to liquify deep discount mortgages (by "selling" them to an affiliate that in turn uses them to collateralize securities) without recognizing a loss, and the ability to match cash flows with debt service to mitigate interest rate risk. CMOs offer substantial flexibility in tailoring maturities and average lives to meet investor demands. They also provide for the first time, through the prioritization of cash flows, a measure of call protection for taxable mortgage-backed securities.[23]

The fertility of the pay-through bond concept is by no means limited to the mortgage markets. Corporations are increasingly using such bonds to turn various types of financial assets into securities, thereby "cleaning-up" their balance sheets, creating liquidity, and leaving unimpaired their usual sources of financing. Because the issuing entity has no liabilities other than its debt securities (hence, it is often called "fireproof"), the credit rating of its securities is tied not to that of the original corporations, but to that of the companies obligated to provide the payments on the assets or that have guaranteed the payments. Hence, the use of pay-through bonds often offers corporations cost savings compared to bank borrowings or traditional debt offerings. Some of the assets that have been securitized as pay-through bonds include car loans, bank loans guaranteed by the Small Business Administration, trade receivables, and leases.[24]

(f) HYBRID AND ESOTERIC SECURITIES

The traditional forms of corporate securities—stocks, bonds, notes, and warrants—are increasingly being forced to share the financial limelight with new, unique, and often complex securities. For the purposes of this book, it is sufficient merely to call attention to some of the more important of these new corporate securities, and to note that their tax

---

[22]F. FABOZZI, *supra* note 15, at 168–69.

[23]*Id.* at 152.

[24]Shapiro, *supra* note 12, at 197.

treatment (as far as we now know) is dependent on the rules and principles discussed in later chapters.

Among the most interesting of the new crop of corporate securities are the following:

- Mandatory convertible notes (essentially long-term notes that can be exchanged at maturity for cash, debt, or stock)[25]
- Adjustable rate preferred stock (ARPs) and a very recent variation, auction rate preferred stock (the dividends on the stock are reset periodically to provide rates close to the money market rate, but not so frequently as to lose the intercorporate dividends received deduction)[26]
- "Puttable" stock (typically offered to the public as a unit consisting of stock plus "rights" to sell the stock back to the company for cash, debt, or additional common stock)[27]
- Stock with dividends pegged to the performance of a subsidiary rather than of the parent corporation (most notably General Motors' Class E shares, the dividends on which are tied to the performance of Electronic Data Systems, Inc.)
- Stock accompanied by a contingent promissory note (a way, through a type of put option, to guarantee a specified compound annual return)
- Convertible exchangeable preferred stock (preferred stock that converts into debt rather than into equity)[28]
- Contingent takedown options on debt securities, typically issued in units consisting of a bond together with a usually detachable option or warrant to purchase a second identical option ("double-up" option) or a different bond[29]

---

[25]Mandatory convertible debt is issued primarily by bank holding companies. The notes are treated as debt for tax purposes, Rev. Rul. 85-119, 1985-30 I.R.B. 21, but as equity (often primary capital) for regulatory purposes. *See* section 28.3(c); section 28.3(d); *see also* Saunders, *Lord, Make Me Chaste, But Not Just Yet*, FORBES, Sept. 9, 1985, at 56.

[26]*See* section 15.7; section 22.9; section 28.3(c). *See generally* Selby, *The Cheapest Equity Around*, INSTITUTIONAL INVESTOR, Oct. 1984, at 287. In the case of auction rate preferred stock, a Dutch auction is used so that all holders are paid the lowest rate that encompasses a sufficient number of the bids made by current and potential holders to cover all outstanding shares. *See, e.g.* Weyerhauser Company, Prospectus (Nov. 8, 1985).

[27]*See, e.g.*, Fertility and Genetics Research Inc., Prospectus (Dec. 6, 1985); Gearhart Industries, Prospectus (May 16, 1985).

[28]*See, e.g.*, Chubb Corp., Prospectus (March 26, 1985); Household Finance Corporation, Prospectus (Dec. 17, 1985).

[29]*See generally*, Kopprasch, *Contingent Takedown Options on Fixed Income Securities*, in THE HANDBOOK OF FIXED INCOME SECURITIES 565. (F. Fabozzi & I. Pollack eds. 1983).

- Debt securities with early redemption (put) options (the right to resell the bond or note on "active" dates to the issuer at the strike price)[30]
- Debt securities (from bonds to commercial paper) carrying various types of issuer credit-enhancement (the security is likely to involve asset-backed securities but the key component is a bank letter of credit or an insurance company guarantee of all or part of the debt)[31]

(g) LIMITED PARTNERSHIP INTERESTS

Although limited partnership interests are assignable[32] and generally treated as securities for federal securities law purposes,[33] restrictions are typically imposed on their transferability (by the agreement of limited partnership) to assure the limited partnership's compliance with Treasury regulations specifying the necessary conditions for partnership tax treatment.[34] Nevertheless, beginning in the early 1980s, the notion of publicly traded limited partnerships began to attract a good deal of attention.[35] The trading of such interests is essentially identical to trading of stock,[36] and therefore, the principal focus of concern is the tax status of the issuing partnerships.

(h) TRUST INTERESTS

Publicly traded trust interests can be attractive vehicles for corporations to use to spin-off to their stockholders nonoperating mineral interests (e.g., royalty or net profit interests in oil, gas, or minerals), royalty rights on patents, and other passive interests. To establish a so-called royalty

---

[30]*See generally*, Kopprasch, *Early Redemption (Put) Options on Fixed Income Securities*, in THE HANDBOOK OF FIXED INCOME SECURITIES, *supra* note 29, at 613–26.

[31]*See generally*, Gregg, *Bolstering Corporate Credit*, INSTITUTIONAL INVESTOR, Apr. 1985, at 151.

[32]ULPA § 19(1) (1916); Revised ULPA § 702 (1976).

[33]Joint Release of Maryland Division of Securities, Virginia Division of Securities, Public Service Commission of the District of Columbia and the Securities and Exchange Commission, SEC Rel. No. 4877 [1966–1967 Transfer Binder] FED. SEC. L. REP. ¶ 77,462 (Aug. 8, 1967).

[34]Treasury regulations provide that a business organization will be classified as an association, taxable as a corporation, if it possesses a majority of the following corporate attributes: continuity of life, centralization of management, limited liability, and free transferability of interests. Treas. Reg. § 301.7701-2(a)(3) (1983).

[35]*See, e.g., Publicly Traded Limited Partnerships: An Emerging Financial Alternative to the Public Corporation*, 39 BUS. LAW 709 (1984).

[36]A number of limited partnerships, including Apache Petroleum Co., are listed on the NYSE. *See* section 25.8.

trust, a publicly traded corporation typically transfers nonoperating interests to a grantor trust,[37] either directly or through a sale of the property to the trust. These grantor trusts are of two kinds: distribution trusts and financing trusts. A distribution trust is formed by a corporation to hold nonoperating interests that have been contributed to it. The units in the trust, represented by publicly traded certificates of beneficial interest, are then distributed pro rata to the corporation's stockholders.[38] A financing trust is formed by a corporation to hold nonoperating interests that have been sold to the trust. The trust, in turn, sells certificates of beneficial interest, typically in conjunction with a public offering of the corporation's stock, to obtain the funds needed to pay the corporation for the property it has purchased.[39]

The units or certificates of beneficial interest in the trust are "securities" subject to the securities laws. These trust interests trade on stock exchanges and in the over-the-counter market independently of the corporation's stock. There is an active secondary market in trust interests.[40]

A corporation may create a royalty trust for a number of reasons. First, contributions or sales of assets to a trust will reduce the corporation's size, thereby (perhaps) increasing its earnings or making it a more attractive (or less) attractive merger or takeover candidate. Second, the corporation may use a financing trust to raise additional capital. And third, the trust vehicle may provide stockholders with increased value.

From a stockholder's perspective, beneficial interests in a publicly traded trust offer several attractions. First, a royalty trust provides a vehicle for direct ownership of passive nonoperating interests without tax at the entity level.[41] Second, beneficial interests provide the holders with a way to "divide" their prior stock interests, giving them increased flexibility and liquidity. Third, certain tax benefits may be available to owners of beneficial interests.[42] Fourth, in certain circumstances, the stockholders may realize a greater return through the direct ownership

---

[37]For a discussion of grantor trusts, see section 25.9(a) and section 28.4(b)(1).

[38]Hineman, *An Update on Oil and Gas Royalty Trusts*, 1 J. TAX OF INVESTMENTS 250–51 (1984).

[39]*Id.* at 251.

[40]For example, on the NYSE there is active trading in the Houston Oil Royalty Trust, Mesa Royalty Trust, Sabine Royalty Trust, Great Northern Iron Ore Properties, and First Union Real Estate Equity and Mortgage Investments.

[41]*See* section 25.9(a).

[42]*See* section 25.9(a); section 25.9(b).

of trust interests than they could through their stock interests in the corporation.[43]

The IRS policy of ruling favorably on the tax status of grantor trusts has encouraged corporations to transfer nonoperating interests directly to stockholders by means of the trust vehicle. Some changes made by the DRA[44] have reduced (but not eliminated) the attraction of establishing royalty trusts. For a discussion of the tax considerations affecting publicly traded trusts, see section 25.9.

§ 1.2 TYPES OF MARKETS

Secondary trading markets for corporate securities are basically of two types: exchange markets and the over-the-counter market.[45] Corporate securities can also be purchased and sold in transactions privately negotiated by the parties.

Even though the exchange markets and the over-the-counter market are similar in their purposes and functions, these markets have substantially different trading mechanisms and practices. The following sections highlight these differences.

(a) EXCHANGE TRADING

Stock exchanges must be registered with the SEC as national securities exchanges.[46] Stock exchanges are generally auction markets growing out of what originally were call markets.[47] People would gather at one place and each security was called, in turn, during a specified trading session, thereby establishing the price for that security until it was called again.[48]

Trading in a security on a stock exchange is centralized at a post on its trading floor.[49] Trading is now continuous rather than on a call

---

[43]*Restructuring Big Oil*, Bus. WEEK, Nov. 14, 1983, at 138.

[44]DRA, Pub. L. 98–369, 98 Stat. 494 (1984).

[45]For an excellent, although somewhat dated analysis of secondary corporate securities markets, see REPORT OF THE SPECIAL STUDY OF THE SECURITIES MARKETS OF THE SECURITIES AND EXCHANGE COMMISSION, H. R. Doc. No. 95, Pt. 2, 88th Cong., 1st Sess. (1963) [hereinafter referred to as "Special Securities Study"].

[46]SEA § 6, 15 U.S.C. § 78f (1982).

[47]Special Securities Study, *supra* note 45, at 8.

[48]*Id.*

[49]*Id.*

basis.[50] In a continuous auction process, all buyers and sellers (or their brokers) in a security are concentrated in one place (i.e., post), at which trades occur by open outcry, thereby allowing potential buyers to seek the lowest prices at which to buy securities and sellers to seek the highest prices at which to sell securities. Orders sent to the stock exchange are executed at the post in accordance with the terms of the order.

Stock exchanges only permit members to trade on the floor of the exchange.[51] Members active on the floor (such as specialists, market makers, and floor brokers) effect as principal or agent all trades executed on the exchange.[52] Exchange members can trade for their own accounts as traders or dealers; customer orders are executed on stock exchanges by brokers, and the customers pay brokerage commissions to the firms acting as their brokers.[53] All national exchange members must be registered with the SEC as broker-dealers.[54] Exchange members are thus subject to the rules and regulations imposed by both the exchanges of which they are members and the SEC.

Securities may be traded on a stock exchange only if they have been listed, that is, the corporate issuer has applied to the exchange for and obtained its approval to have the securities registered for trading, or the exchange has extended to them unlisted trading privileges, that is, the exchange has applied to the SEC and the SEC has granted the exchange the right to trade the securities even though the issuer has not chosen to list its securities on that exchange.[55] Issuers of listed securities have a contractual relationship with the exchange (or exchanges) on which their securities are listed. Through this contract ("listing agreement") the exchange imposes regulations, for example, regarding stockholder voting rights, directly on the issuers of securities traded on the exchange.[56]

(b) OVER-THE-COUNTER MARKETS

Securities transactions not occurring on an exchange are viewed as taking place in the over-the-counter market. In an exchange market (1) all trading occurs face-to-face at a single location, and (2) a significant

---

[50]*Id.*

[51]*See id.*

[52]*Id.* at 9.

[53]*See id.* at 9. For a discussion of market participants, see generally Part Two.

[54]SEA § 15, 15 U.S.C. § 78o(a)(1) (1982).

[55]SEA §§ 12(a), (f), 15 U.S.C. §§ 78l(a), (f) (1982).

[56]Special Securities Study, *supra* note 45, at 11.

portion of transactions involve brokers as agents, on both sides of the trade. By way of contrast, the firms in the over-the-counter market conduct business from their various offices, that is, "upstairs" (off the exchange floor), communicate with each other by means of quotation display systems and the telephone, and execute the vast majority of trades as dealers, that is, as principals, rather than as agents.[57] Market makers in the over-the-counter market stand ready to buy and sell specific securities for their own accounts.[58] Over-the-counter firms that do not make a market (i.e., that do not have an inventory) in a particular security generally handle customers' orders by purchasing or selling the securities for the firms' own account from a market maker and then selling or purchasing the securities as principal (not as an agent) to or from customers.[59] On all principal trades, the customer pays a markup or markdown to or from the market maker's quotation.[60] Over-the-counter market makers and the brokers who represent customers must register with the SEC as broker-dealers[61] and become members of the NASD.[62]

The over-the-counter market is relied on heavily for the distribution of new and secondary issues of securities. In the new corporate issue market, "[t]he over-the-counter broker-dealer stands between investor and issuer to execute the transaction and arrange for the transfer of monies and securities."[63] In the primary (initial) market, underwriters facilitate the initial sale of securities by acting as dealers for firm commitment underwritings or as brokers for best efforts underwritings. Underwriters participate in the over-the-counter market, are registered with the SEC as broker-dealers, and are members of the NASD.[64]

§ 1.3   TYPES OF TRANSACTIONS

The manner in which security transactions settle is often relevant for tax purposes. For example, gain on securities sold by a cash basis taxpayer is reported as of the settlement date, while loss is reported as of

---

[57]*Id.* at 8.

[58]*Id.*

[59]*Id.* at 9.

[60]*Id.*

[61]SEA § 15a, 15 U.S.C. § 78o(a)(1) (1982).

[62]SEA § 15b(8), 15 U.S.C. § 78o(b)(8) (Supp. I 1983).

[63]Resch, *The Over-the-Counter Market*, in THE STOCK MARKET HANDBOOK 168 (F. Zarb and G. Kerekes eds. 1970).

[64]For a discussion of underwriters, see section 6.7.

the trade date. The trade date is the day on which the securities transaction occurs. The settlement date is the day on which the transaction is to be settled, that is, the date delivery and payment is due. Trade dates and settlement dates also are relevant to determine a taxpayer's holding period for securities.

(a) REGULAR WAY

Unless otherwise specified, a corporate securities transaction, whether on an exchange or in the over-the-counter market, settles regular way, which means that settlement is due on the fifth business day following the trade date.[65] Regular way trades on exchanges are reported on the tape, that is, a moving display of last sale data, and a substantial number of regular way trades in the over-the-counter market are reported on the tape or through interrogation devices (data retrieval systems capable of displaying last sale data). Regular way trades are viewed as the norm in the securities market.

(b) CASH

Transactions for cash are expected to settle on the trade date. Because of immediate settlement, the purchaser often must pay the seller a premium over the regular way market price. Due to this pricing difference, cash transactions are not reported on the tape or through interrogation devices. The cash market for corporate securities is often used in tender offer situations, where the purchaser wants to acquire securities for tender less than five business dates before the proration date. A cash trade can assure the purchaser possession of the securities in time to tender.

(c) DELIVERY AGAINST PAYMENT

A delivery against payment or COD transaction typically is used in connection with the purchase of securities by institutional investors that are prohibited by state law or their state or federal regulators from delivering funds without receiving the purchased securities. Delivery of the securities, normally within 35 calendar days, is made to the purchaser's bank or other agent, which pays for the securities at that time. COD trades are in the normal course and do not affect the price of the securities. Such transactions are reported on the tape and are available

[65] 2 NYSE Guide (CCH) Rule 64, ¶ 2064 (Feb. 9, 1968).

through interrogation devices. Delivery against payment transactions also are referred to as "delivery versus payment," "delivery against cash," and "cash on delivery" transactions.

(d) NEXT DAY DELIVERY

Although the rules of the stock exchanges and the NASD do not specifically allow settlement of a trade on the day after the trade, next day delivery transactions do occur. In fact, the NYSE currently is participating in a pilot program to permit next day settlement.[66] Delivery of the securities and payment are both made on the first business day after the trade date.

(e) DELIVERY BETWEEN NEXT DAY AND REGULAR WAY

Settlement can also be set for a date between next day settlement (the next business day after the trade) and regular way settlement (five business days after the trade). Referred to as "trade-plus-two," "trade-plus-three," or "trade-plus-four," these specialized settlement dates are not set out in the rules of the stock exchanges or NASD, but nevertheless are used by market participants.[67] Trades for settlement in less than five business days are not reported on the tape or available through interrogation devices.

Such special settlement dates are used, for example, by market participants who want to obtain a stock dividend without the risks of ownership of the securities. In general, a dividend is paid to the holders of record on the record date (i.e., the date on which the corporation identifies the stockholders who are eligible for a dividend). Although he may not be a stockholder of record on the record date, a purchaser whose transaction has settled on or prior to the record date is entitled to be paid the dividend by the record holder. Because regular way trades settle five business days after the trade date, a stock normally begins to trade ex-dividend (i.e., where the purchaser does not acquire the right to the dividend) beginning on the fourth business day before the record date. Accordingly, by using special settlement dates a person could purchase stock four business days prior to the record date for settlement two business days after the trade date and simultaneously sell the same stock ex-dividend in a regular way transaction, that is, for settlement

---

[66]SEC Release No. 34-21985 (Apr. 25, 1985).

[67]The MSE has proposed amendments to its rules to provide for trade-plus-two, three, or four settlement dates.

in five business days. Such a person would be viewed as the owner of the stock on the record date and, therefore, would be entitled to receive the dividend, but because the regular way trade settles after the record date, he would be able to deliver the stock without any obligation to deliver the dividend.

(f) SELLER'S OPTION (DEFERRED DELIVERY) OR BUYER'S OPTION (DEFERRED PAYMENT)

Depending on where the securities are being traded, a seller's option to defer delivery or a buyer's option to defer payment may be permitted within certain time constraints. For example, on the NYSE, a seller's option transaction can be structured to settle on any day after the trade date plus five days and before the expiration of the seller's option, which cannot be more than 60 days following the trade date.[68] The seller's option permits the seller to deliver the securities at any time between the sixth day after the trade date and the date specified in the contract. On stock exchanges that permit buyer's options, a buyer is allowed to refuse the seller's delivery of securities at any time prior to the date specified in the contract.

A sale might not be deemed to have taken place until the settlement date. Therefore, a seller's option trade may allow a seller to take advantage of the current market price while extending his holding period in the securities for up to 60 days.[69] Similarly, under a seller's option transaction, dividends payable to holders as of a date after the trade date—but before the settlement date—are paid to the seller unless the parties agree otherwise. Seller's option trades are not reported on the tape.

A buyer's option trade allows the buyer an opportunity to take advantage of the current market price without being viewed as the owner until settlement.

(g) WHEN-ISSUED

When-issued trading is trading in securities that have not yet been issued, conducted in contemplation of their issuance. For example, a broker-dealer contracts to sell securities of another broker-dealer or to an ordinary customer "when, as and if issued." If the contemplated

---

[68]2 NYSE GUIDE (CCH) Rule 64(3), ¶ 2064 (Feb. 9, 1968).

[69]*But see* section 15.2(a)(5).

securities are issued according to their terms, the seller delivers and the buyer pays; if the securities are not issued as contemplated, the parties are returned to the status quo.

For tax purposes, the buyer is not the owner of the to be issued security until the trade has been settled; however, for both tax and securities law purposes (e.g., the SEC's short sales rule),[70] the when-issued contract is itself a security.[71] Settlement of when-issued transactions between broker-dealers or those trading in a cash account[72] is required within seven business days of the date the issuer made the securities available for delivery to purchasers.[73] Ordinary investors purchasing or selling when-issued securities in a margin account[74] are treated as purchasing or selling issued securities[75] and must pay the required margin within seven business days after the trade date.[76]

Because of restrictions imposed by the securities laws, the great bulk of when-issued trading occurs in connection with various types of exchange offerings, such as the recent American Telephone and Telegraph divestiture, various rights offerings, stock dividends, and bankruptcy reorganizations.

(h) WHEN-DISTRIBUTED

When-distributed trading anticipates the distribution to the public of an issued security that is held in only a few hands. Whereas when-issued trading occurs in contemplation of a primary offering by the issuer, when-distributed trading occurs in contemplation of a secondary distribution by one or more existing security holders. The when-distributed contract is very much like the when-issued contract, except that the contingency governing performance is not issuance but distribution. As is the case with when-issued securities, the securities subject to when-distributed trading may never be distributed by the securities holders. If the securities are not distributed, the contract is void and there are no continuing obligations on the part of either the purchaser or seller. If the securities are distributed, settlement between broker-dealers or

---

[70] 17 C.F.R. §§ 240.3b-3, .10a-1 (1985); 12 C.F.R. § 220.5(b) (1985).

[71] *See* 17 C.F.R. §§ 240.3b-3, .10a-1 (1985) (governing short sales under the SEC rules), 12 C.F.R. § 220.8(b)(1)(ii)(1985) (governing cash accounts under FRB rules).

[72] *See* section 1.4(a).

[73] 12 C.F.R. § 220.8(b)(1)(ii) (1985).

[74] *See* section 1.4(b).

[75] 12 C.F.R. § 220.5(a) (1985).

[76] 12 C.F.R. § 220.8(b)(1)(ii) (1985).

those trading in a cash account[77] must occur within seven business days of the date the securities were distributed pursuant to a published plan.[78]

(i) INSTALLMENT SALES

A transaction in which the parties have agreed to all the terms, with the sales price to be paid in one or more installments, is an installment transaction. Installment sales typically are privately negotiated. In recent years, some tender offers have been structured as installment sales for tax purposes where tendering stockholders received back debt securities viewed as installment obligations.[79] Installment sales generally involve a sale of a security by a customer to a securities firm that agrees to pay the sales price to the customer over time. (The firm, of course, turns around and sells the securities in the open market.) The customer in such a transaction is a general creditor of the firm until he is paid in full. The firm's obligation to the customer may be unsecured or secured by unregistered exempted securities.[80]

§ 1.4 CREDIT REGULATION

An investor, trader, or dealer can buy securities for cash or on credit, that is, on margin. The procedures governing the purchase and sale of securities by or through registered broker-dealers and the extension of credit on securities generally are established by the Board of Governors of the Federal Reserve System (FRB) under the authority granted to it in Section 7 of the SEA.[81] Although both the financial relations between registered broker-dealers and their customers and the extension of credit on securities are governed by regulations promulgated by the FRB, the SEC enforces these regulations. (In practice, the SEC leaves enforcement of Regulation U, governing extension of credit by banks, to the federal and state bank examining authorities.)

Regulation T, governing the extension of credit by broker-dealers, provides that all financial relations between a customer and a broker-dealer must be recorded in a margin account, a cash account, or one of

---

[77]*See* section 1.4(b).

[78]12 C.F.R. § 220.8(b)(1)(iii) (1985).

[79]For tax purposes, certain freely tradeable debt securities are treated as cash payments, not installment obligations. For a discussion of debt securities, see generally Chapter 27.

[80]*See generally* 12 C.F.R. § 220.15 (1985) (prescribing certain restrictions on borrowings by creditors).

[81]15 U.S.C. § 78g (1982 & Supp. II 1984).

six special-purpose accounts.[82] For tax purposes the cash account and margin account are the most important of the Regulation T accounts, and a short description of both follows.

(a) CASH ACCOUNT

Purchases for cash are usually made in the cash account.[83] Typically, institutions such as banks, insurance companies, tax-exempt organizations, and pension funds that are required by law to pay 100 percent for their securities positions maintain cash accounts. Other institutions and individuals may maintain cash accounts to effect delivery against payment or COD transactions, which are not permitted in a margin account.

Cash account transactions generally must be fully paid for within seven business days from the trade date.[84] If full cash payment is not received within seven business days after the date of purchase and the sum due from the customer exceeds $500, the broker-dealer is required promptly to cancel or otherwise liquidate the transaction.[85] In addition, if a customer sells nonexempted securities before paying for them in full, his "privilege of delaying payment beyond the trade date" must be withdrawn for 90 calendar days.[86] This 90-day rule does not apply, however, if either full payment is received (including any checks or cleared drafts) within seven days of the trade date or the security was deposited in another broker-dealer's cash account that has sufficient funds to pay for the security.[87]

Among the exemptions to the seven-day rule is a provision for COD transactions. Under this exemption, the customer must pay the broker either on delivery or within 35 calendar days of trade date, whichever is earlier.[88] The broker-dealer may seek an extension of either the seven-day or 35-day period from the appropriate self-regulatory agency.[89] Extensions of time for payment typically are granted if requested in good faith.

Short sales cannot be effected in a cash account.

---

[82] 12 C.F.R. § 220 (1985).
[83] 12 C.F.R. § 220.8 (1985).
[84] 12 C.F.R. § 220.8(b)(1) (1985).
[85] 12 C.F.R. § 220.8(b)(4) (1985).
[86] 12 C.F.R. § 220.8(c)(1) (1985).
[87] 12 C.F.R. § 220.8(c)(2) (1985).
[88] 12 C.F.R. § 220.8(b)(1) (1985).
[89] 12 C.F.R. § 220.8(d) (1985).

(b) MARGIN ACCOUNT

The margin account is the principal customer account for margin trading. A customer who buys on credit pays only part of the purchase price in cash and receives an extension of credit from the broker-dealer for the unpaid balance. Usually the broker-dealer, in turn, uses the customer's securities purchased on margin as collateral to finance the balance of the purchase price. (Of course, a customer may also finance his purchase of securities by borrowing against those securities from a bank. Such transactions are governed by FRB Regulation U.)[90]

Trading on margin enables an investor or trader to establish a securities position with a value in excess of the equity committed to establish the position. Such leverage means that bigger percentage gains (or losses) will be generated than on fully paid for (unleveraged) securities positions. Because of the increased risks in margin transactions (for both customer and broker-dealer), two basic requirements are imposed on all margin account trading.

First, the FRB requires that the customer must pay the initial margin in connection with the purchase or short sale of any security other than an exempted security, registered nonconvertible debt security, or OTC margin bond.[91] At present, the initial margin requirement for long margin securities (i.e., registered securities, OTC margin stock, OTC securities designated for trading in the National Market System, and securities issued by open investment companies or investment trusts pursuant to Section 8 of the Investment Company Act of 1940)[92] is 50 percent of the market value of the securities purchased.[93] For exempted securities, registered nonconvertible debt securities, or OTC margin bonds, the margin requirement is to be set by the creditor in good faith.[94] For short nonexempted securities, it is 150 percent of current market value, or 100 percent of current market value if the security is exchangeable or convertible within 90 calendar days without further restriction.[95] Margin may be paid in the form of cash, margin securities, or exempted securities.[96] The broker-dealer must make a new margin calculation each day there is a transaction in a margin account in order to determine

---

[90]For an overview of margin trading, see generally Kerekes, *Principles of Margin Trading,* in THE STOCK MARKET HANDBOOK, *supra* note 63, at 316–24.

[91]12 C.F.R. § 220.18(a)-(b) (1985).

[92]12 C.F.R. § 220.2(o) (1985).

[93]12 C.F.R. § 220.18(a) (1985).

[94]12 C.F.R. § 220.18(b) (1985).

[95]12 C.F.R. § 220.18(d) (1985).

[96]12 C.F.R. § 220.3(e)(1) (1985).

whether additional margin must be requested.[97] In the event that a day's transactions create or increase a margin deficiency, the customer must satisfy the margin call within seven business days unless an extension is granted.[98] If a margin call in excess of $500 is not met in full within the seven-day period (and an extension has not been granted by a self-regulatory organization), the broker-dealer must liquidate securities sufficient to meet the margin call or eliminate any margin deficiency existing on the day such liquidation is required, whichever is less.[99]

Second, the self-regulatory organizations generally require that customers meet strict maintenance margin requirements. Under FRB requirements, no margin calls are required in connection with a customer's account regardless of how much the market falls, provided that the customer has not effected any transaction that creates or increases a margin deficiency. Under the rules of the NYSE, however, a customer must maintain at all times a margin of at least 25 percent of the current market value of the securities long in his account and specified amounts (based on the market value of the securities) for securities short in his account.[100]

Whether considering initial or maintenance margin requirements, margin in a purchase transaction serves as a downpayment on the purchase of the securities, with the remaining funds supplied by the broker-dealer. When securities are bought on margin, credit is extended to the customer who is viewed as the owner of the financed securities.[101] The broker charges interest to the customer on the margin loan and holds the securities as collateral for the loan.

Margin requirements in connection with short sales of securities create, in effect, a performance bond.[102] When a customer sells securities short, the broker-dealer borrows the securities for the customer and delivers them to the purchaser. To protect the broker-dealer from losses that might occur from an increase in the price of the securities, the customer must deposit an amount in excess of the current market value of the securities sold short.[103]

---

[97] 12 C.F.R. § 220.4(c)(1) (1985).

[98] 12 C.F.R. § 220.4(c)(3) (1985).

[99] 12 C.F.R. § 220.4(d) (1985).

[100] 2 NYSE GUIDE (CCH) Rule 431(b), ¶ 2431 (Sept. 22, 1983).

[101] STAFF OF THE BOARD OF GOVERNORS OF THE FEDERAL RESERVE BOARD, A REVIEW AND EVALUATION OF FEDERAL MARGIN REGULATIONS 173 (1984).

[102] Id. at 173–74.

[103] 12 C.F.R. §§ 220.5(b)(1), 220.18(d)-(e) (1985). For a discussion of short sales, see generally Chapter 16.

There is a special rule with respect to a short sale against the box.[104] A short sale against the box occurs when a customer sells short a security he owns but uses a borrowed security to make delivery. Such a short sale is treated as a long sale for purposes of computing the equity and required margin.[105]

§ 1.5   CLEARANCE AND SETTLEMENT

Prior to settlement of a securities transaction, both sides must verify all the terms of the trade, that is, the transaction must be "cleared." The clearance procedure is the mechanism by which information regarding the buy and sell sides of a trade are compared to be sure both sides agree as to the parties, quantity, and identity of the securities, and the price. Once compared, trades are sorted and the broker-dealers are advised of their payment or delivery obligations. Exchange and over-the-counter transactions are cleared through the facilities of various clearing organizations.[106]

After clearance, settlement can occur in one of two ways: by a physical exchange of money for securities or by book entry transfers on the books of the appropriate clearing organization.[107] Typically, the clearing organization guarantees performance of a buyer's obligation to pay for securities and a seller's obligation to deliver securities after the settlement date.

[104]*See generally* Chapter 16.

[105]12 C.F.R. § 220.5(b)(2) (1985).

[106]For a discussion of the clearing process for exchange and over-the-counter transactions, see E. GUTTMAN, ISRAELS AND GUTTMAN'S MODERN SECURITIES TRANSFERS S.6-7 to S.6-9 (rev. ed. Supp. 1984).

[107]For a discussion of settlement procedures for exchange and over-the-counter securities, see *id*. at S.6-9 to S.6-12.

Two

Overview of the Government Securities Market

The United States and its agencies issue marketable and nonmarketable securities (collectively "government securities"). Marketable government securities trade primarily over-the-counter and are of two types. The first comprises those securities issued directly by the United States, that is, Treasury bills, notes, and bonds ("Treasury securities" or "governments").[1] The second type of marketable government securities comprises those issued by corporations in which the United States has a direct or indirect interest or whose liabilities are guaranteed by the United States ("agencies").[2] Although the primary trading in governments and agencies does not occur on exchanges, standardized options on and futures contracts for government securities trade exclusively on securities and commodity exchanges.

The principal nonmarketable government securities available to investors are United States savings bonds,[3] retirement plan bonds,[4] and

---

[1] See generally Stigum & Fabozzi, *U.S. Treasury Obligations*, in THE HANDBOOK OF FIXED INCOME SECURITIES 253 (F. Fabozzi & I. Pollack eds. 1983).

[2] See generally Stigum, *Securities of Federal Government Agencies and Sponsored Corporations, supra* note 1, at 270.

[3] 31 C.F.R. pts. 315, 353 (1985).

[4] See generally 31 C.F.R. § 341.0(a) (1985). Retirement plan bonds may be purchased only by bond purchase plans and qualified pension and profit sharing plans. 31 C.F.R. § 341.0(a) (1985).

individual retirement bonds.[5] The Treasury also issues special nonnegotiable securities to foreign central banks, federal agencies and trust funds, and state and local governments. Only government securities available for purchase by private investors are discussed in this book.

Marketable or negotiable government securities form the largest component of the United States financial markets. Government securities are issued to finance the operations of the United States and its agencies, and at present there is more than $770 billion worth of marketable government securities outstanding. Market participants trade (in both outright purchases and sales and financing transactions) hundreds of billions of dollars of such securities every business day. Secondary trading in government securities occurs for speculative and investment reasons, to facilitate short-term borrowings by institutions, and because of FRB open-market operations intended to influence interest rates and the growth of the money supply.[6]

The primary secondary market for negotiable government securities consists of a number of closely linked, albeit separate, over-the-counter trading networks, each specializing in one or more of the various types of government securities. Dealers (both securities firms and banks) that stand ready to buy and sell (i.e., make a market in) government securities are the heart of the government securities market. The general public plays a relatively small role; the principal participants are the dealers and institutional investors of all sorts.

As of this writing, the government securities market is not directly regulated by the SEC, the FRB, or the Treasury Department. The SEC exercises some control over the marketplace through its antifraud powers,[7] and the FRB is able to exercise a degree of control over the primary dealers, that is, the 36 securities firms and banks with which the FRB deals directly.[8] However, because of the recent insolvency of several government securities dealers, and the detrimental effect such failures are viewed as having had on the marketplace, Congress is now considering whether to impose a pervasive regulatory scheme on the govern-

---

[5]*See generally* 31 C.F.R. pt. 346 (1985). Individual retirement bonds may be purchased only by individuals for retirement plans. 31 C.F.R. § 346.0 (1985).

[6]For a discussion of the entire government securities market, see M. STIGUM, THE MONEY MARKET (rev. ed. 1983).

[7]Securities Act of 1933 § 17, 15 U.S.C. § 77q (1982); SEA § 10, 15 U.S.C. § 78j (1982).

[8]*Failure of Bevill, Bresler & Shulman, A New Jersey Government Securities Dealer: Hearings Before a Subcomm. of the House Comm. on Government Operations*, 99th Cong. 1st Sess. 162-90 (1985) (statement of E. Gerald Corrigan, President, FRBNY).

ment securities market.[9] Although the regulation of trading in government securities is beyond the scope of this book, direct regulation could modify both the operations of the government securities market and the nature of the trading that takes place, possibly affecting the tax treatment of some transactions.

§ 2.1 TYPES OF SECURITIES

(a) TREASURY SECURITIES

The Treasury issues several types of securities to meet the borrowing needs of the United States. By a significant measure, the Treasury is the largest issuer of debt securities in the world. Most Treasury securities are negotiable, although some, such as savings bonds and special issues sold to foreign central banks and government trust funds, are not negotiable.[10] In recent years, the size of Treasury issues has been increasing rapidly, making the role of the dealers that distribute and make a market in these securities, and of the institutions (including foreign institutions) that purchase these securities, increasingly important.[11] Some of the attractions of Treasury securities for purchasers include low credit risk, high liquidity, and an ability to finance a very high percentage of the purchase price.[12] In addition, interest income earned on Treasury securities is not taxable by state and local governments.[13]

(1) TREASURY BILLS

Treasury bills are noninterest bearing debt obligations that have a maturity of one year or less.[14] Treasury bills are issued at a discount from face value and are redeemed at maturity for face value.[15] The Treasury

---

[9]See, e.g.s, H.R. 2032 and S. 936, 99th Cong., 1st Sess. (1985). See generally REGULATION OF THE GOVERNMENT SECURITIES MARKET, REPORT BY THE SECURITIES AND EXCHANGE COMMISSION TO THE SUBCOMMITTEE ON TELECOMMUNICATIONS, CONSUMER PROTECTION AND FINANCE OF THE COMMITTEE ON ENERGY AND COMMERCE OF THE U.S. HOUSE OF REPRESENTATIVES (June 20, 1985).

[10]McCurdy, The Dealer Market for U.S. Securities, in FINANCIAL MARKETS, INSTRUMENTS AND CONCEPTS 131 (J. Brick ed. 1981).

[11]FEDERAL RESERVE BANK OF RICHMOND, INSTRUMENTS OF THE MONEY MARKET 37-40 (T. Cook & B. Summers eds. 1981).

[12]M. STIGUM, supra note 6, at 31.

[13]31 U.S.C. § 3124 (1982); see section 28.1(a).

[14]31 U.S.C. § 3104 (1982); 31 C.F.R. § 309.1 (1985).

[15]31 C.F.R. §§ 309.1, .2 (1985).

does not set the discount; rather, the FRB conducts competitive auctions for each new issue, with the bills being sold to the highest bidders.[16] Bids (or tenders) may be either competitive or noncompetitive. Noncompetitive bids are accepted at a price equal to the average of the competitive bids accepted by the Treasury.[17] All bills are noncertificated and trade through the FRB book entry system.[18]

(2) TREASURY NOTES

Treasury notes are interest bearing debt obligations[19] issued at or very near face value. They bear fixed interest, which is payable semiannually. Treasury notes mature in one to 10 years.[20] They are redeemed at maturity at face value.[21] Notes are sold by the FRB at competitive auctions similar to those used for Treasury bills; the purchasers, however, bid yields, and those bidding the lowest yields are sold the Treasury notes.[22] The fixed interest coupon rate is based on the weighted average of the yields the Treasury has accepted to the nearest eighth of one percent, provided that the price cannot exceed par. All notes are now noncertificated and trade through the FRB book entry system.[23]

(3) TREASURY BONDS

Treasury bonds are interest bearing obligations[24] issued at or very near face value. They are redeemed at maturity at face value. Negotiable bonds mature more than 10 years from the date of issue. Interest is payable semiannually. Treasury bonds can be issued on a call option basis, whereby the Treasury reserves the right to redeem the bonds on four months' notice. The interest rate on new Treasury bonds is determined at competitive auctions held by the FRB; the purchasers that

---

[16]HOUSE COMMITTEE ON ENERGY AND COMMERCE, GOVERNMENT SECURITIES ACT OF 1985, H.R. REP. NO. 258, 99th Cong., 1st Sess. 13 (1985).

[17]31 C.F.R. § 309.10 (1985). For a description of the characteristics and trading of Treasury bills, see Stigum, *Money Market Instruments, supra* note 1, at 220–32.

[18]Under the book entry system, no certificates are issued for the securities. Rather, ownership records are maintained by the FRB. Banks with accounts at the FRB "hold" the securities and record keeping and transfer are accomplished solely by computer. 31 C.F.R. pt. 350 (1985). *See generally* M. STIGUM, *supra* note 6, at 429–30.

[19]31 U.S.C. § 3103(a) (1982).

[20]31 U.S.C. § 3103(a) (1982); 31 C.F.R. § 344.1(b)(2) (1985).

[21]Stigum & Fabozzi, *U.S. Treasury Obligations, supra* note 1, at 264.

[22]*Id.* at 261–64.

[23]For a discussion of Treasury notes generally, see M. STIGUM, *supra* note 6, at 53–60.

[24]31 U.S.C. § 3102 (1982 & Supp. II 1984).

bid the lowest yields are sold the Treasury bonds.[25] New bonds are issued through the FRB book entry system; older bonds trade in certificated ("physical") form but may be converted to book entry format.

(4) NONMARKETABLE SECURITIES

The most common nonmarketable securities issued by the Treasury are savings bonds. The Treasury currently issues two types: Series EE (which replaced Series E on January 1, 1980)[26] and Series HH (which replaced Series H on January 1, 1980).[27]

The maturity of a Series EE bond is 11 years (in contrast to that of a Series E bond, which was five years). Series EE bonds are zero coupon bonds. That is, interest is not paid currently. Rather, the bonds are issued at a discount (currently 50 percent of face amount) and are redeemable at face amount on maturity. The difference between the redemption value and the purchase price is interest income to the investor. A cash basis taxpayer, however, has an election either to recognize the increase in redemption value in the tax year it accrues or to delay tax liability until the bond is redeemed.[28] Interest income is not taxable at the state or local level. Series EE bonds are issued in registered form[29] and cannot be transferred or pledged as collateral.[30]

Series HH bonds, referred to as "current income bonds," have a maturity of 10 years and pay interest on a current basis, semiannually. At the present time, Series HH bonds are only issued in exchange for Series E and EE bonds.[31] Unlike Series EE bonds, no election is available for holders of Series HH bonds to defer recognition of interest income at the federal level. Interest income is not taxable at the state or local level.[32] Series HH bonds are issued in registered form and cannot be transferred or pledged as collateral.[33]

---

[25] 31 C.F.R. § 340.0 (1985); Stigum & Fabozzi, *U.S. Treasury Obligations, supra* note 1, at 261–64.

[26] 31 C.F.R. §§ 351.0, 353.0 (1985).

[27] 31 C.F.R. §§ 352.0, 353.0 (1985).

[28] *See* section 28.1(a)(2)(i).

[29] 31 C.F.R. § 351.8 (1985); *see* section 28.1(a)(2)(i).

[30] 31 C.F.R. §§ 353.15, .16 (1985). *See generally* Stigum & Fabozzi, *U.S. Treasury Obligations, supra* note 1, at 267–69.

[31] 31 C.F.R. § 352.0 (1985).

[32] 31 C.F.R. § 352.10 (1985); *see* section 28.1(a)(2)(ii).

[33] 31 C.F.R. §§ 353.15, .16 (1984). *See generally* Stigum & Fabozzi, *U.S. Treasury Obligations, supra* note 1, at 268.

(b) FEDERAL AGENCY SECURITIES

Various federal agencies have been established by Congress to assure that credit is available to specific sectors of the economy.[34] These agencies generally borrow funds and, in turn, use these funds to make loans to specific types of borrowers. All federal agencies, except nine with specific legislative authority, do their borrowing from the Federal Financing Bank, a government institution supervised by the Secretary of the Treasury.[35] The nine agencies that are authorized to issue or guarantee securities[36] do so in basically two ways: by issuing conventional debt securities (both discount and interest bearing), and by issuing and guaranteeing various types of MBSs.

Federal agency securities can be attractive to investors for several reasons.[37] First, the credit risk is viewed as minimal because agencies are either explicitly backed or viewed as implicitly backed by the federal government. (Regardless of the formal nature of the backing, it seems extremely unlikely that the federal government would allow a default to occur on any agency security.) Second, even though agency securities are not as liquid as Treasury securities, agency securities are generally more liquid than other types of money market instruments. Third, federal agency securities that are viewed as obligations of the United States are exempt from state and local taxation.[38]

Agency securities are issued through a fiscal agent who sells them to dealers that, in turn, distribute the securities to investors and make a secondary market in them. Because agency securities are issued pursuant to congressional authorization, they, like Treasury securities, are exempt from registration with the SEC.[39] A discussion of the most commonly traded federal agency securities follows.

(1) FHLB SECURITIES

To provide liquidity to the thrift institutions that are its members, the FHLB system issues consolidated bonds and consolidated notes. The

---

[34]*See generally* Howell, *Federally Sponsored Credit Agency Securities, supra* note 11, at 20.

[35]12 U.S.C. §§ 2281–2296 (1982).

[36]The federal agencies now issuing or guaranteeing securities sold to the public are: FHLB, FHLMC, FNMA, Federal Land Banks, Federal Intermediate Credit Banks, Banks for Cooperatives, Farm Credit Banks, SLMA, and GNMA.

[37]*See generally* M. STIGUM, *supra* note 6, at 224–25.

[38]31 U.S.C. § 3124 (1982).

[39]Securities Act of 1933 § 3, 15 U.S.C. § 77c (1982).

bonds have a maturity of a year or more, pay interest semiannually, and are not callable. The notes have maturities between 30 days and one year and are issued at a discount. The bonds and notes are "consolidated" because they are the joint obligation of all 12 Federal Home Loan Banks. FHLB securities are not guaranteed by the United States government. Interest income on FHLB securities is exempt from state and local taxation.[40]

(2) GNMA SECURITIES

GNMA ("Ginnie Mae") is a government corporation within the Department of HUD.[41] Its most significant securities program involves its guarantee of mortgage-backed securities.[42] GNMA does not itself issue MBSs; rather, private mortgage institutions assemble pools of mortgages and then sell securities representing undivided interests in these pools. GNMA guarantees the timely payment of principal and interest on these securities.[43] More than a thousand firms are approved GNMA issuers, and approximately 90 securities dealers market the securities.[44] In 1984, more than $27 billion of GNMA securities were issued.[45]

GNMA guaranteed MBSs are "pass-through" securities; that is, payments of principal and interest on the mortgages in the underlying pools are passed through (minus servicing fees) to the security holders.[46] Interest is paid monthly on the unpaid principal amount of the mortgages at the securities' stated certificate rate (or at an adjustable rate in the case of GNMA's GPM program). Scheduled principal amortization and any prepayments of principal are also paid monthly. Although the stated maturity of a pass-through certificate generally equals that of the longest

---

[40]For FHLB securities generally, see 12 U.S.C. §§ 1451–1459 (1982 & Supp. I 1983 & Supp. II 1984).

[41]On GNMA generally, see 12 U.S.C. §§ 1716–1724 (1982 & Supp. I 1983 & Supp. II 1984).

[42]*See generally* GNMA, U.S. DEPARTMENT OF HOUSING AND URBAN DEVELOPMENT, GNMA MORTGAGE-BACKED SECURITIES 3 (1984).

[43]The authority of GNMA "to guarantee the timely payment of principal and interest on such trust certificates or other securities . . . based on and backed by a trust or pool composed of mortgages . . ." insured by the Federal Housing Administration, the Farmer's Home Administration, or the Veterans Administration is provided at 12 U.S.C. § 1721(g) (1982).

[44]K. LORE, MORTGAGE-BACKED SECURITIES, DEVELOPMENT AND TRENDS IN THE SECONDARY MORTGAGE MARKET ch. 2, at 4 (Clark Boardman, Securities Law Series 1985).

[45]*Id.*

[46]On mortgage pass-through securities generally, see Sullivan, Collins & Smilow, *Mortgage Pass-Through Securities,* in HANDBOOK OF MORTGAGE-BACKED SECURITIES 101 (F. Fabozzi ed. 1985).

component mortgage, actual maturities are generally less because of prepayments.[47]

The two principal GNMA/MBS programs are GNMA I (the original program begun in 1970) and GNMA II (introduced in July 1983). All mortgages in a given pool in the GNMA I program have the same interest rate; mortgages in a pool in the GNMA II program may have interest rates that vary within a one percent range. Checks for principal and interest are mailed to the registered owners by the issuer in the case of the GNMA I program, and by GNMA's collateral paying agent in the case of the GNMA II program. Further, GNMA II pools (unlike GNMA I pools) may have multiple issuers.[48] GNMA has several additional programs,[49] the most significant of which is its GPM program, which is based on graduated payment mortgages.[50] Because payments on the underlying mortgages are not level, GNMA/GPM pass-through securities have smaller payments in the early years that cause the mortgage balance to increase for a period. Given their variable cash flow and initial negative amortization,[51] GNMA/GPM pass-through securities are complex investment vehicles.

All GNMA securities are guaranteed by the United States government as to timely payment of interest and amortized principal (i.e., they are fully modified) and are certificated.[52] Interest on GNMA securities is not exempt from state and local taxation.[53]

(3) FNMA SECURITIES

FNMA ("Fannie Mae") is a federally chartered, private, for-profit corporation that is fully subject to federal income tax. Its stock trades on the NYSE, and 13 of its 18 directors are elected by stockholders. (The remaining five are appointed by the President.) FNMA receives no gov-

---

[47]For a summary of the terms of the various types of GNMA/MBSs, see Senft, *Pass-Through Securities, supra* note 1, 514–26.

[48]For a discussion of the difference between the GNMA I and GNMA II programs, see K. Lore, *supra* note 44, ch. 2, at 5–11.

[49]Sullivan, Collins & Smilow, *Mortgage Pass-Through Securities, supra* note 46, at 103–07.

[50]For a discussion of the terms of GNMA/GPMs, see Senft, *Pass-Through Securities, supra* note 1, at 516–17.

[51]*See generally* Sullivan, Collins & Smilow, *Mortgage Pass-Through Securities, supra* note 46, at 106–07.

[52]Although transactions in GNMA securities now settle through the physical delivery of certificates, there are plans for the immobilization of GNMA certificates in the depository division of the privately owned Mortgage-Backed Securities Clearing Corporation. Zigas, *Ginnie Mae Will Use MBS for Clearance of Its Securities,* THE BOND BUYER, Apr. 11, 1985, at 1, col. 3.

[53]*See* section 28.1(b); section 28.4.

ernment subsidy or appropriations, although the Treasury is authorized to purchase up to $2.25 billion of its debt.[54]

FNMA's basic programs involve the purchase and sale of insured or guaranteed and (since 1970) conventional mortgages.[55] In effect, FNMA buys when mortgage money is in short supply and sells when demand softens.[56] FNMA's primary means of financing its mortgage purchase activities is through the sale of debentures and short-term discount notes. FNMA debentures are noncertificated and trade through the FRB book entry system.[57] Interest is paid semiannually. FNMA securities are not guaranteed by the United States government, and interest income from them is not exempt from state or local taxation.

Since 1981, FNMA has been an issuer of mortgage-backed pass-through securities. It issues MBSs basically in two ways: directly to purchasers, or in "swap" transactions whereby it exchanges its pass-through securities (backed by the mortages it is receiving) with participating lenders.[58] The "swapped" securities may then be held or sold by the lenders. Interest and principal payments on FNMA/MBSs are made monthly. Interest rates on the mortgages in a pool may vary but must be between 0.5 percent and 2.5 percent higher than the coupon rate.[59] FNMA guarantees timely payment of principal and interest, that is, the pass-through securities are fully modified. FNMA pass-through securities are registered, and, since May 1, 1985, are issued in book entry form through the FRB's wire system.[60]

(4) FHLMC SECURITIES

FHLMC ("Freddie Mac") is a federally chartered agency established in 1970 to provide liquidity to the residential mortgage market.[61] Its nonvoting common stock is held by the 12 Federal Home Loan Banks; its preferred stock is held by savings and loan associations; and since Jan-

[54]On FNMA generally, see 12 U.S.C. §§ 1716–1723h (1982 & Supp. I 1983 & Supp. II 1984).

[55]On FNMA mortgage purchase programs, see generally Thygerson, *Federal Government-Related Mortgage Purchasers*, in THE HANDBOOK OF MORTGAGE BANKING, A GUIDE TO THE SECONDARY MORTGAGE MARKET 60–64 (1985); K. LORE, *supra* note 44, ch. 2, at 15–24.

[56]M. STIGUM, *supra* note 6, at 218.

[57]Stigum, *Securities of Federal Government Agencies and Sponsored Corporations*, *supra* note 1, at 278.

[58]*See generally* K. LORE, *supra* note 44, ch. 2, at 19–24.

[59]On the terms of FNMA/MBSs, see generally Senft, *Pass-Through Securities*, *supra* note 1, at 523–25.

[60]K. LORE, *supra* note 44, at 2–23.

[61]Emergency Home Finance Act of 1970, Pub. L. 91-351, § 303, 12 U.S.C. § 1452, *amended by* Pub. L. 96-153, § 316(b), 93 Stat. 1101, 1118 (1979), *amended by* Pub. L. 98-369, § 177(a), 98 Stat. 494, 709 (1984).

uary 1985, its participating preferred stock trades on the NYSE. As of 1984, FHLMC is fully subject to federal income tax.[62]

FHLMC buys mortgages only from federally insured financial institutions and FHA mortgagees approved by HUD.[63] FHLMC finances its mortgage purchase activities in two ways.[64] The first, and less significant, is through the sale of discount notes and debentures. (This program was not begun until 1981.) FHLMC discount notes are sold with maturities of one year or less. FHLMC debentures are noncertificated and trade through the FRB book entry system.[65] FHLMC securities are not guaranteed by the United States government and interest income from them is not exempt from state or local taxation.[66]

The second financing technique employed by FHLMC is the sale of MBSs. FHLMC currently sells two types of MBSs, both of which are issued in registered form.[67] The first is a pass-through security called a mortgage participation certificate ("PC"). The monthly payments and other features of PCs are similar to GNMA pass-through certificates. Unlike GNMA pass-throughs, however, PCs are issued by FHLMC rather than individual mortgage lenders. The holder of a PC has an undivided interest in a pool of conventional (30- or 15-year) level payment residential mortgages previously purchased by FHLMC.[68] The underlying pool may contain mortgages issued at different interest rates. FHLMC issues PCs by selling them directly to investors ("standard program") or by "swapping" them for pooled mortgages with mortgage originators ("guarantor program"). FHLMC/PCs are guaranteed by FHLMC as to timely payment of interest but only eventual (i.e., within one year) payment of principal, thus, the securities are modified pass-throughs, not fully modified.[69] PCs are being converted to book entry.[70]

The second type of mortgage-related security issued by FHLMC is a collateralized mortgage obligation ("CMO"). The CMO is a pay-through obligation rather than a pass-through obligation. That is, the CMO con-

[62]DRA, Pub. L. 98-369, § 177, 98 Stat. 494, 709–12 (1984); see section 22.9(d).

[63]*Federal Secondary Mortgage Finance Programs*, 3 HOUS. & DEV. REP. (BNA) 70:0012 (Aug. 15, 1977).

[64]*See generally* K. LORE, *supra* note 44, ch. 2, at 24–29.

[65]M. STIGUM, *supra* note 6, at 221.

[66]*See* section 22.9(d); section 25.5(b).

[67]FHLMC has in the past issued a third type of MBS, guaranteed mortgage certificates or GMCs. *See generally* M. STIGUM, *supra* note 6, at 220–21. FHLMC has not issued GMCs since 1979. Senft, *Pass-Through Securities, supra* note 47, at 523.

[68]On the terms of PCs generally, see Senft, *Pass-Through Securities, supra* note 1, at 522–23; Sullivan, Collins & Smilow, *Mortgage Pass-Through Securities, supra* note 46, at 104–05, 108.

[69]*See generally* M. STIGUM, *supra* note 6, at 220–21.

[70]K. LORE, *supra* note 44, ch. 2, at 30.

stitutes an obligation or debt of FHLMC (secured by a pool of mortgage loans pledged as collateral) rather than an undivided beneficial ownership interest in the mortgage loan pool.[71] Begun in 1983 by FHLMC, CMOs are perhaps the most important development in the mortgage-backed securities area in recent years.[72]

The key feature of a CMO is that it is issued with two or more (typically four) classes (or "tranches"), each tranche having a different interest rate and scheduled maturity. Accordingly, CMOs are often referred to as multiclass pay-through bonds.[73] Unlike GNMA/MBSs and FHLMC/PCs, interest and principal on the collateral mortgage pool for FHLMC/CMOs is not passed through pro rata to the security holders. Rather, each tranche of a CMO is assigned a separate priority (in the trust indenture) with respect to receipt of the cash flow from the pledged collateral.[74] Interest rates and maturities of a CMO, therefore, are not tied to the interest rates or maturities of the mortgage loans serving as collateral.

The first or shorter-term tranches are allocated initial priorities to assure early maturity. The last tranche, called an "accreting or accrual bond," "compound interest bond," "zero coupon CMO," or "Z bond," normally does not pay interest or principal until maturity. Cash flow from the collateral underlying a CMO is used first to pay current interest on the interest bearing tranches; excess cash flow is allocated to repay the first tranche. After repayment of the first tranche, the process is repeated until all tranches have been paid in full.

One of the principal attractions of the CMO is the ability of the issuer, in this case FHLMC, to allocate cash flow to meet the investment objectives of different investors and provide a measure of call protection for investors desiring longer maturities.[75] FHLMC/CMOs, sometimes called "fast pay/slow pay" bonds, may be structured to provide investors a wide array of choices of expected average lives and discounts from par.

(5) FARM CREDIT AGENCIES' SECURITIES

The United States Farm Credit System consists of Federal Land Banks, Federal Intermediate Credit Banks, and Banks for Cooperatives.[76] At

---

[71] *See generally id.* ch. 3, at 17–21; Sullivan, Miller & Kiggins, *Mortgage-Backed Bonds, supra* note 46, at 167–200.

[72] K. LORE, *supra* note 44, ch. 3, at 17.

[73] Sullivan, Miller & Kiggins, *Mortgage-Backed Bonds, supra* note 46, at 167.

[74] FHLMC/CMOs generally use mortgages as collateral; private CMOs now typically use GNMA/MBSs or FHLMC/PCs as collateral. *Id.* at 172.

[75] *Id.* at 176.

[76] *See generally* Stigum, *Securities of Federal Government Agencies and Sponsored Corporations, supra* note 1, at 281–84.

present, the only securities issued by the three Farm Credit Banks are Consolidated Systemwide discount notes and bonds. Interest income on these notes and bonds is exempt from state and local taxation.[77] Prior to 1977, the individual components of the Farm Credit System also issued securities. Federal Land Banks issued Consolidated Federal Farm Loan bonds, interest on which is exempt from state and local taxation.[78] Federal Intermediate Credit Banks (the only privately owned members of the Farm Credit System) issued consolidated collateral trust debentures, interest on which is not exempt from state and local taxation.[79] And Banks for Cooperatives issued consolidated collateral trust debentures, interest on which is exempt from state and local taxation.[80] None of these securities are guaranteed directly or indirectly by the United States government.

(6) SLMA SECURITIES

SLMA ("Sallie Mae") is a government sponsored corporation established to administer student loans guaranteed by the United States government.[81] Although SLMA is authorized to borrow from the Federal Financing Bank (its obligations being guaranteed by the Department of Health, Education, and Welfare), it also issues securities directly to the public.[82] The most important of these securities for investors are short-term floating rate notes. SLMA issues notes monthly. Interest is exempt from state and local taxation.[83]

§ 2.2   TYPES OF TRANSACTIONS

(a) OUTRIGHT PURCHASES AND SALES

Government securities can be purchased or sold in outright transactions. Regular way settlement for government securities depends upon the type of security. Wireable securities (i.e., noncertificated securities that trade through the FRB book entry system, other than FNMA and

---

[77] 12 U.S.C. §§ 2055, 2079, 2134 (1982).

[78] 12 U.S.C. § 2055 (1982).

[79] *See generally* 12 U.S.C. §§ 2071–2098 (1982).

[80] 12 U.S.C. § 2134 (1982).

[81] 20 U.S.C. § 1087-2 (1982).

[82] 20 U.S.C. § 1087-2(h) (1982).

[83] *See generally* 20 U.S.C. § 1087-2 (1982).

FHLMC/MBSs) typically settle the next business day. FNMA and FHLMC securities and physical securities other than GNMAs typically have a corporate settlement cycle, that is, five business days. GNMAs generally settle once each month. There is also a cash (i.e., same day settlement) market for government securities. As with other forms of contracts generally, special settlement terms can be negotiated between the parties.

(b) FORWARD TRANSACTIONS

There is an active forward market for certain government securities, particularly GNMA/MBSs and FHLMC/PCs. (In addition, the trading of government securities on a when-issued basis is, in effect, a type of forward trading.)[84] Forward contracts are privately negotiated agreements for the purchase or sale of a specified type of government security at a fixed price for delivery at an agreed upon date in the future. Generally, forward contracts once made are not freely transferable. The parties to a forward contract usually intend settlement to occur through actual delivery of the underlying government security.

Typically, no consideration is paid by one party to the other upon entering into a forward contract for government securities. Payment is to be made in full at delivery. Under such an arrangement, each party assumes the entire risk of the other party's default and failure to perform the agreement.[85] In recent years, however, there has been a growing trend among dealers to require mark-to-market payments or margin payments on forward contracts.

A forward contract for government securities ordinarily can be closed before maturity only by offset or cancellation, both of which require the consent of the other party. In an offsetting transaction, a taxpayer who had, for example, entered into a long contract, would terminate his obligation by entering into a short contract with the same party for the same securities on the same delivery date. Because the two contract obligations "offset" one another, neither party is obligated to go through the formality of taking or making delivery. The taxpayer's gain or loss is measured by the difference between the two contract prices for the government securities. The other way of closing a forward contract requires the other side to the transaction to "cancel" the contract. Under current law, the taxpayer's gain or loss on cancellation is capital gain or loss for taxpayers who are neither dealers nor hedgers, and is ordinary

---

[84]*See* section 2.2(d).

[85]*See generally* REPORT OF THE JOINT TREASURY-SEC-FEDERAL RESERVE STUDY OF THE GOVERNMENT-RELATED SECURITIES MARKETS, 96TH CONG., 2D SESS. (Comm. Print 1980).

income for dealers and hedgers. It is not settled whether pre-ERTA gain or loss on cancellation was always ordinary.[86]

(c) REPURCHASE AGREEMENTS AND REVERSE REPURCHASE AGREEMENTS

Repurchase agreements ("repos") and reverse repurchase agreements ("reverse repos" or "reverses") are essentially secured loans.[87] In a repo, the borrower sells securities and agrees to repurchase equivalent securities from the other party (i.e., the lenders) at a future date. The securities are either repurchased at the same price, with charges representing an agreed upon interest rate added to the principal at the maturity of the contract, or at a (predetermined) price higher than the sale price. A reverse repo is simply a repo looked at from the lender's side; for example, a dealer lending money and receiving securities has entered into a reverse repo. Repos and reverse repos can be overnight, for a longer specified period (term repos), or open. Open repos generally can be terminated by either side on one business day's notice. The lender (i.e., the party who has purchased the securities) may or may not take physical possession of the securities and, depending on the terms of the agreement and the type of securities involved, may or may not reregister the securities in his name.

The use of purchase and sale terminology in repo transactions, rather than the terminology of secured loans serves a number of purposes. First, repos, unlike secured loans, may be closed out in the event of bankruptcy without violation of the automatic stay.[88] Second, the use of purchase and sale terminology permits municipalities and the FRB to "lend" money that they otherwise could not.[89] Finally, purchases and sales provide participants greater flexibility with less paperwork than secured loans. Because of these advantages, repos and reverses are extensively used by dealers to finance government securities positions, by the FRB to increase or decrease bank revenues, and by institutional investors and state and local governments to borrow and lend money.[90]

Despite the sale and repurchase terminology, a repo transaction is on one side a loan and on the other a borrowing. The securities sold are collateral for the loan; the party making the loan (i.e., taking in or

---

[86]*See generally* Chapter 46.

[87]M. STIGUM, *supra* note 6, at 396.

[88]11 U.S.C. § 362(b) (Supp. II 1984).

[89]*E.g.,* 12 U.S.C. § 1464(c) (Supp. I 1983 & Supp. II 1984).

[90]For a discussion of repos and reverse repos, see M. STIGUM, *supra* note 6, at 395.

purchasing securities) has an asset and the party borrowing (i.e., selling securities) has a liability. The profit or loss on a repo transaction should be treated as interest income or interest expense.[91]

(d) WHEN-ISSUED

There is an active when-issued or wi market for Treasury and agency securities. When-issued trading occurs during the period between the announcement of an auction of Treasury bills, notes, or bonds and the day on which they are actually issued, that is, the settlement date. For notes and bonds that are sold through yield auctions, trading before the auction necessarily involves trading coupon securities without knowing the coupon. Trades made on a yield basis prior to auction must be priced after the auction, based on the coupon determined at the auction.[92]

Federal agency securities trade on a when-issued basis from several days to two weeks after they are priced and sold. The period for when-issued trading for agency securities was much longer when actual certificates were printed and issued. Now, however, most agency securities, except GNMAs, are issued in book entry form.[93]

(e) ZERO COUPON SECURITIES

Zero coupon securities or zeros are Treasury notes and bonds that have had their coupons removed. This "stripping" creates two different types of securities: the principal or corpus, which is sold as a discounted instrument paying no interest, and the coupons, each of which can be sold separately at a different price based on its own maturity and consequent yield.

Trading in zeros started in 1982 with private securities firms selling receipts against the "stripped bond" and each coupon payment.[94] These "private" zeros include Merrill Lynch's TIGRs and Salomon Brothers' CATS. On February 15, 1985 the Treasury began issuing zero coupon bonds directly, its so-called STRIPS.

Zeros are attractive for a number of reasons. First, they provide a guaranteed reinvestment rate over the life of the bond. Second, there

---

[91]*See* section 27.10.

[92]*See generally* M. STIGUM, *supra* note 6, at 432–34, 442–43, 451–52.

[93]*Id.* at 466.

[94]On zeros generally, see M. STIGUM, *supra* note 6, at 460–62.

is no call factor. And third, they offer the ability to accomplish innovative financing objectives such as "defeasance" (retiring outstanding fixed-income debt by matching it to the cash flow from the new securities), "immunization" (producing a portfolio of bonds with no reinvestment risk), and "dedication" (matching cash flows over a future liability stream).[95] Because of their tax treatment,[96] zeros are particularly attractive to foreign investors and United States tax-exempt investors.

§ 2.3 CREDIT REGULATION

The FRB does not have rule making authority with respect to the extension or maintenance of credit on exempted securities.[97] Consequently, Regulation T (which relates to the extension of credit by broker-dealers) and Regulation U (which relates to the extension of credit by banks)[98] provides that initial margin for the purchase of an exempted security is set by the creditor in good faith.[99] In general, an exempted security is defined to include a direct obligation of, or obligation guaranteed as to principal or interest by, the United States government, and certain federal agency securities.[100] All of the securities discussed in this chapter (except privately sponsored zeros) are exempted securities. The initial margin for a short sale of an exempted security is 100 percent of its current market value plus whatever additional amount the broker may require for his protection.[101]

Under the maintenance margin requirements of the NYSE, customers of members using margin accounts must maintain equity in their accounts of not less than five percent of the principal amount of Treasury securities and agency securities unconditionally guaranteed by the United States.[102] The minimum margin on other agency securities is 15 percent of the principal amount of the obligation or 25 percent of the market value, whichever amount is less, unless, upon written application, the

[95]*Interest Rate Markets Become Real Zoo*, FUTURES, Nov. 1985, at 68.

[96]*See* section 27.5.

[97]SEA § 7, 15 U.S.C. § 78g(a) (1982).

[98]*See generally* section 1.4.

[99]12 C.F.R. §§ 220.18(b), 221.8(b) (1985).

[100]SEA § 3(a)(12), 15 U.S.C. § 78c(a)(12) (1982).

[101]12 C.F.R. § 220.18(e) (1985).

[102]2 NYSE GUIDE (CCH) Rule 431(c)(2)(A), ¶ 2431 (Sept. 22, 1978).

exchange grants a lower requirement.[103] The NASD's maintenance margin requirements are somewhat different.[104]

§ 2.4 CLEARANCE AND SETTLEMENT

Except for older certificated bonds, Treasury securities clear and settle through the FRB book entry system. Under the book entry system, member banks hold securities in accounts at the FRB.[105] Because only banks can have such accounts, all dealers and other investors in Treasury securities must have accounts either directly or indirectly with such clearing banks. Transfer of securities in the book entry system is initiated by wire and effected on the FRB's computers. Most agency securities, other than GNMAs, are now issued in book entry form and cleared and settled in much the same way as Treasury securities. GNMAs and other certificated MBSs are cleared and settled by physical delivery or through the facilities of the MBSCC and its depository division.

---

[103]*Id.* Rule 431(c)(2)(B), ¶ 2431.

[104]*See Rules of Fair Practice,* NASD MANUAL (CCH) ¶ 2180A, § 4 (Apr. 13, 1984).

[105]M. STIGUM, *supra* note 6, at 429.

Three

Overview of the Municipal Securities Markets

§ 3.1 IN GENERAL

Debt securities issued by state and local governments and their agencies (referred to as "municipal securities" or "munis") are typically either notes, short-term obligations sold in anticipation of obtaining tax revenues or other funds, or long-term obligations issued to either finance capital projects or governmental programs, or refinance or refund short-term anticipation obligations or long-term obligations.[1] In general, municipal securities are either general obligation bonds or revenue bonds. For general obligation bonds, the payment of principal and interest is secured by the state or local government's pledge of its full faith, credit, and taxing power. Revenue bonds, on the other hand, provide for payments of principal and interest from revenues received from the facilities or projects that are financed with the proceeds of the bonds.

Most municipal securities are interest bearing, although they can also be issued in discount form. Because of the risk that a municipality will be unable to pay its obligations when due, the credit ratings of municipal issuers play a major role in the interest rates on municipal securities.

[1] For a discussion of municipal securities, see generally R. Lamb & S. Rappaport, Municipal Bonds (1980); Public Securities Association, Fundamentals of Municipal Bonds (rev. ed. 1982); M. Stigum, The Money Market (rev. ed. 1983) 649–70; The Municipal Bond Handbook (in two volumes) (F. Fabozzi, S. Feldstein, F. Zarb & I. Pollack eds. 1983).

Municipalities with strong credit ratings can issue securities with lower interest rates and, hence, have lower borrowing costs. In general, publicly offered municipal securities are rated for creditworthiness by Moody's Investors Service and Standard & Poor's.

A major attraction for purchasers of municipal securities is that interest income is exempt from federal income taxation[2] and may be exempt from state taxation. The federal tax exemption and, if available, the state tax exemption generally allow municipal securities to be issued at lower yields than government securities.[3] For municipal securities issued after 1982, securities with a maturity at issuance in excess of 12 months are subject to federal income taxation on interest income unless the securities are issued in registered form.[4]

Despite the broad tax exemption contained in the Code, interest on certain municipal securities (e.g., industrial development bonds, mortgage subsidy bonds, and bonds that are deemed to be arbitrage bonds) might not be exempt from tax. In addition, proposals are frequently introduced in Congress to repeal or limit the tax exemption for certain municipal securities.[5] Recently, certain municipal securities have been structured and issued as taxable, rather than tax-exempt, securities. For example, in December of 1985, Los Angeles County refinanced part of its capital requirements by selling taxable securities.[6] Simply stated, the Los Angeles County securities are taxable because they do not meet statutory arbitrage restrictions, which classifies the securities as so-called arbitrage bonds.[7]

New issues of municipal securities are offered for sale through public offerings and private placements. Most states require their general obligation bonds to be issued through a competitive bidding procedure, although competitive bidding is not usually required for revenue bonds.[8] Although municipal securities are subject to the antifraud provisions of the Securities Act, they are exempt from the registration requirements

[2]See section 28.2(b). Congressional proposals would eliminate many of the tax benefits presently available to owners of certain municipal securities. See, e.g., Tax Reform Act of 1985, H.R. 3838, 99th Cong., 1st Sess. (1985).

[3]See generally Chapter Two.

[4]I.R.C. § 103(j); see section 27.11; section 28.2(b)(1)(i)(b).

[5]See, e.g.s, 1985 Tax Reform, President's Tax Proposals to the Congress for Fairness, Growth, and Simplicity, STAN. FED. TAX REP. (CCH) Rep. No. 25, Extra Ed., ch. 11 (May 29, 1985); Tax Reform Act of 1985, supra note 2, § 701.

[6]See Carlson, Los Angeles County Discovers Benefits in Taxable Securities, Wall St. J., Dec. 10, 1985, at 33, col. 1. In addition, the Indiana Housing Authority also issued taxable securities in December of 1985.

[7]For a discussion of arbitrage bonds, see section 28.2(b)(1)(i)(e).

[8]Feldstein & Fabozzi, Tax-Exempt Securities, in THE HANDBOOK OF FIXED INCOME SECURITIES 404 (F. Fabozzi & I. Pollack eds. 1983).

imposed on the offering of securities.[9] However, the Municipal Securities Rule Making Board (the self-regulatory organization for municipal securities brokers and dealers) has issued rules of practice that impose financial disclosure requirements for municipal securities.[10] The secondary market for municipal securities is the over-the-counter market, which consists of a number of closely linked brokers and dealers who specialize in municipal securities. The municipal securities market is regulated by the SEC, NASD, FRB, bank regulatory agencies, and the Municipal Securities Rule Making Board.

§ 3.2   TYPES OF SECURITIES

(a)   GENERAL OBLIGATION BONDS

General obligation bonds are secured by the issuing municipality's general taxing powers.[11] Some general obligation bonds are also secured by certain identified fees or charges, which provide an additional source of revenue to secure the bonds. Interest on general obligation bonds is tax-exempt.[12]

(b)   REVENUE BONDS

Revenue bonds are usually issued by a municipality to finance or refinance a particular project.[13] The municipality pledges the revenues generated by the project to meet interest and principal payment obligations, but it does not pledge its full taxing power in support of its payment obligations. Interest on revenue bonds is tax-exempt.[14]

(c)   INDUSTRIAL DEVELOPMENT BONDS

IDBs are a type of revenue bond issued by a municipality for industrial or commercial purposes, where a major part of the project or facility

---

[9]Securities Act of 1933 § 3(a)(2), 15 U.S.C. § 77c(a)(2) (1982).

[10]*See generally* Mitchell, *Disclosure and the Municipal Bond Industry*, in 1 THE MUNICIPAL BOND HANDBOOK, *supra* note 1, at 623.

[11]*See generally* R. LAMB & S. RAPPAPORT, *supra* note 1, pt. 2; Kahn, *The Legal Framework for General Obligations Bonds*, in 2 THE MUNICIPAL BOND HANDBOOK, *supra* note 1, at 87.

[12]*See* section 28.2(b)(1).

[13]*See generally* R. LAMB & S. RAPPAPORT, *supra* note 1, pt. 3; Buschman & Gibbons, *The Legal Framework for Revenue Bonds*, in 2 THE MUNICIPAL BOND HANDBOOK, *supra* note 1, at 98.

[14]*See* section 28.2(b)(1).

is leased, owned, or used by a private business and the payment of principal or interest is secured at least in a major part by the project, facility, or revenues of a nonexempt trade or business.[15] The attraction of IDB financing for a private business is that the cost of borrowing is substantially lower than it would be with other types of financing. For a discussion of IDBs, see section 28.2(a)(3).

(d) MORTGAGE SUBSIDY BONDS

Mortgage subsidy bonds are securities issued by a municipality where a significant portion of the proceeds are used directly or indirectly to provide mortgages or other financing for owner occupied residences.[16] Interest on mortgage subsidy bonds issued after April 24, 1979 is generally taxable unless the securities meet a comprehensive list of requirements with respect to the type of residence, its location, the aggregate amount of bonds, and arbitrage limits.[17] For a discussion of tax-exempt mortgage bond issues—qualified mortgage bonds and qualified veterans' mortgage bonds—see section 28.2(a)(4).

§ 3.3 FINANCING ENHANCEMENTS

Historically, municipal securities have been issued with either a serial maturity (where a portion of the debt is retired each year) or a term maturity (where the entire debt is paid at maturity or is subject to mandatory sinking fund payments prior to maturity).[18] Recently, municipalities seek to encourage investment through the use of financing enhancements, ranging from prepayment opportunities to credit enhancements.[19] Some of the more common financing enhancements for municipal securities include the following:

---

[15]See section 23.4(b); section 28.2(a)(3); *see also* Weinberg & Stock, *Industrial Development Bonds: Overview in Light of the Tax Reform Act of 1984,* 1 REAL EST. FIN. L. J. 115 (1985); Drucker & Segal, *Industrial Development Bonds—A Justifiable Sunset?* 4 MUN. FIN. J. 267 (1983); R. LAMB & S. RAPPAPORT, *supra* note 1, ch. 11.

[16]I.R.C. § 103A(b)(1).

[17]*See generally* I.R.C. § 103A.

[18]Feldstein & Fabozzi, *Tax-Exempt Securities,* in THE HANDBOOK OF FIXED INCOME SECURITIES, *supra* note 8, at 380.

[19]*See generally* Petersen & Hough, *Marketing Considerations in the Use of Creative Capital Financing Techniques,* 4 MUN. FIN. J. 117 (1983).

- Securities with put option features provide an owner the right to return the securities, usually at par, before their normal maturity.[20] Put options are attractive to purchasers as protection against rising interest rates.[21]
- Securities with warrants entitle the owners to purchase additional securities at a fixed discount amount during a specified period. Warrants are attractive to purchasers as protection against falling interest rates. They typically provide the owners with the right to buy more securities at the original terms for which the warrants were distributed.[22]
- Securities backed by insurance, guarantees, or letters of credit assure the owners of better credit risks.[23]
- Variable rate bonds (also referred to as "flexible rate" or "floating rate" bonds) have floating interest rates, generally tied to money market rates, that change on a weekly or monthly basis. Variable rate bonds are most attractive to purchasers when interest rates are increasing.[24]
- Stepped coupon securities have interest coupons that increase over the life of the bond. Starting at lower rates in the early years, these securities pay significantly higher rates in later years. At the date of this writing, stepped coupon securities have not been very successful.[25]
- Zero coupon municipal securities are issued at a deep discount and pay no interest to the owner until maturity.[26] Zero coupon securities are particularly attractive to purchasers who want to use the proceeds on maturity to fund fixed obligations.[27]

---

[20]*See* section 28.2(b)(1)(i)(c).

[21]*See generally* Feldstein & Fabozzi, *Option Tender or Put Bonds,* in 2 The Municipal Bond Handbook, *supra* note 1, at 317.

[22]*See generally* Feldstein & Fabozzi, *Municipal Bonds with Warrants,* in 2 The Municipal Bond Handbook, *supra* note 1, at 360.

[23]*See generally* Hicks, *Letter-of-Credit-Backed Bonds,* in 2 The Municipal Bond Handbook, *supra* note 1, at 330; *see* section 28.2(b)(1)(d).

[24]*See generally* Longley, *Variable Rate Bonds and Zero-Coupon Bonds,* in 1 The Municipal Bond Handbook, *supra* note 1, at 374.

[25]*See generally* Petersen & Hough, *supra* note 19, at 122–23; Roberts & Rudolph, *The "Stepped Coupon"—A New Method of Structuring Bond Issues,* 3 Mun. Fin. J. 17 (1982); Greenberg, *Stepped Coupon Bond Issues—Another Viewpoint,* 3 Mun. Fin. J. 141 (1982).

[26]*See* section 27.5(b).

[27]*See generally* Feldstein & Fabozzi, *Zero-Coupon Bonds,* in 2 The Municipal Bond Handbook, *supra* note 1, at 341.

Four

Overview of the Commodity Markets

The trading of agricultural products, energy production materials, metals, foreign currencies, and financial instruments constitute the commodity markets. There are spot and forward ("cash") markets for commodities, as well as futures markets.[1] The cash markets are dominated by dealers, commercial firms, primary producers, and users of the commodities. The futures markets are also used by these firms, although speculators (i.e., traders and investors) are the key participants in the futures markets.[2]

Regulation of the commodity markets and enforcement of the commodity laws are vested in the CFTC,[3] various commodity exchanges, and the NFA.[4] The states are authorized to enforce the CEA and the CFTC's rules.[5] The CEA appears to prohibit the states from enacting their own substantive commodity regulations by providing exclusive jurisdiction in the CFTC.[6] Several states have disputed the exclusive jurisdiction claim,[7] and have adopted rules promulgated by the North American Securities Administrators Association and the Central Secu-

---

[1] The recently developed exchange-traded commodity option market is discussed in section 5.3(a).

[2] For a discussion of market participants, see generally Chapter 6.

[3] CEA §§ 2(a)(1)(B), 2(a)(2)-(11), 7 U.S.C. §§ 2a, 4a (1982 & Supp. I 1983).

[4] CEA § 17, 7 U.S.C. § 21 (1982 & Supp. I 1983).

[5] CEA § 6d, 7 U.S.C. § 13a-2 (1982 & Supp. I 1983).

[6] CEA § 2(a)(1)(B), 7 U.S.C. § 2a (1982 & Supp. I 1983).

[7] See CEA § 12, 7 U.S.C. § 16(e) (Supp. I 1983).

rities Administrators Council governing the sale of commodity pool interests in such states.[8]

Regulation of the commodity markets is generally limited to the operations of the futures markets and the participants in these markets. Congress has generally exempted from the CEA's regulatory scheme commercial merchandising transactions in physical commodities in which delivery is delayed or deferred ("forward contracts").[9]

The commodity firms that provide brokerage services to the public, that is, FCMs and IBs, are subject to direct regulation by the CFTC. These firms are the commodity industry's counterpart of the securities industry's broker-dealers. FCMs and IBs must be members of the NFA, which is responsible for their registration and general oversight.[10] The commodity exchanges are charged with the duty of regulating their members and the transactions executed on their markets.[11] Each of the commodity exchanges has an affiliated clearing organization that regulates the clearing members of that exchange.[12]

§ 4.1 TYPES OF COMMODITIES

The CEA defines the term "commodity" to include 24 specified agricultural products "and all other goods and articles, except onions,"[13] and "all services, rights, and interests in which contracts for future delivery" ("futures contracts" or "futures") are traded.[14] By including within the statutory definition of "commodity" the phrase "all services, rights and interests" in which futures contracts are traded, the CEA in effect converts anything into a commodity if futures contracts for it are

---

[8]*See generally* North American Securities Administrators Association, Registration of Commodity Pool Programs, 1 BLUE SKY L. REP. (CCH) ¶ 5335-40A (Jan. 1, 1984); Central Securities Administrators Council, Registration of Commodity Pool Programs, 1 BLUE SKY L. REP. (CCH) ¶ 5441 (Jan. 24, 1978).

[9]CEA § 2(a)(1)(A), 7 U.S.C. § 2 (Supp. I 1983).

[10]CEA § 17, 7 U.S.C. § 21(m) (1982); NFA By-law 1101 (1983).

[11]17 C.F.R. pt. 8 (1985).

[12]*See* section 4.5(b).

[13]This peculiar exception was enacted to conform the CEA to a criminal statute enacted because speculative activity in the onion futures market was found to cause unwarranted fluctuations in the cash price of onions. SENATE COMMITTEE ON AGRICULTURE AND FORESTRY REPORT, TRADING IN ONION FUTURES—PROHIBITION, S. REP. No. 1631, 85th Cong., 2d Sess., *reprinted in* 1958 U.S. CODE CONG. & AD. NEWS 4210 (providing the rationale for adopting the criminal statute).

[14]CEA § 2(a)(1)(A), 7 U.S.C. § 2 (Supp. I 1983).

traded. For example, GNMAs are securities; however, there is trading in futures contracts for GNMAs. Hence, GNMAs are securities *and* commodities.

The CFTC's jurisdiction turns on whether or not a commodity is involved. If a product, good, or right is a commodity, the CFTC has exclusive jurisdiction over transactions in (1) futures contracts for the commodity, (2) option contracts on the commodity (unless the commodity is a security), and (3) option contracts on futures contracts for the commodity.[15] The CFTC also has jurisdiction over so-called leverage transactions in commodities.[16] With respect to the cash markets for commodities, the CFTC's authority is generally limited to enforcement actions against persons for the manipulation of commodity prices.[17] This power apparently does not extend to foreign currencies, government securities, mortgages, and mortgage purchase commitments, security rights, and other specified financial instruments.[18]

§ 4.2 TYPES OF MARKETS

(a) CASH MARKETS

The cash markets for commodities are various and enormous. The term "cash" refers to commodities purchased and sold for either immediate ("spot") or deferred ("forward") delivery.[19] Some cash markets for specific commodities are highly developed, while others are merely informal trading relationships.[20] Cash markets are off-exchange markets used primarily by merchants, producers, processors, commercial consumers, and dealers. The cash markets have no central clearing facilities. They may be organized and centralized (e.g., the stockyards), built around dealers (e.g., the precious metals markets), or exist solely because of merchant to merchant negotiation. The cash markets are, most simply, the markets in which commodities are traded by those that have them and those that want them.

---

[15] CEA § 2(a)(1)(B), 7 U.S.C. § 2a(ii) (Supp. I 1983).

[16] CEA § 19, 7 U.S.C. § 23(a) (1982).

[17] CEA §§ 6(b), 9, 7 U.S.C. §§ 9, 13(b) (Supp. I 1983).

[18] CEA § 2(a)(1), 7 U.S.C. § 2 (Supp. I 1983).

[19] CBT, COMMODITY TRADING MANUAL 7 (1985).

[20] For example, because of the high volume of trading by speculators and commercial users, a sophisticated network has developed in the metals market. This is in contrast to the simpler relationship that exists between a farmer and a grain elevator.

(b) EXCHANGE MARKETS

All futures contracts for commodities must be executed on an organized exchange or board of trade that has been designated by the CFTC as a "contract market."[21] The restriction of futures trading to contract markets is intended to provide and support an institutional framework for competitive price discovery and efficient risk shifting.[22] Because of the "contract market monopoly" of futures trading,[23] the commodity exchanges are central to the growth and development of the commodities industry. As of June 1, 1985 there were 12 domestic commodity exchanges trading 88 different futures contracts.

A commodity exchange may trade a futures contract only if that exchange has been designated as a contract market for that commodity. Among the designation requirements is a CFTC determination that designation is not contrary to the public interest.[24] This standard is generally understood to mean that the trading of the contract must serve an economic purpose, for example price discovery or hedging.[25]

The commodity exchanges exercise self-regulatory jurisdiction over their members, subject to the CFTC's oversight. Only members may trade on the floor of a commodity exchange.[26] Members may trade as principals (i.e., traders) or agents (i.e., brokers). Brokers must register with the CFTC.[27] All purchases and sales of a particular futures contract must take place in the trading "pit" designated by the exchange for the trading of that commodity and must be executed "openly and competitively by open outcry."[28] Unlike stock exchanges, commodity exchanges have no specialists and no central repository for limited price orders.

§ 4.3 TYPES OF TRANSACTIONS

(a) SPOT TRANSACTIONS

"The vast majority of mercantile transactions in commodities" are done in the spot market, that is, the market for immediate or near immediate

[21]CEA § 4, 7 U.S.C. § 6(a) (Supp. I 1983).

[22]*See. e.g.*, 41 Fed. Reg. 20,860 (1976).

[23]For a discussion of the contract market monopoly, see 1 P. JOHNSON, COMMODITIES REGULATION 206-13 (1982).

[24]CEA § 5(g), 7 U.S.C. § 7(g) (1982).

[25]1 P. JOHNSON, *supra* note 23, at 76 n.3, 214.

[26]CEA § 4, 7 U.S.C. § 6 (Supp. I 1983).

[27]*Id.*

[28]17 C.F.R. § 1.38(a) (1985).

delivery.[29] The parties to the transaction negotiate all the terms of the purchase and sale, not just the price and delivery date as they do in a futures transaction. Specifically, the parties must agree on the amount and grade of the commodity. The amount need not be in standard units as is required for futures contracts nor is the grade predetermined as it is for futures. Typically, neither party makes any payment upon entering into an outright purchase and sale. Payment is due only upon delivery. In spot transactions, margin (i.e., money or collateral deposited for the purposes of assuring peformance) generally is not required because full payment is expected within a short period of time. The risk associated with a substantial swing in the market value of the commodity between the trade date and the delivery date is borne by the parties to the transaction without the intermediation of a clearing organization of the sort that is so important for futures trading.[30]

The CFTC's Office of General Counsel recently defined a spot contract as a contract between a producer and a merchant to make or take immediate delivery of a commodity at a price to be agreed upon at a later time.[31] The contract offered a minimum price guarantee to the short position in return for a premium that allows the short position time to decide whether to take the guaranteed minimum price or try to obtain a higher final price based on either the contract's pricing formula or the cash market price for the commodity. Because both parties are obligated to perform under the contract and delivery is scheduled to occur at the time the contract is entered into, the CFTC's Office of General Counsel views such a contract as a spot contract.[32]

(b)　FORWARD TRANSACTIONS

Forward contracts are privately negotiated agreements for deferred (i.e., forward) delivery of a commodity.[33] Forward contracts usually involve a delivery more than one month after the trade date. They are used by producers to assure the future sale of their products and by users to assure future supplies. Unlike futures, parties entering into forward contracts generally intend to make and take delivery.[34]

---

[29]1 P. JOHNSON, *supra* note 23, at 28.

[30]*See* section 4.5; *see also* LTR 8527041 (Apr. 8, 1985).

[31]Characteristics Distinguishing Cash and Forward Contracts and "Trade" Options, 50 Fed. Reg. 39,656, 39,660 (1985).

[32]A spot contract is not an option (which is only limitedly permitted by the CEA) because the short position's right to demand a price is inseparable from the actual delivery of the commodity between the parties. *See* section 5.2(b).

[33]*See* section 4.2(a); *see also* LTR 8527041 (Apr. 8, 1985).

[34]*See* CBT, *supra* noted 19, at 7-8.

Parties to forward contracts may or may not use margin deposits or other means (e.g., performance bonds or letters of credit) to reduce the risk of open transactions. Forward contracts in GNMAs and other mortgaged-backed securities typically will involve mark-to-market payments, and initial and variation margin is common in forward contracts in precious metals.

Although forward contracts and futures contracts are similar in several ways, for example, they can both be used to hedge the risk of an adverse price movement inherent in waiting until a future date to buy or sell a commodity, the distinctions between them are more important for tax purposes.

1. Forward contracts are negotiated agreements for the purchase and sale of a commodity. The parties to the agreement determine the precise amount, grade, and delivery date of the commodity.[35] Futures contracts are standardized contracts for specified quantities of a specified quality of a commodity.

2. Futures contracts are traded on established exchanges in an active auction market. Forward contracts are private agreements made by means of informal trading networks and markets.

3. Forward contracts are not generally assignable or capable of being closed out by offset without the agreement of both parties. Futures contracts may be liquidated by offset without the other party's consent.[36]

4. The parties to a forward contract look only to each other for performance. A clearing organization becomes the other side of all futures contracts, thereby guaranteeing performance.[37]

5. The parties to a forward contract generally intend settlement to occur through actual delivery of the underlying commodity. Typi-

[35] A forward contract can require delivery of a specified quantity and grade of a commodity on a particular date without an established price. In such a case, the contract specifies a method by which the final price is to be determined (e.g., using a particular futures contract as a base price). The forward contract can guarantee a minimum price for the commodity in return for a premium to be deducted from the final price. Thus, while the pricing formula or subsequent market price specified in the contract may entitle the short position to demand a higher price for the commodity, regardless of market changes, the short position never receives less than the minimum price. The CFTC's Office of the General Counsel has taken the position that this kind of contract is a forward contract, within the forward contract exemption of CEA § 2(a)(1)(A), 7 U.S.C. § 2 (Supp. I 1983). The contract's predominant feature is its use by producers and merchants to market a commodity through actual delivery. Characteristics Distinguishing Cash and Forward Contracts and "Trade" Options, *supra* note 31, at 39,660.

[36] For a discussion of how futures contracts are offset, see section 4.3(c).

[37] *See* section 4.5(b).

cally, the parties to a futures contract intend to close out their positions by offset prior to delivery.

6. Margin or a security deposit is a matter of negotiation between the parties to a forward contract. Margin, set by the commodity exchanges, is required to establish and maintain a futures contract position.[38]

7. Forward contracts are generally excluded from regulation under the CEA.[39] Futures are subject to the full regulatory authority of the CFTC.

(c) FUTURES TRANSACTIONS

Futures contracts are standardized executory contracts to purchase or sell for a fixed price a specified quantity and grade of a commodity at a specified time in the future. The months when the contracts mature and the dates for delivery within the specified delivery months also are standardized. Each domestic commodity exchange establishes the specifications for those futures contracts traded through its facilities. The only negotiable portions of a futures contract are the price and the delivery month.[40] Unless closed out by offset, that is, by establishing an identical but opposite position, futures contracts are settled by delivery (or receipt) of the underlying commodity (or cash).

Futures positions are established[41] when one party agrees to sell a commodity ("short position") and make delivery of it in the specified contract month, and the other party agrees to accept delivery and pay for the commodity ("long position"). The price at which futures contracts are entered into ("contract price") is established by open outcry on the floor of an exchange between exchange members acting as traders or brokers. Upon entering into a futures contract, neither party pays any consideration to the other. Rather, under the prevailing margining system each party makes an initial margin payment, that is, a security deposit, to his FCM when opening a futures contract position.[42]

---

[38]*See* section 4.4.

[39]CEA § 2(a)(1)(A), 7 U.S.C. § 2 (Supp. I 1983), provides that "[t]he term 'future delivery' [as that term is used in setting out the requirements of the CEA] shall not include any sale of any cash commodity for deferred shipment or delivery."

[40]Futures contracts for any particular commodity are distinguished by the month in which delivery is required. For example, "March corn" refers to corn for delivery in March.

[41]The number of futures contracts in a commodity that have been entered into and not yet closed by offset or settlement constitute the open interest in that commodity.

[42]For certain exchange members trading for their own accounts, initial margin may be zero. For a discussion of margin, see section 4.4(b).

As the price of the underlying commodity moves, the price of the futures contract is likely to move as well.[43] The long incurs a profit from an increase in the price of the commodity and the short incurs a loss. Conversely, the long incurs a loss as the commodity's price falls, while the short incurs a profit.

Open futures contracts can be closed out by delivery or payment at maturity or by establishing an opposite and equal futures position ("closing transaction").[44] For example, a speculator with a long position of one December corn (i.e., an obligation to accept delivery of 5000 bushels of No. 2 yellow corn at a designated delivery point in December) can close that position at any time prior to the last trading day for the contract by selling one December corn contract. Gain or loss on the closing transaction is the difference between the contract price of the opening transaction and the contract price of the closing transaction. In this example, the opening transaction was a long position, so the trade is profitable if the closing transaction's contract price is greater than the opening transaction's contract price. If the opening transaction had been a short position, the trade would have been profitable if the contract price of the opening transaction was greater than the contract price of the closing transaction. Upon effecting a closing transaction, the party owes or is owed the difference between the price he paid for the long contract and the price he received for the short contract.

Of course, not all futures transactions are simply outright purchases or sales. Some futures transactions are entered into for the purpose of hedging, that is, to attempt to lock in the future sale price of existing inventory or the cost of future supply.[45] Profit and loss on the two sides of a hedge should ideally match. That is, the side on which the gain or loss on the futures position is when it is closed out should equal the side on which gain or loss on the physical position is when it is disposed of (for a long position) or acquired (for a short position). The fact that the sides of a hedge seldom match has led to extreme complications in the rules governing the taxation of hedging transactions.[46]

Spreading is another example of the use of futures transactions for a purpose other than outright speculation on the price movement of a commodity. A spread involves the purchase of one futures contract and

---

[43]In some commodities, such as corn, the futures market price is the basis for determining the cash market price.

[44]Very few futures contracts are held to maturity.

[45]For a discussion of hedging, see section 6.4.

[46]*See generally* Chapter 21.

the sale of another nonoffsetting contract in the expectation that the price relationships between the two contracts will change such that a subsequent offsetting sale and purchase will yield a net profit.[47] In a spread, the purchased contract is viewed as "cheap," the sold contract as "expensive." Generally, the buy and sell transactions are executed simultaneously and can often be executed at a "difference"; that is, the two contracts can be bought or sold as a pair at the price differential between them.

Spreads can be intramarket (e.g., the simultaneous purchase of September wheat and sale of December wheat on the CBT), intermarket (e.g., the purchase of September wheat on the CBT and the sale of September wheat on the KCBT), intercommodity (e.g., the purchase of September wheat and sale of September corn), or commodity-product (e.g., the purchase of September soybeans and the sale of September soybean oil or meal). Profit or loss on a spread depends upon whether the price spread between the futures contracts making up the spread widens or narrows and which way the spreader had anticipated the spread would move.[48]

(d) CASH AND CARRY TRANSACTIONS

Cash and carry transactions involve an outright purchase of a commodity in the cash market and the sale of a futures or forward contract for that commodity. There are various reasons for such transactions, but the common element is that the taxpayer bears the cost of carrying the cash position while maintaining a futures or forward position that offsets the position. If the cash and carry position arises out of an intramarket spread[49] by the taxpayer taking delivery on the long position while maintaining the short position, the transaction is often referred to as a "full carry straddle."

The cash and carry technique is used generally with commodities that exhibit a price differential between delivery months that is primarily a function of the cost of interest and other carrying charges. The preferred commodities for cash and carry transactions are those that can be stored or warehoused easily and are acceptable to satisfy the delivery obligations under the short position. Historically, silver has been the most commonly used commodity for cash and carry transactions.

---

[47]CBT, *supra* note 19, at 356.

[48]*See generally* section 35.1.

[49]*See* section 4.3(c).

(e) LEVERAGE TRANSACTIONS

Leverage transactions are a unique type of contract for the purchase of a commodity, usually a precious metal, on a deferred delivery basis. Leverage contracts are off-exchange contracts that are sold to customers by firms called "leverage transaction merchants" ("LTMs"). In a typical leverage transaction the customer makes a down payment with the LTM, for example, 30 percent of the total purchase price, for a specified amount of a commodity. The customer also pays the LTM a commission, for example, two percent of the purchase price, and during the life of the contract pays the LTM finance or leverage charges as well as service fees.

Leverage contracts are for a fixed term, which may be 20 years or more. The customer is under no obligation to take delivery until the contract expires, provided that all fees are paid and margin calls are met. The customer may demand delivery at any time or elect to resell the contract to the LTM at the then prevailing market price.

Regulation of leverage transactions is vested in the CFTC, which in 1985, after years of debate, adopted comprehensive regulations governing the sale of leverage contracts by LTMs. These regulations include registration of LTMs and their associated persons with the CFTC,[50] disclosure obligations,[51] financial net worth requirements,[52] and sales practice requirements.[53] Registration of LTMs is limited to those firms that were engaged in the leverage transaction business on June 1, 1978 (in the case of contracts for gold, silver, and bulk coins) or February 2, 1979 (in the case of contracts for all other commodities).[54]

(f) EXCHANGE OF FUTURES FOR PHYSICALS

EFPs are hybrid cash futures transactions. They are an exception to the rule that all futures transactions must be executed in the pit by open and competitive outcry.[55] Although the definition of an EFP varies from exchange to exchange,[56] the basic transaction involves two distinct but related trades: a purchase and sale of a physical commodity and the

---

[50] 17 C.F.R. §§ 3.17, .18 (1985).

[51] 17 C.F.R. § 31.11 (1985).

[52] 17 C.F.R. § 31.9 (1985).

[53] 17 C.F.R. § 31.19 (1985).

[54] These dates correspond to the CFTC's moratoriums on entry into the leverage transaction business. 17 C.F.R. §§ 31.1, .2 (1985).

[55] CEA § 4b, 7 U.S.C. § 6(b) (1982); 17 C.F.R. § 1.38(a) (1985). EFPs are negotiated off of the floor when the exchange is closed.

[56] *Compare* NYME Rule 150.14 (1985) *with* COMEX Rule 4.36 (1982).

sale and purchase of at least one established futures contract.[57] If both parties to the EFP initially held (opposite) futures positions, the transaction results in the transfer of the physical commodity and termination of both parties' futures contract obligations. If only one party to the EFP initially held a futures position, that position is transferred to the other party, who thereby assumes all obligations associated with it.

EFPs are employed primarily by commercial firms seeking to use futures contracts as a hedge against cash market risk. The flexible EFP delivery mechanism and the ability to negotiate the price and grade of the physical commodity actually purchased and sold allows such firms to tailor the contracts on which they take delivery to their particular needs while still hedging effectively in the futures markets. Regulation of EFPs is vested in the exchanges, which have issued rules requiring EFP participants to document their transactions and to make their documents available to the exchanges on request.[58]

§ 4.4 MARGIN REQUIREMENTS

(a) CASH MARKET

Margin (i.e., a security or good faith deposit) is a matter for negotiation between the parties to a cash market transaction in commodities. Typically, margin is not required for spot transactions. Margin may be required for forward contracts, depending on the nature of the commodity and the sophistication and financial strength of the participants. When margin is required, the amount, time of payment, and frequency of recalculation are all matters for negotiation. Enforcement of margin requirements in the cash markets is a private matter arising out of the terms of the contract.

(b) FUTURES MARKET

Margin is a key financial safeguard to performance on futures contracts. Margin on futures contracts ("futures margin") is required of both sides. It represents a performance bond, good faith deposit, or earnest money.[59]

---

[57]*See, e.g.*, NYME Rule 150.14(A) (1985).

[58]*See e.g.s*, NYFE Rule 432(e) (1985); COMEX Trading Rule 4.36(f) (1982); CME Rule 538(4) (1982); *see also* 17 C.F.R. § 1.38(b) (1985). There is now a 24-hour EFP market for metals. One consequence is around the clock availability of quotations on the price differential between the cash and futures markets.

[59]STAFF OF THE BOARD OF GOVERNORS OF THE FEDERAL RESERVE SYSTEM, A REVIEW AND EVALUATION OF FEDERAL MARGIN REGULATIONS 57 (1984) [hereinafter referred to as "FRB Margin Study"].

Margin for the long side is designed to assure that adequate funds are available when the position is closed or delivery is taken. Margin for the short side is designed to assure that if delivery must be made, the commodity can be acquired for delivery or if the position is closed, that any loss will be covered.

If a customer defaults on his futures obligation, his FCM must assume responsibility for the position. If the FCM defaults, the responsibility becomes that of the clearing organization[60] and utimately, based on the terms of the exchange's rules, that of the membership as a whole. Futures margin, therefore, is required for the protection of FCMs, clearing organizations, and the futures market as a whole.[61]

Unlike margin in the securities markets, futures margin is not viewed as a partial payment for the underlying commodity.[62] By the same token, because the opening of a futures position does not involve a transfer of ownership of the underlying property (nor an entitlement to any income or benefits from the underlying property), no one is viewed as extending credit to anyone else in connection with such transactions.[63] Margin deposits are not recorded as a down payment of the purchase price of the commodity and, indeed, under law remain the property of the depositor as long as the futures position is open.[64]

Margin is imposed at three levels in the futures market. First, the commodity exchanges set minimum margin requirements for the customer accounts carried by their members. Second, firms carrying customer accounts (i.e., the FCMs) may impose such additional margin requirements on their customers as they believe appropriate. And third, commodity clearing organizations impose margin requirements on their members ("clearing members"). For convenience, margin required by exchanges and FCMs will be referred to as "customer margin" and that required by clearing organizations as "clearing margin." Because commodity exchange members who trade through FCMs generally are subject to different margin requirements than public customers, it is useful to recognize a subdivision of customer margin that will be referred to as "member margin." These three types of margin—customer margin, member margin, and clearing margin—are discussed in the following subsections.

---

[60]1 P. JOHNSON, *supra* note 23, at 32.

[61]*See* FRB Margin Study, *supra* note 59, at 58.

[62]Margin in a securities transaction is treated as a loan, that is, an extension of credit by a securities broker to its customer. *See* section 1.5.

[63]FRB Margin Study, *supra* note 59, at 57.

[64]CEA § 4d(2), 7 U.S.C. § 6d(2) (Supp. I 1983).

(1) CUSTOMER MARGIN

Persons trading futures contracts, other than exchange members, must trade directly or indirectly through an FCM. Public customers of an FCM are subject to the customer margin requirements of the exchange on which their futures contracts are traded and to such additional margin as their FCM may demand.[65]

Customer margin is a deposit made by the customer with his FCM. It is required of both sides to a futures contract, and it is designed to prevent adverse consequences in the event a customer fails to meet his obligations. In receiving a margin deposit, the FCM has not been paid a down payment from its customer nor has it extended credit to its customer for the balance of the contract price. The payment and receipt of futures margin, therefore, is not viewed as a financing transaction.[66] Interest may or may not be paid by the FCM to the customer on his margin deposit. This depends largely on the size of the margin deposit and the bargaining power of the customer. It may also be governed by exchange rules.[67]

Customer margin is not generally set by the CFTC.[68] Rather, each commodity exchange sets minimum margin requirements for positions established through its facilities.[69] The required level of margin varies among futures contracts. The margin level generally is set based on the historical price volatility of the futures contract. Futures contracts with a history of rapid price movements typically carry higher margin requirements than futures contracts with more stable prices. Margin levels may change as the volatilities of a futures contract change. In periods of high price volatilities (e.g., the silver market during 1980), exchange imposed margin requirements for customers are almost always raised.[70] Required margin levels also may vary depending upon the length of time before the contract matures and the nature of the transaction (i.e.,

---

[65]There is some question as to precisely who must be treated as a public customer. 1 T. RUSSO, REGULATION OF THE COMMODITIES, FUTURES AND OPTIONS MARKETS ch. 1, at 38 (Regulatory Manual Series 1984). For our purposes, viewing all persons other than exchange members as public customers will suffice.

[66]See Smith, *The Custom of Margin Calls and Closing Out Commodity Futures Accounts Lacking Sufficient Margin—The Rule of Unwritten Law*, 13 SEC. REG. L. J. 99-104 (1985).

[67]See, e.g., CBT Rule 431.02(5) (1985), which prohibits the payment of interest to customers on initial margin.

[68]The CFTC can establish margin levels only in emergency situations. CEA § 8a(9), 7 U.S.C. § 12a(9) (Supp. I 1983).

[69]FRB Margin Study, *supra* note 59, at 61.

[70]*Id.* at 62.

hedge position, speculative position, or spread).[71] Margin levels on futures contracts can be changed at any time, even during the course of a trading day.[72]

All open futures contracts must be marked-to-market daily; that is, the value of the futures contracts must be recalculated based on the closing or settlement price for that contract on that day. A loss during a day on a futures position must be paid (through the clearing organization) to the profitable, opposite position before the start of trading on the following day. In other words, gains are credited to and losses are debited from all open futures positions each day.[73] The consequences of this mark-to-market process can best be seen by discussing more specifically the two types of customer margin requirements: initial margin and maintenance margin.

(i)   Initial Margin

Prior to accepting an order for an opening futures transaction (or within a "reasonable" time thereafter), an FCM must receive from a customer the amount of initial or original margin prescribed by the exchange.[74] Although an FCM cannot accept less than the prescribed initial margin, an FCM is free to require higher margin deposits from its customers.[75]

Initial margin varies from contract to contract and among types of positions in futures contracts. For example, on the CBT, the initial margin on a speculative position in corn is $500 per contract, that is, 5000 bushels. A speculative position in wheat requires an initial margin of $750 per contract, that is, 5000 bushels. Initial margin on a hedge position in corn is $300 per contract and in wheat $500 per contract. Initial margin on an intermarket spread between corn and wheat is $750 per paired contracts.[76]

On all exchanges, customers are permitted to deposit cash or Treasury securities for initial margin. Beyond that, exchanges have different rules as to the types of assets permissible for margin purposes.[77] As a general rule, FCMs will only accept cash or carry equivalents, such as Treasury bills, as initial margin. Credits in a customer's account in excess of

[71]*Id.*

[72]*E.g.,* CME Rule 828(A) (1978).

[73]FRB Margin Study, *supra* note 59, at 59.

[74]*E.g.,* CBT Rule 431.02(12) (1985).

[75]FRB Margin Study, *supra* note 59, at 61.

[76]CBT Rule 431.03(4) (1985).

[77]The CFTC allows FCMs to accept assets other than cash for margin purposes provided that they are valued at less than their face value. *See* 17 C.F.R. § 1.17(c)(5)(viii) (1985).

required initial margin can generally be used as part of the initial margin on new positions.[78] Generally, customers may not make withdrawals from accounts containing less than the required initial margin.[79]

(ii) Maintenance Margin

Each exchange requires its members to mark the positions of their customers to the market on a daily basis. Any loss in a customer's account reduces the amount of the initial margin deposit (just as a gain creates a credit in excess of the deposit). The exchanges also establish maintenance margin levels.[80] If the equity[81] in a customer's account falls below the maintenance margin level because of the mark-to-market process or otherwise, the customer generally must bring the equity in the account back to the level of required initial margin.[82] If the customer does not meet the margin call promptly, the FCM may (but is not obligated to) close out some or all of the customer's open futures positions to bring the account's equity into balance with the required margin for the account.[83]

By way of example, the maintenance margin on a speculative position in corn is $300 per contract.[84] If a customer purchased one contract for September corn at $2.30 per bushel, he would be required to deposit $500 initial margin or $.10 per bushel. If the price of corn declines by $.04, his equity in the account will have declined to $300 ($500 minus (5000 × .04)), the maintenance margin level. The FCM is then required (if it has not done so already) to issue a margin call, and the customer is required to deposit with the FCM (at least) an additional $200 of margin to restore the account to the initial margin level.

Customer margin payments in excess of required initial margin deposits are generally referred to as "additional margin."[85] Because of the volatility of the futures market, a customer may be required, either

---

[78]*E.g.*, CBT Rule 431.02(12) (1985).

[79]*E.g.*, CBT Rule 431.02(13) (1985).

[80]Generally, maintenance margin is approximately 75 percent of initial margin. *E.g.*, COMEX Margin Rule 6.03 (1984).

[81]Equity is generally defined to include cash, other property deposited in the account, and realized and unrealized gains and losses from futures contract transactions.

[82]*E.g.*, CBT Rule 431.02(14) (1985).

[83]1 T. Russo, *supra* note 65, ch. 2, at 9; *e.g.*, CBT Rule 430.00 (1985).

[84]*E.g.*, CBT Rule 431.03 (1985).

[85]Although such customer payments are sometimes referred to as variation margin payments, this is not technically correct. A variation margin call is in intraday call by a clearing organization for additional margin from a clearing member. CBT, *supra* note 19, at 358.

pursuant to exchange rules or simply because of the concern of his FCM, to make deposits of additional margin substantially in excess of his initial margin deposit.

(2) NONCLEARING MEMBERS

Members of a commodity exchange who are not members of the affiliated clearing organization must trade through, that is, have their accounts carried by, an FCM that is a member of the clearing organization ("clearing members").[86] However, unlike nonmember customers of an FCM, an exchange member whose account is carried by a clearing member is not generally required by the exchange to deposit initial margin. Rather, his transactions for his own account need only be "margined to the market";[87] that is, on a daily mark-to-market basis, a nonclearing member is expected merely to maintain a positive equity in his account. However, if the clearing member is willing to take a charge against its required net capital in the amount of any deficit in the nonclearing member's account,[88] the clearing member is not required by exchange rule or the CFTC to force the nonclearing member to maintain a positive equity in his account.[89]

(3) CLEARING MARGIN

All futures clearing organizations require their members to maintain margin deposits to secure the members' obligations on the futures contracts open with the clearing organization.[90] Each clearing organization requires its members to make an initial, original, or standing margin deposit (which is not necessarily the same as the amount of, and should not be confused with, a customer's required initial margin) in connection with every position in its clearing account. Most clearing organizations impose initial margin requirements based on the clearing member's net long or short position in each commodity.[91] Certain clearing organizations, however, require margin deposits on both long (buy side) and short (sell side) positions.[92]

[86] 1 P. JOHNSON, *supra* note 23, at 99.

[87] *E.g.*, CBT Rule 431.01 (1985).

[88] *See* 17 C.F.R. § 1.17(c)(5)(viii) (1985).

[89] *See, e.g.*, CBT Rule 431.00 (1985).

[90] Clearing margin is not generally held directly by the clearing organization but by approved banks in special margin accounts. *E.g.*, CBTCC Bylaws 604, 605 (1982).

[91] *See, e.g.*, CBTCC Bylaw 601 (1982).

[92] *See, e.g.*, CME Rule 808 (1982). For a discussion of the difference between net and gross margining systems, see 1 T. RUSSO, *supra* note 65, ch. 2, at 11.

Initial clearing margins are fixed by the clearing organizations and are subject to change at any time. Initial margins are normally uniform for all clearing members, although the clearing organizations have the authority to selectively increase them when confronted with unique risks.[93] Because margin requirements can affect trading activity,[94] it is in the interest of the clearing organizations generally to keep margins as low as possible consistent with prudent risk management.

Initial clearing margins are administered as follows.[95] At the end of each trading day the clearing organization prepares and distributes two basic statements for each member: (1) statement of trades and positions and (2) statement of original margin.[96] The statement of trades and positions shows all trades made that day by the member (and its customers) and all of the member's open positions. For each trade made that day the statement calculates the difference, if any, between the trade's contract price and that day's settlement price of the commodity. For each open position the statement calculates the difference, if any, between the previous day's settlement price and that day's settlement price. Where the member is the seller and the contract price (or the prior day's settlement price for an open position) is less than that day's settlement price, the member is required to pay the difference to the clearing organization and the clearing organization is required to pay that amount to the buyer. Similarly, where the member is the buyer and the contract price (or the prior day's settlement price for an open position) is more than that day's settlement price, the member is required to pay the difference to the clearing organization and the clearing organization is required to pay that amount to the seller. A member's statement of trades and positions shows its net "pay" or "collect"; that is, the amount it owes or is owed by the clearing organization. This amount, the daily variation settlement[97] or settlement variation,[98] must be settled in cash with the clearing organization before the opening of trading the next day. The funds collected from the members with net losses necessarily equals the funds paid to the members with net gains.

[93]*E.g.,* CBT, *supra* note 19, at 29; CME Rule 824 (1982).

[94]1 P. JOHNSON, *supra* note 23, at 35.

[95]The terms used and the procedures described in this and the following paragraph are based on the Bylaws of the CBTCC. Although not precisely identical, all other clearing organizations operate in an essentially similar manner. *See generally* 1 T. RUSSO, *supra* note 65, ch 2, at 6, 8.

[96]The Clearing House of the Chicago Mercantile Exchange ("CMECH") and other commodity exchanges combine these two reports into one. On the CMECH, the report is called a recap ledger. CME Rule 812 (1982).

[97]CBTCC Bylaw 509 (1982).

[98]CME Rule 823 (1982).

Because gains and losses in the futures market always net to zero, the market is often referred to as a "zero-sum game."[99]

The daily variation settlement or mark-to-market payments between clearing members and the clearing organization are *not* margin payments. They are simply part of the daily settlement process in the futures market.[100] Margin requirements for clearing members are the amounts required by the clearing organization in addition to the daily mark-to-market payments. These margin requirements are basically of two types: initial and variation. Initial margins are calculated on the second daily report the clearing member receives, that is, the statement of original margins. This statement calculates the initial margin required on each trade made that day and each position open during that day and the member's net surplus of, or deficit in, its deposits of such margins.[101] Any deficit in a member's initial margin deposit must be covered before the beginning of trading the next day. Initial margin may be posted by a deposit of cash and Treasury securities, and in the case of some clearing organizations, letters of credit and clearing corporation stock.[102]

The required mark-to-market payments and the daily calculation of required initial margin assure—barring the default of a clearing member—that at the beginning of every trading day the clearing organization neither owes nor is owed any money by its members and that it is holding the full amount of required initial margin. Ordinarily, these initial margins are sufficient to protect the clearing organization against daily price movements. However, any market move against a clearing member's position reduces the "cushion" provided by its initial margin deposit. In the event of a severe market movement or anticipated market movement, the clearing organization can issue a margin call on a clearing member during the trading day. This is the second type of margin. Such an intraday demand for a variation deposit,[103] emergency margin,[104] or super-margin must be met by the clearing member in cash within one hour of the time the margin call is made by the clearing organization.[105] Variation deposits are viewed as payments on account of that day's business; that is, they appear as credits on that day's statement of trades and positions, and do not serve to increase the clearing member's initial margin deposit.

[99]1 P. JOHNSON, *supra* note 23, at 34 n.9.

[100]*E.g.*, CBTCC Bylaw 509 (1982).

[101]*E.g.*, CBTCC Bylaw 510 (1982).

[102]1 T. RUSSO, *supra* note 65, ch. 2 at 7; *e.g.*, CBT, *supra* note 19, at 29.

[103]CBTCC Bylaw 603 (1982).

[104]CME Rule 828 (1978).

[105]*E.g.*, CBT, *supra* note 19, at 29.

§ 4.5 CLEARANCE AND SETTLEMENT

(a) CASH MARKETS

The procedures for clearance and settlement in the cash commodity markets vary from commodity to commodity. As a general rule, settlement procedures are established by contractual arrangements directly between the parties. Obvious exceptions to this are the established settlement arrangements in effect at stockyards and the cash markets conducted on several commodity exchanges.

(b) FUTURES MARKETS

The heart of the clearance and settlement mechanism for the futures market—and of the overall financial integrity of the futures market—is the clearing organization. Each commodity exchange has or is affiliated with a clearing organization. Only members of the commodity exchange may be members of the clearing organization, but not all exchange members are clearing members. A clearing organization will only deal with its members and, accordingly, a clearing member must be involved on each side of every futures contract.

A commodity clearing organization typically clears trades as follows.[106] The clearing members representing the buyer and seller of a futures contract each report the trade to the clearing organization on the day of the trade. If the trade reports match, the clearing organization accepts the trade, and this is confirmed to the clearing members on their report of trades and positions.[107] If the trade reports do not match, the clearing organization reports an out-trade, which must then be resolved between the clearing members before it can be resubmitted for settlement. Resolved out-trades are cleared "as of" the trade day.

Once a clearing organization accepts a futures trade, the buyer is deemed to have bought the commodity from the clearing organization, and the seller is deemed to have sold such commodity to the clearing organization.[108] By interposing itself as principal to both sides of every trade, the clearing organization becomes the ultimate guarantor of all cleared futures contracts.[109]

---

[106]For variations on this pattern, see 1 T. Russo, *supra* note 65, ch. 2, at 2–5.

[107]*E.g.*, CBTCC Bylaw 511 (1982).

[108]*E.g.*, CBTCC Bylaw 501 (1982).

[109]1 P. Johnson, *supra* note 23, at 519.

Cleared futures contracts are settled the day after the trade date. This is conducted through the daily mark-to-market process described in section 4.4(b). Based on the net pay or collect stated on its daily statement of trades and positions, a clearing member is either required to make a payment to the clearing organization or it receives a payment from the clearing organization. The result of this daily settlement procedure, which must always net to zero, is that at the beginning of each trading day no clearing member owes any other clearing member anything on any open futures position. This daily settlement or mark-to-market system occurs between clearing members and not with public customers or nonclearing members. Settlement between customers and their FCMs takes place in accordance with the margin process described in section 4.4(b)(1).

Once a futures position is opened it may be closed by offset or delivery. Offset closes approximately 98 percent of all futures contracts. Because the clearing organization has interposed itself as the other side of all futures positions, anyone holding a futures position can liquidate the contract prior to the last day of trading by effecting an equal but opposite trade. As the Bylaws of the CBTCC provide:

[W]here, as the result of substitution . . . any member has bought from the Clearing Corporation any amount of a given commodity for a particular delivery, and subsequently, and prior to such delivery, such member sells to the Clearing Corporation any amount of the same commodity for the same delivery, the subsequent transaction shall be deemed pro tanto a settlement or adjustment of the prior transaction, except [that customer trades will not offset the clearing member's own trades]. In like manner, where a member sells, and subsequently, and before delivery, such member buys the same commodity for the same delivery, the second transaction shall be deemed pro tanto a settlement or adjustment of the prior transaction, except [that customer trades will not offset the clearing member's own trades]. Thereupon, such member shall become liable to pay the loss or entitled to collect the profit, as the case may be, upon such adjusted transactions, and shall be under no further liability to receive or make delivery with respect thereto. For purposes of this Bylaw, the first trades made shall be deemed the first trades offset.[110]

The method of accomplishing delivery on futures contracts varies from exchange to exchange and from contract to contract.[111] Essentially, the clearing organization matches short positions desiring delivery with

---

[110]CBTCC Bylaw 504 (1982).

[111]1 T. Russo, *supra* note 65, ch. 2, at 13.

long positions desiring to take delivery. In doing so, the clearing organization steps out of the middle of these trades and establishes a direct
contractual relationship between the clearing members. Although the
contract on which delivery is to be made or accepted is a customer's,
the clearing member is responsible for completion of the contract in
the event of the customer's default.[112]

---

[112]*E.g.*, CBT Rule 1054.00 (1979).

Five

Overview of the Option Markets

§ 5.1 INTRODUCTION

Options on securities and commodities are a very old, if historically suspect, trading vehicle.[1] Trading in options on stock began in the United States in the late eighteenth century, but it was not until 1973, with the registration of the CBOE and the introduction of standardized options,[2] that options began to attract large numbers of public participants.[3] In 1981 the CFTC authorized exchange trading of options on futures, and in 1982 the CFTC extended this "pilot" program to include options on physical commodities.[4] At the present time, standardized options are traded on five securities exchanges, 10 commodities exchanges, and through the NASDAQ system of the NASD. The interests underlying these options range from common stock to gold and from foreign currencies to corn.

From the perspective of the buyer (i.e., the "holder" or a person with a "long" position), an option is a contract in accordance with which he has the right, but not the obligation, for a specified period of time, to buy or sell a specified amount of the underlying interest at a fixed or

---

[1]For a brief history of options trading, see G. GASTINEAU, THE STOCK OPTIONS MANUAL 15-20 (2d ed. 1979).

[2]SEA Release No. 9985 [1972–1973 Transfer Binder], FED. SEC. L. REP. (CCH) ¶ 79,212 (Feb. 1, 1973).

[3]For an analysis of option trading volume before and after 1973, see G. GASTINEAU, *supra* note 1, at 21.

[4]47 Fed. Reg. 56996 (1982); 46 Fed. Reg. 54500 (1981).

determinable price. From the perspective of the seller (i.e., the "writer" or a person with a "short" position), an option is a contract in accordance with which he is obligated to perform if and when the holder exercises the option. A call option conveys to the holder the right to buy (and obligates the writer to sell) the underlying interest. A put option conveys to the holder the right to sell (and obligates the writer to buy) the underlying interest. Calls and puts are the two "types" of options.[5]

Whether dealing with puts or calls, or viewing options from the perspective of the writer or holder, every option contract has six key terms:

1. *Underlying interest:* The nature of the property (e.g., IBM stock, Treasury bonds with an 11¾ percent coupon, or a futures contract for No. 2 yellow corn) underlying (i.e., covered by) the option

2. *Unit of trading:* The number or quantity of the underlying interest covered by one option

3. *Expiration date and time:* The time on the date on which the option ceases to exist (i.e., the time and date on which the option no longer confers any rights on the holder)

4. *Striking or exercise price:* The price at which the holder has a right to buy or sell the underlying interest

5. *Adjustment procedure:* The manner in which the number of option contracts or the unit of trading is adjusted for such changes in the underlying interest as a stock split, an alteration of exchange rates, or a change in the composition or method of calculating an index

6. *Premium:* The price that the buyer of an option pays and the seller of an option receives for the rights conveyed by the option

These six terms point up a fundamental distinction between conventional options and standardized options. Conventional options (including trade and dealer options in the commodities area)[6] are unique, nonfungible contracts; they are the only type of options that were traded prior to the establishment of the CBOE, and they continue to trade today, albeit to a relatively limited extent and primarily between institutional and professional investors.[7] The buyer and seller must ne-

---

[5]For a basic description of the function and operation of options, see generally AMEX, CBOE, NASD, NYSE, PHLX & OCC, CHARACTERISTICS AND RISKS OF STANDARDIZED OPTIONS (1985). This booklet is prepared by OCC, the NASD, and the five securities option exchanges in accordance with Rule 9b-1 under the SEA.

[6]*See* 17 C.F.R. §§ 32.4, 32.12 (1985).

[7]*See generally* REPORT OF THE SPECIAL STUDY OF THE OPTIONS MARKET TO THE SECURITIES EXCHANGE COMMISSION, 96TH CONG., 1ST SESS. 73-76 (Comm. Print 1978) [hereinafter referred to as "Special Options Study"]; G. GASTINEAU, *supra* note 1, at 20-27.

gotiate all six terms to create a conventional option. This negotiation typically takes place through broker-dealers operating in the over-the-counter market. Because the terms of these options are individually negotiated, there is no active "secondary market" for conventional options. Holders and writers cannot generally close out their positions by offsetting purchases and sales with third parties, but must look to their original counterparties if they wish to get out of their positions prior to expiration or exercise. Further, given the "customized" nature of conventional options, the writer and holder remain paired during the life of the option, and the holder must look exclusively to his writer (typically backed by the guarantee of a NYSE member firm) for performance on exercise.

In contrast to conventional options, standardized options (i.e., all options traded on stock and commodity exchanges and through the NASDAQ system of the NASD) require the parties to negotiate only one term of the option contract—the premium. All other terms are standardized by the exchange or association that regulates the trading of that option.[8] For example, standardized options on stock expire on the Saturday after the third Friday in the designated expiration month;[9] the unit of trading is 100 shares of common stock of the designated company; available exercise prices are fixed by the exchange or association and end in $5, $2.50, or $0; no adjustment is made for ordinary cash dividends (although the holder is entitled to the dividend if he exercises prior to the ex-dividend date); and the exercise price or the number of underlying shares may be adjusted in accordance with the rules of OCC to take account of stock distributions and capital transactions.[10]

Because the terms (other than premiums) of standardized options are uniform, an active secondary market is possible. Any option with a common expiration date and exercise price is interchangeable with any other similar option. Therefore, an option holder (or writer) can economically close out his position prior to exercise or expiration by selling an option with the same terms as the one he bought, or buying an option with the same terms as the one he sold. However, for an option holder (or writer) to close out his position actually as well as economically,

---

[8]For a history of the development of the standardized option market, see J. SELIGMAN, THE SEC AND THE FUTURE OF FINANCE ch. 2 (1985).

[9]For a description of the exercise procedures for options overlaying securities, see generally OCC, OPERATIONS MANUAL § I, at 21 (Aug. 1983).

[10]OCC By-Laws art. VI, § 11 (1985).

one additional factor is needed: the interpositioning of a clearing organization between buyers and sellers. Unlike the relationship of the parties to a conventional option, the writer of a standardized option owes an obligation not to the person to whom he sold the option, but to the clearing organization for that option. Likewise, the option holder looks not to his seller for performance on exercise, but to the clearing organization. For standardized options, a clearing organization rather than an individual firm stands as both the guarantor of every contract and the opposite party to every trade.[11]

The standardization of terms and intermediation of a clearing organization allow options to trade in addition to simply being created and exercised. For example, if a writer wishes to close out a position without waiting for exercise or expiration, he can buy an option identical to the one he wrote. Because both his initial sale (an "opening transaction") and his subsequent purchase (a "closing transaction") are with the same party (i.e., the clearing organization), the two trades offset or cancel one another, leaving only a dollar difference (i.e., the profit or loss) to be settled between the writer and the clearing organization.

The existence of a secondary market gives holders and writers of standardized options (in contrast to holders and writers of conventional options) two ways to make a profit (or incur a loss): (1) by exercising (or waiting until expiration), and (2) by closing the position by offset prior to exercise or expiration. In the first case, it is the movement (or lack of movement) in the value of the underlying interest that determines profit and loss. The underlying interest must move up (in the case of a call) or down (in the case of a put) for the holder to profit and remain the same or move down (for a call) or up (for a put) for the writer to profit. In the second case, it is the movement of the value of the option itself that determines profit or loss. This distinction—between profit and loss based on the value of the underlying interest and profit and loss based on value of the option—highlights the two components of option valuation: intrinsic value and time value.[12] Intrinsic value de-

---

[11]*See generally* CBTCC, A Party to Every Trade (n.d.).

[12]Unless specifically noted to the contrary, the discussion in the text refers only to so-called American-style options and not to so-called European-style options. An American-style option may be exercised by the holder at any time after it is purchased until it expires. A European-style option may be exercised only during a specified period, which may be as short as a day, just before the option expires. During the time a European-style option cannot be exercised, it has no intrinsic value and its market price depends only on the likelihood that the option may ultimately be exercisable at a profit. On the distinction between American and European options, see generally AMEX, CBOE, NASD, NYSE, PHLX & OCC, *supra* note 5, at 10-12. At present, the only standardized European-style options traded in the United States are the foreign currency options traded on the CBOE.

SPECIAL SUPPLEMENT FOR

TAXATION OF SECURITIES, COMMODITIES, AND OPTIONS

by

Andrea S. Kramer

To bring your reference fully in line with major 1986 tax legislation on transactions in securities, commodities, and options, a special supplement analyzing these changes will be prepared and sent to all subscribers without charge.

Used in conjunction with this landmark reference, the special supplement will assist you in smoothly handling the transition between the old rules and the new as well as providing on-going assistance in this complex area of tax practice.

JEANNE LITTAS, *Editor*
John Wiley & Sons, Inc.
605 Third Avenue
New York, N.Y. 10158

pends upon the ability to exercise an option.[13] It reflects the amount, if any, by which the market price of the underlying interest is more (in the case of a call) or less (in the case of a put) than the exercise price of the option. An option with intrinsic value is said to be in-the-money while one without intrinsic value is said to be out-of-the-money. Time value depends on the availability of a secondary market. It is whatever value an option has in addition to its intrinsic value. Time value reflects what a buyer would be willing to pay for the option in the hope that at some time prior to expiration its value will increase because of a favorable change in the price of the underlying interest.[14]

§ 5.2   CLASSES OF OPTIONS

A class of options consists of all put and call contracts on the same underlying interest. A series of options is all contracts of the same class having the same expiration date and exercise price.[15] There are now numerous option classes overlaying various financial instruments and other interests. Certain of these options are traded as "securities" regulated by the SEC while the others are traded as "commodities" regulated by the CFTC. Unfortunately, the security/commodity distinction is not based on economic function, investment appeal, or clear legal principles.[16]

(a)   SECURITY OPTIONS

There has been a proliferation of security options since the CBOE commenced trading in stock options in 1973. Options on securities, options on groups or indexes of securities, and options on foreign currencies that are traded on securities exchanges are themselves securities and are subject to the SEC's regulations.[17] All standardized security options

---

[13]Hence, European-style options have no intrinsic value except during their exercise period; whereas American-style options ordinarily trade for no less than their intrinsic value prior to expiration.

[14]For a brief discussion of the determinants of option value, see L. McMILLAN, OPTIONS AS A STRATEGIC INVESTMENT, A COMPREHENSIVE ANALYSIS OF LISTED STOCK OPTION STRATEGIES 9-15 (1980).

[15]For a description of the presentation of option price information in financial tables, see J. COX & M. RUBINSTEIN, OPTIONS MARKETS 29-32 (1985).

[16]For a discussion of the so-called Shad-Johnson accord and the subsequent legislation that led to the regulatory division between the SEC and CFTC of standardized options, see L. LOSS, FUNDAMENTALS OF SECURITIES REGULATION 37-40 (Supp. 1985).

[17]SEA § 3(a)(10), 15 U.S.C. § 78c(a)(10) (1982).

are registered with the SEC[18] and are "issued" by OCC.[19] A brief discussion of the broad categories of security options follows.[20]

(1) STOCK OPTIONS

Standardized stock options overlay both listed stocks and (since June 1985) unlisted stocks traded in the NASDAQ market. These options trade on securities exchanges and options on unlisted stocks also trade in the NASDAQ market. Each standardized stock option covers 100 shares of the underlying stock (unless adjusted). The exercise price is stated in dollars per share, as is the premium. Conventional stock options are also available.[21]

(2) DEBT OPTIONS

Standardized debt or interest rate options are currently traded on Treasury bonds, notes, and bills. These options trade exclusively on registered securities exchanges. Treasury bond and note options cover specific issues of bonds or notes (e.g., the five-year 9⅞ percent Treasury notes). Treasury bill options cover the "current" bill with a full 13 weeks remaining to maturity as of the time exercise is settled (i.e., the options are really on an interest rate rather than a specific security). In addition to these debt options, the option exchanges have filed proposals to trade European-style options that will generally correspond to Treasury bond and note futures contracts traded on certain futures exchanges. These European-style options will include a "market basket" delivery feature upon exercise.

Exercise prices for bond and note options are expressed as a percentage of par value (e.g., 101 represents a right to buy the underlying bond for $101,000 plus accrued interest). Exercise prices for bill options are expressed as complements of discount rates (i.e., 100 minus the annualized discount rate). Premiums for bond and note options are expressed in 32nds, with each ½₂ representing ½₂ of one percent of the unit of trading (i.e., $100,000). Premiums for bill options are expressed on an annualized basis in basis points, with each basis point repre-

---

[18]*See* 17 C.F.R. § 240.12a-6 (1985).

[19]*See* Form S-20, Securities Act Release No. 6426, 47 Fed. Reg. 41950 (1982).

[20]For an overview of security options, see generally CBOE, UNDERSTANDING OPTIONS (1984).

[21]*See generally id. See* Carasick, *Mechanics and Regulation of Options Trading,* in HANDBOOK OF FINANCIAL MARKETS 570, 575-76 (F. Fabozzi & F. Zarb eds. 1981).

senting ¹⁄₁₀₀ of one percent of the principal amount covered by the option (i.e., $1,000,000).[22]

(3) FOREIGN CURRENCY OPTIONS

Despite the fact that foreign currencies are not themselves securities, options on foreign currencies are "securities" if the options are traded on a national securities exchange.[23] At this writing, security options are traded on Deutsch marks, Swiss francs, British pounds, Canadian dollars, Japanese yen, and French francs. Contract sizes vary (from 25,000 British pounds to 12.5 million Japanese yen). The foreign currency options traded on the PHLX are American-style options; the foreign currency options traded on the CBOE are European-style options, exercise of which is permitted only on the last trading day before expiration. Exercise prices and premiums are stated in U.S. cents (or fractions of U.S. cents) per unit of foreign currency.[24] Proposals are pending before the SEC for the trading of options on the European Currency Unit ("ECU"), but objections have been raised that the CFTC, rather than the SEC, has jurisdiction over such options.

(4) INDEX OPTIONS

An index (in the context of security options) is a measure of the value of a group of stocks or other securities. Options on such an index of securities (as opposed to futures on such an index or options on futures on such an index) are themselves securities subject to the SEC's regulations.[25] At present, security options overlaying 12 different indexes are traded. The most successful of these are the S&P 100 Index and the S&P 500 Index (both traded on the CBOE), the Major Market Index (traded on the AMEX), the Value Line Composite Index (traded on the PHLX), and the NYSE Composite Index (traded on the NYSE). Stock indexes are calculated in different ways; some are "value weighted," others simply divide aggregate stock prices by number of stocks (disregarding number of shares), and still others average percentage price changes of all stocks included in the index. The unit of trading for indexes is not tied to a particular number of shares but rather to a "multiplier" (e.g., the multiplier for the S&P 100 Index is 100; that for

---

[22]*See generally* CBOE, UNDERSTANDING INTEREST RATE OPTIONS (1985).

[23]SEA § 3(a)(10), 15 U.S.C. § 78c(a)(10) (1982).

[24]*See generally* OCC, *supra* note 5, ch. 7.

[25]SEA § 3(a)(10), 15 U.S.C. § 78c(a)(10) (1982).

the S&P 500 Index is 500). The premium for an index option is expressed in points and fractions of points. The total dollar premium for a single index option is determined by multiplying the quoted premium by the applicable index multiplier. Exercise prices for index options are expressed in points and fractions of points. The manner in which adjustments are made to index options are critical to pricing continuity and are in the control of the index publishers, the trading market, and OCC.[26]

(b) OPTIONS ON COMMODITIES

Commodity options refer to both options on physical commodities, often called "cash options," and options on futures contracts or "futures options." Trading of commodity options on domestic agricultural commodities was prohibited in 1936 with the adoption of the CEA.[27] Because of widespread fraud and abuse in options trading on nonagricultural commodities in the 1970s, on June 1, 1978, the CFTC banned all trading in commodity options,[28] except for so-called trade options (i.e., those sold to commercial users of the underlying commodity)[29] and dealer options (i.e., options on physical commodities sold by persons meeting certain established criteria).[30] The CFTC's action was confirmed by the 1978 amendments to the CEA.[31] In 1981, the CFTC adopted comprehensive rules governing the trading on domestic commodity exchanges of options on futures contracts.[32] In 1982, the CFTC amended its rules to permit exchanges to trade options on physical commodities.[33] At present, all exchange trading of commodity options is pursuant to what the CFTC has called a "pilot option program."[34] This program now permits each exchange to trade eight nonagricultural commodity options of which no more than two may be on physical commodities,[35] plus two options on agricultural commodities.[36] The CFTC has proposed

[26]*See generally* AMEX, CBOE, NASD, NYSE, PHLX & OCC, *supra* note 5, ch. 5; CBOE, INDEX OPTIONS FOR PORTFOLIO MANAGERS (1985); AMEX, MAJOR MARKET INDEX OPTIONS (1983).

[27]Act of June 15, 1936, ch. 545, §§ 4c, 5, 49 Stat. 1491, 1492. *See generally* Lower, *The Regulation of Commodity Options*, 1978 DUKE L. J. 1095-1111.

[28]43 Fed. Reg. 16153 (1978).

[29]17 C.F.R. § 32.4 (1985).

[30]17 C.F.R. § 32.12 (1985); *see* CEA § 4c(d)(1), 7 U.S.C. § 6c(d)(1) (Supp. I 1983).

[31]Futures Trading Act of 1978 § 4c(c), 7 U.S.C. § 6c(c) (Supp. I 1983).

[32]46 Fed. Reg. 54500 (1981).

[33]47 Fed. Reg. 56996 (1982).

[34]46 Fed. Reg. 54500, 54501 (1981).

[35]17 C.F.R. § 33.4(a)(6)(ii) (1985); 50 Fed. Reg. 51671 (1985); 50 Fed. Reg. 45811 (1985).

[36]49 Fed. Reg. 2752, 2756 (1984).

to eliminate the pilot nature of options trading on nonagricultural futures contracts and to remove the numerical limitation on the number of such options that an exchange could trade.[37] The trading of commodity options other than on exchanges is prohibited except for trade options and dealer options, neither of which include options on agricultural commodities.[38]

The first futures options—on Treasury bonds and sugar—began trading in October, 1982 on the CBT and the CSC.[39] Since that time, commodity options have established themselves as an important trading vehicle.[40] At the present time, futures options are traded on financial instruments (including Treasury bonds and notes), agricultural products (including sugar and corn), metals (including gold and silver), foreign currencies, and indexes (including the S&P 500 Stock Index and NASDAQ 100 Index). Cash options are traded only on gold.

Cash options or options on physicals are similar to securities options in that upon exercise the holder receives and the writer delivers actual property or cash. (For example, the gold contract on the ACC settles in cash; the settlement amount being the dollar difference between the afternoon London gold fixing price on the business day following the submission of the exercise notice and the exercise price of the contract, multiplied by 100.)[41] A futures option is somewhat different, because a long call that is exercised becomes a long futures position and a short call that is assigned becomes a short futures position. Likewise, a long put becomes a short futures contract position and a short call becomes a long futures contract position. This is so because upon exercise, a call writer must sell a futures contract to the call holder and a put writer must buy a futures contract from a put holder. The exercise of the option occurs by "book entry in the clearing organization of positions in the underlying futures contracts,"[42] and, therefore, apart from increasing open interest in the underlying futures contract, does not affect futures market operations.

Futures options trade in the same delivery months as the underlying futures and have expiration cycles based on the expiration cycles of the underlying futures. This means that a July sugar option is an option to

---

[37] 50 Fed. Reg. 35247, 35248 (1985).

[38] 50 Fed. Reg. 39656, 39659 (1985).

[39] CFTC News Release No. 980-82 (Aug. 31, 1982).

[40] At present, there are 26 exchange-traded commodity options. The CFTC has recently increased the number of nonagricultural options that may be traded on each commodity exchange from five to eight. 50 Fed. Reg. 45811 (1985).

[41] ACC, GOLD OPTIONS (n.d.).

[42] 17 C.F.R. § 33.4(a)(1)(ii) (1985).

buy (in the case of a call) or sell (in the case of a put) a July futures contract for 112,000 lbs. of sugar. The July sugar option does not expire in July but in the preceding month; specifically, the Saturday following the second Friday of June.[43] A similar scheme is followed for all futures options now traded.[44]

As with all options, opening and closing transactions in commodity options involve the transfer of a premium payment. Premiums in commodity options are quoted in one of two ways: in points that are valued in dollars or in dollars. An example of the point system is options on the S&P 500 Stock Index futures. These options are quoted in decimals, with each full point worth $500 and each .05 of a point worth $25. Options on Treasury bond futures are also quoted in points but expressed as fractions, with each 64th of a point equal to 1/64 of one percent of a $100,000 Treasury bond futures contract (i.e., 1/64 equals $15.63). An example of the dollar system is options on gold futures and gold, both of which are quoted in dollars per ounce. Because there are 100 troy ounces in the COMEX gold futures contract and the ACC cash commodity contract for gold, a premium of $10 represents $1000. Likewise, options on foreign currency futures are quoted in "American terms" (i.e., dollars per pound, mark, franc, etc.). Thus a premium of "50" for an option on the Swiss franc futures contract is $.50 per franc, which represents a premium of $625 ($.0050 × 125,000 SF = $625).[45]

§ 5.3   TYPES OF MARKETS

(a)   EXCHANGE MARKETS

Standardized options—both security options and commodity options—trade on registered exchanges. Exchange trading commenced in 1973 for security options and in 1982 for commodity options. All standardized exchange traded options trade in basically the same manner (i.e., by open outcry at a central location on a "floor"). There are, however, differences in the actual conduct of that trading. For example, some

[43]Expiration and Exercise of Options, CSC Rule 10.10 (July 31, 1983).

[44]For example, options on Treasury bonds traded on the CBT expire at 10:00 A.M. on the first Saturday following the last day of trading, and cease trading at 12:00 P.M. on the first Friday preceding, by at least five business days, the first notice day for the corresponding Treasury bond futures contract, which is always in the month prior to the futures contract delivery month. CBT Rules 2808.01, 2809.01, 2813.01 (Apr. 1, 1985).

[45]For a general discussion of commodity options, see INDEX AND OPTION MARKET DIVISION OF CME, OPTIONS ON FUTURES (1983); CSC, UNDERSTANDING OPTIONS ON FUTURES (1982).

exchanges have specialists and others do not;[46] all security exchanges have, while no commodity exchange has, a repository for limit orders;[47] commodity exchanges treat all transactions on an equal footing, while securities exchanges are required to give public orders priority in execution to members' proprietary trades;[48] and futures options and their underlying futures trade on the same exchange, whereas stock options and their underlying stocks have been prohibited from being traded on the same exchange.[49]

Beside the variations in trading rules on the various exchanges, there are significant differences in the processes by which securities and commodity exchanges obtain the authority to trade options. To be traded on a securities exchange, an option must be "listed" on that exchange.[50] In addition, because security options are themselves securities, their issuer (i.e., OCC) must register the options under the Securities Act.[51] Furthermore, pursuant to Section 9(b) of the SEA, the SEC requires that before a broker or dealer may accept an option order from a customer

---

[46]*Compare* CBOE Rule 8.1, *reprinted in* CBOE CONST. & RULES (CCH) ¶ 2271 (May 1, 1973) (the CBOE has a competitive market maker system) *with* AMEX By-Law art. 1, § 1(u) *reprinted in* AM. STOCK EX. GUIDE (CCH) ¶ 13,011 (1985) (the AMEX assigns a specialist to each option class) and CBT Rule 301.00 (Nov. 1, 1983) (no commodity exchange uses a specialist system).

[47]*Compare* CBOE Rule 7.1, *reprinted in* CBOE CONST. & RULES (CCH) ¶ 2221 (Jan. 11, 1979) (the CBOE and the other securities options exchanges have a mechanism to "protect" limit orders against inferior executions) *with* CME Rule 540 (Dec. 1982) (the CME, like the other commodity exchanges, provides no such mechanism).

[48]*Compare* SEA § 11(a)(1), 15 U.S.C. § 78k(a)(1) (1982), and 17 C.F.R. § 240.11a1-1(T) (1985) (requiring members' proprietary trades originated on the floor to yield "priority, parity, and precedence" in execution to public orders) *with* 17 C.F.R. § 1.38 (1985) (requiring all purchases and sales of commodity options to be executed "openly and competitively").

[49]*Compare* 17 C.F.R. § 33.4(a) *with* Special Options Study, *supra* note 7, at 870-925. *But see* SEA Release No. 22026 (May 8, 1985), 50 Fed. Reg. 20310 (1985); SEA Release No. 22439 (Sept. 20, 1985); 50 Fed. Reg. 39191 (1985) (authorizing a "pilot program" to commence in 1986 for the side-by-side trading of stock and options).

[50]SEA § 12(a), 15 U.S.C. § 78(*l*) (1982), requires the exchange to comply with the registration requirements of SEA § 12(b). *See* 17 C.F.R. § 240.12a-6 (1985). The multiple trading of securities options has been a matter of considerable debate. Special Options Study, *supra* note 7, at 800-70. At present, the options exchanges use a "lottery" system to allocate options on listed stocks thereby precluding multiple trading of all but a few of these options. SEA Release No. 22026 (May 8, 1985), *supra* note 49, at 20318-19. No such allocation system exists for options on unlisted stocks or other security options. *Id.* at 20334.

[51]*See* Form S-20, *supra* note 19 (prescribing context of registration statement); 17 C.F.R. § 230.153(b) (1985) (providing that prospectuses need not be delivered directly to investors but may be delivered to the exchange trading the options); 17 C.F.R. § 230.134a (1985) (permitting dissemination of educational materials without deeming these materials to be a prospectus).

it must have furnished the customer with an "option disclosure document" prepared by the security options markets.[52]

In contrast to the essentially disclosure oriented regulatory scheme for standardized security options,[53] commodity options regulation turns in large part on consideration of economic utility. An exchange trading commodity options is deemed to be a contract market subject to all of the regulatory requirements applicable to a contract market.[54] To commence trading in a commodity option, an exchange must "demonstrate" that the option is likely to serve a "legitimate economic purpose," that "commercial interests" have participated in the formulation of the contract, and that the market for the underlying future or physical commodity is liquid and will not be disrupted by options trading.[55] The CFTC has also imposed disclosure obligations on FCMs.[56] The specifically required risk disclosure statement is a pro forma document set out in full text in a CFTC regulation.[57] This document advises prospective customers to obtain certain additional information about options trading from their FCMs, which FCMs are required to provide.[58]

(b) OVER-THE-COUNTER MARKETS

In May 1985, the SEC approved the NASD's proposal to trade standardized options through its NASDAQ system.[59] In September 1985, standardized over-the-counter options began to trade on the NASDAQ 100 Index. At present, these are the only standardized over-the-counter security options; the NASD, however, has proposed to commence NASDAQ trading in options on a large number of unlisted stock.[60]

---

[52]17 C.F.R. § 9b-1 (1985). The most recent option disclosure document, AMEX, CBOE, NASD, NYSE, PHLX & OCC, *supra* note 5, is dated September 1985 and was prepared by the five security option exchanges, the NASD, and OCC. For a discussion of the interrelationships between the registration requirements under the Securities Act and the operation of Rule 9b-1, see SEA Release No. 19055 (Sept. 16, 1982), 47 Fed. Reg. 41950 (1982).

[53]*But see* SEA Release No. 15575 (Feb. 22, 1979), 44 Fed. Reg. 11876 (Mar. 2, 1979) establishing a pervasive customer protection scheme for security options which goes well beyond traditional disclosure concepts.

[54]17 C.F.R. § 33.2 (1985).

[55]17 C.F.R. § 33.4(a)(5) (1985).

[56]17 C.F.R. § 33.7(a) (1985).

[57]17 C.F.R. § 33.7(b) (1985). For the policy considerations behind the CFTC's decision to prescribe the precise language of its risk disclosure statement, see 43 Fed. Reg. 31886, 31887 (1978).

[58]17 C.F.R. § 33.7(c) (1985). The Futures Industry Association has prepared an Options on Futures Risk Disclosure statement for use by FCMs generally.

[59]SEA Release No. 22026 (May 8, 1985), 50 Fed. Reg. 20310 (1985).

[60]*Id.*

The over-the-counter trading of standardized security options differs from exchange trading in the absence of an auction mechanism and the lack of centralized limit order protection (which is also true of options traded on more than one exchange). However, the characteristics of the options traded through NASDAQ and on the exchanges are identical (i.e., all are issued by OCC), as are the disclosure and customer protection requirements.

Conventional security options trade exclusively in the over-the-counter market. The over-the-counter market was once the only market for trading security options, but with the success of standardized exchange traded options, there is now a relatively small conventional security options market.[61] Conventional security options are individually negotiated between the parties. Although standardized terms were generally in place for such options prior to 1973,[62] because the market now primarily serves investors and dealers looking for tailor-made contracts, little generalization about terms is currently possible.

There is a very limited secondary market for conventional security options. Generally, however, the writer is willing to accommodate the holder's desire to liquidate his position. For example, if a conventional option has no intrinsic value immediately prior to expiration, the writer normally will buy the option for a nominal price (e.g., $1) as a service to the customer. This practice enables the customer to establish a specific date for his loss for tax purposes. If the option is "in-the-money," the holder may exercise the option, or the writer may be willing to buy it back. In the latter case, while the dollar amount of profit will remain the same, the investor may obtain long-term capital gain treatment if the option has been held for the required period of time.[63]

Conventional (i.e., over-the-counter) commodity options are of only two types: trade options[64] and dealer options.[65] Trade options are cash options on nonagricultural commodities[66] that must be sold to "a producer, processor, or commercial user of, or a merchant handling the commodity or the products or by-products thereof," who is entering into the transaction "solely for purposes related to its business as such."[67]

---

[61]For a discussion of the over-the-counter options market prior to the establishment of the CBOE, see Farmer, *Options*, in STOCK MARKET HANDBOOK 298 (F. Zarb & G. Kerekes eds. 1970); G. GASTINEAU, *supra* note 1, at 20-27.

[62]Farmer, *supra* note 61, at 300.

[63]Carasick, *Mechanics and Regulation of Options*, *supra* note 21, at 576.

[64]CEA § 4c(c), 7 U.S.C. § 6c(c) (Supp. I 1983).

[65]CEA § 4c(d), 7 U.S.C. § 6c(d) (Supp. I 1983).

[66]50 Fed. Reg. 39656 (1985).

[67]17 C.F.R. § 32.4(a) (1985).

Dealer options are also cash options on nonagricultural commodities,[68] but may only be written by persons domiciled in the United States who on May 1, 1978 were in the business of both "granting options on a physical commodity" and "buying, selling, producing or otherwise utilizing that commodity" and who meet net worth, segregation, record keeping, and other requirements.[69] Although dealer options may be offered and sold (but not written) by FCMs (who are subject to CFTC imposed disclosure requirements),[70] because of the limitations on who may hold trade options and who may write dealer options there is no meaningful secondary market for conventional commodity options.[71]

§ 5.4   TYPES OF TRANSACTIONS

Market participants use a wide variety of option trading strategies. The more common strategies include buying and selling call options, buying and selling put options, and entering into various spreads, straddles, and combinations. This section briefly discusses certain common option strategies and identifies the market participants that are most likely to use them.[72]

(a)   BUYING OR SELLING CALL OPTIONS

A call option gives the purchaser the right to buy the underlying interest for the strike price at any time prior to expiration. The purchaser pays a premium to the writer for granting the option.[73]

---

[68]17 C.F.R. § 32.12(a) (1985).

[69]Id. On dealer options generally, see T. RUSSO, 1 REGULATION OF THE COMMODITIES FUTURES AND OPTIONS MARKETS ch. 7 (Regulatory Manual Series 1985).

[70]17 C.F.R. § 33.12(f) (1985).

[71]For a history of the trade and dealer options exceptions from the option ban in CEA 4c(c), 7 U.S.C. § 6c(c) (Supp. I 1983), and a discussion of the CFTC's pending proposals for additional regulation of these options, see 50 Fed. Reg. 10786 (1985).

[72]For a description of the most common option strategies, their "payoff diagrams" (i.e., diagrams relating profit or loss from a position if held to expiration to the price of the underlying interest at expiration), and their "decay" characteristics (i.e., the effects of time decay on the total option premium involved in the position), see Becker & Deglar, 19 Option Strategies and When to Use Them, FUTURES, June 1984, at 46; see also Special Options Study, supra note 7, at 106-14.

[73]See generally CBOE, ARE CALL OPTIONS FOR YOU? (1977).

(1) CALL BUYING

Call options are generally bought in the hope that the underlying interest—and therefore the options themselves—will increase in value. The options may then be sold or exercised before the expiration date for a profit. If the call is exercised, the holder must pay the strike price (through the clearing organization) to an option seller in exchange for the underlying interest. By exercising a profitable call option prior to expiration, however, the holder loses any time value left in the option. Further, the transaction costs in exercising the option and selling the underlying interest (assuming the option does not settle for cash) are typically higher than those involved in simply selling the option. As might be expected, therefore, a very small percentage of standardized call options are actually exercised.

The benefits of call buying include leverage and limited risk. Leverage is available because a call buyer can benefit from an increase in the value of the underlying interest with the investment of only a fraction of the cost of the underlying interest. Risk is limited because an option buyer can never lose more than the premium he paid to acquire the option (which will be less than the value of the underlying interest). Of course, in percentage terms the possible loss on an option may often be greater than the loss that would have been sustained if the underlying interest had been held directly. The call option buyer can lose his entire investment if the value of the underlying interest does not increase, but this is an unlikely result if the investor holds the underlying interest.

Call purchases can be used in conjunction with positions in the underlying interests. For example, it is useful to recognize that (1) a long call combined with an equal short position in the underlying interest (sometimes called a "synthetic put") limit the risk of the short sale to a fixed amount, and (2) long calls combined with a short position in the underlying interest of a lesser amount (e.g., in a ratio of 2:1) (sometimes called a "simulated straddle") limit loss potential while offering unlimited profit potential if the value of the underlying interest rises *or* falls far enough.

(2) CALL SELLING

A writer of a call obligates himself to deliver the interest underlying the option to a holder if and when he is assigned (i.e., the clearing organization allocates an exercise notice to him). When the writer delivers the underlying interest, he receives the exercise price. It is convenient to distinguish two types of call sales: sales by persons who do not own the interest underlying the option (uncovered calls), and sales by persons who do own the underlying interest (covered calls). A combination of these two types of positions (e.g., writing one covered and one uncovered call with the same strike price and expiration date on the same underlying interest) is referred to as "ratio writing."[74]

(i) Uncovered Calls

A seller of an uncovered call is often referred to as being "naked." Naked call selling is similar to selling the underlying interest short, in that the risk is theoretically unlimited. Unlike a short sale, however, the naked call writer's potential profit is limited to the amount of the premium. In general, a naked call seller does not want the calls to be exercised, because if the market price for the underlying interest increases and the call is exercised, the writer must obtain the underlying interest at a price that is likely to be above the exercise price. The uncovered call seller will always profit, however, if the exercise price plus the premium he received (minus transaction costs) is less than the market price for the underlying interest at the time of exercise.

(ii) Covered Calls

An owner of an interest underlying options may write calls on that interest to increase income or to protect against a decline in the value of the interest. The writer receives the premium, and provided the underlying interest is not "called away," by writing calls he can increase his yield. Further, by writing calls an interest holder can partially protect against a decline in the value of the interest. Of course, the "cost" of writing covered calls is the loss of profit potential on the underlying interest in the event of a substantial increase in its market value. In this regard, it should be recognized that the payoff diagram (i.e., a diagram relating profit or loss from a position if held to expiration to the price of the underlying interest at expiration) for a one-to-one long stock/short call position has the same shape as that for a short put.[75]

To illustrate the use of covered calls, assume an investor owns 1000 shares of XYZ stock for which he paid $50 per share. Assume further that the September 50 call option on XYZ stock can be written for a premium of $5 per share. The investor writes 10 calls against his XYZ

---

[74]*See generally* CBOE, CALL OPTION WRITING STRATEGIES (1975).
[75]J. COX & M. RUBINSTEIN, *supra* note 15, at 8-9.

stock (each call covering 100 shares). When the option trade settles the next day, the investor's account is credited with $5000 of premium income, minus commission costs. This premium income belongs to the seller irrespective of whether his stock is called away. If the price of the stock does not go above $55 (i.e., the strike price plus the premium) the investor has increased his yield from his underlying securities investment. Further, any cash dividends paid on his XYZ stock prior to assignment belong to him.[76] If the value of XYZ stock declines, the covered call writer is "protected" down to 45, because the five-point decrease in stock value would be offset by the $5000 premium for writing the 10 options.[77]

(iii) Ratio Writing

Ratio writing is simply writing calls on a greater amount of the underlying interest than one actually owns. For example, an investor owning 100 shares of stock and writing two options would be engaged in ratio writing. This combined position creates a profit range (i.e., the range between the downside break even point and the upside break even point) such that the investor will profit as long as the price of the underlying interest does not experience an extreme change in either direction. A "ratio write" will produce greater profit than either covered or naked writing if the underlying interest remains relatively unchanged prior to expiration, but it also has significant downside risk (loss of the entire value of the stock less premium received) and unlimited upside risk.

(b) BUYING OR SELLING PUT OPTIONS

A put option gives the purchaser the right to sell the underlying interest at the exercise or strike price at any time prior to expiration. The purchaser pays a premium to the writer for granting the option. The price relationship between put premiums and the value of the underlying interest are the opposite of the call premium relationship; as the value of the underlying interest decreases, the put premium tends to increase.[78]

---

[76]If a call is exercised before the ex-dividend date, the exercising call holder is entitled to the dividend even if the writer does not receive notice of assignment until after that date.

[77]For a detailed discussion of covered call writing, see L. McMillan, *supra* note 14, ch. 2.

[78]*See generally* CBOE, Are Put Options For You? (1977).

(1) PUT BUYING

Put options are generally bought in the hope that the underlying interest will decline in value during the option's life, thereby making the option more valuable. In other words, buying puts is simply the opposite of buying calls; it is a leveraged means of profiting from a decline in the price of stock or other interests. Buying puts is similar to selling short with the following differences: long puts have a known risk, are not subject to margin calls, provide greater leverage than short selling, and the buyer of a put is not obligated to pay dividends on the underlying stock.

An owner of an interest underlying puts might buy puts as protection (i.e., to hedge) against a decrease in the price of the underlying interest. If the underlying interest declines in value, the put holder can exercise his option and sell the interest at the strike price. Unlike "hedging" a long interest with short calls, a long interest/long put "hedge" takes all risk (beyond the cost of the put) out of the position. Similarly, by combining a long put with a covered write, the large potential loss in the covered write position (i.e., if the price of the underlying interest declines by more than the amount of the call premium) is eliminated.[79]

(2) PUT SELLING

A writer of a put option is generally seeking to earn premium income. A person who believes the value of the underlying interest will remain the same or decline can sell put options; his maximum profit equals the premium received and his downside risk is limited only by the fact that the value of the underlying interest cannot go below zero. In this regard it should be recognized that writing uncovered puts is equivalent in terms of profit and loss characteristics (but obviously not in terms of the amount of investment required or right to dividends) to writing covered calls.

Puts can also be used to buy the underlying interest. A person who does not want to purchase the underlying interest at the current market price can write a put option in the hope of acquiring the underlying property at a lower price. (Looked at from this perspective, writing puts is similar to entering limit orders to buy the underlying interest.) If the put is exercised, the cost of the underlying interest to the put seller is

---

[79]For a discussion of put buying strategies, see generally CBOE, BUYING PUTS, STRADDLES AND COMBINATIONS (1977).

the exercise price minus the premium. If the put is not exercised, the put writer nevertheless has earned the premium.[80]

(c) SPREAD TRANSACTIONS

A spread is a transaction involving the purchase and sale of call options or put options on the same underlying interest. The basic objective of a spread transaction is to reduce the risk of a simple long or short option position to a known, predetermined amount. The expected profit arises from the belief that the option purchased is undervalued relative to the option sold.

The basic spreads can be classified as vertical (or money, price, or perpendicular) spreads, horizontal (or time or calendar) spreads, and diagonal spreads. In a vertical spread, one option is bought and another sold, both with the same underlying interest and expiration date but with different exercise prices. In a horizontal spread, one option is bought and another sold, both with the same underlying interest and exercise price but with different expiration dates. In a diagonal spread, one option is bought and another sold, both with the same underlying interest but with different exercise prices and different expiration dates. The terms vertical, horizontal, and diagonal arise from the manner in which option prices are printed in newspaper tables (e.g., exercise prices are printed vertically).

Spreads may be opened or closed by using a single order. In doing so, the customer must specify the price at which the spread is to be executed (i.e., the spread price is the difference in the prices of the two option series) and whether that price is a credit (i.e., cash inflow to the spreader) or a debit (cash outflow from the spreader). In a so-called credit spread, the short option is at a higher price than the long option. In a so-called debit spread, the long option costs more than is received for the short option. Of course, it is also possible to "leg" into a spread, that is, to place separate buy and sell orders (at the same or different times) for the long and short components (i.e., the "legs") of the spread.[81]

(1) VERTICAL SPREADS

One enters a vertical spread based on the belief that the relationship between strike prices for options expiring at the same time on the same

[80]For a discussion of put selling strategies, see generally CBOE, WRITING PUTS, STRADDLES AND COMBINATIONS (1978).

[81]For a discussion of spreading, see generally, AMEX, SPREADING STRATEGIES (1975).

underlying interest are out of line (i.e., over valued or under valued), and the option trader's opinion of how they are out of line will determine the nature of the spread he puts on.

(i) Bull Spreads

In a bull (or purchased) spread, a person buys a put or call at one strike price and sells another put or call on the same underlying interest with the same expiration date at a higher strike price. A bull spread is always put on at a debit if calls are used and a credit if puts are used, and tends to be profitable if the underlying interest goes up in price. The spread has a maximum profit (for calls equal to the difference in strike prices minus the net debit; for puts equal to the net credit) and a maximum loss (for calls equal to the net debit; for puts equal to difference in strike prices minus the net credit).

(ii) Bear Spreads

In a bear (or sold) spread, a person buys a put or call at one strike price and sells a put or call on the same underlying interest with the same expiration date at a lower strike price. A bear spread is always put on at a credit if calls are used and a debit if puts are used, and tends to be profitable if the underlying interest goes down in price. The spread has a maximum profit (for calls equal to the net credit; for puts equal to the difference between strike prices minus the net debit) and a maximum loss (for calls equal to the difference between strike prices minus the net credit; for puts equal to the net debit).

(iii) Butterfly Spreads

A butterfly spread consists of puts or calls for the same underlying interest with three different strike prices. A long butterfly (i.e., one in which the middle two options are short and the "wings" are long) is put on at a debit. A short butterfly (i.e., one in which the middle two options are long and the "wings" are short) is put on at a credit. A long butterfly spread is a combination of a bear spread (e.g., one long option and one short option at a lower strike price) and a bull spread (e.g., one long option and one short option at a higher strike price) with the two short options being written at the same strike price.[82] In other words, a long butterfly involves writing two calls (or two puts) at the same strike price, buying one call (or one put) at a lower strike price, and buying another call (or put) at a higher strike price. A long butterfly requires only a small investment to establish and has a very limited risk (i.e., the amount of the debit). The long butterfly will produce a profit[83] if the price of the underlying interest remains close to the strike price of the written options. For ordinary investors, a butterfly can involve high commission costs, and for that reason may be an attractive trading strategy only for professional market participants.

(2) HORIZONTAL SPREADS

A horizontal spread is a spread between options with the same strike price but different expiration dates. For example, a horizontal spread would be established by buying July ABC 50 options and selling January ABC 50 options. The basic assumption underlying the horizontal spread is that as time passes the spread will widen (i.e., the spread between two distant expiration months will be less than that between two nearby expiration months). Horizontal spreads can be used to profit from little or no movement in the price of the underlying interest (neutral spread), an increase in the price of the underlying interest (bull spread), or a decrease in the price of the underlying interest (bear spread).[84]

(3) DIAGONAL SPREADS

A diagonal spread is a combination of vertical and horizontal spreads, and involves the purchase and sale of options of the same class but with different expiration dates and different strike prices. Any type of spread

---

[82]Alternatively, a butterfly spread can be viewed as a variable or ratio spread (e.g., two short options at the same strike price and one long option at a lower strike price) with "an insurance policy" (i.e., the addition of a higher priced long option). CBOE, REFERENCE MANUAL I-12 (1982). For example, in a credit ratio spread consisting of one long XYZ 50 and two short XYZ 60, the upside risk is unlimited. By adding another long option (for example, one XYZ 70) the maximum loss is limited to the amount of the debit for the entire position.

[83]Maximum profit on a long butterfly is equal to the difference between the strike prices minus the net debit. Maximum profit on a short butterfly is equal to the net credit at which the spread is established.

[84]For a discussion of the uses and advantages of horizontal spreads, see M. ANSBACHER, THE NEW OPTIONS MARKET 159-67 (2d ed. 1979).

(e.g., bull, bear, butterfly, ratio, or backspread)[85] can be "diagonalized." For example, a call spread can be diagonalized by purchasing longer term options and selling shorter term options. This technique has the effect of making the call spread slightly more bearish at the expiration of the near term option.[86]

(d) STRADDLE AND COMBINATION TRANSACTIONS

A combination involves options of different types (i.e., puts and calls) on the same underlying interest. A straddle is a kind of combination: specifically, a long or short position in both puts and calls with the same expiration date and exercise price. Straddles are generally purchased by persons anticipating a substantial price movement in the underlying interest who do not know (or care about) the direction of that movement. Conversely, straddles are generally sold by persons who do not anticipate any substantial price movement. Straddles can be bullish or bearish, depending on the exercise prices of the options in relation to the price of the underlying interest when the position is established. For example, buying a straddle with an exercise price close to the price of the underlying interest would be bullish because only a small upward price movement is necessary to break even. Straddles may be written covered or uncovered.[87]

Other combinations involve puts and calls on the same underlying interest with differing terms. For example, a "strangle" involves a long call and a long put with the same expiration date but different exercise prices. (The maximum potential loss in buying a strangle is typically less than that involved in buying a straddle; for the strangle, however, that loss will be realized if the underlying interest is anywhere between the two strike prices at expiration.) A "condor" (if it is long) involves the sale of a strangle and the purchase of an additional put and call. (The additional put and call eliminate the potentially unlimited risk of selling a strangle. The same risk limiting technique could be used with a straddle.) Many other combinations are used.[88]

---

[85]A backspread or reverse ratio spread is often used by professionals. A backspread using calls, for example, involves selling a call and buying a greater number of calls at a higher strike price.

[86]On the use and theory of diagonal spreads, see L. McMillan, *supra* note 14, ch. 14.

[87]On straddles generally, see L. McMillan, *supra* note 14, at 271-78, 292-304.

[88]On combinations generally, see CBOE, *supra* note 82, at M-5 to M-9.

(e) ARBITRAGE TRANSACTIONS

Option arbitrage techniques "involve buying one side of an equivalent position and simultaneously selling the other side."[89] Option arbitrage techniques are generally used by market participants with low transaction costs and direct access to the floors of security and commodity exchanges.

(1) DISCOUNTING

Discounting (or put and call) arbitrage involves buying either a put or call option at a discount (e.g., buying a call that is selling at a discount from parity) and simultaneously taking an opposite position in the underlying interest (e.g., going short the stock). The option is then exercised and the position in the underlying interest closed out for a profit equal to the amount of the discount.[90]

(2) DIVIDEND ARBITRAGE

There are several types of dividend arbitrage. The most common involves buying, prior to an ex-dividend date, both a put option (with time value less than the amount of a forthcoming dividend) and the underlying stock. The arbitrageur collects the dividend, exercises the put, and sells the stock at the strike price (without the dividend).

(3) CONVERSIONS AND REVERSE CONVERSIONS

A conversion transaction consists of buying the interest underlying an option and also buying a put and selling a call with the same terms on that interest.[91] Once established, a conversion's profit or loss is fixed. If the short call is overvalued relative to the corresponding long put, the conversion is a risk-free way of capturing the disparity. To make the same point another way, if the cost of carrying the entire position to expiration is less than the credit at which the option position can be established, the conversion transaction has a locked in profit.[92]

A reverse conversion is the mirror image of a conversion. It consists

---

[89]L. McMILLAN, *supra* note 14, at 370.

[90]Special Options Study, *supra* note 7, at 158.

[91]It should be noted that the long stock/short call position (sometimes called a "short synthetic put") is equivalent to selling a put.

[92]*See generally* Special Options Study, *supra* note 7, at 149-51.

of selling (short) the interest underlying an option and also selling a put and buying a call with the same terms on that interest.[93] The reverse conversion is used if the call is undervalued relative to the put. The position will be profitable if the interest earned on the short stock sale exceeds the net cost (i.e., debit) of establishing the option position.[94]

(4) BOX SPREADS

Basically, a box spread consists of buying and selling equivalent spreads. For example, the purchase of a call bull spread and the purchase of a put bear spread[95] would comprise a box spread. In this example, if the two spreads are purchased for less than the difference in the strike prices, the arbitrageur will have locked in a risk-free profit. A box spread, like a conversion or reverse conversion, has a value at expiration totally independent of the price of the underlying interest. Any time a "box" can be purchased for (i.e., both call and put spreads can be done at a debit) less than the difference in strike prices, the position will be profitable (disregarding transaction and carrying costs). Conversely, any time a box can be sold for (i.e., both call and put spreads can be done at a credit) more than the difference in strike prices, the position will be profitable.[96]

§ 5.5 MARGIN

(a) SECURITY OPTIONS

All security options are securities and, therefore, subject to the FRB's margin regulations.[97] Options may be purchased by a customer of a broker-dealer in a margin account or cash account, but in either case the customer must pay 100 percent of the premium.[98] Long options may not be borrowed against at a bank (i.e., they have no loan value).[99] Customers' short option transactions, other than covered calls and "cov-

---

[93]It should be noted that the short stock/long call position (sometimes called a "long synthetic put") is equivalent to buying a put.

[94]*See generally* Special Options Study, *supra* note 7, at 151-53.

[95]This position consists of a long call at, say, 50, a short call at, say, 60, a long put at 60, and a short put at 50.

[96]*See generally* L. McMillan, *supra* note 14, at 384-87.

[97]SEA §§ 3a(10), 7, 15 U.S.C. §§ 78c(a)(10), 78g (1982 & Supp. II 1984).

[98]12 C.F.R. § 220.18(e) (1985).

[99]12 C.F.R. § 221.8(c) (1985).

ered" puts, must be done in a margin account.[100] An exemption to this prohibition is made for long options held by registered market makers and specialists.[101]

Effective September 30, 1985, the FRB delegated all margin setting responsibility for short positions in options (both conventional and standardized) to the exchanges and the NASD.[102] The SEC has approved a uniform method of determining margin requirements for all customer short positions in standardized options.[103] This so-called premium-plus method basically provides that a customer with a short position must at all times have on deposit with his broker-dealer 100 percent of the current option premium plus a specified percentage of the current market value of the underlying interest (e.g., 15 percent in the case of equity securities, five percent in the case of broad-based indexes, and four percent in the case of foreign currencies), minus the amount the option is out-of-the-money. Under the premium-plus method, the margin can in no event be less than the premium marked-to-market plus a minimum specified percentage (five percent in the case of equity securities, two percent in the case of broad based indexes, and .75 percent in the case of foreign currencies).[104] Adjustments are made for spread positions.[105] No margin requirements are imposed on covered calls or short puts for which the broker-dealer is holding the full amount of the exercise price in cash or government securities.[106]

(b) COMMODITY OPTIONS

Commodity options are not subject to the FRB's margin authority. In contrast to futures contracts, commodity options are subject to the control of the CFTC.[107] The CFTC currently prohibits the margining of long option premiums. The CFTC requires a customer (whether a member or nonmember) to pay the full amount of the premium to his FCM, the FCM to pay that amount to its clearing firm (if it does not clear itself), and the clearing firm to pay that amount to the clearing organization.[108]

---

[100]*See* 12 C.F.R. §§ 220.5(c), .8(a)(3) (1985).

[101]12 C.F.R. § 221.5(c)(10) (1985).

[102]12 C.F.R. § 220.18(f) (1985); 50 Fed. Reg. 26355 (1985).

[103]SEA Release No. 22469, 50 Fed. Reg. 40633.

[104]*See, e.g.s,* CBOE Rules 12.3, 21.25, 22.11, 24.11 (Jan. 31, 1986).

[105]*Id.*

[106]12 C.F.R. § 220.8(a)(3) (1985).

[107]17 C.F.R. § 1.41(a)(2)(viii) (1985); 47 Fed. Reg. 56996, 57003 (1982).

[108]17 C.F.R. § 33.4(a)(2) (1985).

Various proposals are now before the CFTC to permit so-called futures style margining of long commodity option positions.[109] In accordance with these proposals, the buyer would be required initially to pay only a portion of the premium with additional amounts due (up to the full amount of the premium) if and as the position moved against the holder.

Margin requirements for short commodity option positions are set by the commodity exchanges, subject to review and approval by the CFTC.[110] Margin requirements are not uniform from exchange to exchange, although the general requirement is that the customer must post an amount equal to the required margin on the underlying futures contract[111] plus the premium marked-to-market minus all or a percentage of the amount by which the option is out-of-the-money.[112] Option-against-option spreads and option-against-futures spreads have lesser margin requirements.[113] In September 1985, the CFTC proposed guidelines for exchange margin requirements that would explicitly recognize the appropriateness of a "delta" margining system as well as other "methods of risk assessment."[114]

§ 5.6   CLEARANCE AND SETTLEMENT

All standardized security options are issued and guaranteed by OCC, a clearing organization regulated by the SEC. All standardized commodity options are issued by the clearing organization for the commodity exchange on which the options trade. All standardized options settle on the business day next following trade day (i.e., on "T plus 1"). This means that options must be paid for in full on the business day following the day on which they are purchased.

Each clearing organization sets its own margin requirements (subject to SEC and CFTC control) for clearing members. These requirements are not uniform or necessarily the same as the requirements with respect to the margins that the customers of the clearing members must deposit with these members.[115] OCC, for example, does not require its members

---

[109]See, e.g., 49 Fed. Reg. 8937 (1984).

[110]CEA §§ 4c(c), 5a(12), 7 U.S.C. §§ 6c(c), 7a(12) (Supp. I 1983).

[111]In the case of the ACC's cash option, a corresponding amount is fixed by the exchange.

[112]See, e.g., CME, A GUIDE TO MARGINS FOR OPTIONS ON FUTURES (1985).

[113]Id.

[114]50 Fed. Reg. 31625 (1985).

[115]Compare AMEX, CBOE, NASD, NYSE, PHLX & OCC, supra note 5, § B, at 1-15 with CBTCC Rules 601-608.1 (Sept. 15, 1982).

to deposit premiums with it for long option positions,[116] whereas the CFTC requires the commodity clearing organizations to receive the full amount of the premium paid by customers on long commodity options.[117]

Upon exercise of a standardized security option, it is assigned the next day on a random basis to a clearing member with a short position. The clearing member, in turn, assigns the exercise to one of its customers, who then assigns it to the ultimate customer. Delivery and payment with respect to stock underlying an option is due on the fifth business day following the day on which the exercise notice was properly tendered.[118] Settlement takes place through a clearing organization for the specific stock involved.[119] Delivery of foreign currencies pursuant to an assignment of an option takes place on the fourth business day (which is also a foreign business day) following the day the exercise notice was properly tendered,[120] at a bank in the country of origin of the currency.[121] Delivery and payment with respect to index options occurs in cash through OCC[122] on the business day following the day an exercise notice is properly tendered.[123]

Settlement of futures option exercises occurs on the business day following the day on which an exercise notice is properly tendered. Settlement occurs through the clearing organization, which establishes the new futures positions for the exercising and assigned option participants.[124] Assignment of exercise notices by the commodity clearing organization must be random as must be the assignment of such notices by FCMs to their customers.[125]

Settlement of conventional stock option exercises generally occurs on the fifth business day following the day on which the option is exercised.[126] Settlement of conventional commodity options (i.e., trade and dealer options) occurs in accordance with their terms.

---

[116]*See* OCC Rule 614(a), *reprinted in* CBOE CONST. & RULES (CCH) ¶ 4114 (June 26, 1985) (allowing clearing members to establish an option pledge account at a bank for the purpose of borrowing against long options).

[117]17 C.F.R. § 33.4(a)(2) (1985).

[118]OCC Rule 902, *reprinted in* CBOE CONST. & RULES (CCH) ¶ 4172 (Sept. 5, 1980).

[119]OCC Rule 913, *reprinted in* CBOE CONST. & RULES (CCH) ¶ 4183 (Oct. 29, 1982).

[120]OCC Rule 1604(a), *reprinted in* CBOE CONST. & RULES (CCH) ¶ 4367 (Nov. 21, 1982).

[121]OCC Rule 1606(c), *reprinted in* CBOE CONST. & RULES (CCH) ¶ 4369 (Aug. 29, 1984).

[122]OCC Rule 1806(a), *reprinted in* CBOE CONST. & RULES (CCH) ¶ 4429 (Feb. 4, 1983).

[123]OCC Rule 1805, *reprinted in* CBOE CONST. & RULES (CCH) ¶ 4428 (Feb. 4, 1983).

[124]*See* INDEX AND OPTIONS MARKET DIVISION OF CME, *supra* note 45, at 17.

[125]*See* CBT Rule 490.08 (Apr. 1, 1985).

[126]*E.g.,* OCC Rule 913, *reprinted in* CBOE CONST. & RULES (CCH) ¶ 4183 (Oct. 29, 1982).

Part Two

Taxation of Market Participants

Market participants fall into five general tax categories: investors, traders, dealers, hedgers, and brokers. Investors intend to profit from changes in the market price of their investments. Traders are professional investors who trade more frequently than investors, albeit for substantially the same purpose. Dealers trade as principals for their own accounts, performing a merchandising function by buying from and selling to their customers in the ordinary course of business. Hedgers use the markets to protect the price at which they will acquire or sell their inventories, as well as to assure a market for their products. And brokers act as their customers' agents, earning commission income from their brokerage activities.

Distinctions between the types of market participants are important from a tax standpoint. The tax category a particular participant falls into determines which tax rules apply. For gains on securities, commodities, and equity options held for over six months, noncorporate investors and traders generally are taxed at long-term capital gain rates of up to 20 percent, short-term capital gains are taxed at rates of up to 50 percent.[1] Under current law, a noncorporate taxpayer can deduct from his gross income 60 percent of the amount of any net long-term capital gain, thereby reducing the effective tax rate on such gain to a

---

[1]*See generally* Chapter 13.

maximum rate of 20 percent.[2] Investors and traders also are eligible for the "special tax treatment" available to section 1256 contracts.[3] Dealers, on the other hand, are taxed at ordinary income rates of up to 50 percent for their dealer activities, although they can obtain capital gain treatment on appropriate investment assets.[4]

Part Two of this book addresses in detail the taxation of market participants. Chapter Six provides an overview, in summary fashion, of the various types of participants. The remaining chapters in Part Two discuss relevant tax rules that relate to each type of market participant.

---

[2]On the other hand, net short-term and net long-term capital losses are deductible only to the extent the taxpayer has capital gains, plus $3000 of ordinary income. In addition, only 50 percent of net long-term capital losses can be used as a deduction against ordinary income. Therefore, $2 of net long-term capital loss produces a $1 deduction against ordinary income, limited to the $3000 cap.

[3]*See* Part Nine.

[4]*See* Part Four.

Six

Overview of Market Participants

§ 6.1 INVESTORS

Investors intend to derive a profit from changes in the market price of their security, commodity, or option positions. Investors simply intend to buy low and sell high, speculating that they will profit from increases in the market value of their long positions and decreases in the market value of their short positions.

Whether a taxpayer is classified as an investor is a question of fact.[1] Neither the Code nor Treasury regulations define investor, so one must look to case law. First, investors purchase and hold investments for capital appreciation upon sale, and to obtain income primarily generated from interest and dividends.[2] Investors usually do not hold their investments for short-term swings in market prices that influence the value of their investments.[3] Second, devoting substantial attention to their investments is insufficient to convert investors into traders or dealers.[4] In *Higgins v. Comm'r*,[5] the Supreme Court held that a taxpayer who devoted substantial managerial attention to his extensive stock, bond, and real estate investments (and who employed personnel to assist

---

[1]Higgins v. Comm'r, 312 U.S. 212, 217, *reh'g denied*, 312 U.S. 714 (1941).
[2]Chang Hsiao Liang v. Comm'r, 23 T.C. 1040, 1045 (1955).
[3]*Id.* at 1044.
[4]*See* section 6.2; section 6.3.
[5]312 U.S. 212 (1941).

him in such management) was not carrying on a trade or business.[6] Third, taxpayers who do not maintain separate bank accounts, offices, or personnel to assist in trading activities generally are classified as investors.[7] Fourth, although frequency and regularity of trading are factors to be considered, they are not determinative as to whether taxpayers are classified as investors. Large institutions (such as public pension funds) frequently trade securities, commodities, and options actively throughout the day. Even if such institutions have direct communication lines to their broker-dealers or FCMs and engage in a high volume of trading, they still are viewed as investors for tax purposes.

Moreover, dealers can invest in the property that they deal in and be viewed as investors with respect to these transactions. Securities dealers must comply with specific identification requirements to identify certain investment transactions as held for investment rather than held primarily for sale to customers in the ordinary course of business. Special rules imposed on securities dealers require them to maintain separate investment accounts to keep track of specific securities investment transactions.[8] Properly identified investment account positions that are, in fact, investments are eligible for capital asset treatment.[9]

§ 6.2 TRADERS

Traders are professional investors in securities, commodities, or options who are in the trade or business of buying and selling products, with the aim of profiting from favorable changes in the market prices of their positions. Traders seek to profit from increases in the market value of their long positions and decreases in the market value of their short positions. The distinction between traders and investors is not found in the Code or Treasury regulations and is not well defined in the case law. As a result, whether a taxpayer is a trader may ultimately be determined by both the volume of transactions and the taxpayer's ability to establish that his trading activities constitute the active conduct of a trade or business. Traders, unlike investors, are not viewed as passively accumulating earnings; they do not merely oversee their investments. Rather, traders manipulate their holdings to seek the best possible yield. Notwithstanding this somewhat blurred distinction between traders and

[6]*Id.* at 218.

[7]Purvis v. Comm'r, 530 F.2d 1332, 1334 (9th Cir. 1976); Moller v. U.S., 721 F.2d 810 (Fed. Cir. 1983), *cert. denied*, 104 S. Ct. 3534 (1984).

[8]I.R.C. § 1236.

[9]*See* section 9.7.

investors, it is clear that taxpayers who (1) devote most of their working time to the active management of extensive investment portfolios; (2) derive substantially all of their income from this activity; and (3) engage in a large number of transactions are engaged in a trade or business.[10] Traders profit from "the very acts of trading—direct management of purchasing and selling."[11]

Traders, unlike dealers, perform no merchandising functions. They are compensated neither by markups in the price of the property they sell nor by a commission.[12] Rather, traders depend upon a rise in the value of their long positions or a low purchase price to enable them to sell their holdings at a price in excess of cost.[13] Traders buy and sell securities, commodities, and options in continuous and frequent operations for their own accounts, with income principally derived from these purchases and sales. Traders simply speculate that they will derive a profit from their positions.

The basic definition of a trader was refined in *Purvis*,[14] which tested the taxpayer's status as a trader by considering whether (1) the taxpayer maintained an office or employed any assistants, (2) the gains or losses from the activity were reported on Schedule C of the taxpayer's tax return, (3) separate bank accounts were maintained for trading activities, and (4) the portfolio was held for a long time with little turnover and with income generated largely from interest and dividends.[15] This four-part test has been quoted with approval by several courts.[16] Other decisions according trader status have emphasized (1) the magnitude and continuous volume of purchases and sales,[17] (2) purchasing through a broker,[18] and (3) spending a large amount of time devoted to investments.[19]

Futures contracts are viewed neither as stock in trade to be sold at a markup nor as inventory items upon which gain or loss is measured at the end of each taxable year.[20] As a result, traders in commodity

---

[10]Levin v. U.S., 597 F.2d 760, 765 (Ct. Cl. 1979).

[11]*Id.* at 765.

[12]Seeley v. Helvering, 77 F.2d 323 (2d Cir. 1935).

[13]Kemon v. Comm'r, 16 T.C. 1026, 1033 (1951).

[14]530 F.2d at 1334.

[15]*Id.*

[16]Spring v. U.S., 38 A.F.T.R. 2d (P-H) 76-5533, 5535 (E.D. Tex. 1976).

[17]Ferguson v. Comm'r, 33 T.C.M. (CCH) 1082, 1083-84 (1974).

[18]Faroll v. Jarecki, 231 F.2d 281 (7th Cir.), *cert. denied*, 352 U.S. 830 (1956).

[19]Chemical Bank & Trust Co. v. U.S., 21 F. Supp. 167, 172-73 (Ct. Cl. 1937).

[20]Seroussi v. Comm'r, 22 T.C.M. (CCH) 1186, 1188–1189 (1963); Estate of Makransky v. Comm'r, 5 T.C. 397, 412 (1945), *aff'd*, 154 F.2d 59 (3d Cir. 1946).

futures contracts historically have been treated as traders for tax purposes.[21]

(a) PROFESSIONAL TRADERS

Traders include within their group certain industry professionals, such as floor traders or upstairs traders. Floor traders are members of a securities or commodity exchange who trade on the floor of these exchanges for their own accounts. While acting as floor traders, they have no responsibility to execute orders for the public or to maintain an orderly market.[22] Upstairs traders are exchange members who trade for their own accounts from their offices off of the trading floor. For tax purposes, the distinction between floor traders and upstairs traders is irrelevant; what is relevant is that the designation has been applied to taxpayers who trade on the exchange floor for their own accounts, as well as taxpayers who trade off of exchange floors.

The large number of separate transactions that floor traders enter into does not reclassify them as dealers for tax purposes. In *Faroll v. Jarecki*,[23] the court held that gains and losses incurred by a trader on the floor of the CBT were capital transactions not derived from sales to customers in the ordinary course of business. This was the holding even though the taxpayer personally was on the trading floor not less than 248 of the days on which the CBT was open for business during the tax year in question and entered into "more than 10,000 separate transactions."[24] This holding has been reaffirmed in several subsequent court decisions.[25] This analysis also has been applied to a floor trader who attempts to profit from the rapid turnover of positions, even though he clearly holds his positions as a source of business income.[26]

(b) OPTION DEALERS

Option dealers, defined as taxpayers registered with appropriate securities exchanges as market makers or specialists in listed options,[27] are

---

[21]*See* section 6.2(c); section 6.3(e).

[22]REPORT OF SPECIAL STUDY OF SECURITIES MARKETS OF THE SECURITIES AND EXCHANGE COMMISSION, H.R. DOC. NO. 95, Pt. 2, 88th Cong., 1st Sess. 47 (1963) [hereinafter referred to as "Special Securities Study"].

[23]231 F.2d at 287-88.

[24]*Id.* at 285.

[25]Vickers v. Comm'r, 80 T.C. 394, 406 n.12 (1983); *Seroussi*, 22 T.C.M. at 1186.

[26]Morris v. Comm'r, 38 B.T.A. 265, 267–68 (1938).

[27]I.R.C. § 1256(g)(8).

now taxed in the same way as traders for their section 1256 contract transactions. The DRA introduced for the first time a statutory definition of option dealers.[28]

Under the law in effect prior to the DRA, market makers and specialists in listed options (collectively referred to as "option market makers") treated themselves as dealers for tax purposes.[29] For tax years beginning after July 18, 1984, however, option market makers (now defined as option dealers) cannot treat themselves as "dealers" with respect to their option transactions that qualify as section 1256 contracts. What is confusing about this definition is that despite the fact that the Code defines these market participants as a type of dealer, it generally treats them as if they are traders with respect to their section 1256 contracts.

Designation as an "options dealer" is important in determining whether a taxpayer is eligible for section 1256 treatment on dealer equity options, even though his trading activities generate capital gains and losses under I.R.C. § 1256.[30] In addition, income from trading section 1256 contracts constitutes "net income from self-employment," which can be used to determine available pension and profit sharing benefits. In other words, pension and profit sharing plans are available to option dealers.

(c) COMMODITY DEALERS

The trader designation for tax purposes applies to commodity dealers, defined as taxpayers actively engaged in trading section 1256 contracts who are registered with a commodity exchange designated as a contract market by the CFTC.[31] The commodity dealer designation applies to taxpayers who historically have viewed themselves as traders, not dealers, and who report gains and losses as capital gains or losses. Despite this confusing designation, the tax treatment of commodity dealers under the current law is generally the same as the tax treatment of traders.

The "commodity dealers" designation applies for taxable years beginning after July 18, 1984. It extends the self-employment tax provisions to the newly defined group and enables them to make pension plan contributions not otherwise available to traders.[32] Under prior law, commodity floor traders did not generate "net income from self-em-

---

[28]DRA, Pub. L. 98-369, § 102(a)(3), 98 Stat. 494, 621 (1984).

[29]*See* section 6.3(c).

[30]*See* section 32.4.

[31]I.R.C. §§ 1374(c)(4)(B)(ii), 1402(i)(2)(B).

[32]DRA, *supra* note 28, at § 102(c).

ployment" for social security tax purposes. As a result, commodity floor traders did not pay self-employment tax and could not establish pension and profit sharing plans available to self-employed people.[33] The DRA amended the definition of self-employment tax to provide that the capital gains or losses of commodity dealers are subject to "net earnings from self-employment" for social security purposes.[34] Therefore, income earned by commodity dealers on trading section 1256 contracts now constitute net earnings from self-employment and are subject to self-employment tax. A portion of the income can be set aside in pension and profit sharing plans.

§ 6.3   DEALERS

Dealers buy and sell property in the normal course of business, generating ordinary income or loss. Dealers act as principals, maintaining an inventory of products with the hope of reselling their inventories at a profit. Dealers perform a merchandising function by purchasing property to sell to customers and selling property desired by customers. It is for a markup or some other dealer concession that dealers conduct business.[35] Frequently, dealers make markets by quoting the bid and asked prices at which they are willing to buy and sell products. Because dealers buy and sell for their own accounts, they assume positions (either long or short) as part of their business activities and trade off of these positions. In theory, a dealer's profit is the markup based on his cost. Constant fluctuations in the market price for securities, commodities, and option products, however, have a major impact on a dealer's profits or losses. As a result, a dealer's profit is significantly affected by market fluctuations.

In addition to acting as principals, dealers can act as agents or brokers and earn ordinary income from brokerage commissions, buying and selling products on behalf of customers. Dealers that act as brokers are compensated in the same manner as brokers.[36]

Whether taxpayers are dealers is a mixed question of law and fact, which depends upon the specific circumstances of each case.[37] Taxpay-

---

[33]Some commodity floor traders did establish corporations and became salaried employees in order to obtain pension and profit sharing benefits. To obtain these pension benefits capital gain from trading was converted into ordinary income from salaries.

[34]DRA, *supra* note 28, § 102(c)(2) (codified at 42 U.S.C. § 411(h) (Supp. III 1985)).

[35]Stephens, Inc. v. U.S., 464 F.2d 53, 57 (8th Cir. 1972), *cert. denied*, 409 U.S. 1118 (1973).

[36]*See* section 6.5.

[37]*Stephens, Inc.*, 464 F.2d at 56.

ers bear the burden of establishing or refuting dealer status.[38] The courts and the IRS have found various combinations of the following factors determinative of dealer status: (1) being licensed as a dealer;[39] (2) having a large volume of sales and purchases;[40] (3) holding oneself out to the public as a dealer;[41] (4) selling shares out of inventory to customers;[42] (5) profiting from commissions rather than from appreciation in the value of the shares;[43] and (6) owning a membership in an exchange.[44]

In determining dealer status, courts have emphasized the difference "between securities held for purposes of resale and those held for purposes of investment."[45] Earlier decisions determined dealer status by weighing investment and speculation against the desire to resell at a profit to anyone who desired to buy.[46] Generally dealers seek profits through sales of inventory to customers rather than through speculation.[47] Infrequent and isolated transactions do not qualify a taxpayer as a dealer.[48]

The remainder of this section discusses dealers in greater detail.

(a) SECURITIES DEALERS GENERALLY

Securities dealers are defined in Treasury regulations as merchants of securities with established places of business. A securities dealer, whether an individual, partnership, or corporation, must be regularly engaged in the purchase and resale of securities to customers. As a merchant, a securities dealer buys and sells securities with a view to the gains and profits that may be derived from these transactions.[49]

---

[38]*See generally* Helvering v. Fried, 299 U.S. 175 (1936) (evidence of maintaining an office, leasing floor space, dealing regularly in different securities, and having between 10,300 and 62,300 securities at the end of each month to sell was sufficient to establish dealer status); *Stephens, Inc.*, 464 F.2d at 57–58 (holding that an "investment company" was not a dealer even though it had acquired corporate stock with the intention of profiting from trading).

[39]Polachek v. Comm'r, 22 T.C. 858, 859 (1954).

[40]Reinach v. Comm'r, 373 F.2d 900, 901-02 (2d Cir.), *cert. denied*, 389 U.S. 841 (1967).

[41]Verito v. Comm'r, 43 T.C. 429, 441–42 (1965).

[42]U.S. v. Chinook Inv. Co., 136 F.2d 984, 984–85 (9th Cir. 1943).

[43]Kemon, 16 T.C. at 1032–1033; *accord*, Brown v. U.S., 426 F.2d 355, 364 (Ct. Cl. 1970).

[44]Securities Allied Corp. v. Comm'r, 95 F.2d 384, 386 (2d Cir.), *cert. denied*, 305 U.S. 617 (1938).

[45]Factor v. Comm'r, 281 F.2d 100, 120 (9th Cir. 1960), *cert. denied*, 364 U.S. 933 (1961).

[46]Comm'r v. Charavay, 79 F.2d 406 (3d Cir. 1935); *Securities Allied Corp.*, 95 F.2d at 386.

[47]Comm'r v. Burnett, 118 F.2d 659, 660–61 (5th Cir. 1941); *see also Higgins*, 312 U.S. at 217–18.

[48]Pan-American Bank & Trust Co. v. Comm'r, 5 B.T.A. 839, 844 (1926).

[49]Treas. Reg. § 1.471-5 (1958).

In *Schafer v. Helvering*,[50] the taxpayer purchased securities for his own account in the hope of then selling them to others at a profit. Because the purchases were not to create an inventory of securities, the Supreme Court held that the taxpayer was not a "dealer in securities" with respect to these particular purchases.[51] The Court also held that the term "dealer in securities" refers to "one who, as a merchant, buys and sells securities to customers for the profit thereon."[52]

Whether a person is engaged in a trade or business is a question of fact that requires an analysis of all the surrounding circumstances.[53] Determination of dealer status is made based on an examination of "the frequency, extent and regularity of [the taxpayer's] securities transactions as well as his intent to derive profit from relatively short-term turnovers."[54] Accordingly, if a taxpayer is regularly engaged in the purchase of securities and their resale to customers, as opposed to investment or speculation, he qualifies as a dealer in securities.

In *Northeastern Surety Co. v. Comm'r*,[55] the Board of Tax Appeals held that the taxpayer was not a dealer in securities because its business consisted largely of writing casualty insurance on taxicabs. The taxpayer purchased and sold securities for its own account, attempting to deduct the amount by which the market value of its securities, which it had inventoried, decreased during the year. The Board pointed out specific factors that led it to conclude that the taxpayer was not a dealer in securities: (1) the taxpayer did not possess any license as required by state or local law to engage as a dealer in the purchase and sale of securities; (2) it did not hold itself out to the public as a dealer in securities; (3) it did not employ personnel to sell securities to customers; and (4) it did not buy securities as merchandise or stock in trade.[56] Because the taxpayer did not qualify as a dealer, it could not write down its securities to market value and take a loss thereon.[57]

(b) STOCK SPECIALISTS

Stock specialists are securities dealers who specialize in one or more of the stocks or securities traded on the floor of a stock exchange. The

---

[50]299 U.S. 171, 174 (1936).

[51]*Id.*

[52]*Id.*

[53]Connelly v. Comm'r, 51 T.C.M. (P-H) 2863, 2865 (1982).

[54]*Purvis*, 530 F.2d at 1334.

[55]29 B.T.A. 297, 299 (1933).

[56]*Id.* at 298.

[57]*Id.* at 300.

specialist system developed out of the continuous auction system in place on stock exchanges, where each security is traded at a designated post on the exchange floor.[58] At each post, one or more exchange members specialize in the stocks traded at the particular post. Such members are registered with the exchange as specialists in their particular stocks[59] and are registered with the SEC as broker-dealers. The specialist system developed to assure that every security traded at a stock exchange can be purchased or sold during normal trading hours and that the price of each transaction bears a reasonable relationship to the immediately preceding transaction.[60] For performing the function of maintaining an orderly market (by buying when there is excess supply and selling when there is excess demand) specialists on a stock exchange are granted certain privileges in dealing in the stock in which they specialize. Accordingly, other brokers and dealers who wish to purchase or sell stock deal through the specialist. A specialist participates in trading as both a broker and dealer in the stock for which he is registered as a specialist.[61] If the market is too thin to assure that an order will be executed at a fair price, "it is the specialist's function to buy or sell for his own account at a fair price, to the extent necessary to maintain a 'fair and orderly market.'"[62] Specialists typically do not trade for their personal investment or speculation, but rather to facilitate the purchase and sale of stock by others.[63]

Although specialists do not have customers in the traditional sense of selling merchandise to the general public, sales to other dealers, brokers, or other types of professional buyers can be considered sales to customers.[64] In fact, the IRS audit manual instructs its agents that specialists on the floor of an exchange are to be treated as dealers in the stock in which they specialize.[65]

A substantial portion of the income earned by specialists usually comes from profits derived from being professional dealers, that is, trading for their own accounts in those securities in which they are

[58] Special Securities Study, *supra* note 22, at 57.

[59] *Id.*

[60] *Id.* at 78.

[61] *Id.* at 47.

[62] *Id.*

[63] *Id.* at 48.

[64] Stokes v. Rothensies, 61 F. Supp. 444, 449 (E.D. Pa. 1945), *aff'd per curiam*, 154 F.2d 1022 (3d Cir. 1946).

[65] Internal Revenue Manual 4232.5, 1 INTERNAL REVENUE MANUAL (AUDIT) (CCH) 7261-61, § 420(2) (Dec. 14, 1976).

registered and selling appreciated inventory.[66] Specialists also act as brokers by holding and executing public orders for a commission.[67] Specialists accept orders from others for execution either by buying or selling the desired securities from their own accounts (dealer function) or by matching the orders of buyers and sellers (brokerage function).[68] In *Helvering v. Fried*,[69] the Supreme Court found that floor specialists are dealers because they (1) have an established place of business; (2) are regularly engaged in the purchase of securities and their sale to customers (i.e., nonspecialist members of the exchange); and (3) purchase and sell securities in anticipation of generating gains or profits. This basic definition of a specialist has also been adopted by the IRS.[70] When performing a dealer function, the specialist is treated as a dealer for tax purposes. When performing a brokerage function, the specialist is not viewed as a dealer.[71]

(c) MARKET MAKERS AND SPECIALISTS IN OPTIONS

Market makers and specialists in options (collectively "option market makers") historically have treated themselves as dealers in securities for both tax and regulatory purposes. DRA, however, requires option market makers to be treated as traders with respect to section 1256 contract positions entered into after July 18, 1984. This section analyzes the law in effect prior to DRA, when option market makers treated themselves as dealers in securities. For a discussion of option market makers under current law, see section 6.3(d).

The distinction between a market maker and a specialist in listed options is a technical one that may not be particularly relevant for tax purposes. Market makers and option specialists, registered with the SEC as broker-dealers, both trade on the floor of option exchanges either for their own accounts or as agents for others. Market makers compete with each other to make markets in the various options traded on the exchange.[72] Under the specialist system, option specialists are assigned

---

[66]*Id.* § 420(4).

[67]*Id.* § 420(3).

[68]*Id.* §§ 420(2), (4).

[69]299 U.S. at 177.

[70]*See* Rev. Rul. 71-30, 1971-1 C.B. 226; Rev. Rul. 60-321, 1960-2 C.B. 166.

[71]Lowell v. Comm'r, 30 B.T.A. 1297, 1301–02 (1934).

[72]REPORT OF THE SPECIAL STUDY OF THE OPTIONS MARKETS TO THE SECURITIES AND EXCHANGE COMMISSION, 96TH CONG., 1ST. SESS. 130 (Comm. Print 1978) [hereinafter referred to as "Special Options Study"].

to a particular options class or classes for which they are obligated to make a market and do not compete with other specialists in those option classes to which they are assigned.[73] Each specialist is the principal dealer responsible for making a market in the options in which he specializes.

The tax treatment of an option market maker's gains and losses from pre-DRA option transactions has seldom been addressed directly by Congress, the courts, or the IRS. Nevertheless, for a number of reasons, the view under pre-DRA law that option market makers were dealers in options who received ordinary gain or loss treatment has been generally accepted. Option market makers historically have been and continue to be viewed as dealers for regulatory purposes, basically because the function of an options market maker is viewed as analogous to that of a specialist on a stock exchange. Sales to other dealers, brokers, or other types of professional buyers can be considered sales to customers.[74]

The only pre-DRA reference in the Code to dealers in options appeared in I.R.C. § 1234(b)(3), which can be read as indirect support for treating option market makers as dealers on the same basis as stock specialists. I.R.C. § 1234(a) addresses the holders of options, while I.R.C. § 1234(b) sets forth certain rules for the tax treatment of grantors (writers) of options. I.R.C. § 1234(b)(3) provides that the rules of I.R.C. § 1234(b) do not apply to "any option granted in the ordinary course of the taxpayer's trade or business of granting options."

In addition, the Report of the Ways and Means Committee on the Tax Reform Act of 1976 interprets the meaning of I.R.C. § 1234(b)(3) as indicating that taxpayers who make a market with respect to particular options receive ordinary gain or loss treatment on their transactions. The Ways and Means Committee Report contains the following statement under the heading "treatment of broker-dealers":

> Gain or loss from transactions in options written in the ordinary course of the taxpayer's trade or business would continue to be treated as ordinary income or loss. . . . The determination as to whether an option is written in the ordinary course of a taxpayer's trade or business, or as an investment, is to be determined under principles similar to those which apply under present law in the case of a broker-dealer in securities. Generally, it is anticipated that persons who are treated as writers of options in the ordinary course of their trade or business will be those who "make a market" with respect to a particular option.[75]

[73]*Id.* at 129.

[74]*Stokes*, 61 F. Supp. at 449.

[75]HOUSE COMMITTEE ON WAYS AND MEANS, TAX TREATMENT OF GRANTOR OF CERTAIN OPTIONS, H.R. REP. NO. 1192, 94TH CONG., 2D SESS. 10 (1976), *reprinted in* 1976-3 C.B. (Vol. 3) 19, 28.

In light of this statement, Congress can be viewed as having accepted, under pre-DRA law, the theory that the tax status of an options market maker should be determined using the same principles as have been applied to specialists in stock. Therefore, option market makers should be classified as dealers with respect to their option activities. Unlike the case of a specialist in stock, however, there is no judicial authority specifically holding that an options market maker was, in fact, a dealer for tax purposes.

It is not clear which short option transactions receive ordinary treatment. Both the Ways and Means Committee Report and the Treasury regulations under I.R.C. § 1234(b)(3) indicate that for an option to be granted in the ordinary course of the taxpayer's business, it must be granted by a broker-dealer.[76] Therefore, it is clear that gain or loss from a closing transaction is considered ordinary where the option is written by a dealer in actual securities (a "broker-dealer" in the language of the Ways and Means Committee) in connection with his trade or business.[77] The question that was not answered, however, was whether under pre-DRA law there was such a thing as a dealer who dealt only in options.[78]

The Ways and Means Committee Report suggests that option professionals with the responsibility of making markets with respect to particular options were dealers under prior law. It does not explain the reasoning leading to this suggestion and does not explain whether an options market maker who trades in options for which he has no market making responsibility should also receive ordinary income treatment. There are two possible explanations for the Ways and Means Committee's position. First, option market makers perform a merchandising function similar to that of securities dealers. Second, option market

[76]Treas. Reg. § 1.1234-3(c) (1979) attempts to elaborate on the meaning of I.R.C. § 1234(b)(3) by providing that the general rules of I.R.C. § 1234(b) will apply—despite the exception in I.R.C. § 1234(b)(3)—to options designated by a dealer in securities as held for investment under the provisions of I.R.C. § 1236. The rationale of these regulations is unclear. Because the writer of an option has no property or right to property that can be sold or exchanged, he may not be viewed as acquiring a security within the meaning of I.R.C. § 1236(c). Rather, the option writer has incurred an obligation.

[77]For example, if a dealer in corporate securities acquires call options on such securities to ensure a source of supply for his sales to customers, then the gains and losses on the offset of those options would clearly be ordinary.

[78]This is not an issue with respect to brokers. Brokers do not carry inventories for sale to customers, but simply execute customers' orders for a fee. Thus, a person who acts exclusively as a broker is an agent who does not hold or write options in a principal capacity.

makers' responsibilities to maintain an orderly market, without more, warrant giving their trades ordinary income treatment.

There are some difficulties with the analysis of treating option market makers as dealers. As a starting point, the Tax Court has held that a taxpayer is not a dealer for tax purposes by virtue of writing options. In *Reinach v. Comm'r,*[79] a professional writer of options deducted his option losses as ordinary losses incurred in his trade or business as a dealer in options. The taxpayer devoted substantially all of his time to the writing of options, constituting the principle source of his income. He maintained an office with a salaried staff, rented private telephone lines to brokers, and over a period of three years, wrote 412 option contracts.[80] The Tax Court held that since the taxpayer held no securities for sale to customers, he was not a dealer in securities and, therefore, his losses were of a capital nature.[81] Moreover, the Tax Court questioned whether the taxpayer's activities in option writing constituted a trade or business as opposed to a mere investment activity.[82] Therefore, while the literal language of I.R.C. § 1234(b)(3) appears to apply to taxpayers who are in the trade or business of writing options (who may or may not be dealers), the Tax Court did not recognize the writing of options, alone, as a trade or business.

Another possible interpretation of the Ways and Means Committee Report is that option market makers should receive ordinary treatment on their option transactions because they have a responsibility to maintain an orderly market, just as floor specialists on a stock exchange have such a responsibility. Moreover, according to the holding in *Helvering v. Fried,* market makers receive ordinary income on the sale of stock purchased to maintain price stability.[83]

---

[79]24 T.C.M. (CCH) 1605 (1965), *aff'd,* 373 F.2d 900 (2d Cir.), *cert. denied,* 389 U.S. 841 (1967).

[80]*Id.* at 1606.

[81]*Id.* at 1614.

[82]*Id.* at 1615.

[83]299 U.S. at 177. Option market makers, in contrast to floor specialists, might not be viewed as having greater access to securities than other market participants. An option market maker's activities might be analogized to the activities of traders on the commodity exchanges (who are not deemed to be selling to customers). It could also be argued that an option market maker's responsibility to maintain an orderly market is not imposed (as in the case of a floor specialist) because he has control over *all* purchases and sales in his specialty stock but because all market professionals on the options exchange floor benefit from the early access to market information. Therefore, it might not follow that ordinary income treatment should be imposed for option market maker transactions because they must trade for their own accounts to maintain an orderly market.

In a TAM, the IRS treated an options market maker as a dealer in options and securities who was required to use an inventory to determine his income.[84] As a consequence, the taxpayer paid tax at ordinary income rates. The IRS noted that a call option gives the option holder the right to purchase stock at a specified price and time. Therefore, a call option is a "right to subscribe to or purchase" stock and falls within the definition of a "security" in I.R.C. § 1236(c).[85] A market maker is a dealer with respect to the call options that he buys and sells and with respect to the underlying securities that he purchases to satisfy his obligations under short call options, because such securities are a necessary part of his stock in trade.[86] The IRS concluded that for purposes of Treas. Reg. § 1.471-5, an options market maker is a securities dealer who derives ordinary income from his transactions in options and securities and who may be compelled to account for inventories in computing his taxable income.[87]

Finally, the tax treatment of option market makers was addressed by the Joint Committee on Taxation in its explanation of the DRA changes. In discussing the extension of section 1256 treatment to certain dealer equity options held by option dealers, the Joint Committee implied that option market makers were treated as realizing ordinary income or loss with respect to their option transactions.[88] The implication follows that under pre-DRA law, it appears that taxpayers who made a market with respect to particular options were treated as granting or acquiring options in the course of a trade or business.[89] The Joint Committee statements support the view that market makers were dealers with respect to their option transactions under the law in effect prior to DRA.

---

[84]TAM 8141035 (June 30, 1981).

[85]*Id.*

[86]*Id.* It makes sense that a taxpayer who is a dealer with respect to options also is a dealer with respect to securities purchased to satisfy his obligations to customers. However, if a taxpayer is an investor or trader with respect to his option transactions, then it also follows that securities purchased to cover or reduce the risk of his speculative activities would be treated as capital assets in his hands, unless he is a dealer in the underlying property.

[87]*Id.*

[88]STAFF OF THE JOINT COMMITTEE ON TAXATION, 98TH CONG., 2D SESS., GENERAL EXPLANATION OF THE REVENUE PROVISIONS OF THE DEFICIT REDUCTION ACT OF 1984 302 (Comm. Print 1984) [hereinafter referred to as "General Explanation of DRA"]; *see also* CONFERENCE REPORT, DEFICIT REDUCTION ACT OF 1984, H.R. REP. No. 861, 98th Cong., 2nd Sess. 899 (1984).

[89]General Explanation of DRA, *supra* note 88, at 302.

(d) OPTION DEALERS

Option dealers who are registered with option exchanges as option market makers or specialists in listed options now are viewed generally as traders with respect to their section 1256 contracts. In addition, their income from section 1256 trading is net income from self-employment for social security purposes. It is eligible for contribution to pension and profit sharing plans. Finally, only option dealers are eligible to receive section 1256 treatment on dealer equity options. For a discussion of option dealers under current law, see section 6.2(b). For a discussion of option dealers under prior law, see section 6.3(c). For a discussion of dealer equity options, see section 32.4.

(e) COMMODITY DEALERS

Commodity traders registered with a commodity exchange designated by the CFTC as a contract market are now defined as "commodity dealers."[90] This new definition, however, does not convert capital assets into ordinary income property.[91] The major effect of this change is that commodity dealers now have "net income from self-employment" for social security purposes, which is eligible for contribution to pension and profit sharing plans.[92] For a discussion of commodity dealers, see section 6.2(c).

§ 6.4 HEDGERS

Hedgers use the markets to protect the price at which they will acquire products they need in their businesses and to assure a market to sell their inventories, thereby generating ordinary income or loss treatment on their hedging transactions.[93]

Traditionally, hedgers have used the futures markets to hedge their ordinary income positions in the underlying property. With so many new types of financial products now available, the products and markets

---

[90]I.R.C. §§ 1374(c)(4)(B)(ii), 1402(i)(2)(B).

[91]I.R.C. § 1256(f)(3)(C).

[92]DRA, *supra* note 28, § 102(c)(2) (codified at 42 U.S.C. § 411(h) (Supp. III 1985)).

[93]STAFF OF THE JOINT COMMITTEE ON TAXATION, 97TH CONG., 1ST SESS., GENERAL EXPLANATION OF THE ECONOMIC RECOVERY TAX ACT OF 1981 299 (Joint Comm. Print) [hereinafter referred to as "General Explanation of ERTA"].

used by hedgers have expanded in recent years. Although all of the court cases decided to date only discuss futures contract hedge transactions, the analysis in these cases applies equally as well to other products. Hedge transactions can be established using options and other types of property, as well as futures contracts. In fact, the economic literature acknowledges the expanding use of options and other products in hedge transactions.[94]

Hedging depends on all relevant facts and circumstances. In general, however, a taxpayer who uses a futures contract, option, forward contract, or other position to lock in the purchase or sale price of a product used in the ordinary course of his business is deemed to be a hedger under the Corn Products doctrine.[95] Moreover, hedge property must be disposed of shortly after the purpose for which the hedge was established is accomplished. The taxpayer cannot change his reason for holding the property to an investment motive.[96]

A difficult issue arises in applying the Corn Products doctrine to purchases of securities if the taxpayer has mixed business and investment motives for purchasing the securities. Where the taxpayer has a mixed motive, the cases have concluded that capital, not ordinary, gain results.[97] In *Union Pacific Railroad v. U.S.*,[98] the Court of Claims took the position that stock is a capital asset even if held predominately for a business purpose.

(a) ECONOMIC ANALYSIS

Economists have different views as to what transactions qualify for hedging status. One view characterizes hedging as a risk transfer mechanism with risk transferred from those who are more risk averse (i.e.,

---

[94]A. WOLF, AN AGENT HEDGING WITH COMMODITY OPTIONS: OPTIMAL CHOICE OF OPTIONS, AND PORTFOLIO ANALYSIS 56 (Center for the Study of Futures Markets, Columbia Business School, Working Paper Series #CSFM-70, 1983); R. ANDERSON & JEAN-PIERRE DANTHINE, CROSS HEDGING (Center for the Study of Futures Markets, Columbia Business School, Working Paper Series #CSFM-24, 1980).

[95]Corn Products Refining Co. v. Comm'r, 350 U.S. 46 (1955), *reh'g denied*, 350 U.S. 943 (1956).

[96]Gulftex Drug Co. v. Comm'r, 29 T.C. 118, 121 (1957), *aff'd per curiam*, 261 F.2d 238 (5th Cir. 1958); Rev. Rul. 58-40, 1958-1 C.B. 275.

[97]Continental Illinois National Bank and Trust Co. of Chicago v. Comm'r, 69 T.C. 357, 374-76 (1977), *acq.* 1978-2 C.B. 1; W.W. Windle Co. v. Comm'r, 65 T.C. 694, 704 (1976), *appeal dismissed*, 550 F.2d 43 (1st Cir.), *cert. denied*, 431 U.S. 966 (1977); Rev. Rul. 78-94, 1978-1 C.B. 58, *revoking* Rev. Rul. 75-13, 1975-1 C.B. 67.

[98]524 F.2d 1343, 1355-57 (Ct. Cl. 1975), *cert. denied*, 429 U.S. 827 (1976), *aff'd*, 77-1 U.S. Tax Cas. (CCH) ¶ 9247 (1977).

hedgers) to those who are less risk averse (i.e., speculators).[99] Another view is that hedgers and speculators rely on different information about how prices are distributed.[100] A third view defines a hedger as someone who uses the futures market to hedge a position in an underlying commodity; a speculator does not have a physical commodity position. In fact, a hedger never actually shifts risk; he offsets the risk of price level changes:

> To hedge is to assume a position in futures equal and opposite to an already existing cash position. While in broad context the essence of hedging is risk shifting, the hedger should realize that he does not actually shift risk; he offsets the risk of price level change. He does not cease to speculate; he takes on an additional speculation. Because the additional speculation is opposite in short futures when he is long cash and long futures when he is short cash—profits and losses, because of changes in *price levels*, cancel and leave only profits and losses that result from changes in *price relationships*. The hedger should be under no illusion that he has no market position; he has two where previously he had only one.[101]

These economic views provide some indications of when a transaction is a hedge. They do not account for the diversity of hedging transactions and the sophistication of hedgers.

(b) FACTS AND CIRCUMSTANCES

Whether a taxpayer's transactions qualify as hedges depends upon all of the facts and circumstances. Factors taken into account include whether (1) the transaction is an integral part of the taxpayer's trade or business, (2) the transaction is entered into to provide price protection, and (3) a true risk is offset or reduced by the transaction. Early IRS pronouncements[102] and numerous court decisions have held that futures contracts entered into by a taxpayer to protect against price fluctuations in the value of inventory to be purchased or sold are a form of insurance. Therefore, gains and losses are ordinary, rather than capital, in nature. The concept of a hedge includes transactions that constitute an integral part of the taxpayer's business and which provide price protection or insurance for the taxpayer.[103]

[99]J. KEYNES, A TREATISE OF MONEY 2 (1930); J. HICKS, VALUE AND CAPITAL (2d ed. 1946).

[100]Working, *The Theory of the Price of Storage*, AMERICAN ECONOMIC REVIEW 1254 (Dec. 1949), *reprinted in* CBT, SELECTED WRITINGS OF HOLBROOK WORKING 25 (1977).

[101]T. HIERONYMUS, ECONOMICS OF FUTURES TRADING FOR COMMERCIAL AND PERSONAL PROFIT 175 (2d ed. 1977).

[102]G.C.M. 17322, XV-2 C.B. 151 (1936), *superseded by* Rev. Rul. 72-179, 1972-1 C.B. 57; Rev. Rul. 60-24, 1960-1 C.B. 171.

[103]*Corn Products*, 350 U.S. at 50.

With a hedge, there must be a correlative price relationship between the price of the actual commodity (referred to as the "hedged property") and the price of the offsetting position (referred to as the "hedge position").[104] As long as the prices of the hedged property and the hedge position move in inverse relation to each other, the hedge position and the hedged property do not have to be in the same commodity.[105] In other words, the taxpayer must maintain a balanced position and must not lose money on both the hedged property and the hedge position.[106] If a transaction does not provide price protection or price insurance, the taxpayer might not be viewed as a hedger.

A hedger is protected against adverse price changes only if the price of the property to be hedged and the hedge itself move in the opposite direction and at the same rate. This means that hedgers theoretically accept some risk, referred to as "basis risk," when they enter into hedge transactions.[107] A taxpayer is not a hedger if he enters into a futures contract position for delivery before or after the sale of the actual commodity.[108] In addition, if the size of the hedge position represents far more than the amount actually needed in the business, the taxpayer might not be viewed as a hedger.[109] Hence, the timing and size of the transaction determines whether a transaction is a true hedge. Some examples of transactions that are not hedges under the particular facts and circumstances follow.

Example 6-1

A farmer grows wheat that he expects to harvest in September. He enters into a short futures contract position to sell wheat in May. Because he

---

[104]Stewart Silk Corp. v. Comm'r, 9 T.C. 174, 178 (1947).

[105]Kurtin v. Comm'r, 26 T.C. 958, 961 (1956).

[106]Meade v. Comm'r, 42 T.C.M. (P-H) 205, 212 (1973); Patterson v. Comm'r, 50 T.C.M. (P-H) 122, 124 (1981).

[107]Basis is the difference at any point in time between the cash price of a particular commodity at a specific location and the futures price of the commodity. This difference is due to many factors and varies from one location to another. Fluctuations in the basis tend to be more stable than fluctuations in cash or futures prices. In a hedge, a taxpayer substitutes a basis risk for a price level risk, thereby substituting the risk that the price between the hedged property and the hedge will fluctuate for the risk of an adverse movement in the price of the property itself. Changes in the basis determine whether the taxpayer has made a profit or a loss on a transaction. By hedging, a taxpayer replaces the major risk of cash price fluctuation with a different, usually smaller risk—that of basis change.

[108]Hendrich v. Comm'r, 49 T.C.M. (P-H) 1448, 1452 (1980).

[109]Lewis v. Comm'r, 49 T.C.M. (P-H) 1501, 1505 (1980).

will not have any wheat to deliver against his May futures contract position, he is not a hedger.

Example 6-2

A farmer has planted and is cultivating a soybean crop that he estimates will yield 10,000 bushels of soybeans. He enters into a futures contract position to sell 100,000 bushels of soybeans. Only 10 percent of his futures contract position could be viewed as a hedge. He clearly is not a hedger with respect to 90 percent of his futures contract position. It is possible that the farmer is not viewed as a hedger at all, because the futures contract position is 10 times greater than his anticipated harvest. He might be viewed as a speculator for the entire short futures contract position.

(c) BUYING AND SELLING HEDGES

There are two forms of hedges—the long (or "buying") hedge and the short (or "selling") hedge. Under traditional analysis, a buying hedge is established by a buyer of a commodity to protect against (1) the risk of a price rise in the cost of the property he must acquire for use in the future, or (2) an adverse currency fluctuation between the date the hedge is established and the date he must purchase the commodity. In addition, a buying hedge is established by a seller of a commodity to protect against a price decline. "The buying hedge secures a fixed margin of profit for the hedging entity tied to a fixed price contract by guaranteeing either a supply of materials at a fixed cost or the profit to offset the additional cost of obtaining these materials."[110]

A selling hedge, on the other hand, generally is used by the producer of a product to protect against (1) the risk of a fall in the price at which he will sell his actual product, or (2) an adverse currency fluctuation of a commodity owned by the taxpayer. A "selling hedge is used to protect investments which a hedging entity has already made where there is guaranteed no fixed price on the item to be sold. This is the basis for the characterization of hedging as insurance."[111]

In general, buying and selling hedges can be established using futures contracts, forward contracts, call options, and put options. The following section briefly describes how various types of property can be used to establish hedge transactions, providing some examples.

---

[110]G.C.M. 38178 (Nov. 27, 1979).
[111]*Id.*

(1) BUYING HEDGES

A buying hedge protects the taxpayer who needs a continuous supply of the hedged property against a rise in the price of the hedged property. Typical users are processors, builders, exporters, and all sorts of dealers. In general, a hedger establishes a buying hedge by (1) acquiring a long futures contract position; (2) establishing a long call option position, providing him the option to acquire the underlying property during the option period at the strike price; or (3) selling a put option granting the holder the right to acquire the underlying property during the option period at the strike price. If prices for the hedged property increase, the profit on the hedge position offsets the higher price that the hedger must pay to acquire the hedged property. If prices decline, the hedger loses money on the hedge and profits from the lower price at which he can acquire the hedged property.

Call options can be used to establish a buying hedge.[112] It is likely that a long call option position initially costs more to establish than a futures contracts position because the taxpayer has to pay the option premium. Once established, however, an option position enables the taxpayer to limit his loss to the premium if the price of the underlying property increases. In addition, long option positions do not require margin deposits and once established can be less expensive to maintain than futures positions.

Another hedge strategy involves the sale of a put option. The put seller receives the option premium. If the market remains stable or increases, the put expires worthless. The seller keeps the entire option premium, which partially offsets the loss on his cash position.

Example   6-3

On October 1st, a dealer in XYZ stock agrees to sell a block of XYZ stock for $150 per share for delivery December 1st. The dealer does not have the XYZ stock in his inventory. To protect against an increase in the price of XYZ stock prior to December 1st, the dealer enters into a long call option position, granting him the option to acquire XYZ stock on December 1st at the strike price of $150.[113] This transaction is a buying hedge. If the price of XYZ stock increases, the dealer limits his loss to the option premium paid to acquire the long call position. If the price of XYZ stock falls, the dealer lets the option expire worthless,

---

[112]For a discussion of call options, see section 5.4(a).

[113]Because there are no futures contracts on individual equity stocks, the dealer cannot establish a long futures contract position.

profiting from his ability to deliver XYZ stock at a price in excess of its market value.

Example 6-4

If a government securities dealer has a commitment to sell government securities at a fixed price in the future, he may want to protect himself against declining interest rates and rising securities prices. He reduces these risks by buying futures contracts or call options to cover his short commitments. This is a buying hedge. The long futures contract or call option position allows the dealer to profit in an advancing government securities market, thereby offsetting possible losses on short cash commitments.

Example 6-5

A manufacturing company uses silver to make its products. During periods when silver prices are low, the manufacturer purchases long silver futures contracts or acquires call options (granting it the right to purchase, for the option strike price, silver during the option period). If the price of silver increases, the manufacturer can take delivery pursuant to the long futures contracts or exercise its option to acquire silver at the strike price. This is not a hedge because the manufacturer is not hedging an established or determined cash position. Rather, the manufacturer is speculating on the price of silver to assure itself an adequate supply of silver to make its products at the lowest possible price. The result would be different if the manufacturer was buying silver to meet known future needs.

Example 6-6

A textile manufacturer agrees to sell cotton goods in the future, which requires more cotton than the amount of cotton on hand or the amount that can be immediately purchased at a favorable price. To protect itself against a rising cotton market (during the months between the date of the cotton goods order and the agreed delivery date), the manufacturer enters into long futures contracts for cotton. As the manufacturer buys spot cotton from time to time to manufacture the goods specified in its orders, the long futures contracts are disposed of by a closing transaction. This is a buying hedge.[114]

[114]Rev. Rul. 72-179, 1972-1 C.B. 57.

(2) SELLING HEDGES

A selling hedge protects the value of a hedger's existing inventory or protects against currency fluctuations. Typically, selling hedgers are farmers, processors (who process and sell a property that can be hedged), merchandisers (involved in the purchase and sale of the property to be hedged), importers, and dealers of all sorts. A selling hedge is used as a temporary substitute for the sale of the actual property in the market. In many cases, the user of a selling hedge owns (or is obligated to acquire) the actual property, but will not sell it until a future date.

In general, a taxpayer establishes a selling hedge by (1) selling futures contracts obligating him to deliver the underlying property at a future date; (2) establishing a long put option position, giving him the option to sell the underlying property during the option period at the strike price; or (3) selling call options granting the other side the option to buy the underlying property during the option period at the strike price.

Put options can be used to establish a selling hedge.[115] A taxpayer with a long position in property can purchase a put option either to hedge the downside risk or effectively lock in an unrealized profit on the long position. In a declining market, a long put position provides a selling floor for the hedged property. When a taxpayer acquires puts he maintains all upside appreciation on the underlying property (minus the option premium and any transaction costs). If the price of the underlying long position increases, the taxpayer allows the put to expire worthless and his profit on the underlying property is reduced by the cost of the option premium.

Where a hedger expects that the market will remain relatively stable or decline, a hedger can sell a call option and receive the option premium. If the market remains stable or declines, the call option expires worthless and the seller keeps the entire premium received from the sale of the call option. The call option seller loses money on his cash position, which may be only partially offset by the option premium.

Example 6-7

A corn farmer with a corn crop planted and under cultivation sells corn futures contracts or buys a put option granting him the right to sell corn in a quantity equal to his expected crop, at the strike price. This is a selling hedge. The farmer has set the lowest price at which he will deliver his crop. If he has sold a futures contract, he can deliver into

---

[115]For a discussion of put options, see section 5.3(b).

the contract or purchase an offsetting contract and sell in the cash market. If he has bought a put option and the price of corn rises, he can let the option expire worthless and sell his corn in the cash market, giving up only the option premium.

If he has bought a put and the price of corn falls, he can either (1) sell the put at a profit and sell his corn in the cash market at a lower price; (2) exercise the put, offset the ensuing short futures position at a profit, and sell his corn in the cash market at a lower price; or (3) exercise his put and deliver his corn into the ensuing short futures position.

Example 6-8

A manufacturer buys quantities of spot cotton that will be on hand for some months before being manufactured into goods and sold. To protect himself from losses if the cotton market declines during this period, the manufacturer sells futures contracts for the delivery of equivalent amounts of cotton a few months in the future. From time to time, as the cotton is used to manufacture cotton goods, the short futures contracts are concurrently disposed of by closing transactions. This is a selling hedge.[116]

Example 6-9

A dealer in XYZ stock, with XYZ stock in his inventory, wants to protect himself against losses if XYZ stock declines in value. The dealer enters into a long put option position to sell XYZ stock at the strike price at any time until the option expires. This is a selling hedge. If the stock price declines, the dealer exercises his put option and sells the stock for the strike price. If the stock price increases, the dealer limits his loss to the cost of the option premium by simply allowing the put option to expire worthless.

Example 6-10

On February 1st a government securities dealer holds a portfolio of Treasury bonds that he plans to sell in March. When interest rates increase, bond prices fall, so the dealer wants protection against an increase in interest rates. The dealer decides to hedge his bond portfolio either by selling futures contracts or by establishing a short call options position. This is a selling hedge. If interest rates increase, the loss on the Treasury bonds can be partially offset by the gain on the futures

[116]Rev. Rul. 72-179, 1972-1 C.B. 57.

contract position or by exercising the option to sell the bonds at the strike price. If interest rates fall, the dealer makes money on the bonds and loses money on the futures contract position. (He would allow an options position to expire worthless.)

(d) INTEREST RATE HEDGES

With the introduction of interest rate sensitive products, such as futures contracts and options on government securities, certificates of deposit, and commercial paper, risks from fluctuations in interest rates can be minimized with hedge transactions intended to protect profits (or minimize losses) from interest rate fluctuations.

Interest rate hedge transactions are used by securities dealers, banks, insurance companies, real estate developers, and other taxpayers who borrow or lend money and want to limit their interest rate risks. As with hedges generally, a taxpayer can establish a buying or a selling interest rate hedge, depending on his position as a borrower or lender. A buying hedge reduces the risk of falling interest rates. By entering into a long futures contract, long call option, or short put option position on a financial instrument, a taxpayer can generate a profit to offset the impact of a decline in interest rates on his business.[117] If interest rates fall, the taxpayer loses money on the cash assets comprising this underlying business activity and profits on the futures contract or options position. If interest rates increase, the taxpayer makes money on the underlying cash assets (e.g., by generating a higher yield due to a higher interest rate) and loses money on the futures contract or options position.

To lock in a return, a taxpayer might establish a selling hedge by entering into a short futures contract position or a long put option position. If interest rates increase, the taxpayer loses money on the underlying business activity (due to an increase in cost), and makes money on the futures contract or option position. If interest rates fall, the taxpayer makes money on the cost savings for the underlying activity and loses money on the futures contract or option position.

Example   6-11

A construction company needs to borrow a fixed amount of money in the future and wants to lock in an interest rate for the loan it must obtain. To eliminate the risk of rising interest rates, the company can either sell futures contracts or purchase a put option position. This is

---

[117]*See* section 6.4(c).

a selling hedge. If interest rates increase, the company profits on the short futures contract position or long put option position, which offsets the increased interest cost on the loan it eventually obtains. On the other hand, if interest rates fall, the cost savings on the loan is reduced by the loss on the futures contract or option position.

Example 6-12

In the course of its business, an insurance company enters into an agreement to pay a 10 percent fixed interest rate on an annuity contract purchased by the customer. This 10 percent rate is acceptable to the company because it believes that it can find an investment that returns a greater interest rate. If such an investment is not available, the company loses some or all of its anticipated profit. To avoid the risk of falling interest rates, the company can enter into a long futures contract position or purchase a call option on a financial instrument that it believes will generate a profit to offset any decline in interest rates. This is a buying hedge. Both the futures position and the call option position eliminate the risk of falling interest rates. If interest rates fall, the higher cost of the annuity is compensated for by an offsetting profit on the futures or option positions. If interest rates increase, a loss on the futures or option position is added to the interest paid on the annuity, thereby increasing the borrowing cost and preserving the anticipated profit. The yield on the investment reflects the higher interest rate.

Example 6-13

On March 1st, when the current interest rate is 11.2 percent, a bank agrees to lend money payable on April 1st over a five year period with a 12 percent yield. To lock in its spread, the bank can either enter into a short futures contract position or a long put option position on a financial instrument that it believes will minimize the impact of fluctuations in interest rates. This is a selling hedge. If five-year interest rates rise, the actual cost to the bank of the fixed rate loan is higher than it expected at the time the loan was made. Profit on the futures or option position reduces the cost of the loan, preserving the bank's profit. If interest rates fall, the cost savings on the loan are reduced by the losses on the futures contract or option position.

Case law developed around agricultural hedges, so there is no comparable case law as to interest rate hedge transactions. To date, there is neither judicial authority nor formal IRS policy on interest rate hedging. However, a G.C.M.[118] and a private letter ruling[119] each provide some guidance on interest rate hedges, indicating that the government recognizes such hedges are appropriate. In the G.C.M., a REIT that derived its income primarily from making real estate construction and development loans secured by mortgages on the property was viewed as a hedger for its futures contract transactions.[120] To reduce the impact of fluctuations in short-term interest rates on the REIT's income, the REIT traded established futures contract positions on government securities and commercial paper. The G.C.M. compared the REIT's cost of money to raw materials used in a business with inventories. "The characterization of the REIT's futures trading as hedging is based on an analogy between a REIT, whose primary business is making mortgage and construction loans in which cash is the raw material, and businesses involving other raw materials futures which have been held to be purchased for hedging."[121] Futures contracts in government securities and commercial paper can provide price protection as bona fide hedges.

The G.C.M. limited its conclusion to purchases or sales of futures contracts by the REIT if the REIT had not lent money at a fixed interest rate and borrowed money to cover these loans at a fixed interest rate.[122] If the costs were fixed on both sides, the REIT would not have any interest rate risks to hedge. "The insurance factor . . . integral to hedging is absent if the REIT's procurement costs and sales receipts are both fixed, guaranteeing a fixed profit margin, or both open, allowing a profit to be made under any circumstances."[123]

In a private letter ruling, the IRS ruled that commercial paper futures contracts entered into by a taxpayer in the business of making loans qualify as hedge transactions.[124] The taxpayer made loans to third parties, primarily financed through issuance of its commercial paper. To protect itself from interest rate fluctuations, the taxpayer purchased financial futures contracts, and the IRS ruled that the taxpayer's purchases were hedges.

What sorts of transactions qualify as interest rate hedges is not clear. Even with this uncertainty, interest rate hedges should be exempt from

---

[118]G.C.M. 38178 (Nov. 27, 1979).
[119]LTR 8435054 (May 29, 1984).
[120]G.C.M. 38178 (Nov. 27, 1979).
[121]*Id.*
[122]*Id.*
[123]*Id.*
[124]LTR 8435054 (May 29, 1984).

application of the Straddle Rules and from section 1256 treatment.[125] One technical problem is that the General Explanation of ERTA assumes that gain and loss on the disposition of hedged property and hedges must be ordinary to qualify for the statutory hedging exemption.[126] When a liability is hedged, as in the case of many interest rate hedges, the liability technically is not "property" in the hands of a taxpayer. In fact, borrowings and obligations do not generate either ordinary or capital gain or loss. This ambiguity should not be used to deny hedge treatment under appropriate circumstances. It is important to note that even with this uncertainty the IRS has treated financial futures contract transactions as hedges. The IRS acknowledged that in addition to gain or loss on the futures contracts being ordinary, gain or loss on the lapse, cancellation, or other disposition of the taxpayer's commercial paper borrowings should be treated as ordinary income or loss.[127] "[G]ain or loss on futures contracts purchased as hedges against [the taxpayer's] commercial paper must be characterized as ordinary gain or loss because [the taxpayer's] hedges are to help protect itself against ordinary losses on its commercial paper."[128]

In addition, the Committee on Commodities and Financial Futures of the Tax Section of the New York State Bar Association stated that obligations and liabilities should qualify as hedging transactions if the payment itself gives rise to an ordinary deduction, or if on a hypothetical repayment of the principal amount of the liability or obligations at an amount above par there is an ordinary deduction.[129] "Under this test an issuer could generally hedge indebtedness for borrowed money. Obligations incurred to acquire ordinary income property and section 1231 property (without regard to the [long-term capital gain] holding period) would be deemed automatically to meet this test."[130]

§ 6.5 BROKERS

Brokers act as their customers' agents and charge a negotiated commission for executing these transactions. They do not act as principals

---

[125]*See generally* Chapter 21.

[126]General Explanation of ERTA, *supra* note 93, at 299; *see generally* Chapter 19.

[127]LTR 8435054 (May 29, 1984).

[128]*Id.*

[129]Committee on Commodities and Financial Futures of the Tax Section of the New York State Bar Association, *Recommendations for Proposed Tax Straddle Regulations Under Sections 1092 and 1256*, 23 TAX NOTES, 973, 982 (1984).

[130]*Id.* at 982.

and do not take title to the particular securities or commodities positions they buy and sell. Instead, they simply act to put buyers together with sellers for a fee.

Many market participants only act as brokers on a part-time basis and fall into one of the other tax categories (e.g., trader or dealer) the rest of the time. For example, floor traders, specialists, market makers, and underwriters frequently act as brokers when not trading in a principal capacity for their own accounts.

§ 6.6   UNDERWRITERS

Underwriters facilitate the initial sale of securities by acting as dealers (in a principal capacity) or as brokers (in an agency capacity). When acting as dealers, underwriters purchase new securities from the issuers of the securities and resell them in the open market. With a firm commitment underwriting, the underwriter can lose money from securities not sold at the public offering price. On the other hand, in a best efforts underwriting, the underwriter acts as the issuer's broker without guaranteeing the sale of the securities. The underwriter is simply paid a fee for securities sold with no obligation to pay for any securities not sold in the best efforts underwriting.

§ 6.7   ARBITRAGEURS

Arbitrageurs attempt to profit from price distortions within a market ("intramarket") or between markets ("intermarket") by establishing certain kinds of long and short positions (purchases and sales). Arbitrageurs establish positions they believe are not properly priced, hoping to profit when and if reasonable relationships between the prices of the positions are reestablished. They buy property that is selling too cheaply and sell it in another market where the price is higher. Certain arbitrage positions provide an opportunity for risk free profit if the prices are not "in line." For example, if a price relationship between an option and the underlying property is not in line, an arbitrageur would establish a long and short position, expecting to profit once the proper price relationship is reestablished.

Another form of arbitrage, referred to as "risk arbitrage," is conducted in anticipation of, or upon the announcement of, a possible corporate merger or tender offer. "Risk arbitrage has its roots in classic arbitrage. The arbitrageur bids for announced takeover targets that he believes are undervalued in the marketplace relative to their ultimate value."[131] Purchasing stock in a corporation to be acquired in a merger or selling stock in the acquiring corporation are risk arbitrage positions. The risk arbitrageur speculates that the stock of the corporation to be acquired will increase in value or the stock of the acquiring corporation will go down in value. Risk arbitrageurs take the risk that the proposed merger or tender offer will not go through.

For tax purposes, arbitrageurs generally are viewed as traders (or investors), rather than dealers. As a result, such transactions usually generate capital gain or loss.

§ 6.8 FINANCIAL INSTITUTIONS

Various Code provisions provide special rules for banks and other financial institutions. Some of the special rules are mentioned in various parts of this book. One significant distinction between certain financial institutions and other market participants is that commercial banks, mutual savings banks, savings and loans, and small business investment companies cannot obtain capital gain or loss on the sale or exchange of bonds, debentures, notes, or certificates of indebtedness.[132] Such assets are never considered to be capital assets in their hands.[133] This limitation on capital asset treatment applies even if the financial institution would otherwise be classified as an investor[134] or trader[135] in such property. In many ways, the taxation of banks and financial institutions is beyond the scope of this book. For an excellent discussion of the income taxation of banks and other financial institutions, see *Federal Income Taxation of Banks and Financial Institutions* (M. Wakely ed. 1978).

§ 6.9 REGULATED INVESTMENT COMPANIES

The tax treatment of regulated investment companies is discussed in various parts of this book. This section mentions the major statutory

---

[131]I. BOESKY, MERGER MANIA, ARBITRAGE: WALL STREET'S BEST KEPT MONEY-MAKING SECRET xiii (1985).

[132]I.R.C. § 582(c)(1).

[133]*Id.*

[134]*See* section 6.1.

[135]*See* section 6.2.

requirements for qualification as a regulated investment company, and the tax treatment for different types of distributions from regulated investment companies.

The special tax treatment for regulated investment companies is provided in I.R.C. §§ 851–855. Regulated investment companies are typically structured as corporations or trusts, which allows for flow-through treatment to the extent that their earnings are distributed to their shareholders. This means that corporate tax is not imposed on a regulated investment company's distributed earnings. Despite this flow-through for earnings, however, regulated investment companies are not treated as partnerships or grantor trusts. For example, losses are not deductible to their shareholders,[136] and tax is imposed at the company level on any taxable income.[137]

Regulated investment companies can be (1) corporations or trusts registered under the Investment Company Act of 1940 as management companies or unit investment trusts,[138] (2) common trust funds maintained by a bank, or (3) certain companies established prior to 1936 that are exempt from registration.[139] Regulated investment companies that hold municipal securities (frequently referred to as "municipal bond funds") are usually structured as unit investment trusts.[140]

To qualify as a regulated investment company, an entity must meet the following requirements. First, the company must elect to be treated as a regulated investment company.[141] Second, at least 90 percent of the company's gross income must be derived from dividends, interest, payments with respect to certain security loans, and gains from securities transactions.[142] Third, less than 30 percent of the company's gross income must be derived from the sale or other disposition of securities held for less than three months.[143] Fourth, at the close of each quarter of the company's taxable year, at least 50 percent of the value of its total assets must be represented by cash, cash items (including receiv-

---

[136]I.R.C. § 852.

[137]I.R.C. § 852(b)(1); *see also* section 28.2(d)(3).

[138]I.R.C. § 851(a)(1).

[139]I.R.C. § 851(a)(2).

[140]A unit investment trust, which maintains a fixed investment portfolio, is the most popular vehicle for holding municipal securities. Although additional securities cannot be added to the portfolio, distressed securities can be sold to minimize losses. *See* Asinof, *Municipal-Bond Funds Offer Tax-exemption, Diversification and Minimum—but Some—Risk*, Wall St. J., Mar. 21, 1983, at 38. For a discussion of municipal bond funds, see section 28.2(d)(3).

[141]I.R.C. § 851(b)(1).

[142]I.R.C. § 851(b)(2).

[143]I.R.C. § 851(b)(3).

ables), government securities, securities of other regulated investment companies, and securities of corporations where the company's total investment does not exceed five percent of the value of the total assets of the taxpayer and does not constitute more than 10 percent of the voting securities of a corporate issuer.[144] Fifth, not more than 25 percent of the value of its total assets is invested in the securities of (1) any one issuer (except for government securities or the securities of other regulated investment companies), or (2) two or more issuers if 20 percent or more of the issuers are "controlled" by the company and they are engaged in the same, a similar, or a related trade or business.[145] And sixth, the company must distribute 90 percent of its ordinary income as dividends for the year.[146]

If a company meets the requirements set out above, in computing its taxable income it is entitled to a dividends paid deduction for the dividends it distributes to its shareholders during the taxable year.[147] In addition, a regulated investment company can distribute capital gain dividends under certain circumstances,[148] so that it is not taxed on the amount of capital gain dividends distributed to its shareholders. Finally, exempt-interest dividends can be paid to a company's shareholders on interest earned from tax-exempt securities under certain circumstances.[149]

Shareholders are taxed on distributions received from a regulated investment company in one of three ways. First, ordinary income dividends are treated as dividend income and are included in a shareholder's gross income.[150] (Unless otherwise designated by a regulated investment company, all distributions are treated as ordinary income dividends.) Second, capital gain dividends from transactions that result in long-term capital gains to the company are treated as long-term capital gains to the shareholder, regardless of how long the shareholder has owned his shares in the company.[151] Third, exempt-interest dividends, earned on tax-exempt securities owned by the company retain their tax-exempt status under certain circumstances.[152]

---

[144]I.R.C. §§ 851(b)(4)(A), 851(e).
[145]I.R.C. §§ 851(b)(4)(B), 851(c).
[146]I.R.C. § 852(a)(1).
[147]See generally I.R.C. §§ 561–562.
[148]I.R.C. § 852(b)(3).
[149]I.R.C. § 852(b)(5); see section 28.2(d)(3).
[150]Treas. Reg. § 1.852-4(a)(1) (1984).
[151]I.R.C. § 852(b)(3)(B); Treas. Reg. § 1.852-4(b)(1) (1984).
[152]I.R.C. § 852(b)(5); see section 28.2(d)(3).

Seven

Investors

Investors obtain capital gain or loss on their investments, that is, capital assets.[1] The Code does not specifically define capital assets. Instead, it identifies those assets that are not capital assets, implicitly providing that all other assets are capital assets. To determine whether an investor holds capital assets, one must look to the definition in I.R.C. § 1221, which lists those assets that are not capital assets, including property held by the taxpayer (1) as stock in trade, (2) as inventory, or (3) primarily for sale to customers in the ordinary course of business.[2] Because investors do not hold their investment assets for such business reasons, their securities, commodities, and option positions are capital assets.[3] In addition, investors obtain 60/40 treatment on their section 1256 contracts.[4]

This chapter discusses deductible expenses of investors. It also discusses limitations on deductions for expenses attributable to tax-exempt income as well as limitations on interest deductions.

§ 7.1 SECTION 212 EXPENSES

(a) IN GENERAL

Deductions are available to noncorporate investors under I.R.C. § 212 for expenses paid or incurred (1) for the production or collection of

[1] For a discussion of investors, see section 6.1.

[2] I.R.C. § 1221(1).

[3] Masonite Corp. v. U.S., 426 F. Supp. 469, 470 (S.D. Miss. 1977); Weiss v. Comm'r, 24 T.C.M. (CCH) 79, 84 (1965).

[4] *See generally* Part Nine.

income;[5] (2) for the management, conservation, or maintenance of property held for the production of income;[6] or (3) in connection with the determination, collection, or refund of any tax.[7] These expenses, loosely referred to as "section 212 expenses," are deductible by noncorporate investors. Reasonable amounts paid or incurred by a fiduciary of an estate or trust for administrative expenses (including fiduciary fees and expenses of litigation) are also deductible under I.R.C. § 212.[8] In contrast, investment expenses incurred by a corporation are not deductible under I.R.C. § 212.[9] Expenses incurred with respect to investment activities of corporations are not deductible under I.R.C. § 212 because that section is only available to individuals.[10]

For purposes of I.R.C. § 212, "income" is defined broadly to include not only current income but also income realized in a prior year or which may be realized in a subsequent year. Similarly, "income" is not confined to recurring items and applies to the prospect of gain from the disposition of property.[11] This means that section 212 expenses are deductible even if income is not generated in the taxable year for which the deduction is taken, and even if the property currently is not productive or there is no likelihood that the property will be sold at a profit (or will otherwise produce income).[12] In addition, section 212 expenses are deductible if the property is held merely to minimize a loss.[13]

Deductible section 212 expenses must be ordinary and necessary under all of the circumstances, considering both the type of investment and its relationship to the taxpayer.[14] Hence, such expenses must be reasonable in amount and must bear a reasonable relation to the production or collection of taxable income or to the management of property held for the production of income.[15] In addition, no deduction is allowed for any amount allocable to the production or collection of tax-

[5] I.R.C. § 212(1).
[6] I.R.C. § 212(2).
[7] I.R.C. § 212(3).
[8] Treas. Reg. § 1.212-1(i) (1975).
[9] A corporation is not an "individual" within the meaning of the Code. In defining a "person," I.R.C. § 7701(a)(1) distinguishes a corporation from an individual, thereby indicating that the two concepts (person and individual) are distinct unless otherwise specified.
[10] It is believed that corporations can deduct investment expenses under I.R.C. § 162(a). B. BITTKER & J. EUSTICE, FEDERAL INCOME TAXATION OF CORPORATIONS AND SHAREHOLDERS 5.03.12 (1979 ed.).
[11] Treas. Reg. § 1.212-1(b) (1975).
[12] Id.
[13] Id.
[14] Treas. Reg. § 1.212-1(d) (1975).
[15] Id.

exempt income (except for tax-exempt interest) or for any amount allocable to the management, conservation, or maintenance of property held for the production of income not included in gross income.[16] Furthermore, deductions are not allowed for any expenses that are disallowed by any Code provisions, even if such expenses are paid or incurred for one of the purposes specified in I.R.C. § 212.[17]

(b) ALLOCATION TO TAXABLE AND NONTAXABLE INCOME

Taxpayers cannot deduct expenses allocable to income wholly exempt from tax, except for tax-exempt interest expenses.[18] This means that an investor who incurs expenses attributable to taxable and nontaxable income must allocate those expenses between taxable and nontaxable income.[19] If an allocation between taxable and nontaxable income is required but not made, none of the expenses are deductible. For a discussion of nondeductible expenses attributable to tax-exempt income and the allocation between taxable and nontaxable income, see section 7.3.

(c) TYPES OF COVERED EXPENSES

Investors not engaged in a trade or business for purposes of I.R.C. § 162 must claim expenses incurred in purchasing and selling securities, commodities, and options either as itemized deductions (where allowable under I.R.C. § 212) or as deductions to capital gains and increases to capital losses.[20] Fees for investment advice, custodial fees, clerical help, and similar expenses incurred in connection with investments usually are deductible section 212 expenses.[21] In addition, expenditures for periodicals and books that deal with the markets are deductible,[22] although expenses to research facts concerning a corporation in which a taxpayer holds securities are not deductible.[23] Salaries, investment ad-

---

[16]I.R.C. § 265; *see also* section 7.3.

[17]Treas. Reg. § 1.212-1(e) (1975).

[18]I.R.C. § 265(1).

[19]Mallinckrodt v. Comm'r, 2 T.C. 1128, 1148 (1943), *aff'd*, 146 F.2d 1 (8th Cir.), *cert. denied*, 324 U.S. 781, *reh'g denied*, 325 U.S. 892 (1945).

[20]*See generally* Part Three.

[21]Rev. Rul. 75-523, 1975-2 C.B. 257; Treas. Reg. § 1.212-1(g) (1975).

[22]Hale v. Comm'r, 44 T.C.M. (CCH) 1116, 1119–20 (1982).

[23]Nichols v. Comm'r, 22 T.C.M. (CCH) 698 (1963).

vice, and fees and commissions of trustees of certain revocable trusts are deductible if such expenses are allocable to taxable income.[24]

(1) BUYING AND SELLING COSTS

Buying, managing, and selling expenses (other than those fees and commissions that must be capitalized) are deductible section 212 expenses. Commissions and fees to execute purchases are capitalized and added to the cost of the property,[25] while selling commissions are treated as an offset against the selling price.[26] One-time fees, however, such as brokerage, legal, accounting, and similar expenses paid to acquire or dispose of an asset, are not viewed as ordinary and necessary section 212 expenses and, therefore, must be capitalized.[27]

(2) INVESTMENT ADVISORY FEES

Investment advisory fees are deductible section 212 expenses if incurred to produce or collect income or to manage or maintain property held to produce income.[28] Such fees must be ordinary and necessary in light of the taxpayer's investment objections and portfolio.

(3) LITIGATION EXPENSES

Litigation expenses to rescind a transfer of stock are deductible.[29] Such litigation expenses are viewed as ordinary and necessary expenses under I.R.C. § 212.[30]

(4) PROXY CONTESTS

Proxy contest expenses generally are deductible.[31] The IRS supports a deduction if the proxy fight is sufficiently related to the production of

---

[24]*Mallinckrodt*, 2 T.C. at 1148.

[25]Comm'r v. Covington, 120 F.2d 768, 770-71 (5th Cir. 1941), *cert. denied*, 315 U.S. 822 (1942).

[26]Spreckels v. Helvering, 315 U.S. 626, 630 (1942); Estate of Milner v. Comm'r, 1 T.C.M. (CCH) 513 (1943); *cf.* Rev. Rul. 74-384, 1974-2 C.B. 152.

[27]Woodward v. Comm'r, 397 U.S. 572, 576 (1970); Honodel v. Comm'r, 722 F.2d 1462, 1466, 1468 (9th Cir. 1984).

[28]Rev. Rul. 73-13, 1973-1 C.B. 42; Treas. Reg. § 1.212-1(g) (1975).

[29]Megargel v. Comm'r, 3 T.C. 238, 250-51 (1944).

[30]*Id.*

[31]Graham v. Comm'r, 326 F.2d 878, 879 (4th Cir. 1964); Surasky v. U.S., 325 F.2d 191, 195–96 (5th Cir. 1963).

income.[32] Proxy contest expenses are deductible even if the anticipated proxy contest does not materialize.[33] A taxpayer's single effort to secure the proxies of other stockholders, however, has been held to be nondeductible.[34]

(5) TRAVEL AND TRANSPORTATION EXPENSES

Under certain circumstances, travel expenses are deductible as section 212 expenses. Those travel expenses incurred by an investor to make on site investigations of corporations in which he is buying and selling stock generally are not deductible.[35] In one case, however, the Tax Court noted that a taxpayer who made scheduled visits to corporations in which he had substantial ownership interests might be deductible if the taxpayer established that the visits were not disguised personal trips.[36]

Transportation expenses to visit a broker for investment consultation are deductible,[37] but transportation expenses to visit a broker's office to view quotation display systems cannot be deducted.[38]

(6) HOME OFFICE EXPENSES

Home office expenses can only be deducted by taxpayers in a trade or business. As a result, home office expenses of an investor (even a full-time investor) are not deductible.[39] In addition, an investor cannot deduct expenses attributable to the portion of his residence used for investment activities.[40] To obtain deductions for the use of a taxpayer's own residence, the taxpayer must be both in a trade or business and use that portion of the residence exclusively and on a regular basis for business purposes.[41]

---

[32]Rev. Rul. 64-236, 1964-2 C.B. 64.

[33]Nidetch v. Comm'r, 37 T.C.M. (CCH) 1309 (1978).

[34]Dyer v. Comm'r, 352 F.2d 948, 952 (8th Cir. 1965).

[35]Kinney v. Comm'r, 66 T.C. 122 (1976); Weinstein v. U.S., 420 F.2d 700, 701–02 (Ct. Cl. 1970).

[36]*Kinney*, 66 T.C. at 126.

[37]Henderson v. Comm'r, 27 T.C.M. (CCH) 109, 111 (1968).

[38]Walters v. Comm'r, 28 T.C.M. (CCH) 22, 24–25 (1969).

[39]Moller v. U.S., 721 F.2d 810, 815 (Fed. Cir. 1983), *cert. denied*, —U.S.—, 104 S. Ct. 3534 (1984).

[40]I.R.C. § 280A(a).

[41]I.R.C. § 280A(c).

(7) EXPENSES TO REPLACE LOST CERTIFICATES

Fees paid to purchase an indemnity bond and other expenses that relate to such a purchase are deductible if the expenses are required to replace lost stock certificates.[42]

(8) SERVICE CHARGES

Service charges paid to a bank to participate in an automatic dividend reinvestment plan are deductible section 212 expenses.[43]

(9) INVESTMENT PROMOTION EXPENSES

Expenses incurred for the creation and promotion of corporations in which a taxpayer is a stockholder are deductible section 212 expenses but only to the extent that a substantial portion of the expenses relate to the production or collection of income.[44]

§ 7.2 INTEREST EXPENSES

(a) IN GENERAL

Interest on indebtedness is deductible if paid or accrued within the taxable year.[45] For a cash basis taxpayer, interest generally can be deducted in the year paid. An accrual basis taxpayer can deduct interest when properly accrued.

For purposes of I.R.C. § 163, the term "interest" denotes that which is paid for the use of borrowed funds or as compensation for the use or forbearance of money.[46] The indebtedness on which such a payment is made must be an "existing, unconditional, and legally enforcible [sic] obligation."[47] In determining whether a payment constitutes interest on indebtedness, economic realities govern over the form of the transaction.[48]

[42]Rev. Rul. 62-21, 1962-1 C.B. 37.

[43]Rev. Rul. 70-627, 1970-2 C.B. 159.

[44]Deely v. Comm'r, 73 T.C. 1081, 1100 (1980).

[45]I.R.C. § 163(a).

[46]Old Colony R. Co. v. Comm'r, 284 U.S. 552, 560 (1932); Deputy v. Du Pont, 308 U.S. 488, 497–98 (1940).

[47]Kovtun v. Comm'r, 54 T.C. 331, 338 (1970), aff'd per curiam, 448 F.2d 1268 (9th Cir. 1971) cert. denied, 405 U.S. 1016 (1972); Titcher v. Comm'r, 57 T.C. 315, 322 (1971).

[48]Knetsch v. U.S., 364 U.S. 361, 365–66 (1960); Goldstein v. Comm'r, 364 F.2d 734, 741 (2d Cir. 1966), cert. denied, 385 U.S. 1005 (1967).

(b) SECURITIES MARGIN ACCOUNTS

Taxpayers who purchase securities on margin own the securities.[49] As a result, customers include in income all dividends paid during the taxable year on the securities in their margin accounts and all interest received on their securities.[50]

A securities margin account establishes a debtor-creditor relationship between the customer and the broker,[51] where the broker lends money to the customer, charging interest for the use of the funds. This interest, subject to the limitations on investment interest, is deductible under I.R.C. § 163.[52] With respect to a cash basis taxpayer, an interest deduction is allowed when the interest is actually or constructively paid by offsetting it with a cash credit in the margin account.[53] Interest expense charged to a margin account is actually or constructively paid "only as the broker receives payments from the taxpayer or makes collections for the account of the taxpayer."[54] Payments made to the broker by collections from a taxpayer's account include (1) the collection of dividends or interest for the account; (2) the sale of securities held by or to be received by the broker; and (3) the deposit of additional cash, whether voluntarily or in answer to a call for additional margin.[55] Hence, interest charges on a margin account are considered paid by a cash basis taxpayer whenever, and to the extent that, cash is credited to the customer's account from additional cash contributions, dividends, interest, or the proceeds from the sale of securities.

(c) FUTURES MARGIN

(1) RECEIPT OR DEPOSIT

Futures margin deposits and credits are not viewed as a loan between a customer who deposits margin with his FCM (or the FCM who, in turn, deposits margin with the clearing organization).[56] Rather, futures margin is viewed as a performance bond, good faith deposit, or earnest money. Opening and holding futures positions does not entail the trans-

---

[49]*See* section 1.4(b).

[50]For a discussion of dividend and interest income, see Part Five.

[51]Rev. Rul. 70-221, 1970-1 C.B. 33.

[52]*See* section 7.2(e).

[53]Rev. Rul. 70-221, 1970-1 C.B. 33; Rev. Rul. 70-647, 1970-2 C.B. 38.

[54]Rev. Rul. 70-221, 1970-1 C.B. 33.

[55]*Id.*

[56]For a discussion of the futures margin system, see section 4.4(b).

fer of ownership of the property underlying the futures contract position and does not entitle the holder of the futures contract position to any income or benefits from the underlying property. As a result, credit is not extended to customers who establish futures contract positions.[57]

Margin on a long position demonstrates a customer's intention to pay the balance of the purchase price when the underlying property is delivered to him.[58] For a short position, the margin deposit demonstrates a customer's ability to deliver the underlying property.[59] Interest is not charged by the customer who deposits commodity margin with an FCM and is not paid by the FCM on excess margin deposits. This general rule also applies to the FCM who deposits margin with a clearing organization.[60] Commodity customers with large margin requirements typically post Treasury bills, collecting the interest that accrues on the Treasury bills.

Under traditional tax doctrines, the receipt of futures margin is not income, and its deposit is not a deductible loss. This is because the term "income" in the Sixteenth Amendment is construed to mean gain derived from property severed from the capital.[61] Without a special Code provision (such as section 1256, which was enacted to mark section 1256 contracts to market), unrealized gains generally are not taxable. A taxpayer realizes taxable income when his futures positions are closed out during the taxable year and when all open positions held at the end of the year are marked-to-market.[62] In addition, gain or loss usually is recognized for tax purposes only upon the sale or other disposition of property.[63] These traditional tax doctrines have been modified for section 1256 contract positions that are open at the end of the year—these positions are marked-to-market.[64]

The only judicial authority that addresses tax treatment for margin and mark-to-market payments on futures contracts is found in *Elkan & Co. v. Comm'r*,[65] where the Tax Court refused to decide whether the

[57]STAFF OF THE BOARD OF GOVERNORS OF THE FEDERAL RESERVE BOARD, A REVIEW AND EVALUATION OF FEDERAL MARGIN REGULATIONS 57 (1984).

[58]*Id.* at 57-58.

[59]*Id.*

[60]*See* section 4.4(b)(3).

[61]Eisner v. Macomber, 252 U.S. 189, 207 (1920). Enrichment through an increase in capital value is not income. *Id.* at 214–15.

[62]*See generally* Part Nine.

[63]I.R.C. § 1001(c); Treas. Reg. § 1.165-1(b) (1977).

[64]I.R.C. §§ 1256(a)(1), 1256(c).

[65]2 T.C. 597 (1943); In *Elkan*, the Tax Court referred to the taxpayer's futures margin and mark-to-market payments as variation margin. This characterization, although not technically correct, does not change the tax result. *See* section 4.4(b)(1).

receipt of margin constituted taxable income because the IRS did not sufficiently establish what the taxpayer's net margin credit actually was.

The issue in *Elkan* was whether unrealized gain on futures contract positions open on the last day of the taxable year should have been included in the taxpayer's income. The taxpayer, a merchant who traded futures contracts throughout the year, maintained an account on its books in which it reflected what it referred to as the "variation margin" credited and charged to carry its futures positions.[66] Until a particular contract was closed out, margin amounts were not reflected in the value of the futures contracts and margin was not credited to the taxpayer's "profit and loss account."[67] Net unrealized profits as of the last day of the taxable year (reflected in the "variation margin account" maintained on the taxpayer's books) were not reported as income.[68] The IRS attempted, in its brief filed after the trial, to include the credits in income. The Tax Court cited *Eisner v. Macomber*[69] for the general proposition that unrealized profit is not taxable.[70] Furthermore, the court refused to decide this issue because it was only "on brief and in the alternative" that the IRS contended for the first time that the net positive balance in the taxpayer's "variation margin account" was taxable income.[71] No cases have directly addressed the taxability of futures margin deposits or mark-to-market payments.

Example   7-1

Assume a taxpayer enters into a futures contract position with the underlying property valued at $100,000. Assume further that this position required an initial margin deposit of $1000. And assume that the value of this futures position increases and a $200 mark-to-market payment is credited to the taxpayer's account. If the taxpayer's agreement with his FCM so permits, he can withdraw the mark-to-market credit even though he still holds the open futures contract position. Tax is not imposed on the withdrawal. If the contract is a section 1256 contract, the taxpayer recognizes taxable income when the contract is closed out or, if it remains open at year-end, when the contract is marked-to-market.

---

[66]*Elkan*, 2 T.C. at 601.
[67]*Id.*
[68]*Id.*
[69]252 U.S. 189 (1920).
[70]*Elkan*, 2 T.C. at 602.
[71]*Id.* at 606–07.

Example 7-2

Given the same facts described in Example 7-1, assume that the futures contract position subsequently increases in value, resulting in an additional $100 mark-to-market credit. This means that the taxpayer's mark-to-market credits total $300. If the taxpayer now closes out his futures contract position, gain on the transaction is the difference between the opening and closing prices for the position. Gain is reported irrespective of whether the taxpayer previously withdrew any of the positive credit balance in his account. The only difference is that the taxpayer receives less cash on closing the transaction if some or all of the mark-to-market credits already have been withdrawn from his account.

(2) BELOW MARKET LOANS

The futures margin system does not create a debtor-creditor relationship between a customer and the FCM (or the FCM and the clearing organization) or vice versa. Interest usually is not collected or charged on margin or mark-to-market payments. In the rare case where a customer receives interest, of course, this is taxable as income. In addition, those customers who deposit Treasury bills and other interest bearing securities as initial margin obtain the interest that accrues on the securities and report this as income.[72] As a result, it is the author's view that interest should not be imputed to futures margin deposits under the below market interest rules imposed by I.R.C. § 7872.

When I.R.C. § 7872 was enacted, Congress was concerned about both the transfer of an economic benefit through the low interest or interest free use of money as a substitute for another payment to the borrower, and the situation where the tax consequences after such a transfer are different from those that would occur if a market interest rate had been charged and the lender actually made a separate payment to the borrower.[73] I.R.C. § 7872 imposes interest on loans between certain related parties that otherwise would circumvent established tax rules, recharacterizing a below market or interest free loan as if a loan had been made at the applicable federal rate.[74] The balance of the loan proceeds is treated as a payment, such as a gift or compensation, by the lender

---

[72]I.R.C. § 61(a)(4).

[73]Conference Report, Deficit Reduction Act of 1984, H.R. Rep. No. 861, 98th Cong., 2d Sess. 1011-1012, *reprinted in* 1984 U.S. Code Cong. & Ad. News 1445, 1699-1700.

[74]*Id.* at 1012.

to the borrower. In addition, the rules also are extended to "tax-avoidance loans"[75] and "other below market loans"[76] with a de minimis exception[77] and a broad grant of regulatory authority to the Treasury to carry out the purposes of the section.[78] It is the author's view that futures margin should not be viewed as a tax-avoidance or a below market loan that is established to circumvent the tax rules.

On August 15, 1985, the Treasury issued proposed and temporary regulations under I.R.C. § 7872.[79] In a request for comments, the Treasury stated that a cash margin deposit made to an FCM or a commodity exchange pursuant to exchange requirements as a condition of trading might be characterized as a compensation-related loan under I.R.C. § 7872(c)(1)(B). The Treasury requested written comments on whether a cash margin transaction should be subject to I.R.C. § 7872 and whether the "interest arrangements" of such transactions have a "significant effect" on the tax liability of the lender or borrower.[80]

An exemption from application of I.R.C. § 7872 is provided for margin on commodity futures and option contracts prior to July 1, 1986. For periods prior to July 1, 1986, exempted loans include all money, securities, and property received by an FCM or by a clearing organization (1) to margin, guarantee, or secure contracts for future delivery on or subject to the rules of a qualified board or exchange or (2) to purchase, margin, guarantee, or secure option contracts traded on or subject to the rules of a qualified board or exchange.[81] For these periods, exempted loans also include all money that may accrue to account holders as the result of such futures and option contracts.[82] This means that until July 1, 1986, futures and commodity option margin, is exempt from the below market loan provisions. At that time, the Treasury will either modify the exemption or make it permanent.

It is the author's belief that this exemption from compensation-related loans should be made permanent. The legislative history states that compensation-related loans with below market rates provide benefits, rather than a fee, for services. In such cases, interest is imputed under I.R.C. § 7872.[83] A customer who deposits margin, whether cash

---

[75]I.R.C. § 7872(c)(1)(D).

[76]I.R.C. § 7872(c)(1)(E).

[77]I.R.C. § 7872(c)(2).

[78]I.R.C. § 7872(g).

[79]Prop. Treas. Reg. § 1.7872-5 (1985); Temp. Treas. Reg. § 1.7872-5T (1985).

[80]Request for Comments on Certain Transactions, 50 Fed. Reg. 33,555 (1985).

[81]Prop. Treas. Reg. § 1.7872-5(b)(13) (1985); Temp. Treas. Reg. § 1.7872-5T(b)(13) (1985).

[82]*Id.*

[83]H.R. REP. No. 861, *supra* note 73, at 1019.

or other property, pays the FCM its regular brokerage charges and other fees. Although some customers have economic leverage to negotiate lower fees (based in part upon the interest free use of their margin deposits by the FCM), the majority of all commodity customers pay commissions and fees without regard to the FCM's interest free use of their funds.[84] Commodity margin deposits should not be viewed as compensation-related and should not be subject to the below market interest rules.

In many cases, a commodity customer cannot withdraw his margin or mark-to-market payments from his account until his positions are closed out. At any time, he can close out all of his positions and withdraw all of his funds. As a result, an FCM has no assurance of any time period during which it can benefit from the deposit of a particular customer's funds. Furthermore, the FCM might need to deposit greater margin and mark-to-market payment amounts with the clearing organization affiliated with the commodity exchange on which the particular contracts are traded. Although FCMs take this benefit into account when establishing commission rates, the situation is different from compensation-related loans with respect to the below market interest rules because there is no guarantee at the outset of the transaction that the FCM will derive any specific economic benefit. The same cannot be said where a low interest or interest free use of money is made available for a period of time agreed to at the outset of the transaction.

In conclusion, it is the author's view that commodity margin payments should not be subject to the below market interest rules because margin does not create a debtor-creditor relationship.[85] Rather, the margin deposit assures that the customer performs his obligations in connection with his open futures and commodity option positions. The FCM (or clearing organization) merely becomes a custodian of the customer's funds. Customers with strong economic power can negotiate lower fees (and can occasionally negotiate interest payment on their excess margin deposits). Other customers who deposit Treasury bills or other interest bearing securities obtain the interest that accrues on their securities. While an FCM might obtain an economic benefit from holding its customer's margin funds (for instance, as a compensating balance at its bank or from investment in interest bearing obligations where the

---

[84]The authority of FCMs to retain interest earned on customer margin funds has been challenged in several pending actions. *See* Craig v. REFCO, Inc., No. 84 C 10900 (N.D. Ill. filed Dec. 26, 1984); *but see* Marchese v. Shearson Hayden Stone, Inc., No. CV 79-0003228 (C.D. Calif. Mar. 4, 1985) (upholding an FCM's right to interest on customer margin).

[85]*See* section 4.4.

interest accrues to the FCM's benefit), commodity margin deposits are made because of established business practices to protect the financial integrity of the futures market. Margin deposits should not be subject to the below market loan rules imposed by I.R.C. § 7872.

(d) PREPAID INTEREST

Prepaid interest cannot be deducted currently. Rather, it must be capitalized by a cash basis taxpayer and deducted as if the taxpayer were on the accrual basis, that is, ratably over the term of the loan.[86] Therefore, an investor cannot prepay interest expenses in one year to obtain an interest deduction if the interest is properly allocable to another tax year.

(e) INVESTMENT INTEREST

Limitations are imposed on deductions for interest incurred to purchase or carry property held for investment. The full amount of interest paid or incurred might not be deductible if the interest is incurred to finance the purchase or maintenance of investment assets.

A noncorporate taxpayer's annual deduction for payments of investment interest is limited to the sum of (1) $10,000 ($5000 in the case of a married taxpayer filing a separate return) plus (2) the amount of net investment income.[87] Net investment income generally consists of gross income (derived from interest, dividends, rents, royalties, and short-term capital gains from the sale of investment property) minus expenses (such as straight-line depreciation attributable to income other than interest expense).[88] The disallowed portion is carried forward to subsequent tax years. Corporations are not subject to this limitation.[89]

Interest incurred for personal reasons or business purposes is not investment interest and, therefore, is not subject to the investment interest limitations. In Rev. Rul. 82-163, the IRS ruled that interest on a second mortgage loan on the taxpayer's home, obtained from an affiliate of a brokerage firm at which the taxpayer has a margin account, is subject to the investment interest limitations if the purpose of the loan is to purchase investment securities.[90] The investment interest limita-

---

[86]I.R.C. § 461(g).
[87]I.R.C. § 163(d).
[88]I.R.C. § 163(d)(3).
[89]I.R.C. § 163(d).
[90]1982-2 C.B. 57.

tions do not apply, however, if the loan proceeds are used for a personal, noninvestment activity.[91]

The investment interest limitation has been imposed on interest incurred to purchase shares of stock in a bank by a partnership in which the taxpayer, who subsequently became the bank's president, was a partner.[92] An investment motive was evidenced by the fact that (1) the partnership's principal activity was making investments; (2) the partnership purchased the stock to obtain a gain on the stock and, in fact, actually reported capital gain on the sale of the stock; (3) the interest on the loan was reported as excess investment interest; and (4) the taxpayer, in his capacity as bank president, directed the bank's operations toward capital growth.[93] To avoid the investment interest limitations, investors might want to assert that their activities qualify for trader rather than investor status and that such interest expense should be allowed as related to a trade or business. The risk of making this argument is that a taxpayer might be required to maintain an inventory that might include interest and other carrying charges.[94] In addition, the IRS might assert that the taxpayer should be viewed as a dealer, subject to ordinary income or loss treatment.[95]

(f) INTEREST AND CARRYING CHARGES ON STRADDLE POSITIONS

Interest and carrying charges allocable to personal property that is part of a straddle must be capitalized.[96] Exceptions to the capitalization requirements include bona fide hedging transactions[97] and straddles of section 1256 contracts that are not part of larger straddles.[98] Investors are not eligible for the hedging exemption for various reasons, not the least of which is the fact that their trading activities generate capital gains and losses. Investors can deduct interest and carrying charges for section 1256 straddles as long as the straddles consist only of such contracts.[99]

---

[91]*Id.*

[92]Miller v. Comm'r, 70 T.C. 448 (1978).

[93]*Id.* at 456–57.

[94]Rev. Rul. 74-226, 1974-1 C.B. 119, *see also* section 43.2.

[95]*See generally* Part Four; section 6.3.

[96]I.R.C. § 263(g)(1).

[97]I.R.C. § 263(g)(3); *see generally* Chapter 21.

[98]I.R.C. § 1256(a)(4); *see* section 43.2.

[99]I.R.C. § 1256(a)(4).

(g) SHAM TRANSACTIONS

Interest deductions are not allowed if incurred for transactions that are shams or have little purpose beyond obtaining a tax deduction.[100] In addition, the taxpayer must prove that the transaction was bona fide and that there was some economic purpose (such as the procurement of a profit) to support the interest deduction.[101]

§ 7.3 EXPENSES RELATING TO TAX-EXEMPT INCOME

Expenses allocable to income (other than tax-exempt interest income) that is wholly exempt from income tax are not deductible.[102] That is, taxpayers generally are denied deductions for interest incurred to purchase or carry tax-exempt securities.[103]

(a) TYPES OF EXPENSES

Expenses otherwise deductible under the Code are not deductible if allocable to income that is wholly exempt from tax.[104] The only exception is for interest income, which means that expenses attributable to earning tax-exempt interest are deductible.[105] Tax-exempt income includes any class of income (irrespective of whether income is received or accrued) that is wholly exempt from income taxes or wholly excluded from gross income under the Code or any other law.[106]

If a taxpayer has both taxable and nontaxable income, expenses must be allocated between the taxable and nontaxable income.[107] As a result, expenses directly allocable to exempt income must be allocated to the exempt income, while expenses directly allocable to nonexempt income must be allocated to nonexempt income.[108] If an expense is indirectly allocable to both exempt and nonexempt income, a reasonable alloca-

---

[100]*Knetsch*, 364 U.S. at 366; *Goldstein*, 364 F.2d at 740.

[101]Julien v. Comm'r, 82 T.C. 492, 509 (1984); Forseth v. Comm'r, 85 T.C. 127 (1985); Hirai v. Comm'r, 48 T.C.M. (CCH) 1134, 1142 (1984).

[102]I.R.C. § 265(1).

[103]I.R.C. § 265(2).

[104]Treas. Reg. § 1.265-1(a)(1) (1958).

[105]*Id.*

[106]Treas. Reg. § 1.265-1(b) (1958).

[107]*Mallinckrodt*, 2 T.C. at 1148.

[108]*Id.*

tion, determined in light of all of the facts and circumstances, must be made.[109] If an allocation is not made, the expenses attributable to non-exempt income are not deductible. The taxpayer must maintain those records necessary to make a proper allocation.[110] A taxpayer with exempt income must submit an itemized statement with his tax return showing, in detail (1) the amount of each class of exempt income, and (2) the amount of allowable expenses allocated to each such class (the amount allocated by apportionment must be shown separately).[111] If an item is apportioned between exempt and nonexempt income, the statement must show the basis of the apportionment and assert that each deduction claimed in the return is not in any way attributable to exempt income.[112]

If tax-exempt securities in a trust produce taxable income or are held for that purpose, termination fees for a fiduciary are deductible.[113] On the other hand, expenses allocable to interest income wholly exempt from federal income taxes are not deductible.[114]

(b) INTEREST ON INDEBTEDNESS ON TAX-EXEMPT SECURITIES

A deduction is not available for interest on any indebtedness incurred or continued to purchase or carry tax-exempt securities (e.g., municipal bonds, Panama Canal loans, so-called three percent bonds, or United States securities issued after September 24, 1917 if the securities were not originally subscribed to by the taxpayer). Obviously, the largest group of tax-exempt securities is municipal securities. For the rules that cover interest on certain governmental obligations in gross income, see I.R.C. § 103 and the Treasury regulations promulgated thereunder.[115]

The IRS announced in Rev. Proc. 72-18[116] that the purpose to carry tax-exempt securities will be deemed to exist with respect to indebtedness incurred to finance a portfolio investment.[117]

[109]Treas. Reg. § 1.265-1(c) (1958); Rev. Rul. 63-27, 1963-1 C.B. 57; Fabens v. Comm'r, 519 F.2d 1310, 1312 (1st Cir. 1975).

[110]I.R.C. § 6001; Treas. Reg. § 1.265-1(d)(2) (1958).

[111]Treas. Reg. § 1.265-1(d)(1) (1958).

[112]Id.

[113]Whittemore v. U.S., 383 F.2d 824, 836 (8th Cir. 1967).

[114]Rev. Rul. 73-27, 1973-1 C.B. 46.

[115]Treas. Reg. § 1.265-2(a) (1967).

[116]1972-1 C.B. 740.

[117]Bradford v. Comm'r, 60 T.C. 253, 260–61 (1973) (which follows Rev. Rul. 72-18).

(1) ALLOWABLE DEDUCTIONS

The following factors have been considered as to whether an interest deduction is available: (1) whether all of an individual's loans are used to finance major, nonrecurring, and long range business opportunities; (2) whether business reasons are the sole motivation for incurring indebtedness; (3) whether only what the investor and his advisor consider an absolute minimum of tax-exempt securities are owned by the taxpayer at the time loans are made; and (4) whether no reasonable person, under the circumstances, would sacrifice the liquidity and security of the taxpayer's position by cashing in the tax-exempt securities.[118]

Interest deductions are allowed to the extent that the loans are supported by collateral other than tax-exempt securities.[119] In addition, interest on installment notes used to purchase securities is deductible if the taxpayer does not incur or continue indebtedness represented by the installment notes to purchase or carry tax-exempt securities.[120]

(2) DISALLOWED DEDUCTIONS

If a taxpayer reasonably can foresee at the time of purchasing tax-exempt securities that a loan probably is required to meet future economic needs of an ordinary, recurrent variety, a deduction is not available.[121] Interest is not deductible if there is "a sufficiently direct relationship" between the interest and tax-exempt securities.[122] If a loan is needed to sustain a taxpayer's business operation, the interest is not deductible to the extent that the indebtedness is continued to enable the taxpayer to retain ownership of tax-exempt securities.[123] In addition, interest on funds borrowed by one spouse and used by the other to purchase tax-exempt securities is not deductible on their joint federal tax return.[124]

---

[118]Ball v. Comm'r, 54 T.C. 1200, 1209 (1970).

[119]Levitt v. U.S., 517 F.2d 1339, 1346–47 (8th Cir. 1975).

[120]Handy Button Machine Co. v. Comm'r, 61 T.C. 846 (1974).

[121]Wisconsin Cheeseman, Inc. v. U.S., 388 F.2d 420, 422–23 (7th Cir. 1968).

[122]McDonough v. Comm'r, 577 F.2d 234, 235 (4th Cir. 1978) (citing Indian Trail Trading Post, Inc. v. Comm'r, 60 T.C. 497, 500 (1973), aff'd, 503 F.2d 102 (6th Cir. 1974)); Wynn v. U.S., 411 F.2d 614 (3d Cir. 1969), cert. denied, 396 U.S. 1008 (1970); Ball, 54 T.C. at 1209; Lang v. Comm'r, 46 T.C.M. (CCH) 335 (1983).

[123]Illinois Terminal Railroad Co. v. U.S., 375 F.2d 1016, 1021 (Ct. Cl. 1967).

[124]Rev. Rul. 79–272, 1979-2 C.B. 124.

(3) REGULATED INVESTMENT COMPANIES

A shareholder of a regulated investment company cannot deduct interest on indebtedness that relates to exempt-interest dividends distributed to him.[125] Regulated investment companies are certain flow-through entities (e.g., corporations or trusts) that qualify for regulated investment company status under the Code, which includes mutual funds and unit investment trusts. Indebtedness is deemed to relate to exempt-interest dividends if the indebtedness either is incurred or continued to purchase or carry shares of stock in a regulated investment company that distributes exempt-interest dividends, as defined in I.R.C. § 852(b)(5).[126] To determine the amount of interest that relates to exempt-interest dividends, the total amount of interest paid or accrued on indebtedness is multiplied by a fraction. The numerator of the fraction is the amount of exempt-interest dividends received by the shareholder. The denominator is the sum of both exempt-interest dividends and taxable dividends received by the shareholder (excluding capital gain dividends received by the shareholder and capital gains required to be included in the shareholder's computation of long-term capital gains under I.R.C. § 852(b)(3)(D)).[127]

(4) DE MINIMIS EXCEPTION

When a taxpayer's investment in tax-exempt securities is insubstantial, the purpose of incurring indebtedness to purchase or carry tax-exempt securities is not inferred in the absence of direct evidence to the contrary.[128] This de minimis exception, available only to taxpayers who are not dealers, applies separate tests for noncorporate and corporate investors. To be insubstantial,[129] a noncorporate taxpayer's investment in tax-exempt securities must not exceed two percent of his average adjusted basis of total portfolio investments and any assets held in the active conduct of a trade or business. In the case of a corporation, an investment in tax-exempt securities is presumed to be insubstantial if the average amount of tax-exempt securities (valued at their adjusted

---

[125]I.R.C. § 265(3); Treas. Reg. § 1.265-3(a) (1979). *See* section 6.9.

[126]Treas. Reg. § 1.265-3(b)(1) (1979).

[127]Treas. Reg. § 1.265-3(b)(2) (1979).

[128]Rev. Proc. 72-18, 1972-1 C.B. 740, *amplified by* Rev. Proc. 80-55, 1980-2 C.B. 849 (which was revoked by Rev. Proc. 81-16, 1981-1 C.B. 688), *clarified by* Rev. Proc. 74-8, 1974-1 C.B. 419.

[129]*Id.*

basis) held during the taxable year does not exceed two percent of the corporation's average total assets (valued at their adjusted basis) held in the active conduct of the corporation's trade or business.[130]

§ 7.4 BOND PREMIUMS

Investors can elect to deduct bond premiums, which are the amounts paid on taxable bonds that are in excess of the face value of the bonds. For tax-exempt bonds, no deduction is allowed for the taxable year.[131] Rather, investors must amortize premiums on tax-exempt bonds on an annual basis so as to reduce their basis.[132] For a discussion of bond premiums, see section 27.4.

§ 7.5 WASH SALES

Investors in stocks and securities are subject to the wash sales rule of I.R.C. § 1091. For a discussion of the wash sales rule, see generally Chapter 17.

§ 7.6 SHORT SALES

Investors are subject to the short sales rule of I.R.C. § 1233 for short sales of capital assets. For a discussion of the short sales rule, see generally Chapter 16.

§ 7.7 STRADDLE RULES

The Straddle Rules of I.R.C. §§ 1092 and 263(g) apply to offsetting positions in personal property. For a discussion of the Straddle Rules, see generally Part 10.

---

[130]*Id.*
[131]I.R.C. § 171(a).
[132]*Id.*; Brown v. U.S., 426 F.2d 355, 366 (Ct. Cl. 1970).

Eight

Traders

Traders obtain capital gain or loss treatment on their security, commodity, and option transactions[1] and 60/40 treatment on their section 1256 contracts.[2] Securities, commodities, and options held by traders are capital assets, so they receive capital gain and loss treatment.[3] Commodity futures contract traders similarly receive capital gain and loss treatment on their transactions.[4] Capital gain or loss results regardless of whether the taxpayer is an individual, partnership, or corporation.[5]

This chapter discusses deductible expenses of traders and limitations on certain deductions.

§ 8.1 EXPENSES OF TRADERS

(a) TRADE OR BUSINESS EXPENSES

Traders are in the trade or business of buying and selling securities, commodities, or options. As a result, expenses attributable to trading

[1]For a discussion of traders, see section 6.2.

[2]*See generally* Part Nine.

[3]Bradford v. U.S., 444 F.2d 1133, 1140 (Ct. Cl. 1971); Huebschman v. Comm'r, 41 T.C.M. (CCH) 474, 476 (1980); Adnee v. Comm'r, 41 T.C. 40 (1963); Kemon v. Comm'r, 16 T.C. 1026 (1951).

[4]Comm'r v. Covington, 120 F.2d 768, 770 (5th Cir. 1941), *cert. denied*, 315 U.S. 822 (1942); Vickers v. Comm'r, 80 T.C. 394, 405 (1983); Seroussi v. Comm'r, 22 T.C.M. (CCH) 1186, 1189 (1963); Polachek v. Comm'r, 22 T.C. 858, 861 (1954); Estate of Makransky v. Comm'r, 5 T.C. 397, 411-12, *aff'd*, 154 F.2d 59 (3d Cir. 1946).

[5]Mirro-Dynamics Corp. v. U.S., 374 F.2d 14 (9th Cir.) *cert. denied*, 389 U.S. 896 (1967); Smith v. Comm'r, 33 T.C. 465 (1959), *rev'd on other grounds, sub nom.* Estate of Smith v. Comm'r, 313 F.2d 724 (8th Cir. 1963).

activities generally are deductible as ordinary and necessary expenses under I.R.C. § 162. Deductible expenses specifically enumerated in the Code include (1) salaries,[6] (2) traveling expenses,[7] and (3) rentals (including office rent) and other payments required to use property not owned by the trader.[8]

(b) TRADE OR BUSINESS DEFINED

The phrase "trade or business" is not defined in the Code or the Treasury regulations; consequently, whether trading activities qualify as a trade or business is a question of fact.[9] Various factors must be considered, although no one factor is dispositive.[10] Elements of a trade or business include (1) activities that occupy "the time, attention and labor" of the taxpayer for the purpose of "a livelihood or profit";[11] (2) the continuity and regularity of the taxpayer's activities; and (3) a profit motive.[12] In *Morris v. Comm'r*,[13] the Board of Tax Appeals held that a taxpayer who participated in a joint venture to trade a particular stock and who executed 600 transactions in a six-month period involving over $5 million was a trader for tax purposes. The trading activity occupied most of the taxpayer's time and constituted most of his income.[14] In contrast, merely holding a brokerage account in which a series of purchases and sales are made is not a sufficient activity to constitute an active trade or business.[15] In looking to trade or business status, the courts have considered maintenance of an office, employment of assistants, and the devotion of extensive time to the continual management of the activity.[16]

---

[6]I.R.C. § 162(a)(1).

[7]I.R.C. § 162(a)(2).

[8]I.R.C. § 162(a)(3).

[9]Higgins v. Comm'r, 312 U.S. 212, 217, *reh'g denied*, 312 U.S. 714 (1941).

[10]Barrett v. Comm'r, 58 T.C. 284, 288 (1972), *acq.* 1974-1 C.B. 1.

[11]Flint v. Stone Tracy Co., 220 U.S. 107, 171 (1910).

[12]Schley v. Comm'r, 19 A.F.T.R. 2d (P-H) 1031 (1967). Activities not engaged in for profit (i.e., hobbies) do not qualify as a business under I.R.C. § 162 or as income-producing activities under I.R.C. § 212.

[13]38 B.T.A. 265, 267–68 (1938).

[14]*Id.* at 268; *see also* Kunau v. Comm'r, 27 B.T.A. 509 (1933) (where the Board of Tax Appeals held that a trust making numerous purchases and sales generating a $2 million profit over two years was actively conducting a trade or business).

[15]Coulter v. Comm'r, 32 B.T.A. 617 (1935).

[16]Purvis v. Comm'r, 530 F.2d 1332, 1334 (9th Cir. 1976) (where the court found that the frequency, extent, and regularity of the taxpayer's securities transactions did not qualify him as a trader).

An activity constitutes a trade or business when substantial portions of a trader's total income or losses are derived from the activity.[17]

(c) DEDUCTIBLE EXPENSES

Business expenses are deductible by a trader. Such expenses include ordinary and necessary expenditures directly connected with and pertaining to the taxpayer's trade or business. The full amount of these expenses are deductible, even if the expenses exceed the gross income derived during the taxable year from such business.[18] Business expenses include the costs of expenses; certain noncapitalized commissions;[19] labor;[20] supplies;[21] incidental repairs;[22] operation of automobiles used in the trade or business; traveling while away from home solely in the pursuit of the trade or business;[23] advertising and other promotion that do not need to be capitalized; insurance to protect against fire, storm, theft, accident, or other similar losses in the case of a business; and rent for the use of business property.[24]

A deduction otherwise allowable under I.R.C. § 162 can be denied if the deduction is against public policy. Deductions are not allowed for illegal bribes, kickbacks, and other such payments,[25] fines and penalties,[26] or antitrust damages.[27]

(d) COMMISSIONS ON PURCHASES AND SALES

A trader's fees and commissions to execute purchase and sale transactions are not deductible. For purchases, such fees and commissions are

---

[17]Levin v. U.S., 597 F.2d 760 (Ct. Cl. 1979).

[18]Treas. Reg. § 1.162-1(a) (1975).

[19]*But see* I.R.C. § 263 and the Treasury regulations thereunder for rules governing when commissions must be capitalized; *see also* section 8.1(d).

[20]Treas. Reg. § 1.162-7 (1958).

[21]Treas. Reg. § 1.162-1(a) (1975).

[22]Treas. Reg. § 1.162-4 (1958).

[23]Treas. Reg. § 1.162-2 (1958).

[24]Treas. Reg. § 1.162-1(a) (1975).

[25]I.R.C. § 162(c); Treas. Reg. § 1.162-18 (1975).

[26]I.R.C. § 162(f); Treas. Reg. § 1.162-21 (1975).

[27]I.R.C. § 162(g); Treas. Reg. § 1.162-22 (1972).

added to the cost of the property;[28] sales commissions are offset against the selling price.[29]

Under the rules of the security and commodity exchanges, floor traders can generally buy and sell positions either for their own accounts or as agents or brokers for customers.[30] This means that floor traders earn ordinary income from brokerage commissions obtained by executing transactions that are totally unconnected with trading for their own accounts. Nevertheless, such traders cannot offset the commissions they pay to other brokers for their own trading activities from those brokerage commissions earned by executing orders for customers.[31]

(e) INVENTORIES UNAVAILABLE

Because a trader is not a dealer, a trader cannot use the inventory methods available to dealers.[32] As a result, traders must identify all purchases and sales to compute gain or loss.[33]

§ 8.2 INTEREST EXPENSES

(a) IN GENERAL

Interest on indebtedness generally is deductible if paid or accrued within the taxable year. A cash basis taxpayer can deduct interest in the year paid.[34] An accrual basis taxpayer deducts interest when it is accrued.

(b) SECURITIES MARGIN ACCOUNTS

The tax treatment of securities margin accounts of traders is identical to that of investors. For a discussion of the tax treatment of investors, see section 7.2(b).

---

[28]*Covington*, 120 F.2d at 770.

[29]Spreckels v. Helvering, 315 U.S. 626, 629 (1942); Comm'r v. Levis' Estate, 127 F.2d 796, 797 (2d Cir.), *cert. denied*, 314 U.S. 645 (1942).

[30]*See* section 6.2(a).

[31]Helvering v. Winmill, 305 U.S. 79, 83-84 (1938); *Spreckels*, 315 U.S. at 630.

[32]Seeley v. Helvering, 77 F.2d 323 (2d Cir. 1935); *see* section 9.6; *but see* Rev. Rul. 74-226, 1974-1 C.B. 119.

[33]*See generally* Chapter 18.

[34]I.R.C. § 163(a).

(c) FUTURES CONTRACT MARGIN

The tax treatment of futures margin accounts of traders is identical to that of investors. For a discussion of the tax treatment of futures margin accounts, see section 7.2(c).

(d) PREPAID INTEREST

Prepaid interest must be capitalized by a cash basis taxpayer, including a trader, and deducted as if the taxpayer were on the accrual basis, that is, ratably over the term of the loan.[35] Therefore, a trader who reports income on the cash basis cannot prepay interest expenses in one year to obtain an interest deduction if such expenses are properly allocable to another tax year.

(e) INVESTMENT INTEREST

If interest is incurred to purchase or carry property held for investment, a deduction can be limited under I.R.C. § 163(d). For a discussion of investment interest limitations generally, see section 7.2(e). Because traders are in a trade or business, interest incurred to finance their trading operations should be deductible without regard to the investment interest limitations. Interest expenses incurred in investment activities, of course, remain subject to the investment interest limitations. Although I.R.C. § 163(d)(3)(D) does not explicitly exclude from the definition of investment interest interest on property held for use in a trade or business, such interest is explicitly excluded from the definition of investment income and investment expense.[36] As a result, it is possible to assert that interest incurred in a trade or business is investment interest, even though interest incurred to purchase or carry trade or business property generally is viewed as deductible from gross income. A possible reading of the statutory limitations on deducting investment interest is that it extends to all taxpayers who have an investment motive for holding property. This position has been advanced by the IRS in recent audits and cases pending before the Tax Court. Under the IRS analysis, whether a taxpayer has investment interest does not revolve around whether the taxpayer is in a trade or business. The key questions are whether the property is held for an investment motive and whether property is actively used in the taxpayer's trade or business.

---

[35]I.R.C. § 461(g).
[36]I.R.C. §§ 163(d)(3)(C), (B).

This analysis forces the taxpayer to assert that he does not have an investment motive and that the interest was incurred to finance property or trading activity used in his trade or business. It is possible that the taxpayer could lose capital gain on the sale of the property if he successfully argues that the property was held for business, rather than investment, purposes.

(f) INTEREST AND CARRYING CHARGES ON STRADDLE POSITIONS

Interest and carrying charges allocable to personal property that is part of a straddle must be capitalized.[37] Exceptions to the capitalization requirements are provided for bona fide hedging transactions[38] and straddles of section 1256 contracts that are not part of larger straddles.[39] Traders, with trading activities that generate capital gains and losses, are not eligible for the hedging exemption. Traders in section 1256 contracts can deduct interest and carrying charges incurred on straddle positions if the straddles consist entirely of section 1256 contracts.

(g) SHAM TRANSACTIONS

Interest is not deductible if the expenses are incurred for transactions that are shams or have little purpose beyond obtaining a tax deduction.[40] Transactions must be bona fide and there must be some economic purpose (such as the procurement of a profit) to support the interest deduction.[41]

§ 8.3 EXPENSES RELATING TO TAX-EXEMPT INCOME

(a) TYPES OF EXPENSES

Traders, like investors, cannot deduct expenses allocable to income (other than tax-exempt interest income) that is wholly exempt from income

---

[37] I.R.C. § 263(g).

[38] *See generally* Chapter 21.

[39] I.R.C. § 1256(a)(4); *see* section 44.7.

[40] Knetsch v. U.S., 364 U.S. 361, 366 (1960); Goldstein v. Comm'r, 364 F.2d 734, 740 (2d Cir. 1966).

[41] Julien v. Comm'r, 82 T.C. 492, 509 (1984); Forseth v. Comm'r, 85 T.C. 127 (1985); Hirai v. Comm'r, 48 T.C.M. (CCH) 1134, 1143 (1984).

tax.[42] In addition, traders cannot deduct interest expenses incurred to purchase or carry tax-exempt securities.[43]

(b) INTEREST ON INDEBTEDNESS ON TAX-EXEMPT SECURITIES

As in the case of investors, traders cannot deduct interest on any indebtedness incurred or continued to purchase or carry tax-exempt securities. For a discussion of the limitations on expenses relating to interest on indebtedness of tax-exempt securities, see section 7.3(b). If the trader can establish that the indebtedness was not "incurred or continued to purchase or carry" the tax-exempt securities, an interest deduction is available.[44] Because the restrictions contained in I.R.C. § 265(2) apply only to indebtedness incurred to purchase or carry tax-exempt securities, such a purpose might not be present if the trader, actively engaged in a trade or business, did not incur the indebtedness to finance tax-exempt securities.[45] Finally, it should be noted that the de minimis exception does apply to traders.[46]

§ 8.4 BOND PREMIUMS

Traders can elect to deduct bond premiums, which are the amounts paid for taxable bonds in excess of face value. Traders cannot deduct bond premiums on tax-exempt bonds, but must reduce the basis of the bonds on an annual basis by nondeductible amortizable amounts.[47] For a discussion of bond premiums, see section 27.4.

§ 8.5 WASH SALES

Traders in stocks and securities are subject to the wash sales rule of I.R.C. § 1091. For a discussion of the wash sales rule, see generally Chapter 17.

[42]I.R.C. § 265(1).

[43]I.R.C. § 265(2). For a discussion of the limitations on expenses relating to tax-exempt income, see section 7.3.

[44]I.R.C. § 265(2).

[45]See Bradford v. Comm'r, 60 T.C. 253, 258 (1973); Rev. Proc. 72-18, 1972-1 C.B. 740. For a discussion of allowed and disallowed deductions, see section 7.3.

[46]See section 7.3(b)(4).

[47]I.R.C. § 171(a); Brown v. Comm'r, 426 F.2d 355, 366 (Ct. Cl. 1970).

§ 8.6   SHORT SALES

Traders are subject to the short sales rule of I.R.C. § 1233 for short sales of capital assets. For a discussion of the short sales rule, see generally Chapter 16.

§ 8.7   STRADDLE RULES

The Straddle Rules of I.R.C. §§ 1092 and 263(g) apply to offsetting positions in personal property. For a discussion of the Straddle Rules, see generally Part Ten.

Nine

Dealers

Dealers obtain ordinary income and loss on security, commodity, and option positions that are part of their trade or business activities.[1] Because dealers hold their positions as stock in trade, inventory, and primarily for sale to customers in the ordinary course of business, their positions are not capital assets.[2]

This chapter discusses the tax treatment of dealer expenses and certain tax provisions relevant to dealers.

§ 9.1   EXPENSES OF DEALERS

(a)   TRADE OR BUSINESS EXPENSES

Dealers, like traders, are in a trade or business and, therefore, can deduct their ordinary and necessary business expenses under I.R.C. § 162(a). As a result, dealers are entitled to the same trade or business deductions available to traders. For a detailed discussion of those expenses allowed as deductions under I.R.C. § 162, see section 8.1.

(b)   DEDUCTIBLE SELLING EXPENSES

Unlike other taxpayers, dealers can deduct the costs of selling property as business expenses.[3] Dealers are exempt from the general rule that

---

[1] For a discussion of dealers, see section 6.3.

[2] I.R.C. § 1221(1).

[3] Treas. Reg. § 1.162-1(a) (1975).

commissions on both purchases and sales are to be treated as direct adjustments to the profit or loss arising from the particular sales in which the commissions are paid. This is because dealers frequently buy property in large quantities while making numerous sales, thereby leaving it difficult to apply each selling commission to each purchase and sale. Consequently, securities dealers can treat selling commissions as ordinary and necessary business expenses. Similarly, commodity dealers should also be allowed to treat fees and commissions incurred with respect to their commodity positions as ordinary and necessary business expenses. Both securities and commodities dealers should be able to add their fees and commissions to the cost of property in purchase transactions and deduct their fees and commissions as ordinary and necessary business expenses in sale transactions.[4]

(c) FUTURES CONTRACT TRANSACTIONS

For futures contract transactions, fees and commissions generally are payable on the delivery of the underlying commodity or when the futures position is closed out by entering into a closing transaction. Hence, only one commission, referred to as a "round turn commission," is paid for both the opening and closing transaction. There is no established precedent on whether a dealer can deduct round turn fees and commissions as ordinary and necessary business expenses or as reductions in the profit or increases in the loss of futures contract positions. It appears likely, however, that fees and commissions for futures transactions cannot be deducted as ordinary and necessary business expenses. For those futures contract transactions that are not hedges and that generate capital gains and losses, a dealer's inability to deduct fees and commissions could have a significant tax effect.

§ 9.2 INTEREST EXPENSES

Dealers generally are subject to the same rules with respect to interest deductions as those applicable to traders. For a discussion of these rules, see section 8.2.

---

[4]*See* I.R.C. § 162(a).

§ 9.3 EXPENSES RELATING TO TAX-EXEMPT INCOME

(a) TYPES OF EXPENSES

Dealers cannot deduct expenses that are allocated to income wholly exempt from income tax.[5] For a discussion of these limitations, see section 7.3(b).

(b) INTEREST ON INDEBTEDNESS ON TAX-EXEMPT SECURITIES

(1) GENERAL RULE

Dealers cannot deduct interest incurred or continued to purchase or carry tax-exempt securities.[6] If the dealer can establish that the indebtedness was not incurred or continued to purchase or carry tax-exempt securities, an interest deduction is available.[7] If the dealer is actively engaged in a trade or business and the indebtedness is not incurred to finance tax-exempt securities, a deduction might be available.[8] For a discussion of allowable and nonallowable deductions, see section 7.3(b).

(2) DE MINIMIS EXCEPTION UNAVAILABLE

The de minimis exception (i.e., the amount below which investments in tax-exempt securities are presumed to be insubstantial), is not available to dealers in tax-exempt securities. For a discussion of the de minimis exception, see section 7.3(b)(4). Noncorporate dealers cannot deduct such interest even if they hold tax-exempt securities in an amount less than two percent of their average portfolio investments and assets held to conduct an active business.[9] Similarly, corporate dealers cannot deduct such interest even if they own tax-exempt securities in an amount

---

[5]I.R.C. § 265(1).

[6]For a discussion of the limitations on expenses relating to interest on indebtedness on tax-exempt securities, see section 7.3.

[7]*See* I.R.C. § 265(2).

[8]Bradford v. Comm'r, 60 T.C. 253, 258 (1973); Rev. Proc. 72-18, 1972-1 C.B. 740, *amplified by* Rev. Proc. 80-55, 1980-2 C.B. 849 (which was revoked by Rev. Proc. 81-16, 1981-1 C.B. 688), *clarified by* Rev. Proc. 74-8, 1974-1 C.B. 419.

[9]Rev. Proc. 72-18, 1972-1 C.B. 740.

less than two percent of their average total assets used to conduct an active business.[10]

(3) SPECIAL RULES FOR FINANCIAL INSTITUTIONS

Banks and certain financial institutions can deduct 80 percent of their interest expenses allocable to indebtedness to purchase or carry tax-exempt securities.[11] Under current law, banks[12] can deduct 80 percent of their interest expense attributable to indebtedness (including deposits and other short-term obligations) incurred or continued to purchase or carry tax-exempt securities acquired after 1982.[13] A statutory presumption establishes a ratio used to treat a portion of the bank's indebtedness as allocable to tax-exempt securities.[14] The ratio is the amount for the taxable year that the average adjusted basis of tax-exempt securities acquired after 1982 bears to the average adjusted basis of all assets held by the bank.[15] Under Treasury regulations (yet to be promulgated), banks can establish another allocation method.

Because banks can deduct 80 percent of their financing to purchase or carry tax-exempt obligations, bank dealers can carry municipal securities (and other tax-exempt securities) without the tax penalty placed on other dealers and taxpayers. If "the bank has taxable income, financing its position in [municipal securities] will yield the bank a positive carry under all money market conditions."[16]

Nonbank dealers cannot deduct their interest expense to finance tax-exempt securities, so that nonbank dealers can finance tax-exempt securities only at a negative spread. To avoid a negative spread, nonbank dealers can do one of two things. First, a nonbank dealer can sell his

---

[10]*Id.*

[11]I.R.C. § 291(a)(3). On December 15, 1980, the IRS issued Rev. Proc. 80-55, 1980-2 C.B. 849, which would have increased the amount of tax paid by a bank that owned municipal securities. Rev. Proc. 80-55 ruled that if a bank uses municipal securities as collateral for bank time deposits, the bank will be treated as having borrowed with the intent to buy or carry tax-exempt securities. On April 8, 1981, Rev. Proc. 80-55 was withdrawn in IRS News Release No. IR-81-42 (Apr. 9, 1981) and was then revoked by Rev. Proc. 81-16, 1981-1 C.B. 688. In a joint statement, Assistant Secretary for Tax Policy John B. Chapoton and IRS Commissioner Roscoe L. Egger acknowledged that the revenue procedure was contrary to past rulings and that the IRS would continue to examine the matter and consider offering a legislative solution.

[12]As defined in I.R.C. §§ 581 and 593(a) to include banks, trust companies, domestic building and loan associations, mutual savings banks, and cooperative banks.

[13]I.R.C. § 291(e)(1)(B).

[14]I.R.C. § 291(e)(1)(B)(ii).

[15]*Id.*

[16]M. STIGUM, THE MONEY MARKET 667 (rev. ed. 1983).

tax-exempt securities to a bank for purposes of carry. "Under such an arrangement, the nonbank dealer sells his securities to a bank at par and then buys them back from the bank, again at par, as he sells them."[17] Second, a nonbank dealer can open a joint trading account with a bank. "The bank carries the securities and gets the benefit of positive carry. The bank also assumes underwriting responsibility, and the bank and nonbank dealer split the underwriting profit or loss."[18]

§ 9.4 BOND PREMIUMS

(a) GENERAL RULE

Amortization of bond premiums by securities dealers is not required for bonds held for sale to customers in the ordinary course of business.[19] This general rule applies irrespective of whether the bonds are taxable or tax-exempt. For a discussion of bond premiums, see section 27.4.

(b) TAX-EXEMPT SECURITIES

Special provisions are available to dealers in tax-exempt securities. Dealers in tax-exempt securities can deduct bond premiums on certain tax-exempt securities.[20] Securities dealers can be placed in substantially the same position as investors and traders by application of I.R.C. §§ 171(e) and 1016(a)(5). For a discussion of bond premiums, see section 27.4.

A special rule is imposed for inventories not valued at cost. Dealers who inventory their securities at market or at the lower of cost or market must reduce their cost of securities sold each year by an amount equal to the annual premium amortization required for such securities.[21] In addition, any dealer who does not maintain inventories or who inventories his securities at cost must reduce his cost basis for all such securities sold during the year by an amount equal to the annual premium amortization applicable to the securities.[22]

An adjustment rule covers the situation in municipal bond underwritings where the prevailing interest rates decrease immediately after

[17]*Id.*
[18]*Id.*
[19]Brown v. U.S., 426 F.2d 355, 358 (Ct. Cl. 1970).
[20]I.R.C. §§ 75, 171(e).
[21]I.R.C. § 75(a)(1). For a discussion of inventory methods, see section 20.2.
[22]I.R.C. § 75(a)(2).

subscription by the dealers and prior to resale to the public. To take advantage of the adjustment rule, a dealer must dispose of a tax-exempt security either within 30 days after acquisition, or the security, at the time acquired by the dealer, must have more than five years to run to its earliest call or maturity date. Furthermore, the tax-exempt security must be sold at a profit (without regard to accrued interest) or, in case of another type of disposition, its fair market value at the time of disposition (without regard to accrued interest) must be higher than its cost to the dealer.[23] Because this adjustment rule is intended solely to prevent loss deductions resulting from "premium runoff," it seems fair not to require any such adjustment if the securities are sold at a profit. For securities with more than five years until maturity or call that are not sold at a gain, the entire amortization during the period the securities are held reduces the cost of the securities sold in the year of sale.[24]

§ 9.5   ACCOUNTING METHODS

In general, dealers compute taxable income using the same methods regularly employed in keeping their books.[25] Permitted methods include the cash receipts and disbursements method ("cash basis"), the accrual method, and any other method allowed by I.R.C. § 446 or a combination of allowed methods approved by the Treasury.[26] In cases where inventories are required, the accrual method of accounting also is required.[27] As a result, dealers with mandatory inventories must use the accrual method to compute taxable income. For a discussion of accounting methods, see section 20.1.

§ 9.6   INVENTORY METHODS

Dealers who are required to maintain inventories must consider the methods available for valuation of the inventory as well as cost flow assumptions. For a discussion of inventory methods, see section 20.2.

[23]I.R.C. § 75(b)(1).
[24]I.R.C. § 75(a).
[25]I.R.C. § 446(a).
[26]I.R.C. § 446(c).
[27]Treas. Reg. § 1.446-1(c)(2)(i) (1973).

§ 9.7 SECURITIES DEALER INVESTMENT ACCOUNTS

(a) STATUTORY REQUIREMENTS

Under general tax principles, property held primarily for sale to customers in the ordinary course of business is excluded from the capital asset designation, while property held for investment is generally a capital asset. A more restrictive requirement is imposed for dealers in securities who want to obtain capital gain on the sale of investment securities. Dealers in securities can segregate a portion of inventory property as held for investment and can maintain a separate investment account to derive capital gain treatment from specific investment account transactions. Investment securities can be used as collateral for loans without affecting their investment status.[28]

To obtain capital asset treatment, a securities dealer must comply with the requirements of I.R.C. § 1236. Gain from the sale or exchange of a security is not considered as gain from the sale of a capital asset *unless* (1) before the close of the day on which the security was acquired (or in the case of a stock specialist, before the close of the seventh business day following the acquisition) it was clearly identified in the dealer's records as a security held for investment and (2) the security was not, at any time after the close of such day, held primarily for sale to customers.[29] For purposes of I.R.C. § 1236, the term "security" includes stock, notes, bonds, debentures, or any interest in or right to subscribe to or purchase any of the foregoing,[30] which should be read to include stock rights and options.

(b) STATUS AS TRADER OR INVESTOR

A dealer in securities may be a trader or investor with respect to investment account securities. He does not automatically become a trader with respect to securities positions identified as held for investment, although he may become a trader if he also performs no merchandising function with respect to the securities, offers no service for which he would be entitled to a markup in the price of the securities, and segregates those securities held for investment from his general trading account.[31] A dealer might also be an investor with respect to his in-

---

[28]Rev. Rul. 73-403, 1973-2 C.B. 308.

[29]I.R.C. §§ 1236(a), (d).

[30]I.R.C. § 1236(c).

[31]Bradford v. U.S., 444 F.2d 1133, 1141 (Ct. Cl. 1971); *see generally* Chapter 8; *cf.* Nielsen v. U.S., 212 F. Supp. 801, 803 (M.D. Tenn. 1962), *aff'd*, 333 F.2d 615 (6th Cir. 1964).

vestment account if he holds the securities primarily for interest and dividends or long-term appreciation.[32]

(c) IDENTIFICATION REQUIREMENTS

Investment securities must be clearly identified. The dealer must keep a separate accounting for investment and dealer securities. He must make appropriate entries in his books of accounts by either (1) indicating with such entries, to the extent feasible, the serial number or other characteristic symbol imprinted upon the security; or (2) adopting some other method of identification satisfactory to the IRS.[33] In Rev. Rul. 64-160,[34] the IRS amplifies the Treasury regulation provision that allows adoption of any method of identification satisfactory to the IRS. It also provides identification instructions to clearing companies that perform a clearing function and maintain a clearing facility for participating dealers.[35] Separate investment accounts must be maintained by the clearing depository.[36] Rev. Rul. 64-160 imposes other recordkeeping procedures to insure clear identification.[37]

With respect to book entry securities, additional identification procedures are contained in Rev. Rul. 67-419,[38] Rev. Rul. 69-416,[39] Rev. Rul. 71-15,[40] and Rev. Rul. 73-37.[41]

Securities acquired through the exercise of options must also conform to the identification requirements of I.R.C. § 1236.[42] For options acquired after September 22, 1982, a dealer must identify an option to acquire securities as being held for investment by the close of the business day on which the option was acquired if the securities received upon exercise of the option are eligible for capital treatment.[43]

---

[32]See generally Chapter 7.
[33]Treas. Reg. § 1.1236-1(d)(1) (1964).
[34]1964-1 C.B. 306.
[35]Id.
[36]Id.
[37]See id.
[38]1967-2 C.B. 265.
[39]1969-2 C.B. 159.
[40]1971-1 C.B. 149.
[41]1973-1 C.B. 374.
[42]I.R.C. § 1236(e), as amended by TCA '82, Pub. L. No. 97-448, § 105(d)(1), 96 Stat. 2365, 2387.
[43]Id.

(d) INCORRECT IDENTIFICATION

Incorrect identification can result in ordinary income or capital loss on disposition of a security. Failure to segregate certain stocks clearly held as investments might not mandate ordinary treatment (i.e., ordinary loss) where the facts indicate that the stocks were held for investment.[44]

(e) VOLUMINOUS TRANSACTIONS

The fact that a dealer conducts voluminous transactions in his investment account while also acting as a dealer with respect to the same securities might have his investment account transactions reclassified as dealer activities.[45]

(f) STRADDLES BETWEEN INVESTMENT ACCOUNTS AND DEALER ACCOUNTS

The IRS has asserted in a TAM that a securities dealer who creates what is essentially a balanced position between dealer and investment securities cannot under certain circumstances obtain capital asset treatment on the investment account position and ordinary treatment on the dealer account position.[46] Consequently, if any investment positions offset positions held in the dealer account, capital gain treatment might not be available to the offsetting positions held in the investment account. In addition, the offsetting positions may be subject to the Straddle Rules and the requirement to capitalize interest and carrying charges.[47]

§ 9.8 WASH SALES

Dealers of stock and securities are specifically exempt from the wash sales rule of I.R.C. § 1091 for their inventory securities. For a discussion

[44]Stephens, Inc. v. U.S., 464 F.2d 53, 61–62 (8th Cir. 1972), *cert. denied*, 409 U.S. 1118 (1973).

[45]*Cf.* LTR 7107230380A (July 23, 1971) (where the IRS determined from the investment opportunities to the dealer and from the difference in holding periods of capital assets from ordinary business assets that a reclassification was not in order).

[46]TAM 8131008 (April 4, 1981).

[47]*See generally* Part Ten; section 43.2. The IRS ruled that a specialist and market maker on an options exchange who created a call spread on stock options in his trading account could not transfer the appreciated long position to his investment account prior to expiration of the pre-ERTA 30-day look-back period under I.R.C. § 1236 to qualify for capital treatment. *See also* Rev. Rul. 71-30, 1971-1 C.B. 226.

of the wash sales rule, see generally Chapter 17. Dealers otherwise exempt from the wash sales rule might be subject to the modified wash sales rule under I.R.C. § 1092(b)(1). For a discussion of the modified wash sales rule, see section 42.3.

§ 9.9   SHORT SALES

Dealers are not subject to the short sales rule of I.R.C. § 1233 for their inventory securities. For a discussion of the short sales rule, see generally Chapter 16. For a discussion of the modified short sales rule, see section 42.4.

§ 9.10   STRADDLE RULES

The Straddle Rules of I.R.C. §§ 1092 and 263(g) apply to offsetting positions in personal property that are not qualified hedging transactions. For a discussion of the Straddle Rules, see generally Part Ten. For a discussion of hedging transactions, see generally Chapter 21.

§ 9.11   UNDERWRITERS

(a)   STOCK WARRANTS, OPTIONS, AND CONVERTIBLE SECURITIES

In connection with certain securities underwritings, the underwriters obtain warrants, options, or convertible securities to buy stock of the corporation, either at the public offering price or at a higher price.[48] Such warrants, options, or convertible securities, referred to as "underwriters' options," can be obtained from either the issuing corporation or its controlling stockholders. If issued in connection with or in relation to the offering of securities, underwriters' options are compensation[49] subject to I.R.C. § 83 and the Treasury regulations issued thereunder.

An underwriter who demonstrates that he neither rendered nor was obligated to render substantial services in consideration for the granting of the option might be able to obtain capital gain or loss on the sub-

---

[48]For a discussion of underwriters, see section 6.6.

[49]*Review of Corporate Financing*, NASD Sec. Dealers Man. (CCH) ¶ 2151.02 (July 13, 1984).

sequent sale or exercise of the option.[50] The underwriter would have to show that there was no reason for the warrants, options, or convertible securities to have been granted as compensation.[51] In other words, the underwriters' options would need to be unrelated to the offering.[52]

Warrants, options, and convertible securities issued to underwriters in best efforts underwritings might not have any ascertainable value.[53] On the other hand, warrants, options, and convertible securities issued in firm commitment underwritings might have an ascertainable value, because the underwriter might be in a position to establish a reasonable value for the property.[54]

(b) INVESTMENT ACCOUNTS

Under certain circumstances, underwriters, much like other dealers in securities, can place stock obtained prior to an underwriting in which it participates in an investment account and obtain long-term capital gain.[55] To obtain capital asset treatment, contingencies would need to exist that could make a successful underwriting impossible. If contingencies are not present and it is clear that the stock offering will be underwritten, capital gain treatment is not available.[56]

---

[50]Treas. Reg. § 1.61-15(b)(2) (1978).

[51]*Id.*

[52]*See id.*

[53]Victorson v. Comm'r, 326 F.2d 264, 266 (2d Cir. 1964).

[54]*Id.* at 267. *See* Weigl v. Comm'r, 84 T.C.—, No. 66 (1985), Tax Ct. Rep. (CCH) Dec. ¶ 42,124 (May 30, 1985).

[55]Berckmans v. Comm'r, 20 T.C.M. (CCH) 458, 468 (1961); *see also* section 9.7.

[56]Husted v. Comm'r, 47 T.C. 664, 679 (1967).

Ten

Hedgers

Hedgers obtain ordinary income or loss on their security, commodity, and option hedge transactions. In addition, those transactions that qualify as hedging transactions under the Code are exempt from both the Straddle Rules and section 1256 treatment.[1]

Under traditional hedge analysis, hedgers seek to protect the price at which they will acquire their inventories and to assure that a market will be available to sell their inventories. In other words, hedgers attempt to shift some commercial risks by entering into a hedging transaction. A taxpayer who uses a futures contract or option position to lock in the purchase or sales price of a commodity used in the ordinary course of business is deemed to be a hedger under the Corn Products doctrine.[2]

This chapter discusses the tax treatment of hedgers' expenses and certain tax provisions applicable to hedgers.

§ 10.1 EXPENSES OF HEDGERS

Hedgers, like dealers and traders, are in a trade or business and can deduct their ordinary and necessary business expenses under I.R.C. § 162(a).[3] It is also well established that losses on closing futures contract hedges are deductible under I.R.C. § 165(a).[4] Of course, this anal-

---

[1]For a discussion of hedgers, see section 6.4; Chapter 21.

[2]Corn Products Refining Co. v. Comm'r, 350 U.S. 46, 51 (1955).

[3]I.R.C. § 162(a).

[4]I.R.C. § 165(a); Rev. Rul. 72-179, 1972-1 C.B. 57.

ysis applies equally well to hedging transactions involving other types of property. In fact, the Senate Finance Committee Report to ERTA acknowledges that "[h]edging transactions are varied and complex. They may be executed in a wide range of property and forms, including options, futures, forwards, other contract rights, and short sales."[5]

Hedgers use futures, forwards, and option positions as insurance to protect their inventories and products. They can claim certain expenses as deductions to arrive at adjusted gross income.[6] For fees and commissions incurred to execute physical commodity transactions, a hedger should be able to treat them in the same manner available to dealers in securities and real estate. Therefore, fees and commissions should be added to the cost of property for purchases and deducted as business expenses for sales.[7]

It is not clear whether a hedger can deduct as business expenses round turn commissions and fees paid to execute futures contract hedge transactions (which are paid on the delivery of the underlying commodity or when the futures contract position is closed out by entering into a closing transaction), or whether the hedger must treat the fees as reductions in the profit or increases in the loss of futures contract positions. Because hedges generate ordinary income and loss, this distinction affects the timing of a deduction for hedge transactions that qualify for the hedging exemption. The requirement to capitalize interest and carrying charges for straddle positions does not apply to hedges qualifying for the hedging exemption.[8] These expenses are deductible to arrive at adjusted gross income.[9] For futures contract transactions that do not qualify for the hedging exemption (and therefore subject to the loss deferral rules of I.R.C. § 1092[10] and the requirement to capitalize interest and carrying charges under I.R.C. § 263(g)),[11] the distinction between taking a business deduction and adjusting profit and loss can distort the timing for a deduction.

[5]FINANCE COMMITTEE REPORT, ECONOMIC RECOVERY ACT OF 1981, 97th Cong., 1st Sess. 159, *reprinted in* 1981 U.S. CODE CONG. & AD. NEWS 258.

[6]*See* I.R.C. § 162(a); *see also* Chapter 9.

[7]*See* I.R.C. § 162(a)(1); *see also* section 9.1.

[8]I.R.C. § 263(g)(3).

[9]*See* section 43.2.

[10]*See generally* Part Ten.

[11]*See* section 43.2.

§ 10.2   INTEREST COSTS

Hedgers generally are subject to the same rules with respect to interest deductions as those that apply to traders and dealers. For a discussion of these rules, see section 8.2. Hedgers, however, are exempt from the requirement to capitalize interest and carrying charges for those transactions that qualify for the hedging exemption under I.R.C. § 1256(e)(2).[12]

§ 10.3   STRADDLE RULES AND SECTION 1256 TREATMENT

Positions in personal property that are part of hedging transactions as defined in the Code are explicitly exempted from both section 1256 treatment[13] and the Straddle Rules (which consists of the loss deferral rule, the requirement to capitalize interest and carrying charges, the modified wash sales rule, and the modified short sales rule).[14] This means that gain or loss on hedging transactions can be reported when a position is closed, used to adjust basis (where appropriate), or deferred in accordance with the taxpayer's normal accounting practices. Open section 1256 positions are not marked-to-market at the end of the taxable year, and losses need not be deferred under the loss deferral rule.

The analysis used to determine whether a transaction qualifies as a hedge eligible for the statutory hedging exemption is identical for both section 1256 and non-section 1256 positions. Section 1256 hedge positions are exempt from section 1256 treatment under I.R.C. § 1256(e), while hedges involving non-section 1256 positions are exempt from the Straddle Rules under I.R.C. § 1092(e). Hedging transactions also are exempt from the requirement to capitalize interest and carrying charges under I.R.C. § 263(g)(3).[15] If a transaction does not qualify for the statutory hedging exemption, the positions are subject to section 1256 treatment and the Straddle Rules generally.

---

[12]*See generally* Chapter 21; section 43.2; section 44.2.

[13]*See generally* Part Nine.

[14]*See generally* Part Ten.

[15]*See* section 43.2.

Eleven

Brokers

Brokers, as agents for their customers, charge brokerage commissions to their customers for executing transactions. They generate ordinary gain or loss on their commission income. For a discussion of brokers, see section 6.5.

This chapter discusses certain expenses of brokers.

§ 11.1 EXPENSES OF BROKERS

Brokers of securities, commodities, and options are all entitled to deductions for ordinary and necessary business expenses under I.R.C. § 162. For a detailed discussion of deductible expenses, see section 8.1.

§ 11.2 ORDER ERRORS AND DIFFERENCES

Due to the tremendous volume of transactions conducted by brokers, errors do occur in filling orders, and differences do occur in the reconciliation or matching of property that the broker purchases and sells on behalf of his customers. In general, these discrepancies result in ordinary income or loss. In Rev. Rul. 79-80,[1] the IRS analyzed such errors in the context of securities brokers. Although the IRS only addressed securities brokers, the analysis applies equally as well to brokers

[1] 1979-1 C.B. 86.

of commodities and options. The tax treatment of order errors and discrepancies are discussed below.

(a) ORDER ERRORS

Order errors usually include those situations where (1) the wrong property is purchased or sold, leaving the broker short (long) in the correct property and long (short) in the wrong property; (2) an incorrect quantity is purchased or sold, forcing the broker either to buy more property to correct a shortage or to sell some of the excess property; (3) the trade cannot be settled because the other side of the trade has no record of a purchase or sale executed on the same terms as the broker believed the trade was executed; and (4) the trade cannot be settled because the broker has no record of a purchase or sale executed on the same terms as those the customer believed the trade was executed.[2] In all of these examples, the broker realizes a gain or sustains an economic loss, as measured by the difference between his purchase or sales price at the time of the error and the purchase or sales price at the time the error is corrected.

Mistakes in executing orders do not have an investment motive, because in each situation it is the broker's intention to perform a service for a customer and not to acquire ownership of the property. As a result, gain or loss on acquisitions or subsequent sales of properties from order errors is ordinary, not capital.

(1) DEDUCTIBLE BUSINESS EXPENSES

Expenditures to correct order errors that do not result in the acquisition of property are deductible as ordinary and necessary business expenses under I.R.C. § 162.[3] These expenditures are deductible when the broker actually corrects the error (by a purchase or sale of the correct property) or the amount of the expense is fixed with reasonable accuracy. Order errors that do not result in acquisitions of property are deductible under I.R.C. § 162 in the taxable year when the error is corrected, when an offer to compromise is accepted, or a court action is adjudicated. Expenditures to correct order errors are incurred when the parties agree to a compromise.[4] Expenditures to correct order errors involving litigation are not incurred until the controversy is adjudicated.

[2]*Id.*

[3]*Id.*

[4]*Id.* (citing American Hotels Corp. v. Comm'r, 46 B.T.A. 629, 631 (1942), *aff'd on other grounds*, 134 F.2d 817, 819 (2d Cir. 1943)).

(2) DEDUCTIBLE LOSSES

Expenses to correct order errors in which the broker acquires property are deductible as losses under I.R.C. § 165(a).[5] Expenditures to correct order errors of this type are not deductible business expenses under I.R.C. § 162, because they result in property held solely for sale. Errors that result in acquisition of property include (1) purchasing the wrong property; (2) replacing the property after selling the wrong one; (3) purchasing more than the correct amount of property; (4) selling more than the correct amount and purchasing replacement property; (5) buying property for a customer who cannot subsequently be identified; and (6) selling property for a customer who cannot subsequently be identified.

(b) DISCREPANCIES

Another category of errors, referred to as "discrepancies," includes differences that usually are discovered through audits by independent accountants, inventory reviews, and vault counts.[6] These discrepancies are usually caused by (1) transferring property to a transfer agent for registration, who fails to return it; (2) mismatching property; (3) accidentally receiving property owned by others; (4) transmitting the wrong property to others, resulting in a shortage of one type and an overage of another; (5) overdelivering to others; (6) bookkeeping errors; and (7) failing to detect order errors. Discrepancies result in ordinary income or loss.

[5]*See id.*
[6]*Id.*

Part Three

Taxation of Capital Transactions

Part Three deals with the taxation of capital transactions, which have been afforded special tax treatment since the Revenue Act of 1921. Fundamental tax concepts, such as capital assets, short-term and long-term capital gain and loss, basis, holding periods, and identification of assets are discussed in Part Three.

In addition, various steps taken to compute gain or loss on capital transactions are discussed. First, the amount of gain or loss realized on the transaction is computed. Second, the amount of gain or loss to be recognized on the transaction is determined. Third, the character of the gain or loss, as either long-term or short-term, is ascertained.

Twelve

General Principles

§ 12.1 CAPITAL ASSETS

Gains and losses from the sale or exchange of assets held for investment are treated as capital gains and losses. A sale generally occurs with the transfer of property for cash or its equivalent. An exchange generally occurs with a reciprocal transfer of property, not simply a transfer of property for money.

To obtain capital gain or loss, there must be a sale or exchange of a capital asset, defined as property (whether or not connected with a trade or business) other than the types of property specifically enumerated in I.R.C. § 1221.[1] Unless a security, commodity, or option position held by a taxpayer falls within one of the enumerated categories, it is a capital asset and its sale or exchange generates capital gain or loss. As a result, capital assets do not include within their definition ordinary income property.[2]

§ 12.2 SECTION 1256 CONTRACTS

Section 1256 contracts are marked-to-market, which means that un-realized gains and losses on such contracts are reported at the end of the taxable year on open, not just closed, positions. Section 1256 con-tracts are marked-to-market at their fair market values on the last busi-ness day of the taxable year as if they are 60 percent long-term and 40

[1]I.R.C. § 1221.
[2]*See generally* Part Four.

percent short-term capital gain or loss.[3] For a discussion of section 1256 contracts, see generally Part Nine.

§ 12.3 AMOUNT REALIZED

The first step in computing capital gain or loss is to determine the total amount of consideration received from the sale or exchange of the capital asset in cash, services, or property. Services and property are valued at their respective fair market values. To arrive at net proceeds, all costs incurred in connection with the sale or exchange (e.g., commissions, finders' fees, accounting, and legal fees) are deducted from the amount of the total consideration received from the sale or exchange.[4] Once net proceeds are determined, they are compared with the taxpayer's adjusted basis for the asset that is disposed of,[5] and the difference between the net proceeds and the adjusted basis represents the amount of gain or loss realized by the taxpayer.[6] If net proceeds exceed the taxpayer's basis, the taxpayer realizes a gain on the sale or exchange. If net proceeds are less than the taxpayer's basis, the taxpayer realizes a loss on the transaction.

§ 12.4 AMOUNT RECOGNIZED

Realized gain or loss is not necessarily the amount to be taken into account in computing taxable income. Rather, the amount of gain or loss that is taken into account for tax purposes is the amount recognized on the sale or exchange.[7] As a result, to determine the tax effect of capital gain or loss, one must determine the amount of realized gain or realized loss to be recognized for tax purposes. In case sales, the entire amount of gain or loss is recognized and must be brought into income. In certain exchanges of property, however, the transaction can qualify for either total or partial nonrecognition under specific Code provisions.[8]

[3]I.R.C. § 1256(a).
[4]Giffin v. Comm'r, 19 B.T.A. 1243, 1246 (1930).
[5]*See generally* Chapter 14.
[6]I.R.C. § 1001(a).
[7]I.R.C. § 1001(c).
[8]*See*, e.g., I.R.C. §§ 351, 354–356, 1031, 1036, 1037.

§ 12.5 TIME OF REPORTING INCOME, GAIN, DEDUCTIONS, OR LOSSES

(a) INCOME

A cash basis taxpayer includes in income all dividends, interest, and gains on the sale or exchange of securities, commodities, and options in the year in which the cash or other property is received.[9] For example, income from a cash dividend is included in income when the payment is received by the stockholder, not when it is declared or issued by the corporation.[10] A noncash dividend is valued as of its date of distribution, even if the property is received by the stockholder at a later date (or in a subsequent tax year) and even if it is not included in income until a subsequent year.[11] For a discussion of dividend and interest income, see generally Part Five.

(b) GAIN

Special rules apply to gain on securities traded on a stock exchange or in the over-the-counter market. Gain on the sale or exchange of securities is usually taxed when the sales proceeds are received by the taxpayer, not on the date the transaction is entered into. With respect to publicly traded securities sold on a stock exchange or in the over-the-counter market, the settlement date, not the trade date, determines the date when the sales proceeds are taxable.[12] Gain on closing a short sale or a short options position is reported on the settlement date when the property is delivered, even if it occurs in a subsequent tax year.[13]

    Certain tax planning opportunities are available to cash basis investors and traders.[14] A taxpayer who wants to lock in a sales price for securities but also wants to recognize the gain on the sale in a subsequent tax year can sell the securities for deferred delivery in the next year[15] or on the installment method,[16] thereby reporting gain in the subsequent

---

[9]Treas. Reg. § 1.446-1(c)(1) (1973).

[10]Rev. Rul. 68-126, 1968-1 C.B. 194; Treas. Reg. § 1.451-2(b) (1979).

[11]Treas. Reg. § 1.301-1(b) (1979).

[12]Taylor v. Comm'r, 43 B.T.A. 563, 568 (1941), *aff'd*, Helvering v. Taylor, 128 F.2d 885 (2d Cir. 1942); Rev. Rul. 72-381, 1972-2 C.B. 233. For a discussion of settlement procedures for corporate securities see section 1.5.

[13]*See generally* I.R.C. §§ 1233, 1234; *see also* Chapter 16.

[14]*See* section 6.1; section 6.2.

[15]*See* section 1.3(f).

[16]I.R.C. § 453; *see* section 1.3(i).

tax year. On the other hand, if the taxpayer wants the gain recognized in the year of the trade, the taxpayer can enter into a trade that settles for cash in a cash transaction[17] or elect out of the installment method, which is otherwise available to the taxpayer.[18]

(c) DEDUCTIONS

For cash basis taxpayers, expenses are deductible when paid, not when incurred. Taxpayers on the accrual basis of reporting income deduct such expenses when incurred and properly accrued. For a discussion of deductible expenses for the different types of market participants, see generally Part Two.

(d) LOSSES

Special loss rules apply to publicly traded securities sold on a stock exchange or in the over-the-counter market. Losses on the sale or exchange of securities generally are deductible on the trade date, even if delivery of the securities and receipt of the proceeds occurs in a subsequent tax year.[19]

A current loss deduction is not delayed until a loan is repaid if funds are borrowed.[20] In *Page v. Rhode Island Hospital Trust Co.*,[21] however, a taxpayer gave promissory notes to his broker instead of posting required margin payments to his margin account. The court denied a loss deduction to the taxpayer until the promissory notes were repaid in later years.[22] The court stated that for a loss to be deductible it must be paid in cash or its equivalent and there must be an actual depletion of the taxpayer's property.[23] A mere promise to pay is not viewed as a cash payment and a deduction is not available until the taxpayer pays cash or his property is depleted.[24]

In *Bramer v. U.S.*,[25] the court acknowledged that (1) a cash basis

---

[17]*See* section 1.3(b).

[18]Rev. Rul. 82-227, 1982-2 C.B. 89.

[19]Rev. Rul. 70-344, 1970-2 C.B. 50.

[20]Larkin v. Comm'r, 46 B.T.A. 213, 220, *appeal dismissed*, 129 F.2d 1020 (1942).

[21]88 F.2d 192 (1st Cir. 1937).

[22]*Id.* at 194.

[23]*Id.* at 193.

[24]*Id.* at 193 (citing Hart v. Comm'r, 54 F.2d 848, 852 (1st Cir. 1932)).

[25]259 F.2d 717, 721 (3d Cir. 1958).

taxpayer can deduct a loss only if he has satisfied the obligation arising from the transaction; (2) a loss is deductible in the year paid, even if paid with borrowed funds; and (3) a deduction cannot be postponed to the year in which repayment of the borrowed funds is made. The insolvent taxpayer in *Bramer* owed his broker money for stock that had become worthless.[26] An independent third party (the "guarantor") had previously pledged stock, on behalf of the taxpayer. When notified that the broker planned to sell the guarantor's stock to reduce the taxpayer's deficit in his margin account, the guarantor paid the broker the market value of his stock for its return. Although the insolvent taxpayer gave his promissory note to the guarantor, this transaction was not viewed as a loan;[27] the guarantor simply stepped into the shoes of the broker. The taxpayer did not have a deductible loss in the year he gave his promissory note to the guarantor.[28] He could deduct a loss when he paid the guarantor, but not when he gave his promissory note to the guarantor. Substitution of the taxpayer's promissory note for the existing obligation to his broker was not viewed as a payment of the sort necessary to obtain a current loss deduction.[29] However, in a recent Tax Court memorandum decision, *Estate of Hirsch v. Comm'r*,[30] a cash basis taxpayer was allowed a deduction for losses on speculative commodities trading in the year incurred, even though the funds used by the taxpayer to make the margin payments were borrowed and the taxpayer could not pay the entire debt out of his own assets.

Loss on closing a short sale of property or a short options position is reported as of the settlement date, that is, when the property is delivered, even if this occurs in a different taxable year.[31]

§ 12.6   APPLICATION OF LOSS DEFERRAL RULE

All taxpayers, except hedgers with respect to hedging transactions that qualify for the statutory hedging exemption,[32] are subject to the loss

---

[26]*Id.* at 719.

[27]*Id.* at 720.

[28]*Id.* at 722.

[29]*Id.* at 721.

[30]46 T.C.M. (CCH) 559, 562–64 (1983).

[31]*See generally* I.R.C. §§ 1233–1234; *see generally* Chapter 16.

[32]*See generally* Chapter 21.

deferral rule imposed by I.R.C. § 1092(a)(1)(A). The loss deferral rule applies to losses incurred on positions in personal property if the taxpayer holds offsetting positions with inherent gains.[33] This means that losses are deferred on loss positions that are closed out until the offsetting gain positions also are closed out. For a discussion of the loss deferral rule, see generally Part Ten.

---

[33]I.R.C. § 1092(a)(1).

Thirteen

Computation of Gains or Losses

To compute gain or loss on capital transactions, the character of the gain or loss must be characterized as either long-term or short-term. This chapter discusses steps to compute gain or loss on capital transactions.

§ 13.1 LONG-TERM AND SHORT-TERM TRANSACTIONS

To determine the tax effect of a sale or exchange of a capital asset, it is necessary to ascertain whether the gain or loss is treated as a long-term or short-term capital gain or loss. This determination is based on the taxpayer's holding period for the property. For a discussion of holding periods, see generally Chapter 15.

Gains and losses on capital assets acquired between June 23, 1984 and December 31, 1987 are long-term if the assets were held for more than six months.[1] Capital assets sold after 1977 which were acquired prior to June 23, 1984 or after December 31, 1987 generate long-term capital gain or loss only if held for more than 12 months.[2] Hence, short-term capital gains and losses result from the sale or exchange of capital

---

[1] I.R.C. §§ 1222(3), (4).
[2] I.R.C. § 1222 (1976), *amended by* DRA, Pub. L. 98-367, § 1001(a), 98 Stat. 494, 1011 (1984).

assets acquired between June 23, 1984 and December 31, 1987 if held for less than six months.[3]

Futures contracts traded on and subject to the rules of a commodity exchange that are (1) not section 1256 contracts and are (2) not subject to the Mark-to-Market Rule, generate long-term capital gain if held for more than six months.[4]

§ 13.2   SECTION 1256 CONTRACTS

Section 1256 contracts are taxed at the end of the taxable year as if their unrealized gains or losses are 60 percent long-term and 40 percent short-term capital gain or loss, irrespective of how long the taxpayer actually held the section 1256 positions.[5] Losses on closed section 1256 positions can be deferred under the modified short sales rule if unrealized gain positions consist of non-section 1256 contracts that offset those positions in which the loss is incurred.[6] For a discussion of the loss carry-back rules available to section 1256 contracts, see section 33.4.

§ 13.3   NONCORPORATE TAXPAYERS

To determine the tax treatment for noncorporate taxpayers (i.e., for individuals, estates, and trusts) of long-term and short-term capital transactions, it is necessary to first net all the long-term transactions (including gains and losses) against each other and then all the short-term transactions (including gains and losses) against each other. The two resulting numbers are referred to as "net long-term capital gain or loss" and "net short-term capital gain or loss," respectively.

(a)   CAPITAL GAIN

(1)   NET SHORT-TERM CAPITAL GAIN

Net short-term capital gains are first reduced by any net long-term capital losses and capital loss carry-overs. Any net short-term capital gain remaining after being reduced by net long-term capital losses and

[3]I.R.C. §§ 1222(1), (2).
[4]*See generally* Part Nine.
[5]*See id.*
[6]*See* section 42.4.

capital loss carry-overs is included in gross income and taxed to non-corporate taxpayers in the same way as ordinary income.[7]

(2) NET LONG-TERM CAPITAL GAIN

(i) Capital Gains Deduction

Noncorporate taxpayers deduct from gross income 60 percent of the excess of net long-term capital gain over net short-term capital losses.[8] This capital gains deduction is subtracted from gross income before determining the taxpayer's adjusted gross income for the year.[9] Because the capital gains deduction is a tax preference item, it is included in the alternative minimum tax computation.[10]

(ii) Alternative Minimum Tax

An alternative minimum tax is imposed on noncorporate taxpayers if their alternative minimum tax exceeds their regular income tax for the year. Alternative minimum taxable income is defined as adjusted gross income, determined without regard to a net operating loss deduction, reduced by certain deductions and increased by the sum of all tax preference items.[11] One of the tax preference items used to compute the alternative minimum tax is the capital gains deduction, which excludes 60 percent of the excess of the net long-term capital gains from taxation.[12] A flat 20 percent tax is imposed on alternative minimum taxable income in excess of $40,000 for joint returns, $20,000 for married persons filing separate returns, and $30,000 for single returns.[13]

Another tax preference item includes interest deductions on repurchase agreements (referred to as "repos") that exceed 60 percent of a taxpayer's adjusted gross income.[14] In *Wallach v. U.S.*, the United States Court of Claims granted an IRS motion for summary judgment on the grounds that there was no genuine issue in the case and that repo interest deductions that exceeded 60 percent of the taxpayers' adjusted gross

[7]*See* I.R.C. § 61(a)(3).

[8]I.R.C. § 1202.

[9]I.R.C. § 62(3).

[10]*See* section 13.3(a)(2)(ii). Tax preference items, which are added to adjusted gross income to compute alternative minimum tax, include such items as the excess of accelerated over straight line depreciation on real and personal property.

[11]I.R.C. § 55(b).

[12]I.R.C. § 57(a)(9)(A).

[13]I.R.C. §§ 55(a), (f).

[14]I.R.C. §§ 55, 57; for a discussion of repos, see section 2.2(c).

income were tax preference items.[15] The taxpayers engaged in repo transactions in 1978 and 1979. They purchased Treasury securities, federal agency securities, and a bank certificate of deposit with a total purchase price of $12,760,000 from a securities dealer. They paid $229,000, borrowed the rest of the purchase price, and immediately sold the securities back to the dealer, subject to their obligation to repurchase the securities at the same price. The "yield to maturity" on the securities was fixed and did not fluctuate, although the taxpayers' borrowing costs fluctuated. During both 1978 and 1979, the taxpayers' interest expense on the repo transaction exceeded their repo interest income (by $95,000 in 1978 and $322,000 in 1979). The taxpayers' total repo interest expense for 1978 and 1979, when added to their other deductions, resulted in their adjusted itemized deductions for each year to exceed 60 percent of their adjusted gross income. The Court of Claims found, as a matter of law, that these excess deductions were tax preference items.

(b) CAPITAL LOSS

Net capital loss of noncorporate taxpayers is deductible to the extent of net capital gain (irrespective of whether the losses and gains are long-term or short-term). An additional deduction is available for excess net capital losses, which are deductible up to the lesser of (1) $3000;[16] (2) the taxpayer's taxable income (defined to exclude capital gains or losses and the deduction for personal exemptions),[17] reduced by the zero bracket amount (but not below zero); or (3) the sum of (a) the excess of net short-term capital loss over net short-term capital gain and (b) one-half of the excess of net long-term capital loss over net short-term capital gain.[18] In other words, net capital losses generally are deductible against ordinary income in an amount up to $3000, but a taxpayer needs $2 of net long-term capital loss to reduce ordinary income by $1. Married persons filing separate tax returns can deduct only one-half of the otherwise deductible amount (i.e., $1500 of ordinary income)[19] and neither spouse can use up the other's losses if separate returns are filed.[20]

---

[15]Eli Wallach and Anne (Jackson) Wallach v. U.S., 8 Cl. Ct. 631 (1985).
[16]I.R.C. §§ 1211(b)(2)(B), 1212(b)(2).
[17]I.R.C. § 1211(b)(3).
[18]I.R.C. § 1211(b)(1)(A).
[19]I.R.C. § 1211(b)(2).
[20]See Treas. Reg. § 1.1211-1(b)(6)(iii); Helvering v. Janney, 311 U.S. 189, 194-95 (1940); see also section 13.3(d).

Short-term capital loss, including short-term capital loss carry-overs, is deducted against ordinary income up to the applicable amount (i.e., $3000 or $1500 for married persons filing separately) for the year.[21] If there are no short-term capital losses or they are less than the applicable amount, long-term capital losses can be used on a 50 percent basis to offset ordinary income.[22]

(c) CAPITAL LOSS CARRY-OVERS

Capital losses of noncorporate taxpayers cannot be carried back to prior years except for the carry-back allowed for RFC losses.[23] Net capital losses, however, that are not deductible in the taxable year when the losses are incurred can be carried forward indefinitely from one year to the next.[24] Capital losses carried forward retain their original character as long-term or short-term capital loss. In other words, unused net short-term capital losses are carried forward as short-term losses until they are used up, while unused net long-term capital losses are carried forward as long-term losses until they are used up.[25] Losses carried forward are combined with losses in the same category (i.e., short-term or long-term) for the succeeding taxable year as if the losses carried forward were incurred in the succeeding taxable year.[26]

(d) JOINT RETURNS

Married persons can file joint tax returns. Gains and losses of both spouses are reported on the same return and are aggregated for tax purposes. Both spouses are viewed as one taxpayer and the rules for determining capital gains and losses apply as if the taxpayers were one taxpayer.[27] Losses of one spouse can be used to offset the gains of the other. It does not matter that one spouse has only losses while the other has only gains.[28]

Treasury regulations provide specific rules for allocating capital loss carry-overs between spouses in those situations where joint returns are

---

[21]I.R.C. § 1211(b)(1).

[22]I.R.C. § 1211(b)(1)(c)(ii).

[23]For a discussion of the special carry-back rules available to noncorporate taxpayers for section 1256 contracts, see section 33.4.

[24]I.R.C. § 1212(b)(1).

[25]I.R.C. § 1212(b).

[26]I.R.C. § 1212(b)(1).

[27]*Janney*, 311 U.S. at 192.

[28]*Id.* at 194–95.

filed. With respect to capital loss carry-overs generated prior to the year of filing a joint return, both spouses can include such capital losses on the joint return as long-term or short-term capital losses, as the case may be.[29] For separate returns filed in subsequent tax years, capital loss carry-overs generated from joint return years must be allocated between the spouses on the basis of their respective capital gains and losses.[30] If separate returns are filed for all taxable years, the capital losses of each spouse are reported on the return of the spouse who incurred the capital loss.[31]

(e) INCOME AVERAGING

Income averaging is available to ease the tax burden of high income years for those taxpayers with incomes that vary widely from year to year.[32] Certain noncorporate taxpayers (defined for income averaging purposes as individuals who are citizens or residents of the United States)[33] with substantial net long-term or net short-term capital gains (as well as most other types of ordinary income) can use income averaging to compute their taxable income. Income averaging views the income to be averaged as if it was earned over a four-year period.[34] The base period for income averaging is now three years (reduced from four years under the law in effect prior to the DRA), and the benefits of income averaging apply only to so much of the taxable income of the computation year as exceeds 140 percent of the average base period income (increased from 120 percent under the law in effect prior to the DRA).[35]

§ 13.4   CORPORATE TAXPAYERS

To determine the tax treatment for corporate taxpayers of long-term and short-term capital transactions, it is necessary (as with noncorporate taxpayers) to first net all the long-term transactions (including gains and losses) against each other and then net all the short-term trans-

---

[29]Treas. Reg. § 1.1212-1(c)(1)(i) (1980).
[30]Treas. Reg. § 1.1212-1(c)(1)(iii) (1980).
[31]Treas. Reg. § 1.1212-1(c)(1)(v) (1980).
[32]I.R.C. § 1302(a).
[33]I.R.C. § 1303(a).
[34]I.R.C. § 1302(c).
[35]I.R.C. § 1301.

actions (including gains and losses) against each other. "Net long-term capital gain or loss" and "net short-term capital gain or loss" are the two resulting numbers.

(a) CAPITAL GAIN

(1) NET SHORT-TERM CAPITAL GAIN

Net short-term capital gain of corporations is first reduced by any net long-term capital loss. Whatever net short-term capital gain remains thereafter is treated as ordinary income. Although no statutory provision specifically says that net short-term capital gain is taxed as ordinary income, this treatment results because I.R.C. § 1201, which provides an alternative tax for net long-term capital gain, does not apply to net short-term capital gain.[36]

(2) NET LONG-TERM CAPITAL GAIN

Unlike the capital gains deduction available to noncorporate taxpayers, which allows them to exclude up to 60 percent of their net long-term capital gain, corporations cannot deduct any portion of their long-term capital gain from gross income. Rather, corporations include net capital gain in gross income (in the same way as other income) unless they elect to be taxed at a flat 28 percent tax rate for capital gains.[37] This alternative rate only benefits corporations with incomes taxable at rates above 28 percent. In other words, if a corporation's net long-term capital gain exceeds its short-term capital loss, the net long-term capital gain is added to the corporation's taxable income, and taxed at regular corporate rates (i.e., 15 percent for the first $25,000 of taxable income; 18 percent for the second $25,000; 30 percent for the third $25,000; 40 percent for the fourth $25,000; 46 percent on taxable income in excess of $100,000; and for a corporation with taxable income in excess of $1 million, the amount of tax determined under the progressive rates is increased by the lesser of five percent of such excess or $20,250).[38] Otherwise, a corporation can elect to apply the flat 28 percent alternative tax rate to its net long-term capital gain. Unless a corporation's overall tax rate exceeds 28 percent, this alternative rate does not provide a

[36]I.R.C. § 1201.
[37]I.R.C. § 1201(a).
[38]I.R.C. § 11(b).

lower overall tax for net long-term capital gain than the regular tax computation otherwise available for the corporation's other taxable income.[39]

(b) CAPITAL LOSS

A corporation's capital loss is only deductible to the extent of the corporation's capital gain.[40] Unused capital loss cannot be used to offset any ordinary income (not even to the limited extent available to non-corporate taxpayers).[41] Corporate capital losses, on the other hand, can be carried back for three years and carried forward for five years as short-term capital losses.[42] Losses that are carried back or carried forward are reduced by capital gains in the order in which the capital losses were incurred—the oldest capital losses are used up first.[43] In addition, a capital loss cannot be carried back if it would create a net operating loss for the year.[44] And, if a corporation has an operating loss and a capital loss, the capital loss must be carried back first to a year in which capital gain can be offset and any gains remaining can be offset by net operating losses.[45]

(c) ADD-ON MINIMUM TAX

If a corporation's tax preference items exceed the greater of $10,000 or the corporation's regular income tax for the year, a minimum tax of 15 percent is imposed on a corporation in addition to its other taxes.[46] The corporate minimum tax is referred to as an "add-on tax" because it is imposed on top of all other taxes. Corporate tax preference items used

---

[39]*Compare* I.R.C. § 11(b) (the corporate tax rate) *with* I.R.C. § 1201(a)(2) (the alternative corporate tax rate).

[40]I.R.C. § 1211(a).

[41]*See* section 13.3(b).

[42]I.R.C. § 1212(a).

[43]This follows from the fact that a loss cannot be carried back more than three years and that the taxpayer would presumably want to make use of the loss before it was no longer available.

[44]I.R.C. § 1212(a)(1)(A)(ii).

[45]Treas. Reg. § 1.1212-1(a)(3)(iv), Example (3). (1980).

[46]I.R.C. § 56(a). A corporation's minimum tax base (subject to a 15 percent add-on minimum tax) is equal to the sum of the corporation's tax preferences reduced by the greater of $10,000 or the full amount of its income tax. Corporate tax preferences include accelerated cost recovery deductions on real property and certain intangible drilling costs.

to compute the add-on minimum tax are not the same tax preference items as those items that apply to noncorporate taxpayers.[47]

A corporation with a net capital gain can treat as a tax preference item an amount equal to the product obtained by multiplying the net capital gain by a certain fraction.[48] The numerator of the fraction is the highest tax rate specified in I.R.C. § 11(b), minus the alternative tax rate under I.R.C. § 1201(a). The denominator of the fraction is the highest tax rate specified in I.R.C. § 11(b).[49] If the alternative tax method available under I.R.C. § 57(a)(9)(B) is used by the corporation, approximately 39 percent of its long-term capital gains are treated as tax preference items. At current tax rates the fraction is 18/46, which is approximately 39 percent.

---

[47]*Compare* I.R.C. § 291 (corporate tax preference items) *with* I.R.C. § 57 (noncorporate tax preference items).

[48]I.R.C. § 57(a)(9)(B).

[49]*Id.*

Fourteen

Basis

§ 14.1 IN GENERAL

To determine the gains or losses from capital transactions, the tax basis for the asset sold or exchanged must be ascertained. This is because the amount of gain or loss realized on a sale or exchange is the difference between an asset's adjusted basis and the net value of the consideration received for its sale or exchange. Usually an asset's basis is its cost, although special basis rules apply to acquisitions that are other than by purchase. Of course, an asset's basis might be adjusted (referred to as "adjusted basis") by certain subsequent transactions. Still, it is up to the taxpayer to establish the tax basis of the assets that he sells or exchanges. If the taxpayer cannot establish the basis, the IRS can impose a lower (or zero) basis on the assets.[1]

§ 14.2 DETERMINATION OF COST BASIS (PURCHASE)

A capital asset that is purchased by the taxpayer generally has a basis equal to its acquisition cost, which includes those commissions and fees paid to purchase the asset.[2] As with all types of acquisitions, the purchase price can be paid in cash, property, services, or in satisfaction of an existing debt obligation.

---

[1]*See* Eder v. Comm'r, 9 T.C.M. (CCH) 98, 100–01 (1950); Biggs v. Comm'r, 27 T.C.M. (CCH) 1177 (1968).

[2]*See* section 7.1(c)(1).

The tax basis for a cash purchase equals the money paid for the asset.[3] Exceptions to this general rule include, for example, bulk purchases and wash sales. If the agreement to acquire several assets does not allocate the purchase price among the different assets (i.e., a "bulk purchase"), the taxpayer must allocate the purchase price (based upon the relative market values of the assets acquired at the time of the purchase) among all of the assets purchased in the bulk purchase package.[4] For a discussion of the rules on the basis of securities acquired in wash sales, see section 14.4(d).

§ 14.3 DETERMINATION OF BASIS OTHER THAN COST

(a) GIFTS

When a taxpayer receives securities, commodities, or option positions as a gift, the taxpayer's basis in the gift (including a transfer made into a trust) is for all purposes (except determining loss on the gift's disposition) the same as the donor's adjusted basis at the time of the gift.[5] This substituted basis rule applies to gifts acquired after 1920. Gifts acquired before 1921 receive a stepped-up basis equal to the fair market value of the property at the time of the gift.[6]

To determine a loss, however, the donee's basis in the gift is the lesser of the donor's basis or the fair market value of the gift at the date the gift was made.[7] Accordingly, if the gift is sold by the donee for an amount less than the amount of his basis—but for no more than the gift's fair market value on the date the gift was made—neither gain nor loss is realized on the transaction.[8]

If a gift tax is paid on a gift made after September 2, 1958 and before January 1, 1977, the donee's basis for the gift is increased by the amount of the gift tax paid.[9] If a gift tax is paid on a gift made on or after January 1, 1977, the donee's basis is increased by the proportionate part of the gift tax allocated to the appreciation (if any) of the gift over its value

---

[3]Treas. Reg. § 1.1012-1(a) (1980).

[4]Strauss v. Comm'r, 168 F.2d 441 (2d Cir.), *cert. denied*, 335 U.S. 858 (1948), *reh'g denied*, 335 U.S. 888 (1948); Alamo Broadcasting Co. v. Comm'r, 15 T.C. 534 (1950); Pierce v. U.S., 49 F. Supp. 324 (Ct. Cl. 1943).

[5]I.R.C. § 1015(a).

[6]I.R.C. § 1015(c).

[7]Treas. Reg. § 1.1015-1(a)(1) (1971).

[8]Treas. Reg. § 1.1015-1(a)(2) (1971).

[9]I.R.C. § 1015(d)(1)(A).

as of the date when the gift is made.[10] In either case, since September 2, 1958, a gift's basis cannot be increased above its fair market value at the time the gift is made. Consequently, a gift tax adjustment has no effect on an asset with a fair market value that is less than its respective tax basis as of the date the gift is made.[11]

(b) ACQUISITION FROM A DECEDENT

The basis of property received from a decedent through an inheritance or a bequest is adjusted to the fair market value of the asset as of the estate valuation date[12] or the alternative valuation date, if so elected by the executor of the estate.[13] In addition, when the alternative valuation date is elected and property is distributed to a beneficiary between the date of death and the alternative valuation date, the fair market value on the date of actual distribution becomes the property's basis. This stepped-up basis rule applies irrespective of how long the asset was held by the decedent and irrespective of the asset's basis in the decedent's hands. Assets receive a stepped-up basis even if the estate is not subject to tax and even if the decedent made a short sale of the asset that was not closed out at the decedent's death.[14]

Various basis adjustment and valuation rules apply to property received from a decedent who died after December 31, 1976 and before November 7, 1978.[15] For example, if property was acquired from a decedent who died during this period, the executor of the estate could have irrevocably elected to have the basis of the property acquired from the decedent valued at the property's basis immediately before the decedent's death.[16]

§ 14.4   ADJUSTED BASIS

The original cost basis for property might not represent a taxpayer's current basis in the assets. Certain transactions adjust a taxpayer's basis up or down. In general, basis adjustments are made with respect to

[10]I.R.C. § 1015(d)(6)(A).

[11]I.R.C. § 1015(d)(1)(A).

[12]I.R.C. § 1014(a)(1).

[13]I.R.C. §§ 1014(a)(2), (3).

[14]Rev. Rul. 73-524, 1973-2 C.B. 307.

[15]I.R.C. § 1023, prior to repeal by the Crude Oil Windfall Profit Tax Act of 1980, Pub. L. No. 96-223 § 401(a), 94 Stat. 229, 299 (1980).

[16]See Temp. Treas. Reg. § 7.1023(b)(3)-1 (1978).

nontaxable transactions to insure that the gain or loss realized upon the subsequent disposition of the asset is correct and reflects the fact that gain or loss was not recognized. A taxpayer's adjusted basis for property sold or exchanged is compared with the net proceeds realized upon the sale or exchange to determine whether a gain or loss is realized on the transaction.[17]

Basis is adjusted, for example, to reflect depreciation deductions and certain other nontaxable transactions. The following section, however, limits its discussion to those transactions between a stockholder and a corporation that result in an upward or downward adjustment to the stockholder's stock basis. Typically, a basis adjustment is made when the stockholder makes an additional capital contribution to the corporation or when he receives a corporate distribution that is neither a dividend nor interest income.

(a) CAPITAL CONTRIBUTIONS

A stockholder's basis for stock is generally increased by whatever additional amounts he contributes to the capital of the corporation.[18] If a stockholder contributes noncash property to a corporation that he does not control,[19] his stock basis is increased by the fair market value of the property he contributed.[20] If the stockholder contributes noncash property to a controlled corporation under I.R.C. § 351, however, his basis in the stock is increased by his adjusted basis in the property immediately prior to the contribution.[21]

If a stockholder forgives a debt owed to him by the corporation, the forgiveness of the debt is viewed as a capital contribution to the corporation in an amount equal to his basis in the debt.[22] As a result, the stockholder's basis in the stock is increased by his basis in the debt he forgives.

---

[17]I.R.C. § 1001.

[18]Treas. Reg. § 1.118-1 (1956).

[19]I.R.C. § 368(c).

[20]Chesshire v. Comm'r, 11 T.C.M. (CCH) 146, 147 (1952); International Trading Co. v. Comm'r, 17 T.C.M. (CCH) 521 (1958), aff'd, 275 F.2d 578 (7th Cir. 1960), and aff'd, Comm'r v. Shapiro, 278 F.2d 556 (7th Cir. 1960); Gardens of Faith, Inc. v. Comm'r, 23 T.C.M. (CCH) 1045 (1964), aff'd per curiam, 345 F.2d 180 (4th Cir.), cert. denied, 382 U.S. 927 (1965).

[21]See Rev. Rul. 70-291, 1970-1 C.B. 168; but see Haft v. Comm'r, 20 B.T.A. 431 (1930).

[22]Kasle v. U.S., 75 F. Supp. 341 (N.D. Ohio 1947); Treas. Reg. § 1.61-12 (1980).

(b) STOCK DIVIDENDS

When a corporation distributes shares of its own stock to its stockholders, gain or loss generally is not recognized by the stockholders.[23] Rather, nontaxable stock dividends (referred to as "new stock") receive an allocation of the stockholder's basis in his original stock holdings (referred to as "old stock") prior to the distribution of the nontaxable stock dividend, provided that the dividend is paid on old stock with an adjusted basis above zero.[24] A stockholder allocates his adjusted basis between the fair market value of the old stock as it was before the dividend and the fair market value of the new stock received as the dividend. In other words, the allocation is made in proportion to the relative fair market values of the old stock and new stock at the time of the dividend.[25]

In general, a stock dividend issued by a corporation in its own stock is nontaxable under I.R.C. § 305(a), subject to various exceptions under I.R.C. § 305. One taxable type of dividend, for example, is stock issued in another corporation. In all cases, the basis of the stock received in the distribution equals the dividend income received by the stockholder.[26]

(c) NONTAXABLE STOCK RIGHTS

If a corporation issues stock rights that allow its stockholders to purchase additional shares of stock, the stock rights usually are nontaxable. Stock rights are taxed in the same manner as stock dividends under I.R.C. § 305.[27]

Special rules do apply, however, with respect to certain stock rights. If a stockholder's nontaxable stock rights expire unexercised, the rights are disregarded for tax purposes and no basis adjustment or allocation is made with respect to the stock rights.[28] If stock rights are exercised or disposed of, however, three rules determine basis. First, if the value of the stock rights at the time of their distribution is greater than or equal to 15 percent of the value of the old stock with respect to which

---

[23]See I.R.C. § 305(a); *but see* I.R.C. § 305(b) (for exceptions to the nonrecognition provisions).

[24]Treas. Reg. § 1.307-1 (1955).

[25]*Id.*

[26]I.R.C. § 1012.

[27]*See* section 14.4(b).

[28]Lineaweaver v. Comm'r, 3 T.C.M. (CCH) 331 (1944); St. Louis Union Trust Co. v. Comm'r, 30 B.T.A. 370 (1934), *acq.* XIII-1 C.B. 14 (1934).

they are distributed, the basis of the old stock is allocated between the old stock and the stock rights in proportion to their respective fair market values as of the date the stock rights were distributed.[29] Second, if the stock rights are worth less than 15 percent of the fair market value of the old stock with respect to which they are distributed, the stock rights are deemed to have a zero basis, unless the stockholder elects to allocate the basis of the old stock between the old stock and the stock rights in proportion to their respective fair market values as of the date the stock rights were distributed.[30] Such an election to allocate basis is made on the stockholder's tax return for the year in which the stock rights are distributed and, once made, the election is irrevocable.[31] If an election to allocate basis is made, any gain or loss is determined in reference to the allocated basis amount.[32] Third, if and when the stock rights are exercised, the basis of the stock acquired by such exercise is the sum of the price actually paid for the stock plus the amount, if any, allocated to the stock rights from the basis of the old stock on which the stock rights were issued.[33]

(d) WASH SALES

The basis of stock or securities, the acquisition of which resulted in a disallowance of loss under the wash sales rule, takes as its basis the basis of the stock or securities that were sold.[34] The basis is adjusted for differences, if any, between the selling price of the old property and the purchase price of the new property.[35] For a discussion of wash sales, see generally Chapter 17.

(e) MODIFIED WASH SALES RULE

The modified wash sales rule is applied to positions in personal property that are part of a straddle. This rule may affect the basis of property. For a discussion of the modified wash sales rule, see section 42.3.

---

[29] I.R.C. § 307(a); Treas. Reg. § 1.307-1(a) (1955).

[30] I.R.C. § 307(b)(1); Treas. Reg. § 1.307-2 (1955).

[31] I.R.C. § 307(b)(2); Treas. Reg. § 1.307-2 (1955).

[32] *Id.*

[33] *Special Ruling* [1954–1955 Transfer Binder] STAND. FED. TAX REP. (CCH) ¶ 37,383 (Oct. 11, 1955).

[34] I.R.C. § 1091(d).

[35] *Id.*

(f) DISTRIBUTIONS IN EXCESS OF EARNINGS AND PROFITS

If a corporation distributes cash or property to its stockholders in excess of its accumulated and current earnings and profits, the distribution is a return of capital or paid-in surplus; it is not a dividend. Such a distribution is applied against and reduces a stockholder's basis in his stock.[36]

(g) MISCELLANEOUS CORPORATE TRANSACTIONS

A taxpayer's basis in stock or securities is also subject to adjustment in the following circumstances:

1. A taxpayer receives stock in a tax-free spinoff of a controlled corporation.[37]
2. A taxpayer is allocated undistributed capital gains of a regulated investment company.[38]
3. A taxpayer receives tax-exempt interest on any bond to the extent of the amortizable bond premiums.[39]
4. A transaction is subject to the wash sales rule.[40]
5. A taxpayer recognizes interest income and correspondingly receives annual adjustments for OID on debt securities.[41]
6. A taxpayer continues to hold stock in a corporation that is subject to a partial liquidation.[42]
7. A taxpayer receives a deemed dividend distribution.[43]
8. A taxpayer receives income from the redemption of stock of a related corporation.[44]
9. A dealer in tax-exempt securities receives payments on municipal bonds.[45]

---

[36]I.R.C. §§ 301(c)(2), 1016(a)(4).

[37]I.R.C. § 355.

[38]I.R.C. § 852(b)(3)(D)(iii).

[39]I.R.C. § 1016(a)(5); *see* section 27.4.

[40]I.R.C. § 1091(d); *see generally* Chapter 17.

[41]I.R.C. § 1272(d)(2).

[42]I.R.C. § 304.

[43]I.R.C. § 305(b).

[44]I.R.C. § 304.

[45]I.R.C. § 75(a).

10. A taxpayer benefits by a partial pro rata surrender of the stock of a corporation because the surrender reduces the capital of the corporation.[46]

11. A taxpayer receives from a decedent stock in a foreign investment company.[47]

12. A taxpayer is required to recognize his pro rata share of "subpart F income," stock, and other property in a controlled foreign corporation.[48]

§ 14.5 BUYING AND SELLING COMMISSIONS

Commissions on the purchase of securities, commodities, and options are not deductible and must be added to the cost of the property acquired by the taxpayer. This is the case for all taxpayers, including dealers in the property.[49] Selling commissions reduce the sales price of property for traders and investors. Dealers, on the other hand, can deduct commissions on sales of securities (and possibly commodities) as ordinary and necessary business expenses.[50]

§ 14.6 BASIS REDUCTION FOR EXTRAORDINARY DIVIDENDS

As a general rule, stockholders do not reduce their tax basis in their shares of stock in a corporation when they receive dividends from the corporation. Congress viewed this as a substantial tax advantage to corporate stockholders who sold their stock shortly after receiving a dividend that qualifies for the dividends received deduction.[51] A corporate stockholder who sells stock shortly after meeting the requisite holding period to obtain the dividends received deduction frequently

---

[46]Rev. Rul. 70-291, 1970-1 C.B. 168, *amplified by* Rev. Rul. 82-112, 1982-1 C.B. 59; Hellman v. Helvering, 68 F.2d 763 (D.C. Cir. 1934); Kistler v. Burnet, 58 F.2d 687, 688 (D.C. Cir. 1932).

[47]I.R.C. § 1246(e)(1).

[48]I.R.C. § 961.

[49]Helvering v. Winmill, 305 U.S. 79, 84 (1938); Woodward v. Comm'r, 397 U.S. 572, 575 (1970).

[50]*See* section 7.1(c)(1); section 8.1(d); section 9.1(b).

[51]*See* section 22.9.

obtains both a low tax rate on the dividend and a capital loss on the sale of the stock (assuming the stock's price declines after the corporation pays the dividend). To remove this tax advantage, a basis reduction is now required of corporate stockholders to the extent of nontaxed extraordinary dividends on stock held for less than one year (referred to as a "one-year holding period.")[52]

I.R.C. § 1059, effective for distributions made after March 1, 1984, discourages certain corporate transactions Congress viewed as abusive.[53] For purposes of the basis adjustment, an extraordinary dividend is defined as any dividend (including distributions in redemption of stock treated as dividends under I.R.C. § 301)[54] that equals or exceeds (1) five percent of the corporation's basis in preferred stock,[55] (2) 10 percent of the corporation's basis in common stock,[56] and (3) dividends with ex-dividend dates within a 365 day period that in the aggregate exceed 20 percent of the corporation's basis.[57] In addition, dividends with ex-dividend dates within an 85-day period are aggregated.[58]

In addition, dividends are aggregated under this provision if received by (1) the taxpayer, (2) a person from whom the taxpayer acquired the stock if the taxpayer's basis is determined in whole or in part by reference to the basis of the stock in the hands of such person, or (3) a person to whom the taxpayer transferred the stock if the transferee's basis in the stock is determined by reference to the basis of such stock in the hands of the taxpayer.[59]

The nontaxed portion of an extraordinary dividend by which the basis is reduced is the excess, if any, of the amount of the extraordinary dividend over the taxable portion of the dividend.[60] The taxable portion of the extraordinary dividend is includible in gross income, reduced by the amount of any deduction for dividends received.[61]

The one-year holding period is computed subject to the same rules that apply to the holding period requirements to obtain the dividends

---

[52]I.R.C. § 1059(a).

[53]See STAFF OF THE JOINT COMMITTEE ON TAXATION, 98TH CONG., 2D SESS., GENERAL EXPLANATION OF THE REVENUE PROVISIONS OF THE DEFICIT REDUCTION ACT OF 1984, 136 (Joint Comm. Print 1984) [hereinafter referred to as "General Explanation of DRA"].

[54]Id. at 141.

[55]I.R.C. § 1059(c)(2)(A).

[56]I.R.C. § 1059(c)(2)(B).

[57]I.R.C. § 1059(c)(3)(B).

[58]I.R.C. § 1059(c)(3)(A).

[59]I.R.C. § 1059(c)(3)(C); General Explanation of DRA, supra note 53, at 140.

[60]I.R.C. § 1059(b)(1).

[61]I.R.C. § 1059(b)(2).

received deduction.[62] This means that the corporate stockholder cannot sell the stock short, grant an option to buy substantially identical stock, or diminish its risk of loss in holding the stock by holding one or more positions of substantially similar or related property.[63] For a discussion of the holding period requirements, see section 15.7 and section 22.9. Solely for purposes of I.R.C. § 1059, the fair market value and not the tax basis of distributions of appreciated property is used to compute the basis reduction.[64]

The Treasury is authorized to issue regulations to carry out the purposes of I.R.C. § 1059.[65] When the regulations are issued, it is assumed that they will encompass stock dividends, stock splits, reorganizations, and similar transactions.[66]

[62]I.R.C. § 1059(d)(3).
[63]I.R.C. § 246(c)(4).
[64]I.R.C. § 1059(d)(2).
[65]I.R.C. § 1059(e).
[66]*Id.*

Fifteen

Holding Period

Determination of a taxpayer's holding period for a capital asset is necessary to ascertain whether its sale or exchange generates long-term or short-term gain or loss.[1] The taxpayer must establish the length of time he has held the asset to meet the long-term holding period requirement.[2] A capital asset held for more than the long-term holding period generates long-term capital gain or loss, while an asset held for less than the long-term holding period generates short-term capital gain or loss. Assets acquired between June 23, 1984 and December 31, 1987 must be held for more than six months to obtain long-term treatment. All other assets must be held for more than 12 months to obtain long-term capital gain. A special rule is imposed for section 1256 contracts that are capital assets in the hands of the taxpayer. Irrespective of the taxpayer's holding period, section 1256 contracts receive 60 percent long-term and 40 percent short-term capital gain or loss.

Holding period provisions relevant to securities, commodities, and options are discussed in this chapter.

§ 15.1   COMPUTATION OF HOLDING PERIOD

(a)   ACQUISITION AND DISPOSITION DATES

The period during which a taxpayer owns a capital asset is measured in full calendar months rather than weeks or days. As a result, if the

---

[1] *See generally* Chapter 13.

[2] Taylor v. Comm'r, 76 F.2d 904 (2d Cir.), *cert. denied*, 296 U.S. 594 (1935), *reh'g denied*, Peeless Stages v. Railroad Com., 296 U.S. 663 (1936).

holding period includes more than the number of full calendar months required to obtain long-term gain, there is no question but that long-term capital gain is available. Assets with more than six month holding periods (for example, assets held for seven full calendar months) clearly qualify for long-term treatment. Similarly, assets with more than 12 month holding periods (for example, assets held for 13 full calendar months) qualify for long-term treatment.

Example   15-1

The holding period for a more than six month capital asset that begins in February and ends in September qualifies for long-term treatment.

If the holding period is one calendar month short of the required number of full calendar months, although the holding period includes fractional parts of both the month at the beginning and the month at the end of the taxpayer's holding period, it must be determined whether these fractional parts add up to a full month or not. For example, if one of the months that is overlapped is August and the other is February, should the standard for determining whether the fractional parts add up to a month be 31 days or 28 days, respectively? Obviously, a method to compute the holding period is required. The general rule is that the term "month" denotes a calendar month (regardless of whether it has 28, 29, 30, or 31 days). Consequently, a month terminates on the day of the succeeding calendar month that numerically corresponds with the day of its beginning, less one. The only exception is where there is no corresponding day (for example, if the month begins on January 30), in which case the period terminates on the last day of the succeeding month (February 28 unless it is a leap year).[3]

Example   15-2

The holding period of a more than six month capital asset that begins on March 15th and ends on September 16th qualifies for long-term capital gain.

As a general rule, the date a capital asset is acquired is not included in the computation of the holding period, while the date the asset is

[3]Caspe v. U.S., 82-1 U.S. Tax Cas. (CCH) ¶ 9247 (S.D. Iowa 1982) (citing I.T. 3985, 1949-2 C.B. 51), *aff'd*, 694 F.2d 1116 (8th Cir. 1982).

disposed of is included in the computation.[4] Calculation of the holding period also is not affected by holidays or weekends.

Example   15-3

A capital asset with a holding period that begins on March 23rd and is sold on September 29th has a holding period that runs from March 23rd to September 29th.

(b) METHOD OF COMPUTATION

The holding period for capital assets is computed in months and fractions of months, without regard to the number of days in the month.[5] This means that a capital asset is held for exactly six months (or 12 months) on the same calendar day of the sixth (or twelfth) calendar month that corresponds with the acquisition date, since the date of acquisition is not included in calculating the period.[6] Consequently, the asset becomes a long-term asset on the day after the same numbered day in the sixth (or twelfth) month.

Example   15-4

A *more than six month* capital asset acquired on February 25th with a holding period that commences on February 26th becomes a long-term asset on August 27th of the same year.

Example   15-5

A *more than twelve month* asset acquired on February 16th with a holding period that commences on February 17th becomes a long-term asset on February 18th of the succeeding year.

There is a special rule for capital assets purchased on the last day of the month. Such assets become long-term assets only on the first day of the seventh (or thirteenth) succeeding month, without regard to the number of days in the month.[7]

[4]Rev. Rul. 66-97, 1966-1 C.B. 190; Weir v. Comm'r, 10 T.C. 996 (1948), *aff 'd per curiam,* 173 F.2d 222 (3d Cir. 1949); Anderson v. Comm'r, 527 F.2d 198 (9th Cir. 1975).
[5]Rev. Rul. 66-7, 1966-1 C.B. 188.
[6]Rev. Rul. 70-598, 1970-2 C.B. 168.
[7]Rev. Rul. 66-7, 1966-1 C.B. 188.

Example   15-6

A *more than six month* asset with a holding period that commences on February 28th becomes a long-term asset on September 1st.

Example   15-7

A *more than twelve month* asset with a holding period that commences on February 28th becomes a long-term asset on March 1st of the succeeding year. If the succeeding taxable year is a leap year, however, the asset becomes long-term on February 29th of the succeeding year.

If a cash basis taxpayer sells property in one taxable year, but neither delivers the property nor receives the sales proceeds until the second taxable year, the holding period rule is different from the general rule used to determine when to report gain. Although the year in which the sales proceeds are received usually determines the taxable year in which to report the gain, the year in which the sale occurs—not when the sales proceeds are received—usually determines the holding period.[8]

(c) WORTHLESS SECURITIES

Losses on worthless securities are treated as losses that occur on the last day of the taxable year in which the securities become worthless.[9] The actual date on which the securities become worthless is not relevant when determining loss.

§ 15.2 DETERMINATION OF ACQUISITION AND DISPOSITION DATES

(a) PURCHASE FROM ANOTHER HOLDER

(1) GENERAL RULE

The date when a capital asset is acquired for computation of the holding period is based on the date that title to the asset passes to the purchaser under state law. Also relevant is when the parties intend ownership of

---

[8]Rev. Rul. 78-270, 1978-2 C.B. 215.
[9]I.R.C. § 165(g)(1).

the asset to be transferred.[10] Frequently, the holding period begins the day after the purchase contract has been entered into, even if the asset has not been delivered or the purchase price has not been paid.[11] Of course, if the parties do not intend a sale to occur until the asset is delivered or payment is received, the holding period does not begin until these conditions are satisfied.[12] If an asset is placed in an escrow account until certain conditions are satisfied, the sale is not viewed as complete until the conditions are performed; the holding period does not begin to run until the sale is complete.[13] In the case where the seller does not own the asset, but enters into an executory contract to sell the asset, the purchaser's holding period does not commence until the seller can deliver the asset.[14]

(2) YEAR-END TRANSACTIONS

There are various techniques available to taxpayers to accelerate or defer gain on year-end transactions. These techniques are discussed below.

(i) Installment Transactions

An important tax benefit is available for taxpayers who agree to sell an asset in the current taxable year but receive at least one payment for the asset in the next taxable year. Under I.R.C. § 453(b)(1), such an arrangement is an installment sale, defined as a disposition of property where at least one payment is received in a taxable year after the year of disposition.[15] The only exceptions are for the disposition of personal property either on an installment plan by a dealer[16] or for property required to be in the taxpayer's inventory if held at the close of the taxable year.[17]

Gain on an installment sale is taken into account under the install-

[10]*See* Merrill v. Comm'r, 40 T.C. 66, 74 (1963), *aff'd per curiam,* 336 F.2d 771 (9th Cir. 1964); Bradford v. U.S., 444 F.2d 1133, 1144 (Ct. Cl. 1971); Boykin v. Comm'r, 344 F.2d 889 (5th Cir. 1965).

[11]Marsh v. Comm'r, 12 T.C. 1083, 1088 (1949), *acq.* 1949-2 C.B. 3; McKean v. Comm'r, 6 T.C. 757, 761-62 (1946), *acq.* 1947-1 C.B. 3.

[12]Shillinglaw v. Comm'r, 99 F.2d 87 (6th Cir. 1938), *cert. denied,* 306 U.S. 635 (1939).

[13]Dyke v. Comm'r, 6 T.C. 1134, 1140 (1946), *acq.* 1946-2 C.B. 2.

[14]Armstrong v. Comm'r, 6 T.C. 1166, 1174 (1946), *aff'd,* 162 F.2d 199 (3d Cir. 1947); Otto v. Comm'r, 37 B.T.A. 479 (1938), *remanded,* 101 F.2d 1017 (4th Cir. 1939).

[15]I.R.C. § 453(b)(1).

[16]I.R.C. § 453(b)(2)(A).

[17]I.R.C. § 453(b)(2)(B).

ment method,[18] defined as "a method under which the income recognized for any taxable year from a disposition is that proportion of the payments received in that year which the gross profit (realized or to be realized when payment is completed) bears to the total contract price."[19] Installment treatment is automatic unless the taxpayer elects out, thereby reporting the entire gain on Schedule D of his tax return. If the taxpayer elects to report the gain in the year of the sale, he must do so on or before he has to file his tax return for the taxable year in which the disposition occurred.[20] A late election will be allowed, however, if the IRS determines that the taxpayer has good cause for failing to make a timely election.[21] In all events, the election must be made on a trade by trade basis and is revocable only with the consent of the Treasury.[22]

The advantages to the taxpayer in electing out of the installment method will, of course, depend on his financial situation for the taxable years in question. Some examples of when an election is financially advantageous to the taxpayer follow:

Example   15-8

Assume a taxpayer is a cash basis taxpayer on the calendar year. On December 31st he sells a security on a stock exchange at a gain. On January 5th of the next year, pursuant to the rules of the stock exchange, the taxpayer delivers the security and receives payment. Assume that the taxpayer's taxable income for the first year is unusually low. As a result, the taxpayer can benefit by expressly "electing out" of the installment method. He includes the gain in his taxable income for the earlier year.

Example   15-9

Assume an investor realized a short-term capital gain of $8000 on a year-end transaction that settles in the next taxable year along with a long-term capital loss of $8000. If the short-term gain is reported in the next taxable year, only 50 percent (or $4000) of the long-term loss is deductible from ordinary income in the year of disposition. By electing

---

[18] I.R.C. § 453(a).
[19] I.R.C. § 453(c).
[20] I.R.C. § 453(d)(1); Temp. Treas. Reg. § 15A.453-1(d)(3)(i) (1981).
[21] Temp. Treas. Reg. § 15A.453-1(d)(3)(ii) (1981).
[22] I.R.C. § 453(d)(3).

out of the installment method, the taxpayer offsets 100 percent (or $8000) of the long-term capital loss against the short-term gain, which might have otherwise been taxed as ordinary income in the second year.

When a taxpayer sells stock at the end of one year in a regular way transaction and receives payment when the trade settles in the next taxable year, the taxpayer can elect out of the installment method and include the gain in his income in the year of the sale.[23] In such a case, the taxpayer recognizes gain on the sale in accordance with his method of accounting.[24] Cash basis taxpayers recognize gain in the year of the sale.[25] Because an installment obligation is considered to be property,[26] the fair market value of an installment obligation must be taken into account in the taxable year when it arises, that is, the year in which the contract to sell securities is entered into.[27] For a taxpayer using the accrual method of accounting, the total amount of the installment obligation is treated as the amount realized in the year of the sale.[28]

Because the installment sale provisions of I.R.C. § 453 anticipate a gain from a sale, no election is necessary where a loss results. Moreover, losses resulting from the sale of stocks and bearer bonds are deductible in the tax year in which the contract is entered into even if delivery is made the following year.[29]

(ii) Escrow Accounts

A taxpayer can sell an asset on the condition that the proceeds be paid into an escrow account and not be disbursed to him until the subsequent tax year. In this situation, the taxpayer's motive is to defer gain from the sale to a subsequent taxable year. If the only condition for an arm's length escrow agreement is that funds will not be dispensed until a later date and the seller does not receive any economic benefit from the amounts in escrow, judicial decisions allow a taxpayer to defer the gain on the sale to a subsequent taxable year.

---

[23]Rev. Rul. 82-227, 1982-2 C.B. 89.
[24]Temp. Treas. Reg. § 15A.453-1(d)(2)(i) (1981).
[25]Rev. Rul. 82-227, 1982-2 C.B. 89; *see* Temp. Treas. Reg. § 15A.453-1(d)(2)(ii)(A) (1981).
[26]*Id.*
[27]Rev. Rul. 82-227, 1982-2 C.B. 89.
[28]Temp. Treas. Reg. § 15A.453-1(d)(2)(ii)(A) (1981).
[29]Rev. Rul. 70-344, 1970-2 C.B. 50.

In *Reed v. Comm'r*,[30] the court reversed a Tax Court decision in which proceeds from the sale of securities were paid into an escrow account on December 27th. The escrow provided for disbursement to the seller on January 3rd of the subsequent year. The court held that the escrow arrangement constituted an arm's length, bona fide modification of the sales agreement rather than a self-imposed limitation by the taxpayer (which would have been ineffective).[31] The modification was viewed as effective and legally binding prior to the time when the taxpayer had the right to demand immediate payment under the purchase agreement.[32] In contrast, the Tax Court in *Vaughn v. Comm'r*[33] held that the taxpayer had constructively received the proceeds from the sale of certain stock. The Tax Court found that the taxpayer could have insisted that the buyer transfer the sales proceeds into escrow instead of using the proceeds to make payments on certain other obligations.

In addition, in *Busby v. U.S.*,[34] an escrow agreement that had no conditions for disbursement except for the passage of time could defer gain on a sale. It appears that the test the courts should follow is that a seller cannot directly or indirectly control the proceeds or possess the economic benefit therefrom.[35]

(3) TAXABLE TRANSACTIONS

Assets received in taxable purchases, exchanges, reorganizations, distributions, and liquidations usually receive both a new tax basis and a new holding period in the hands of the taxpayer.[36] In addition, the holding period generally begins on the date of the transaction.

(4) TAXABLE DISTRIBUTIONS OF PROPERTY AND STOCK RIGHTS

Taxable property dividends and stock rights are treated as purchases for purposes of determining a taxpayer's holding period. As a result, the holding period of property or stock rights received from a corporation

---

[30]723 F.2d 138 (1st Cir. 1983).

[31]*Id.* at 143.

[32]*Id.*

[33]81 T.C. 893 (1983).

[34]679 F.2d 48 (5th Cir. 1982).

[35]*Vaughn*, 81 T.C. at 909.

[36]*See generally* Chapter 14.

in a taxable distribution begins the day following the distribution to the taxpayer.

(5) STOCK AND SECURITIES IN TRANSACTIONS OTHER THAN CASH TRANSACTIONS

The trade date for securities traded in the over-the-counter market or on a stock exchange is generally considered to be both the acquisition date and the sales date for computation of the holding period.[37] This means that the holding period begins and ends on the trade date, even though the securities are delivered and paid for on the settlement date.[38] This rule usually applies regardless of whether the securities are traded on a stock exchange or in the over-the-counter market.

There may be some exceptions. In *Otto v. Comm'r,*[39] the Board of Tax Appeals held that the taxpayer did not acquire securities on the date he placed his order to buy securities with his broker-dealer in the over-the-counter market. In reaching this decision, the court considered that (1) no stock was acquired by the broker-dealer on the trade date, (2) the broker-dealer did not have the stock needed to cover the taxpayer's order in inventory, and (3) the stock was not acquired by the broker-dealer until a full month later.[40]

Cash transactions for stock and securities settle on the trade date.[41] The seller's holding period ends at that time. Other types of transactions on exchanges and in the over-the-counter market have settlement dates from one day to 60 days after the trade date.[42] Although there are no judicial decisions or Treasury pronouncements on point, the seller's holding period may be extended until the settlement date if the intention of the parties is not to pass title until the settlement date. For seller's option transactions on the NYSE, for example, which settle at the seller's option within 60 days, the seller's holding period may be extended to the agreed settlement date.[43]

Securities purchased by a bank on behalf of its customers who par-

---

[37]Rev. Rul. 66-97, 1966-1 C.B. 190.
[38]Rev. Rul. 70-598, 1970-2 C.B. 168; Rev. Rul. 70-344, 1970-2 C.B. 50; Rev. Rul. 66-97, 1966-1 C.B. 190.
[39]37 B.T.A. at 483.
[40]*Id.*
[41]*See* section 1.3(b).
[42]*See generally* section 1.3.
[43]*See* section 1.3(f).

ticipate in an automatic investment service have an acquisition date when the bank makes the purchase for the customers' accounts.[44]

(6) WHEN-ISSUED SECURITIES

Trading in when-issued securities technically involves two separate transactions, that is, trading in the actual contracts to acquire the securities on a when, as and if issued basis, as well as acquisition or sale of the actual securities pursuant to the when-issued contract.[45] The purchase and sale of the actual securities pursuant to a when-issued contract takes place on the settlement date. The holding period for securities acquired pursuant to a when-issued contract begins on the date the securities are actually acquired, not when the taxpayer purchases the when-issued contract.[46] In addition, if the taxpayer disposes of a when-issued contract prior to delivery of the actual securities, long-term or short-term capital gain or loss results (depending upon the holding period of the when-issued contract).[47]

If securities subject to a when-issued contract are issued, the holder of a short position must acquire the newly issued securities (either directly from the issuer or by a purchase in the open market) and deliver them to the long position at the agreed to price. Obviously the holder of the short contract position holds the actual securities for less than the long-term holding period. His gain or loss is short-term (even if he held the contract for more than the long-term holding period).[48] In addition, the holding period of a long contract position is not tacked onto the holding period of the securities delivered. Instead, the holding period for securities delivered pursuant to a when-issued contract begins on the day after the securities are issued; no actual sale of stock takes place until the new stock is issued.[49]

(b) TREASURY SECURITIES

The acquisition date for Treasury securities (i.e., Treasury bills, notes, and bonds) purchased at auctions is the date on which the Treasury notifies the successful competitive and noncompetitive bidders of ac-

---

[44]Rev. Rul. 75-548, 1975-2 C.B. 331.

[45]*See* section 1.3(g).

[46]*See* I.T. 3721, 1945 C.B. 164.

[47]Stavisky v. Comm'r, 34 T.C. 140, 144 (1960), *aff'd*, 291 F.2d 48 (2d Cir. 1961); I.T. 3721, 1945 C.B. 164; Rev. Rul. 57-29, 1957-1 C.B. 519.

[48]Shanis v. Comm'r, 19 T.C. 641, 650 (1953), *aff'd per curiam*, 213 F.2d 151 (3d Cir. 1954).

[49]*See* I.T. 3721, 1945 C.B. 164.

ceptance through news releases.[50] The acquisition date of Treasury notes sold on a subscription basis at a specified yield is the date the subscription is submitted.[51]

(c) DIRECT PURCHASES OF SECURITIES FROM THE ISSUING CORPORATION

(1) SUBSCRIPTION FOR SECURITIES

For stock acquired by subscription, the date on which the taxpayer becomes a stockholder in a corporation, under state law, usually is the date that the taxpayer's holding period commences.[52] The Tax Court has held that a subscriber for stock becomes a stockholder on the date the subscription is accepted by the corporation, even if the stock certificate is not issued on the same date.[53] Conversely, if the terms of the subscription agreement provide that the agreement is not binding until the securities are issued, the holding period does not commence until the securities are issued.[54]

(2) EXERCISE OF WARRANTS OR OPTIONS

There is a split among the jurisdictions as to the acquisition date for securities received from the exercise of a warrant or option issued directly by a corporation to the taxpayer. It is clear that the holding period commences with the passage of the benefits and burdens or incidents of ownership of the property involved. There is disagreement on when such passage takes place. If the date the securities are issued is viewed as the acquisition date, then the holder must actually acquire, in accordance with the provisions of the warrant or option, actual ownership of the underlying securities.[55] If the acquisition date is viewed as the date the holder gives notice of his exercise of the warrant or option, the holding period commences when the holder acquires significant con-

---

[50]Rev. Rul. 78-5, 1978-1 C.B. 263.

[51]*Id.*

[52]Bacon v. Comm'r, 4 T.C.M. (CCH) 868, 874 (1945), *aff'd per curiam*, 158 F.2d 981 (9th Cir. 1947).

[53]*Id.*

[54]Sommers v. Comm'r, 22 B.T.A. 1241 (1931), *aff'd*, 63 F.2d 551 (10th Cir. 1933).

[55]Stanley v. U.S., 436 F. Supp. 581, 583 (N.D. Miss. 1977), *aff'd*, 599 F.2d 672 (5th Cir. 1979); *see generally* McFeely v. Comm'r, 296 U.S. 102 (1935) (holding that the date of acquisition of personal property passing from a decedent is the date of death); Helvering v. San Joaquim Fruit & Investment Co., 297 U.S. 496 (1936) (holding that real property is acquired when a lease containing an option is exercised).

tract rights to the securities and that unless the contract is breached, he will own the securities.[56] The holding period of securities acquired by the exercise of warrants or options issued by a corporation generally begins on the date the warrants are exercised.[57]

(3) EXERCISE OF STOCK RIGHTS

The holding period for securities purchased by the exercise of stock rights, that is, equity interests derived from stock ownership, begins on the date the stock rights are exercised.[58]

§ 15.3 TACKED HOLDING PERIOD

In some cases a taxpayer's holding period for a capital asset includes the holding period of some other property or, in the case of some securities, the same security held by another person. Some of the situations where another holding period is tacked, that is, added onto the holding period of property held by a taxpayer, are discussed in this section.

(a) EXCHANGED SECURITIES

In those cases where a security received in an exchange has the same tax basis (in whole or in part) in the taxpayer's hands as the basis of the asset exchanged, the taxpayer's holding period for the security received includes the holding period for the capital asset (or I.R.C. § 1231 asset) given up in the exchange.[59] The holding period for the security received is tacked onto the holding period for the asset exchanged, even if the taxpayer receives money or other property (referred to as "boot") as well as securities in the exchange.

(1) REORGANIZATIONS

The holding period of securities received by a taxpayer in a corporate reorganization qualifying under I.R.C. §§ 354 and 356, includes the holding period of the securities surrendered pursuant to the reorganization

---

[56]Swenson v. Comm'r, 309 F.2d 672, 673–74 (8th Cir. 1962); Becker v. Comm'r, 378 F.2d 767, 769 (3d Cir. 1967).

[57]Becker, 378 F.2d at 769; Rev. Rul. 72-71, 1972-1 C.B. 99.

[58]I.R.C. § 1223(6).

[59]I.R.C. § 1223(1).

plan.[60] This is because I.R.C. § 358(a) provides for a substituted basis for securities acquired pursuant to such reorganizations. And, in general, whenever there is a change in basis without a recognition of gain or loss, the holding period of the new securities is tacked onto the holding period of the old securities.

(2) STOCK FOR STOCK IN THE SAME CORPORATION

Gain or loss is not recognized under I.R.C. § 1036 if common or preferred stock is exchanged solely for common or preferred stock, respectively, in the same corporation.[61] A substituted basis is provided in such a situation.[62] As a result of the nonrecognition and substitution of basis provisions, the holding period of securities exchanged in a transaction qualifying under I.R.C. § 1036 is tacked onto the holding period of the securities acquired in the transaction.

(3) STOCK ACQUIRED FROM CONVERTIBLE SECURITIES

The holding period of securities received upon conversion of convertible securities includes the holding period of the securities that were converted.[63] If the taxpayer pays cash to the corporation as well as surrenders the convertible security, the holding period of the new securities received by the taxpayer is split. The portion of each share of stock represented by the cash payment receives a new holding period, while the portion of each share of stock represented by the convertible securities receives a tacked holding period.[64]

(4) TRANSFERS TO CONTROLLED CORPORATIONS

If securities are received by a taxpayer in exchange for property transferred to a controlled corporation in a tax-free incorporation or contribution to capital under I.R.C. § 351, the securities obtain a substituted basis under I.R.C. § 358(a). Moreover, the securities have a holding period that includes the holding period for the property transferred to the corporation by the taxpayer.[65]

---

[60]I.R.C. § 1223(1).
[61]I.R.C. § 1036.
[62]I.R.C. § 1031(d).
[63]Rev. Rul. 62-153, 1962-2 C.B. 186.
[64]Rev. Rul. 62-140, 1962-2 C.B. 181.
[65]I.R.C. § 1223(1).

(b) COMMODITIES ACQUIRED PURSUANT TO FUTURES CONTRACTS

The holding period of property acquired by taking delivery under a long section 1256 contract position begins to run on the date of delivery.[66] Thus, a taxpayer who acquires property pursuant to a futures contract subject to the provisions of section 1256 does not include the period that he held the section 1256 position in his holding period of the underlying property.

On the other hand, the holding period for property acquired pursuant to a long futures contract that is not governed by section 1256 includes the period the long contract was held if the long contract is a capital asset in the hands of the taxpayer.[67] This tacked on holding period applies, for example, to futures contracts traded on foreign exchanges not designated as qualified boards or exchanges by the Treasury and to futures contracts that are part of a section 1256(d) identified mixed straddle where an identified mixed straddle election is in effect.[68]

(c) TACKING ON A HOLDING PERIOD OF ANOTHER PERSON

As a general rule, a taxpayer's holding period for a capital asset includes the holding period of another person if that other person's tax basis is carried over to the taxpayer and becomes, in whole or in part, the taxpayer's basis.[69]

(1) GIFTS

The holding period for assets acquired as a gift after 1920 usually includes the donor's holding period.[70] This is because the donor's basis must be used (in whole or in part) to determine the taxpayer's gain or loss on the transaction. The donor's holding period is tacked, even if the taxpayer is required to pay a gift tax.[71] There is an exception for losses. If the taxpayer claims a loss upon the disposition of a gift that had a fair market value at the time of the gift which was lower than

[66]I.R.C. § 1223(8).
[67]Id.
[68]See section 45.2.
[69]I.R.C. § 1223(2).
[70]Id.
[71]Comm'r v. Turner, 410 F.2d 752, 753 (6th Cir. 1969).

the donor's basis, the taxpayer's holding period begins with the day following the date of the gift.[72]

(2) PARTNERSHIP TRANSACTIONS

The general rule with respect to partnership distributions of capital assets to partners is to tack onto the holding period during which the partnership held the capital assets.[73] This rule does not apply to assets distributed upon termination of a partnership where one partner purchases the partnership interest from another partner.[74] In addition, a partner's basis in property contributed to a partnership is carried-over to the partnership and the partner's holding period is tacked onto the holding period of the property.[75]

(3) TRANSFERS TO CONTROLLED CORPORATIONS

Capital assets transferred to a controlled corporation in a tax-free transfer under I.R.C. § 351 and for which the carry-over basis provisions of I.R.C. § 362(a) apply have a tacked holding period.[76]

(4) CORPORATE LIQUIDATIONS

If the liquidation of a corporate subsidiary qualifies for the parent corporation to receive a carry-over basis for the subsidiary's assets, the subsidiary's holding period is tacked onto the holding period of the parent.[77] In addition, if a corporate subsidiary distributes assets to its parent corporation as a dividend and the basis of the assets is carried over to the parent (provided the fair market value of the assets exceeds the asset's basis in the hands of the subsidiary), the subsidiary's holding period in the assets is tacked onto its parent's holding period.[78]

Property received in a one-month liquidation under I.R.C. § 333 obtains a carry-over basis and a tacked holding period that includes the

---

[72]Treas. Reg. § 1.1223-1(b) (1980).

[73]I.R.C. § 735(b).

[74]Rev. Rul. 55-68, 1955-1 C.B. 372; McCauslen v. Comm'r, 45 T.C. 588, 592 (1966).

[75]I.R.C. §§ 723, 1223; cf. Edwards v. Hogg, 214 F.2d 640 (5th Cir. 1954).

[76]I.R.C. § 1223(1); Dairy Queen of Oklahoma, Inc. v. Comm'r, 18 T.C.M. (CCH) 322, 325 (1959).

[77]See I.R.C. § 1223.

[78]Rev. Rul. 70-6, 1970-1 C.B. 172.

taxpayer's holding period in the stock cancelled or redeemed in the liquidation.[79]

(5) DISTRIBUTIONS BY ESTATES AND TRUSTS

The holding period of capital assets received from an estate or trust depends upon whether the beneficiary's basis equals the fair market value of the assets (referred to as "stepped-up basis") or is determined with reference to the basis in the hands of the estate or trust prior to the distribution (referred to as "carry-over basis").[80] If assets in the hands of a beneficiary have a carry-over basis, the holding period of the estate or trust is tacked onto the beneficiary's holding period.[81]

In general, the date that the assets are, in fact, distributed to the beneficiary is not relevant in determining the beneficiary's holding period.[82]

§ 15.4 HOLDING PERIOD DETERMINED BY REFERENCE TO OTHER PROPERTY

(a) NONTAXABLE STOCK DIVIDENDS, STOCK RIGHTS, AND STOCK SCRIP

Nontaxable stock dividends and stock rights are viewed as being part of the stock with respect to which they are issued. The tax basis of the new stock (or stock rights) received in the distribution is determined by allocating between the old stock and new stock (or stock rights) the adjusted basis of the old stock.[83] Similarly, the holding period for non-taxable stock dividends or stock rights includes the holding period of the stock.[84]

The holding period for stock scrip, which represents a fractional share of stock, depends upon the manner in which the stock scrip is acquired

---

[79]I.R.C. § 334(c).

[80]For a discussion of the basis rules, see section 14.3(b).

[81]I.R.C. § 1223(2); Rev. Rul. 72-359, 1972-2 C.B. 478.

[82]Brewster v. Gage, 280 U.S. 327, 335 (1930).

[83]I.R.C. § 307; *see* section 14.4(b); section 14.4(c).

[84]I.R.C. § 1223(5); Rev. Rul. 72-71, 1972-1 C.B. 99.

by the taxpayer. Stock scrip issued in lieu of fractional shares as part of a stock dividend is not taxable until sold and has a tacked holding period that includes the holding period of the stock with respect to which it is issued.[85] Stock scrip received as a taxable dividend, in lieu of accrued interest, or in another taxable transaction is treated as income in the year received[86] and obtains a new holding period.

(b) WASH SALES

For securities acquired in wash sales subject to I.R.C. § 1091, the holding period rules are somewhat modified. If a taxpayer sells securities at a loss and also purchases substantially identical securities, the loss might be disallowed under the wash sales rule of I.R.C. § 1091.[87] If the loss is disallowed, the holding period for the loss securities is tacked onto the taxpayer's holding period for the substantially identical property.[88] To the extent that the holding periods for the loss securities and substantially identical securities overlap, the holding period for the loss securities is not tacked onto the holding period of the substantially identical securities. This assures that the holding period for the loss securities is not counted twice.

A fractional month computation of a holding period is allowed for wash sales. This is because the holding period for wash sales of securities is based on the aggregate of the holding period before the sale and the holding period after the purchase.[89] The sum of these two fractional periods must add up to more than six months or more than 12 months (depending upon the required holding period) for substantially identical property to obtain a long-term capital gain or loss.

(c) SHORT SALES

The short sales rule provided under I.R.C. § 1233 establishes separate rules for determining a taxpayer's holding period. For a discussion of the short sales rule, see generally Chapter 16.

---

[85]Rev. Rul. 69-202, 1969-1 C.B. 95.

[86]Andrews v. Comm'r, 135 F.2d 314, 317 (2d Cir. 1943), *cert. denied,* 320 U.S. 748 (1943); Patterson v. Anderson, 20 F. Supp. 799, 801 (S.D.N.Y. 1937).

[87]*See generally* Chapter 17.

[88]I.R.C. § 1223(4).

[89]I.R.C. § 1223(4).

(d) MODIFIED WASH SALES AND SHORT SALES RULES

The modified wash sales and short sales rules established under I.R.C. § 1092(b) prescribe special holding periods for positions in personal property that are parts of straddles. For a discussion of the modified wash sales and short sales rules, see generally Chapter 42.

§ 15.5 SECTION 1256 CONTRACTS

Section 1256 contracts that are capital assets in the hands of a taxpayer generate, without regard to the taxpayer's holding period, 60 percent long-term and 40 percent short-term capital gain or loss. For a discussion of section 1256 contracts, see generally Part Nine. Property acquired pursuant to the exercise of or delivery under a long section 1256 contract position obtains a new holding period and does not get a tacked holding period that would include the time during which the taxpayer held the long section 1256 contracts.[90]

§ 15.6 REGULATED INVESTMENT COMPANIES

Special holding period requirements apply to taxpayers who own shares in a regulated investment company after they receive a capital gain dividend from the company. To obtain a short-term capital loss on the sale of shares in a regulated investment company that has paid a capital gain dividend, the taxpayer must hold the shares (without any offsetting short position) for at least 31 days.[91] This holding period requirement is designed to prevent a taxpayer who holds shares in a regulated investment company from creating short-term capital losses by purchasing shares in a regulated investment company immediately prior to an ex-dividend date and selling the shares immediately after the ex-dividend date, thereby reporting a short-term capital loss on the sale and long-term capital gain on the dividend.[92]

[90]I.R.C. § 1223(8).
[91]I.R.C. § 852(b)(4).
[92]For a discussion of this technique, see section 22.9.

§ 15.7 INTERCORPORATE DIVIDENDS

In order for a corporate taxpayer to obtain a deduction for intercorporate dividends received from another corporation under I.R.C. §§ 243, 233, or 245, the corporate taxpayer must hold the stock with respect to which the dividend is received for more than 45 days.[93] Furthermore, in the case of any stock with a preference in dividends, the required holding period to obtain the dividends received deduction is increased to more than 90 days.[94] For a discussion of the dividends received deduction, see section 22.9. To determine the holding period of a corporation's stock, several rules are applied. First, the day that the stock is disposed of, but not its day of acquisition, is taken into account.[95] Second, no day that is more than 45 days (or 90 days in the case of stock with a dividends preference) after the date the stock becomes ex-dividend is taken into account.[96] And third, the tacked on holding period rule of I.R.C. § 1223(4) for wash sales of securities is not applied.[97] The 46-day period (or 91-day period for certain preferred stock) does not include any period during which the taxpayer reduces the risk of loss from holding the stock by (1) entering into a short sale, acquiring an option to sell, or entering into a binding contract to sell substantially identical stock or securities; (2) granting an option to buy substantially identical stock or securities, subject to an exception for qualified covered call options,[98] without regard to the requirement that gain or loss on the option not be ordinary; or (3) being prescribed by Treasury regulations, by reason of holding one or more other positions in substantially similar or related property.[99]

The DRA amendments to the dividends received deduction contemplate that the regulations setting forth the application of the rule for substantially similar or related property will be effective as of July 18, 1984, but that the regulations will be applied to other transactions on

---

[93]I.R.C. § 246(c)(1)(A).

[94]I.R.C. § 246(c)(2).

[95]I.R.C. § 246(c)(3)(A).

[96]I.R.C. § 246(c)(3)(B).

[97]I.R.C. § 246(c)(3)(C); *see* section 15.4(b).

[98]*See* section 44.3.

[99]I.R.C. § 246(c)(4); STAFF OF THE JOINT COMMITTEE ON TAXATION, 98th CONG. 2D SESS., GENERAL EXPLANATION OF THE REVENUE PROVISIONS OF THE DEFICIT REDUCTION ACT OF 1984 142 (Joint Comm. Print 1984) [hereinafter referred to as "General Explanation of DRA"].

a prospective basis.[100] The Joint Committee Report on the DRA provides examples of the types of transactions that are within the scope of the rule for substantially similar or related property. First, a short sale of common stock when the taxpayer holds convertible preferred stock of the same issuer and the price changes of the convertible preferred stock and common stock are related qualify as substantially similar or related property.[101] Second, the short sale of a convertible debenture while holding stock into which the debenture is convertible is substantially similar or related property.[102] Third, the short sale of convertible preferred stock while holding common stock is substantially similar or related property.[103] Fourth, a short position in a regulated futures contract on a stock index (or option to sell the regulated futures contract or index itself) while holding the stock of an investment company whose principal holdings mimic the performance of the stocks is substantially similar or related property.[104]

The Joint Committee Report on the DRA, in its examples of transactions established after July 18, 1984 that are within the scope of the rule for substantially similar or related property, provides that a deep-in-the-money option to buy a stock index regulated futures contract or the stock index, itself, is substantially similar or related to the stock of an investment company whose principal holdings mimic the performance of the stocks included in the index.[105] In Rev. Rul. 80-238,[106] the IRS ruled that writing call options on stock held by a corporate taxpayer does not reduce the corporation's holding period for purposes of I.R.C. § 246(c)(1)(A). Short call option positions are treated as a short sale of substantially identical securities and the corporation is not under a contractual obligation to sell the stock.[107] Writing call options does not place the writer in a risk free position. The ruling was limited to calls that were not in-the-money because the IRS believed that the exercise of in-the-money calls may be virtually guaranteed and the element of risk is either greatly reduced or eliminated.[108] The Joint Committee Report on the DRA views deep-in-the-money call options as substan-

---

[100]*Id.* at 143.
[101]*Id.*
[102]*Id.*
[103]*Id.*
[104]*Id.*
[105]*Id.*
[106]1980-2 C.B. 96.
[107]*Id.*
[108]*Id.*

tially similar to the underlying property for transactions entered into after July 18, 1984. The DRA contemplates that Treasury regulations setting forth the application of the rule for substantially similar or related property will be effective as of July 18, 1984, but that Treasury regulations (when promulgated) will be applied to other transactions on a prospective basis.[109] It is important to note that the Joint Committee Report makes it clear that "[n]o inference was intended regarding the circumstances under which the dividends received deduction would be disallowed under prior law where taxpayers wrote in-the-money calls with respect to stock they held."[110]

In LTR 8610016,[111] the IRS ruled that the convertible features on CAPS are not to be treated as options for tax purposes. As a result, the intercorporate dividends received deduction is available to corporate CAPS owners.

§ 15.8   SECURITIES LENDING TRANSACTIONS

If a taxpayer (referred to as a "lender") lends his securities in a transaction that qualifies for nonrecognition of gain or loss under I.R.C. § 1058 and identical securities are returned to him, his holding period for the securities delivered back to him includes both his holding period for the original securities and the period during which his original securities were lent.[112] If the terms of a loan transaction qualify under I.R.C. § 1058 but the borrower does not return identical securities or otherwise defaults under the agreement, the lender's holding period terminates on the date of the default and the borrower's holding period begins on that date.[113] A transfer that does not qualify under I.R.C. § 1058 is treated as a sale on the date of the transfer. As a result, if the transfer of securities does not comply with I.R.C. § 1058, the lender's holding period terminates on the day when the securities are transferred to the borrower and the borrower's holding period begins on that date.[114]

---

[109]General Explanation of DRA, *supra* note 99, at 143.

[110]*Id.*

[111](Nov. 29, 1985).

[112]Prop. Treas. Reg. § 1.1223-2(a) (1983). For a discussion of security loan transactions, see generally Chapter 24.

[113]Prop. Treas. Reg. § 1.1223-2(b)(2) (1983).

[114]Prop. Treas. Reg. § 1.1223-2(b)(1) (1983).

Sixteen

Short Sales of Capital Assets

The short sales rule was enacted to prevent a taxpayer from reporting a capital gain at long-term rates after making a short sale and holding it open for the long-term holding period.[1] Prior to enactment of the short sales rule, a taxpayer could sell property substantially identical to his long position, thereby locking in a predetermined gain on the long position. And without a short sales rule, a taxpayer could keep the short position open for the long-term holding period to assure long-term gain on the property sold short. The result was the same if the initial transaction was a short sale.[2]

§ 16.1 COORDINATION WITH MODIFIED SHORT SALES RULE

If a short sale is entered into as part of a straddle,[3] the modified short sales rule under I.R.C. § 1092(b) is applied in lieu of the short sale provisions of I.R.C. § 1233. Property subject to the short sales rule does not include any position to which the modified short sales rule applies.[4]

[1] SENATE FINANCE COMMITTEE REPORT, REVENUE ACT OF 1950, S. REP. NO. 2375, 81st Cong., 2d Sess. 44, *reprinted in* 1950 U.S. CODE CONG. & AD. NEWS 3053, 3231.

[2] *Id.* For a discussion of the trading tactics currently used by some short sellers, see The Wall St. J., Sept. 5, 1985, at 1, col. 6.

[3] *See generally* Part Ten.

[4] I.R.C. § 1233(e)(2).

As a result, the scope of the short sales rule is limited to short sales not otherwise covered by the modified short sales rule; it still applies to short sales of stock. With the DRA's expansion of the Straddle Rules to stock options and certain stock positions,[5] the scope of the short sales rule has been substantially reduced. For a discussion of the modified short sales rule, see section 42.4. In addition, qualified covered calls[6] are exempt from the Straddle Rules and, therefore, the modified short sales rule.

Many transactions previously subject to the short sales rule are instead subject to the modified short sales rule. Hence, many of the issues over whether certain securities products are "property" subject to the short sales rule are of historical significance only. For example, the issue of whether options were subject to the short sales rule was important in pre-DRA planning. If an options position was not viewed as a security, the short sales rule did not apply. Now that stock options are subject to the Straddle Rules, such positions are "property" for purposes of the Straddle Rules. They are now subject to the modified short sales rule, which applies the principles of I.R.C. § 1233 to straddle transactions.[7]

§ 16.2   OPERATION OF SHORT SALES RULE

The short sales rule, in fact, comprises three separate rules, which are referred to in this book as Rules 1, 2, and 3. Rule 1 provides that gain from closing a short sale is short-term capital gain even if the property used to close the short sale is a long-term capital asset in the hands of the taxpayer.[8] Rule 2 provides that the holding period of substantially identical property begins on the earlier to occur of the closing of a short sale or the disposition of the property.[9] Rule 3 provides that any loss on closing a short sale is a long-term loss if substantially identical property has been held for the long-term holding period and the property delivered to close the short sale was held for less than the long-term holding period.[10] These rules (collectively referred to as the "short sales rule") are discussed in this chapter.

---

[5]*See* section 36.2(c).
[6]*See* section 44.3.
[7]I.R.C. § 1092(b)(1).
[8]I.R.C. § 1233(b)(1).
[9]I.R.C. § 1233(b)(2).
[10]I.R.C. § 1233(d).

(a) SHORT SALE DEFINED

A short sale is a contract for the sale of property that the seller does not own or that is not delivered at the settlement date.[11]

Example   16-1

A taxpayer sells 100 shares of XYZ stock for $1000. He does not own the stock so he borrows stock from a lender (typically through his broker) to deliver to the buyer on the settlement date. The taxpayer has made a short sale. Three months later he buys 100 shares of XYZ stock in the stock market and closes the short sale by delivering the identical shares back to the lender.

A short sale against the box is a short sale that is entered into when the seller owns the property sold short but does not intend to deliver it to cover the sale.

Example   16-2

A taxpayer owns 100 shares of XYZ stock. He sells short 100 shares of XYZ stock and borrows stock from a lender (typically through his broker) to deliver to the buyer on the settlement date. The taxpayer has made a short sale against the box. Three months later the taxpayer closes the short sale by delivering his shares of XYZ stock to the lender.

With a short sale, property is borrowed to deliver to the buyer at the settlement date.[12] The short sale is ultimately closed by either a market purchase or, in the case of a short sale against the box, by the delivery of the property not previously delivered to the buyer.[13] It is possible with a short sale against the box for a taxpayer to lock in a gain (or loss) in one year, while deferring recognition of the gain (or loss) until the second year.

Example   16-3

A taxpayer owns 100 shares of XYZ stock with a tax basis of $50 per share. On November 1st, XYZ stock is trading at $100 per share, which the taxpayer believes is high in relation to XYZ's true value. The tax-

[11]Provost v. U.S., 269 U.S. 443, 450–51 (1926).
[12]See generally Chapter 24.
[13]See Provost, 269 U.S. at 453; Rev. Rul. 72-478, 1972-2 C.B. 288.

payer believes the stock will decline in value. Although he wants to lock in a gain of $50 per share, he does not want to report the gain until the next taxable year. The taxpayer sells short 100 shares of XYZ stock for $100 per share (i.e., he does not deliver the shares he owns). In the second year he closes out the short sale with the shares he owns.[14] The $50,000 gain, although fixed in the first year, is not taxable until the short sale is closed in the second year.

Whether a short sale is subject to the short sales rule depends on the facts and circumstances of each case. Some applications of the short sales rule are mentioned in the remainder of this section. A taxpayer who sold put options on British pounds to his broker more than six months after the original short sale, but before the short sale closed, was subject to the short sales rule.[15] The sale was not viewed as bona fide. Although the broker closed the short sale, the taxpayer remained fully liable for any loss and the broker had no economic exposure on the transaction.[16] The covering purchase of British pounds was viewed as the acquisition of substantially identical property, thereby producing short-term capital gain.[17] The short sales rule did not apply to a corporation that sold foreign currency forward contracts held for more than six months.[18] The sales were bona fide; the seller had no continuing liability, and the seller never held, at the time of or after the short sale, substantially identical property.[19] In addition, the short sales rule, not I.R.C. § 1242 (granting ordinary loss on stock in a small business investment company), applies when a taxpayer acquires substantially identical stock to close a short sale in a small business investment company.[20] The short sales rule also applies to the short sale of regulated investment company shares.[21]

(b) PROPERTY SUBJECT TO THE SHORT SALES RULE

Capital assets are defined generally as all classes of property not specifically enumerated in I.R.C. § 1221. It does not include inventory,

[14]To avoid application of the wash sales rule, the taxpayer must not enter into any other transactions in XYZ stock within 30 days before or 30 days after the short sale is closed. *See* section 17.3(f).

[15]La Grange v. Comm'r, 26 T.C. 191 (1956).

[16]*Id.* at 197.

[17]*See id.*

[18]American Home Products Corp. v. U.S., 601 F.2d 540, 548 (Ct. Cl. 1979).

[19]*Id.* at 547; *accord* Carborundum Co. v. Comm'r, 74 T.C. 730, 737-38 (1980).

[20]Rev. Rul. 63-65, 1963-1 C.B. 142. *See* section 25.6.

[21]*Id. See* section 6.9.

property used in a trade or business, copyrights, and accounts or notes receivable acquired in the ordinary course of a trade or business.[22] Property subject to the short sales rule is limited to securities (including when-issued securities) and futures contracts that are capital assets in the hands of the taxpayer. In addition, because the short sales rule does not include any property subject to the Straddle Rules (which includes the modified short sales rule),[23] property otherwise subject to both the short sales rule and modified short sales rule is only subject to the modified short sales rule. Hence, the short sales rule only applies to stock, securities, and futures contracts (if any) not subject to the modified short sales rule.

(c) CLOSING A SHORT SALE

A short sale remains open until the short seller delivers the property to the lender.[24] Loss on a short sale is determined in the year the property is delivered and not the year when the short seller borrows property to cover the short position. In other words, loss on the short sale is fixed when the short sale is closed by delivering property to replace property borrowed to cover the short position;[25] no gain or loss is realized until the short seller closes the transaction.[26] The IRS has ruled that if a short seller dies before delivering property to close a short sale, the short sale is not closed until the decedent's estate or the beneficiary delivers the property.[27] In addition, the unrealized gain or loss at the decedent's death is not treated as "income in respect of a decedent" under I.R.C. § 691.[28]

The conversion of convertible preferred stock into when-issued common stock prior to closing a short sale is not the acquisition of substantially identical property within the meaning of the short sales rule if certain conditions are met.[29] First, the taxpayer must have sold short when-issued common stock while he holds (or later acquires) preferred stock. And second, the preferred stock must be convertible into stock that is substantially identical to the when-issued common stock he sold

---

[22]I.R.C. § 1221.

[23]I.R.C. § 1233(e)(2)(A); *see* section 42.4.

[24]Treas. Reg. § 1.1233-1(a)(1) (1980).

[25]Hendricks v. Comm'r, 51 T.C. 235, 241 (1968), *aff'd*, 423 F.2d 485 (4th Cir. 1970).

[26]Comm'r v. Levis's Estate, 127 F.2d 796, 797 (2d Cir.), *cert. denied*, 314 U.S. 645 (1942).

[27]Rev. Rul. 73-524, 1973-2 C.B. 307.

[28]*See generally* I.R.C. § 691.

[29]Rev. Rul. 62-153, 1962-2 C.B. 186.

short.[30] If preferred stock and the when-issued common stock are substantially identical at the time of the short sale (or at the time the preferred stock is acquired if acquired after the short sale but prior to closing the short sale), then Rule 1 and Rule 2 are applied to adjust the character and holding period of the gains or losses.[31]

§ 16.3 CHARACTER OF GAINS, LOSSES, AND HOLDING PERIOD

(a) GAINS ON SHORT SALES

Under Rule 1 any gain on closing a short sale is treated as gain from the sale or exchange of a short-term capital asset, notwithstanding the period of time the property used to close the short sale was actually held by the taxpayer.[32] Gain on substantially identical property in excess of the amount needed to cover the short sale is not subject to the short sales rule.[33]

(b) HOLDING PERIOD

Under Rule 2 the holding period of substantially identical property held or acquired within the prohibited period does not begin until the date the short sale is closed or on the first to occur of the date of sale, gift, or other disposition of the property.[34] The holding period adjustment is made in the order the property was acquired in an amount equal to the property sold short.

(c) LOSSES ON SHORT SALES

If a taxpayer holds substantially identical property for more than the long-term holding period on the date of a short sale, Rule 3 requires that any loss on closing the short sale is a long-term capital loss.[35] The character of any loss on substantially identical property used to close a short sale in excess of the short sale amount is not affected.[36]

[30]*Id.*
[31]*Id.*
[32]I.R.C. § 1233(b)(1).
[33]I.R.C. § 1233(e)(1).
[34]I.R.C. § 1233(b)(2); *see* section 15.4(c).
[35]I.R.C. § 1233(d).
[36]I.R.C. § 1233(e)(1).

Example 16-4

Assume that a taxpayer (1) buys 100 shares of ABC stock at $10 per share on February 1st, (2) sells short 100 shares of ABC stock at $16 per share on July 1st, (3) closes the short sale on August 1st (with 100 shares of ABC stock purchased on that date at $18 per share), and (4) on August 2nd sells the 100 shares of ABC stock purchased on February 1st at $18 per share. The $200 loss incurred on closing the short sale is a short-term capital loss. The holding period of the 100 shares of stock purchased on February 1st and sold on August 2nd begins to run on August 2nd (the date the short sale is closed). The $800 gain realized upon the sale of the stock purchased on February 1st is a short-term capital gain.

§ 16.4 PROPERTY COVERED

The short sales rule applies only to stock and securities (including when-issued securities)[37] and futures contracts that are capital assets in the hands of the taxpayer.[38] It does not apply to physical commodities. The remainder of this section discusses property interests technically covered by the short sales rule. However, because certain positions are subject to the modified short sales rule, these rules apply instead of the short sales rule. For a discussion of the modified short sales rule, see section 42.4. For a detailed discussion of substantially identical property, see section 17.9.

(a) STOCK OR SECURITIES

"Stock or securities" is not defined for purposes of the short sales rule. It is defined, however, for purposes of a security dealer's investment account. It includes shares of stock in any corporation, certificates of stock or interest in any corporation, notes, bonds, debentures, or evidences of indebtedness, or any evidence of an interest in or right to subscribe to, or purchase, any of the foregoing.[39] In addition, I.R.C. § 1233(e)(4) (addressing application of the short sales rule to dealers) defines "stock" in essentially the same manner. The phrase "stock or securities" appears in numerous other Code provisions and Treasury regulations for purposes of corporate transactions. For example, the

---

[37]*See* section 1.3(g).

[38]I.R.C. § 1233(e)(2)(A).

[39]I.R.C. § 1236(c). For a discussion of investment accounts, see section 9.7.

same definition is used in I.R.C. §§ 351, 354 and 361.[40] For purposes of corporate transactions, short-term notes are not viewed as securities, that is, equity interests.[41]

Warrants and stock rights are also viewed as securities for a security dealer's investment account, although they are not securities for purposes of I.R.C. §§ 351, 354, and 361.[42] It is not clear from reading the statutory provision whether I.R.C. § 1233 contemplates the inclusion of warrants and stock rights in the short sales rule, although I.R.C. § 1233 does include when-issued securities.[43] However, it is not logical for Congress to have included when-issued securities under the short sales rule without including warrants and stock rights. Therefore, it is safe to assume that the broader definition of a security more closely reflects the types of securities subject to the short sales rule.

(b) WHEN-ISSUED SECURITIES

When-issued securities are subject to the short sales rule.[44] In addition, the contracts to sell securities on a when-issued basis (short position) are considered to be short sales. Performance under or assignment of when-issued securities contracts are viewed as the closing of a short sale.[45] The Tax Court has similarly concluded that a short sale includes a sale of when-issued securities.[46] When-issued securities may be subject to the modified short sales rule.[47]

(c) OPTIONS

The acquisition of a put option (long position) granting the holder the right to sell property at a fixed price is considered a short sale.[48] The exercise or failure to exercise a long put option position is treated as

---

[40]*See* Lloyd-Smith v. Comm'r, 116 F.2d 642, 643 (2d Cir.), *cert. denied*, 313 U.S. 588 (1941).

[41]Pinellas Ice & Cold Storage Co. v. Comm'r, 287 U.S. 462, 468-69 (1933); Treas. Reg. § 1.368-1(b) (1980).

[42]Treas. Reg. § 1.351-1(a)(1) (1967).

[43]I.R.C. § 1233(e)(2).

[44]I.R.C. § 1233(e)(2)(A); *see* section 1.3(g).

[45]S. Rep. No. 2375, *supra* note 1, at 87.

[46]*See* Stavisky v. Comm'r, 34 T.C. 140, 144 (1960).

[47]When-issued securities are interests in securities and the exception from application of the Straddle Rules for certain stock positions is limited to stock, not interests in stock. *See* section 36.2(c); section 42.4.

[48]I.R.C. § 1233(b).

the closing of a short sale.[49] Option positions are subject to the modified short sales rule.[50]

Example   16-5

A taxpayer owns stock that he has held for less than the long-term holding period. He acquires a put option (long position). The taxpayer's holding period in the underlying stock is lost and does not start until he disposes of the put.

The acquisition of a put is not considered to be a short sale for purposes of reclassifying losses as long-term under Rule 3 and its exercise or failure to exercise is not a closing of a short sale.[51] Call options are not viewed as substantially identical property, so call options are not subject to the short sales rule.[52]

The purchase of a put option to sell stock acquired upon the exercise of a restricted stock option is not a disposition of the stock.[53] Rather, a disposition occurs when the put is exercised.[54] With respect to call options, a long call option position is not substantially identical to the underlying securities for purposes of the short sales rule.[55] Consequently, the holding period of the call option is not affected by short sales of the underlying securities. Option positions generally are subject to the modified short sales rule,[56] although qualified covered calls are exempt from the Straddle Rules, including the modified short sales rule.[57]

(d) MARRIED PUT TRANSACTIONS

The married put exception, enacted in 1954, allows a taxpayer to avoid the Rule 2 termination of the holding period of underlying stock that otherwise occurs when buying a put. As a result, a taxpayer with a married put transaction can receive long-term capital gain on the un-

---

[49]I.R.C. § 1233(b); Treas. Reg. § 1.1233-1(c)(3) (1980); Rev. Rul. 78-182, 1978-1 C.B. 265.

[50]*See* section 42.4.

[51]I.R.C. § 1233(d); Treas. Reg. § 1.1233-1(c)(4) (1980).

[52]*See* section 17.9(f).

[53]Rev. Rul. 59-242, 1959-2 C.B. 125.

[54]*Id.*

[55]Rev. Rul. 58-384, 1958-2 C.B. 410.

[56]*See* section 42.4.

[57]I.R.C. § 1092(c)(4); *see* section 44.3.

derlying property even though he has reduced his risk of loss on owning such property. The taxpayer can earn any future appreciation in the underlying property and the put provides him with some price insurance if it declines in value. At this writing it is unclear whether this exception is available for put options subject to the Straddle Rules.[58]

Put options eligible for the married put exception are exempt from the short sales rule if two conditions are met. First, the taxpayer must acquire property identified as property intended for use in exercising the put option on the same day that the put is purchased.[59] If the option itself does not specifically identify the property intended to be used in exercising the option, the taxpayer's records must identify the position within 15 days after the property is acquired.[60] Second, if the put is exercised, the property so identified is delivered under the option.[61] If the option is not exercised, its cost is added to the basis of the property with which the option is identified.[62]

(e) FUTURES CONTRACTS

The short sales rule applies to futures contracts that have identical delivery months if the contracts are capital assets in the hands of the taxpayer. Futures contracts requiring delivery in one calendar month are not viewed as substantially identical to futures contracts requiring delivery in another calendar month. As a result, such futures contracts are not subject to the short sales rule.[63] For example, futures contracts in May wheat are not substantially identical to futures contracts in July wheat.[64] Because all futures contracts are section 1256 contracts, futures contracts are subject to section 1256 treatment and straddles consisting of the futures contracts are not subject to the modified short sales rule.[65] Futures contracts that are part of mixed straddles may be subject to the modified short sales rule.[66]

Although futures contracts are not defined for purposes of the short sales rule, the Code and Treasury regulations refer to "futures trans-

[58]*See* section 44.4.
[59]I.R.C. § 1233(c).
[60]Treas. Reg. § 1.1233-1(c)(3) (1980).
[61]I.R.C. § 1233(c).
[62]Special Ruling, 9 STAND. FED. TAX REP. (CCH) ¶ 6596 (Sept. 7, 1973).
[63]I.R.C. § 1233(e)(2); *see* section 4.3(c).
[64]Treas. Reg. § 1.1233-1(d)(2)(i) (1980).
[65]I.R.C. § 1233(e)(2)(B); Treas. Reg. § 1.1233-1(d)(2)(i) (1980).
[66]*See* section 44.7; Chapter 45.

actions in any commodity on or subject to a board of trade or commodity exchange" as property that is covered by the short sales rule.[67]

(1) HEDGES

Futures contracts for commodities that are not generally used as hedges for each other (such as corn and wheat) are not viewed as substantially identical property.[68] Treasury regulations suggest, however, that those commodities that are generally used as hedges for each other are considered as substantially identical.[69]

(2) DIFFERENT BROKERS

The mere fact that futures contracts are traded through different brokers does not remove them from the scope of the term "substantially identical property."[70] As a result, all of a taxpayer's positions are considered in the aggregate.

(3) DIFFERENT MARKETS

Futures contracts traded in different markets can be viewed as "substantially identical property."[71] The primary factor in determining substantial identity is the historical similarity in the price movements in the markets.[72]

(4) FUTURES ARBITRAGE TRANSACTIONS

A taxpayer establishes a futures arbitrage transaction if he enters into two futures contract transactions on the same day—one requires delivery in one market and the other requires delivery of the same (or substantially identical) commodity in the same delivery month in a different market.[73] If the taxpayer subsequently closes both positions on the same day, the short sales rule is not applied.[74] The provision covering

---

[67]*See* section 42.4.

[68]*Id.*

[69]*Id.* For a discussion of hedging transactions, see section 6.4.

[70]Treas. Reg. § 1.1233-1(d)(2)(i) (1980).

[71]*Id.*

[72]*Id.*

[73]I.R.C. § 1233(e)(3).

[74]*Id.*; Treas. Reg. § 1.1233-1(d)(2)(ii) (1980).

arbitrage operations in stocks or securities under I.R.C. § 1233(f) does not apply to futures arbitrage operations.[75] Instead, I.R.C. § 1233(e)(3) applies.

This futures arbitrage provision is basically irrelevant now that section 1256 treatment applies to all futures contracts traded on domestic commodity exchanges.[76] As a result, all gain or loss is marked-to-market at year–end and the short sales rule is irrelevant.[77] In addition, futures contracts that are part of mixed straddles are subject to the modified short sales rule.

(f) COMMODITIES

Physical commodity transactions are not subject to the short sales rule.[78] Physical commodities are not "property" for I.R.C. § 1233 purposes. A purchase of a spot or a cash commodity and a sale of a futures contract is outside the scope of the short sales rule. As a result, such transactions were used under pre-ERTA law to defer current taxation. Under current law, however, to the extent a physical commodity is sold short, the modified short sales rule applies.[79]

§ 16.5 SUBSTANTIALLY IDENTICAL PROPERTY

The term "substantially identical property" is not defined in I.R.C. § 1233 for purposes of the short sales rule. Treasury regulations provide that the term is to be applied according to the facts and circumstances of each case.[80] In addition, the concept of substantially identical property is to be applied similarly to the way it is applied for wash sales.[81] Although the short sales rule borrows the wash sales definition of substantially identical property, the short sales rule includes futures contracts not covered by the wash sales rule.

---

[75]See section 16.10.

[76]See generally Part Nine.

[77]Straddles consisting exclusively of section 1256 contracts are exempt from the Straddle Rules. See section 44.7.

[78]See section 43.2.

[79]I.R.C. § 1092(b)(1).

[80]Treas. Reg. § 1.1233-1(d)(1) (1980).

[81]Id. See section 17.9.

§ 16.6 EXPENSES AND PAYMENTS

(a) EXPENSES

Certain items, such as, payments for dividends, interest, and other distributions, are paid to a lender of securities for the use of securities borrowed to cover short sales.[82] The lender generally treats these payments as a fee for the temporary use of the property and reports them as ordinary income.[83] These expenses are deductible by the borrower under certain circumstances. Dividends paid by a borrower of securities in a short sales transaction can be ordinary and necessary business expenses or section 212 expenses.[84] Payments in the ordinary course of business are deductible under I.R.C. § 162(a), while payments that qualify as section 212 expenses are deductible under I.R.C. § 212.[85] However, these expenses must be capitalized in certain circumstances. For a discussion of when these expenses must be capitalized, see section 16.6(e). For a discussion of the impact of short sales on the dividends received deduction for corporate lenders, see section 22.9.

If the motive behind a short sale is tax avoidance rather than a profit, expenses are not deductible under any circumstances.[86] For a dealer or trader, such expenses do not qualify as ordinary and necessary business expenses under I.R.C. § 162; for an investor, they do not qualify as expenses paid or incurred for the production of income under I.R.C. § 212.[87]

(b) PREMIUMS

Loan premiums paid in connection with stock borrowed to cover short sales are deductible.[88]

---

[82]For the tax treatment of payments made to the lender of securities, see generally Chapter 24.

[83]Prop. Treas. Reg. § 1.1058-1(d) (1983).

[84]Comm'r v. Wilson, 163 F.2d 680, 682 (9th Cir. 1947).

[85]*See* section 6.1; section 6.2.

[86]*See* Gold v. Comm'r, 41 T.C. 419, 428 (1963).

[87]*See* Hart v. Comm'r, 41 T.C. 131 (1963), *aff'd*, 338 F.2d 410 (2d Cir. 1964); Shapiro v. Comm'r, 40 T.C. 34 (1963).

[88]Rev. Rul. 72-521, 1972-2 C.B. 178.

(c) STOCK DIVIDENDS AND LIQUIDATING DIVIDENDS

A borrower of securities who pays a lender an amount in lieu of a complete or partial liquidating distribution actually discharges all or part of his obligation to the lender of the securities.[89] The additional shares purchased in the case of a nontaxable stock dividend and the payment in the case of a liquidating dividend are payments to replace principal amounts loaned. The amount paid by the taxpayer to replace the underlying property is a capital expenditure and is not deductible. Payments in lieu of a liquidating dividend are not viewed as a carrying charge (e.g., interest) on the outstanding balance of borrowed securities, because a stock dividend or liquidating dividend requires a borrower to compensate the lender for the reduction in capital represented by each share of stock to be returned.[90]

Corporations might not be entitled to a deduction for payments made in lieu of liquidating dividends unless they are dealers in securities. In *Main Line Distributors, Inc. v. Comm'r,*[91] the court held that for a corporation to be able to deduct amounts paid in lieu of liquidating dividends, it must be a dealer in securities (or its trading of securities must constitute a trade or business). The court found that Main Line was not a dealer in securities, and the liquidating distribution was not an ordinary and necessary expense incurred in the course of its trade or business.[92] The court implied that if the corporation had been a dealer in securities, an ordinary deduction would have been available.[93]

(d) CASH DIVIDENDS

Payments in lieu of cash dividends from a borrower of securities on a short sale must be capitalized under the provisions of I.R.C. § 263(h).[94] For transactions entered into prior to July 18, 1984, a deduction was available to the borrower of securities. The IRS has ruled that a borrower can deduct amounts equal to cash dividends received by the borrower when paid upon closing a short sale as required by I.R.C. § 1058.[95]

[89]1955 Production Exposition, Inc. v. Comm'r, 41 T.C. 85, 89-90 (1963).

[90]Rev. Rul. 72-521, 1972-2 C.B. 178.

[91]321 F.2d 562, 566 (6th Cir. 1963).

[92]*Id.*

[93]*See id.*

[94]For a discussion of the capitalization requirement, see section 16.6(e).

[95]Rev. Rul. 62-42, 1962-1 C.B. 133; *see* Comm'r v. Wiesler, 161 F.2d 997, 1000 (6th Cir. 1947); *see also* Chapter 24.

(e) CAPITALIZATION OF SHORT SALE PAYMENTS IN LIEU OF DIVIDENDS

(1) GENERAL REQUIREMENTS

Prior to the DRA, amounts paid for the use of stock or to reimburse the lender for dividends paid on borrowed stock were deductible expenses.[96] A dealer or trader would deduct these expenses as ordinary and necessary business expenses under I.R.C. § 162(a), while an investor would deduct these expenses under I.R.C. § 212.[97] The DRA requires capitalization of certain payments made in lieu of dividends for certain short sales of stock. Payments made in lieu of regular dividends on stock sold short after July 18, 1984 are only deductible if the short sale is closed out more than 45 days after the date of the short sale.[98] If the short sale is closed out within the 45-day period, however, the basis of the stock used to close the short sale is increased by the payment amount that is not deductible.[99]

Allowable deductions for short sale payments made by investors are treated as investment interest expenses subject to investment interest expense limitations.[100] Interest expenses related to purchasing and carrying tax-exempt securities, however, are not deductible.[101]

(2) EXTRAORDINARY DIVIDENDS

Payments made in lieu of extraordinary dividends are not deductible unless the short sale period is held open for more than one year.[102] An extraordinary dividend is any dividend on a share of stock that equals or exceeds the amount realized on the short sale of the stock by (1) five percent for preferred stock dividends, (2) 10 percent for any common stock dividends, and (3) 20 percent for aggregate dividends in a 365-day period.[103] I.R.C. § 1059(c) defines an extraordinary dividend as any

---

[96]For a discussion of the tax treatment to lenders of securities, see generally Chapter 24.

[97]See Comm'r v. Wiesler, 161 F.2d at 1000; Dart v. Comm'r, 74 F.2d 845, 847 (4th Cir. 1935); Rev. Rul. 72-521, 1972-2 C.B. 178; Rev. Rul. 62-42, 1962-1 C.B. 133. Contra Comm'r v. Levis's Estate, 127 F.2d at 797.

[98]See I.R.C. § 263(h)(1).

[99]I.R.C. § 263(h)(1).

[100]I.R.C. § 163(d)(3)(D)(ii); section 7.2(e); section 8.2(e); section 9.2.

[101]I.R.C. § 265(2); section 7.3; section 8.3; section 9.3.

[102]I.R.C. § 263(h)(2).

[103]I.R.C. §§ 263(h)(3), 1059(c).

dividend that equals or exceeds the so-called threshold percentage of the taxpayer's adjusted basis in the stock. For purposes of I.R.C. § 263(h)(2), the amount realized on the short sale of the stock is substituted for the adjusted basis requirement of I.R.C. § 1059(c).[104] For extraordinary dividends, the period during which a deduction is not available for payments made in lieu of a dividend is extended from 45 days to one year after the short sale date.[105] Failure to meet the required time period to hold a short sale open forces the expenses to be added to the basis of the stock used to close the short sale. Because substantial economic risks are involved in keeping a short sale open for more than one year, I.R.C. § 263(h)(2) may stop the use of short sales in the case of extraordinary dividend situations.

(3)   SUSPENSION OF HOLDING PERIOD

Where the risk of loss on holding a position is diminished because the taxpayer holds substantially similar property or an option to buy (or is under a contractual obligation to buy) substantially identical stock or securities, the running of the 45-day period is suspended for ordinary dividends (or the one year period for extraordinary dividends). The holding period does not commence running again until the taxpayer no longer holds substantially identical or similar stock or securities.[106] For a discussion of reduced risk while holding substantially similar property, see section 15.7 and section 22.9.

(4)   SHORT STOCK REBATES

Short sale payments are added to the basis of stock used to close a short sale if the payments or other distributions exceed the amount of income from the short stock rebate received by the taxpayer, and then only if the following two requirements are met. First, the amount received must exceed the amount that is treated as ordinary income by the taxpayer.[107] Second, the income must be received by the taxpayer "as compensation for the use of any collateral with respect to any stock used in a short sale."[108] A deduction is allowable to the extent of ordinary income from

---

[104]I.R.C. § 263(h)(3); *see* section 14.6.

[105]I.R.C. § 263(h)(2).

[106]I.R.C. § 263(h)(4).

[107]I.R.C. § 263(h)(5)(A).

[108]*Id.*

amounts paid by the broker for the use of the collateral.[109] This exception is not available for payments or other distributions made with respect to an extraordinary dividend.[110]

Example   16-6

A taxpayer purchases a call option, sells stock short and sells a put option, all in the same corporation. He incurs interest expense on the call position and earns income from the short stock position (the short stock rebate received, less any payments made in lieu of dividends). The taxpayer holds a mixed straddle.[111] Any interest expense on the call position that needs to be capitalized under I.R.C. § 263(h) is first offset by the short stock rebate.

(5)   APPLICATION BEFORE STRADDLE CAPITALIZATION REQUIREMENT

Finally, the provisions of I.R.C. § 263(h) (requiring capitalization of certain short sale payments in lieu of dividends) are applied to short sales before application of I.R.C. § 263(g) (requiring capitalization of straddle interest and carrying charges).[112] Only after I.R.C. § 263(h) is applied to short sales payments are the provisions of I.R.C. § 263(g) applied.

§ 16.7 MATCHING PROPERTY

When the short sales rule is applied, it is limited to an equal quantity of substantially identical property and does not apply to gain or loss attributable to property that exceeds the quantity sold short.[113] Gain or loss from a short sale is determined by matching the short sales price against the covering purchase.[114] Matching applies even if a taxpayer owns substantially identical stock held in a margin account maintained with the same broker who executed the short sale.[115] The holding period adjustment provision under Rule 2 is applied to substantially identical

---

[109]*See* I.R.C. § 263(h)(5).

[110]I.R.C. § 263(h)(5)(B).

[111]*See generally* Chapter 45.

[112]I.R.C. § 263(h)(6).

[113]I.R.C. § 1233(b)(2).

[114]Bingham v. Comm'r, 27 B.T.A. 186, 190 (1932).

[115]*Id.* at 189.

property in the chronological order when it was acquired, up to the amount of the property sold short.[116]

§ 16.8   SPOUSES

Under the short sales rule, the term "taxpayer" is read as the "taxpayer or his spouse" if legally married.[117] Transactions of both spouses are viewed in the aggregate. An individual who is legally separated from the taxpayer is not viewed as the taxpayer's spouse.

§ 16.9   DEALERS

Dealer transactions generally are exempt from the short sales rule,[118] because such transactions generate ordinary, not capital, income, or loss. The short sales rule applies to dealers in securities if, on the date of a short sale of stock, substantially identical property that is a capital asset has been held for not more than the long-term holding period (currently six months) and the short sale is not closed within 20 days after the date it is entered into.[119] This rule is designed to prevent dealers from manipulating inventory and investment positions to circumvent the short sales rule, while providing them 20 days to close a short sale. The short sales rule applies if the short sale remains open for more than 20 days.

The term "dealer in securities" has the same meaning as it does for a dealer's investment account in I.R.C. § 1236.[120] Stock is defined as any "share or certificate of stock in a corporation, any bond or other evidence of indebtedness which is convertible into any such share or certificate, or any evidence of an interest in, or right to subscribe to or purchase, any of the foregoing."[121] In addition, the provisions of the married put exception[122] apply to dealers in securities subject to the short sales rule.[123]

[116]See section 16.2; section 16.3(b); section 15.4(c).
[117]I.R.C. § 1233(e)(2).
[118]See section 16.2(b).
[119]I.R.C. § 1233(e)(4)(A).
[120]Id.
[121]I.R.C. § 1233(e)(4)(B)(ii).
[122]See section 16.4(d).
[123]I.R.C. § 1233(e)(4)(B)(ii).

§ 16.10   SECURITIES ARBITRAGE TRANSACTIONS

Special rules apply to securities arbitrage transactions that limit application of the short sales rule.[124] Arbitrage involves the purchase and sale of securities (and rights to acquire them) to seek a profit from a difference between the price of the securities purchased and the price of the securities sold.[125] Treasury regulations limit securities arbitrage operations covered by I.R.C. § 1233(f) to stock, securities, and rights to acquire stocks and securities.[126] Commodity futures arbitrage is addressed in I.R.C. § 1233(e)(3).[127] For a securities arbitrage transaction, the property purchased can be identical to the property sold or, if not identical, its acquisition entitles the taxpayer to acquire property that is identical.[128] This expands the general definition of substantially identical property to include options that are not otherwise so viewed for short sales or wash sales purposes.[129]

A taxpayer holds substantially identical property at the close of any business day if (1) he owns other property acquired for arbitrage (whether or not substantially identical), or (2) he has entered into any contract in an arbitrage transaction to receive or acquire substantially identical property.[130] A taxpayer must identify the arbitrage transaction on his records the day it is entered into or as soon thereafter as is practicable.[131] The arbitrage provisions of I.R.C. § 1233(f) continue to apply to property properly identified as part of an arbitrage transaction even if the taxpayer eventually sells the property outright and does not use it to complete the arbitrage transaction.[132]

It is unclear how the arbitrage rules apply to those transactions subject to the modified short sales rule.[133] The author believes that the arbitrage transaction rules should remain in place. The remainder of this section discusses the special short sales rules applicable to securities arbitrage in greater detail.

---

[124]*See* I.R.C. § 1233(f); section 6.7.

[125]I.R.C. § 1233(f)(4); Treas. Reg. § 1.1233-1(f)(3) (1980).

[126]Treas. Reg. § 1.1233-1(f)(3) (1980).

[127]*See* section 16.4(e)(4).

[128]*Id.*

[129]*See* Rev. Rul. 58-384, 1958-2 C.B. 410; *see* section 16.5; section 17.9.

[130]Treas. Reg. § 1.1233-1(f)(2) (1980).

[131]I.R.C. § 1233(f)(4); Treas. Reg. § 1.1233-1(f)(3) (1980).

[132]Treas. Reg. § 1.1233-1(f)(3) (1980).

[133]*See* section 16.1; section 42.1.

(a) HOLDING PERIOD

The holding period adjustment provision of Rule 2 is applied first to substantially identical securities acquired for arbitrage operations held at the close of business on the day the short sale is made.[134] If the quantity sold short exceeds the substantially identical assets acquired for arbitrage operations, Rule 2 is applied to any other substantially identical assets held by the taxpayer.[135] This means that the holding period of the substantially identical property is deemed to begin on the closing of the short sale or the disposition of the property, whichever occurs first.

(b) DEEMED SHORT SALE

If substantially identical property acquired for arbitrage transactions is disposed of without closing the short sale (i.e., a net short position is created), a short sale in the amount of the net short position is deemed made on the day the net short position is established.[136] The holding period adjustment under Rule 2 is applied to any substantially identical property not acquired for arbitrage operations "to the same extent as if the taxpayer, on the day such net short position is created, sold short an amount equal to the amount of the net short position in a transaction not entered into as part of an arbitrage operation."[137]

Example   16-7

On August 13, 1957, a taxpayer buys 100 convertible bonds of X Corporation for purposes other than arbitrage operations. The bonds are convertible into common stock of X Corporation on the basis of one bond for one share of stock. On November 1, 1957, the taxpayer sells short 100 shares of common stock of X Corporation in a transaction identified as part of an arbitrage operation. On the same day he buys another 100 bonds of X Corporation in a transaction identified and intended to be part of the same arbitrage operation. The bonds acquired on both August 13, 1957 and November 1, 1957 are, on the basis of all the facts, substantially identical to the common stock of X Corporation. On December 1, 1957, the taxpayer closes the short sale with 100 shares

---

[134]I.R.C. § 1233(f)(1).

[135]Id.

[136]I.R.C. § 1233(f)(2).

[137]Treas. Reg. § 1.1233-1(f)(1)(ii) (1980).

of common stock of X Corporation acquired on that day. The holding period of the bonds acquired on November 1st begins on December 1st. The holding period is unaffected for the bonds acquired on August 13th. There is also no effect on the holding period of the bonds acquired on August 13th[138] if instead of purchasing the 100 shares of common stock of X Corporation on December 1, 1957, the taxpayer had converted the bonds acquired on November 1st into common stock and, on December 1, 1957, used the stock so acquired to close the short sale.

Example 16-8

Assume the same facts as in Example 16-6, except that the taxpayer, on December 1st, sells the bonds acquired on November 1st (or converts such bonds into common stock and sells the stock), but does not close the short sale. The sale of the bonds (or stock) creates a net short position in assets acquired for arbitrage operations that is deemed to be a short sale made on December 1st. Accordingly, the holding period of the bonds acquired on August 13th begins on the date the short sale is closed or on the date of sale, gift, or other disposition of such bonds, whichever date occurs first.[139]

(c) ARBITRAGING SECURITIES NOT SUBSTANTIALLY IDENTICAL

The short sales rule applies only to transactions involving substantially identical property. Securities of one corporation are not ordinarily considered to be substantially identical to the securities of another corporation. There are situations, however, where the securities are considered substantially identical.[140] For example, when-issued securities of a successor corporation might be viewed as substantially identical to the securities to be exchanged in a reorganization.[141]

Arbitraging securities that are not substantially identical can be utilized if a taxpayer is willing to hold investment securities for more than the long-term holding period in a corporation that has announced merger plans. This technique for converting short-term capital gain to long-term capital gain can be utilized if two corporations plan to merge and

---

[138]Treas. Reg. § 1.1233-1(f)(1)(iii), Example (1) (1980).
[139]Treas. Reg. § 1.1233-1(f)(1)(iii), Example (2) (1980).
[140]Treas. Reg. § 1.1233-1(d)(1) (1980).
[141]Treas. Reg. § 1.1233-1(c)(6), Example (6) (1980).

it is anticipated that the shares of one corporation will be exchanged for the shares of the other. Prior to shareholder approval of the merger, the securities in the two corporations are not identical for application of the short sales rule. In addition, there can be other contingencies, even after stockholder approval, that might prevent a merger. The fact that securities subsequently become substantially identical is immaterial for purposes of the short sales rule if they were not substantially identical at acquisition. The exchange of securities pursuant to the merger does not bring the short sales rule into play. There is an economic risk to such arbitrage trading because the anticipated merger may not be completed upon the terms originally contemplated.

Example   16-9

Assume that in a proposed merger the shares in one corporation will be exchanged evenly with shares in the second corporation. If one corporation's securities are selling for less per share than the securities of the other corporation, the taxpayer could buy those securities selling for less per share and sell short those securities selling for more. Closing the long position against the short position once the long-term holding period is met results in long-term capital gain to the extent of the initial spread between the price of the two securities. The short position can be covered through a market purchase, resulting in a short-term capital loss that would offset the short-term capital gain. The net economic gain equals the initial price spread, but the character of the gain can be short-term or long-term depending on the taxpayer's holding period.

§ 16.11   HEDGES

The short sales rule does not apply to futures contracts used to hedge the underlying property.[142] In addition, transactions that qualify for the statutory hedging exemption are exempt from the modified short sales rule.[143] A hedge, a form of price insurance using a balanced market position to avoid the risk of a change in the market price of commodities, occurs when futures contract transactions constitute an integral part of a manufacturing business.[144] The determinative issue is whether the

[142]I.R.C. § 1233(g); *see generally* Chapter 21; section 6.4.
[143]*See generally* Chapter 21.
[144]*See* Corn Products Refining Co. v. Comm'r, 350 U.S. 46, 50 (1955).

purchases and sales of futures contracts are important and necessary to the successful operation of the business.[145] If the facts support a finding that the futures contracts are integral to the operation of the business, then gains or losses are ordinary, not capital.[146] The taxpayer bears the burden of proving that losses resulting from the purchase and sale of futures contracts were incurred to protect against price fluctuation.[147]

Various types of hedging transactions are discussed extensively in section 6.4. The remainder of this section briefly highlights some judicial decisions that may be of particular interest for short sales purposes. Futures contracts must be connected to the taxpayer's business. Capital gain or loss results on currency positions that were entered into to protect stock investments in foreign subsidiaries and not to protect the taxpayer's business.[148] For a futures transaction to constitute a legitimate hedge there must be some relationship between the taxpayer's business and the futures contract traded. A taxpayer was allowed an ordinary loss deduction on the sale of stock of an oil producer where the taxpayer originally purchased the stock to ensure a continuous supply of oil to its customers.[149] The Tax Court determined that ordinary income resulted when a newspaper entered into long-term contracts to obtain newsprint paper to hedge against increases in the price of the paper and subsequently sold the contracts at a gain to other publishers.[150] The Tax Court allowed an ordinary loss deduction to a wool distributor who entered into a currency futures contract to protect the value of foreign inventory from a possible devaluation of currency that could precipitate an immediate decline in market value.[151] A soybean farmer who purchased futures contracts that neither assured a source of supply nor protected against risk of price changes had a capital loss; the taxpayer merely sold soybeans due to lack of storage space and then bought futures contracts and closed the positions out one month later.[152]

[145]*See id.*

[146]*Accord* Grote v. Comm'r, 41 B.T.A. 247, 249 (1940); Weiler v. U.S., 187 F. Supp. 742, 748 (M.D. Pa. 1960); Rev. Rul. 72-179, 1972-1 C.B. 57.

[147]*See* W. H. Wilson, Inc. v. Comm'r, 5 T.C.M. (CCH) 592 (1946), *aff'd per curiam*, 161 F.2d 556 (4th Cir.), *cert. denied*, 332 U.S. 769 (1947).

[148]Hoover Co. v. Comm'r, 72 T.C. 206, 236-37 (1979).

[149]FS Services, Inc. v. U.S., 413 F.2d 548, 555 (Ct. Cl. 1969).

[150]Mansfield Journal Co. v. Comm'r, 31 T.C. 902, 909 (1959), *aff'd*, 274 F.2d 284 (6th Cir. 1960).

[151]Wood Distributing Corp. v. Comm'r, 34 T.C. 323, 332 (1960).

[152]Patterson v. Comm'r, 50 T.C.M. (P-H) 122 (1981); *see also*, Estate of Laughlin v. Comm'r, 30 T.C.M. (CCH) 227 (1971); Oringderff v. Comm'r, 48 T.C.M. (P-H) 391 (1979), *aff'd*, 48 A.F.T.R. 2d (P-H) 5908 (10th Cir. 1981); Bronner v. Comm'r, 52 T.C.M. (P-H) 287 (1983).

In addition, the Tax Court held that it is not necessary for a taxpayer to cover every purchase of inventory with corresponding futures contracts. As long as a risk of price fluctuation affects inventory, outstanding futures contracts are viewed as purchased to ensure against risk of loss.[153]

Futures contracts used in a hedging transaction are not immediately converted into a speculative transaction when the inventory being hedged is sold. Rather, they need only be closed out within a reasonable time.[154] Furthermore, closing the futures contracts within the same tax year has been viewed as reasonable. A taxpayer can enter into a short position even if no commodity to cover the position exists before the position is taken.[155] He need only show that the purpose of the short position is to offset expected production risk. The fact that a commodity is not on hand when a futures contract is entered into, however, is evidence that the transaction is not a hedge.[156]

---

[153]Stewart Silk Corp. v. Comm'r, 9 T.C. 174, 179 (1947).

[154]Fulton Bag & Cotton Mills v. Comm'r, 22 T.C. 1044, 1052 (1954).

[155]Battelle v. Comm'r, 47 B.T.A. 117, 127 (1942).

[156]Comm'r v. Farmers & Ginners Cotton Oil Co., 120 F.2d 772, 775 (5th Cir.), *cert. denied*, 314 U.S. 683 (1941).

Seventeen

Wash Sales of Stock or Securities

§ 17.1 PURPOSE OF THE WASH SALES RULE

The wash sales rule was enacted to prevent taxpayers from reporting so-called artificial losses by selling securities for a loss at the end of one taxable year and repurchasing the same (or substantially identical) securities in the succeeding taxable year.[1] Congress believed that reporting a tax loss in the first year without a substantial change in investment position failed to reflect economic reality.[2] Since its enactment, the wash sales rule has been extended to include contracts and options to acquire substantially identical stock or securities and to short sales.

§ 17.2 COORDINATION WITH THE STRADDLE RULES

When the Straddle Rules[3] were extended in 1984 to options and certain stock positions,[4] it was unclear whether the wash sales rule, the modified wash sales rule, or both applied to stock or securities positions that were part of a straddle. Because some transactions clearly fell within

[1]HOUSE WAYS AND MEANS COMMITTEE REPORT, INTERNAL REVENUE BILL OF 1921, H.R. REP. NO. 350, 67th Cong., 1st Sess. 11 (1921).

[2]SENATE FINANCE COMMITTEE REPORT, INTERNAL REVENUE BILL OF 1921, S. REP. NO. 275, 67th Cong., 1st Sess. 14 (1921).

[3]*See generally* Part Ten.

[4]*See* section 36.2(c).

the statutory language of both rules, the issue of the coordination of these rules had to be addressed in Treasury regulations or further legislation. On January 14, 1986, the Treasury amended the temporary regulations issued in 1985 under I.R.C. § 1092(b) to "coordinate" the application of the wash sales rule, modified wash sales rule, and the loss deferral rule for stock and securities positions. The amended temporary regulations, which apply retroactively to dispositions of loss positions on or after January 24, 1985,[5] provide that I.R.C. § 1092(b) applies in lieu of I.R.C. § 1091 to defer losses incurred from the disposition of stock and securities positions in a straddle.[6] As a result, the wash sales rule contained in I.R.C. § 1091 applies after January 24, 1985 only to stock or securities positions that are not part of a straddle (e.g., outright stock or securities positions and the short sale of stock).[7] The temporary regulations that were issued to coordinate application of the wash sales rule with both the modified wash sales rule and loss deferral rule are discussed in detail in Chapter 42.

The temporary Treasury regulations provide that the wash sales rule only applies to stock and securities positions when the Straddle Rules do not apply. Nevertheless, the wash sales rule remains relevant for three reasons. First, it applies after January 24, 1985 to stock or securities positions that are not part of a straddle. Second, it applies to all stock or securities positions prior to January 24, 1985. Third, the definition of the term "substantially identical" as used in the temporary regulations has the same meaning as in I.R.C. § 1091(a).[8]

§ 17.3   OPERATION OF THE WASH SALES RULE

(a) IN GENERAL

Losses (other than by a dealer in the ordinary course of business) otherwise allowable under I.R.C. § 165 are not deductible if the wash sales rule applies. It applies if two conditions are met. First, it applies if the loss is from a sale or other disposition of stock or securities. And second, it applies if, within a period beginning 30 days before and ending 30 days after the date of the disposition ("61-day prohibited period"), the

[5]T.D. 8070, 1986-12 I.R.B. 6.

[6]Temp. Treas. Reg. § 1.1092(b)-1T(e) (1986).

[7]For a discussion of application of the Straddle Rules to certain stock positions, see section 36.2.

[8]Temp. Treas. Reg. § 1.1092(b)-5T(p) (1986).

taxpayer has either acquired substantially identical securities (by a purchase or in a taxable transaction) or has entered into a contract or option to acquire substantially identical securities.[9] This means that there is a 61-day prohibited period in which the taxpayer may be subject to the wash sales rule. Issues concerning wash sales of stock or securities are discussed in the remainder of this chapter. It is important to remember that even if losses are allowed under the wash sales rule, they may be disallowed under the modified wash sales rule.[10]

Example 17-1

A taxpayer sells 100 shares of ABC stock for a $3000 loss. He purchases 50 shares of ABC stock 10 days later. The wash sales rule applies because the taxpayer acquired substantially identical property within the 61-day prohibited period. The loss on the old ABC stock is denied, and the taxpayer's basis in the new ABC stock is adjusted to reflect the difference between its purchase price and the sales price of the old ABC stock.[11] In addition, the taxpayer's holding period for the old ABC stock is added to the holding period of the new ABC stock.[12]

Example 17-2

On September 21st a calendar year taxpayer purchases 100 shares of common stock in XYZ corporation for $5000. On December 21st he purchases 50 shares of substantially identical stock for $2750 and on December 27th he purchases 25 additional shares for $1125. Then, on January 3rd of the next year the taxpayer sells the 100 shares purchased on September 21st for $4000. The portion of the $1000 loss attributable to the purchase of the 75 additional shares ($3750 minus $3000, or $750) is not deductible because the shares were purchased within the 61-day prohibited period. The loss on the remaining 25 shares ($1250 minus $1000, or $250) is deductible under I.R.C. § 1091.[13] The basis and the

---

[9]I.R.C. § 1091(a). A wash sale affords the taxpayer the opportunity to correct a mistake if he prematurely realized a loss on stock or securities. A wash sale puts the taxpayer in substantially the same tax position he was in before the loss was realized.

[10]*See* section 42.1; section 42.3.

[11]*See* section 17.3(c).

[12]*See* section 17.3(d).

[13]For possible application of the modified wash sales rule, see section 42.1 and section 42.3.

holding period of the newly acquired shares are adjusted in accordance with the provisions discussed in section 14.4 and section 15.4.

(b) MATCHING DISPOSITIONS AND ACQUISITIONS

The method of matching sales and acquisitions under the wash sales rule is set forth in Treas. Reg. § 1.1091-1(b). It provides that the wash sales rule applies to losses sustained within a taxable year from the sale or disposition of securities in the order in which the securities were disposed of (beginning with the earliest disposition). If the order of disposition cannot be determined, the securities are considered to have been disposed of in the order they were originally acquired, that is, on a FIFO basis (beginning with the earliest acquisition).[14]

Example   17-3

A taxpayer purchases 100 shares of XYZ stock on March 15th for $100 per share and 100 more shares on April 1st for $50 per share. On December 1st the taxpayer sells the 200 shares for $25 per share. In addition, on December 10th he repurchases 100 shares. The $75 per share loss on the first acquisition is disallowed, but the $25 per share loss on the second disposition is deductible under I.R.C. § 1091.[15]

This method of determining the amounts of losses to be disallowed on disproportionate sales and acquisitions of stock or securities has been approved by the Board of Tax Appeals. When 500 shares of stock were sold at a loss less than 30 days after 200 shares of stock were purchased, the Board of Tax Appeals disallowed the amount of the loss that was proportionately applicable to 200 shares of stock using the FIFO method.[16] Application of the FIFO rule with the wash sales rule was not viewed as inconsistent.[17]

If there is a bona fide sale of securities to reduce a taxpayer's position (even if purchased in one lot) within 30 days after the securities are purchased, the wash sales rule is not applied.[18]

[14]Treas. Reg. § 1.1091-1(b) (1967).

[15]For possible application of the modified wash sales rule, see section 42.1 and section 42.3.

[16]Coulter v. Comm'r, 32 B.T.A. 617, 618 (1935).

[17]*Id.*

[18]Rev. Rul. 56-602, 1956-2 C.B. 527. The wash sales rule has been applied, however, to separate lots purchased in the same month where the last purchase is sold at a loss at the end of the same month. Rev. Rul. 71-316, 1971-2 C.B. 311.

(c) BASIS ADJUSTMENTS

If the acquisition of stock or securities results in the nondeductibility of a loss, the basis is adjusted by the difference, if any, between the price at which the property is acquired and the price at which the other substantially identical securities are sold.[19]

Example 17-4

A taxpayer owns 100 shares of XYZ stock with a $100,000 basis. The shares are sold for $90,000. The taxpayer purchases 100 shares within 20 days for $100,000. The wash sales rule applies to deny the $10,000 loss on the sale of the old XYZ stock. In addition, the basis of the new XYZ stock is adjusted to reflect the loss that is denied. The taxpayer's basis in the new XYZ stock is $110,000.

(d) HOLDING PERIOD

If a loss is disallowed under the wash sales rule, the holding period of the property sold is added to the holding period of the newly acquired substantially identical property.[20] In other words, the holding period, like the artificial loss, is carried over to the new property.

Example 17-5

Assume the facts are the same as Example 17-4. The taxpayer's holding period in the new XYZ stock includes his holding period in the old XYZ stock. If the old XYZ stock was held for five months prior to its sale, five months are tacked onto the holding period of the new XYZ stock.

(e) DATE LOSS SUSTAINED

For wash sales, a purchase of stock occurs on the date the contract is entered into (e.g., the trade date) even though the stock is not delivered until a later date (e.g., the settlement date). Similarly, a sale of stock occurs when the equitable interest in the stock is transferred.[21] A loss incurred from the sale of a block of stock (lot) cannot be deducted or

---

[19]I.R.C. § 1091(d); Treas. Reg. § 1.1091-2 (1971); *see* section 14.4(d).
[20]I.R.C. § 1223(4); *see* section 15.4(b).
[21]Rev. Rul. 59-418, 1959-2 C.B. 184.

used to reduce any gain on identical lots sold on the same day if the seller acquired identical stock within the prohibited period.[22]

(f) SHORT SALES COVERAGE

The wash sales rule treats a short sale as if it were an actual sale.[23] Losses realized on closing short sales of securities are denied if within the 61-day prohibited period either substantially identical securities are sold or another short sale of substantially identical securities is entered into.[24] The 61-day prohibited period is tested against the closing date for the short sale so that losses realized on closing a short sale are disallowed under the wash sales rule if within 30 days before or after the closing of a short sale the taxpayer acquires substantially identical securities or enters into another short sale. For transactions entered into after July 18, 1984, wash sales coverage of short sales more closely parallels the operation of the short sales rule.[25]

By way of background, short sales are subject to the wash sales rule under I.R.C. § 1091(e), enacted as part of DRA. This provision does not follow the position taken in Treas. Reg. § 1.1091-1(g). The regulation provides that if a taxpayer owns property substantially identical to the property sold on the date of a short sale (i.e., short sale against the box), the short sale is deemed closed for wash sales purposes at the time of the short sale, not when the short sale is closed by delivery of the securities sold short to the lender. Treas. Reg. § 1.1091-1(g) was issued in response to *Doyle v. Comm'r*,[26] which allowed a deduction for losses sustained on the delivery of stock to close a short sale against the box where the taxpayer had acquired identical stock more than 30 days prior to closing the short sale. In *Doyle*, the taxpayer purchased 3700 shares of stock in the early part of 1953.[27] In November of 1953 she deposited the shares of stock with her broker as collateral for the purchase of an additional 3700 shares of identical stock and made a short sale of 3700 shares of the same stock.[28] Prior to the end of 1953 she covered the short sale with the stock she had purchased at the beginning of the year, leaving her with the shares purchased in November. Because

---

[22]Rev. Rul. 70-231, 1970-1 C.B. 171, *superseding* I.T. 1353, I-1 C.B. 150 (1922).

[23]*See* section 16.2(a).

[24]I.R.C. § 1091(e).

[25]For a discussion of short sales, see generally Chapter 16.

[26]286 F.2d 654, 659-60 (7th Cir. 1961).

[27]*Id.* at 656.

[28]*Id.*

the short sale was closed with shares purchased outside of the 61-day prohibited period, the court found that the wash sales rule was not violated.[29] The court suggested that this apparent "loophole" be closed by legislation.[30] Treas. Reg. § 1.1091-1(g) (issued by the Treasury in an attempt to prevent this result) shifted the 61-day prohibited period for wash sales to the date the short sale occurred instead of when the short sale is closed, and still applies for transactions entered into after May 2, 1967 and before July 18, 1984. This regulation created a conflict between the provisions of the wash sales rule and the short sales rule, which has been resolved by enactment of I.R.C. § 1091(e) for transactions entered into after July 18, 1984. Transactions outside of the 61-day prohibited period are subject to the short sales rule.

Example 17-6

A taxpayer who holds 10 shares of ABC stock sells 10 shares short at a loss of $100. The taxpayer has made a short sale against the box. By delivering ABC stock to the lender within 15 days after the short sale is closed, the taxpayer either makes a second short sale or simply sells outright 10 shares of ABC stock. The $100 loss on the first short sale is denied under the wash sales rule.

(g) BURDEN OF PROOF

Once the IRS determines that the wash sales rule applies to deny a loss, the taxpayer generally bears the burden of proof that the operative provisions of the wash sales rule have not been met. The taxpayer must show that no contract or option to reacquire substantially identical property was established within the 61-day prohibited period.[31]

§ 17.4 COVERED PERSONS

Numerous court decisions have made it clear that all taxpayers other than those specifically excluded from the statutory definition are subject to the wash sales rule. All taxpayers, except dealers in securities who sustain losses in the ordinary course of business, are subject to the wash

---

[29] *Id.* at 658.

[30] *Id.* at 659.

[31] Mellon v. Comm'r, 36 B.T.A. 977, 1053 (1937); Metropolitan Commercial Corp. v. Comm'r, 22 T.C.M. (CCH) 533, 540 (1963).

sales rule.[32] In addition, noncorporate traders are not subject to the wash sales rule for transactions entered into prior to January 1, 1985.[33]

An investor, regardless of the number of purchases and sales, is not exempt from the wash sales rule.[34] If Congress had intended the word "dealer" to include an investor, "it would have used language to aptly convey that thought";[35] the intention of Congress was to the contrary.[36] Similarly, banks that are not securities dealers remain subject to the wash sales rule.[37] Moreover, losses sustained by a mutual life insurance company that was not a dealer on the sale of stock from its general asset account are not deductible if the company purchases substantially identical stock and allocates it among segregated asset accounts within the prohibited period.[38]

§ 17.5 EXEMPTIONS

(a) DEALERS

The only current exemption from the wash sales rule is for dealers in securities who sustain losses in transactions made in the ordinary course of business. For a discussion of dealers, see section 6.3. If both the wash sales rule and the modified wash sales rule[39] could apply to a transaction, it is possible that a dealer otherwise exempt from the wash sales rule (because he is a dealer and the transaction is entered into in the ordinary course of business) could be subject to the modified wash sales rule (because his transaction does not qualify as a hedge eligible for the statutory hedging exemption).

(b) NONCORPORATE TRADERS PRIOR TO
JANUARY 1, 1985

Prior to January 1, 1985, the wash sales rule did not apply to losses of noncorporate traders for transactions in the ordinary course of busi-

---

[32]See section 6.3.

[33]I.R.C. § 1091(a) (1982), amended by DRA, Pub. L. 98-369, § 106(b), 98 Stat. 494, 629 (1984); see section 17.5(b).

[34]Donander Co. v. Comm'r, 29 B.T.A. 312, 314-15 (1933).

[35]Id. at 315.

[36]Accord Nevitt v. Comm'r, 20 T.C. 318, 322 (1953).

[37]Merchants National Bank v. Comm'r, 9 T.C. 68, 70 (1947).

[38]Rev. Rul. 74-4, 1974-1 C.B. 51.

[39]See generally Chapter 42.

ness.[40] This exemption for noncorporate traders was eliminated by the DRA to remove the disparity in treatment between corporate and non-corporate traders.[41] Corporate taxpayers could only deduct losses incurred in the ordinary course of the corporation's business as a securities dealer. Treasury regulations specifically provided that the wash sales rule did not apply to a noncorporate taxpayer as long as the sale or other disposition of securities was made in connection with his trade or business.[42] For a discussion of traders, see section 6.2.

The fact that noncorporate traders were exempt from the wash sales rule for pre-DRA transactions is of particular importance to option market makers under pre-DRA law. Such taxpayers viewed themselves as securities dealers and conducted their options and securities transactions without regard to the wash sales rule.[43] The IRS has questioned whether certain market makers were dealers with respect to certain of their option transactions under pre-DRA law. In fact, this issue has been raised on audit and in cases docketed in Tax Court. If a noncorporate market maker is found not to have been a dealer for pre-DRA transactions, the exemption for noncorporate traders can be of critical importance.[44]

(c) TRANSACTIONS IN THE ORDINARY COURSE OF BUSINESS

Dealers (and noncorporate traders for pre-1985 transactions) must sustain losses in the ordinary course of business to avoid application of the wash sales rule. Judicial decisions in the wash sales area appear analogous to the "active conduct of a trade or business" test under I.R.C. § 162.[45] The Board of Tax Appeals held that a taxpayer who participated in a joint venture to trade a particular stock and who executed 600 transactions in a six-month period involving $5 million was in the active conduct of a trade or business.[46] The activity occupied most of his time

---

[40]I.R.C. § 1091(a) (1982), *amended by* DRA, *supra* note 33, at § 106(b); HOUSE CONFERENCE REPORT, DEFICIT REDUCTION ACT OF 1984, H.R. REP. NO. 861, 98th Cong., 2d Sess. 915-16 (1984).

[41]H.R. REP. NO. 861, *supra* note 40, at 915-16.

[42]Treas. Reg. § 1.1091-1(a) (1967).

[43]For a discussion of market makers under pre-DRA law, see section 6.3(c).

[44]It is possible that certain option transactions (e.g., closing a short option position and then reestablishing the short position within the 61-day prohibited period) are exempt from the wash sales rule. For wash sales purposes, options might not be securities but only substantially identical property for purposes of denying losses on wash sales of securities.

[45]*See* section 8.1; section 9.1.

[46]Morris v. Comm'r, 38 B.T.A. 265 (1938), *acq.* 1938-2 C.B. 22.

and constituted most of his income.[47] Merely maintaining a brokerage account does not constitute an active trade or business.[48] In addition, the courts have looked to whether the taxpayer maintains an office, employs assistants, or devotes an extensive amount of time to the market.[49] It is safe to say that a taxpayer is in a trade or business if a substantial portion of his total income or loss is derived from the activity.[50]

§ 17.6 STOCK OR SECURITIES

(a) DEFINITION

Unlike the short sales rule, the wash sales rule applies only to stock or securities, not futures contracts.[51] Although the phrase "stock or securities" appears with slightly different meanings in numerous Code provisions, it is not defined in I.R.C. § 1091. It is clear, however, that certain contracts or options to acquire stock are viewed as securities for purposes of the wash sales rule.[52] For a securities dealer's investment account, a security is defined in I.R.C. § 1236(c) to include shares of stock in any corporation, certificates of stock or interests in any corporation, notes, bonds, debentures, evidences of indebtedness, or any evidence of an interest in or right to subscribe to or purchase any of the foregoing. For corporate tax purposes, I.R.C. §§ 351, 354, and 361 use a narrow definition of a security. Short-term notes (considered to be debt, not equity interests, under the corporate tax provisions) are treated as securities for a dealer's investment account. In addition, warrants and stock rights are excluded from the corporate tax definition of a security[53] but are included in the dealer investment account definition. It appears likely that the broader definition of securities contained in I.R.C. § 1236(c) more closely defines the types of property Congress intended to be covered by the wash sales rule. In fact, the term "security" is given the

---

[47]*Accord* Kunau v. Comm'r, 27 B.T.A. 509 (1933), *acq.* XII-1 C.B. 7 (1933) (which held that a trust making numerous purchases and sales that generated a $2 million profit over two years was actively conducting a trade or business).

[48]Coulter v. Comm'r, 32 B.T.A. at 617.

[49]*See* Levin v. U.S., 597 F.2d 760, 765 (Ct. Cl. 1979); Purvis v. Comm'r, 530 F.2d 1332, 1334 (1976); *see* section 6.1; section 6.2.

[50]*See Levin,* 597 F.2d at 765.

[51]*See generally* Chapter 16.

[52]*See* Rev. Rul. 56-406, 1956-2 C.B. 523.

[53]Treas. Reg. § 1.351-1(a)(1) (1967).

same definition under the modified wash sales rule as under I.R.C. § 1236(c).[54]

(b) PROPERTY NOT DEEMED "STOCK OR SECURITIES"

(1) FUTURES CONTRACTS

The wash sales rule does not apply to futures contracts because futures contracts are not securities.[55] In *Smith v. Comm'r*,[56] the first case to address the deductibility of commodity straddle losses under pre-ERTA law, the Tax Court stated that the wash sales rule "has no application to the field of commodities futures trading." Moreover, neither a non-statutory wash sales rule nor the step transaction doctrine could be applied to disallow futures contract straddle losses.[57] Although futures contracts can be substantially identical property for short sale purposes, futures contracts are not securities for wash sale purposes.[58]

Futures contracts are now subject to section 1256 treatment, so gains and losses are marked-to-market at year-end at 60/40 rates.[59] With section 1256 treatment there is no opportunity for "artificial losses" of the type the wash sales rule was enacted to prohibit. Those futures contracts that are part of mixed straddles (i.e., straddles where at least one but not all of the positions are section 1256 contracts) generally are subject to the Straddle Rules and the modified wash sales rule.[60]

(2) FOREIGN CURRENCY TRANSACTIONS

Foreign currency transactions are not subject to the wash sales rule. The IRS has held that currency in its usual sense means gold, silver, and other metals or paper used as a circulating medium of exchange, but does not include bonds, evidences of indebtedness, other personal property, or real estate. Foreign currency is not, therefore, considered to be a security for wash sales purposes and losses from the disposition

---

[54]Temp. Treas. Reg. § 1.1092(b)-5T(q) (1986).

[55]Rev. Rul. 71-568, 1971-2 C.B. 312; *see also* Corn Products Refining Co. v. Comm'r, 215 F.2d 513, 517 (2d Cir. 1954), *aff'd,* 350 U.S. 46 (1955); Sicanoff Vegetable Oil Corp. v. Comm'r, 27 T.C. 1056, 1066 (1957), *rev'd on other grounds,* 251 F.2d 764 (7th Cir. 1958); *cf.* Trenton Cotton Oil Co. v. Comm'r, 148 F.2d 208, 209 (6th Cir. 1945).

[56]78 T.C. 350, 388 (1982).

[57]*Id.* at 388.

[58]*See* section 16.4(e).

[59]*See generally* Part Nine.

[60]*See generally* Chapter 42; Chapter 45.

or conversion of foreign currency are not subject to the wash sales rule.[61] Certain foreign currency contracts are subject to section 1256 treatment.[62] Those foreign currency contracts that are section 1256 contracts and that are part of mixed straddles might be subject to the Straddle Rules and the modified wash sales rule.[63]

(3) SECURITIES AND COMMODITY EXCHANGE MEMBERSHIPS

Memberships in securities and commodity exchanges, although capital assets, are not viewed as securities subject to the wash sales rule.[64] Nevertheless, a loss deduction on a sale of a commodity exchange membership was disallowed where the taxpayer had purchased another membership eight days before the sale. The taxpayer was viewed as not having incurred a real economic loss.[65]

§ 17.7 SALES OR DISPOSITIONS

For the wash sales rule to apply, there must be a sale or disposition of securities at a loss. A sale or disposition is read broadly to include any transaction in which a loss is recognized by the taxpayer. The sale of securities purchased on margin, for example, is a sale even if it is made pursuant to the broker's right to sell the securities if they decline in value and the taxpayer fails to make additional payments.[66]

§ 17.8 ACQUISITION OF SUBSTANTIALLY IDENTICAL SECURITIES (OR A CONTRACT OR OPTION TO ACQUIRE SECURITIES)

For the wash sales rule to apply, the taxpayer must acquire (or have entered into a contract or option to acquire) substantially identical

---

[61]Rev. Rul. 74-218, 1974-1 C.B. 202.

[62]See generally Part Nine.

[63]See generally Chapter 42; Chapter 45.

[64]Under certain circumstances, sales of exchange memberships can generate ordinary income or loss. See Becker Warburg Paribas Group, Inc. v. U.S., 514 F. Supp. 1273, 1279-80 (N.D. Ill. 1981).

[65]Horne v. Comm'r, 5 T.C. 250, 255-56 (1945).

[66]Rev. Rul. 71-316, 1971-2 C.B. 311. The terms "disposing, disposes, or disposed" are defined broadly for purposes of the modified wash sales rule under I.R.C. § 1092(b) to include "the sale, exchange, cancellation, lapse, expiration, or other termination." Temp. Treas. Reg. § 1.1092(b)-5T(a) (1986).

securities within the 61-day prohibited period.[67] The acquisition (or the contract or option to acquire) must be in a transaction where the entire amount of gain or loss is recognized.[68] Securities received as a gift or through a nontaxable transaction are not considered to be an acquisition. Issues involving methods of acquisition are discussed in the remainder of this section.

Example   17-7

A taxpayer acquires 50 shares of ABC stock as a gift and within 20 days sells 50 shares of ABC stock that he previously owned for a $30,000 loss. The taxpayer is not viewed as having acquired substantially identical property for purposes of the wash sales rule. Shares acquired by a gift are not considered to be an acquisition.[69]

The taxpayer must know of the possibility of acquiring substantially identical securities and must acquire substantially identical securities. In *Gutmann v. Comm'r*,[70] the taxpayer surrendered stock to the issuing corporation in payment of an outstanding debt. Without the taxpayer's knowledge the corporation's treasurer inserted in the minutes of the directors meeting that an option had been granted allowing the taxpayer to repurchase the same shares.[71] This grant was not made known to either the taxpayer or the corporation's directors until three months later.[72] The Board of Tax Appeals held that there was no contract before the option was ratified by the directors (or if the option was a gift and informed ratification assumed, the gift was not complete until the taxpayer accepted it).[73] The taxpayer was not aware of the option until more than two months after he surrendered the stock and recognized the loss.[74] The taxpayer was not found to have entered into a contract or option to acquire substantially identical stock.[75]

Gutmann is consistent with other court decisions addressing the acquisition of (or contract or option to acquire) substantially identical

---

[67]I.R.C. § 1091(a).

[68]*Id.;* Treas. Reg. § 1.1091-1(f) (1967).

[69]For possible application of the modified wash sales rule, see generally Chapter 42.

[70]38 B.T.A. 679, 681 (1938).

[71]*Id.* at 682.

[72]*Id.* at 682-83.

[73]*Id.* at 686.

[74]*Id.*

[75]*Id.*

securities. The courts require a volitional act on the part of the taxpayer. In other words, if the taxpayer attempts to circumvent the wash sales rule, the courts seek to limit a loss deduction. Although an attempt to circumvent the wash sales rule need not be intentional,[76] the taxpayer must know that there is a possibility that he might acquire substantially identical securities and that possibility does materialize.[77]

(a) SUBSCRIPTION RIGHTS

The IRS has applied the wash sales rule to a taxpayer who purchased shares with subscription rights to acquire additional shares of stock substantially identical to stock sold at a loss.[78] The taxpayer exercised the subscription rights and within 30 days sold an amount equivalent to the original shares sold at a loss.[79] The wash sales rule applied to the new stock just as if the new stock had been purchased in the open market.[80] Although the principal motive for acquiring stock with subscription rights is not to replace stock sold at a loss, all purchases of substantially identical stock within the 61-day prohibited period are covered by the wash sales rule.[81] In other words, the taxpayer's motive is irrelevant.

(b) STOCK BONUS SHARES

An employee who receives, pursuant to a stock bonus plan, substantially identical shares of his employer's stock for services rendered has made an acquisition that falls within the scope of the wash sales rule.[82] Therefore, any loss sustained from disposing of old bonus shares within 30 days after receiving additional bonus shares is disallowed as a wash sale.[83] The basis of the new shares is adjusted to reflect the disallowance of the loss.[84]

---

[76]See, e.g., Rev. Rul. 71-316, 1971-2 C.B. 311 (where there is no indication that the taxpayer acted intentionally).

[77]In light of the holding of Estate of Estroff v. Comm'r, 52 T.C.M. (P-H) 2751 (1983), the portion of the Gutmann decision that rests on the unenforceability of the treasurer's grant of the option is less significant. Gutmann is distinguishable from Estroff, and it supports the proposition that if the taxpayer has no knowledge of another's actions (which could imply either an actual or tacit agreement), an essential element of a wash sale is missing.

[78]Rev. Rul. 71-520, 1971-2 C.B. 311.

[79]Id.

[80]Id.

[81]Id.

[82]Rev. Rul. 73-329, 1973-2 C.B. 302.

[83]Id.

[84]For a discussion of basis adjustments, see section 14.4(d).

(c) STOCK OPTION PLANS

An employee's right to purchase his employer's stock under a restricted or qualified stock option plan is subject to the wash sales rule. The employee is treated as having entered into an option to acquire stock as of the date the option is granted.[85] In addition, stock acquired pursuant to exercise of the option is acquired for wash sales purposes on the date the stock certificates are issued.[86] In any case where the stock represented by a restricted stock option has resulted in a nondeductible loss on the exercise of the option under the wash sales rule, the shares cannot be used to deny a loss incurred within 61 days of the issuance of the stock.[87] Although the IRS can only use the substantially identical property analysis once to deny a loss, it has two separate opportunities to apply the wash sales provision.

(d) UNENFORCEABLE AGREEMENTS

The IRS and the Tax Court have ignored the issue of whether an oral agreement is enforceable under local law, implicitly acknowledging that the wash sales rule is not subject to technical manipulations to avoid its application. Losses recognized on "sales" subject to a handshake or the wink of an eye are subject to the wash sales rule even though the agreement to repurchase the securities is legally unenforceable.

In *Estate of Estroff v. Comm'r*,[88] the Tax Court denied a loss deduction of a taxpayer who orally agreed to sell stock to a friend with the understanding that the stock would be repurchased. The wash sales rule prevents tax evasion by deducting losses that do not reflect economic realities. In *Estroff*, the taxpayer loaned the "purchaser" the amount of money needed to purchase the stock.[89] The market value for the stock increased but the taxpayer repurchased the stock 34 days later at the price for which he sold it.[90] The "loan" was repaid with the sales proceeds, although the purchaser kept the dividend paid on the stock during the period he "owned" it.[91] The Tax Court looked to the taxpayer's relative cost in forgoing the dividend compared to the savings that

---

[85]Rev. Rul. 56-452, 1956-2 C.B. 525.
[86]*Id.*
[87]*Id.*
[88]52 T.C.M. (P-H) at 2752.
[89]*Id.*
[90]*Id.* at 2752-53.
[91]*Id.* at 2753.

resulted if the loss were allowed. The court viewed the dividend merely as a device to make the transaction look real.[92]

(e) PUT OPTIONS

The IRS applied the wash sales rule to a taxpayer who sold stock at a loss and, within the 61-day prohibited period, sold a put option obligating him to purchase substantially identical stock from the holder of the put option.[93] The exercise price of the put at the time it was sold exceeded the fair market value of the stock, so it was likely that the put would be exercised.[94] Because the put option is, in substance, a contract to acquire stock, the wash sales rule is applied; substance controls over form.[95] The DRA makes all options and certain stock positions[96] subject to the Straddle Rules[97] and the modified wash sales rule.[98] The modified wash sales rule of I.R.C. § 1092(b)(1) applies to certain put option transactions.

§ 17.9 SUBSTANTIALLY IDENTICAL PROPERTY

A wash sale is a transaction in which substantially identical property is acquired within the 61-day prohibited period. The term "substantially identical property" is not defined in I.R.C. § 1091 or in the Treasury regulations.[99] Rather, it is applied according to the facts of each case.[100] Substantial identity covers something less than a precise correspondence.[101] It is sufficient that there be economic correspondence, notwithstanding slight differentiations.[102] The scope of the term substantially identical is important for two reasons. First, the wash sales rule applies to stock, securities, and substantially identical property not part of a straddle. Second, the definition of substantially identical stock or

---

[92]*Id.*

[93]Rev. Rul. 85-87, 1985-25 I.R.B. 6.

[94]*Id.*

[95]*Id.*

[96]*See* section 36.2(c).

[97]*See generally* Part Ten.

[98]*See* section 42.3.

[99]In fact, Treas. Reg. § 1.1233-1(d) (1980) provides that for purposes of the short sales rule, the term substantially identical property has the same meaning as for wash sales.

[100]Treas. Reg. § 1.1233-1(d)(1) (1980).

[101]Hanlin v. Comm'r, 108 F.2d 429, 430 (3d Cir. 1939).

[102]*Id.*

securities in the modified wash sales rule, which applies to stock or securities positions that are part of a straddle, is the same as it is for wash sales purposes.[103] Some IRS rulings and judicial decisions analyzing substantially identical property are discussed in the remainder of this section.

(a) CONVERTIBLE SECURITIES

When preferred stock, bonds, or debentures are convertible into common stock of the same corporation, the relative values, price changes, and other circumstances can make the convertible securities substantially identical to the common stock into which they are convertible.[104] Convertible preferred stock is treated as substantially identical to the common stock into which it can be converted if it (1) has the same dividend restrictions and same voting rights as the common stock, (2) sells at prices that do not vary significantly from the conversion ratio, and (3) is not restricted as to convertibility.[105] Moreover, convertible preferred stock is viewed as an option to acquire stock of the issuing corporation if it is convertible at the holder's election without any restrictions.[106] In addition, for purposes of the attribution rules of I.R.C. § 318(a)(4), a convertible debenture is viewed as an option to acquire stock.[107]

(b) WARRANTS

Warrants can be subject to the wash sales rule. If a taxpayer sells common stock at a loss and simultaneously purchases warrants for common stock of the same corporation, the loss is disallowed under the wash sales rules.[108] The warrant is viewed as a contract or option to acquire substantially identical property. Conversely, if a taxpayer sells a warrant at a loss and simultaneously purchases common stock of the same corporation, the loss generally is allowed unless "the relative values and price changes are so similar as to make the warrants fully convertible securities and therefore substantially identical with shares of common stock."[109]

---

[103]Temp. Treas. Reg. § 1.1092(b)-5T(p) (1986). *See generally* Chapter 42.
[104]Treas. Reg. § 1.1233-1(d) (1980).
[105]Rev. Rul. 77-201, 1977-1 C.B. 250.
[106]*Id.*
[107]Rev. Rul. 68-601, 1968-2 C.B. 124.
[108]Rev. Rul. 56-406, 1956-2 C.B. 523.
[109]*Id.*

In discussing the predecessor Code provision to the short sales rule, the Senate Finance Committee and House Ways and Means Committee stated in their reports that "[n]o general definition of substantially identical property is given ... since it is believed that the term must be applied in accordance with the actual circumstances of each transaction."[110] Relying on this general statement from the legislative history, G.C.M. 28274,[111] which underlies Rev. Rul. 56-406,[112] concludes that the definition of substantial identity as it relates to a warrant and the underlying stock of the issuing corporation depends upon relative values and price changes. It is possible to have a warrant that is traded on a stock exchange or over-the-counter at prices substantially equal to the current value of the underlying stock. Under such circumstances the warrant is considered to be a fully convertible security.

In 1983 a proposed revenue ruling stated that a stock warrant and the underlying stock are always substantially identical for wash sales purposes.[113] The IRS General Counsel's Office recommended that the proposed ruling not be published because the presumption of substantial identity was inconsistent with the legislative history as to the meaning of substantially identical property.[114] As a result, the principles of G.C.M. 28274 continue to be followed; a sale of a warrant does not disallow loss under the wash sales rule when the underlying stock is purchased within the prohibited period unless the relative values and price changes of the stock and warrant are so similar that the warrant is viewed as substantially identical to the underlying stock.[115]

(c) VOTING TRUST CERTIFICATES

A taxpayer who sold voting trust certificates representing shares of common stock and within the 61-day prohibited period purchased common stock in the same corporation made a wash sale.[116] Although the trust certificates were subject to the trust agreement until actual delivery of the stock, the taxpayer was viewed as the beneficial owner of the stock

---

[110]HOUSE WAYS AND MEANS COMMITTEE REPORT, REVENUE ACT OF 1950, H.R. REP. NO. 2319, 81st Cong., 2d Sess. 96 (1950).

[111]G.C.M. 28274 (June 14, 1954).

[112]1956-2 C.B. 523.

[113]This proposed ruling, had it been adopted, would have revoked Rev. Rul. 56-406, 1956-2 C.B. 523, to the extent it concluded that a loss is allowable where a taxpayer sells warrants at a loss and then purchases common stock of the corporation.

[114]G.C.M. 39036 (Sept. 22, 1983).

[115]Id.

[116]Kidder v. Comm'r, 30 B.T.A. 59, 61 (1934).

and he had a right to receive dividends.[117] Moreover, the taxpayer entered into the trust voluntarily,[118] and there was a sufficient approximation of economic attributes to constitute substantially identical property.[119] The fact that the taxpayer had no right to independently vote the certificates was not sufficient to treat the property as anything but substantially identical.[120]

(d) REORGANIZATIONS

The securities of one corporation are not generally considered substantially identical to the securities of another corporation.[121] In certain situations, however, the securities might be viewed as substantially identical once all of the facts are considered.[122] No decisions or rulings state whether the securities of corporations involved in a reorganization should be treated as substantially identical. The legislative history accompanying the predecessor Code provision to the short sales rule states that except for when-issued stock, the stock of one corporation is not substantially identical to the stock of another corporation.[123]

(e) WHEN-ISSUED SECURITIES

When-issued securities are subject to the wash sales rule.[124] In addition, the IRS General Counsel's Office has approved a proposed revenue ruling applying the wash sales rule to when-issued securities.[125] At this writing the ruling has not been issued. In addition, when-issued securities of a successor corporation can be substantially identical to the securities to be exchanged for the when-issued securities in a reorganization.[126] The IRS has ruled that a taxpayer did not acquire substantially identical stock when he converted preferred stock into common prior to closing a short sale of when-issued common stock.[127]

---

[117]*Id.*

[118]*Id.*

[119]*Id.*

[120]*Id.*

[121]Treas. Reg. § 1.1233-1(d)(1) (1980).

[122]*Id.*

[123]SENATE FINANCE COMMITTEE REPORT, REVENUE ACT OF 1950, S. REP. NO. 2375, 81st Cong., 2d Sess. 44, *reprinted in* 1950 U.S. CODE CONG. & AD. NEWS 3053, 3231.

[124]*See* I.T. 3858, 1947-2 C.B. 71.

[125]G.C.M. 37332 (Nov. 25, 1977).

[126]*See* Treas. Reg. § 1.1233-1(c)(6), Example (6) (1980).

[127]Rev. Rul. 62-153, 1962-2 C.B. 186.

(f) PUBLICLY TRADED OPTIONS

Call options and the securities underlying them are not substantially identical property.[128] However, G.C.M. 37332[129] suggested that this view be reconsidered on the grounds that the option, as a contract right to acquire property at a fixed price, should be substantially identical to the property itself. The IRS General Counsel's Office stated that if a taxpayer acquires a put option, which constitutes a short sale, and subsequently acquires a call option on the same security, gain is fixed and risk is eliminated before the expiration of the put period.[130] At the date of this writing, no formal ruling has asserted that call options are substantially identical to the underlying securities. Rev. Rul. 80-238,[131] which addresses the holding period requirement for the corporate dividends received deduction, does assert, however, that a call option can be a contractual obligation to sell stock or securities.[132]

Writing call options on stock is not a short sale of substantially identical stock or securities for purposes of reducing a corporate stockholder's holding period for the intercorporate dividends received deduction.[133] The IRS stated in that ruling that the result should be different if the corporation writes in-the-money calls.[134] The IRS views exercise of such options as virtually guaranteed and the element of risk as greatly reduced or eliminated.[135]

The IRS has taken a first step towards treating options and the underlying stock as substantially identical.[136] The IRS ruled that a put option and the underlying property were substantially identical where a taxpayer sold stock at a loss and within the 61-day prohibited period also sold a put option, obligating him to purchase substantially identical stock at a price which, in light of existing market conditions, created no substantial likelihood that the put would not be exercised.[137] Therefore, based on the value of the put option at the time of purchase, the

[128]Rev. Rul. 58-384, 1958-2 C.B. 410.

[129]G.C.M. 37332 (Nov. 25, 1977).

[130]*Id.*

[131]1980-2 C.B. 76.

[132]*See* section 15.7; section 22.9.

[133]Rev. Rul. 80-238, 1980-2 C.B. 96. The ruling also says that the legislative history of I.R.C. § 246(c) indicates that for purposes of I.R.C. § 246(c)(3), a call option is not a contractual obligation to sell stock or securities.

[134]*Id.*

[135]*Id.*

[136]Rev. Rul. 85-87, 1985-25 I.R.B. 6.

[137]*Id.*

IRS treated the taxpayer as having acquired within the prohibited period a contract or option to acquire substantially identical property to that previously sold.[138] Consequently, the IRS concluded that the taxpayer could not take a loss deduction on the initial sale of the stock.

(g) SUBSTANTIALLY IDENTICAL DEBT SECURITIES

Debt securities are treated as substantially identical if they are not substantially different in any material feature or several material features considered together.[139] Debt securities purchased must be compared to their terms when purchased, while debt securities sold must be compared to their terms when sold.[140] Identical market values and interest rates on a particular date do not necessarily establish substantial identity between debt securities.[141] Debt securities with the same interest rates, face amounts, acceptability to secure deposits of public money, eligibility for restricted investment by commercial banks, and only nominal differences between their sale and purchase prices have been found to be substantially identical. Debt securities were substantially identical where the earliest call dates and maturity dates differed by six months, even though the securities sold were in registered form and the securities purchased were in bearer form.[142]

Municipal securities of the same obligor with the same par values, unit selling prices, interest rates, issue dates, and authorizing ordinances have been held to be substantially identical even though their maturity dates were different by four to 10 months, approximately 16 years in the future.[143] In addition, Federal Land Bank securities issued by the same bank with the same values, authorizing ordinances, unit prices, redeemability (after six months) at the obligor's option, and different maturity dates have been found to be substantially identical.[144] Because the debt securities had different maturity dates, the court placed more emphasis on the similarity of redemption provisions, viewing that factor as more significant than the difference in maturity dates.[145]

---

[138]*See id.*
[139]Rev. Rul. 58-211, 1958-1 C.B. 529.
[140]*Id.*
[141]*Id.*
[142]*Id.*
[143]*Hanlin,* 108 F.2d at 431-32.
[144]*Id.*
[145]*Id.* at 432.

In Frick v. Driscoll,[146] the court held that municipal securities of the same obligor with the same interest rates, sale and purchase prices, and average issue and due dates were substantially identical. This decision has far reaching implications because the court, in determining the substantial identity issue, lumped all maturity dates together to arrive at an average, and averaged all issue and due dates to compare substantial identity.[147] This averaging process eliminated any individual discrepancies that might otherwise be considered substantial.[148] Furthermore, because the court averaged all of the factors, it could not recognize and apply the FIFO principles of matching sales with purchases. Averaging of items when comparing sales and purchases allows the IRS a great deal of flexibility in determining substantial identity.

(h) DEBT SECURITIES THAT ARE NOT SUBSTANTIALLY IDENTICAL

Even if debt securities are issued by the same governmental agency, they might not be viewed as substantially identical if they have different issue dates, maturity dates, interest rates, interest payment dates, or callable features.[149] Highway authority bonds with interest rates of 3.45 percent and 4.5 percent and a maturity date 40 years in the future have not been viewed as substantially identical, because the different interest rates were considered to be a materially different feature.[150]

Debt securities of different local housing authorities issued pursuant to agreements with the Federal Public Housing Administration are not substantially identical. Each housing authority is different from the others and is the primary obligor on its own securities.[151] In addition, Federal Land Bank bonds issued by different banks but with the same par values, unit prices, interest rates, and maturity dates (over 20 years in the future varying by only six months) have been held to be different from each other (and not substantially identical) where the bonds were secured by different collateral.[152]

Debt securities that differ in their annual interest rates, maturity

---

[146]29 A.F.T.R. (P-H) 1298, 1303 (1941), *rev'd in part on other grounds*, 129 F.2d 148 (3d Cir. 1942).

[147]*Id.* at 1305.

[148]*See id.*

[149]*See* Rev. Rul. 58-210, 1958-1 C.B. 523; Rev. Rul. 58-211, 1958-1 C.B. 529.

[150]Rev. Rul. 60-195, 1960-1 C.B. 300.

[151]Rev. Rul. 59-44, 1959-1 C.B. 205.

[152]*Hanlin*, 108 F.2d at 431.

dates, and use in payment of federal estate taxes have been held not to be substantially identical. In addition, the IRS has ruled that 6⅜ percent Treasury bonds maturing in 1982 (which were not redeemable at par value with accrued interest and could not be used to pay estate taxes) were not substantially identical to 4¼ percent Treasury bonds maturing in 1992 (which were redeemable at par value with accrued interest and could be used to pay estate taxes).[153] Because the Treasury bonds had different annual interest rates, maturity dates, and whether they could be used to pay estate taxes, these bonds were not substantially identical even though they were from the same issuer. The Board of Tax Appeals has held that municipal bonds of the same obligor are not substantially identical where (1) the issue dates differed by not less than 53 months, (2) the maturity dates differed by not less than 65 months, (3) the interest payment dates differed from May and November to March and December, (4) the market prices differed by 1⅜ percent, and (5) one lot was registered and the other lot was coupon-bearing, with the nearest maturity date 23½ years after the purchase.[154]

§ 17.10   RELATED PARTIES

Although the wash sales rule does not prevent indirect sales or acquisitions, the courts have been quick to use other provisions to prevent abuses. It is not clear whether the wash sales rule is interpreted broadly to apply to any sale and reacquisition that directly benefits the selling taxpayer or whether some income shifting is acceptable. This section discusses some of the problems raised by related party transactions.

(a)   HUSBANDS AND WIVES

Losses generated by indirect sales between related persons have been disallowed under I.R.C. § 267 (denying losses with respect to related party transactions) and its predecessor Code provision. In one case, a husband who managed his wife's assets instructed his broker to sell certain stock from one account and simultaneously repurchase an equal number of shares of the same stock for another account.[155] Disallowance under I.R.C. § 267 does not depend on simultaneous execution and

[153]Rev. Rul. 76-346, 1976-2 C.B. 247.
[154]Campbell v. Comm'r, 39 B.T.A. 916, 921 (1939), *aff'd sub nom.* Comm'r v. Gambrill, 112 F.2d 530 (2d Cir. 1940), *rev'd on other grounds sub nom.* Helvering v. Campbell, 313 U.S. 15 (1941).
[155]McWilliams v. Comm'r, 331 U.S. 694 (1947).

includes all sales (even if made on different securities exchanges).[156] It is important to note that if losses are disallowed under I.R.C. § 267, the result can be much more severe than if the losses are disallowed under the wash sales rule. I.R.C. § 267 does not allow any basis adjustments or the tacking of holding periods. Additionally, I.R.C. § 267 has no 61-day prohibited period upon which to test related party transactions; it operates on the facts of each case. If it appears that the taxpayer intends to acquire substantially identical property, the time period does not matter.

The proper treatment of purchases of substantially identical property between a husband and wife depends upon the bona fides of the transaction. The purchase of stock by a taxpayer's spouse outside of the 61-day prohibited period after the taxpayer sold substantially identical stock has not subjected losses to the wash sales rule.[157] Some courts have held losses sustained by one spouse on the sale of securities are deductible on a joint return even where the other spouse, within the 61-day prohibited period, acquired substantially identical property.[158] The loss on a sale through a broker was deductible even though an equal number of the same shares was simultaneously purchased by a business associate of the taxpayer and subsequently transferred to the taxpayer's spouse, who paid for them with her own funds.[159]

Where one spouse repurchased securities with money furnished by the other spouse, the transactions were found not to be bona fide.[160] Furthermore, sales were not bona fide where the same securities were purchased at the taxpayer's orders in the name of his spouse, and the evidence failed to show that the taxpayer was not the real purchaser.[161] The Board of Tax Appeals held in a memorandum decision that where a taxpayer disposed of stock and on the same day his wife purchased the same number of shares, depositing them in their joint names, one-half of the loss was disallowed as a wash sale.[162]

---

[156]Shethar v. Comm'r, 28 T.C. 1222, 1226 (1957).

[157]Corbett v. Comm'r, 16 B.T.A. 1231, 1233 (1929).

[158]See Fawsett v. Comm'r, 31 B.T.A. 139, 142 (1934); Gummey v. Comm'r, 26 B.T.A. 894, 896 (1932). Contra Brochon v. Comm'r, 30 B.T.A. 404, 408 (1934).

[159]Young v. Comm'r, 34 B.T.A. 648, 652-53 (1936).

[160]Singer v. Comm'r, 32 B.T.A. 177, 180 (1935); Belden v. Comm'r, 30 B.T.A. 601, 603-04 (1934); Brochon, 30 B.T.A. at 406-07.

[161]Estate of Mitchell v. Comm'r, 37 B.T.A. 161, 167 (1938); Morse v. Comm'r, 34 B.T.A. 943, 945-46 (1936).

[162]Harvey v. Comm'r, 2 B.T.A.M. (P-H) 639, 640 (1933).

(b) PARENTS AND CHILDREN

The wash sales rule was not applied to a taxpayer who sold securities at a loss and lent money to his son on the next day to purchase a like amount of the same securities. The taxpayer took the securities as collateral for his son's promissory note.[163] The taxpayer subsequently cancelled the note and obtained the securities. The court found the taxpayer had not purchased the securities through his son but rather had legitimately lent money to his son to enable him to profit from an expected price rise.[164] The taxpayer cancelled the promissory note after the price actually dropped. The initial sales transaction was not subject to the wash sales limitations.[165]

(c) BROTHERS AND SISTERS

The wash sales limitation was not applied to a taxpayer who reported a loss from the sale of securities, the proceeds of which he gave to his sister as a gift even though she used the money to purchase substantially identical securities.[166] The court found that the taxpayer's sister was acting in her own interest and not indirectly for the taxpayer's benefit.[167]

(d) CONTROLLED CORPORATIONS

A loss was denied where a taxpayer sold securities and 15 days later his wholly owned corporation purchased substantially identical securities in his name.[168] In another case, a taxpayer who sold securities and ordered his controlled corporation to purchase substantially identical securities purchased the securities from his corporation outside of the 61-day prohibited period. Nevertheless, the sale was found to be part of a plan to circumvent the wash sales rule. The controlled corporation acted as the taxpayer's agent and no real change in economic position occurred.[169] The Board of Tax Appeals held that where a tax-

---

[163]Cole v. Helburn, 4 F. Supp. 230, 232 (W.D. Ky. 1933).

[164]*Id.*

[165]*Id.*

[166]Comm'r v. Johnston, 107 F.2d 883, 885 (6th Cir. 1939).

[167]*See id.*

[168]Kaplan v. Comm'r, 21 T.C. 134, 141-42 (1953).

[169]Shoenberg v. Comm'r, 77 F.2d 446, 449 (8th Cir. 1935); Comm'r v. Dyer, 74 F.2d 685, 686 (2d Cir.), *cert. denied,* 296 U.S. 586 (1935).

payer acquired stock of a new corporation and the next day sold other stock to that new corporation, the indirect interest in the stock sold was not substantially identical to the taxpayer's interest in the stock held prior to sale.[170] As a result, losses on the sale of the original stock were allowed.

(e) TRUSTS AND ESTATES

A trust under the sole control of a taxpayer who repurchases securities substantially identical to securities previously sold comes within the wash sales limitation. A loss deduction is denied to the taxpayer because the taxpayer and the trust are deemed to be identical.[171] A loss was allowed to an estate when securities were sold to a corporation controlled by the beneficiaries of the estate even though the beneficiaries owned stock in the controlled corporation. No one beneficiary owned proportionately more than a 50 percent interest in the corporation.[172]

[170]Knox v. Comm'r, 33 B.T.A. 972, 975 (1936).
[171]Security First Nat'l Bank of Los Angeles v. Comm'r, 28 B.T.A. 289, 313-15 (1933).
[172]Estate of Ingall v. Comm'r, 45 B.T.A. 787, 793 (1941), *aff'd*, 132 F.2d 862 (6th Cir. 1943).

Eighteen

Identification of Capital Assets

§ 18.1 IN GENERAL

A taxpayer's ability to identify the specific property that he wants to sell or transfer can have enormous tax implications. It is up to the taxpayer to maintain records that allow him to specifically identify the property that he intends to sell or transfer.

Methods of identifying property vary with specific types of property. Typically, physical commodities are easily identified by warehouse receipts or other documents of title. Futures contracts and exchange-traded option positions frequently are closed out on a FIFO basis, which assumes that the first property purchased is the first property sold. Thus, the property on hand at year-end is assumed to be the property most recently purchased by the taxpayer. Under certain circumstances, it may be possible to specifically identify those futures and option positions to be closed out.[1] For stock and securities positions, FIFO is imposed unless the securities are specifically identified by the taxpayer and the taxpayer complies with the identification requirements contained in the Treasury regulations. If the identification requirements

[1]Perlin v. Comm'r, 86 T.C. ___, No. 25 (Mar. 19, 1986). In *Perlin*, the Tax Court noted that, under the CFTC's regulations, a trader is permitted to specifically identify the position that he wishes to close out and it is only if no such identification is made that the clearing organization will offset the positions on a FIFO basis. The court held that the taxpayer's use of special instructions was consistent with the requirements of these regulations and was perfectly valid for tax purposes.

are not met, however, the taxpayer is deemed to sell his securities on a FIFO basis.

If a taxpayer owns several of the same assets that were acquired at different times and at different prices (i.e., that were acquired in more than one lot), he might want to identify a particular asset or lot as the one for sale. A taxpayer might want to minimize his gain by selling those assets with the highest basis, or he might want to report a loss by selling an asset with a basis in excess of the anticipated sales price, if such an asset is available. In addition, a taxpayer's holding period for a capital asset determines whether the gain or loss on the sale or transfer is long-term or short-term.[2] The importance of identifying the appropriate asset cannot be underestimated. It is in the taxpayer's interest to maintain adequate records to allow for specific identification.

Several issues with respect to the identification of securities are discussed in the remainder of this chapter.

§ 18.2   IDENTIFICATION OF SECURITIES

A major difficulty in identifying assets arises when a taxpayer wants to dispose of only a portion of identical securities that were acquired in more than one lot on different dates and at different prices. If the taxpayer cannot adequately identify the lot (or lots) of securities that he intends to sell, Treasury regulations impose the FIFO method of identification on him, so that those securities sold are deemed to be the securities held by the taxpayer for the longest time. The identification requirements imposed by the Treasury regulations are discussed in the remainder of this section.

(a)   SPECIFIC IDENTIFICATION REQUIREMENTS

(1)   REGISTERED SECURITIES

As a starting point, securities that are registered in the taxpayer's name can be held by the taxpayer or held in the custody of the taxpayer's broker or other agent. When the taxpayer has possession of securities registered in his name, proper identification should be relatively easy. If, on the other hand, the securities are purchased through a broker or another agent that retains possession of the securities, the confirmation statement covering the transaction will identify the securities purchased. The rules for properly identifying securities registered in the

[2]*See generally* Chapter 15.

taxpayer's name, when held by the taxpayer or his broker or agent, are discussed below. For a discussion of securities held in street name, see section 18.2(a)(2).

(i) In General

Securities that are "adequately identified" can be specifically identified as the ones for sale.[3] In general, when securities (such as stocks, bonds, and convertible securities) are registered in the taxpayer's name and then are sold or transferred, the certificates or bonds actually delivered are treated for tax purposes as the securities sold by the taxpayer.[4] Indeed, the certificates conclusively identify the securities represented, even if the taxpayer intended to deliver other securities.[5] Hence, delivery of the proper certificates is imperative for those securities registered in the taxpayer's name. Identification of the securities by the taxpayer in his own records is not sufficient if those securities are not the ones for which certificates are actually delivered.[6]

(ii) Mistaken Delivery by Broker or Agent

Taxpayers sometimes leave certificates representing securities registered in their own names in the custody of their brokers or other agents for safekeeping or in a margin account. To adequately identify the securities represented by these certificates, the taxpayer must provide his broker or agent with specific instructions as to which securities are to be sold. Furthermore, the broker or other agent must follow the taxpayer's instructions and must actually deliver the correct certificates. Specific instructions are not recognized for tax purposes if the taxpayer's broker or agent does not, in turn, follow the instructions.[7] In all cases where the securities are registered in the taxpayer's name, those securities represented by the certificates that are actually delivered are the ones conclusively deemed to be sold for tax purposes.

(iii) Single Certificate Representing Several Lots

Complications in specifically identifying securities result if a taxpayer has a single stock certificate, which represents prior acquisitions of two

---

[3]Treas. Reg. § 1.1012-1(c)(1) (1980).
[4]Treas. Reg. § 1.1012-1(c)(2) (1980).
[5]*Id.*
[6]Kluger Associates, Inc. v. Comm'r, 69 T.C. 925 (1978), *aff'd*, 617 F.2d 323 (2d Cir. 1980).
[7]Davidson v. Comm'r, 305 U.S. 44, 46 (1938).

or more lots of securities acquired at different times and at different prices, and he wants to sell only a particular lot (or lots) but not all of the shares represented in the single certificate. A taxpayer can identify the particular securities he wants his broker or other agent to sell out of a single certificate if two requirements are met. First, the taxpayer must advise the broker or other agent of either the date he acquired the particular lot to be sold or the price he paid for the particular lot.[8] Second, the taxpayer must receive back from the broker or other agent a written confirmation that specifies with sufficient detail those securities that were sold.[9] Alternatively, if the taxpayer wants to sell or transfer particular securities out of a single certificate without using a broker or other agent, he must maintain a written record of the particular securities that he intends to transfer or sell.[10]

(2) STREET NAME SECURITIES

It is quite common for a taxpayer's securities to be registered in the name of a broker, rather than in the taxpayer's own name. Such securities, referred to as "street name" securities, legally belong to the taxpayer, who has all of the rights of ownership. The broker merely acts as a nominee. Because securities held in street name are not in the taxpayer's name or possession, it is impossible for a taxpayer to physically identify them. As a result, such securities are adequately identified if the taxpayer (1) specifies in writing to the broker the sequence in which the securities are to be sold; (2) identifies by either the date of acquisition or his original cost, the particular securities he wants to sell; and (3) within a reasonable time after the sale, receives back from the broker a written confirmation acknowledging his sales instructions.[11] If these conditions are met, the taxpayer's identification is sufficient for tax purposes, without regard to which securities are delivered by the broker.

In Rev. Rul. 67-436,[12] the IRS sanctioned an identification procedure used by a corporate taxpayer who left a portfolio of stock, registered in street name, in the custody of a broker who commingled those shares with identical securities owned by other customers. The taxpayer authorized the broker to make certain purchases and sales without first obtaining the taxpayer's prior approval. As a result, although the broker

---

[8]Treas. Reg. § 1.1012-1(c)(3)(ii)(a) (1980); Rev. Rul. 72-415, 1972-2 C.B. 463.
[9]Treas. Reg. § 1.1012-1(c)(3)(ii)(b) (1980); Rev. Rul. 72-415, 1972-2 C.B. 463.
[10]Treas. Reg. § 1.1012-1(c)(3)(ii)(b) (1980); Rev. Rul. 72-415, 1972-2 C.B. 463.
[11]Treas. Reg. § 1.1012-1(c)(3)(i) (1980); Rev. Rul. 61-97, 1961-1 C.B. 394.
[12]1967-2 C.B. 266.

immediately advised the taxpayer of all sales of stock, the securities could not be identified on the trade date. Once advised of the trade, however, the taxpayer would determine from its records what lot of stock it wanted to use for delivery. The IRS ruled that this method of identification was sufficient as long as the taxpayer advised the broker of the stock selection in writing and received back from the broker a written confirmation prior to the settlement date.[13]

(3) SECURITIES HELD BY FIDUCIARIES

Securities held by fiduciaries (i.e., trustees, executors, and administrators) are adequately identified if the fiduciaries specify in the books and records of the trust or estate those securities to be sold, transferred, or distributed.[14] In addition, securities distributed to a beneficiary are adequately identified if the fiduciary (1) identifies the securities distributed to the beneficiary in the books and records of the trust or estate and (2) gives the beneficiary a written statement identifying the particular securities that are distributed to him.[15] Even if the securities actually sold, transferred, or distributed turn out to be different from those that were identified by the fiduciary, a fiduciary's identification is deemed sufficient.[16]

(b) FIRST-IN, FIRST-OUT RULE

If securities are not adequately identified, the taxpayer is presumed to have disposed of the securities on a FIFO basis. This means that the first securities acquired by the taxpayer are deemed to be the first securities sold for determining both the basis and holding period of the securities.[17] Of course, if the taxpayer does not want to sell his securities on the FIFO basis, application of the FIFO rule could produce adverse tax consequences.

When imposing the FIFO rule, the date used to determine which securities were acquired first is the date the holding period begins for the securities and includes any tacked holding periods.[18] For example, securities received as a gift are acquired on the date the donor received

---

[13]*Id.*
[14]Treas. Reg. § 1.1012-1(c)(4)(i) (1980).
[15]Treas. Reg. § 1.1012-1(c)(4) (1980).
[16]Treas. Reg. § 1.1012-1(c)(4)(ii) (1980).
[17]Treas. Reg. § 1.1012-1(c)(1) (1980).
[18]For a discussion of holding period computations, see section 15.1.

the securities.[19] Securities acquired on margin and held in a margin account are viewed as sold under the FIFO rules in the order purchased, even if placed in the margin account in a different order.[20]

(c) STOCK DIVIDENDS AND STOCK SPLITS

If a taxpayer receives stock as a noncash dividend or as a stock split ("new stock"), the shares so received are allocated generally to the lots of stock already owned by the taxpayer ("old stock").[21] The taxpayer can, with adequate identification, sell the new stock (with a tacked holding period which relates to the old stock), irrespective of whether the new shares are received in a single certificate or in separate certificates.[22] If the taxpayer does not adequately identify the new stock, the FIFO rule treats the stock sold as being allocated to the stock held by the taxpayer for the longest time, including any dividend or stock received in a stock split that relates to the oldest shares.[23]

(d) NONTAXABLE EXCHANGES

Securities received in nontaxable exchanges (e.g., tax-free reorganizations and recapitalizations) are allocated to the various lots of securities surrendered by the taxpayer in exchange for the new securities.[24] If adequate identification is not made by the taxpayer, however, securities received in the same corporation are allocated on a FIFO basis.[25]

The FIFO rule is not applied to securities received in a nontaxable exchange if the securities received are in a corporation that is different from the corporation whose old shares were surrendered in the ex-

[19]Richardson v. Smith, 23 A.F.T.R. (P-H) 1264, 1270 (D.C. Conn. 1938), *rev'd on other grounds*, 102 F.2d 697 (2d Cir. 1939); *cf.* Hanes v. Comm'r, 1 T.C.M. (CCH) 634, 638 (1943).

[20]Forrester v. Comm'r, 32 B.T.A. 745, 749 (1935).

[21]For a discussion of those situations where the holding period of securities received in a nontaxable distribution is tacked onto the taxpayer's old holding period, see section 15.3.

[22]Ford v. Comm'r, 33 B.T.A. 1229 (1936), *acq.* 1937-1 C.B. 9; Willock v. Comm'r, 6 T.C.M. (CCH) 487 (1947); Rev. Rul. 56-653, 1956-2 C.B. 185.

[23]Fuller v. Comm'r, 81 F.2d 176 (1st Cir. 1936); Kraus v. Comm'r, 88 F.2d 616, 617 (2d Cir. 1937); Epstein v. Comm'r, 36 B.T.A. 109 (1937), *acq.* 1938-1 C.B. 10.

[24]Block v. Comm'r, 148 F.2d 452 (9th Cir. 1945); for a discussion of those situations where the holding period for securities received in an exchange is tacked with another holding period, see section 15.3(a).

[25]Keller v. Comm'r, 86 F.2d 265, 266 (8th Cir. 1936), *cert. denied*, 300 U.S. 373 (1937); *see Kraus*, 88 F.2d at 617.

change. Rather, the total cost basis for the lots surrendered is allocated pro rata among all of the new shares received in the exchange.[26]

(e) BOOK ENTRY SECURITIES

A sale or transfer of book entry securities made after December 31, 1970 is adequately identified if the taxpayer specifies the securities to be sold by the unique lot number that he has assigned to the lot from which the securities are to be sold.[27] For sales or transfers made after December 31, 1970, a book entry security is defined as (1) a transferable Treasury bill, note, certificate of indebtedness, or bill issued under the Second Liberty Bond Act, or (2) a bill, note, bond, certificate of indebtedness, debenture, or similar obligation that is subject to 31 C.F.R. Part 306 (or other comparable federal regulations) and which is issued by any department or agency of the federal government, FNMA, Federal Home Loan Banks, FHLMC, the Federal Land Banks, the Federal Intermediate Credit Banks, the Bank for Cooperatives, or the Tennessee Valley Authority.[28]

Specification of securities to be transferred generally is made by the taxpayer with a written instruction.[29] If the book entry is made by an FRB bank in the name of the taxpayer, additional requirements are imposed. First, the taxpayer in whose name the book entry is made must list the lot numbers for all book entry securities sold or transferred on that date.[30] Second, the list must be mailed to or received by the appropriate FRB bank on or before the next business day.[31] And third, the taxpayer must assign lot numbers in numerical sequence to all successive purchases of securities of the same series and maturity date that were purchased at different prices.[32] Purchases of securities at the same price on the same date may be included within the same lot.

With respect to a book entry made by an FRB bank after December 31, 1970, the Treasury regulations also provide that the taxpayer's written instructions must be confirmed by a written acknowledgment from the FRB bank or the person through whom the taxpayer sells or transfers the securities. The acknowledgment must include the amount and de-

[26]Comm'r v. Von Gunten, 76 F.2d 670, 671 (6th Cir. 1935); Helvering v. Stifel, 75 F.2d 583, 584 (4th Cir. 1935); Rev. Rul. 55-355, 1955-1 C.B. 418.

[27]Treas. Reg. § 1.1012-1(c)(7) (1980).

[28]Treas. Reg. §§ 1.1012-1(c)(7)(iii)(a)(1), (b) (1980).

[29]Treas. Reg. § 1.1012-1(c)(7)(i) (1980).

[30]Treas. Reg. § 1.1012-1(c)(7)(i)(b) (1980).

[31]*Id.*

[32]Treas. Reg. § 1.1012-1(c)(7)(i) (1980).

scription of the securities sold or transferred and the date of the transaction.[33] If the book entry is made by an FRB bank prior to January 1, 1971, the FRB bank must furnish the taxpayer with a serially numbered advice of transaction.[34]

Identification requirements for book entry securities have been addressed in several revenue rulings, some of which are mentioned here. Rev. Rul. 73-37[35] provides rules for identification of book entry securities that have unique lot numbers assigned to them at the time of purchase. Rev. Rul. 71-21[36] provides a means for verifying specifically identified book entry securities owned as investments. And, in Rev. Rul. 73-31,[37] the IRS acknowledged that book entry securities in dealer inventories present the same identification problems as investment securities.

(f) REGULATED INVESTMENT COMPANY SHARES

The tax basis of shares in a regulated investment company (e.g., a mutual fund or a unit investment trust) is generally determined in the same manner as the tax basis of shares of stock in any other corporation. Additional shares that are acquired by the taxpayer through reinvestment of dividends (including capital gain dividends) have a tax basis equal to the amount of dividend income taxed to the taxpayer. This is because the shares are acquired in a taxable transaction.[38] Similarly, when a regulated investment company elects, under I.R.C. § 852(b)-(3)(D)(iii), to treat undistributed capital gains as distributions to its shareholders, this election increases the taxpayer's basis in his shares.

To determine a taxpayer's basis in the shares of a regulated investment company, the taxpayer can use the specific identification method (if the shares are adequately identified) or the FIFO method.[39] An additional method is provided, on an elective basis, for regulated investment company shares left by the taxpayer with a custodian or agent in an account maintained specifically for the acquisition or redemption of

---

[33]Treas. Reg. § 1.1012-1(c)(7)(ii)(a) (1980).

[34]Treas. Reg. § 1.1012-1(c)(7)(ii)(b) (1980).

[35]1973-1 C.B. 374.

[36]1971-1 C.B. 221.

[37]1973-1 C.B. 217; for a discussion of specific identification by dealers, see section 20.2(c).

[38]A shareholder's tax basis in the shares credited to his account is the fair market value of those shares on the dividend payment date, even though the shares may have been purchased at a discount or premium. Rev. Rul. 79-42, 1979-1 C.B. 130; Rev. Rul. 78-375, 1978-2 C.B. 130; Rev. Rul. 76-53, 1976-1 C.B. 87.

[39]*See* section 18.2.

the shares in that company for taxable years ending on or after December 31, 1981. In such a case, a taxpayer can elect to determine the cost or other basis of the regulated investment company shares on an average basis.[40]

Two methods are available to average a taxpayer's regulated investment company share basis: the double-category method and the single-category method. The double-category method is discussed in Treas. Reg. § 1.1012-1(e)(3), while the single-category method is discussed in Treas. Reg. § 1.1012-1(e)(4). An election to adopt either method is made on the taxpayer's tax return for the first taxable year ending on or after December 31, 1970 for which the taxpayer wants the election to apply.[41] It is up to the taxpayer to maintain all of the records that are necessary to substantiate the average basis (or bases) used on his tax return.[42] Once made, the average basis election applies to all of the taxpayer's shares in the regulated investment company (except for certain shares that were acquired by gift) if the shares are left with custodians or agents.[43] The election cannot be revoked without the prior consent of the IRS.[44]

[40]Treas. Reg. § 1.1012-1(e)(1)(i) (1980).
[41]Treas. Reg. § 1.1012-1(e)(6)(i) (1980).
[42]Id.
[43]Treas. Reg. § 1.1012-1(e)(6)(ii) (1980).
[44]Id.

Part Four

Taxation of Ordinary Income Transactions

Nineteen

General Principles

§ 19.1 ORDINARY INCOME OR LOSS

Ordinary income or loss is generated from the sale or exchange of property that is not a capital asset in the hands of the taxpayer. As a result, the definition of ordinary income property is important to determine whether an asset generates ordinary income or loss. Ordinary income is defined as any gain from the sale or exchange of property that is neither a capital asset nor business property described in I.R.C. § 1231(b).[1] Ordinary loss is defined as any loss from the sale or exchange of property that is not a capital asset.[2]

Ordinary income property includes those assets that are held by dealers as stock in trade, inventory, and primarily for sale to customers in the ordinary course of business.[3] Similarly, hedgers purchase securities, commodities, or option positions for business purposes, rather than for investment, which are excluded from capital asset treatment.[4] Ordinary income property includes property purchased to acquire or assure a

---

[1]I.R.C. § 64; *see* section 6.8 for a special rule for financial institutions.

[2]I.R.C. § 65.

[3]I.R.C. § 1221(1); *see generally* section 6.3; Chapter Nine.

[4]*See* Corn Products Refining Co. v. Comm'r, 350 U.S. 46, 52-53 (1955), *reh'g denied*, 350 U.S. 943 (1956); *see generally* Chapter 21.

source of inventory.[5] Furthermore, ordinary income or loss results from property (other than I.R.C. § 1231(b) assets) held for business purposes.[6]

Ordinary income or loss on the sale or exchange of ordinary income property is taken into account for computing taxable income. This means that gain or loss from the sale or exchange of ordinary income property is added to or deducted from a taxpayer's ordinary income from other sources.

§ 19.2   APPLICATION OF LOSS DEFERRAL RULE

All taxpayers, except hedgers with respect to those hedging transactions that qualify for the statutory hedging exemption,[7] are subject to the loss deferral rule imposed by I.R.C. § 1092(a)(1)(A). The loss deferral rule defers losses incurred on positions in personal property if the taxpayer holds offsetting positions with inherent gains.[8] Losses are deferred until the offsetting gain positions are closed out. For a discussion of the loss deferral rule, see generally Part Ten.

§ 19.3   AMOUNT REALIZED

The first step in computing gain or loss is to determine the total amount of consideration received from the sale or exchange of property in cash, services, or other property. Services and property are valued at their respective fair market values. In general, net proceeds are compared with the taxpayer's adjusted basis for the property that is disposed of,[9] and the difference between net proceeds and the adjusted basis represents the amount of gain or loss realized by the taxpayer.[10] If the net proceeds exceed the taxpayer's basis, the taxpayer realizes income on the sale or exchange. If the net proceeds are less than the taxpayer's basis, the taxpayer realizes a loss on the transaction. A taxpayer using an inventory method must use it to determine property sold.[11]

[5]See Western Wine & Liquor Co. v. Comm'r, 18 T.C. 1090, 1099 (1952), appeal dismissed, 205 F.2d 420 (8th Cir. 1953), acq. 1958-1 C.B. 6; Bagley & Sewall Co. v. Comm'r, 20 T.C. 983, 989 (1953), aff'd, 221 F.2d 944 (2d Cir. 1955), acq. 1958-1 C.B. 3; Waterman, Largen & Co. v. U.S., 419 F.2d 845, 851-52 (Ct. Cl. 1969), cert. denied, 400 U.S. 869 (1970).

[6]See section 6.3.

[7]See generally Chapter 21.

[8]I.R.C. § 1092(a)(1)(A).

[9]See generally Chapter 14.

[10]I.R.C. § 1001(a).

[11]See section 20.2.

§ 19.4 AMOUNT RECOGNIZED

Gain or loss realized on a sale or exchange of property is not necessarily the amount to be taken into account in computing taxable income. Rather, the amount of gain or loss that is taken into account for tax purposes is the amount recognized on the sale or exchange.[12] As a result, to determine the tax effect of a gain or loss, one must calculate the amount of realized gain or realized loss to be recognized for tax purposes. In cash sales, the entire amount of gain or loss is recognized and must be brought into income. In certain exchanges of property, however, the transaction can qualify for either total or partial nonrecognition under specific Code provisions.[13]

§ 19.5 SECTION 1256 CONTRACTS

Ordinary income property that is a section 1256 contract position and that is not eligible for the statutory hedging exemption under I.R.C. § 1256(e) is marked-to-market at its fair market value on the last business day of the tax year at ordinary income rates.[14] The 60/40 Rule does not apply to section 1256 contracts that are not capital assets. For a discussion of section 1256 contracts, see generally Part Nine.

§ 19.6 POSSIBLE APPLICATION OF THE WASH SALES RULE

It is possible that the wash sales rule imposed by I.R.C. § 1091 may be applied to taxpayers who generate ordinary income or loss on their securities transactions but who are not dealers. For a discussion of the wash sales rule, see generally Chapter 17.

---

[12]I.R.C. § 1001(c).
[13]*See generally* I.R.C. §§ 351, 354–356, 1031, 1036.
[14]I.R.C. § 1256(f)(2).

Twenty

Identification of Ordinary Income Property

In certain cases, dealers (and hedgers) are required to maintain inventories for property held for sale to customers in the ordinary course of business that clearly reflects income. In addition, those taxpayers who maintain inventories must also report their income on the accrual method, rather than on the cash basis. Accounting and inventory methods for ordinary income property are discussed in this chapter.

§ 20.1   ACCOUNTING METHODS

(a)   IN GENERAL

In general, dealers compute taxable income using the same methods regularly employed in keeping their books.[1] Permitted methods include the cash basis, the accrual method, and any other permitted method.[2] In cases where inventories are mandatory, the accrual method of accounting also is required.[3] Dealers with inventories must use the accrual method to compute taxable income.

[1] I.R.C. § 446(a).
[2] I.R.C. § 446(c).
[3] Treas. Reg. § 1.446-1(c)(2)(i) (1973).

Dealers who engage in more than one active trade or business can use different accounting methods for each separate and distinct business,[4] as long as the accounting methods clearly reflect income.[5] In other words, a dealer can use the accrual method for those activities that require inventories and the cash basis method for brokerage and other businesses that do not require the maintenance of inventories. To treat different business activities as separate and distinct, separate books and records must be maintained.[6] Also, to avoid a possible audit challenge to the use of different methods for separate business activities, some dealers conduct their different business activities in wholly separate business entities.

(b) FUTURES CONTRACTS

Commodity dealers (and hedgers) can value commodities actually on hand at the close of the taxable year at market value.[7] They can take into account gains or losses at year-end based upon the market value of open futures contracts that are hedges against cash positions or against forward sales or purchases.[8] Nevertheless, a commodities dealer (or hedger) cannot take into account in his year-end inventory open futures contract positions, because title to the underlying commodities does not pass to the taxpayer until delivery.[9] Open futures contracts form no integral part of the cost of the commodities included in the physical inventory and cannot be used to reflect unrealized gains and losses.[10] Section 1256 contract positions that are not hedge transactions (as defined in I.R.C. § 1256(e)) are marked-to-market at year-end at ordinary income rates for noncapital assets. For a discussion of section 1256 treatment, see generally Part Nine. Losses on such transactions also might be subject to the modified wash sales rule.[11]

(c) ON-CALL CONTRACTS

On-call contracts, that is, contracts that assure a source of supply but do not fix the price at which the commodity will be sold, are commonly

---

[4]I.R.C. § 446(d).
[5]Treas. Reg. § 1.446-1(d)(1) (1973).
[6]Treas. Reg. § 1.446-1(d)(2) (1973).
[7]Rev. Rul. 74-226, 1974-1 C.B. 119.
[8]Rev. Rul. 74-223, 1974-1 C.B. 23.
[9]Rev. Rul. 74-227, 1974-1 C.B. 119.
[10]*Id.*
[11]*See* section 42.3.

used in the cotton industry. The price remains open until the seller exercises a call right granted by the contract. In *Molsen v. Comm'r*,[12] the Tax Court approved the cotton industry practice of accounting for the cost of goods sold by valuing an ending cotton inventory at market and accruing to the cost of purchases the additional amounts that would be payable under unfixed, delivered, on-call purchase contracts at the end of the year.[13] The court viewed on-call contracts as an exception to the doctrine that requires all events to be fixed and a transaction to be closed for tax purposes. Molsen invalidates the IRS position stated in Rev. Rul. 81-298[14] that cotton merchants could not include the additional amounts (if any) payable under on-call purchase contracts in the cost of cotton purchases unless the cotton producers had called the prices during the taxable year. This ruling was contrary to the long-standing practice of cotton merchants. The Tax Court stated that "the unique accounting needs and practices of the cotton merchants have similarly led to a deviation from the general rules governing the valuation of inventories and the calculation of income."[15] The Tax Court found the IRS's proposed treatment of unfixed, delivered, on-call contracts inconsistent with the treatment of hedging transactions entered into by cotton merchants, because on-call contracts (although not technically hedge transactions) appear to function in much the same way as a hedge.[16] The court held that the taxpayer's accounting method clearly reflected income and that the IRS had abused its discretion in trying to change the taxpayer's accounting method.[17]

§ 20.2 INVENTORY METHODS

Two components make up every inventory method: valuation basis and cost flow assumptions. Once an inventory method is adopted it cannot be changed without prior consent of the IRS.[18] Securities, commodities, or options not held for sale to customers in the ordinary course of business (i.e., held as investment property) cannot be included in the dealer's

---

[12]85 T.C. 485 (1985).
[13]*Id.* at 497.
[14]1981-2 C.B. 114.
[15]*Molsen*, 85 T.C. at 504.
[16]*Id.* at 507.
[17]*Id.* at 509.
[18]I.R.C. § 446(e).

inventory. Regardless of the inventory method employed by a dealer, the opening inventory in the first year must be valued at cost.[19]

(a) VALUATION BASES

Valuation bases most commonly used by business concerns are (1) cost or (2) lower of cost or market.[20] Dealers in securities and commodities can value their inventories at the market value,[21] even though it may exceed their cost.

(b) COST FLOW METHODS

With respect to inventory cost flow techniques, the three main methods are: FIFO,[22] specific identification,[23] and LIFO.[24] The FIFO method assumes that the first items purchased are the first items sold; hence, the items on hand at year-end are those most recently purchased. The LIFO method assumes the opposite; the items on hand at year-end are those first purchased, and the ones sold during the year are those most recently purchased. The LIFO method matches current (usually higher) costs with current revenues. When prices are rising the use of the LIFO method can significantly reduce a dealer's taxable income. In addition, a dollar-value method of valuation, rather than a unit-value method, can be used in conjunction with the LIFO method.[25] The specific identification method makes no assumption about the flow of property; rather, it allows the taxpayer to specifically identify those items sold and those on hand at year-end.[26]

Once a dealer uses LIFO, FIFO, or specific identification, he generally has the option of valuing the property (whose identity is determined based on either the assumptions of LIFO or FIFO or on the actual physical identification of specific securities) at cost, the lower of cost or market, or at market.[27] For LIFO, however, only cost is appropriate.[28]

[19]Claude Neon Electrical Products Corp. v. Comm'r, 35 B.T.A. 563, 566 (1937).

[20]Treas. Reg. § 1.471-2(c) (1973).

[21]Treas. Reg. § 1.471-5 (1958); Rev. Rul. 74-227, 1974-1 C.B. 119.

[22]See generally Treas. Reg. § 1.471-2(d) (1973) (providing that an inventory method must be applied consistently to the entire inventory except for those goods inventoried under LIFO).

[23]Id.

[24]Treas. Reg. § 1.472-1(a) (1961).

[25]Treas. Reg. § 1.472-8(a) (1982).

[26]See section 18.2(a).

[27]Treas. Reg. § 1.471-5 (1958); Rev. Rul. 74-227, 1974-1 C.B. 119.

[28]Treas. Reg. § 1.472-2(b) (1981).

(c) SPECIFIC IDENTIFICATION

The specific identification method is expressly authorized for tax purposes. Treas. Reg. § 1.471-2(d) provides that:

> [w]here the taxpayer maintains book inventories in accordance with a sound accounting system in which the respective inventory accounts are charged with the actual cost of the goods purchased or produced and credited with the value of goods used, transferred, or sold, calculated upon the basis of the actual cost of the goods acquired during the taxable year . . . the net value as shown by such inventory accounts will be deemed to be the cost of the goods on hand.[29]

Treas. Reg. § 1.471-2(d) provides that the specific identification method is an appropriate and acceptable method for assessing the tax consequences of inventory accounts. In addition, Treas. Reg. § 1.471-5 provides that a "[d]ealer in securities in whose books of account separate computations of the gain or loss from the sale of various lots of securities sold are made on the basis of the cost of each lot shall be regarded, for the purposes of this section, as regularly inventorying his securities at cost."[30] This provision authorizes a dealer in securities to make separate computations of gain or loss based upon the cost of each particular security. In other words, a dealer in securities can specifically identify the particular security that is being sold.

Rev. Rul. 73-31[31] specifies the tax records that a dealer in securities must maintain to specifically identify inventoried securities transferred to a book entry system maintained by an FRB Bank. In the ruling, the taxpayer, a dealer in securities, used the cost method to value the securities in his inventory. Cost was determined by specifically identifying the securities purchased, sold, and inventoried. The dealer maintained records by specific certificate numbers and actually transferred the specified certificates when a sale was made. The IRS ruled that specific identification of inventoried book entry securities presents the same need of a verification method as did the specific identification of book entry securities owned as investments.[32] Rev. Rul. 71-21[33] provides a means of independently verifying specifically identified book entry securities owned as investments. Sufficient independent verification of book entry securities for specific identification is met by a procedure instituted to meet the requirements of Treas. Reg. § 1.1012-1(c)(7)(i),

---

[29]Treas. Reg. § 1.471-2(d) (1973).
[30]Treas. Reg. § 1.471-5 (1958).
[31]1973-1 C.B. 217.
[32]*Id.*
[33]1971-1 C.B. 221, *amplified by* Rev. Rul. 73-37, 1973-1 C.B. 374.

which basically requires the taxpayer either to specify (1) the particular security to be sold or transferred or (2) the unique lot number that the taxpayer has assigned to the lot containing the security to be sold or transferred.[34]

In a 1971 private letter ruling,[35] a dealer in Treasury bills used the cost method of inventory valuation. In most cases, FIFO was used to determine which particular securities were sold. However, in some cases the dealer used the specific identification method to determine which securities were sold. The IRS stated that Rev. Rul. 71-21[36] details the means of specifically identifying book entry securities owned as investments. "Specific identification of inventoried securities presents the same need of a verification method."[37] Tax records similar to "those detailed in Rev. Rul. 71-21 are appropriate for specific identification of inventoried securities."[38] Therefore, the specific identification method of accounting is available to inventoried securities.

The IRS Manual provides a checklist of questions for IRS agents conducting audits of securities dealers. The following questions about inventory methods are asked: "If the firm is a dealer, which inventory method is used for its dealer securities—cost, cost or market whichever is lower, or market value? In conjunction therewith is FIFO or LIFO followed?"[39] In addition, the IRS Manual states that while most dealers in securities follow a FIFO basis, more and more are adopting a LIFO basis of inventory valuation.[40] This assumes that only two inventory costing methods are available to dealers in securities, which is in direct contravention of the Treasury regulations. This appears to be an oversight by the writers of the IRS Manual, rather than a limitation as to the inventory costing methods available to dealers in securities. It does, however, indicate the possibility of a challenge to specific identification upon audit.

(d) SHORT POSITIONS

As a necessary part of their businesses, dealers frequently sell securities, commodities, and option positions short. Consequently, dealers often

---

[34]Treas. Reg. § 1.1012-1(c)(7)(i) (1980); Rev. Rul. 71-21, 1971-1 C.B. 221, *amplified by* Rev. Rul. 73-37, 1973-1 C.B. 374.

[35]LTR 7101131330A (Jan. 13, 1971).

[36]1971-1 C.B. 221.

[37]LTR 7101131330A (Jan. 13, 1971).

[38]*Id.*

[39]1 INTERNAL REVENUE MANUAL (AUDIT) (CCH) 7261-10, ¶ 142(2)(e) (Dec. 14, 1976).

[40]*Id.* at 7261-50, ¶ 315(1).

have open short positions at the end of their taxable years. Irrespective of the inventory method used by a dealer, short positions are not included in a dealer's inventory and are not subject to the dealer's valuation basis or cost flow methods.[41] Short positions generally are viewed as liabilities, not as inventory assets.

§ 20.3   CLEAR REFLECTION OF INCOME

An inventory method must clearly reflect income to be recognized for tax purposes. Inventories are taken on such a basis and as conforming as nearly as possible to the best accounting practices in the trade or business that will most clearly reflect the income.[42]

Case law is not in agreement as to what accounting method is sufficient to clearly reflect income. In *Wood v. Comm'r*,[43] a dealer in securities treated each lot of securities purchased separately and applied the proceeds of the sale of any portion of a lot to the cost of the entire lot, thereby reducing the cost of the remaining securities in the lot and the cost of the securities on hand at the end of each tax year.[44] This method, which was successfully challenged by the IRS, resulted in no profit on the sale of any portion of the securities until the entire lot was disposed of.[45] The court held that the dealer's method did not clearly reflect income for the tax year, and under these circumstances the FIFO method could be used to determine the cost of securities on hand at the close of the taxable year.[46]

As long as the taxpayer's method of maintaining an inventory clearly reflects his income, the IRS may not disregard it simply because it deviates slightly from one of the three inventory costing methods (i.e., FIFO, LIFO, and specific identification) available to dealers. Any variation must be practiced consistently. The crucial point is that the basis of inventory valuation chosen by a taxpayer clearly reflects income.

In *Huntington Securities Corp. v. Busey*,[47] the court acknowledged that if a taxpayer's method of accounting clearly reflects income, the taxpayer has wide discretion in following the accounting method of his choice. The court did state, however, that neither the taxpayer nor the

---

[41]*See* section 20.2(a) and section 20.2(b).

[42]I.R.C. § 471.

[43]197 F.2d 859 (5th Cir. 1952).

[44]*Id.* at 860-61.

[45]*Id.* at 861.

[46]*Id.*

[47]112 F.2d 368, 370 (6th Cir. 1940).

IRS has unlimited discretion.[48] If the taxpayer's method of accounting clearly reflects income, I.R.C. § 471 (which provides the general rule for inventories) is mandatory on both the taxpayer and the IRS "that taxable income must be determined in accordance therewith."[49] The selection of a system of accounting is exclusively the taxpayer's, and provided it clearly reflects income, the method must be recognized by the IRS.[50] In addition, the court defined the word "clearly" as plainly, honestly, straightforwardly, and frankly; not as "accurately," which in its ordinary use means precisely and exactly.[51]

The taxpayer in *Huntington* valued its inventory by using the profit realized from the sale of lots of identical securities to reduce the cost of the remaining identical securities, or, where losses were realized on the sale of such securities, by adding such losses to the cost of the remaining securities.[52] This method clearly indicated the cost and sale price of all of the securities for each annual accounting period.[53] Although the court acknowledged that this method of valuing inventories was not accurate, the court held it clearly reflected income, which is all that it believed was required under the Code.[54] In addition, the court defined the phrase "basis of keeping accounts" as the general bookkeeping system followed by the taxpayer.[55] Indeed, the court implied that, although the taxpayer's method of accounting was not accurate, it was not to be disregarded because it clearly reflected income.[56] Because *Huntington* did not directly involve inventory cost flow issues (such as FIFO, LIFO, and specific identification), it did not directly involve valuation basis issues (such as cost, the lower of cost or market, or market value). By using profit to reduce the basis of the remaining unsold securities, the case did involve, as the court noted, the "basis of keeping accounts," for both the cost flow methods and the valuation basis methods.[57] Consequently, the case might be read as allowing cost flow and pricing methods that closely reflect income, even if those methods are not otherwise accurate.

---

[48] *Id.*
[49] *Id.*
[50] *Id.*
[51] *Id.*
[52] *Id.* at 369–70.
[53] *Id.* at 370.
[54] *Id.* at 370–71.
[55] *Id.* at 371.
[56] *See id.* at 370–71.
[57] *Id.* at 371.

In *Koebig & Koebig, Inc. v. Comm'r*,[58] the court discussed the taxpayer's use of the accrual method of accounting, noting that the accrual method does not always result in a precise matching of income and expenses. Precise matching is not necessary for a clear reflection of income; "the vital point is consistency."[59] The court held that because the taxpayer's method of accounting clearly reflected income, the IRS could not reconstruct the taxpayer's income on some other basis to secure more favorable tax results.[60]

In *Caldwell v. Comm'r*,[61] however, the court held that the phrase "clearly reflects income" means that income should be reflected with as much accuracy as standard accounting practices permit, and not merely that the taxpayer keeps his books fairly and honestly.

[58]23 T.C.M. (CCH) 170, 181 (1964).
[59]*Id.*
[60]*Id.* at 182.
[61]202 F.2d 112, 115 (2d Cir. 1953).

Twenty-one

Hedging Transactions

§ 21.1 INTRODUCTION

Hedging transactions are entered into by hedgers primarily to protect the price at which they acquire their raw materials and inventories and to assure a market to sell their inventories. For a discussion of hedgers generally, see section 6.4. In addition, those hedging transactions that qualify for the statutory definition of a hedging transaction under I.R.C. § 1256(e)(2) are exempt from (1) section 1256 treatment,[1] (2) the loss deferral rule,[2] and (3) the requirement to capitalize interest and carrying charges.[3] This chapter discusses the statutory hedging exemption. It also identifies the consequences of entering into transactions that do not qualify for the statutory exemption.

§ 21.2 DEFINITIONS FOR EXEMPT HEDGE

Positions in personal property that are part of hedging transactions as defined in the Code are explicitly exempt from section 1256 treatment[4] and the Straddle Rules (including the loss deferral rule, the modified wash sales rule and short sales rules, and the requirement to capitalize interest and carrying charges).[5] This means that gain or loss on hedging

[1] I.R.C. § 1256(e)(1).
[2] I.R.C. § 1092(e).
[3] I.R.C. § 263(g)(3).
[4] See generally Part Nine.
[5] See generally Part Ten.

transactions can be taken into income when a position is closed, used to adjust basis (where appropriate) or deferred in accordance with the taxpayer's normal accounting practices. Open section 1256 positions are not marked-to-market at the end of the taxable year. Losses need not be deferred under the loss deferral rule, and interest and carrying charges are currently deductible. If a transaction fails to qualify for the statutory hedging exemption, the positions remain subject to section 1256 treatment (for section 1256 contracts that are capital assets in the hands of the taxpayer) and the Straddle Rules generally.

The analysis used to determine whether a transaction qualifies for the statutory hedging exemption is identical for both section 1256 and non-section 1256 positions, because hedging transactions for both purposes are defined in I.R.C. § 1256(e).

Although a formal hedging election is not required, several requirements must be met for a transaction to qualify for the hedging exemption. First, the transaction must be entered into in the normal course of the taxpayer's trade or business.[6] Second, the transaction must be entered into primarily to reduce the risks of certain price changes, interest rate changes, or currency fluctuations.[7] Third, gain or loss on hedging transactions must be treated as ordinary income or loss.[8] Fourth, the taxpayer must identify the transaction as a hedge on his books before the end of the day the transaction is entered into (or an earlier time if prescribed by Treasury regulations).[9]

A syndicate, defined as any partnership or other enterprise that allocates 35 percent or more of its losses to limited partners or limited entrepreneurs, cannot qualify for the statutory hedging exemption.[10] Limited partners and limited entrepreneurs of entities that are not syndicates are subject to certain rules that limit the deductibility of losses incurred on hedging transactions entered into by their flow-through entities.[11]

Once a taxpayer identifies a transaction as a hedging transaction, it can never result in capital gain.[12] Improper identification precludes capital gain treatment even if the personal property (as identified in

---

[6]*See* section 21.3(a).

[7]*See* section 21.3(b).

[8]*See* section 21.3(c).

[9]*See* section 21.3(d).

[10]I.R.C. § 1256(e)(3); *see* section 21.4(b).

[11]*See* section 21.4(c).

[12]I.R.C. § 1256(f)(1); *see* section 21.6.

I.R.C. § 1092(d)(1)) was a capital asset and otherwise would have been eligible for capital asset treatment. Difficult issues are raised when the property to be hedged does not qualify as personal property because it is not actively traded. Finally, if a transaction does not comply with the specific requirements of I.R.C. § 1256(e)(2)—but is subject to ordinary income treatment under the Corn Products doctrine—the transaction, nevertheless, generates ordinary income or loss although it remains subject to the Straddle Rules and section 1256 treatment.[13] In other words, the gains and losses from a Corn Products hedge transaction are always ordinary, rather than capital, even if the transaction does not qualify for the statutory hedging exemption. And, the positions that do not qualify as a hedge can be used to defer loss, change holding periods, and require capitalization of interest and carrying charges on offsetting positions.

Despite the statutory definition provided in I.R.C. § 1256(e), defining hedges and hedging transactions are not simple matters. The pre-ERTA case law continues to apply to determine whether gain or loss on a transaction is ordinary income or loss and whether the transaction constitutes an integral part of the taxpayer's business.[14] Whether a transaction qualifies as a hedge can be somewhat hard to pin down, because it depends on the facts and circumstances of the individual taxpayer.[15]

The Senate Finance Committee Report of ERTA acknowledged that "[h]edging transactions are varied and complex. They may be executed in a wide range of property and forms, including options, futures, forwards, and other contract rights and short sales."[16] This broad view of a hedge is appropriate because such transactions, depending upon the taxpayer's business, can encompass various sorts of property and a wide range of activities. The broad scope of hedging includes short ("selling") hedges and long ("buying") hedges.[17] In addition, interest rate hedges, entered into to reduce the risk of interest rate fluctuations on obligations or borrowings, are eligible for the hedging exemption.[18]

---

[13]Corn Products Refining Co. v. Comm'r, 350 U.S. 46 (1955).

[14]JOINT COMMITTEE ON TAXATION, 97TH CONG., 2D SESS., GENERAL EXPLANATION OF THE ECONOMIC RECOVERY TAX ACT OF 1981 300 (Joint Comm. Print 1981) [hereinafter referred to as "General Explanation of ERTA"].

[15]See section 6.4.

[16]FINANCE COMMITTEE REPORT, ECONOMIC RECOVERY TAX ACT OF 1981, S. REP. NO. 144, 97th Cong., 1st Sess. 159, reprinted in 1981 U.S. CODE CONG. & AD. NEWS 105, 258.

[17]See section 6.4(c).

[18]See section 6.4(d).

§ 21.3 STATUTORY REQUIREMENTS

A transaction must meet four requirements to qualify as a hedging transaction.[19] First, the transaction must be entered into by the taxpayer in the normal course of his trade or business.[20] Second, the transaction must be entered into primarily to reduce the risk of certain price changes, interest rate changes, or currency fluctuations.[21] Third, gain or loss on the transaction must be treated as ordinary income or loss.[22] Fourth, the transaction must be clearly identified as a hedge before the close of the day it was entered into (or earlier if prescribed by regulations).[23] The following section discusses these requirements in detail.

(a) NORMAL COURSE OF BUSINESS

A hedging transaction must be entered into in the normal course of the taxpayer's trade or business.[24] Investment activities and speculative transactions are not in the normal course of business and do not qualify for the hedging exemption.[25] Because taxpayers can be viewed as dealers, hedgers, traders, or investors for certain types of activities, whether a transaction is entered into in the normal course of business is based on all of the facts and circumstances.[26] What category the taxpayer falls into determines whether the transaction is entered into in the normal course of business and qualifies for the hedging exemption.

Example   21-1

On October 1st, a United States importer agrees to pay for goods to be shipped to the United States in a foreign currency upon delivery. The importer does not want to assume the risk of currency fluctuations. He decides to establish a hedge, so he enters into a long futures contract position or a long call option position to insulate him from such fluctuations. This transaction is entered into in the normal course of the importer's business.

---

[19]I.R.C. § 1256(e)(2).
[20]I.R.C. § 1256(e)(2)(A).
[21]I.R.C. §§ 1256(e)(2)(A)(i), (ii).
[22]I.R.C. § 1256(e)(2)(B).
[23]I.R.C. § 1256(e)(2)(C).
[24]I.R.C. § 1256(e)(2)(A).
[25]*See generally* Section 6.4.
[26]*See* section 6.4(b).

Example 21-2

A grain elevator operator owns 100,000 bushels of corn. Any gain or loss on the sale of the corn is ordinary, not capital. If the price of corn increases, the operator makes money on the corn in his inventory. If the price of corn declines, the operator loses money on his inventory. To reduce the risk of a decline in the price of corn, the operator sells corn futures contracts obligating him to sell approximately 100,000 bushels of corn for delivery in the future. This transaction is entered into in the normal course of the operator's business.

(b) PRIMARILY TO REDUCE CERTAIN RISKS

A hedging transaction must be entered into primarily to reduce the risk of price changes or currency fluctuations with respect to property held or to be held by the taxpayer,[27] or to reduce the risk of interest rate or price changes or currency fluctuations with respect to borrowings made (or to be made) or obligations incurred (or to be incurred).[28] Transactions entered into in the normal course of business to make a profit, but not primarily to reduce risk, do not qualify as hedges, except when entered into by banks.[29] This means that taxpayers (other than banks) who enter into positions to pursue a profit and not to reduce risk are not engaged in hedging transactions.

Because the risks of price and interest rate changes are inherent in most purchase and sale transactions—whether for current or deferred delivery—a taxpayer can establish hedge positions that offset and reduce these risks.

Example 21-3

A government securities dealer with $10 million of Treasury bills in his inventory could establish a hedge by entering into a short futures contract position to sell $10 million of Treasury bills. However, if the dealer establishes a short position to sell contracts with an underlying value of $20 million of Treasury bills, the dealer does not have a cash market position to support half of his short position as a hedge. The entire short position was not entered into primarily to reduce the risk of interest

---

[27]I.R.C. § 1256(e)(2)(A)(i).
[28]I.R.C. § 1256(e)(2)(A)(ii).
[29]*See* section 21.5.

rate or price changes. Half of the position may, however, qualify as a hedge.

_____

Example   21-4

_____

A silver refinery that enters into a short silver futures contract position to profit from a fall in the price of silver has not entered into a hedging transaction—the transaction was not entered into primarily to reduce certain business risks.

_____

(c) ORDINARY INCOME OR LOSS

Gain or loss on hedging transactions must be treated as ordinary income or loss.[30] As a starting point, this means that hedging transactions must be entered into in the ordinary course of business, not for investment or speculative purposes. To determine whether the transaction generates ordinary income or loss, one must look to the case law prior to enactment of I.R.C. § 1256(e). Cases and rulings established guidelines as to when transactions qualify for ordinary income or loss. IRS pronouncements[31] and numerous court decisions held that futures contracts entered into by a taxpayer to protect against price fluctuations in the value of inventory to be purchased or sold were a form of insurance. Therefore, gains and losses were ordinary, rather than capital, in nature. Hedging transactions are an integral part of the taxpayer's business and provide price protection or insurance for the taxpayer.[32]

The legislative history on ERTA provides that "[g]ain or loss on dispositions of both the hedged property and the hedge itself must be ordinary."[33] This requirement should not preclude interest rate hedge transactions, where the borrowings and obligations that a taxpayer may seek to hedge do not generate any gain or loss, either capital or ordinary. For example, when a liability is hedged, as in many interest rate hedges, the liability technically is not property in the hands of a taxpayer. Borrowings and obligations generate neither ordinary nor capital gain

[30]I.R.C. § 1256(e)(2)(B).
[31]G.C.M. 17322, XV-2 C.B. 151, _superseded by_ Rev. Rul. 72-179, 1972-1 C.B. 57; Rev. Rul. 60-24, 1960-1 C.B. 171.
[32]_Corn Products Refining Co._, 350 U.S. at 50.
[33]General Explanation of ERTA, _supra_ note 14, at 299.

or loss. In fact, interest rate hedgers generally produce ordinary income or loss only through interest rate adjustments. In spite of this, interest rate hedges should qualify as hedges under the appropriate facts and circumstances. For a detailed discussion of interest rate hedges, see section 6.4(d).

The IRS has viewed certain commercial paper transactions as hedges.[34] To reconcile the statutory requirement for ordinary income or loss, the IRS acknowledged that in addition to ordinary income or loss on the futures contracts, gain or loss on the lapse, cancellation, or other disposition of the taxpayer's commercial paper borrowings could be treated as ordinary income or loss.[35] "[G]ain or loss on futures contracts purchased as hedges against [the taxpayer's] commercial paper must be characterized as ordinary gain or loss because [the taxpayer's] hedges are to help protect itself against ordinary losses on its commercial paper."[36] In addition, a G.C.M. reported that the United States money market (where cash is the commodity) is affected by factors similar to other commodity markets (where goods are the commodities), so the fluctuations affecting a taxpayer's loan business, for example, also affect debt instruments.[37] As a result, offsetting positions in debt instruments can provide the taxpayer's loan business with price protection of the type that constitutes a hedge.[38]

(d) IDENTIFICATION

A transaction qualifies as a hedge if it is clearly identified as a hedging transaction before the close of the day on which it is entered into (or an earlier time if required by Treasury regulations).[39] At the date of this writing, Treasury regulations have not been promulgated to specify the time and form necessary to identify hedging transactions. In addition, the Treasury has broad authority to impose identification deadlines earlier than by the close of the day on which the position is acquired,[40] to reduce the opportunity for unwarranted tax benefits due to substan-

---

[34]LTR 8435054 (May 29, 1984).

[35]Id.

[36]Id.

[37]See G.C.M. 38178 (Nov. 27, 1979).

[38]Id.

[39]I.R.C. § 1256(e)(2)(C).

[40]Id. CONFERENCE REPORT, DEFICIT REDUCTION ACT OF 1984, H.R. REP. No. 861, 98th Cong., 2d Sess. 906 (1984).

tial price movements within the course of a day.[41] The Treasury can exempt particular classes of taxpayers from this earlier identification.[42]

A hedger may need to provide detailed information as to what part of a particular transaction is a hedge and what part is the hedged property, along with additional backup materials. The Senate Finance Committee Report on ERTA implies that property being hedged ("hedged property") as well as the hedging contracts ("hedge") must be identified on the taxpayer's records.[43] Of course, detailed identification maintained by the taxpayer can be used when a taxpayer is audited to ascertain whether the transaction qualified as a hedging transaction. The Treasury also has authority to provide for a method of identification other than on the taxpayer's own records.[44]

Certain taxpayers may not need to specifically identify every hedge position they establish. The House Ways and Means Committee Report, the Senate Report, and the General Explanation of ERTA all state that the Treasury regulations (when issued) should allow taxpayers such as banks and securities dealers to minimize bookkeeping identification requirements in as many cases as practicable "[i]n situations where hedging transactions are numerous and complex but opportunities for manipulation of transactions are minimal."[45] The General Explanation of ERTA assumes that banks and securities dealers with thousands of hedging transactions should not be required to identify the individual transactions as hedges or hedged property.[46] Taxpayers with a minimal opportunity for manipulation of their positions should be able to establish hedged accounts, so that all ordinary income transactions will not require specific identification to qualify as hedging transactions. Hedged accounts for certain taxpayers were also addressed in the DRA Conference Committee Report. It states that "[i]t is contemplated that any additional identification requirements for the hedging exemption that may be imposed under the regulations will be consistent with the intended application of the identification rule for the hedging exemption

---

[41]*Id.* at 900.

[42]*Id.* at 907.

[43]S. REP. NO. 144, *supra* note 16, at 151.

[44]H.R. REP. NO. 861, *supra* note 40, at 906.

[45]General Explanation of ERTA, *supra* note 14, at 300; S. REP. NO. 144, *supra* note 16, at 159; REPORT OF THE COMMITTEE ON WAYS AND MEANS, TAX INCENTIVE ACT OF 1981, H.R. REP. NO. 201, 97th Cong., 1st Sess. 200-01 (1981).

[46]General Explanation of ERTA, *supra* note 14, at 290.

expressed in the report of the Senate Finance Committee in 1981."[47] Of course, if hedged accounts are available to banks and securities dealers, such accounts should also be available to commodity dealers with hedging transactions too numerous to identify.

If dealer activities and other ordinary income transactions are not conducted and identified separately from capital transactions (e.g., investment account transactions) or a danger of manipulation between accounts is possible, more detailed identification records might be required.[48]

Of course, unless Treasury regulations are issued to authorize hedged accounts, compliance with the literal language of the statutory hedging exemption requires identification of hedge transactions before the close of the day on which they are entered into.

§ 21.4   LIMITATIONS

(a)   WHO CAN QUALIFY

It is not clear under the Code whether a taxpayer can treat positions held by others as a hedge. Under I.R.C. § 1256(e), a hedging transaction is defined as a transaction "entered into by the taxpayer." For purposes of defining a straddle, however, a taxpayer is treated "as holding any position held by a related person."[49]

If only the taxpayer who entered into all of the positions can qualify for the hedging exemption, then offsetting positions taken by two corporate members of an affiliated group that files a consolidated return might not be eligible for the hedging exemption—even though these positions would otherwise be treated as a straddle. Because corporations filing consolidated returns under I.R.C. § 1501 are treated as "related persons" under I.R.C. § 1092(d)(4), it should be possible to assert that the hedging exemption is available to the members of the consolidated group even if different members of the group hold the positions making up the straddle. It is unclear whether the hedging exemption can be applied broadly. Treasury regulations are needed to clarify who can qualify for the hedging exemption.

---

[47]H.R. REP. No. 861, *supra* note 40, at 906.

[48]General Explanation of ERTA, *supra* note 14, at 300.

[49]I.R.C. § 1092(d)(4)(A); *see generally* Chapter 39.

(b) SYNDICATES

The hedging exemption is not available to a syndicate, defined as any partnership or other enterprise which allocates more than 35 percent of its losses during the taxable year to limited partners or limited entrepreneurs.[50] This provision was enacted to prevent possible manipulation of the hedging exemption by tax shelters structured as limited partnerships.[51] Section 1256 positions held by a syndicate are marked-to-market, unless excluded as an identified section 1256(d) mixed straddle for which the one-time mixed straddle election is in effect. If the section 1256 contracts are capital assets in the hands of the syndicate, gain or loss on the section 1256 contracts are marked-to-market at year-end at 60/40 rates. On the other hand, if the section 1256 contracts are ordinary income assets, the positions are marked-to-market at year-end at ordinary income rates. Of course, the modified wash sales and short sales rules may require deferral of a loss that is marked-to-market.

The term "limited entrepreneur" was introduced into the Code initially to deny farm losses to certain enterprises with passive investors.[52] A limited entrepreneur is defined as someone who has an interest in an enterprise other than as a limited partner and who does not actively participate in its management.[53] Treasury regulations proposed under I.R.C. § 464 (for purposes of farm syndicates) state that a limited entrepreneur is someone with an interest other than as a limited partner who does not actively participate in the management of the enterprise.[54] This implies that to not be viewed as a limited entrepreneur, an active participant under the I.R.C. § 464(e) standard might need to actively participate in the enterprise. On the other hand, for purposes of I.R.C. § 1256(e) an active participant might need to actively participate in the entity. Because the definition is vague, it is unclear whether such a designation applies to certain general partners in partnerships. The standard for when a taxpayer is a limited entrepreneur is not clear. Literal application of the proposed Treasury regulations might require a general partner to actively participate in both the enterprise, as provided in I.R.C. § 464(e), and the entity, as might be required in I.R.C.

---

[50]I.R.C. § 1256(e)(3).

[51]General Explanation of ERTA, *supra* note 14, at 300.

[52]WAYS AND MEANS COMMITTEE REPORT, TAX REFORM ACT OF 1976, H.R. REP. NO. 658, 94th Cong., 2d Sess. 107, *reprinted in* 1976 U.S. CODE CONG. & AD. NEWS 3002.

[53]I.R.C. § 464(e)(2); Prop. Treas. Reg. § 1.464-2(a)(3) (1983); I.R.C. § 1256(e)(3); *see also* General Explanation of ERTA, *supra* note 14, at 301.

[54]Prop. Treas. Reg. § 1.464-2(a)(3) (1983).

§ 1256(e). This seems inappropriate, however. It is the author's view that both requirements should not be imposed and that general partners not be viewed as limited entrepreneurs.

The Code provides that certain interests held by limited partners or limited entrepreneurs are attributable to active management. This means that such interests are not counted towards the 35 percent allocation of losses necessary to define an entity as a syndicate. Active interests include the following. First, an interest held by an individual during any period he actively participates in the management of the entity is an active interest.[55] Second, an interest held by the spouse, children, grandchildren, or parents of an individual who actively participates in the management of the entity is an active interest.[56] A legally adopted child is treated as a child by blood.[57] Third, an interest held by an individual who actively participated in the management of the entity for at least five years is an active interest.[58] Fourth, an interest held by the estate of an individual who actively participated in the entity for at least five years, and an interest held by the estate of the spouse, children, grandchildren, or parents of such an individual is an active interest.[59] Fifth, certain other interests can be designated by the Treasury as not used for tax avoidance purposes.[60] It is not clear if this authority can be exercised through regulations or must be exercised on a case-by-case basis.[61] Nonpassive interests are not counted to convert an entity to a syndicate.

(c) HEDGING LOSSES OF LIMITED PARTNERS AND LIMITED ENTREPRENEURS

For taxable years beginning after December 31, 1984, limited partners and limited entrepreneurs are subject to restrictions on the deductibility of hedging losses allocable to them from the hedging entity.[62] This limitation is separate from the provision that precludes syndicates from

---

[55] I.R.C. § 1256(e)(3)(C)(i).

[56] I.R.C. § 1256(e)(3)(C)(ii).

[57] I.R.C. § 1256(e)(3)(C).

[58] I.R.C. § 1256(e)(3)(C)(iii).

[59] I.R.C. § 1256(e)(3)(C)(iv).

[60] I.R.C. § 1256(e)(3)(C)(v).

[61] REPORT OF THE COMMITTEE ON WAYS AND MEANS, TECHNICAL CORRECTIONS ACT OF 1982, H.R. REP. NO. 794, 97th Cong., 2d Sess. 23 (1982); S. REP. NO. 592, 97th Cong., 2d Sess. 26, reprinted in 1982 U.S. CODE CONG. & AD. NEWS 4172.

[62] I.R.C. § 1256(e)(5).

reporting hedging transactions.[63] Rather, it applies to taxpayers who are allocated losses from bona fide hedging transactions from entities that are not syndicates and, therefore, eligible at the entity level for the hedging exemption. If an entity is a syndicate, none of its participants qualify for the hedging exemption—a limitation on deducting hedging losses is not necessary. If an entity is not a syndicate but has limited partners or limited entrepreneurs, the flow-through of losses to such limited partners or limited entrepreneurs is restricted under I.R.C. § 1256(e)(5). The loss restriction is intended "to prevent the passthrough of ordinary losses to limited investors from hedging transactions of traders who qualify as dealers in the underlying property."[64]

Deductible hedging loss for a limited partner or limited entrepreneur is limited to the taxable income from the trade or business to which the hedge relates.[65] Taxable income for purposes of this provision does not include items attributable to hedging transactions.[66] In addition, the General Explanation of DRA makes it clear that "[t]axable income as so determined is to be separately computed for partners and S corporation shareholders with such limited interests."[67] Hedging loss is defined as the excess of the deductions attributable to hedging transactions (determined without regard to the rule limiting losses) over the income received or accrued by the limited partner or limited entrepreneur from hedging transactions during the taxable year.[68]

The General Explanation of DRA also indicates that the limitation on the deductibility of any loss from a hedging transaction in the conduct of the trade or business should be interpreted broadly.[69] Dealers in securities frequently engage in many aspects of the securities business. In their capacity as brokers and best efforts underwriters they earn commission income. As block traders or firm commitment underwriters they earn income on the spread between the purchase price and the sales price. Dealers obtain income not only from purchases and sales but also from interest, dividends, and fees from lending securities. It is possible to assert that all such income items should be viewed as having been derived from the active trade or business of the securities dealer

---

[63]See section 21.4(b).

[64]JOINT COMMITTEE ON TAXATION, 98TH CONG., 2D SESS. GENERAL EXPLANATION OF THE REVENUE PROVISIONS OF THE DEFICIT REDUCTION ACT OF 1984 315 (Joint Comm. Print 1985) [hereinafter referred to as "General Explanation of DRA"].

[65]I.R.C. § 1256(e)(5)(A)(i).

[66]Id.

[67]General Explanation of DRA, supra note 64, at 315.

[68]I.R.C. § 1256(e)(5)(D).

[69]General Explanation of DRA, supra note 64, at 315.

and should be treated as taxable income attributable to the trade or business against which hedging losses are allowed.[70]

Example   21-5

A limited partner in a securities dealer partnership can deduct hedging losses sustained by the partnership's municipal bond operations against profits from the partnership's other securities operations. The limited partner cannot deduct the hedging losses against his dividend income.[71]

In the case of a hedging transaction involving property other than stock or securities, this loss limitation applies only to limited partners and limited entrepreneurs who are individuals or C corporations where five or fewer individuals own, directly or indirectly at any time during the last half of the taxable year, more than 50 percent of the value of the stock.[72] A broader application (and hence a broader limitation on losses) is applied to hedge transactions involving stock and securities. All limited partners and limited entrepreneurs who participate in a securities venture that enters into hedges with stock and securities positions are subject to the loss limitation provision, irrespective of whether the limited partners and limited entrepreneurs are individuals or C corporations.

Hedging losses disallowed for any taxable year are carried forward and treated as a deduction in the first succeeding taxable year, subject once again to the limitation on hedging losses.[73] This means that hedging losses can be carried forward indefinitely, unless and until the losses are utilized against taxable income derived from the trade or business to which the hedging transaction relates. Hedging losses not currently deductible cannot be reallocated to other participants in the entity (who would not have their losses limited) and cannot be used by other participants to increase their net losses from hedging transactions.

If real economic losses result from hedging transactions, limited partners and limited entrepreneurs can deduct these losses currently under an exception to the loss limitation provision. This is because I.R.C. § 1256(e)(5)(B) provides that overall economic losses from hedging transactions are deductible if the hedging loss exceeds the aggregate

---

[70]For a discussion of dealers, see section 6.3.
[71]General Explanation of DRA, *supra* note 64, at 315.
[72]I.R.C. § 1256(e)(5)(C).
[73]I.R.C. § 1256(e)(5)(A)(ii).

unrecognized gains from hedging transactions "as of the close of the taxable year attributable to the trade or business in which the hedging transactions were entered into." Hence, a hedging loss is deductible to the extent there is a real economic loss associated with the trade or business. Hedging gains are defined as those gains relating to the same trade or business in which the hedging losses were incurred.[74] Unrecognized gain, defined the same way as in the Straddle Rules under I.R.C. § 1092(a)(3),[75] is the amount of gain that would be taken into account on a position if it were sold at its fair market value on the last day of the taxable year.[76] In the case of any position for which gain has been realized but not recognized, unrecognized gain is the amount of the realized gain.[77]

§ 21.5   SPECIAL RULES FOR BANKS

A bank, defined generally to include a bank or trust company where (1) a substantial part of its business consists of receiving deposits and making loans and discounts and (2) it is subject by law to supervision and examination by state or federal bank regulators,[78] is allowed a special, somewhat relaxed definition for hedging transactions.[79] As long as a hedging transaction is entered into in the normal course of the bank's business, the bank need not meet the "primary purpose" tests of I.R.C. §§ 1256(e)(2)(A)(i) and (ii).[80] A bank's hedging transactions need not have as their primary purpose reducing the risk of price, interest rate, or currency fluctuations as is otherwise required for other hedgers.[81] The special rule for banks is intended to bring within the hedging exemption—and hence take out of section 1256 treatment—certain business activities (such as forward trading of foreign currencies) that are regularly conducted by banks, even though not conducted primarily to reduce risks.[82]

A transaction entered into by a bank qualifies as a hedging transaction

---

[74]General Explanation of DRA, *supra* note 64, at 315.

[75]I.R.C. § 1256(e)(5)(E).

[76]I.R.C. § 1092(a)(3)(A)(i).

[77]I.R.C. § 1092(a)(3)(A)(ii).

[78]I.R.C. § 581.

[79]I.R.C. § 1256(e)(4).

[80]*See* section 21.3(b).

[81]I.R.C. § 1256(e)(2)(A).

[82]General Explanation of ERTA, *supra* note 14, at 299.

if it is entered into in the normal course of the bank's business and the gain or loss on the transaction is treated as ordinary. A bank can enter into qualified hedges in the normal course of business to produce profits, not to reduce risks.

Banks also may be able to avoid the specific identification requirements imposed on other hedges while still qualifying for the hedging exemption.[83] The Senate Report and the General Explanation of ERTA both state that Treasury regulations (when issued) should allow banks to minimize bookkeeping identification requirements in as many cases as practicable in situations where hedging transactions are numerous and complex but opportunities for manipulation of transactions are minimal.[84] The legislative history of ERTA assumes that banks, with thousands of hedging transactions, should be allowed to identify their ordinary income accounts as hedged accounts without identifying the individual transactions in those accounts as hedges or hedged property. A bank should be allowed under the regulations to designate an account for its ordinary income transactions as a hedged account where the account "is managed and recorded independently and separately" from other "capital asset accounts" and "there is little danger of manipulation" to convert ordinary income to capital gain. The General Explanation of ERTA explained that the deferral opportunities of banks are limited because federal regulatory agencies impose standard accounting practices on banks.[85] The concept of hedged accounts for banks was approved by the DRA Conference Committee.[86] To date, Treasury regulations have not been issued establishing the requirements for maintaining hedged accounts, so technical compliance with the statutory hedging exemption still requires specific identification of hedges and hedged property.

§ 21.6 CAPITAL GAIN UNAVAILABLE

Once personal property, as defined in I.R.C. § 1092(d)(1), is identified as part of a hedging transaction, it automatically becomes ineligible for capital gain treatment—even if the transaction ultimately does not qualify as a hedge under the statutory provisions and even if it otherwise

---

[83]*See* section 21.3(d).

[84]General Explanation of ERTA, *supra* note 14, at 300; S. REP. No. 144, *supra* note 16, at 159.

[85]General Explanation of ERTA, *supra* note 14, at 300.

[86]H.R. REP. No. 861, *supra* note 40, at 906.

would have qualified for capital asset treatment.[87] Improper identification precludes capital gain treatment, so any gain on the property receives ordinary income treatment. On the other hand, any loss on property classified improperly as a hedge is either capital or ordinary, depending upon the character of the property. General tax rules apply so that a capital loss is not converted into an ordinary loss and an ordinary loss is not converted into a capital loss. In addition, those section 1256 contracts that are not eligible for the statutory hedging exemption but which generate ordinary income under the Corn Products doctrine[88] are subject to the Mark-to-Market Rule but not 60/40 treatment.[89]

In addition, if an incorrect identification was not due to a reasonable cause, the taxpayer could be subject to the penalty under I.R.C. § 6653(f). Such a penalty would apply only if the transaction should have been reported under I.R.C. § 1092(a)(3)(B).[90]

It is not clear upon reading the Code whether United States businesses can maintain capital gain treatment on the stock of their foreign subsidiaries and the net worth of foreign branches that contain a variety of assets if these subsidiaries and branches "hedge" such assets against value changes in the U.S. dollar as it moves up or down against other currencies. The risk of currency fluctuations would be reflected in the shares of stock and debt in foreign subsidiaries or in I.R.C. § 1231 business assets held by the United States business or its foreign subsidiary. In general, neither stock and debt in a foreign corporation nor I.R.C. § 1231 assets generate ordinary income. The General Explanation of ERTA states that gain or loss on the disposition of both a hedge and the hedged property must be ordinary.[91] In addition, I.R.C. § 1256(f)(1) provides that gain from any property once identified as part of a hedge can never be considered a capital asset if such property was at any time personal property as defined in I.R.C. § 1092(d)(1).[92]

Senators Moynihan and Dole, however, discussed the issue of hedging foreign exchange risks for multinational businesses on the United States Senate floor on July 28, 1981, and acknowledged that the hedging exemption was intended to apply to U.S. taxpayers who hedge their in-

---

[87]I.R.C. § 1256(f)(1).

[88]*Corn Products Refining Co.*, 350 U.S. at 53–54.

[89]I.R.C. § 1256(f)(2). *See generally* Part Nine.

[90]*See* section 41.1.

[91]General Explanation of ERTA, *supra* note 14, at 299.

[92]*See* section 36.2.

vestments in foreign subsidiaries and branches without converting stock, debt, or I.R.C. § 1231 assets to ordinary assets.[93] Such assets are not personal property, as defined in I.R.C. § 1092(d)(1), because such property is not actively traded. Senator Moynihan used as an example a bank that entered into forward contracts to hedge against foreign exchange risks associated with foreign stock, debt, and I.R.C. § 1231 assets. Senator Moynihan said that it was his understanding that "the forward contracts would be covered by the hedging exemption, and any assets against which the bank is hedging would not be converted from capital assets into ordinary income property."[94] Senator Dole said that Senator Moynihan "is correct in his understanding."[95]

§ 21.7   CLEAR REFLECTION OF INCOME

Application of the hedging exemption cannot be used by taxpayers to override the Code provision that requires a taxpayer's accounting method to clearly reflect income.[96] In other words, the hedging exemption cannot be used by taxpayers to distort their income or defer the payment of tax by "pushing" gains into future tax years. The General Explanation of ERTA points out that the IRS continues to have the power to require taxpayers to employ accounting methods that clearly reflect income and that taxpayers cannot use the hedging exemption to distort their income.[97]

Example 21-6

———————

A taxpayer who enters into transactions that qualify for the hedging exemption habitually closes out all of his loss positions in these hedging transactions prior to the close of the tax year and reestablishes identical positions on the same day. The IRS could assert under I.R.C. § 446(b) that the taxpayer must change his accounting method, because the taxpayer's method of accounting allows him to claim losses at the time closed out while not permitting him to claim these losses if the positions were kept open.

———————

---

[93]127 Cong. Rec. S8643 (daily ed. July 28, 1981).
[94]*Id.*
[95]*Id.*
[96]I.R.C. § 446(b). *See also* section 20.3.
[97]General Explanation of ERTA, *supra* note 14, at 300.

§ 21.8 NONSTATUTORY HEDGES

Hedging transactions that do not qualify for the statutory hedging exemption are subject to section 1256 treatment[98] and the Straddle Rules (including the loss deferral rule, the modified wash sales and short sales rules, and the requirement to capitalize interest and carrying charges).[99]

---

[98]*See generally* Part Nine.
[99]*See generally* Part Ten.

Part Five

Taxation of Dividends, Interest, and Security Loans

Twenty-two

Dividend Income

D ividend income is not limited to an issuer's distribution of cash (or other property) on a pro rata basis to all stockholders. It includes within its scope certain distributions that a taxpayer may not initially consider as dividends:[1] stock redemptions that have the effect of dividends[2] and certain sales or redemptions of shares of preferred stock that were received as stock dividends on common stock.[3]

This chapter discusses certain corporate distributions that are taxed as dividends, highlights special rules, and identifies certain timing and reporting requirements for dividends.

§ 22.1 STATUTORY CONCEPTS

(a) DIVIDENDS

The term "dividend" is defined in I.R.C. § 316(a) as any distribution of property made by a corporation to its stockholders out of current or accumulated earnings and profits.[4] Hence, a corporate distribution is taxable as a dividend only to the extent the corporation has earnings and profits.

---

[1]For an excellent discussion of corporate distributions, see R. WILLENS, TAXATION OF CORPORATE CAPITAL TRANSACTIONS; A GUIDE FOR CORPORATE, INVESTMENT BANKING, AND TAX ADVISERS (1984).

[2]See I.R.C. § 302.

[3]See I.R.C. § 306.

[4]I.R.C. § 316(a); Treas. Reg. § 1.316-1(a)(1) (1984).

(b) PROPERTY

Property is defined as "money, securities, and other property."[5] It does not include stock (or stock rights) in the corporation making the distribution.[6]

(c) EARNINGS AND PROFITS

The phrase "earnings and profits" has no specific statutory definition, although it is central to an understanding of whether a distribution is a dividend. Basically, it is the corporation's earned surplus computed on a tax basis, which is decreased by the amount of money, corporate obligations, and the adjusted basis of other property distributed by the corporation to its stockholders.[7] DRA amendments to the Code are "designed to ensure that a corporation's earnings and profits more closely conform to its economic income."[8]

(d) DISTRIBUTIONS IN EXCESS OF EARNINGS AND PROFITS

Distributions in excess of earnings and profits are not classified as dividends and, therefore, are not taxable as dividends. Rather, such distributions are treated as a return of capital, and are applied against and reduce the recipient stockholder's basis in his stock in the corporation.[9] To the extent that a distribution exceeds the stockholder's adjusted basis in his stock, the excess is treated as either long-term or short-term capital gain or loss, depending on the stockholder's holding period for the stock.[10] In *Johnson v. U.S.*,[11] the court held that non-dividend distributions are made on a share by share, not an aggregate, basis. As a result, a stockholder with different lots of stock applies the stock basis reduction on a share by share basis, possibly reporting gain on some shares even though other shares still have some remaining basis.

---

[5]I.R.C. § 317(a).

[6]*Id.*

[7]I.R.C. § 312(a).

[8]JOINT COMMITTEE ON TAXATION, 98TH CONG., 2D SESS., GENERAL EXPLANATION OF THE REVENUE PROVISIONS OF THE DEFICIT REDUCTION ACT OF 1984 177 (Joint Comm. Print 1984) [hereinafter referred to as "General Explanation of DRA"].

[9]I.R.C. § 301(c)(3).

[10]*Id.*

[11]435 F.2d 1257, 1259 (4th Cir. 1971).

(e) ORDINARY INCOME

I.R.C. § 301(c)(1) provides that the portion of a distribution that qualifies as a dividend under I.R.C. § 316 is to be included in the stockholder's gross income, that is, taxed as ordinary income.

(f) NONCASH DIVIDENDS

I.R.C. § 301 provides the extent to which noncash dividends received by a stockholder are included in ordinary income. The results, which vary for noncorporate and corporate stockholders, are discussed below.

(1) NONCORPORATE STOCKHOLDERS

For noncorporate stockholders, noncash dividends are included in ordinary income at the fair market value of the property that is distributed.[12] In addition, the distributing corporation's earnings and profits are reduced by, among other things, the adjusted basis in the distributed property.[13]

(2) CORPORATE STOCKHOLDERS

For corporate stockholders, noncash dividends generally are included in ordinary income to the extent of the *lesser* of (1) the fair market value of the property received or (2) the property's adjusted basis in the hands of the corporation making the distribution, increased by any gain recognized by the distributing corporation.[14] Special rules are provided for certain distributions made by or received from a foreign corporation.[15]

Pre-DRA law governing distributions by corporations to certain corporate stockholders were viewed by Congress as presenting opportunities for tax avoidance.[16] Under prior law, corporate stockholders could obtain a carry-over of the basis and holding period of property distributed by one corporation to another in the case of a distribution of property other than cash to certain corporate stockholders.[17] In addition, if the stockholder's basis in the distributed property was determined by

---

[12]I.R.C. § 301(b)(1)(A).
[13]I.R.C. § 312(a)(3).
[14]I.R.C. § 301(b)(1)(B).
[15]*See* I.R.C. §§ 301(d)(3), (4).
[16]General Explanation of DRA, *supra* note 8, at 136.
[17]*Id.*

reference to the property's basis in the hands of the distributing corporation, the corporate stockholder's holding period for the property included the period during which the property was held by the distributing corporation. If the basis of the property was determined by its fair market value, the corporate stockholder's holding period in the distributed property generally began under pre-DRA law on the date of distribution.

DRA amends the rules for determining the basis and holding period of property received by a corporate stockholder from a distributing corporation with respect to the distributing corporation's stock. If the corporate stockholder's basis in the property it received is determined by reference to the property's basis in the hands of a distributing corporation and the distributing corporation does not recognize gain on the distribution, the corporate stockholder's holding period does not begin until the date on which the stock with respect to which the distribution was made was acquired by the corporate stockholder.[18] If, however, the distributing corporation recognized a gain on the distribution, the corporate stockholder's basis in the distributed property is treated as the fair market value of the property and not the property's adjusted basis in the hands of the distributing corporation, increased by any gain recognized to the distributing corporation. The stockholder's holding period for the distributed property begins on the date of the distribution.[19]

§ 22.2   STOCK DIVIDENDS AND STOCK RIGHTS

Stock dividends are distributions by a corporation to its stockholders of shares of its own stock. They include distributions of common stock on the same or a different class of common stock, common stock on preferred stock, preferred stock on the same or a different class of preferred stock, and convertible securities on either common or preferred stock. Stock rights generally refer to those rights distributed by a corporation to its stockholders to purchase additional shares of the corporation's own stock. In general, for purposes of I.R.C. § 305 (except for dividend reinvestments in certain public utilities),[20] the term "stock" includes the right to acquire such stock.[21] For a discussion of tax basis,

[18]I.R.C. § 301(e)(2); General Explanation of DRA, *supra* note 8, at 141.
[19]I.R.C. § 301(d)(2)(A); General Explanation of DRA, *supra* note 8, at 141.
[20]I.R.C. § 305(e).
[21]I.R.C. § 305(d)(1).

see generally Chapter 14. For a discussion of holding periods, see generally Chapter 15.

(a) GENERAL RULE

Under I.R.C. § 305(a), gross income does not include the amount of any distribution of the stock (or stock rights) of a corporation made by it to its stockholders with respect to its stock. After stating this so-called general rule, however, I.R.C. § 305(b) provides broad exceptions to this rule of nontaxability. The remainder of this section discusses taxable distributions of stock and stock rights.

(b) TAXABLE DISTRIBUTIONS

The rules for the taxation of stock dividends provided in I.R.C. § 305(b) are generally effective for distributions (or deemed distributions) made after January 10, 1969.[22] The effective dates are deferred, however, for certain distributions that would not have been taxable prior to the 1969 amendments to the Code. Transitional rules for the phase in of the 1969 amendments are complex and provide various effective dates. It is safe to say, however, that the rules do not apply before January 1, 1991 to distributions made on stock outstanding on January 10, 1969.[23]

(1) DISTRIBUTIONS IN LIEU OF MONEY

If, at the election of *any* of the stockholders, a distribution is payable in either stock of the corporation or in property, the distribution is potentially taxable to all stockholders.[24] The distribution is taxable as a dividend regardless of whether (1) the distribution is actually made (wholly or in part) in stock or stock rights; (2) the election is exercised or exercisable before or after the declaration; (3) the terms of the distribution provide that the payment will be made in one medium unless the stockholders specifically request payment in another medium; (4) the election or option is provided in the declaration, corporate charter, or circumstances of the distribution; or (5) all or part of the stockholders are given an election.[25] If the distribution is only partially in lieu of

---

[22]Tax Reform Act of 1969, Pub. L. 91-172, § 421(b)(1), 83 Stat. 487, 615 (1969).

[23]Tax Reform Act of 1969, *supra* note 22, § 421(b)(4).

[24]I.R.C. § 305(b)(1).

[25]Treas. Reg. §§ 1.305-2(a)(1)–(5) (1973).

money, only that portion for which there is an election is treated as a taxable distribution.[26]

(2) DISPROPORTIONATE DISTRIBUTIONS

A distribution of stock and stock rights is taxable as a disproportionate distribution if some stockholders receive property and others receive an increase in their proportionate interests in the corporation's assets and earnings and profits.[27] For example, if a corporation with two classes of common stock pays, as a dividend, cash to one class and its own stock (or stock rights) to the other class, the stock distributed as a noncash dividend is taxable as a dividend.[28]

This rule covers "deemed distributions" where an actual distribution does not occur.[29] Deemed distributions arise whenever a stockholder's proportionate interest in either the assets or the earnings or profits of the corporation increase because of a change in the conversion ratio (for convertible securities), change in the redemption prices, difference between the redemption price and issue price, or redemption that is treated as a distribution under I.R.C. § 301.[30]

(3) MONEY IN LIEU OF FRACTIONAL SHARES

Cash received in lieu of fractional stock dividends is treated as ordinary income.[31] If, however, the stockholders are given an option to buy or sell fractional shares and a stockholder sells fractional shares, the transaction generates capital gain or loss.[32] If a corporation declares a dividend payable in its stock and distributes cash in lieu of fractional shares to which the stockholders otherwise would be entitled, or upon conversion of convertible shares the corporation distributes cash in lieu of fractional shares, the distribution is not taxable as a dividend provided (1) "the purpose of the distribution of cash is to save the corporation the trouble, expense, and inconvenience of issuing or transferring fractional shares (or scrip representing fractional shares);"[33] and (2) the

---

[26]*See* Treas. Reg. § 1.305-2(b), Example (2) (1973).

[27]I.R.C. § 305(b)(2).

[28]Treas. Reg. § 1.305-3(a) (1974).

[29]I.R.C. § 305(c).

[30]I.R.C. § 305(c); *see generally* Treas. Reg. §§ 1.305-3(d), (e) (1974) (for examples of adjustments in the conversion ratio and disproportionate distributions).

[31]*Special Ruling*, 7 STAND. FED. TAX REP. (CCH) ¶ 6301 (Dec. 21, 1960).

[32]Rev. Rul. 69-15, 1969-1 C.B. 95.

[33]Treas. Reg. § 1.305-3(c) (1974).

distribution satisfies either the disproportionate redemption rules of I.R.C. § 302(b)(2) or the "meaningful reduction in proportionate interest" standard of I.R.C. § 302(b)(1), as set forth in *U.S. v. Davis*.[34]

I.R.C. § 302(b)(2) provides that a "substantially disproportionate distribution" is made in part or full payment of stock if immediately after the distribution, the stockholder owns less than 50 percent of the combined voting power of all classes of stock entitled to vote.[35] A substantially disproportionate distribution occurs when the ratio of the voting stock of the corporation owned by the taxpayer immediately after the distribution divided by all of the voting stock of the corporation at the time is less than 80 percent of the ratio of the voting stock of the corporation owned by the stockholder immediately before the distribution divided by the voting stock of the corporation at that time.[36] A substantially disproportionate distribution does not occur, however, where the distribution is made pursuant to a plan the purpose or effect of which (in the aggregate) is not substantially disproportionate to the taxpayer.[37]

In *U.S. v. Davis*,[38] the taxpayer, who (after the application of the attribution rules) was the sole shareholder of a corporation both before and after the redemption of his preferred stock, brought an action for a refund of federal income taxes after the redemption was treated as essentially equivalent to a dividend. The Supreme Court, in holding that the taxpayer was not entitled to the refund, stated that for a distribution to qualify as being made in part or full payment of stock, and not as a dividend, under I.R.C. § 302(b)(1), the "redemption must result in a meaningful reduction of the shareholder's proportionate interest in the corporation."[39] The Court did not state what constitutes a "meaningful reduction" in a stockholder's proportionate interest in the corporation. It is, therefore, an open question whether a minority stockholder can show a meaningful reduction in his proportionate interest by having fractional shares redeemed.

Three final points should be made. First, if a corporation declares a pro rata stock dividend and, with stockholder approval, sells the shares in the open market, and distributes the proceeds to those entitled to a fractional interest, the proceeds are not taxable as ordinary income to

[34] 397 U.S. 301, *reh'g denied*, 397 U.S. 1071 (1970).
[35] I.R.C. §§ 302(b)(2)(A), (B).
[36] I.R.C. § 302(b)(2)(C).
[37] I.R.C. § 302(b)(2)(D).
[38] 397 U.S. at 301.
[39] *Id.* at 313.

the taxpayer.[40] Second, the IRS will not challenge the purpose of a cash payment in lieu of fractional shares if the total amount of the cash distributed is five percent or less of the total fair market value of the stock distributed.[41] And third, a cash payment in lieu of a distribution of fractional shares of common stock by a regulated public utility is treated as if the company had first issued the shares and then redeemed them.[42]

(4) DISTRIBUTIONS OF COMMON AND PREFERRED STOCK

If a corporation distributes preferred stock to some common stockholders and common stock to other common stockholders, the distribution is taxable at ordinary income rates.[43] This results irrespective of whether the preferred stock is convertible into common stock.[44] For example, if a corporation with two classes of common stock (Class A and Class B) pays a common stock dividend of Class A common stock to the holders of Class A common stock and a preferred stock dividend to the holders of Class B common stock, the distributions are taxable under I.R.C. § 305(b)(3).[45]

(5) DISTRIBUTIONS ON PREFERRED STOCK

Distributions made on preferred stock, defined as a class of stock that "enjoys certain limited rights and privileges (generally associated with specific dividend and liquidation priorities) but does not participate in corporate growth to any significant extent,"[46] generally are taxable at ordinary income rates.[47] An exception to taxation is provided for distributions made on convertible preferred stock to increase the conversion ratio solely to compensate for a common stock dividend, stock split, or other similar adjustment.[48]

Reasonable redemption premiums are not viewed as taxable distri-

---

[40]Rev. Rul. 69-15, 1969-1 C.B. 95.

[41]Treas. Reg. § 1.305-3(c)(1) (1974).

[42]LTR 8111056 (Dec. 16, 1980). For a discussion of public utilities, see section 22.4.

[43]I.R.C. § 305(b)(3).

[44]Treas. Reg. § 1.305-4(a) (1973).

[45]Treas. Reg. § 1.305-4(b), Example (1) (1973).

[46]Treas. Reg. § 1.305-5(a) (1974).

[47]I.R.C. § 305(b)(4).

[48]*Id.*

butions of additional stock.[49] If preferred stock can be redeemed after a specified period at a price that is unreasonably higher than the issue price, the difference is viewed as a distribution of additional stock on preferred stock that is constructively received over the period of time when the preferred stock cannot be redeemed.[50] A premium not in excess of 10 percent of the issue price on the stock that is not redeemable for five years is reasonable.[51] A premium in the nature of a penalty for premature redemption is reasonable if it does not exceed the amount the corporation would be required to pay for the right to make a premature redemption given the market conditions existing at the time of issuance.[52]

(6) DISTRIBUTIONS OF CONVERTIBLE PREFERRED STOCK

If convertible preferred stock is distributed, the distribution is taxable unless it can be established (to the satisfaction of the IRS) that the distribution is not disproportionate.[53] A disproportionate distribution is likely to result if (1) the conversion right must be exercised within a relatively short period, and (2) it can be assumed that some stockholders will exercise their conversion rights taking into account such factors as the dividend rate, redemption provisions, marketability of the convertible stock, and conversion price.[54] A distribution is nontaxable if there is no basis on which to predict the time or extent to which the stock will be converted.[55] For example, the conversion right can be exercised over a period of many years and the dividend rate is consistent with market conditions at the time of the distribution.[56]

(7) STOCK RIGHTS TO PURCHASE OTHER PROPERTY

If a corporation distributes stock rights (or options) to purchase other property such as the stock of a subsidiary or affiliated corporation, the distribution is taxable to the stockholders.[57] Noncorporate stockholders are taxed an amount equal to the fair market value on the distribution

---

[49]Treas. Reg. § 1.305-5(b)(2) (1974).
[50]Treas. Reg. § 1.305-5(b)(1) (1974).
[51]Treas. Reg. § 1.305-5(b)(2) (1974).
[52]*Id.*
[53]I.R.C. § 305(b)(5).
[54]Treas. Reg. § 1.305-6(a)(2) (1973).
[55]*Id.*
[56]*Id.*
[57]Rev. Rul. 70-521, 1970-2 C.B. 72.

date of the stock rights and obtain a carry-over basis in the property.[58] Corporate stockholders are taxed on the distribution date at the *lesser* of the fair market value of the property or distributing corporation's tax basis, if any, in the stock rights.[59] The issuance of stock rights to the stockholders of a parent corporation by a wholly owned subsidiary has been viewed by the IRS as a nontaxable transfer of the stock rights to the parent corporation followed by a taxable distribution to the stockholders of the parent corporation.[60]

§ 22.3   PERSONAL HOLDING COMPANIES

A personal holding company is defined in I.R.C. § 542 as a corporation (1) if at any time during the last half of the taxable year more than 50 percent of the value of its stock is owned directly or indirectly by not more than five individuals, and (2) at least 60 percent of its adjusted ordinary gross income is personal holding company income.[61] A personal holding company is subject each year to a penalty tax of 50 percent on its undistributed personal holding company income (defined in I.R.C. § 545).[62] In computing undistributed personal holding company income, a deduction is allowed for all dividends, except preferential dividends (as defined in I.R.C. § 562(c)).[63]

The definition of a dividend (i.e., a distribution out of current and accumulated earnings and profits) is modified for personal holding companies. Personal holding company dividends include distributions made by the personal holding company to its stockholders to the extent of undistributed personal holding company income for the year.[64] Distributions from a personal holding company with taxable income for the year but no earnings and profits qualify for the computation of dividends paid to reduce the 50 percent tax imposed on undistributed personal holding company income as long as the personal holding company is in the process of completely liquidating its assets within 24 months

---

[58]I.R.C. § 301(d)(1).

[59]I.R.C. § 301(d)(2); *see* Redding v. Comm'r, 630 F.2d 1169, 1183 (7th Cir. 1980), *cert. denied,* 450 U.S. 913 (1981); *see also* Rev. Rul. 70-521, 1970-2 C.B. 72.

[60]Rev. Rul. 80-292, 1980-2 C.B. 104.

[61]*See* I.R.C. § 543(a).

[62]I.R.C. § 541.

[63]I.R.C. §§ 562, 563.

[64]I.R.C. § 316(b)(2).

after adopting a plan of liquidation.[65] Any nonliquidating distributions (as well as certain liquidating distributions) of a personal holding company are deemed to be dividends to the extent of the undistributed personal holding company net income computed prior to any deductions for the distributions.[66]

§ 22.4 PUBLIC UTILITIES

A public utility is defined in I.R.C. § 247(b)(1) as a corporation engaged in furnishing telephone service or in the sale of electrical energy, gas, or water (if the rates have been established or approved by a governmental unit). Public utilities are subject to special tax rules.[67] A public utility receives a deduction for dividends paid on some of its preferred stock.[68] The deduction is limited to a computation using dividends and tax rates for the year.[69] Redemption premiums paid on retirement of this preferred stock do not qualify as dividends for this computation.[70]

From 1982 through 1985, stockholders of qualified public utilities who owned less than five percent of the voting stock or value of the corporations were allowed an election to exclude from income qualified common stock dividends received in lieu of cash dividends of up to $750 (or $1500 for joint returns).[71] Such stock dividends have a zero basis.[72] If a stockholder receives a qualified reinvestment dividend and holds it for one year after the date it was distributed, the disposition thereafter of any of his common stock is treated as a capital gain.[73] If, however, any stock received as a qualified reinvestment dividend is disposed of within one year after the stock is distributed, the disposition is deemed to be of ordinary income property taxed at ordinary income rates.[74]

---

[65]I.R.C. § 562(b).

[66]*See* I.R.C. §§ 316(b)(2), 562(b).

[67]*See* I.R.C. § 247.

[68]I.R.C. § 247(a).

[69]*Id.*

[70]Atlantic City Electric Co. v. U.S., 161 F. Supp. 811 (Ct. Cl.), *cert. denied*, 358 U.S. 834 (1958).

[71]I.R.C. § 305(e).

[72]I.R.C. § 305(e)(7).

[73]I.R.C. § 305(e)(9)(A).

[74]I.R.C. § 305(e)(9)(B).

§ 22.5   REGULATED INVESTMENT COMPANIES

Special rules are provided for regulated investment companies and their shareholders.[75] A regulated investment company (which includes within its definition mutual funds and unit investment trusts) is exempt from corporate tax on earnings it distributes to its shareholders. As a result, dividends that represent long-term capital gain to the company are treated as long-term capital gain treatment by the shareholders.

Distributions from a regulated investment company can be classified as a dividend, nonqualifying dividend, capital gain dividend, distribution of tax-exempt interest, or return of capital.[76] A capital gain distribution made by a regulated investment company with a capital loss carry-over for the year is taxed as a capital gain dividend.[77]

Generally, regulated investment companies that distribute their income are not subject to tax because their income is taxed to their shareholders. Under pre-DRA law, shareholders were allowed what Congress believed to be too much of an opportunity to convert short-term capital gain to long-term capital gain. This was because under pre-DRA law a shareholder in a regulated investment company could convert short-term capital gain to long-term capital gain by acquiring shares in a regulated investment company making capital gain distributions if the shares were acquired immediately prior to a capital gain distribution and the taxpayer held the shares of stock for more than 31 days (including the ex-dividend date) prior to liquidating the position.[78] The DRA extended the minimum holding period to more than six months.[79] In determining the holding period for which a taxpayer has held shares of a regulated investment company, rules similar to those of I.R.C. § 246(c) apply.[80] The DRA amendments apply to regulated investment company shares for which the taxpayer's holding period begins after July 18, 1984.[81]

Regulated investment companies generally declare capital gain distributions shortly after year-end and within the first 45 days of the next taxable year. If a shareholder sells the shares immediately after the distribution, he usually will have a loss on the sale because the market

[75]See I.R.C. §§ 851–855; see also section 6.9.

[76]See I.R.C. § 852.

[77]Rev. Rul. 76-299, 1976-2 C.B. 211.

[78]General Explanation of DRA, supra note 8, at 154.

[79]I.R.C. § 852(b)(3)(B), as amended by DRA, Pub. L. 98-369, § 1001(b)(11), 98 Stat. 494, 1011 (1984).

[80]General Explanation of DRA, supra note 8, at 154; see section 15.6; section 15.7.

[81]General Explanation of DRA, supra note 8, at 155.

price of the shares can be expected to drop following the ex-dividend date by an amount approximately equal to the long-term capital gain distribution. If the shares are not held for the six-month holding period, the loss incurred on the sale of the shares is treated as long-term capital loss to the extent of the capital gain dividend.[82] In addition, to the extent allowed by Treasury regulations, an exception is provided for dispositions of stock pursuant to a periodic redemption plan.[83]

Example 22-1

A taxpayer bought shares in a regulated investment company for $103 per share. Within six months he received a long-term capital gain distribution of $5, and subsequently sold each share after six months for $97 (loss of $6). The loss is reported as a $6 short-term capital loss. If, on the other hand, the taxpayer had sold each share within a six month period, the $6 loss would be reported as (1) a $5 long-term capital loss and (2) a $1 short-term capital loss.

§ 22.6   REAL ESTATE INVESTMENT TRUSTS

REITs and their beneficiaries are taxed under I.R.C. §§ 856–859 in a manner that is similar to regulated investment companies and their shareholders. REITs can be established as corporations, trusts, or associations,[84] with no tax imposed at the entity level; income is taxed directly to their beneficiaries. Distributions are taxed as either ordinary income or capital gain in the same manner as distributions from regulated investment companies.[85]

§ 22.7   REPORTING INCOME

(a)   IN GENERAL

Dividends, declared by a corporation's board of directors, are made payable only to the stockholders of record as of a designated date after the dividend is declared (i.e., the record date), and are paid on a fixed

[82]I.R.C. § 852(b)(4)(A).
[83]General Explanation of DRA, *supra* note 8, at 154.
[84]I.R.C. § 856(a).
[85]*See* section 22.5.

date thereafter. Stock on which a dividend has been declared and for which the purchaser of the stock does not receive the dividend when it is distributed on the stock is referred to as sold "ex-dividend." On regular way transactions governed by the rules of a stock exchange (for exchange-traded stock) or the NASD (for over-the-counter stock), a stock generally trades ex-dividend on the fourth business day prior to the record date.[86] Sales not in organized markets and privately negotiated transactions in stock of closely held corporations are subject to rules keyed to the terms of the agreement between the seller and the purchaser.

Both cash basis and accrual basis taxpayers include dividends in income for the years in which the dividends are received.[87] This means that payment of the dividends is the taxable event, although the right to the dividends accrues to the stockholders of record on the ex-dividend date.[88] Dividends are included in income when payment is actually or constructively received even if the dividends are received in the following year.[89]

A dividend of noncash property is valued at its date of distribution, not when it is received, even if this date is a date later than when it is includable in gross income.[90]

(b) SECURITIES MARGIN ACCOUNTS

Taxpayers who own securities purchased on margin and maintained in margin accounts with their brokers must include all dividends paid during the taxable year in income.[91]

(c) SALES AND GIFTS BEFORE EX-DIVIDEND DATE

A seller's regular way sale of stock prior to the ex-dividend date means that the seller is not entitled to the dividend when it is declared and paid. Any increase in the price representing the anticipated dividend only increases the gain (or reduces the loss) on the sale. Similarly, the purchaser of the stock prior to the ex-dividend date in a regular way transaction includes the dividend, when received, in his income in the

---

[86]See section 1.3(a).

[87]Treas. Reg. §§ 1.446-1(c)(1)(i), (ii) (1973); Rev. Rul. 78-117, 1978-1 C.B. 214.

[88]Treas. Reg. § 1.61-9(c) (1964); Rev. Rul. 78-117, 1978-1 C.B. 214.

[89]Treas. Reg. § 1.451-2(b) (1979); Rev. Rul. 68-126, 1968-1 C.B. 194.

[90]Treas. Reg. § 1.301-1(b) (1979).

[91]See Treas. Reg. § 1.61-9(b) (1964).

year paid.[92] In addition, the purchaser cannot deduct any premium paid for the purchase of the stock in anticipation of the dividend and must treat the premium as part of the purchase price.[93] The dividend, when received, is ordinary income.

There are a number of exceptions that apply in transactions that are not regular way transactions. For example, if a seller of stock retains title solely to secure payment of the purchase price with the agreement that dividends paid are to be applied to reduce the amount owed to the seller, the dividends are taxable to the purchaser.[94] In addition, if stock is held as collateral for a loan, dividends are taxable to the borrower at least to the extent that there is no evidence to show that the dividend payments are applied to reduce the loan balance.[95]

In addition, on October 9, 1984 the IRS ruled in a private letter ruling that when common stock is sold seller's option and the corporate seller remains the shareholder of record on the record date and receives the dividend, a corporate seller is entitled to the dividends received deduction pursuant to I.R.C. § 243(a).[96] However, on May 28, 1985 the IRS revoked this private letter ruling without explanation.[97] A possible reason for the IRS's revocation of its initial position is that the taxpayer may have been viewed as holding substantially similar property.[98]

The rules that are applied to sales of stock should apply equally to gifts made prior to the ex-dividend date. In *Estate of Smith v. Comm'r*,[99] the court treated a gift of stock made after the dividend was declared but prior to the record date as taxable to the donor under the assignment of income doctrine. Since the case was handed down, *Smith* has been distinguished on its facts.[100] However, it is not clear if this will become a consistent pattern.[101] A factor that may have been determinative in *Smith* was that the corporation was controlled by the donor.[102]

---

[92]Hastings v. Comm'r, 11 T.C.M. (CCH) 399, 401 (1952); Frieder v. Comm'r, 27 B.T.A. 1239, 1241 (1933); Treas. Reg. § 1.61-9(c) (1964); for a discussion of regular way transactions, see section 1.3(a).

[93]Jemison v. Comm'r, 28 B.T.A. 514, 516 (1933); Treas. Reg. § 1.61-9(c) (1964).

[94]Treas. Reg. § 1.61-9(c) (1964); Rev. Rul. 56-153, 1956-1 C.B. 166; *cf.* Northern Trust Co. of Chicago v. U.S., 193 F.2d 127, 130-31 (7th Cir. 1951), *cert. denied,* 343 U.S. 956 (1952).

[95]Estate of Federman v. Comm'r, 11 T.C.M. (CCH) 686 (1952).

[96]LTR 8503016 (Oct. 9, 1984); *see* section 1.3(f); section 15.7; section 22.9.

[97]LTR 8535010 (May 28, 1985).

[98]*See* section 15.7; section 22.9.

[99]292 F.2d 478 (3d Cir. 1961), *cert. denied,* 368 U.S. 967 (1962).

[100]Cukor v. Comm'r, 27 T.C.M. (CCH) 89, 94 (1968).

[101]*See* Kinsey v. Comm'r, 477 F.2d 1058 (2d Cir. 1973); Hudspeth v. U.S., 471 F.2d 275 (8th Cir. 1972); Rev. Rul. 74-562, 1974-2 C.B. 28; Rev. Rul. 60-331, 1960-2 C.B. 189.

[102]292 F.2d at 478.

(d) SALES AND GIFTS AFTER EX-DIVIDEND DATE

Once a stock trades ex-dividend in a regular way transaction, the seller (i.e., record owner) is entitled to keep the dividend and must include it in his income in the year received.[103]

In a transaction not settled regular way, a father agreed to sell his son both his bonds and his dividends. The Supreme Court held that the dividend was included in the seller's income and the sales price was reduced by the dividend amount.[104]

(e) STOCK HELD IN STREET NAME

For stock held in street name, a corporation's records do not necessarily reflect the person entitled to a dividend. Even so, the corporation pays the dividend to the record owner and files an information return with the IRS showing the dividend payments.[105] The record owner, in turn, files his own information return with the IRS. The information return discloses the actual owner of the stock entitled to the dividends.[106]

(f) CONSTRUCTIVE RECEIPT

A taxpayer can be deemed to constructively receive a dividend that he has not actually received. For example, a local stockholder was found to have constructively received a dividend (although the dividend was not actually received) on the date it was paid because the corporation allowed its local stockholders to pick up their dividend checks at the corporation's office.[107]

(g) DIVIDEND WAIVERS

In cases where the terms of an underwriting arrangement require dividends to be paid on stock after it is sold, controlling stockholders sometimes enter into agreements to irrevocably waive, for the time period specified in the agreement, their rights to the dividends. Of course, dividend waiver agreements only make economic sense to controlling stockholders who remain in control of the corporation after the under-

---

[103]See Treas. Reg. § 1.61-9(c) (1964).
[104]Helvering v. Horst, 311 U.S. 112, 118 (1940).
[105]This information is reported on Form 1099-DIV issued to the broker as a nominee.
[106]This information is also reported on Form 1099-DIV.
[107]Kunze v. Comm'r, 19 T.C. 29, 32 (1952), aff'd per curiam, 203 F.2d 957 (2d Cir. 1953).

writing, so that the bulk of the corporation's increased net worth accrues for their benefit. Dividend waivers are recognized for tax purposes in cases where the dividends are not deemed to be constructively received by the stockholders agreeing to such a waiver.[108] Previously declared dividends cannot be waived for tax purposes. There must be a business purpose for the waiver. For example, a corporation needs the capital to be raised by the stock offering to conduct its business. Further, the waiver must (1) not increase the taxpayer's pro rata share of the dividends paid in the form of increased dividends to his relatives and employees as minority stockholders, and (2) the waiver must not result primarily in benefiting his relatives.[109]

§ 22.8 DIVIDEND EXCLUSION

Noncorporate taxpayers are allowed an exclusion from tax in the amount of $100 ($200 for joint returns) for dividend income.[110] For taxable years beginning after December 31, 1980 and before January 1, 1982 this exclusion was increased to $200 ($400 for joint returns).[111] In certain circumstances, dividends received by persons who are 65 years of age or older (or who are permanently and totally disabled) may be eligible for the credit for the elderly (or disabled).[112]

Some dividends are not eligible for the dividend exclusion. The exclusion is not available in the case of dividends from a mutual savings bank (or cooperative bank, building and loan association, or savings institution), because the entity receives a deduction for dividends paid under I.R.C. § 591.[113] In addition, dividends from corporations exempt from tax under I.R.C. §§ 501 and 521 are not eligible for the dividend exclusion.[114] If less than 95 percent of a regulated investment company's

---

[108]Rev. Rul. 53-45, 1953-1 C.B. 178, *distinguished by* Rev. Rul. 56-431, 1956-2 C.B. 171.

[109]*See* Rev. Rul. 56-431, 1956-2 C.B. 171. Before executing a dividend waiver agreement, a stockholder may want to obtain a private letter ruling. In LTR 8519038 (Feb. 12, 1985), the IRS ruled that a dividend waiver was valid for tax purposes, and the waiving stockholder was not taxed on a pro rata portion of the corporation's payments. In LTR 8519038, the IRS found that there was a bona fide business purpose for the waiver and that the waiving stockholder's spouse and relatives did not own more than 20 percent of the stock held by nonwaiving stockholders.

[110]I.R.C. § 116(a). Dividends paid on FNMA common stock owned by individuals are eligible for the dividend exclusion. Rev. Rul. 56-510, 1956-2 C.B. 168.

[111]I.R.C. § 116(a)(2), *amended by* Pub. L. No. 96-223, § 404(a), 94 Stat. 299, 305 (1980).

[112]I.R.C. § 22.

[113]I.R.C. § 116(c)(1).

[114]I.R.C. § 116(b).

gross income consists of dividends that, if the stockholder received them directly, would qualify for the dividend exclusion, then only that portion of the ordinary dividends paid during the year qualifies for the exclusion.[115]

§ 22.9   INTERCORPORATE DIVIDENDS RECEIVED DEDUCTION

(a)   IN GENERAL

Corporations are allowed a deduction for certain fixed percentages of dividends received from domestic corporations subject to federal income tax as long as the holding period requirement is met.[116] In general, corporations are allowed an 85 percent deduction for dividends received from domestic corporations.[117] The 85 percent dividends received deduction cannot exceed 85 percent of the corporation's taxable income for the year, except in the case of net operating losses where the limitation is not applied.[118]

A special 100 percent exclusion is available for dividends received by a small business investment company operating under the Small Business Investment Act of 1958.[119] In addition, a 100 percent deduction is provided for intercorporate dividends within the same affiliated group (which has the meaning assigned by I.R.C. § 1504(a)),[120] even though the group does not file a consolidated return for the taxable year.[121] For a dividend to qualify for the 100 percent affiliated group deduction, certain requirements must be met. First, the entire affiliated group must join in an election for the taxable year in which the dividend is paid.[122] Such election is made for the affiliated group by means of a statement from the common parent.[123] Second, the recipient corporation and the distributing corporation must be members of the same affiliated group at the close of the day on which the dividend is received.[124] Third, no

[115]I.R.C. §§ 116(c)(2), 854.
[116]See I.R.C. §§ 243–244, 246.
[117]I.R.C. § 243(a)(1).
[118]I.R.C. § 246(b).
[119]I.R.C. § 243(a)(2).
[120]I.R.C. § 243(b)(5).
[121]I.R.C. § 243(a)(3).
[122]I.R.C. § 243(b)(2).
[123]The election can be made at any time if certain conditions specified in Treas. Reg. § 1.243-4(c)(1) (1969) are met.
[124]I.R.C. § 243(b)(1).

member of the group can have consented to an election of multiple surtax exemptions.[125] And fourth, the distribution must be made from the distributing corporation's earnings and profits for a taxable year ending after 1963 on each day of which both the receiving and distributing corporations were members of the same affiliated group.[126] If the dividends are paid by a corporation in the taxable year in which it has made an election under I.R.C. § 936 (possessions corporation credit), the third and fourth requirements need not be met for the dividend to qualify for the 100 percent affiliated group deduction.[127]

The dividends received deduction is reduced with respect to dividends on certain preferred stock of public utilities[128] and certain dividends from mutual savings banks, cooperative banks, building and loan associations, and other savings institutions.[129]

(b) HOLDING PERIOD

No deduction is allowed for any dividends received on any share of stock that is sold or otherwise disposed of if the corporation does not hold the stock for the required holding period. First, the corporate taxpayer must hold the stock on which the dividend is received for more than 45 days.[130] For stock acquired prior to July 19, 1984, the holding period was 15 days.[131] The holding period was increased by the DRA to prevent "dividend stripping" transactions, whereby a corporation would acquire stock shortly before the ex-dividend date, receive a dividend eligible for the dividends received deduction, and then sell the stock after satisfying only a 15-day holding period.[132] The increase in the required holding period obviously makes it more difficult for corporations that actively trade securities to qualify for the dividends received deduction. Second, the corporation cannot sell the stock short or be under an obligation to make related payments on positions in substantially similar or related property.[133] Third, in the case of any stock with a preference in dividends, the corporation must hold the stock for more than 90 days

---

[125]I.R.C. § 243(b)(1)(B)(ii).
[126]I.R.C. § 243(b)(1)(B)(i).
[127]I.R.C. § 243(b)(1)(C).
[128]I.R.C. § 244.
[129]I.R.C. §§ 243(c)(1), 596.
[130]I.R.C. § 246(c)(1)(A).
[131]I.R.C. § 246(c)(1)(A) (1982), *amended by* DRA, *supra* note 79, § 53(b)(1).
[132]*See* General Explanation of DRA, *supra* note 8, at 138.
[133]I.R.C. § 246(c)(1)(B).

to obtain the dividends received deduction.[134] For the manner in which a corporation's holding period is determined, see generally section 15.7.

(1) CALL OPTIONS

In interpreting the holding period requirement of I.R.C. § 246(c)(1)(A) for a taxpayer to obtain the dividends received deduction, the IRS has ruled that writing an at-the-money or out-of-the-money call option on stock held by a corporate taxpayer does not reduce the corporate taxpayer's holding period on the underlying stock.[135] The IRS found that a corporate taxpayer who writes such a call (1) is at the risk of the market, (2) does not hold an option to sell, (3) is not under a contractual obligation to sell, and (4) has not made a short sale of substantially identical stock or securities.[136] Writing the option does not provide the writer with protection against loss (beyond the option premium received) if the stock declines in value.[137] The ruling does not apply to in-the-money call options with a strike price below the market price of the underlying stock on the date that the option is written.[138] The IRS said that the exercise of such options is virtually guaranteed and the element of risk is greatly reduced or eliminated.[139] The Joint Committee Report on the DRA states that the DRA authorization of Treasury regulations (prospective after July 18, 1984) to limit the availability of the dividends received deduction if a corporate taxpayer holds substantially similar or related property cannot be used to ascertain when the dividends received deduction would be disallowed under pre-DRA law for a taxpayer who wrote in-the-money call options.[140] In other words, it is an open question as to whether writing in-the-money call options would reduce a corporate taxpayer's holding period for the dividends received deduction.[141]

---

[134]I.R.C. § 246(c)(2).

[135]Rev. Rul. 80-238, 1980-2 C.B. 96.

[136]*Id.*

[137]*Id.*

[138]*Id.*

[139]*Id.*

[140]General Explanation of DRA, *supra* note 8, at 143.

[141]*See* section 15.7.

(2) SELLER'S OPTION TRANSACTIONS

In LTR 8503016,[142] the IRS ruled that the dividends received deduction was available to a corporate taxpayer who sold stock in a seller's option trade on a stock exchange for settlement in 60 days.[143] This private letter ruling was revoked without any explanation.[144] The IRS's current position might be that selling stock in a seller's option trade is economically equivalent to a short sale of stock or of substantially identical property. Under I.R.C. § 246(c)(1)(B), if the corporation sells the stock short or holds substantially identical property, the dividends received deduction is not available. Substantially identical property has the same meaning as the corresponding term in the wash sales rule[145] and short sales rule.[146] Whether a taxpayer holds substantially identical property is based on all facts and circumstances.[147]

(3) SECURITY LOANS

The IRS has ruled that a lender of stock who receives dividends with respect to stock loaned to cover short sales is not eligible for the dividends received deduction.[148] This view is consistent with the proposed Treasury regulations under I.R.C. § 1058, which provide that payments made to a lender of securities are treated as a fee for the temporary use of property.[149] In a recent technical advice memorandum, the IRS ruled that where a corporation, as part of its securities lending agreements, made loans of common stock to securities brokers for so-called fail sale transactions (i.e., where securities are loaned to brokers to cover sales of stock by sellers who own the shares they are selling but whose certificates are either lost or have not been delivered to the broker prior to settlement), the dividends paid over to the corporation by the brokers were entitled to the dividends received deduction.[150] The IRS reasoned

---

[142](Oct. 9, 1984).

[143]*See* section 1.3(f).

[144]LTR 8535010 (May 28, 1985).

[145]I.R.C. § 1091.

[146]I.R.C. § 1233.

[147]Treas. Reg. § 1.246-3(c)(2) (1960).

[148]Rev. Rul. 60-177, 1960-1 C.B. 9.

[149]Prop. Treas. Reg. § 1.1058-1(d) (1983). For a discussion of security loan transactions generally, see Chapter 24.

[150]TAM 8538001 (June 6, 1985).

that in the case of fail sale transactions, the lender has a contractual right to receive the dividend payments and there is no possibility for two parties to claim dividend treatment on the loaned stock.[151]

To avoid possible loss of the dividends received deduction, a corporate stockholder should avoid lending its shares of stock near the ex-dividend date. Based on the analysis of Rev. Rul. 60-177 and the TAM, it is possible that any stock held by a corporate stockholder in a margin account that is subject to a stock loan agreement entered into between the corporate stockholder and its broker has a risk of not qualifying for the dividends received deduction. If the corporate taxpayer is unable to establish upon audit that the stock was not loaned to a short seller by the broker to cover a short sale, the IRS may seek to deny the dividends deduction.

(c) DEBT FINANCED PORTFOLIO STOCK

Under pre-DRA law, a corporate stockholder was entitled to both the dividends received deduction and an interest deduction on indebtedness incurred to purchase the stock. Congress viewed this as a way for corporations to avoid taxation.[152] As a result, the DRA enacted a new Code provision that reduces the deduction for dividends received on debt financed portfolio stock so that the deduction is available, in effect, only with respect to dividends attributable to that portion of stock that is not debt financed. "Generally this is accomplished by determining the percentage of the cost of an investment in stock which is debt financed and by reducing the otherwise allowable dividends received deduction with respect to any dividends received on that stock by that percentage."[153] Under current law, the dividends received deduction can be reduced for stock with a holding period that begins after July 18, 1984 in taxable years beginning after that date.[154] The dividends received deduction is reduced for debt financed portfolio stock by a percentage related to the amount of debt incurred to purchase the stock.[155] Portfolio stock is defined as any stock that, as of the beginning of the ex-dividend date, is owned by a taxpayer who owns (1) less than 50 percent of the total voting control and total value of the stock, or (2) less than 20 percent of the total voting control and total value of the stock where

---

[151]*Id.*

[152]HOUSE CONFERENCE REPORT, DEFICIT REDUCTION ACT OF 1984, H.R. REP. NO. 861, 98th Cong., 2d Sess. 811 (1984).

[153]General Explanation of DRA, *supra* note 8, at 129.

[154]I.R.C. § 264A; DRA, *supra* note 79, at § 51(a).

[155]I.R.C. § 246A(a).

the stock is owned by five or fewer corporate stockholders.[156] Any deduction will not exceed the amount of any interest deduction (including any deductible short sale expense) allocable to the dividend.[157]

There is a special rule for stock in banks and bank holding companies. Stock in a bank or bank holding company is portfolio stock if as of the beginning of the ex-dividend date the taxpayer owns less than 80 percent of the value of all stock.[158] In determining whether such stock is portfolio stock, a corporation is treated as owning stock of a bank or bank holding company that it has an option to acquire if, as of the beginning of the ex-dividend date for the dividend involved, the taxpayer owns stock having a value equal to at least 80 percent of the value of all the stock of the corporation.[159] Certain preferred stock is not taken into account for purposes of determining whether the taxpayer holds portfolio stock. Nonvoting preferred stock is not taken into account for determining porfolio stock if it is limited and preferred as to dividends, does not participate in corporate growth, has redemption and liquidation rights that do not exceed the paid-in capital or par value represented by such stock (except for a reasonable redemption premium), and is not convertible into another class of stock.[160]

The deduction allowable for dividends received on debt financed portfolio stock is equal to the product of 85 percent and 100 percent minus the average indebtedness ratio,[161] that is, the percentage obtained by dividing the average amount of the portfolio indebtedness with respect to the stock during the base period by the average amount of the adjusted basis of the stock during the base period.[162]

Portfolio indebtedness means any indebtedness, including any amount received from a short sale, directly attributable to an investment in portfolio stock.[163] The directly attributable requirement is satisfied if there is a direct relationship between the debt and investment in portfolio stock.[164] If indebtedness is clearly incurred to acquire dividend paying portfolio stock, or is directly traceable to the acquisition, the indebtedness constitutes portfolio indebtedness.[165] For portfolio stock

---

[156]I.R.C. § 246A(c)(2).

[157]I.R.C. § 246A(e).

[158]I.R.C. § 246A(c)(3).

[159]General Explanation of DRA, *supra* note 8, at 129.

[160]I.R.C. §§ 246A(c)(4), 1504(a)(4).

[161]I.R.C. § 246A(a).

[162]I.R.C. § 246A(d)(1).

[163]I.R.C. § 246A(d)(3)(A).

[164]General Explanation of DRA, *supra* note 8, at 130.

[165]*Id.*

held in a margin account, the margin borrowing constitutes portfolio indebtedness.[166]

The base period is the period from the previous ex-dividend date to the day before the current ex-dividend date. Only indebtedness during the base period is applied to reduce the dividends received deduction. Buying stock within five days of the ex-dividend date results in the indebtedness being outstanding on the settlement date, which is after the ex-dividend date. A reading of the statute is that in such a situation there is no indebtedness during the base period and no reduction in the dividends received deduction.

When the obligor of the indebtedness is someone other than the corporation receiving the dividend, Treasury regulations (when issued), instead of reducing the dividend received deduction, will disallow interest deductions or provide "other appropriate treatment."[167]

Reduction of the dividends received deduction for debt financed portfolio stock does not apply to (1) qualifying dividends (as defined in I.R.C. § 243(b)) eligible for the 100 percent dividends received deduction,[168] or (2) dividends received by a small business corporation operating under the Small Business Investment Act of 1958.[169]

(d) FHLMC DIVIDENDS

Under pre-DRA law, FHLMC was exempt from all federal, state, and local taxation by its enabling legislation.[170] Real property owned by FHLMC was, and still is, subject to state and local taxation. This tax exemption originally was intended to allow FHLMC "to accumulate adequate capital so that it could compete against other entities in the secondary mortgage market, including Fannie Mae, which is a taxable entity. The purpose of this tax exemption was not to provide Freddie Mac with a competitive advantage."[171] Congress found that FHLMC had become highly profitable and had accumulated sufficient capital to compete in the secondary mortgage market.[172] As a result, Congress believed that the tax exemption provided FHLMC a competitive advantage.

[166]*Id.*
[167]I.R.C. § 246A(f).
[168]*See* section 22.9(a).
[169]I.R.C. § 246A(b).
[170]12 U.S.C. § 1452(d) (Supp. II 1984).
[171]General Explanation of DRA, *supra* note 8, at 550.
[172]*Id.*

DRA repeals the federal tax exemption for FHLMC as of January 1, 1985. It does not affect the state or local exemption. Now that FHLMC is taxable, the Code allows the stockholders of the Federal Home Loan Banks (who, in turn, own the stock in FHLMC) a dividends received deduction for that portion of dividends received from a Home Loan Bank that is allocable to dividends paid to the Home Loan Bank by FHLMC out of taxable earnings after December 31, 1984.[173] Specific authorization was required because the Federal Home Loan Banks are tax-exempt entities and dividends paid from tax-exempt corporations do not qualify for the dividends received deduction.

The DRA amendments generally became effective, with special transitional provisions, on January 1, 1985.

---

[173]I.R.C. § 246(a)(2)(B).

Twenty-three

Interest

§ 23.1 IN GENERAL

Gross income includes all income from whatever sources, including interest.[1] Interest, which is not defined in the Code, generally is viewed as a payment for the use of money. It is taxable unless it is specifically exempt from taxation under the Code or another federal statute. In fact, nearly all interest is includable in gross income and is fully taxable.

In general, interest received by or credited to a taxpayer is included in gross income and is fully taxable.[2] Interest income includes, among other things, interest on (1) savings or other bank deposits, (2) coupon bonds, (3) open accounts, (4) promissory notes, and (5) corporate bonds or debentures.[3] In fact, most interest earned on corporate and federal debt securities is taxable. Interest on municipal securities (i.e., state, local, and certain industrial development bonds) is exempt from tax.[4]

An accrual basis taxpayer includes interest in income when all of the events that fix the right to receive the income have occurred and the amount of the payment can be determined with reasonable accuracy.[5] As a result, an accrual basis taxpayer can be required to include in taxable income daily interest earned, even though not yet received or payable at that time.

---

[1] I.R.C. § 61(4).
[2] Treas. Reg. § 1.61-7(a) (1966).
[3] *Id.*
[4] I.R.C. § 103.
[5] Treas. Reg. § 1.446-1(c)(1)(ii) (1973); Treas. Reg. § 1.451-1(a) (1978).

§ 23.2   CONSTRUCTIVE RECEIPT

A cash basis taxpayer includes interest that is accrued or constructively received in income in the year when it is actually or constructively received.[6] Under the doctrine of constructive receipt, a cash basis taxpayer includes interest in gross income when it is credited or held on deposit subject to his call.[7] Interest must be reported when it becomes available, even if it is not collected at that time. For instance, amounts payable on coupon bonds "which have matured and are payable but have not been cashed are constructively received in the taxable year during which the coupons mature, unless it can be shown that there are no funds available for payment of the interest during such year."[8]

§ 23.3   INTEREST EXCLUSION

For taxable years beginning after December 31, 1980 and before January 1, 1982, noncorporate taxpayers were allowed an exclusion from tax in the amount of $100 ($200 for joint returns) for interest income.[9] In certain circumstances, interest income received by persons who are 65 years of age or older (or who are permanently and totally disabled) may be eligible for the credit for the elderly (or disabled).[10]

§ 23.4   TAX-EXEMPT INTEREST

(a)   IN GENERAL

I.R.C. § 103(a) provides a basic exemption from taxation for interest earned on state and municipal debt securities. Interest on debt securities issued by any state, territory, possession of the U.S., District of Columbia, or any political subdivision is exempt from gross income.[11] The exemption also applies to corporations organized by states or municipalities to perform essential government functions such as soil conser-

---

[6]I.R.C. § 451(a); *see* Treas. Reg. § 1.61-7(a) (1966).

[7]Treas. Reg. § 1.451-2(a) (1979).

[8]Treas. Reg. § 1.451-2(b) (1979).

[9]I.R.C. § 116(b)(1), *amended by* Pub. L. No. 96-223, § 404(a), 94 Stat. 299, 305 (1980).

[10]I.R.C. § 22.

[11]I.R.C. § 103(a)(1). For a discussion of tax-exempt interest, see section 28.2(b)(1).

vation districts,[12] turnpike authorities,[13] utility service authorities,[14] transit authorities,[15] but not water system authorities (where interest arises on loans sold out of the Agricultural Credit Insurance Fund on or after January 1, 1971).[16] Interest from tax-exempt securities is includable in a corporation's earnings and profits and constitutes a taxable dividend when distributed to the stockholders.[17]

(b) INDUSTRIAL DEVELOPMENT BONDS

I.R.C. § 103(b)(1) states that except as otherwise provided under that subsection, an "IDB" is not treated as an obligation exempt from taxation under I.R.C. § 103(a). This means that unless an IDB meets one of the specific exemptions set forth in I.R.C. § 103(b), it is not exempt from taxation. Although interest on certain IDBs continue to remain exempt from taxation,[18] the exemption has been curtailed in recent years. For a discussion of the tax treatment of IDBs, see generally section 28.2(a)(3).

(c) REGISTERED FORM

Tax-exempt securities issued after December 31, 1982 must be issued in registered form.[19] Registration is not required, however, for (1) securities not of a type offered to the public;[20] (2) securities with a maturity date at issue of one year or less;[21] (3) securities issued before January 1, 1983, regardless of any right of the holder to convert the obligation into bearer form, whether or not exercised;[22] or (4) certain securities issued to foreign persons.[23]

In general, a tax-exempt security is issued in registered form in either of two ways. First, both principal and any stated interest is transferable

---

[12]See Rev. Rul. 59-373, 1959-2 C.B. 37.
[13]See Rev. Rul. 61-145, 1961-2 C.B. 21; Rev. Rul. 55-76, 1955-1 C.B. 239.
[14]See Rev. Rul. 57-151, 1957-1 C.B. 64.
[15]See Rev. Rul. 73-563, 1973-2 C.B. 24; Rev. Rul. 61-181, 1961-2 C.B. 21.
[16]Rev. Rul. 71-594, 1971-2 C.B. 91.
[17]Treas. Reg. § 1.312-6(b) (1955).
[18]I.R.C. §§ 103(b)(4), (6).
[19]I.R.C. § 103(j); Temp. Treas. Reg. § 5f.103-1(a) (1982).
[20]Temp. Treas. Reg. § 5f.103-1(b)(1) (1982).
[21]Temp. Treas. Reg. § 5f.103-1(b)(2) (1982).
[22]Temp. Treas. Reg. § 5f.103-1(b)(3) (1982).
[23]Temp. Treas. Reg. § 5f.103-1(b)(4) (1982).

only by the surrender of the old security, and either the reissuance of the old security to the new holder or the issuance of a new security to the new holder.[24] Second, the right to principal of, and stated interest on, the security can be transferred only through a book entry system.[25] For a discussion of the registration requirements, see section 27.11 and section 28.2(b)(1)(i)(b).

[24]Temp. Treas. Reg. § 5f.103-1(c)(1)(i) (1982).
[25]Temp. Treas. Reg. § 5f.103-1(c)(1)(ii) (1982).

Twenty-four

Security Loans

Many taxpayers obtain additional income by lending their securities to others, typically their brokers, who use the securities to cover short sales transactions or so-called fail sale situations where the seller does not deliver the securities on the settlement date.[1] Securities lending transactions take place because the borrowers need the actual securities. Typically the broker agrees to fully collateralize the loan (with cash or other securities) and to return identical securities to the lender upon demand or within a short time thereafter. The lender receives a fee as compensation for the use of the securities and an amount equal to any dividends or interest payments made by the issuer of securities during the period when the securities were loaned. Security loans are quite common. Tax-exempt organizations and regulated investment companies frequently lend their portfolio securities positions to earn current income.

§ 24.1 INTRODUCTION

Prior to the enactment of I.R.C. § 1058, there was uncertainty as to the correct tax treatment for securities lending transactions entered into before January 1, 1977.[2] The IRS had stopped issuing rulings on whether

---

[1]*See generally Banking Agencies Adopt Securities Lending Policy*, BANKING EXPANSION REPORTER, July 1, 1985, at 18 (comparing securities lending with repurchase agreements).

[2]SENATE FINANCE COMMITTEE REPORT, INTERNAL REVENUE CODE OF 1954—TELEPHONE COMPANIES—INCOME, S. REP. NO. 762, 95th Cong., 2d Sess. 3, *reprinted in* 1978 U.S. CODE CONG. & AD. NEWS 1286, 1289.

a securities lending transaction constituted a sale or exchange or whether the transaction interrupted the lender's holding period.[3] Prior to its refusal to issue a ruling, the IRS had stated in a widely circulated private letter ruling that a securities lending transaction did not constitute a taxable disposition of the loaned securities and that the transaction did not interrupt the lender's holding period. The private ruling, issued to the NYSE on April 19, 1948, stated that the securities lending transaction described in the ruling was

> not a disposition of property which results in recognized gain or loss for Federal income tax purposes; and that such a transaction does not affect the lender's basis for the purpose of determining gain or loss upon the sale or the disposition of the stock, nor the holding period of the stock in the hands of the lender.[4]

§ 24.2   QUALIFIED LOAN AGREEMENTS

I.R.C. § 1058(a), which applies to security loans after December 31, 1976, provides that if a qualified loan agreement is in place, neither gain nor loss is recognized on the loan of securities if the borrower agrees to return, and does return, identical securities to the taxpayer. For a discussion of the possible application of I.R.C. § 1058 to repo transactions, see section 27.10.

(a) NONRECOGNITION

Under a qualified loan agreement, the lender neither recognizes gain or loss on the exchange of rights nor recognizes gain or loss on the return of securities identical to those securities transferred by the lender.[5]

(b) REQUIREMENTS

A qualified loan agreement must meet several requirements. First, the agreement must provide that identical securities will be returned to the lender.[6] Second, it must require that payments be made to the lender in an amount equivalent to all interest, dividends, and other distributions that the owner of the securities is entitled to receive, during the

---

[3]*Id.* at 4.
[4]*Id.*
[5]Prop. Treas. Reg. § 1.1058-1(a) (1983).
[6]I.R.C. § 1058(b)(1).

period from the transfer of the securities until identical securities are returned to the lender.[7] Third, it cannot reduce the lender's risk of loss or opportunity for gain on the securities transferred back.[8] Fourth, it must meet any other requirements provided in Treasury regulations.[9] Proposed Treasury regulations provide that the agreement must be in writing[10] and must allow the lender to terminate the loan upon notice of not more than five business days.[11]

(c) BASIS

A lender's basis in identical securities returned by the borrower in a qualified loan agreement is the same as the lender's basis in the securities lent.[12] In addition, the proposed Treasury regulations provide that the lender's basis in the contractual obligation (i.e., the loan agreement) he received from the borrower in exchange for the lender's securities is equal to the lender's basis in the securities lent.[13]

(d) HOLDING PERIOD

A lender's holding period for securities received back from the borrower in a qualified loan transaction includes the period during which the lender held the securities transferred to the borrower and the period between the transfer and the date the identical securities were returned to him.[14] In other words, a qualified loan transaction does not interrupt the lender's holding period for securities lent and returned in accordance with the qualified loan agreement.

(e) PAYMENTS TO LENDER

All amounts paid to the lender that are equivalent to interest, dividends, and other distributions that the owner of securities is entitled to are treated as a fee for the temporary use of property.[15] The proposed Treas-

---

[7]I.R.C. § 1058(b)(2).
[8]I.R.C. § 1058(b)(3).
[9]I.R.C. § 1058(b)(4).
[10]Prop. Treas. Reg. § 1.1058-1(b) (1983).
[11]Prop. Treas. Reg. § 1.1058-1(b)(3) (1983).
[12]I.R.C. § 1058(c); Prop. Treas. Reg. § 1.1058-1(c)(1) (1983).
[13]Prop. Treas. Reg. § 1.1058-1(c)(2) (1983).
[14]Prop. Treas. Reg. § 1.1223-2(a) (1983).
[15]Prop. Treas. Reg. § 1.1058-1(d) (1983).

ury regulations state that an amount received by the lender that is equivalent to a dividend paid during the term of the loan does not constitute a dividend to the lender but is taken into account as ordinary income.[16] The payments lose their original character and are treated as fees received by the lender. As a result, a corporate lender generally loses the benefit of the dividends received deduction,[17] and a lender of tax-exempt securities receives ordinary income, not tax-exempt income, during the period the securities are lent under the qualified loan agreement.[18] Both I.R.C. § 1058 and the proposed Treasury regulations are silent as to the appropriate treatment of OID on discount obligations transferred under a qualified loan agreement.

(f) UNRELATED BUSINESS TAXABLE INCOME

Special rules are provided for payments received by tax-exempt organizations involved in an unrelated trade or business, including the lending of securities pursuant to qualified loan agreements. I.R.C. § 512(a)(5) defines "payments made with respect to securities loans." Then, I.R.C. § 512(b) provides that such payments are not used to compute unrelated business taxable income under I.R.C. § 512(a).

(g) MERGERS, RECAPITALIZATIONS, AND REORGANIZATIONS

If a merger, recapitalization, or reorganization (including a reorganization under I.R.C. § 368(a)) of the issuer occurs during the term of a qualified loan agreement, the loan transaction is deemed to terminate immediately prior to the corporate transaction and a second loan transaction, on identical terms to the original loan transaction, is deemed to be entered into immediately following the merger, recapitalization, or reorganization.[19] In other words, the borrower is treated as having returned the securities to the lender immediately prior to the merger, recapitalization, or reorganization and the new securities are deemed to be re-lent to the same borrower in a new, but otherwise identical, qualified loan transaction immediately following the merger, recapi-

[16]*Id.*
[17]Rev. Rul. 60-177, 1960-1 C.B. 9; *see* section 15.7; section 22.9.
[18]Rev. Rul. 80-135, 1980-1 C.B. 18; *see* section 23.4; section 28.2(b)(1).
[19]Prop. Treas. Reg. § 1.1058-1(f) (1983).

talization, or reorganization.[20] If the lender ultimately is repaid with securities identical to the ones originally transferred, the rule that deems a new loan transaction to occur does not apply.[21]

§ 24.3 NONQUALIFIED LOAN TRANSACTIONS

The tax consequences of a nonqualified loan transaction vary depending upon whether the loan transaction ever qualified for I.R.C. § 1058 protection as a qualified loan agreement. If the security loan initially meets the requirements of I.R.C. § 1058(b), but the borrower fails to return to the lender identical securities or otherwise defaults under the terms of the agreement, gain or loss is recognized by the lender on the day the borrower fails to return identical securities.[22] This means that even if the terms of an agreement are proper, but the borrower fails to return identical securities or otherwise defaults, the lender recognizes gain or loss on the day of the default.[23] The lender's holding period for the securities also terminates on the day of the default and the borrower's holding period begins on that date.[24]

If securities were not transferred pursuant to a qualified loan agreement, the transfer does not meet the nonrecognition requirements of I.R.C. § 1058(b) or Prop. Treas. Reg. § 1.1058-1(b). As a result, gain or loss is recognized at the initial transfer in accordance with both I.R.C. § 1001 and Treas. Reg. § 1.1001(a).[25] In this situation, the lender's holding period terminates on the day the securities are transferred and the borrower's holding period begins on that date.[26]

§ 24.4 INTERCORPORATE DIVIDENDS RECEIVED DEDUCTION

The IRS has ruled that dividends received by a lender of stock used to cover short sales are not eligible for the dividends received deduction.[27]

---

[20]*Id.*

[21]*Id.*

[22]Prop. Treas. Reg. § 1.1058-1(e)(2) (1983).

[23]*Id.*

[24]Prop. Treas. Reg. § 1.1223-2(b)(2) (1983).

[25]Treas. Reg. § 1.1058-1(e)(1) (1983).

[26]Prop. Treas. Reg. § 1.1223-2(b)(1) (1983).

[27]Rev. Rul. 60-177, 1960-1 C.B. 9; *see* section 15.7; section 22.9.

This is consistent with the view that payments to a lender are treated as a fee for the temporary use of property.[28] In a recent TAM, the IRS ruled that where a corporation, as part of its securities lending agreements made loans of common stock to securities brokers for fail sale transactions (i.e., where securities are loaned to brokers to cover sales of stock by sellers who own the shares they are selling but whose certificates are either lost or have not been delivered to the broker prior to settlement), the dividends paid over to the corporation by the brokers were entitled to the dividends received deduction.[29] The IRS reasoned that in the case of fail sale transactions, the lender has a contractual right to receive the dividend payments and there is no possibility for two parties to claim dividends on the loaned stock.[30]

[28]*See* section 24.2(e).
[29]TAM 8538001 (June 6, 1985).
[30]*Id.*

Part Six

Taxation of Stock, Other Equity Interests, and Options on Securities

Twenty-five

Stock and Equity Interests

§ 25.1 IN GENERAL

This chapter addresses general tax principles for the taxation of corporate stock, federal agency stock, publicly traded limited partnership interests, and publicly traded trust interests. It also discusses the special tax rules that apply to preferred stock, convertible stock, when-issued securities, small business investment companies, and so-called section 1244 stock. The wash sales rule,[1] the short sales rule,[2] and the Straddle Rules[3] apply to taxpayers holding stock interests unless specific exemptions are available. In addition, investors[4] and traders[5] are subject to the general rules for capital transactions,[6] while dealers[7] and hedgers[8] are subject to the general rules for ordinary income treatment.[9]

---

[1] *See generally* Chapter 17.
[2] *See generally* Chapter 16.
[3] *See generally* Part Ten.
[4] *See* section 6.1.
[5] *See* section 6.2.
[6] *See generally* Part Three.
[7] *See* section 6.3.
[8] *See* section 6.4.
[9] *See generally* Part Four.

§ 25.2   DEBT-EQUITY CONSIDERATIONS

An exhaustive discussion of the considerations for whether a corporation should issue debt or equity interests is beyond the scope of this book.[10] Nevertheless, the following is a brief discussion of debt and equity characteristics that may be useful in determining whether a security identified as an equity interest is actually a debt security for tax purposes or vice versa.[11]

There have been many conflicting judicial decisions as to whether a security is classified as a debt or an equity interest.[12] Recharacterization can have significant, usually detrimental, tax consequences to both the issuer and the owner of the interest.[13] For example, the intercorporate dividends received deduction[14] makes the ownership of equity more attractive than debt interests for corporate stockholders. Recharacterization of an equity interest as a debt interest precludes application of the intercorporate dividends received deduction. In addition, the stock would potentially be subject to the OID and the market discount rules. And, the "dividend" payments are deductible by the issuer as interest, although issuers with net operating losses may not need current interest deductions.

On the other hand, recharacterization of debt interests as equity interests may also create unexpected tax consequences.[15] First, interest is deductible by a corporate issuer of debt securities, while dividends paid on its stock are not. Second, premiums and discounts are not created on the issuance of common stock, although premiums and discounts can result upon the issuance of certain preferred stock and debt securities.[16] Third, the receipt of stock is often eligible for tax-free treatment under the reorganization provisions, but the receipt of debt securities does not qualify for those reorganization provisions that require the

---

[10]*See generally* Taylor, *Debt/Equity and Other Tax Distinctions: How Far Can We Go?* 62 TAXES 848-58 (1984). *See also* Walter & Strasen, *Fox Television Stations, Inc. Increasing Rate Exchangeable Guaranteed Preferred Stock*, 64 *Taxes* 234 (1986).

[11]*See* section 28.3.

[12]*See generally* B. BITTKER & J. EUSTICE, FEDERAL INCOME TAXATION OF CORPORATIONS AND SHAREHOLDERS ¶¶ 4.03-4.05, at 4-8 to 4-16 (4th ed. 1979).

[13]*See* section 28.3(c); section 28.3(d).

[14]*See* section 22.9.

[15]*See* section 28.3(a)(1); section 28.3(c).

[16]Preferred stock can be issued at a discount. If its redemption premium is "unreasonable," the unreasonable portion is deemed to be a dividend that is paid throughout the period the stock cannot be called for redemption. Rev. Rul. 83-119, 1983-2, C.B. 57; Treas. Reg. § 1.305-5(b) (1974).

receipt of voting stock whenever stock is surrendered and debt securities are received.[17] Fourth, payment of the principal amount of a debt security is ordinarily tax-free to the holder, while stock redemptions are often taxable as dividends.

I.R.C. § 385, enacted in 1969 to provide some guidance on whether an interest is classified as either debt or equity, lists some factors to consider as to whether a corporation-stockholder or a debtor-creditor relationship exists. First, is there a written unconditional promise to pay a fixed sum on demand or on a specified date and a fixed rate of interest, in return for an adequate consideration in money or money's worth?[18] Second, is the security subordinated or does it have a preference over any indebtedness of the corporation?[19] Third, what is the corporation's ratio of debt to equity?[20] Fourth, is the security convertible into stock of the corporation?[21] Fifth, what is the relationship between the stockholders and the owners of the interest in question?[22] All of these factors are considered in light of all facts and circumstances.

In addition, I.R.C. § 385(a) specifically authorizes the Treasury to issue debt-equity regulations. At this writing, after several attempts to issue such regulations, all proposed and final regulations have been withdrawn.[23] The only available guidelines as to whether a security is a debt instrument or an equity interest are those listed in I.R.C. § 385(b), IRS pronouncements, and often conflicting judicial decisions.

§ 25.3 TYPES OF CORPORATE STOCK INTERESTS

This section discusses various types of corporate stock interests and tax considerations for these interests. Neither the Code nor the regulations provide a useful definition of "stock." Stock has generally been defined, however, as an equity interest in a corporation, either common or preferred, voting or nonvoting.[24]

[17]I.R.C. § 354(a)(2).
[18]I.R.C. § 385(b)(1).
[19]I.R.C. § 385(b)(2).
[20]I.R.C. § 385(b)(3). In LTR 8523009 (Feb. 25, 1985), the IRS ruled that convertible debt securities issued in a leveraged buy out qualified as debt even though the issuer had an enormous amount of debt compared to equity.
[21]I.R.C. § 385(b)(4).
[22]I.R.C. § 385(b)(5).
[23]The effective date of the final Treasury regulations, issued on December 31, 1980, was continually delayed until the regulations were formally withdrawn on August 5, 1983.
[24]See Mather & Co. v. Comm'r, 171 F.2d 864 (3d Cir. 1949), cert. denied, 337 U.S. 907 (1949).

(a) COMMON STOCK

Stock is frequently classified as common stock for tax purposes if it is an equity interest with an unrestricted right to participate in the growth of a corporation. The right to vote is not determinative.[25] Common stock must have an unrestricted right to share in both dividends and liquidating distributions.[26] Stock with a dividend preference, a priority for payment on liquidation, and equal participation with the other classes of stock in additional distributions, if any, is classified as common stock.[27] Further, the IRS has ruled in a private letter ruling that stock with a dividend preference and a limited right to participate in dividends in excess of its preference is common stock.[28]

(b) PREFERRED STOCK

(1) DEFINED

Preferred stock is defined in the Treasury regulations as a class of stock that in relation to other outstanding classes of stock has certain limited rights and privileges (generally specified dividend and liquidation priorities), and is not expected to participate in corporate growth to any significant extent.[29] Stock that does not participate in corporate growth is classified as preferred stock, even though it is the only class of stock with voting rights.[30] Stock with a liquidation preference limited to par value is classified as preferred stock. A restriction to an ascertainable maximum value for the stock on liquidation indicates that the stock does not have a restricted right to participate in the growth of the corporation.[31] If the right of a class of stock to participate in corporate growth lacks substance, the stock is treated as preferred stock.[32] Even if a stock has a priority right to receive dividends and a priority on liquidation, but it participates with another class of stock on liquidation, it may still be classified as preferred stock (for purposes of distributions

---

[25]Rev. Rul. 75-236, 1975-1 C.B. 106 (stock that does not participate in the growth of a corporation is not common stock, even if it is the only class of stock with voting rights); Rev. Rul. 76-387, 1976-2 C.B. 96 (stock with an unrestricted right to participate in the growth of a corporation is common stock, even if it has no voting rights); LTR 8210065 (Dec. 10, 1981).

[26]Rev. Rul. 79-163, 1979-1 C.B. 131.

[27]Rev. Rul. 81-91, 1981-1 C.B. 123.

[28]LTR 8037096 (June 20, 1980).

[29]Treas. Reg. § 1.305-5(a) (1974).

[30]Rev. Rul. 75-236, 1975-1 C.B. 106.

[31]Rev. Rul. 79-163, 1979-1 C.B. 131.

[32]Treas. Reg. § 1.305-5(a) (1974).

under I.R.C. § 305). Such stock is classified as preferred stock if it is reasonable to anticipate at the time of a distribution that there is little or no likelihood of its participating in current and anticipated earnings beyond its liquidation priority.[33]

(2) DEBT-EQUITY CONSIDERATIONS FOR PREFERRED STOCK

In general, preferred stock is treated as equity if it is clearly labeled as preferred stock and a third party does not guarantee either dividend or redemption payments.[34] Preferred stock with mandatory redemption provisions has been treated as an equity interest in some, although not all, cases.[35] Preferred stock has seldom been reclassified as debt. In *Zilkha & Sons, Inc. v. Comm'r*,[36] the Tax Court rejected the IRS's contention that preferred stock held by the taxpayer represented, in substance, a debt security of the corporation. Similarly, in *Ragland Investment Co. v. Comm'r*,[37] and in *Miele v. Comm'r*,[38] the Tax Court upheld the equity status of preferred stock. However, in Rev. Rul. 80-221,[39] the IRS ruled that preferred stock issued for cash and redeemable for a corporate asset within 13 months after issuance was not preferred stock but merely a device in a step transaction aimed at the sale of the asset.

New types of preferred stock have been issued in recent years,[40] often by corporations with net operating losses or minimal taxable income. These preferred stocks are frequently structured to attract corporate investors who can benefit from the intercorporate dividends received deduction.[41] Examples of new preferred stock products are so-called convertible exchangeable preferred stocks, ARPs, CAPS, and auction

---

[33]Treas. Reg. § 1.305-5(a) (1974).

[34]*See e.g.s*, Elko Lamoille Power Co. v. Comm'r, 50 F.2d 595 (9th Cir. 1931); First Mortgage Corp. of Phila. v. Comm'r, 135 F.2d 121 (3d Cir. 1943); Crown Iron Works Co. v. Comm'r, 245 F.2d 357 (8th Cir. 1957); Ragland Inv. Co. v. Comm'r, 52 T.C. 867 (1969), *aff'd*, 435 F.2d 118 (6th Cir. 1970).

[35]*See e.g.s*, *Crown Iron Works Co.*, 245 F.2d 357; Comm'r v. Meridian & Thirteenth Realty Co., 132 F.2d 182 (7th Cir. 1942).

[36]52 T.C. 607, 618 (1969).

[37]52 T.C. 867 (1969), *aff'd*, 435 F.2d 118 (6th Cir. 1970).

[38]56 T.C. 556, 566 (1971), *aff'd*, 474 F.2d 1138 (3d Cir. 1973).

[39]1980-2 C.B. 107.

[40]*See* section 1.1(f). Fox Television Stations, Inc. issued over $1.1 billion of "preferred stock" in a widely publicized offering. The stock, referred to as "increasing rate exchangeable guaranteed preferred stock," provides for a mandatory cash redemption after 10 years. The issuer's payment obligations are unconditionally guaranteed by affiliates. The prospectus states that legal counsel cannot opine on whether the stock is equity or debt for tax purposes. *See* Fox Television Stations, Inc., Prospectus (Feb. 27, 1986).

[41]*See* section 15.7; section 22.9.

rate preferred stock. Convertible exchangeable preferred stocks, convertible at the option of the issuer into debt securities, provide flexibility for issuers who may not need current interest deductions.[42] Prior to conversion, the owners of the preferred stocks obtain dividends that are usually eligible for the intercorporate dividends received deduction. Conversion of the preferred stock into debt securities provides the issuer with interest deductions (and the debt holders with interest income). ARPs are preferred stocks that provide dividends that adjust periodically to rates that are close to the money market rate. Auction rate preferred stocks (also referred to as "money market preferred stocks" and "market auction preferred stocks") are types of adjustable rate stocks that generally reset dividend rates every 49 days. Dividends are reset using a Dutch auction process whereby holders are paid the lowest dividend rate that encompasses a sufficient number of bids made by current and potential holders to cover all outstanding shares.[43] Typically, ARPs and auction rate preferred stocks may be subject to call by the issuer, but are not subject to mandatory redemption provisions. ARPs and auction rate preferred stocks do not have a fixed maturity date. As a result, it appears unlikely that the IRS could prevail in an attempt to reclassify ARPs as debt securities. CAPS are adjustable rate preferred stocks that are convertible into a number of common shares established by a predetermined cash value.

(i) Mandatory Redemption Provisions

Even though preferred stock is seldom reclassified as debt, simply labeling stock as preferred stock may not be enough to assure that it is treated as an equity interest for tax purposes. To be classified as equity, it is also important that dividends are payable only out of corporate earnings and only if and when declared. Further, rights on default should not be substantially identical to rights typically provided to creditors.

---

[42]*See, e.g.s,* Household Finance Corporation, Prospectus (Dec. 17, 1985); Chubb Corp., Prospectus (March 26, 1985).

[43]In LTR 8529095 (Apr. 25, 1985), the IRS approved the full intercorporate dividends received deduction for dividends paid on ARP stock owned by a regulated investment company. Corporate shareholders of the regulated investment company were eligible for the intercorporate dividends received deduction on dividends paid during the entire period they held the shares as long as they met the 46-day holding period requirement. *Id.* In LTR 8610016 (Nov. 29, 1985), the IRS approved the intercorporate dividends received deduction for dividends paid on CAPS. The conversion feature was not treated as a stock option for tax purposes. *See* section 15.7; section 22.9. A recent ARP offering is the adjustable rate cumulative preferred stock issued by Sun Life Group of America, Inc., Prospectus (Jan. 10, 1986). A recent auction rate preferred stock is the market auction preferred stock issued by Weyerhauser Company, Prospectus (Nov. 8, 1985).

The Treasury's attempts to issue debt-equity regulations under I.R.C. § 385 are instructive in the area of preferred stock with mandatory redemption privileges. Treasury regulations under I.R.C. § 385, which were revised[44] and ultimately withdrawn by the Treasury, took such an expansive view of debt interests that almost everything issued by a corporation could be classified as debt. Classifications of preferred stock as equity depended on the absence of "fixed payments . . . in the nature of either principal or interest."[45] The stock might have been classified as debt if (1) the preferred stock owners could compel the payment of either dividends or sinking fund (i.e., redemption) payments and (2) there were fixed payments.[46] The proposed regulations described preferred stock without any mandatory redemption privileges (frequently referred to as "permanent preferred stock") as "a garden variety preferred stock."[47] In other words, preferred stock with mandatory redemption rights was considered unusual under the proposed regulations. In the final Treasury regulations,[48] which were also withdrawn, the Treasury proposed a "rule of convenience" that would have provided a safe harbor for certain preferred stock subject to mandatory redemption in 10 years or more.[49]

Although it is not clear at what point preferred stock with a mandatory redemption provision may no longer be classified as equity, it is safe to say that a short-term nonvoting preferred stock with an unconditional sinking fund is a debt interest. In *Ragland Investment Co. v. Comm'r*,[50] the Tax Court treated preferred stock with mandatory redemption after four years as equity. The controlling stockholders had agreed to take all necessary actions to cause the corporation to redeem the stock within four years and the stock could be put back to the issuing corporation if the corporation's surplus dropped below 110 percent of the redemption price. In *Ragland*, the Tax Court relied on the facts that the preferred stock owners had a right to elect directors[51] and that dividends were only payable out of corporate earnings.[52]

---

[44]T.D. 7747, 1981-1 C.B. 141; T.D. 7920, 1983-2 C.B. 69.

[45]*Id.*

[46]Under the proposed Treasury regulations, classification of preferred stock as debt or equity depended on "hybrid" instrument rules that examined the relative values of an interest's equity and nonequity features. *Id.*

[47]45 Fed. Reg. 18957 (1980).

[48]T.D. 7920, 1983-2 C.B. 69.

[49]Prop. Treas. Reg. § 1.385-10(b) (1980).

[50]52 T.C. at 879.

[51]*Id.* at 877.

[52]*Id.* at 876–77.

(ii)   Guarantees

It is unclear whether third party guarantees of dividend and redemption payments affect the classification of the stock as equity. A guarantee might reclassify stock as a debt interest because it removes the payment contingencies typical for equity interests. In addition, guarantees may make the owners of the interest appear more like creditors than stockholders. Further, guarantees may preclude availability of the intercorporate dividends received deduction.[53] In *Northern Refrigerator Line, Inc. v. Comm'r*,[54] the taxpayer corporation issued nonvoting preferred stock that provided for both cumulative annual dividends in a predetermined amount and mandatory redemption. In addition, the common stockholder guaranteed the payment of the dividends and the mandatory redemption. The Tax Court held that the issuer could not deduct as interest expense the dividends it paid on the preferred stock because the preferred stock was an equity interest.[55] Other judicial decisions have held that such guarantees converted the stock to debt interests.[56]

Guarantees typically are not available for an indefinite period of time. As a result, if a stock interest also provides other types of stockholder protections (e.g., put options or a mandatory call by the issuer on the lapse of a guarantee), the preferred stock may be reclassified as a debt security.

(iii)   Tax-Free Exchanges

Distinctions between preferred stock and debt are also relevant in determining whether a merger or a corporate acquisition qualifies as a tax-free reorganization under I.R.C. § 368.[57] To qualify for tax-free treatment, the stockholders of the corporation to be acquired must, to some extent, continue to have an interest in the enterprise after the merger.[58]

---

[53]If a corporate stockholder holds positions in substantially similar or related property, the Treasury can issue regulations that suspend the stockholder's holding period for purposes of the intercorporate dividends received deduction. I.R.C. § 246(c)(4)(C). *See* section 15.7; section 22.9.

[54]1 T.C. 824 (1943).

[55]1 T.C. at 830.

[56]*See* Bowersock Mills & Power Co. v. Comm'r, 172 F.2d 904 (10th Cir. 1949); Comm'r v. Palmer, Stacy-Merrill, Inc., 111 F.2d 809 (9th Cir. 1940). *But see* Richmond, Fredericksburg & Potomac R.R. Co. v. Comm'r, 528 F.2d 917 (4th Cir. 1975).

[57]*See* section 25.4.

[58]Cortland Specialty Co. v. Comm'r, 60 F.2d 937 (2d Cir. 1932) *cert. denied*, 288 U.S. 599 (1933).

The IRS has announced that it will consider issuing a favorable ruling on the reorganization status of a merger if 50 percent of the consideration paid to the stockholders of a merging corporation is in the form of common or preferred stock.[59] Hence, if the preferred stock issued by the acquiring corporation is reclassified as debt, more than half of the remaining stockholders of the acquired corporation must receive equity interests in the acquiring corporation for the merger to be treated as a tax-free reorganization.

If stockholders transfer preferred stock that is so-called section 306 stock[60] to their wholly owned corporation in a tax-free exchange for other preferred stock of equal value, the stock remains section 306 stock in the hands of the corporation (irrespective of whether it has earnings and profits).[61] The new stock received by the stockholders is also section 306 stock.[62] The basis of the new stock received by the stockholders is determined by reference to the basis of their old section 306 stock; the new preferred stock remains section 306 stock.[63]

Even if the acquiring corporation's preferred stock is classified as equity, it may not qualify as a present equity interest for purposes of the 50 percent continuity of interest rule. In *McDonald's Restaurants of Illinois, Inc. v. Comm'r*,[64] the taxpayer argued that a purported reorganization failed the continuity of interest requirement because the majority of the stockholders of the acquired corporation had intended to sell the preferred stock that they received in the course of the merger. The Tax Court rejected this argument and distinguished this case from a situation in which the stockholders of the merging corporation had not only intended to sell their preferred stock, but had committed themselves to sell it.[65] The Seventh Circuit Court of Appeals reversed the Tax Court, holding that the step transaction doctrine applied to collapse the merger and the subsequent sale of the stock, thereby making tax-free treatment unavailable.[66] The Seventh Circuit focused on the fact that the "sellers" had negotiated contract rights to require the "buyer" to register the stock received in the exchange to facilitate its sale.[67]

[59]Rev. Proc. 77-37, 1977-2 C.B. 568, *superseded in part by* Rev. Proc. 79-14, 1979-1 C.B. 496.

[60]*See* section 25.3(b)(4).

[61]*See* section 22.1(c).

[62]Rev. Rul. 77-108, 1977-1 C.B. 86.

[63]*Id.*

[64]76 T.C. 972, 988 (1981), *rev'd*, 688 F.2d 520 (7th Cir. 1982).

[65]*McDonald's*, 76 T.C. at 989–90.

[66]*McDonald's*, 688 F.2d at 525.

[67]*Id.*

(3) PREFERRED STOCK REDEMPTIONS

The two major tax questions with respect to preferred stock redemptions are whether mandatory redemption provisions reclassify stock as debt and whether a periodic redemption is subject to the rules of I.R.C. § 305(c), which treats certain transactions as deemed distributions.[68] Preferred stock may still qualify as a stock interest if it is redeemable through a sinking fund or otherwise. The debt-equity considerations for a mandatory redemption of preferred stock are discussed in section 25.3(b)(2).

The remainder of this section addresses the issue of whether a periodic redemption is subject to the deemed distribution rules of I.R.C. § 305(c). In general, a periodic redemption of preferred stock is viewed as a deemed distribution if there is an increase in the proportionate interest of any stockholder in the earnings and profits or assets of a corporation because of the redemption. Further, a redemption may qualify as an increase in the proportionate interest of any stockholder if the redemption removes a priority claim on earnings, thereby increasing a stockholder's interest in the redeeming corporation's earnings and profits. A deemed distribution does not result if a periodic redemption plan is viewed as a security arrangement. In Rev. Rul. 78-115,[69] the IRS ruled that I.R.C. § 305(c) did not apply where one corporation acquired another corporation in exchange for cash and redeemable preferred stock, which was scheduled to be redeemed at a fixed percentage over a period of years. The IRS viewed the preferred stock as a security arrangement because the stock was issued solely to facilitate the corporate acquisition and other forms of financing were not available to the corporate issuer.[70]

(4) PREFERRED STOCK BAILOUTS

I.R.C. § 306 was enacted to stop preferred stock "bailouts" used to avoid ordinary income treatment on the withdrawal of earnings from a corporation.[71] Prior to enactment of I.R.C. § 306, the distribution of preferred stock was a way to withdraw earnings from a corporation at

---

[68]For a discussion of deemed distributions under I.R.C. § 305(c), see section 22.2(b).

[69]1978-1 C.B. 85.

[70]*Id.* The IRS did not apply I.R.C. § 305(c), even though the redemption of preferred stock from a stockholder who also held common stock was likely to be taxable as a dividend, the redemption was not isolated, and the proportionate interests of the nonredeeming stockholders would increase because of the redemption.

[71]From the issuing corporation's perspective, there is no tax advantage to preferred stock over common stock: dividends paid on preferred and common stock are both nondeductible.

capital gain rates. This was because pro rata preferred stock dividends paid to common stockholders avoided dividend treatment.[72]

The tax benefits available with a preferred stock bailout prior to enactment of I.R.C. § 306 were illustrated by *Chamberlin v. Comm'r*,[73] where a corporation with substantial earnings distributed a preferred stock dividend to its stockholders. The stockholders promptly sold the preferred stock, pursuant to a prearranged plan, to a group of insurance companies. The stockholders reported capital gain on their sale of the preferred stock. Some of the insurance companies retained the preferred stock for investment while the issuing corporation redeemed the stock of other insurance companies. The court in *Chamberlin* allowed this result, even though the stockholders were able to convert ordinary income to capital gain.

I.R.C. § 306, enacted in response to *Chamberlin,* provides for ordinary income, with certain exceptions, on sales of preferred stock that qualify as "section 306 stock." Section 306 stock includes stock (other than common stock) that is received by the stockholder in a tax-free transaction.[74] Such tax-free transactions include (1) tax-free stock dividends under I.R.C. § 306, (2) stock received tax-free in corporate reorganizations under I.R.C. § 368, (3) stock received in corporate divisions under I.R.C. § 335, and (4) stock with adjusted bases determined by reference to section 306 stock.

Stock does not qualify as section 306 stock if *no* part of the distribution would have been a dividend at the time of the distribution if money, instead of stock, had been distributed.[75] The presence of *any* earnings and profits[76] taints all stock received and classifies the stock as section 306 stock. Conversely, if the corporation did not have earnings and profits in the year the stock was distributed, the stock is not section 306 stock. (Obviously, there is no reason for stockholders to convert ordinary income to capital gain if the issuing corporation has no earnings and profits in the year the stock is distributed.)

The receipt of section 306 stock is not taxable. Rather, the section 306 classification only affects a stock's tax treatment on disposition. (This is because the purpose of I.R.C. § 306 is to prevent capital gain on the bailout of earnings from corporations.) I.R.C. § 306 applies on the disposition of section 306 stock in two different ways. First, certain

---

[72]For a discussion of dividends, see generally Chapter 22.

[73]207 F.2d 462 (6th Cir. 1953), *cert. denied,* 347 U.S. 918 (1954).

[74]I.R.C. § 306(c).

[75]I.R.C. § 306(c)(2).

[76]*See* section 22.1(c).

rules apply to redemptions of section 306 stock.[77] Second, other rules apply to dispositions of section 306 stock in transactions that are not redemptions.[78]

A redemption of section 306 stock is treated as a distribution of property that is subject to I.R.C. § 301,[79] rather than as a redemption under I.R.C. § 302. As a result, the amount received in redemption of section 306 stock is treated under the same tests for dividends. For a discussion of dividend treatment, see generally section 22.1.

If section 306 stock is exchanged in a tax-free exchange for other preferred stock, the new stock is section 306 stock in the hands of the stockholders.[80] This is because the provisions of I.R.C. § 306(c)(2) (which provides that section 306 stock does not include any portion of a distribution that would have been a dividend at the time of the distribution if money had been distributed in lieu of stock) do not apply to new stock received in exchange for section 306 stock if the basis of the new stock is determined by reference to the stockholder's basis in the section 306 stock.[81] I.R.C. § 306(c)(2) only applies to distributions and not to tax-free exchanges.

For dispositions of section 306 stock in transactions other than redemptions, the amount realized falls into three categories: ordinary income, a tax-free return of basis, and capital gain.[82] In other words, the prospect of ordinary income on the disposition of section 306 stock distinguishes such stock from other stocks.

(c) CONVERTIBLE STOCK

Convertible stock is typically (although not always) preferred stock that is convertible into common stock of the issuing corporation.[83] The taxation of convertible stock is not governed by any single Code provision. Rather, one must look to various Code provisions, Treasury regulations, often conflicting judicial decisions, and IRS pronouncements to ascertain the appropriate tax treatment of convertible stock.[84] This section

---

[77] I.R.C. § 306(a)(2).

[78] I.R.C. § 306(a)(1).

[79] I.R.C. § 306(a)(2).

[80] Rev. Rul. 77-108, 1977-1 C.B. 86.

[81] *Id.*

[82] I.R.C. § 306(a)(1).

[83] For a discussion of convertible securities, see section 1.1(c). For a discussion of convertible debt securities, see section 28.3.

[84] *See generally* Fleischer & Cary, *The Taxation of Convertible Bonds and Stock*, 74 HARV. L. REV. 473-524 (1960–61).

discusses types of convertible stock interests and tax issues that affect convertible stock.

(1) IN GENERAL

Simply stated, conversion is the exchange of one security for another. In general, the act of converting one type of stock into another type of stock in the same corporation is viewed as tax-free to both the issuer[85] and the owner of the stock.[86] Stock conversions have generally been viewed as tax-free even though there is no explicit Code section authorizing such treatment. "[D]espite the absence of any explicit statutory immunity, the authorities available seem to indicate that some type of nontaxable transaction is effected when . . . convertible stock [is transmuted] into another equity interest."[87] However, the provisions of I.R.C. § 305 cast a long shadow on all stock distributions and conversions. Although a full discussion of the rules of I.R.C. § 305 is beyond the scope of this book, it should be pointed out that a distribution of stock pursuant to a conversion privilege or the distribution of convertible stock, itself, may be subject to dividend treatment (rather than I.R.C. § 368(a)(1)(E) recapitalization treatment). A dividend may result if (1) the distribution is pursuant to a plan to periodically increase a stockholder's proportionate interest in the assets or earnings of a corporation, or (2) a stockholder who owns preferred stock with dividends in arrears exchanges his stock for other stock, thereby increasing his proportionate interest in the assets or earnings of the corporation. An increase in a stockholder's interest occurs whenever the fair market value or the liquidation preference of the stock received exceeds the issue price of the stock surrendered.[88]

(2) PREFERRED STOCK CONVERTIBLE INTO COMMON STOCK

The rationale for treating the conversion of preferred stock into common stock of the same corporation as tax-free is that the conversion qualifies as a Type E reorganization (i.e., a recapitalization) under I.R.C. § 368(a)(1)(E).[89] Although the Code does not define "recapitalization," the term has been used to describe a "reshuffling of a capital structure,

---

[85]I.R.C. § 1032.

[86]For a discussion of the rationale for tax-free treatment, see section 25.3(c)(2).

[87]Fleischer & Cary, *supra* note 84, at 477.

[88]I.R.C. §§305(c), (d); Treas. Reg. §§ 1.305-7 (1973).

[89]*See* section 25.4.

within the framework of an existing corporation."[90] When convertible preferred stock sells at a substantial premium geared to the market price of the common stock into which it is convertible, a purchase of the preferred stock may arguably represent an investment in the issuing corporation's common stock. As a result, a subsequent conversion might be regarded, under I.R.C. § 1036, as a tax-free exchange of common for common.[91]

Since 1937, the IRS has taken the position that the exchange of convertible stock for other classes of stock into which it is convertible generates no gain or loss on the conversion.[92] In addition, the Treasury regulations provide examples of recapitalizations that include exchanges of preferred stock for common stock.[93] Further, many judicial decisions have treated exchanges of preferred stock for common stock as Type E reorganizations.[94]

In Rev. Rul. 56-179,[95] the IRS ruled that where a stockholder exercises his right to convert his first preference stock into common stock, no gain or loss is recognized and the conversion is a recapitalization. The corporate issuer gave its first preference stockholders an option to exchange their shares for a package of common stock, debt securities, and accrued dividends in cash, or to receive a stated redemption price plus accrued dividends. The IRS ruled that the transaction was a Type E reorganization.[96]

In Rev. Rul. 77-238,[97] the IRS ruled that the conversion of preferred stock into common stock of equal value of the same corporation is tax-free. Conversion took place pursuant to a provision of the corporation's certificate of incorporation that gave a right to the stockholders to convert their preferred stock into common stock at a specified exchange rate.[98] Further, "[t]he purpose of the conversion privilege is to encourage

---

[90]See Helvering v. Southwest Consolidated Corp., 315 U.S. 194 (1942).

[91]I.R.C. § 1036(a) provides that no gain or loss is recognized if common stock in a corporation is exchanged solely for common stock in the same corporation, or if preferred stock is exchanged solely for preferred stock in the same corporation.

[92]Rev. Rul. 77-238, 1977-2 C.B. 115; Rev. Rul. 72-265, 1972-1 C.B. 222 (superseding G.C.M. 18436, 1937-1 C.B. 101) (for the conversion of debt securities).

[93]Treas. Reg. §§ 1.368-2(e)(2), (3) (1985).

[94]See e.g.s, Muchnic v. Comm'r, 29 B.T.A. 163 (1933); Thermoid Co. v. Comm'r, 4 T.C.M. (CCH) 412 (1945), aff'd, 155 F.2d 589 (3d Cir. 1946).

[95]1956-1 C.B. 187.

[96]Id. (citing I.R.C. § 354(a)(1)).

[97]1977-2 C.B. 115.

[98]Id.

the conversion of the preferred stock into common stock in order to simplify the capital structure of the corporation by eliminating the preferred stock."[99] The IRS ruled that the conversion was in furtherance of a corporate business purpose and was pursuant to a plan of reorganization.[100] The IRS viewed the certificate of incorporation provision as a plan of reorganization. Because a reorganization must have a valid business purpose,[101] however, there is an opportunity for the IRS to challenge a conversion of preferred stock into common stock on the grounds that the requisite business purpose is not met.

(3) COMMON STOCK CONVERTIBLE INTO PREFERRED STOCK

Not all convertible stock interests are preferred stock that is convertible into common stock. In fact, common stock can be convertible into preferred stock. As with convertible preferred stock, the conversion of common stock into preferred stock should be a tax-free Type E reorganization (i.e., a recapitalization) if the reorganization requirements are met and I.R.C. § 305(c) is avoided. For a discussion of stock conversions as reorganizations, see section 25.3(c)(2).

Common stock that is convertible into preferred stock is not viewed as common stock for purposes of I.R.C. § 306.[102] This is because such convertible common stock has obvious bailout potential. Periodically, depending on the profitability of a corporation, some of the common stock could be converted into preferred stock and sold to a third party at capital gain rates. I.R.C. § 306(e)(2) seeks to prevent the possibility of a bailout by providing that common stock that is convertible into preferred stock (or other property) is not common stock for purposes of avoiding application of I.R.C. § 306. Thus, convertible common stock does not fall within the common stock exception of I.R.C. § 306(c) and is subject to section 306 treatment. For a discussion of section 306, see section 25.3(b)(4).

(4) STOCK CONVERTIBLE INTO DEBT SECURITIES

Even if the conversion of stock into debt securities qualifies as a recapitalization under I.R.C. § 368(a)(1)(E), the exchange will be taxable un-

---

[99] *Id.*

[100] *Id.* (citing Rev. Rul. 56-179, 1956-1 C.B. 187).

[101] Treas. Reg. § 1.368-2(g) (1985).

[102] I.R.C. § 306(e)(2); *see* section 25.3(b)(4).

der I.R.C. §§ 354(a)(2)(B) and 356(d) because the debt securities constitute "boot."[103]

Prior to TCA '82, former I.R.C. § 1232(b)(2) excluded evidences of indebtedness issued pursuant to a Type E recapitalization qualifying under I.R.C. § 368(a)(1)(E) from the OID rules of I.R.C. § 1232.[104] As a result, new debt securities issued in the course of recapitalizations would call for the deferral of interest payments without any current income inclusion by the holders. TCA '82 removed the exclusion from the OID rules for debt securities issued in reorganizations.[105]

(5) STOCK CONVERTIBLE INTO STOCK OF ANOTHER CORPORATION

Sometimes stock of one corporation provides rights for conversion into the stock of another corporation. Conversion of such stock is taxable unless the transaction qualifies as a tax-free reorganization.[106] In Rev. Rul. 69-265,[107] the IRS addressed two separate situations. The first raises the question of whether a second-tier subsidiary's acquisition of the assets of an unrelated corporation in exchange for stock in its parent (referred to as the "first-tier subsidiary") qualifies as a Type C reorganization[108] if the stock is convertible into the stock of the parent of the first-tier subsidiary. The IRS ruled that where the stockholders could present their stock directly to the parent for the parent's stock, the conversion right was "other property" that precluded a Type C reorganization.[109] The conversion was treated as a taxable sale pursuant to I.R.C. § 1002.[110] The first-tier subsidiary issued "other property" to the stockholders of the second-tier subsidiary in the form of its own stock plus the right that the parent granted to the first-tier subsidiary stockholders.

In the second situation discussed in Rev. Rul. 69-265, prior to the first date for conversion of the subsidiary's stock into the stock of the parent, the parent transfers sufficient stock to the subsidiary to cover

---

[103]See also Bazley v. Comm'r, 331 U.S. 737 (1947), where the Supreme Court held that an exchange by stockholders of a family corporation of its common stock for debt securities was not a recapitalization as defined in I.R.C. § 368(a)(1)(E).

[104]Rev. Rul. 77-415, 1977-2 C.B. 311, Microdot, Inc. v. U.S., 728 F.2d 593 (2d Cir. 1984).

[105]TCA '82 § 306(a)(9), 96 Stat. 2365, 2403-2404 (1982).

[106]See Rev. Rul. 69-135, 1969-1 C.B. 198; Rev. Rul. 69-265, 1969-1 C.B. 109; Rose v. Trust Co. of Georgia, 77 F.2d 355 (5th Cir. 1935).

[107]1969-1 C.B. 109.

[108]See section 25.4(b).

[109]See section 25.4.

[110]Rev. Rul. 69-265, 1969-1 C.B. 109.

conversions. Those stockholders who wish to convert their stock into the stock of the parent would present their stock to the subsidiary in exchange for stock in the parent. The IRS viewed the right to convert the subsidiary's stock into the stock of the parent as a right to redeem the stock of the subsidiary for specified property (which happens to be stock of the parent).[111] Stock redemptions are subject to the provisions of I.R.C. § 302.[112]

(6) ADJUSTABLE RATE CONVERTIBLE NOTES

ACRNs are identified as debt interests (i.e., notes) but nevertheless have been classified as equity interests.[113] Under most circumstances, ACRNs will be converted into common stock.[114] Moreover, it is to the advantage of the issuing corporation to force conversion in order to avoid payment of additional cash to the ACRN owners. ACRNs usually do not represent a promise to pay a sum certain, because of the high probability of conversion.[115] As a result, "interest" payments are not deductible interest expenses for the issuer and are taxed as dividends to the ACRN owners. A possible advantage of reclassification for corporate ACRN owners is that the "interest" payments can qualify for the intercorporate dividends received deduction.[116]

(7) DISTRIBUTIONS OF CONVERTIBLE PREFERRED STOCK

Distributions of convertible preferred stock to common stockholders are generally taxable as dividends unless it can be established (to the satisfaction of the IRS) that the distributions are not disproportionate.[117] Distributions of convertible preferred stock as dividends have recently been used by corporations as a defensive response to various sorts of takeover tactics, such as two-tier and partial tender offers. Uses of convertible preferred stock dividends in the corporate takeover context include the following. First, convertible preferred stock dividends can assure that stockholders are not "frozen out" if they do not tender during the first stage of a two-tier tender offer that is to be followed by a merger. Second, convertible preferred stock distributions can assure that non-

---

[111]*Id.*

[112]*Id. See generally* Eisenberg, *IRS Position on Right to Convert into Another Corporation's Stock is Confusing,* 33 J. OF TAX. 25-29 (1970).

[113]Rev. Rul. 83-98, 1983-2 C.B. 40.

[114]*Id.*

[115]*Id. But see* LTR 8523009 (Feb. 25, 1985).

[116]*See* section 22.9.

[117]*See* section 22.2(b)(6).

tendering stockholders retain liquidity with respect to their equity interests. Third, the distributions may reduce the possibility of a partial tender offer because the assets of the corporation may not be as readily available to a prospective "raider."

(8) RECEIPT OF CONVERTIBLE STOCK IN RECAPITALIZATIONS

Convertible stock may be received in a Type E reorganization (i.e., a recapitalization) without affecting the tax-free character of the transaction.[118] In Rev. Rul. 69-265,[119] the IRS ruled that a future right to convert stock into stock of a second corporation (which right was not available for at least five years) might not constitute "other property" that taints a Type C reorganization. The characterization depends on the facts and circumstances surrounding the transaction. The IRS further ruled that the right to convert stock is viewed as "other property" if the conversion right is to be entered into directly with the corporation into which the stock is convertible. Conversion is generally taxable where the conversion is into stock of a different corporation.[120] No judicial decisions or IRS pronouncements have ever held a conversion feature to be "other property" in the context of a recapitalization. Nevertheless, it is possible that the IRS could challenge an atypical conversion feature on the grounds that it is "other property."

(d) WHEN-ISSUED SECURITIES

The term "when-issued" securities technically refers to two separate transactions.[121] It refers to both actual contracts to acquire securities on a when, as, and if issued basis, and to the actual securities that may be issued pursuant to the when-issued contract. The purchase and sale of the actual securities pursuant to a when-issued contract takes place on the settlement date. The holding period for securities acquired pursuant to a when-issued contract begins on the date the securities are actually acquired, not when the taxpayer purchases the when-issued contract.[122] In addition, if the taxpayer disposes of a when-issued contract prior to delivery of the actual securities, long-term or short-term

---

[118]Common stock that is convertible into preferred stock is not treated as common stock for purposes of I.R.C. § 306. *See* section 25.3(b)(4).

[119]1969-1 C.B. 109.

[120]Rev. Rul. 69-135, 1969-1 C.B. 198.

[121]*See* section 1.3(g); section 2.2(d).

[122]*See* I.T. 3721, 1945 C.B. 164.

capital gain or loss results (depending upon the holding period of the when-issued contract).[123]

If the securities subject to a when-issued contract are issued, the holder of a short position must acquire the newly issued securities (either directly from the issuer or by a purchase in the open market) and deliver them to the long position at the contract price. Obviously, the holder of the short contract position holds the actual securities for less than the long-term holding period. His gain or loss is short-term (even if he holds the contract for more than the long-term holding period).[124] In addition, the holding period of a long contract position is not tacked onto the holding period of the securities delivered. Instead, the holding period for securities delivered pursuant to a when-issued contract begins on the day after the securities are issued; no actual purchase of stock takes place until the new stock is issued.[125]

If the transaction contemplated in a when-issued contract does not take place and the underlying securities are not issued, the when-issued contracts are cancelled and become worthless. Dealers[126] and hedgers[127] obtain ordinary income or loss. For investors[128] and traders,[129] when-issued contracts are neither "securities" as defined in I.R.C. § 165(g) nor "options" as defined in I.R.C. § 1234. As a result, worthless when-issued contracts do not generate capital loss under those sections. Loss on these contracts may be subject to the provisions of I.R.C. § 1234A, which requires capital gain or loss treatment.[130] The Straddle Rules[131] apply to certain stock positions[132] and when-issued contracts are "interests" in "personal property" that may be "actively traded" (as those terms are all defined for application of the Straddle Rules).[133] For a discussion of I.R.C. § 1234A, see generally Part Eleven.

For application of the wash sales rule, see section 17.9(e); the short

---

[123]Stavisky v. Comm'r, 34 T.C. 140, 144 (1960), aff'd, 291 F.2d 48 (2d Cir. 1961); Rev. Rul. 57-29, 1957-1 C.B. 519; I.T. 3721, 1945 C.B. 164.

[124]Shanis v. Comm'r, 19 T.C. 641, 650 (1953), aff'd per curiam, 213 F.2d 151 (3d Cir. 1954).

[125]See I.T. 3721, 1945 C.B. 164.

[126]See section 6.3.

[127]See section 6.4.

[128]See section 6.1.

[129]See section 6.2.

[130]I.R.C. § 1234A requires capital loss on the cancellation, lapse, expiration, or termination of a right or obligation with respect to personal property that is a capital asset in the hands of the taxpayer.

[131]See generally Part Ten.

[132]See section 36.2(c).

[133]See generally Chapter 36.

sales rule, see section 16.4(b); and the Straddle Rules, see generally Part Ten.

§ 25.4   TAX-FREE EXCHANGES

(a) IN GENERAL

There are many situations in which a taxpayer can receive stock in exchange for stock, securities, or other property without the recognition of gain or loss. A detailed discussion of these Code provisions is beyond the scope of this book. Instead, this section merely identifies some of the most common tax-free exchange provisions that may apply to corporate stock transactions. First, tax-free treatment may be available under any of the various types of reorganizations defined in I.R.C. § 368.[134] Second, exchanges of stock for stock in the same corporation may be tax-free under I.R.C. § 1036. Third, divisive reorganizations and spin-offs can also be tax-free under I.R.C. § 355. Fourth, transfers to controlled corporations may be tax-free under I.R.C. § 351. And fifth, Code provisions may provide tax-free treatment for exchanges of stock and property in radio broadcasting corporations,[135] public utility holding companies,[136] and bank holding companies.[137]

(b) REORGANIZATIONS

Tax-free reorganizations, defined in I.R.C. § 368(a)(1), include eight types of corporate transactions that are identified in this paragraph. It is important to note that the tax-free reorganization provisions are unavailable for exchanges of equity interests other than stock (i.e., trust interests and partnership interests). Type A reorganizations are statutory mergers or consolidations of separate corporations.[138] Type B reorganizations are acquisitions of stock of one corporation solely for voting stock of another corporation.[139] Type C reorganizations are acquisitions of assets of one corporation solely for voting stock of another corporation.[140] Type D reorganizations include transfers of assets to

[134]See generally B. BITTKER & J. EUSTICE, supra note 12, ch. 14; R. WILLENS, TAXATION OF CORPORATE CAPITAL TRANSACTIONS: A GUIDE FOR CORPORATE, INVESTMENT BANKING, AND TAX ADVISERS pt. 3 (1984).

[135]I.R.C. § 1071.

[136]I.R.C. §§ 1081-1083.

[137]I.R.C. §§ 1101-1103.

[138]I.R.C. § 368(a)(1)(A).

[139]I.R.C. § 368(a)(1)(B).

[140]I.R.C. § 368(a)(1)(C).

certain controlled corporations and divisive reorganizations such as spin-offs, split-offs, and split-ups.[141] Type E reorganizations are recapitalizations of a corporation, whereby its stock and debt securities are readjusted as to their terms.[142] Type F reorganizations are changes in the identity, form, or place of organization of one corporation.[143] And Type G reorganizations (added to the Code by the Bankruptcy Tax Act of 1980),[144] allow a corporation's tax-free transfer, pursuant to a bankruptcy reorganization, of part or all of its assets.[145]

(1) BUSINESS PURPOSE REQUIREMENT

There is a judicially imposed requirement that reorganizations must have a business purpose to qualify for tax-free status. This means that a reorganization must be motivated by a purpose other than tax savings. Although the Treasury regulations require reorganizations to be motivated by "business exigencies" and conducted for purposes "germane to the business of the corporations,"[146] the courts have been willing, in the context of closely held corporations, to look to the objectives of the stockholders for a sufficient business purpose.[147]

(2) CONTINUITY OF BUSINESS ENTERPRISE AND CONTINUITY OF INTEREST REQUIREMENTS

For transfers after January 30, 1981, the Treasury regulations require that an acquiring corporation either continue the acquired corporation's business or that the acquiring corporation use a significant portion of the business assets of the acquired corporation in its business.[148] The Treasury regulations provide that this requirement is satisfied if the acquired corporation's historic business is continued or if a significant portion of the acquired corporation's business assets are used in a new business.[149] Using the proceeds from a sale of the acquired corporation's

---

[141]I.R.C. §§ 355, 368(a)(1)(D).

[142]I.R.C. § 368(a)(1)(E).

[143]I.R.C. § 368(a)(1)(F).

[144]Pub. L. 96-589, § 4(a), 94 Stat. 3389, 3401-02 (1980).

[145]I.R.C. § 368(a)(1)(G).

[146]Treas. Reg. §§ 1.355-2(c), 1.368-1(b) (1955 & 1980).

[147]See, e.g.s, Estate of Parshelsky v. Comm'r, 303 F.2d 14 (2d Cir. 1962); Lewis v. Comm'r, 176 F.2d 646 (1st Cir. 1949); Rev. Rul. 75-337, 1975-2 C.B. 124.

[148]Treas. Reg. § 1.368-1(d)(5), Example (4) (1980).

[149]Id.

assets in the acquiring corporation's business does not satisfy this requirement.[150]

The courts and Treasury regulations have also required that the owners of a transferred business must have a continuing proprietary interest in the reorganized business enterprise for the transaction to qualify for reorganization treatment.[151] The Supreme Court recently reaffirmed that there must be a continuity of interest to have a valid tax-free reorganization.[152] In addition, the IRS has announced that it will consider a favorable ruling as to a tax-free reorganization if 50 percent of the consideration paid to the stockholders of an acquired corporation is in the form of stock.[153]

(3) SEPARABLE TRANSACTIONS

In certain circumstances, elements of a reorganization can be treated as separable transactions to preserve tax-free treatment. In Rev. Rul. 69-142,[154] the IRS ruled that a corporation that acquired all of the stock of another corporation in exchange for its voting stock and also exchanged its own debt securities for the outstanding debt securities of the acquired corporation had actually entered into two separable transactions.[155] The exchange of stock for stock qualified as a Type B reorganization, but the exchange of the debt securities was taxable under I.R.C. § 1001.[156] One factor mentioned by the IRS was the fact that a substantial proportion of the debt securities was held by persons who owned no stock in the corporation.

In Rev. Rul. 78-408,[157] the IRS ruled that an exchange of warrants of an acquiring corporation is taxable if the warrants were issued pursuant to a plan of reorganization specifically to be exchanged for the warrants of another corporation in a Type B reorganization. The exchange of the warrants was taxable under I.R.C. § 1001. Under a Type B reorganization, consideration for the acquisition of stock must be solely in stock. The IRS ruled, however, that a plan of reorganization

---

[150]*Id.*

[151]Treas. Reg. § 1.368-2(a) (1976).

[152]*See* Paulsen v. Comm'r, 105 S. Ct. 627 (1985).

[153]Rev. Proc. 77-37, 1977-2 C.B. 568. For a discussion of considerations in establishing continuity of interest, see section 25.3(b)(2)(iii).

[154]1969-1 C.B. 107.

[155]*See, e.g.s*, Rev. Rul. 72-522, 1972-2 C.B. 215; Rev. Rul. 70-269, 1970-1 C.B. 82; Rev. Rul. 70-41, 1970-1 C.B. 77; *cf.* Rev. Rul. 75-360, 1975-2 C.B. 110.

[156]Rev. Rul. 69-142, 1969-1 C.B. 107.

[157]1978-2 C.B. 203.

can be treated as separable transactions under certain circumstances. As a result, a portion of a transaction may be tax-free, while a non-qualifying portion can be taxable. In Rev. Rul. 78-408, the IRS also ruled that because of the substantial split in the ownership of a corporation's stock and warrants, the acquiring corporation was deemed to have acquired the stock of the other corporation solely in exchange for voting stock and pursuant to a Type B reorganization.[158] However, the exchange of the warrants was a taxable transaction; the owners of warrants in the acquired corporation recognized gain or loss on the exchange pursuant to I.R.C. § 1001.

(c) GOVERNMENTAL ORDERS TO REORGANIZE CERTAIN REGULATED INDUSTRIES

Special Code provisions apply to defer the recognition of gain or loss if taxpayers are required to surrender their securities in certain regulated corporations or to receive corporate distributions pursuant to orders issued by the FCC (with respect to radio broadcasting corporations),[159] the SEC (with respect to utility holding companies),[160] or the FRB (with respect to bank holding companies).[161] Detailed requirements are set out with respect to utility holding company adjustments under I.R.C. §§ 1081-1083. In addition, similar requirements are provided in I.R.C. §§ 1101-1103 for certain distributions and exchanges of securities in bank holding companies if required by the Bank Holding Company Act of 1956.[162] A substantially abbreviated set of requirements is provided under I.R.C. § 1071 for changes in the ownership and control of radio broadcasting corporations certified by the FCC.

§ 25.5 FEDERAL AGENCY STOCK

Although many federal agencies are departments of the United States or corporations wholly owned by the United States, several federal agencies issue stock to public stockholders. Although all dividends received on stock of federal agencies issued after March 28, 1942 are taxable,[163]

---

[158]*Id.*

[159]I.R.C. § 1071.

[160]I.R.C. §§ 1081-1083.

[161]I.R.C. §§ 1101-1103.

[162]Bank Holding Company Act of 1956, ch. 240, 70 Stat. 133.

[163]Public Debt Act of 1942, ch. 205, 56 Stat. 189.

dividends received on certain federal agency stocks issued prior to March 28, 1942 are exempt from taxation.[164] Because the intercorporate dividends received deduction is only available for dividends received from taxable domestic corporations, any dividends received from federal agencies not subject to tax are not eligible for the intercorporate dividends received deduction. The remainder of this section discusses FNMA common stock and FHLMC preferred stock, both of which are publicly traded.

(a) FNMA STOCK

(1) IN GENERAL

FNMA common stock is publicly held and trades on the NYSE.[165] FNMA is fully taxable, and dividends received by corporate stockholders are eligible for the intercorporate dividends received deduction.[166]

Lending institutions (e.g., banks, mortgage companies, savings and loan associations, and insurance companies) that sell mortgages to FNMA (referred to as "mortgage seller-servicers") must make nonrefundable capital contributions to FNMA, evidenced by shares of FNMA common stock, in amounts equal to a stated percentage of the unpaid mortgage principal amount sold to FNMA.[167] In addition, although FNMA stock is freely transferable, a prescribed amount of FNMA stock must be held by a mortgage seller-servicer as a condition of servicing mortgages purchased by FNMA, and it must continue to own a minimum amount of FNMA common stock for the life of each mortgage it services for FNMA.[168]

(2) CAPITAL CONTRIBUTIONS TO FNMA

Mortgage seller-servicers must purchase FNMA stock directly from FNMA at a subscription price that is frequently in excess of the market price for the FNMA common stock. As a result, a mortgage seller-servicer can deduct as a business expense under I.R.C. § 162(d) an amount equal to the difference between the subscription price paid as a capital contribution to FNMA for FNMA stock and the market value of the stock as

[164]*I.e.*, stock in Federal Land Banks, National Farm Loan associations, Federal Home Loan Banks, and Federal Reserve banks. Treas. Reg. § 1.103-2 (1956).

[165]*See* section 2.1(b)(3).

[166]Rev. Rul. 56-510, 1956-2 C.B. 168; *see* section 15.7; section 22.9.

[167]12 U.S.C. § 1718(b) (1982). The current requirement is that a mortgage seller-servicer must purchase one share of FNMA stock for each $10,000 of its aggregate outstanding mortgages to be serviced by FNMA. 24 C.F.R. § 81.13(b) (1985).

[168]12 U.S.C. § 1718(c) (1982).

of its issue date.[169] The mortgage seller-servicer's basis in the stock purchased is reduced by any amounts deducted as ordinary and necessary business expenses.[170]

In *Eastern Service Corp. v. Comm'r*,[171] a mortgage seller-servicer unsuccessfully attempted to deduct a portion of the amount it paid to FNMA to purchase FNMA common stock at a subscription price that was *less* than the quoted market price. The mortgage seller-servicer sought a deduction on the grounds that it was required to retain a minimum amount of FNMA stock and that this ownership requirement reduced the stock's fair market value to less than the amount actually paid for the stock. In denying the deduction, the court found that the FNMA stock was freely transferable at all times, and that there were no legal restrictions on transfer.[172] Rather, the only restrictions were the economic incentives of the mortgage seller-servicer to continue to service FNMA mortgages. The court determined that the taxpayer could not discount the fair market value of the FNMA stock because the taxpayer "felt constrained to retain the stock for a substantial period of time."[173] I.R.C. § 162(d) only benefits mortgage seller-servicers that purchase FNMA stock directly from FNMA for more than its market price.

(3) DISPOSITION OF FNMA STOCK

FNMA stock is a capital asset in the hands of investors,[174] traders,[175] and mortgage seller-servicers.[176] It is an ordinary asset in the hands of dealers[177] and hedgers.[178] Treating a mortgage seller-servicer as an investor is in line with Supreme Court cases considering stock ownership requirements of other federally chartered corporations.[179] In *Eastern Service Corp.*, the court considered the legislative history of the stock own-

---

[169]I.R.C. § 162(d).

[170]I.R.C. § 1054.

[171]650 F.2d 379 (2d Cir. 1981).

[172]*Id.* at 384.

[173]*Id.*

[174]*See* section 6.1.

[175]*See* section 6.2.

[176]*Eastern Service Corp.*, 650 F.2d at 385. For a discussion of capital treatment, see generally Part Three.

[177]*See* section 6.3.

[178]*See* section 6.4. For a discussion of ordinary treatment, see generally Part Four.

[179]*See* Comm'r v. Lincoln Sav. & Loan Ass'n, 403 U.S. 345 (1971) (concerning a compulsory payment to the FSLIC as a partial substitute for stock ownership in the FHLB); U.S. v. Mississippi Chemical Corp., 405 U.S. 298 (1972) (concerning the tax treatment of a stock ownership requirement imposed by the Farm Credit Act on agricultural cooperatives that borrow money from banks in the Federal Land Bank system).

ership requirements. It determined that "Congress imposed the stock ownership requirement in part for the purpose of compelling . . . mortgage servicers to acquire a long-term commitment to and interest in FNMA."[180] The required FNMA stock purchases were viewed as capital assets for which a deduction for the cost of the stock is not available.[181]

(b) FHLMC STOCK

FHLMC has three types of stock. First, its nonvoting common stock is held by the 12 Federal Home Loan Banks. Second, its preferred stock is held by savings and loan associations. And third, FHLMC's widely held participating preferred stock trades on the NYSE.[182] As of 1984, FHLMC became fully subject to federal income tax.[183]

With respect to FHLMC stock held by the Federal Home Loan Banks, a special statutory provision authorizes an intercorporate dividends received deduction on dividends paid by FHLMC on its common stock held by the Federal Home Loan Banks if the dividends are paid out of taxable earnings after December 31, 1984.[184] An intercorporate dividends received deduction would otherwise be unavailable because the Federal Home Loan Banks are tax-exempt entities.

§ 25.6 SMALL BUSINESS INVESTMENT COMPANY STOCK

(a) IN GENERAL

Small business investment companies provide equity capital to small businesses through the purchase of convertible debt securities.[185] The Small Business Administration, in turn, makes loans to small business investment companies through the purchase of subordinated debt securities. Losses on small business investment company stock and losses realized by such companies on their portfolio investments are subject to special rules allowing ordinary losses.[186] Small business investment companies are corporations licensed under the Small Business Invest-

---

[180]*Eastern Service Corp.*, 650 F.2d at 385.

[181]For a discussion of the deduction available if the issuance price of FNMA stock is greater than the fair market value of the stock on the date of issue, see section 25.5(a)(2).

[182]For a discussion of FHLMC, see section 2.1(b)(4).

[183]DRA, Pub. L. 98-369, § 177, 98 Stat. 494, 709-12 (1984); *see also* section 22.9(d).

[184]I.R.C. § 246(a)(2)(B); *see* section 22.9(d).

[185]For a discussion of convertible debt securities, see section 28.3.

[186]*See* I.R.C. §§ 1242-1243.

ment Act of 1958[187] and ⸺re subject to the regulations issued by the Small Business Administration.[188] They are private corporations with minimum capital requirements which assure that they maintain paid-in capital and surplus in an amount that is not less than $150,000 (if licensed before October 1, 1979), $500,000 (if licensed between October 1, 1979 and September 30, 1983), and $1,000,000 (if licensed after September 29, 1983), and that is adequate to assure a reasonable prospect that the companies will be operated soundly and profitably.[189]

(b) STOCK IN SMALL BUSINESS INVESTMENT COMPANIES

Losses incurred on small business investment company stock are fully deductible by the company's stockholders if the company's license to operate as a small business investment company is valid at the time of the loss.[190] There is no ceiling on the amount of losses than can be reported as ordinary. If losses exceed a stockholder's income for the year, the losses are treated as business deductions to compute net operating losses that can be carried back or forward.[191]

Gains and losses from small business investment company stocks do not have to be "netted" with each other.[192] This is significant for investors[193] and traders[194] who obtain capital gain and ordinary losses on their small business investment company stock.[195] Dealers[196] and hedgers[197] obtain ordinary income and loss without application of I.R.C. § 1242.

I.R.C. § 1242 is read narrowly, so that ordinary loss is denied unless the applicable Code requirements are complied with. Losses sustained on closing a short sale of small business investment company stock with stock subsequently purchased to close the short sale are not deductible as ordinary losses under I.R.C. § 1242.[198] Instead, investors and traders may treat such losses as short-term under the short sales rule.[199]

---

[187]Pub. L. 85-699, § 301(a), 72 Stat. 689 (1958).

[188]See generally 13 C.F.R. pt. 107 (1985).

[189]13 C.F.R. § 107.101(d)(1) (1985).

[190]Rev. Rul. 62-58, 1962-1 C.B. 158.

[191]I.R.C. § 1242.

[192]Rev. Rul. 65-291, 1965-2 C.B. 290.

[193]See section 6.1.

[194]See section 6.2.

[195]Rev. Rul. 65-291, 1965-2 C.B. 290.

[196]See section 6.3.

[197]See section 6.4.

[198]Rev. Rul. 63-65, 1963-1 C.B. 142.

[199]Id. For a discussion of the short sales rule, see generally Chapter 16.

A taxpayer claiming an ordinary loss on the sale, disposition, or worthlessness of small business investment company stock must file a statement with his tax return containing (1) the name and address of the company that issued the stock, (2) the number of shares on which the loss is claimed, (3) the basis and selling price of the shares on which the loss is claimed, (4) the dates of purchase of the stock, and (5) the dates of sales of the stock or the reason for the stock's worthlessness and approximate date of worthlessness.[200]

(c) PORTFOLIO LOSSES OF SMALL BUSINESS INVESTMENT COMPANIES

If a small business investment company incurs a loss on convertible debt securities (or stock it receives on conversion of convertible debt securities) that it acquired pursuant to the Small Business Investment Act of 1958,[201] the company's loss on the sale, disposition, or worthlessness of the stock is an ordinary loss, even if the debt securities were acquired for investment and are capital assets.[202]

Convertible debt securities acquired by a small business investment company are subject to the provisions of I.R.C. § 582 for taxable years beginning after July 11, 1974 (and for taxable years beginning after July 11, 1969 and before July 11, 1974, if irrevocably elected by the company).[203] This means that where I.R.C. § 582 applies, a small business investment company obtains ordinary income and loss on the sale or exchange of its investments in debt securities.[204]

A small business investment company is eligible for a 100 percent intercorporate dividends received deduction on dividends it receives from domestic corporations.[205]

A small business investment company claiming an ordinary loss on convertible debt securities must file a statement with its tax return containing (1) a statement that the company is a federal licensee under the Small Business Investment Act of 1958, (2) the name and address of the company with respect to whose securities the loss was sustained, (3) the number of shares of stock or the number and denomination of bonds for which the loss is claimed, (4) the basis and selling price of

---

[200]Treas. Reg. § 1.1242-1(c) (1960).

[201]*Supra* note 186, §303.

[202]I.R.C. § 1243.

[203]Treas. Reg. §§ 1.582-1(d), 1.1243-1 (1972).

[204]I.R.C. § 582(c); *see* section 6.8.

[205]I.R.C. § 243(a). For a discussion of the intercorporate dividends received deduction, see section 15.7 and section 22.9.

the securities, (5) the date of the purchase of the stock, and (6) the date of the sale or the reason for the stock's worthlessness and the approximate date of worthlessness.[206]

§ 25.7 SECTION 1244 (SMALL BUSINESS) STOCK

Certain individuals can obtain ordinary losses on the sale, exchange, or worthlessness of common and preferred stock of certain so-called small business corporations.[207] Under I.R.C. § 1244, an ordinary loss is limited to $50,000 for any taxable years ($100,000 if a joint return is filed),[208] provided all of the statutory requirements of section 1244 are met.

    I.R.C. § 1244 treatment has been expanded in recent years. First, it was liberalized in 1978 to increase the amount of stock that can be issued as small business stock, and to increase the amount of section 1244 loss that stockholders can claim annually.[209] Second, the Subchapter S Revision Act of 1982[210] lessens or eliminates many of the technical difficulties in operating a qualified small business corporation as an S corporation under the provisions of subchapter S.[211] Third, "to encourage new venture capital,"[212] Section 1244 status was extended to losses on preferred stock issued after July 18, 1984 and incurred in taxable years ending after that date.[213]

    The major requirements of I.R.C. § 1244 include the following.[214] First, the stock must be stock in a small business corporation, which at the time the stock is issued has an aggregate amount of money and other property received for its stock (as capital contributions and as paid-in surplus) not exceeding $1 million.[215] Second, the stock must be issued

---

[206]Treas. Reg. § 1.1243-1(b) (1972).

[207]I.R.C. § 1244.

[208]I.R.C. § 1244(b).

[209]Revenue Act of 1978, Pub. L. 95-600, § 345, 92 Stat. 2763, 2844-45.

[210]Pub. L. 97-354, 96 Stat. 1669.

[211]*See generally* I.R.C. §§ 1361-1379. The 1982 revisions to subchapter S bring the taxation of S corporations and their stockholders closer to the taxation of partnerships and their partners.

[212]HOUSE WAYS AND MEANS COMMITTEE REPORT, DEFICIT REDUCTION ACT OF 1984, H.R. REP. No. 432, 98th Cong., 2d Sess., 1581, *reprinted in* 1984 U.S. CODE CONG. & AD. NEWS 697, 1208.

[213]DRA, *supra* note 183, § 481.

[214]Section 1244 stock issued prior to July 18, 1984 (the effective date of the DRA) cannot be preferred stock. In addition, stock issued prior to November 6, 1978 (the effective date of the Revenue Act of 1978) must meet more stringent requirements than the requirements mentioned in the remainder of this section.

[215]I.R.C. §§ 1244(c)(1)(A), (3)(A).

for money or property other than stock and securities.[216] Third, the corporation must satisfy a gross receipts test for the five years before the loss is sustained. Under the gross receipts test, the corporation must not derive 50 percent or more of its gross receipts from royalties, rents, dividends, interest, annuities, and sales or exchanges of securities.[217]

If the requirements for I.R.C. § 1244 treatment are met, an individual can treat a loss on section 1244 stock as ordinary. I.R.C. § 1244 treatment is only available to stockholders who are individuals. Stock losses incurred by corporations, trusts, and estates do not qualify as section 1244 stock.[218] There is a special provision, however, for losses sustained on stock held by a partnership. When section 1244 stock is held by a partnership, losses are ordinary to the extent they are allocated to individual partners; I.R.C. § 1244 does not apply to the partnership as a partnership.[219] I.R.C. § 1244 applies only to stockholders who invest capital directly in corporations. It is unavailable to individuals who acquire the stock by purchase, gift, inheritance, or any other way[220] except from an underwriter acting merely as a selling agent (i.e., a best efforts underwriting) for the small business corporation.[221]

§ 25.8   PUBLICLY TRADED LIMITED PARTNERSHIPS

Partnership interests in certain limited partnerships are securities for securities law purposes and trade on stock exchanges and in the over-the-counter market in the same way that stock is traded.[222] Publicly traded partnerships are generally taxed as partnerships, although the IRS may assert in certain circumstances that an organization is an association taxable as a corporation.

Since the first publicly traded limited partnership commenced trading in 1980,[223] the classification of publicly traded limited partnerships as partnerships for tax purposes has been considered and debated by various lawyers' groups, the staff of the Senate Finance Committee, and the House Ways and Means Committee. Some proposals would classify all publicly traded partnerships as corporations, while other proposals

---

[216]I.R.C. § 1244(c)(1)(B).

[217]I.R.C. § 1244(c)(1)(C).

[218]Treas. Reg. § 1.1244(a)-1(b) (1981).

[219]Treas. Reg. § 1.1244(b)-1(a) (1981).

[220]Treas. Reg. § 1.1244(a)-1(b) (1981).

[221]Treas. Reg. § 1.1244(a)-1(b)(2) (1981).

[222]*See* section 1.1(g).

[223]*See* Mack, *Disincorporating America*, FORBES, Aug. 1, 1983, at 76.

would treat all partnerships with more than 100 partners as associations taxable as corporations.[224]

(a) FACTORS IN DETERMINING TAX STATUS

The term "corporation" is defined to include an unincorporated "association" that has corporate characteristics.[225] Although an organization may be a partnership for local law purposes, it may, under certain circumstances, be deemed an "association" and thus be treated as a corporation for tax purposes. The major effect is that unlike a partnership, a corporation is liable for tax on its income and its losses cannot be deducted by its stockholders.[226]

The Treasury has issued regulations specifying the conditions under which an organization is treated as an "association." For a business partnership to be classified as an "association," it must possess at least three of the following four corporate characteristics: (1) continuity of life, (2) centralized management, (3) transferable interests, and (4) limited liability.[227] However, the Treasury regulations also make clear that partnerships governed by the Uniform Partnership Act and the ULPA, or their local equivalents, are rarely treated as "associations."

In *Zuckman v. U.S.*[228] and *Larson v. Comm'r*,[229] the courts undertook in-depth analyses of the Treasury regulations as they apply to limited partnerships having corporations as their sole general partners. In each case, the courts refused to accept the IRS's contention that the limited partnerships involved should have been classified as "associations" and upheld the partnership status of those organizations.

The remainder of this section discusses the four corporate characteristics as they apply to limited partnerships.

(1) CONTINUITY OF LIFE

The major questions with respect to continuity of life are whether acts by or conditions of the general partners cause dissolution of the entity and whether the partnership terminates at a date certain. An organi-

---

[224]For a summary of many of these proposals, see Hobbet, *Limited Partnerships: Associations or Partnerships?* 22 SAN DIEGO L. REV. 105 (Jan.–Feb. 1985). Sheppard, *Rethinking Limited Partnership Taxation*, 30 TAX NOTES 877 (1986).

[225]I.R.C. § 7701(a)(3).

[226]*See generally* B. BITTKER & J. EUSTICE, *supra* note 12, § 2.04 at 2-11.

[227]Treas. Reg. §§ 301.7701-2(a)(1), (3) (1983).

[228]524 F.2d 729 (Ct. Cl. 1975).

[229]66 T.C. 159 (1976).

zation is deemed to lack continuity of life if, under local law, the death, insanity, bankruptcy, retirement, resignation, or expulsion of any member causes a dissolution of the organization.[230] In the case of the withdrawal of a sole general partner (or the withdrawal of all the general partners), dissolution cannot be avoided.[231] Furthermore, under the rule announced in *Glensder Textile Co. v. Comm'r*,[232] and expressly adopted by the Treasury regulations, the reservation in the limited partnership agreement of a power in the remaining members to continue the partnership constitutes only a "contingent continuity of existence" insufficient to satisfy the standard in the Treasury regulations.[233] The Treasury regulations therefore state flatly that a limited partnership organized under the ULPA does not have continuity of life.[234] This conclusion has been accepted readily by the courts. In both *Zuckman* and *Larson*, the courts determined, as a matter of law, that the limited partnerships they examined lacked the corporate characteristic of continuity of life.

(2) CENTRALIZED MANAGEMENT

An organization is deemed to have centralized management if any person or group of persons has continuing exclusive authority to make the management decisions necessary to conduct the business of the entity.[235] The Treasury regulations take the position that a limited partnership organized under the ULPA does not have centralized management unless "substantially all" of the interests in the partnership are owned by the limited partners.[236] The general partners are charged with the management of the venture. If the general partners own an insubstantial economic interest in the partnership, this fact is taken as an indication that they have undertaken their management responsibilities in a representative capacity on behalf of the limited partners.

Although the phrase "substantially all" is not defined in the Treasury regulations, the regulations provide an example which indicates that where 94 percent of the interests in a partnership are owned by the limited partners, the partners are deemed to own substantially all of the partnership.[237] In *Zuckman*, the Court of Claims held that the limited

---

[230]Treas. Reg. § 301.7701-2(b)(1) (1983).

[231]*Zuckman*, 524 F.2d at 735.

[232]46 B.T.A. 176 (1942).

[233]Treas. Reg. § 301.7701-2(b)(1) (1983).

[234]Treas. Reg. § 301.7701-2(b)(3) (1983).

[235]Treas. Reg. § 301.7701-2(c)(1) (1983).

[236]Treas. Reg. § 301.7701-2(c)(4) (1983).

[237]Treas. Reg. § 301.7701-3(b)(2), Example (2) (1960).

partners' ownership of 61 percent of all interests did not create centralization of management, although the court suggested that 90 percent control would suffice.[238]

(3) FREE TRANSFERABILITY OF INTERESTS

An organization has the corporate characteristic of transferability of interests if each of its members has the power, without the consent of other members, to substitute for himself, in the same organization, a person who is not a member.[239] The ULPA provides that a limited partner's interest in the assets and profits of the partnership is assignable but that the assignee does not succeed to all of the rights and privileges of a partner unless the assignee's admission as a substituted limited partner is approved by all of the members.[240]

The Treasury regulations make clear that the characteristic of free transferability of interests does not exist if each member can, without the consent of other members, assign only his right to share in profits but cannot so assign his rights to participate in the management of the organization.[241] Therefore, a partnership organized under the ULPA that provides in its partnership agreement that the consent of the general partners must be secured before an outsider can become a substituted limited partner does not have free transferability of interests. Free transferability does not result merely because the limited partners can assign their interests in the profits of the venture. In Rev. Rul. 77-137,[242] however, the IRS ruled that where an assignee acquires substantially complete dominion and control over a limited partnership interest, he must report the distributive share of partnership items of income, gain, loss, and deduction attributable to the assigned interest in the same manner as would be required if the assignee were a substituted limited partner. Although Rev. Rul. 77-137 is not directly applicable to the issue of transferability of interests, the ruling equates, at least under some circumstances, the assignment of partnership interests and the transfer of limited partner status.

---

[238]524 F.2d at 742.

[239]Treas. Reg. § 301.7701-2(e)(1) (1983).

[240]ULPA § 19 (1916). *But see* Evans v. Comm'r, 447 F.2d 547, 552 (7th Cir. 1971), where the court held that a taxpayer who transferred his entire partnership interest to his wholly owned corporation was no longer a partner for income tax purposes, even though the remaining partner in the partnership did not consent to having the corporation as a new partner.

[241]Treas. Reg. § 301.7701-2(e)(1) (1983).

[242]1977-1 C.B. 178.

(4) LIMITED LIABILITY

An organization has the corporate characteristic of limited liability if no member is personally liable for the debts and liabilities of the organization.[243] In a limited partnership, only the general partners are liable for amounts beyond their capital contributions to the partnership. The Treasury regulations authorize the use of a corporation as a general partner. The regulations provide that a limited partnership organized under the ULPA lacks limited liability unless the general partners do not have substantial assets and are merely "dummies" acting as agents of the limited partners.[244] Both the *Zuckman* and *Larson* courts held that in order to have limited liability, a limited partnership must fail both the "substantial assets" and "dummy" tests.[245]

In *Larson*, the Tax Court found it unnecessary to determine whether the sole corporate general partner had "substantial assets" because the facts revealed that it was not a "dummy," but was, rather, the moving force behind the enterprise.[246] In *Zuckman*, the Court of Claims went further and found the reasoning of the Treasury regulations to be incorrect. The court in *Zuckman* held that where the sole corporate general partner of a limited partnership has no assets, then only two alternatives may follow: If the general partner is not a "dummy," it is liable for partnership debts and limited liability does not exist. If, on the other hand, the general partner is found to be a "dummy," then, under the ULPA, the limited partners for whom it acts as agent are liable for the debts of the partnership and limited liability still does not exist.[247] The Court of Claims concluded that a limited partnership organized under the ULPA cannot have limited liability inasmuch as at least one of its members bears at all times personal liability.[248]

(b) ADVANCE RULING REQUESTS

Under the reasoning of the Treasury regulations, a limited partnership organized pursuant to the ULPA lacks limited liability if its general partners own "substantial assets." The Treasury regulations, however, do not define the phrase "substantial assets." The only authority that

---

[243]Treas. Reg. § 301.7701-2(d)(1) (1983).
[244]Treas. Reg. § 301.7701-2(d)(2) (1983).
[245]*Zuckman*, 524 F.2d at 741; *Larson*, 66 T.C. at 180.
[246]*Larson*, 66 T.C. at 181.
[247]*Zuckman*, 524 F.2d at 741.
[248]*Id.*

addresses this point is a revenue procedure in which the IRS outlines the requirements for obtaining an advance ruling on the issue of partnership status.

Rev. Proc. 72-13[249] provides that, in a situation where a corporation serves as the sole general partner of a limited partnership, the IRS will not issue an advance ruling as to partnership status unless the corporate general partner has a net worth, at all times, equal to the lesser of (1) 15 percent of the total contributions to the partnership or $250,000 if such contributions total less than $2.5 million, or (2) 10 percent of the contributions if they total over $2.5 million. Although Rev. Proc. 72-13 does not necessarily represent the audit position of the IRS, it does provide a useful indication of how the IRS interprets the "substantial assets" requirement of the Treasury regulations. The capitalization requirement introduced by Rev. Proc. 72-13 provides that a corporate general partner must maintain the prescribed net worth continuously, thus indicating that if at any time during the partnership's operations the general partner ceases to have sufficient net worth, the entity may become an association taxable as a corporation.

Additional prerequisites for an IRS ruling are provided in Rev. Proc. 74-17.[250] It applies to ruling requests made by any limited partnership, whether or not it has a sole corporate general partner, and sets forth three additional conditions necessary to obtain a favorable ruling on partnership classification:

1. The interests of all of the general partners, taken together, in each material item of partnership income, gain, loss, deduction, or credit must be equal to at least one percent of each such item at all times during the existence of the partnership. In determining the existence of the one percent interest, any interests of the general partners as limited partners are not taken into account.[251]

2. The aggregate deductions to be claimed by the partners as their distributive shares of partnership losses for the first two years of the limited partnership's operation must not exceed the amount of their equity capital invested in the limited partnership. (This requirement is relevant to tax shelter entities, where an allocation of nonrecourse liabilities may be made to a limited partner to create a basis for his partnership interest that may allow a deduction in excess of his investment during the first two years.)[252]

---

[249] 1972-1 C.B. 735.
[250] 1974-1 C.B. 438.
[251] *Id.*
[252] *Id.*

3. A creditor who makes a nonrecourse loan to a limited partnership must not acquire or have the right to acquire, as consideration for the loan, capital or property of the limited partnership, other than as a secured creditor.[253]

§ 25.9   PUBLICLY TRADED TRUST INTERESTS

Certain beneficial interests in trusts are securities and trade on stock exchanges and in the over-the-counter market in the same way stock is traded. These trusts, frequently referred to as "royalty trusts," are attractive vehicles for corporations to use to spin off to their stockholders nonoperating mineral interests, royalty rights on patents, and other passive interests. Basically, there are two types of royalty trusts: distribution trusts (set up by corporations that transfer assets to the trusts and distribute the beneficial interests to the stockholders)[254] and financing trusts (set up to purchase the assets from the corporations).[255] For a discussion of royalty trusts generally, see section 1.1(h).

(a)   TAX STATUS AS A TRUST

The major tax consideration with a publicly traded royalty trust is whether the trust is taxable as a trust or characterized as an association taxable as a corporation.[256] To avoid tax at the entity level, the grantor trust structure is generally preferred.[257] A grantor trust is ignored for tax purposes. Its beneficial interest owners ("certificate owners"), not the trust, are subject to tax.

For tax purposes, the term "corporation" includes an unincorporated "association" that has corporate characteristics.[258] Grantor trusts are also structured to avoid classification as an association taxable as a corporation. Although an entity may be a trust (or a partnership) for local law purposes, it can, under certain circumstances, be deemed an association and treated as a corporation for tax purposes. An investment trust, such as a royalty trust, is treated as an association if there is a

---

[253]*Id.*

[254]*See* section 1.1(h).

[255]*Id.*

[256]*See generally* Gelinas, *Mineral Royalty Trust Transactions: The Use of the Grantor Trust to Avoid Corporate Income Tax,* 37 TAX LAW REV. 225-249 (Winter, 1982); *Pickens-Gulf Royalty Trust Dispute Puts Spotlight on Subchapter C Reforms,* 22 TAX NOTES 5-7 (1984).

[257]*See generally* I.R.C. §§ 671-679.

[258]I.R.C. § 7701(a)(3).

power under the trust agreement to vary the investments.[259] Hence, the enabling documents for the trust must provide that the trustee has no power to vary the investments. The trustees can only exercise ministerial powers and vary the trust assets by disposing of such assets. For example, the IRS ruled in a private ruling that a distribution trust created by Mesa Petroleum Co. is a trust for tax purposes.[260] In addition, the IRS has announced that it will rule on the classification of royalty trusts in situations where the corporation retains working interests (as opposed to passive nonoperating interests) in oil and gas property.[261]

A trust qualifies as such for tax purposes if the trustee's power is limited to collecting revenues, paying expenses, and dispersing proceeds.[262] In fact, various trust provisions allow a minimal level of activity on the part of the trustee. In LTR 8331065,[263] the IRS characterized a distribution trust as a trust for tax purposes where the trustee was prohibited from engaging in any business, commercial, or investment activities. The trustee did not have power to vary the trust's investments[264] and was permitted to sell property only with the approval of a majority of the outstanding beneficial interest owners. In addition, minor activities on the part of trustees have been approved by the IRS in published rulings in the MBS area.[265] For example, the IRS has ruled that a trust that holds mortgages and makes quarterly distributions to the certificate owners can reinvest the monthly payments it receives on the mortgages held in the pool in certain high quality debt obligations if the obligations (1) mature prior to the next trust distribution date and (2) are held to maturity.[266] Finally, the IRS has allowed a trustee of a mortgage pool two years to accept new mortgages in exchange for mortgages initially included in the trust which did not conform to representations and warranties, without subjecting the trust to taxation as a corporation.[267]

A trust is treated as a grantor trust if the grantor holds "the beneficial

---

[259]Comm'r v. North American Board Trust, 122 F.2d 545 (2d Cir.), *cert. denied*, 314 U.S. 701 (1941); Treas. Reg. § 301.7701-4(c) (1986).

[260]LTR 8223015 (Feb. 26, 1982); *see also* LTR 8331065 (May 2, 1983) (where the IRS also ruled that a distribution trust was a trust for tax purposes).

[261]Rev. Proc. 83-11, 1983-1 C.B. 674.

[262]*See* Royalty Participation Trust v. Comm'r, 20 T.C. 466 (1953), *acq.* 1953-2 C.B. 6.

[263](May 2, 1983).

[264]LTR 8331065 (May 2, 1983).

[265]*See* section 28.4(b)(1); section 28.4(c).

[266]Rev. Rul. 75-192, 1975-1 C.B. 384.

[267]Rev. Rul. 71-399, 1971-2 C.B. 433. It is unclear whether an exchange period that extends beyond two years might change the tax result.

enjoyment of the corpus or the income therefrom" and has the power to dispose of the corpus without the approval or consent of any adverse party.[268] The equitable ownership of each separate nonoperating interest, patent, or royalty is deemed transferred on a pro rata basis to certificate owners who own an undivided interest in each asset. The certificate owners compute their tax liability by including in income all items of income, deductions, and credits attributable to their pro rata interests.[269] Certificate owners (whether on the cash or accrual method of accounting) report income at the time the payments are received by the trust, even if distributions are not made to them at that time. The trustee is viewed simply as an agent acting on behalf of the certificate holders. This tax result has been confirmed in numerous revenue rulings in the mortgage pool area with respect to pass-through MBS certificates.[270]

For trust interests to be actively traded, the subsequent owners of the trust interests must succeed to all of the tax attributes available to the initial certificate owners. This carry-over treatment has been approved in some situations by the IRS.[271]

The cost depletion deduction for oil and gas property held by a grantor trust is determined at the level of the certificate owners.[272] On the other hand, the depletion allowance is determined at the trust level, based on the adjusted basis of the property.[273] Unless the trust is a grantor trust, subsequent certificate owners cannot deduct cost depletion.[274]

---

[268]I.R.C. § 674(a).

[269]Treas. Reg. § 1.671-3(a) (1969); Rev. Rul. 70-545, 1970-2 C.B. 7.

[270]See generally Rev. Rul. 84-10, 1984-1 C.B. 155; Rev. Rul. 81-204, 1981-2 C.B. 157; Rev. Rul. 81-203, 1981-2 C.B. 137; Rev. Rul. 80-96, 1980-1 C.B. 317; Rev. Rul. 77-349, 1977-2 C.B. 20; Rev. Rul. 74-300, 1974-1 C.B. 169; Rev. Rul. 74-221, 1974-1 C.B. 365; Rev. Rul. 74-169, 1974-1 C.B. 147; Rev. Rul. 72-376, 1972-2 C.B. 647; Rev. Rul. 70-544, 1970-2 C.B. 6; Rev. Rul. 61-175, 1961-2 C.B. 128.

[271]See Rev. Rul. 61-175, 1961-2 C.B. 128; LTR 8331065 (May 2, 1983). In LTR 8113068 (Dec. 31, 1980), the IRS ruled that the Houston Oil Royalty Trust (now traded on the NYSE) is a grantor trust. Although the ruling does not differentiate between initial certificate holders and transferees, the ruling should apply to transferees as well as initial holders of beneficial interests.

[272]Prop. Treas. Reg. § 1.613A-3(f) (1977). The Code permits taxpayers owning certain mineral property to claim depletion deductions based on their cost of the property or (subject to certain limitations) a percentage of the gross income from the property, whichever is greater. I.R.C. §§ 612-613A. Cost depletion permits a deduction for a portion of the taxpayer's cost for the investment during the production period. Percentage depletion is based on the gross income of the property, without regard to the taxpayer's basis in the property.

[273]Rev. Rul. 74-530, 1974-2 C.B. 188.

[274]LTR 8411017 (Dec. 7, 1983).

Subsequent certificate owners, however, can use their cost for the beneficial interests as the basis for cost depletion.[275]

(b) USE OF TRUSTS TO MAXIMIZE STOCKHOLDERS' RETURN

A corporation with nonoperating income from trade or business assets can create a distribution trust[276] in the form of a grantor trust to transfer the nonoperating interests to the trust. The trustee collects the income, pays trust expenses, and distributes the proceeds to the owners of the trust interests. There is no tax at the entity level. This technique has become very popular with corporations with minimal or no earnings and profits (frequently because of intangible drilling and development cost deductions).[277] The tax consequences to the stockholders on the creation of a royalty trust are discussed briefly below.[278]

A noncorporate stockholder is treated as having received a distribution in an amount equal to the fair market value of the property received.[279] The distribution is treated as a dividend only if the distributing corporation has current or accumulated earnings and profits.[280] To the extent the fair market value of the assets distributed exceeds the distributing corporation's earnings and profits, the excess first reduces a noncorporate stockholder's basis in his shares of stock in the distributing corporation.[281] Once his basis is reduced to zero, any additional amounts are taxable as either long-term or short-term capital gain.[282]

For corporate stockholders, a distribution is treated as equal to the lesser of (1) the fair market value of the property, or (2) the adjusted basis of the property in the hands of the distributing corporation, increased by any gain recognized to the distributing corporation.[283] Once the amount of the distribution is determined, the distribution is treated as a dividend to the extent of current and accumulated earnings and profits of the distributing corporation. A corporate stockholder may be

---

[275]Gelinas, *supra* note 256, at 274.

[276]*See* section 1.1(h).

[277]*See* section 22.1(c).

[278]I.R.C. § 311(d)(1), as amended by TEFRA, imposes gain recognition on a distributing corporation in the case of most appreciated property distributions made on or after June 14, 1984.

[279]I.R.C. § 301(b)(1)(A).

[280]*See* section 22.1.

[281]I.R.C. § 301(c)(2).

[282]I.R.C. § 301(c)(3).

[283]I.R.C. § 301(b)(1)(B); *see* section 22.1.

eligible for the 85 percent intercorporate dividends received deduction.[284] An excess distribution reduces the corporate stockholder's basis in its shares of stock in the distributing corporation. Once reduced to zero, any additional amounts are taxed as capital gain.[285]

(c) SPECIAL CONSIDERATIONS FOR EMPLOYEE BENEFIT PLANS

Because pension and profit sharing trusts invest in oil and gas properties,[286] royalty trust interests can also be attractive investments. Although pension and profit sharing plans that meet all of the Code requirements are exempt from tax under I.R.C. § 501(a), they are subject to tax on "unrelated business income."[287] Passive royalty income and income from other nonoperating interests (i.e., where the owner does not participate in the management of the property and has no out-of-pocket liability for the expenses of operating the property), are not from a trade or business and, hence, are not unrelated business income.[288] Royalties and nonoperating interests are passive nonbusiness investments. Thus, the definition of unrelated business taxable income specifically excludes "all royalties (including overriding royalties) whether measured by production or by gross or taxable income from the property, and all deductions directly connected with such income."[289] The debt financed income rules, which impose tax on certain investments of tax-exempt entities,[290] should not apply in the royalty trust context unless trust interests are purchased on margin or with borrowed funds.[291]

(d) RECENT DEVELOPMENTS

Several recent legislative developments significantly reduce the benefits of establishing distribution type royalty trusts where a corporation distributes nonoperating interests to a trust formed for the benefit of its

---

[284]See section 15.7; section 22.9.

[285]I.R.C. §§ 301(c)(2), (3).

[286]Jansson, *Prospecting for Oil and Gas*, INSTITUTIONAL INVESTOR, Apr. 1981, at 91.

[287]I.R.C. § 501(b).

[288]Rev. Rul. 69-574, 1969-2 C.B. 130.

[289]I.R.C. § 512(b)(2).

[290]I.R.C. § 514.

[291]See Rev. Rul. 74-197, 1974-1 C.B. 143.

stockholders.[292] Some changes made by the DRA[293] limit some of the attractions of distribution type trusts. First, to be eligible for the intercorporate dividends received deduction, stock held by corporate stockholders must now be held for 46 days (rather than 16 days for the pre-DRA dividends).[294] Second, a distributing corporation must increase its earnings and profits (for distributions made in taxable years beginning after September 30, 1984), by gain realized on a distribution even if the gain is not recognized for tax purposes.[295] And third, with certain statutory exceptions, a distributing corporation recognizes income when it distributes appreciated property to its stockholders on or after June 14, 1984.[296] The amount of gain is the difference between the adjusted basis of the property distributed and its fair market value.[297]

With the DRA changes, many of the major benefits of distribution type royalty trusts may have been removed. First, a distributing corporation may be unwilling to establish a royalty trust if it is taxed when it distributes appreciated property to the trust. Second, the attraction of a royalty trust may be greatly reduced if the stockholders have increased future dividend income because the distribution of the nonoperating property to the trust increases the earnings and profits of the distributing corporation.[298]

§ 25.10 STRADDLE RULES

Prior to January 1, 1984, corporate stock was not subject to the Straddle Rules.[299] This was changed by the DRA, which repeals the blanket ex-

---

[292]See e.g., STAFF OF SENATE COMM. ON FINANCE, 98TH CONG., 2D SESS., PRELIMINARY REPORT ON THE REFORM AND SIMPLIFICATION OF THE INCOME TAXATION OF CORPORATIONS (Comm. Print 1983).

[293]DRA, Pub. L. 98-369, §§ 53 and 54, 98 Stat. 494, 565-571 (1984).

[294]See section 15.7; section 22.9.

[295]I.R.C. § 312(n).

[296]I.R.C. § 311(d)(1).

[297]Id.

[298]Legislative proposals would further reduce the attraction of establishing royalty trusts. For example, the Tax Reform Act of 1985, H.R. 3838, §§ 303 and 312, proposes a reduction in the amount of the intercorporate dividends received deduction and a repeal of the General Utilities doctrine. Tax Reform Act of 1985, H.R. 3838, § 331, proposes to repeal General Utilities & Operating Co. v. Helvering, 296 U.S. 200 (1935). See also Saunders, A Nasty Little Time Bomb, FORBES (Jan. 13, 1986) 286; Pickens-Gulf Royalty Trust Dispute Puts Spotlight on Subchapter C Reforms, supra note 256.

[299]I.R.C. § 1092(d)(1) (1982).

emption for corporate stock positions established after December 31, 1983.[300] As a result, certain stock positions are now subject to the Straddle Rules. For a discussion of the Straddle Rules, see generally Part Ten. For a discussion of the application of the Straddle Rules to certain stock positions, see section 36.2(c).

[300]DRA, *supra* note 183, § 101(b)(1).

Twenty-six

Options on Stock

§ 26.1 TYPES OF STOCK OPTIONS

Types of stock option products continue to increase at an explosive rate. As a result, market participants can choose from an increasing selection of stock related products and trading markets. For a discussion of the option markets, see generally Chapter Five. For a discussion of option classes, see section 5.2.

One of two tax systems apply to stock options and narrow based index options, depending on whether the taxpayer is an investor,[1] market maker, or specialist in options (i.e., an options dealer): equity option treatment or section 1256 treatment.[2] Stock options are equity options, which means they are not eligible for section 1256 treatment unless they are held by so-called option dealers.[3] Certain options on stock products, such as broad based stock index options, are classified as nonequity options and are subject to section 1256 treatment. This following section discusses the major tax designations for options on stock and stock products.

(a) LISTED OPTIONS

A listed option is any option (other than a right to acquire stock from the issuer)[4] that is traded on or subject to the rules of a qualified board

---

[1]*See* section 6.1.

[2]*See* section 6.2(b); section 6.3(d); section 26.4; section 32.4.

[3]For a discussion of section 1256 treatment, see generally Part Nine.

[4]For a discussion of warrants and stock rights, see section 1.1(d), section 26.1(e), and section 26.3(e).

or exchange.[5] The term "qualified board or exchange" is defined to include (1) a national securities exchange registered with the SEC; (2) a commodity exchange registered with the CFTC; or (3) another exchange, board of trade, or market designated by the Treasury.[6] Listed options include options on property other than stock.

(b) UNLISTED OPTIONS

All options that do not qualify as listed options are considered to be unlisted options. Listed options are discussed in section 26.1(a).

(c) EQUITY OPTIONS

Generally, an option is an equity option if (1) it is an option to buy or sell stock, or (2) its value is determined directly or indirectly by reference to any stock, group of stocks, or stock index.[7] An option is excluded from the definition of an equity option, however, if the CFTC has designated a contract market for trading such options, or if the Treasury has determined that trading such options meets the requirements for CFTC designation.[8]

(d) SECTION 1256 OPTIONS

Nonequity options[9] and dealer equity options[10] comprise section 1256 options. Options on stock are, by definition, equity options. Nevertheless, options on stock are section 1256 contracts if they qualify as dealer equity options.[11] Dealer equity options must meet the following requirements. First, they must be listed options.[12] Second, they must be equity options.[13] Third, they must be purchased or granted by an options dealer in the normal course of his options business.[14] And fourth, they must be listed on a qualified board or exchange (i.e., a national securities

[5]I.R.C. § 1256(g)(5).
[6]I.R.C. § 1256(g)(7).
[7]I.R.C. § 1256(g)(6)(A).
[8]I.R.C. § 1256(g)(6)(B).
[9]*See* section 32.3.
[10]*See* section 32.4.
[11]*Id.*
[12]I.R.C. § 1256(g)(4).
[13]*Id.*
[14]*Id.*

exchange, commodity exchange, or other market designated by the Treasury)[15] on which the options dealer is registered.[16]

(e) WARRANTS

Warrants are options to acquire stock that are issued directly by corporations with stocks that are subject to the options.[17] Warrants are frequently issued by corporations in connection with financings (as "sweeteners" to induce lenders to agree to lower interest rates than would otherwise be available to the corporation), reorganizations, and corporate acquisitions.[18]

§ 26.2 PRE-DRA TRANSACTIONS

When ERTA[19] was enacted in 1981, certain stock options with exercise periods that were shorter than the then current long-term capital gain holding period were exempt from the Straddle Rules.[20] This exemption for so-called short-term stock options was removed by the DRA.[21] All options (including options on stock), irrespective of their exercise periods, are now subject to the Straddle Rules.[22] Specific exemptions from the Straddle Rules are provided for options that are part of (1) straddles made up exclusively of section 1256 contracts,[23] (2) hedging transactions,[24] and (3) qualified covered call transactions.[25]

(a) OPTION SPREAD TRANSACTIONS

After enactment of ERTA and prior to the DRA, the major concern with those option transactions exempt from the Straddle Rules was the use

---

[15]I.R.C. §§ 1256(g)(4), (7); *see* section 32.1(b).

[16]I.R.C. § 1256(g)(4); *see* section 6.2(b); section 6.3(d).

[17]For a discussion of warrants, see section 1.1(d).

[18]*See generally* Reiling, *Warrants in Bond-Warrant Units: A Survey And Assessment,* 70 MICH. L. REV. 1411 (1972).

[19]ERTA, Pub. L. 97-34, 95 Stat. 172 (1981).

[20]I.R.C. § 1092(d)(2)(B)(ii) (1982), *amended by* DRA, Pub. L. 98-369, § 101(a)(1), 98 Stat. 494, 616 (1984); *see* section 44.6.

[21]DRA, *supra* note 20, § 101(a)(1).

[22]For a discussion of pre-DRA law, see section 44.6.

[23]*See* section 44.7.

[24]*See generally* Chapter 21; section 44.2.

[25]*See* section 44.3.

of exchange-traded stock options to defer the payment of tax on capital gains (for investors[26] and traders)[27] and ordinary income (for hedgers,[28] market makers, and specialists in listed options).[29] Deferral was available through the use of option spread transactions.[30] Tax deferral was available—subject, of course, to IRS attack—because under pre-DRA law the Straddle Rules only applied to stock options with exercise periods in excess of the long-term capital gain holding period. Exchange-traded stock options had maximum exercise periods of approximately nine months, which was less than the then current one year period for long-term capital treatment.[31]

In 1983, an official of the Treasury delivered a statement at a Senate Finance Committee hearing on tax shelters in which one of the items he mentioned was the Treasury's concern about tax abuses in the options market. It was the Treasury's position that "Congress should re-examine the exemption of exchange-traded stock options from the loss deferral rules."[32] The Treasury official reported that "since the enactment of ERTA, we have seen substantial indications that investors are attempting to defer the taxation of income through tax straddles in exchange-traded stock options."[33] Straddle transactions identified by the Treasury took two forms. First, limited partnerships were structured as market maker firms to produce ordinary tax losses that would be used to offset ordinary income from unrelated businesses and professions.[34] Second, investors and traders would establish offsetting positions in stock options ("typically with deep-in-the-money options with a smaller time premium and more predictable response to price fluctuations in the underlying stock")[35] to defer short-term capital gains by incurring short-term capital losses.

[26]See section 6.1.

[27]See section 6.2.

[28]See section 6.4.

[29]See section 6.3(c).

[30]The tax issues with respect to option spread transactions and commodity spread transactions are similar in many ways. For a discussion of commodity spread transactions, see generally section 35.1.

[31]Certain unlisted options had option terms of more than the pre-DRA long-term capital gain holding period of more than one year. As a result, such options were subject to the Straddle Rules.

[32]*Abusive Tax Shelters: Hearing Before the Subcomm. on Oversight of the Internal Revenue Service of the Senate Comm. on Finance*, 98th Cong., 1st Sess. 69 (1983) (statement of Robert Woodward, Acting Tax Legislative Counsel, Department of the Treasury), *reprinted in* 20 Tax Notes (BNA) 83, 85 app. (1983).

[33]*Id.*

[34]*Id.*

[35]*Id.*

In connection with the same Senate Finance Committee hearings on tax shelters, the Joint Committee on Taxation published a report to serve as background for the hearings.[36] Several passages in the Joint Committee Report addressed concerns with option transactions. First, in connection with a general discussion of the problem of straddles and the legislative solution enacted by ERTA, the Joint Committee Report states that "[b]ecause short-term stock options are excepted from [the Straddle Rules], straddle transactions in these options have become widely used since the enactment of ERTA."[37] Second, in mentioning the scope of the hedging exemption provided by ERTA,[38] the Joint Committee Report expressly referred to syndicates[39] and observed that "[t]axpayers are attempting to structure transactions to qualify losses not entered into in the normal course of business as ordinary losses."[40] In addition, the Report mentioned concerns about the use of foreign corporations for tax deferral, conversion, and avoidance.[41]

(b) AUDIT ISSUES

The IRS has attacked pre-DRA option spread transactions on much the same grounds it has attacked pre-ERTA commodity spreads. The IRS has asserted the same arguments it advanced in Rev. Rul. 77-185[42] and *Smith v. Comm'r*[43] to deny stock option losses incurred in one tax year while the taxpayer holds offsetting positions in options or stock.[44] Unlike pre-ERTA commodity transactions, however, pre-DRA stock option transactions are not covered by the so-called amnesty provision granted for certain pre-ERTA commodity transactions by Section 108 of the DRA.[45] In fact, with Section 108 unavailable for pre-DRA option transactions, taxpayers who have their pre-DRA option transactions challenged may need to meet the difficult to establish profit motive standard,

---

[36] STAFF OF THE JOINT COMMITTEE ON TAXATION, 98TH CONG., 1ST SESS., BACKGROUND ON TAX SHELTERS, in *Abusive Tax Shelters: Hearing Before the Subcomm. on Oversight of the Internal Revenue Service of the Senate Comm. on Finance*, 98th Cong., 1st Sess. (1983) [hereinafter referred to as "Joint Committee Report"].

[37] *Id.* at 12.

[38] *See generally* Chapter 21.

[39] *See* section 21.4(b).

[40] Joint Committee Report, *supra* note 36, at 13.

[41] *Id* at 36–38.

[42] 1977-1 C.B. 48, *amplified by* Rev. Rul. 78-414, 1982-2 C.B. 213.

[43] 78 T.C. 350 (1982).

[44] For a discussion of Rev. Rul. 77-185, 1977-1 C.B. 48, see section 35.2(a). For a discussion of *Smith v. Comm'r*, see section 35.2(b).

[45] *See* section 35.2(c).

announced in *Fox v. Comm'r*,[46] that their transactions were entered into *primarily* to realize an economic profit.

One of the audit issues for option spreads is whether certain types of transactions (e.g., butterfly spreads[47] or boxes)[48] were entered into with the requisite profit motive. For example, the IRS has asserted that butterfly spreads are noneconomic on the grounds that taxpayers must pay three sets of commissions to put on and take off butterfly positions.[49] Market makers, however, do not pay brokerage commissions and their expenses for executing transactions are minimal when compared to those of investors and traders. As a result, butterfly spreads may turn out to be unprofitable for certain nonprofessionals, but may be profitable for market professionals. (In fact, market makers continue to actively trade butterfly spreads, and their trading strategy has not changed significantly since the DRA tax changes.) The IRS has also asserted in some cases that the so-called at risk rules of I.R.C. § 465 limit a taxpayer's ability to deduct losses on option transactions.[50]

An additional issue raised on the audits of certain taxpayers is whether option market makers were dealers under pre-DRA law for certain op-

---

[46]82 T.C. 1001, 1021 (1984).

[47]*See* section 5.4(c)(1)(iii).

[48]*See* section 5.4(e)(4).

[49]The IRS has cited as support for its position G. GASTINEAU, THE STOCK OPTIONS MANUAL 121 (2d ed. 1979).

[50]The at risk rules may not apply in many cases. First, the legislative history to the Tax Reform Act of 1976 (Pub. L. 94-455, 90 Stat. 1520) and the Revenue Act of 1978 (Pub. L. 95-600, 92 Stat. 2763) supports the position that I.R.C. § 465 was *never* intended to apply to option market makers in the course of their business activities. *See* SENATE FINANCE COMMITTEE REPORT, TAX REFORM ACT OF 1976, S. REP. NO. 938, 94th Cong., 2d Sess. 45–48 *reprinted in* 1976 U.S. CODE CONG. & AD. NEWS 3439, 3481–83 (referring generally to tax shelters, nonrecourse financing, and limited partnerships); HOUSE WAYS AND MEANS COMMITTEE REPORT, REVENUE ACT OF 1978, H.R. REP. NO. 1445, 95th Cong., 2nd Sess. 67–69, *reprinted in* 1978 U.S. CODE CONG. & AD. NEWS 7046, 7103–05 (covering tax treatment of investors rather than those engaged in a business); HOUSE CONFERENCE REPORT, REVENUE ACT OF 1978, H.R. REP. NO. 1800, 95th Cong., 2d Sess. 219–20, *reprinted in* 1978 U.S. CODE CONG. & AD. NEWS 7198, 7222–23 (covering tax treatment of investors rather than those engaged in a business). Second, even if I.R.C. § 465 is applied to options trading of certain taxpayers, there should be no limitation on losses in certain circumstances. I.R.C. § 465(b)(1) provides that amounts considered at risk from an activity include (1) amounts of money and the adjusted basis of other property contributed to the activity, and (2) amounts borrowed with respect to the activity. If I.R.C. § 465 is applicable, the IRS's first hurdle would be to define the "activity" from which losses would be limited to the "amounts considered at risk"; that would be simple for a nonprofessional trader holding *one* straddle from which the maximum economic loss would be, for example, $50, but what about a market maker whose total exposure during the course of a year in all his trades (tax motivated and otherwise) exceeds $100 million? Unless the IRS can define the "activity" as including only the tax spreads, the market maker's at risk amount could be $100 million.

tion transactions.[51] In light of this IRS position, the pre-DRA exemption from the wash sales rule for noncorporate traders[52] may be vital for option market makers (who viewed themselves as dealers under pre-DRA law) if they are subsequently reclassified as traders or investors for certain pre-DRA option transactions.

§ 26.3 EQUITY OPTIONS

(a) IN GENERAL

Equity options can be either listed options (i.e., options traded on or subject to the rules of a national securities exchange, a board of trade designated as a contract market by the CFTC, or a market designated by the Treasury),[53] or unlisted options (i.e., all options that are not listed options).[54] Whether options are listed is irrelevant for those equity options that are not dealer equity options.[55] Types of equity options include, for example, options on individual corporate stock, options on a narrow based index of transportation stocks,[56] and options on a narrow based index of technology stocks.[57] For a discussion of the types of options and option trading strategies, see generally Chapter Five.

The general tax rules for capital or ordinary treatment apply to equity options. This means that investors[58] and traders[59] incur capital gains or losses on their equity option transactions, while dealers in the underlying stocks[60] and hedgers[61] incur ordinary income or loss on their equity option transactions. Option dealers, that is, market makers and specialists in options,[62] are taxed in accordance with section 1256 on

[51]*See* section 6.3(c).

[52]*See* section 17.5(b).

[53]I.R.C. § 1256(g)(5); *see* section 26.1(a).

[54]*Compare* I.R.C. § 1256(g)(6) *with* I.R.C. § 1256(g)(3) *and* I.R.C. § 1256(g)(4). *See* section 26.1(b).

[55]*Compare* I.R.C. § 1256(g)(6) *with* I.R.C. § 1256(g)(4). *See* section 26.4; section 32.4.

[56]*See* section 5.2(a)(4).

[57]Narrow based index equity options are covered by the rules applicable to stock options even though they are settled in cash. I.R.C. § 1234(c)(2). In Rev. Rul. 86-8, 1986-4 I.R.B. 6, the IRS ruled that the high technology index traded on the PSE is a nonequity option within the meaning of I.R.C. § 1256(g)(3).

[58]*See* section 6.1.

[59]*See* section 6.2.

[60]*See* section 6.3; section 33.2(a).

[61]*See* section 6.4.

[62]*See* section 6.2(b); section 6.3(d).

their dealer equity option transactions.[63] For a discussion of the general tax principles that apply to capital transactions, see generally Part Three. For a discussion of the general tax principles that apply to ordinary income transactions, see generally Part Four. In addition, option transactions may be subject to rules that defer loss or change the character of gain or loss. For a discussion of these rules as they apply to options, see section 26.3(f).

The remainder of this section addresses the tax treatment of purchasers and sellers of equity options (both puts and calls) who are not option dealers. For a discussion of market makers and specialists in options, see section 26.4 and section 32.4.

(b) EQUITY CALL OPTIONS

(1) PURCHASERS OF EQUITY CALLS

A taxpayer realizes no taxable gain or loss on the purchase of an option, and does not incur a deductible expense. The ultimate tax treatment for an option depends on whether it is sold, disposed of, lapses, or is exercised. I.R.C. § 1234(a)(1) provides, in the case of the purchaser of an option, that gain or loss attributable to the sale or exchange of, or loss attributable to the failure to exercise, a long call or put option is considered gain or loss from the sale or exchange of property with the same character as the property to which the option relates would have in the hands of the taxpayer.[64]

(i) Option Premiums, Commissions, and Fees

The option premium paid to purchase an option represents the cost of the option. It is a nondeductible capital expenditure[65] that is carried in a deferred account as an incomplete transaction until the position is closed.[66] Commissions and fees paid to purchase an option are part of the option premium and are also not deductible.[67] In other words, all amounts paid to acquire options are nondeductible capital expendi-

---

[63]*See* section 32.4.

[64]This provision was enacted in 1954 to prevent dealers in property from obtaining capital treatment on the sale of options in such property. HOUSE WAYS AND MEANS COMMITTEE REPORT, INTERNAL REVENUE CODE OF 1954, H.R. REP. No. 1337, 83rd Cong., 2d Sess. A278–79, *reprinted in* 1954 U.S. CODE CONG. & AD. NEWS 4019, 4420–21.

[65]Rev. Rul. 78-182, 1978-1 C.B. 265.

[66]Rev. Rul. 71-521, 1971-2 C.B. 313.

[67]Rev. Rul. 58-234, 1958-1 C.B. 279, *clarified by* Rev. Rul. 68-151, 1968-1 C.B. 363.

tures.[68] Premiums, commissions, and fees comprise a taxpayer's basis in the option, which is an intangible property right.

(ii) Dispositions

On the sale of an unlisted option or a closing transaction for a listed option, an investor or trader incurs capital gain or loss (long-term or short-term depending on his holding period for the option).[69] In addition, dealers in options (i.e., market makers and specialists in options) are subject to section 1256 treatment for transactions that qualify as dealer equity options.[70] Finally, hedgers[71] obtain ordinary income and loss on their equity option transactions.

Gain is realized to the extent that the sales price or closing transaction price exceeds a taxpayer's basis in the option. Loss is realized to the extent that the taxpayer's basis in the option (i.e., the premium paid plus commissions and fees paid to acquire the option) exceeds the sales price or closing transaction price.[72] Gain or loss on transactions that are not hedges or dealer transactions is short-term or long-term depending on the taxpayer's holding periods.[73]

(iii) Lapse of Long Call Option Positions Without Exercise

If a long option position lapses (i.e., expires without being exercised or sold), it is deemed to have been sold or otherwise disposed of on the date it expires.[74] The cost of the premium (plus any commissions and other fees) is treated as a capital loss for investors and traders, long-term or short-term depending on the taxpayer's holding period for the option prior to expiration.[75] Hedgers and dealers in the underlying stock obtain an ordinary loss on the lapse of long call option positions.[76]

(iv) Exercise of Long Call Option Positions

When the holder of a long call position exercises the option and purchases the underlying stock, he does not realize gain. Rather, his basis

---

[68]*Id.*

[69]Rev. Rul. 78-182, 1978-1 C.B. 265; I.R.C. § 1234(a)(1); Treas. Reg. § 1.1234-1(a)(1) (1979).

[70]*See* section 32.4.

[71]*See* section 6.4.

[72]Rev. Rul. 78-182, 1978-1 C.B. 265; I.R.C. § 1234(a).

[73]Treas. Reg. § 1.1234-1(a)(1) (1979).

[74]I.R.C. § 1234(a)(2); Treas. Reg. § 1.1234-1(b) (1979).

[75]Rev. Rul. 78-182, 1978-1 C.B. 265; I.R.C. § 1234(a); Treas. Reg. § 1.1234-1(b) (1979).

[76]I.R.C. § 1234(a)(3).

in the option (i.e., the premium, commissions, and fees) is added to the tax basis of the stock he acquires.[77] In addition, the taxpayer's holding period for the stock begins on the day following the date the long call position is exercised.[78] The holding period of the stock does not include the period during which the taxpaper held the call option.[79]

(2) SELLERS OF EQUITY CALLS

(i) Receipt of Premiums

The seller of an option does not incur taxable income on receipt of an option premium.[80] Receipt of a premium is not a taxable event. Instead, the premium is carried in a deferred account as an incomplete transaction until the option is exercised,[81] sold or terminated in a closing transaction,[82] or lapses.[83]

(ii) Commissions and Fees

Commissions and fees paid by a seller of an option reduce the total option premium received for selling the option.[84]

(iii) Lapse of Short Option Positions Without Exercise

If a short position lapses (i.e., expires without being exercised or sold), the premium income (reduced by any commissions and fees paid to establish the position) is treated as income to the writer (short position) on the date of lapse. Investors and traders recognize a short-term capital gain, while hedgers and dealers in the underlying stock recognize ordinary income.[85] Gain is included in the taxpayer's income for the year that includes the date the option expires.[86]

---

[77]Rev. Rul. 78-182, 1978-1 C.B. 265; Rev. Rul. 58-234, 1958-1 C.B. 279.

[78]Weir v. Comm'r, 10 T.C. 996, 1000–01 (1948), *aff'd per curiam*, 173 F.2d 222 (3d Cir. 1949).

[79]Rev. Rul. 78-182, 1978-1 C.B. 265.

[80]Rev. Rul. 78-182, 1978-1 C.B. 265; Rev. Rul. 58-234, 1958-1 C.B. 279; *see also* Rev. Rul. 72-198, 1972-1 C.B. 223, *modified by* Rev. Rul. 77-40, 1977-1 C.B. 248.

[81]*See* section 26.3(b)(1)(i).

[82]*See* section 26.3(b)(1)(ii).

[83]*See* section 26.3(b)(1)(iii).

[84]Rev. Rul. 58-234, 1958-1 C.B. 279.

[85]Rev. Rul. 78-182, 1978-1 C.B. 265; I.R.C. § 1234(b).

[86]Rev. Rul. 78-182, 1978-1 C.B. 265.

(iv) Exercise of Call Options

When a purchaser exercises a call option, the seller is obligated to sell the underlying stock to the purchaser at the option's strike price. To determine the total amount realized on the sale, the seller adds the amount of the option premium (minus any commissions and fees paid to sell the option) to the strike price (i.e., the sale price of the stock). The taxpayer has a gain on exercise of the option if the total amount realized exceeds his basis in the stock sold. On the other hand, he incurs a loss if his basis in the stock sold exceeds the total amount realized on the sale. For investors and traders, gain or loss is capital; long-term or short-term depending on the taxpayer's holding period for the stock sold, without regard to the holding period of the option sold.[87] Taxpayers who sell calls as part of a covered call transaction may be subject to the Straddle Rules unless the transaction qualifies as a qualified covered call.[88]

(c) EQUITY PUT OPTIONS

There is no tax effect on the purchase of a call option. A taxpayer realized no taxable gain or loss on the purchase of an option and does not incur a deductible expense. The ultimate tax result depends on whether the option is sold, lapses, or is exercised.

(1) PURCHASERS OF EQUITY PUTS

(i) Option Premiums, Commissions, and Fees

A put purchaser is subject to the same tax treatment as a call purchaser for the premiums, commissions, and fees he pays. These amounts are carried in a deferred account until the option is disposed of, expires, or is exercised. For a discussion of these rules, see section 26.3(b)(1)(i).

(ii) Dispositions

A put purchaser is generally taxed in the same way as a purchaser of a call option on the sale of an unlisted put option or closing transaction for a listed put option. For a discussion of the tax rules on the disposition of long positions, see generally section 26.3(b)(1)(ii). On the sale of an

[87]*Id.*; *but see* section 26.3(f).
[88]*See* section 44.3.

unlisted put or a closing transaction for a listed put (except for a so-called married put transaction),[89] any gain is treated as short-term for investors or traders if (1) as of the date a put option was acquired a taxpayer owned the underlying stock for less than the long-term capital gain holding period, or (2) he acquired the underlying stock during the period after the put was acquired but before the put was sold.[90]

(iii)   Lapse of Long Option Positions Without Exercise

Except in the case of so-called married put transactions,[91] the tax rules that apply to purchasers of call options apply to purchasers of put options who allow their option positions to lapse (i.e., expire without being exercised or sold). For a discussion of these tax rules, see section 26.3(b)(1)(iii).

(iv)   Exercise of Long Put Option Positions

When a long put option position is exercised, the option purchaser (long position) sells the underlying stock to the option seller (short position). The sale of the underlying stock on the exercise of a put option position is taxable. Basically, the taxpayer subtracts the option premium from the strike price (i.e., the amount he receives for the stock) to determine the total amount realized on the sale of the stock.[92] Capital gains result for investors and traders, while ordinary income results for hedgers and dealers in the underlying stock. If the amount realized exceeds a taxpayer's tax basis in the stock, he has a gain. If his tax basis in the stock exceeds the amount realized, he has a loss on the sale of his stock.[93]

For put options that are capital assets in the hands of a taxpayer, a capital gain realized on the exercise of a put (which is not part of a so-called married put transaction)[94] is short-term under the short sales rule if (1) as of the date the put was acquired the underlying stock had been held for less than the long-term holding period, or (2) the underlying stock was acquired after the put was purchased but on or before

---

[89]*See* section 16.4(d).

[90]Rev. Rul. 78-182, 1978-1 C.B. 265; I.R.C. § 1233(b). *See generally* Chapter 16; Chapter 42.

[91]*See* section 16.4(d).

[92]Rev. Rul. 58-234, 1958-1 C.B. 279.

[93]Rev. Rul. 78-182, 1978-1 C.B. 265; Rev. Rul. 71-521, 1971-2 C.B. 313.

[94]*See* section 16.4(d).

the date the put was exercised.[95] Because such option and stock positions established in taxable years ending after December 31, 1983 are subject to the Straddle Rules,[96] the modified short sales rule now applies to terminate a taxpayer's holding period.[97]

(2)   SELLERS OF EQUITY PUTS

(i)   Receipt of Premiums

The seller of a put option is subject to the same tax treatment as a seller of a call option; he does not incur taxable income on the receipt of an option premium.[98] For a discussion on the receipt of premiums, see section 26.3(b)(2)(i).

(ii)   Commissions and Fees

Commissions and fees paid by a seller of an option reduce the total option premium received for selling the option.[99]

(iii)   Lapse of Short Put Option Positions Without Exercise

The lapse (i.e., expiration without exercise) of a short put option position is subject to the same tax rules as apply to the lapse of a short call option position. Lapse results in a taxable gain for the seller. For a discussion of these tax rules, see section 26.3(b)(2)(iii).

(iv)   Assignment of Put Options

The writer of a put realizes no gain or loss when he purchases the stock underlying his short put option position. Instead, his basis in the stock is reduced by the amount of the option premium he received when he originally sold the put options.[100] In addition, his holding period for the underlying stock begins on the date the stock is purchased pursuant to exercise of the option.[101]

[95]Rev. Rul. 78-182, 1978-1 C.B. 265; I.R.C. § 1233(b). *See generally* Chapter 16.

[96]*See generally* Part Ten.

[97]*See* section 42.3; *see also* section 44.4.

[98]Rev. Rul. 78-182, 1978-1 C.B. 265; Rev. Rul. 58-234, 1958-1 C.B. 279; *see also* Rev. Rul. 72-198, 1972-1 C.B. 223.

[99]Rev. Rul. 58-234, 1958-1 C.B. 279.

[100]*Id.*

[101]Rev. Rul. 78-182, 1978-1 C.B. 265; *cf.* Weir v. Comm'r, 10 T.C. at 1000–01.

(d) SELLERS OF PUT AND CALL STRADDLES

If the seller of a straddle (i.e., a combination of a put option and call option where both positions are for the same option period and exercisable at the same market price) sells the components of the spread for separate identifiable premiums, the seller must utilize the separate premiums received for the put and call options in determining the respective gains and losses for each option.[102] If the put and call options are sold for a single premium, the seller must either allocate the premium among the component options according to the relative market value of each component or allocate 55 percent of the premium to the call and 45 percent to the put.[103]

(e) WARRANTS

(1) WARRANT OWNERS

(i) Acquisition of Warrants

If warrants are acquired by a stockholder in a corporate distribution, the transaction is taxable if the distribution is a taxable dividend.[104] If warrants are acquired in a nontaxable distribution, there is no immediate taxation, and the tax basis for the warrants is based on an allocation of the basis in the old stock in accordance with the fair market value of the old stock and the warrants.[105] If warrants are acquired in a taxable transaction, the amount that is included in the stockholder's income is the fair market value of the warrants on the date of distribution.[106] The fair market value is also the tax basis for the warrants. In general, basis is only allocated to warrants if they are exercised or sold and their value is de minimis, provided an express election is made.[107]

Warrants acquired by a purchase, gift, or inheritance are not taxed on their acquisition. The tax basis of such warrants is determined in accordance with the general rules for tax basis. For a discussion of the tax basis of warrants acquired by purchase, see section 14.2. For a

---

[102]Rev. Rul. 78-182, 1978-1 C.B. 265.

[103]*Id. See also* Rev. Proc. 65-29, 1965-2 C.B. 1023, declared obsolete (which authorized the allocation of premium in these proportions).

[104]*See generally* Chapter 22.

[105]*See* section 14.4(c).

[106]Treas. Reg. § 1.305-1(b) (1973).

[107]I.R.C. § 307(b); *see* section 14.4(c).

discussion of warrants acquired by gift, see section 14.3(a). For a discussion of warrants acquired from a decedent, see section 14.3(b).

(ii) Disposition, Lapse, or Exercise of Warrants

In many ways, the tax treatment of a warrant holder is the same as the tax treatment for purchasers of equity call options.[108] Because warrants are specifically excluded from the statutory definition of listed options under I.R.C. § 1256(g)(5),[109] warrants purchased by option dealers do not qualify for section 1256 treatment as dealer equity options.[110]

The major tax issue with respect to warrants[111] is calculating the premiums paid by purchasers to acquire warrants that are not traded in established markets. For those warrants that are traded on stock exchanges (e.g., Pan Am Corp., Occidental Petroleum Corp., Trans. World Corp., and Commonwealth Edison Company) the determination of the premium is easy.

Warrants issued with debt securities as part of an investment package can be difficult to value. The amount paid for warrants bought as part of a package with debt securities is determined based on the interest rate at which the debt securities would have been issued without the warrants.[112] If convertible debt securities are part of the investment package, the price payable at redemption is generally deemed to be the issue price and no portion of the amount paid for the convertible securities is allocable to warrants.[113]

Premium valuation questions also arise with respect to warrants issued in connection with corporate reorganizations or to underwriters for services performed for corporate issuers.[114] Valuation for purposes of determining the premium (including compensation for services rendered) can be based on various valuation formulas.[115]

---

[108]See generally Rev. Rul. 70-521, 1970-2 C.B. 72; Rev. Rul. 63-225, 1963-2 C.B. 339; I.R.C. § 1234. For a discussion of the tax treatment of equity call option purchasers, see section 26.3(b)(1).

[109]See section 26.1(a).

[110]See section 26.1(d); section 32.4.

[111]See section 1.1(d); section 26.1(e).

[112]Treas. Reg. § 1.1232-3(b)(2)(ii) (1980).

[113]Treas. Reg. § 1.1232-3(b)(2)(i) (1980); see generally section 28.3.

[114]For a discussion of underwriters' options, see section 9.11(a).

[115]See Weigl v. Comm'r, 84 T.C. 1192 (1985). See generally Shelton, *The Relation of the Price of a Warrant to the Price of its Associated Stock*, (Pts. 1 & 2) 23 FIN. ANALYSIS J., May-June 1967, at 143, and 23 FIN. ANALYSIS J., July-Aug 1967, at 88.

(2) WARRANT ISSUERS

Under current laws, corporate issuers do not recognize any gain or loss with respect to the acquisition or lapse of their warrants. This rule applies after July 18, 1984.[116] A corporation may issue options to buy or sell its stock (including treasury stock) on a tax-free basis.[117]

For warrants acquired or lapsed prior to July 19, 1984, the tax treatment of the corporate issuer was unclear. Prior to 1972, many commentators assumed that the amounts received by a corporate issuer for its warrants were a contribution to capital and therefore not taxable.[118] In 1972, however, the IRS issued a ruling (applying pre-1976 law) that stated that a corporate issuer realized income (ordinary income under I.R.C. § 1234(b) prior to its amendment in 1976)[119] on the lapse of its warrants in the amount of the fair market value of the warrants at the time they were issued.[120]

(f) APPLICATION OF RULES DEFERRING LOSS OR CHANGING CHARACTER OF GAIN OR LOSS

(1) STRADDLE RULES

The Straddle Rules apply generally to equity option positions established after December 31, 1983 in taxable years ending after that date.[121] The Straddle Rules include the loss deferral rule, the modified wash sales rule, the modified short sales rule, and the requirement to capitalize interest and carrying charges. These rules can apply to defer loss and to change the character of gain or loss. For a discussion of the Straddle Rules, see generally Part Ten. For application of the Straddle Rules to option positions, see section 36.4(b).

There are exemptions from the Straddle Rules that may apply to certain option transactions. First, short call option positions that qualify

---

[116]DRA, *supra* note 20, § 57(a) (codified at I.R.C. § 1032(a)).

[117]I.R.C. § 1032(a).

[118]*See generally* B. BITTKER & J. EUSTICE, FEDERAL INCOME TAXATION OF CORPORATIONS AND SHAREHOLDERS ¶ 4.06, at 4–27 (1971 ed.).

[119]Tax Reform Act of 1976, *supra* note 50, §§ 1402(b)(1)(U), (b)(2), 2136(a) (amending I.R.C. § 1234(b)).

[120]Rev. Rul. 72-198, 1972-1 C.B. 223; Rev. Rul. 77-40, 1977-1 C.B. 248 (ruling that Rev. Rul. 72-198 only applies to warrants issued after April 24, 1972); Rev. Rul. 78-73, 1978-1 C.B. 265 (ruling that Rev. Rul. 77-40 is amplified to make it clear that Rev. Rul. 72-198 does not apply to warrants issued after April 24, 1972 if issued pursuant to a legally enforceable contract on April 24, 1972 and at all times thereafter); Rev. Rul. 80-134, 1980-1 C.B. 187.

[121]DRA, *supra* note 20, § 101(e).

for the covered call exemption are exempt from the Straddle Rules.[122] Second, hedging transactions that meet the statutory hedging exemption are exempt from the Straddle Rules.[123] Third, it is possible, although not assured, that the married put exception provided in the short sales rule[124] is available as an exemption from the Straddle Rules.[125]

(2) WASH SALES RULE

The modified wash sales rule applies to positions that are part of a straddle. In many cases the wash sales rule of I.R.C. § 1091[126] may also apply. Some transactions technically fall into both the wash sales and the modified wash sales rules. Temporary Treasury regulations make it clear that the modified wash sales rule takes precedence over the wash sales rule.[127]

(3) SHORT SALES RULE

The modified short sales rule applies to positions that are part of a straddle. In many cases the short sales rule of I.R.C. § 1233 could also apply. However, the short sales rule of I.R.C. § 1233[128] provides that "property" subject to the short sales rule does not include any position to which the modified short sales rule applies.[129] As a result, the modified short sales rule takes precedence over the short sales rule. The short sales rule can be read narrowly. It may, in fact, be limited to short sales of stock.[130]

§ 26.4 SECTION 1256 OPTIONS

Certain options are subject to section 1256 treatment, which means that they are marked-to-market at year-end and those options that are capital assets are taxed as 60 percent long-term and 40 percent short-term capital gain or loss. For a discussion of section 1256 treatment, see generally Part Nine.

[122]*See* section 44.3.

[123]*See generally* section 6.4; Chapter 21; section 44.2.

[124]*See* section 16.4.

[125]*See* section 44.4.

[126]*See generally* Chapter 17.

[127]*See* section 42.1; section 42.3.

[128]*See generally* Chapter 16.

[129]I.R.C. § 1233(e)(2).

[130]*See* section 16.1.

Options that are eligible for section 1256 treatment are nonequity options and dealer equity options. For a discussion of nonequity options, see section 32.3. For a discussion of dealer equity options, see section 32.4. Once section 1256 applies to an options position, spreads consisting exclusively of section 1256 positions are not subject to the Straddle Rules.[131] Spreads and other offsetting positions where at least one, but not all, of the positions are section 1256 contracts are referred to as "mixed straddles," subject to the various mixed straddle rules.[132] Hedging transactions that qualify for the statutory hedging exemption are exempt from the Straddle Rules.[133]

---

[131]*See* section 44.7.
[132]*See generally* Chapter 45.
[133]*See generally* Chapter 21.

Part Seven

Taxation of Debt Securities and Options on Debt Securities

Twenty-seven

General Principles for Taxation of Debt Securities

§ 27.1 IN GENERAL

This chapter addresses general tax principles for the taxation of debt securities. It discusses the special tax rules that apply to tax-exempt securities and to short-term obligations. The wash sales rule,[1] the short sales rule,[2] and the Straddle Rules[3] apply to taxpayers holding debt securities unless specific exemptions are available. In addition, investors and traders are subject to the general rules for capital transactions,[4] while dealers, hedgers, and certain financial institutions are subject to the general rules for ordinary income transactions.[5]

§ 27.2 ORIGINAL ISSUE DISCOUNT

OID is the difference between the issue price of a debt security and its stated redemption price at maturity.[6] The concept is that if a debt

[1]*See generally* Chapter 17.
[2]*See generally* Chapter 16.
[3]*See generally* Part Ten.
[4]*See generally* Part Three.
[5]*See generally* Part Four.
[6]I.R.C. § 1273(a)(1).

security is originally issued at a price that is less than its redemption value at maturity, this discount amount is a form of interest that must be included in the owner's income. It can be deducted by the issuer. The discount is allocated over the life of the security through a series of adjustments to the security's issue price. The method used to adjust the issue price depends on the date the security was issued and whether it is a corporate, government, short-term, or tax-exempt security. OID on a security is carried over from one purchaser to the next. The OID rules have changed in many ways since enactment of the 1954 Code. They were first applied to corporate securities in 1969, to government securities in 1982, and were amended in 1984 to treat all taxable securities in the same way. In addition, there are special rules for short-term securities and tax-exempt securities. This section discusses OID.

(a) CORPORATE AND GOVERNMENT DEBT SECURITIES ISSUED AFTER JULY 1, 1982

Holders of either corporate or government debt securities issued after July 1, 1982 with a term to maturity exceeding one year must include in income the sum of the daily portion of OID determined for each day during the taxable year the security is held by the taxpayer.[7] The issuer's interest deduction is also subject to these rules.[8] For taxable securities, OID is ignored under a di minimus exception if the difference is less than .25 percent per year of the stated redemption price at maturity when multiplied by the number of complete years to maturity.[9] For debt securities issued before January 1, 1985, OID is allocated over the life of the security through a series of adjustments to the issue price for each "bond period" (i.e., the first one-year period beginning on the security's issue date and each subsequent anniversary, or the shorter period to maturity for the last period). The increase in the adjusted issue price for any bond period is allocated ratably to each day in the bond period.[10] In the case of securities issued after December 31, 1984, the adjustments are made on the basis of six-month "accrual periods" that end on the day in the calendar year that corresponds to the maturity date or the date six months before the maturity date.[11] Each adjustment is allocated ratably to each day in the period, which is included in the

[7] I.R.C. § 1272(a)(1).
[8] I.R.C. § 163(e).
[9] I.R.C. § 1273(a)(3).
[10] I.R.C. § 1272(a)(3).
[11] I.R.C. § 1272(a)(5).

taxpayer's income for each day he holds the securities during the taxable year.[12]

The adjustment to a debt security's issue price, which is made each "bond period" or "accrual period" (whichever is applicable), increases the issue price as adjusted from the previous period. The adjustment made each period equals the adjusted issue price of the debt security at the beginning of the period multiplied by the security's yield to maturity minus the interest payable during the period.[13]

A subsequent owner of an OID security who purchased it for more than the debt security's adjusted issue price (i.e., the issue price plus the daily portions of OID for all days prior to the purchase) is allowed an offset to the amount of OID included in income. For securities purchased before July 19, 1984, this "acquisition premium" is allocated on a straight-line basis over the number of days remaining to maturity. For securities purchased after July 18, 1984, the excess purchase price is amortized by reducing the daily portion of OID by the amount that would be the daily portion multiplied by a fraction reflecting the ratio of the acquisition premium to the total unaccrued OID at purchase.[14]

The taxpayer's basis in a security is increased by the amount of OID included in his income.[15] Gain on the sale or redemption of debt securities is treated as interest to the extent of OID minus the portion of OID previously included in income if there was an intention (at the time of issuance) to call the debt security before maturity.[16] Redemptions pursuant to a mandatory sinking fund may evidence an intent to call debt securities before maturity. A mandatory sinking fund could also accelerate the inclusion of OID under the rules that apply to debt securities with serial maturity provisions as well. The amount of gain realized on the exchange of OID debt securities issued with an intention to call the securities before maturity is not taxed as ordinary income if the gain is otherwise nonrecognized because of a nonrecognition provision such as I.R.C. § 354(a).[17]

A corporate issuer with debt securities that were issued at a discount outstanding in registered form must furnish the registered owner and the IRS with an information statement on IRS Form 1099-OID for the calendar year if there is at least $10 of OID for the calendar year.[18] Because the amount of OID includable in the owner's gross income is

[12]I.R.C. § 1272(a)(1).
[13]I.R.C. § 1272(a)(3).
[14]I.R.C. § 1272(a)(6).
[15]I.R.C. § 1272(d)(2).
[16] I.R.C. § 1271(a)(2)(A).
[17]Rev. Rul. 75-39, 1975-1 C.B. 272.
[18]Treas. Reg. § 1.6049-6(a) (1983).

treated as interest, it is subject to backup withholding, with the amount to be withheld limited to cash payments made to payees (e.g., payments of stated interest and payments on redemption or maturity).[19]

(b) CORPORATE DEBT SECURITIES ISSUED AFTER MAY 27, 1969 AND BEFORE JULY 2, 1982

The owner of corporate debt securities with maturities in excess of one year issued after May 27, 1969 and before July 2, 1982, must include in income the "ratable monthly portion" of OID (i.e., OID divided by the number of complete months from the date of issuance through the day before the stated maturity) multiplied by the number of complete months and fractions thereof that he held such securities during the taxable year.[20] The basis of the security is increased by the amount of OID that was included in his income.[21]

In the event of a sale or exchange of corporate debt securities issued after May 27, 1969, the purchaser of a security is treated as stepping into the shoes of the first owner. Thus, the untaxed balance of the OID that is not includable in the income of the prior owner or owners is included in the income of the subsequent owner ratably over the remaining life of the security. The amount is prorated on a daily basis for corporate and government securities issued after July 1, 1982,[22] and on a monthly basis for corporate securities issued after May 27, 1969 and before July 2, 1982.[23] If the subsequent owner purchases a debt security for an amount in excess of its adjusted basis in the hands of the prior owner or owners of the security, however, the ratable amount of the excess is allowed as a reduction or offset. This is accomplished by allowing the subsequent holder the option of determining his ratable monthly portion by dividing the amount by which the debt security's stated redemption price at maturity exceeds the security's cost to him by the number of complete months plus any fractional months from the date he purchased the security and ending on the day before maturity.[24] Subsequent holders are treated in a similar manner.[25]

---

[19]Temp. Treas. Reg. § 35a.9999-2(A-15) (1983). The time and the manner of backup withholding for OID depends on the type of security on which the OID is earned. *See generally* I.R.C. § 3406 and the temporary Treasury regulations issued thereunder.

[20]I.R.C. § 1272(b)(1); Treas. Reg. § 1.1232-3A(a)(2) (1975).

[21]I.R.C. § 1272(d)(2).

[22]I.R.C. § 1272(a)(1).

[23]I.R.C. § 1272(b)(1).

[24]I.R.C. § 1272(b)(4); Treas. Reg. §§ 1.1232-3A(a)(2), (3) (1975).

[25]I.R.C. § 1272(b)(4); Treas. Reg. §§ 1.1232-3A(a)(2), (3) (1975).

Any corporate issuer with any debt securities outstanding in registered form issued after May 27, 1969 at a discount must furnish the registered owner and the IRS with an information statement[26] for the calendar year if there is at least $10 of OID for the calendar year and the term of the security is more than one year.[27]

(c) CORPORATE DEBT SECURITIES ISSUED BEFORE MAY 28, 1969 AND GOVERNMENT DEBT SECURITIES ISSUED BEFORE JULY 2, 1982

For corporate debt securities issued after December 31, 1954 and before May 28, 1969, and for government securities issued after December 31, 1954 and before July 2, 1982, the holder pays no tax on the OID until the security is sold, exchanged, or redeemed.[28] This provision allowed a cash basis taxpayer the opportunity to defer discount income until he was actually paid. Upon sale or redemption of such securities, any gain is treated as ordinary income to the extent of an amount equal to the OID multiplied by a fraction the numerator of which is the number of full months the owner holds the security and the denominator of which is the number of months from issuance to maturity.[29] For investors[30] and traders,[31] any excess gain is capital gain (long-term or short-term depending on the taxpayer's holding period).[32] Dealers,[33] hedgers,[34] and certain financial institutions[35] report ordinary income on the entire gain.

(d) SHORT-TERM CORPORATE AND GOVERNMENT OBLIGATIONS

OID on a short-term security is generally not included in income by a cash basis taxpayer prior to sale or redemption unless the taxpayer elects to include OID in income as it accrues.[36] Under the law in effect

---

[26]This statement is provided on IRS Form 1099-OID.

[27]Treas. Reg. § 1.6049-6(a) (1983).

[28]I.R.C. § 1271(c)(2).

[29]I.R.C. § 1271(c)(2); Treas. Reg. § 1.1232-3(c) (1980).

[30]See section 6.1.

[31]See section 6.2.

[32]I.R.C. § 1271(c)(2)(A).

[33]See section 6.3.

[34]See section 6.4.

[35]See section 6.8.

[36]I.R.C. §§ 1281, 1282(b)(2), 1283(c).

prior to the DRA, the Code exempted short-term government securities payable without interest and due in one year or less (i.e., Treasury bills)[37] from the periodic inclusion of OID for all taxpayers.[38] A similar exemption from the OID rules was available for the obligations of natural persons,[39] and tax-exempt securities.[40] In addition, interest on indebtedness incurred to purchase or carry securities eligible for these exemptions was currently deductible against unrelated income.[41]

The DRA changes these provisions for securities acquired by certain taxpayers after July 18, 1984. Acquisition discount (i.e., the difference between the stated redemption price at maturity and the taxpayer's basis in the security)[42] on short-term securities must now be accrued if the securities are held by (1) a taxpayer using the accrual method of accounting;[43] (2) a bank;[44] (3) a taxpayer who holds the securities primarily for sale to customers in the ordinary course of business;[45] (4) a taxpayer who identifies the securities as being part of a hedging transaction;[46] (5) a regulated investment company;[47] (6) a common trust fund;[48] (7) a partnership, S corporation, trust, or other flow-through entity if more than 20 percent of the value of the entity is owned for 90 days by taxpayers who are subject to the rule for mandatory accrual;[49] and (8) any flow-through entity that is formed or availed of to avoid mandatory accrual.[50] A "short-term obligation" is defined as any bond, debenture, note, or certificate or other evidence of indebtedness with a fixed maturity date not more than one year from the date of issue.[51] Acquisition discount accrued on a daily basis is computed so that each

---

[37]*See* section 2.1(a)(1).

[38]I.R.C. § 1232A(a)(2)(C) (1983), *repealed by* DRA, Pub. L. 98-369, § 42(a)(1), 98 Stat. 494, 556 (1984).

[39]I.R.C. § 1232A(a)(2)(A) (1983), *repealed by* DRA, *supra* note 38, § 42(a)(1).

[40]I.R.C. § 1232A(a)(2)(B)(ii) (1983), *repealed by* DRA, *supra* note 38, § 42(a)(1). For a discussion of tax-exempt securities, see section 28.2.

[41]I.R.C. § 163(a).

[42]I.R.C. § 1283(a)(2).

[43]I.R.C. § 1281(b)(1).

[44]*Id.*

[45]*Id.*

[46]*Id.*

[47]*Id.*

[48]*Id.*

[49]I.R.C. §§ 1281(b)(2)(C), (D).

[50]I.R.C. § 1281(b)(2)(A).

[51]I.R.C. § 1283(a)(1)(A).

daily portion is equal to the amount of the discount divided by the number of days from the day after the acquisition to the maturity date.[52]

A taxpayer's ability to currently deduct interest is also limited for indebtedness incurred to purchase or carry securities not subject to mandatory accrual. If a taxpayer is not subject to mandatory accrual, his "net direct interest expense" (defined as the excess of interest paid or accrued to carry a security over the interest or OID included in income from the security)[53] with respect to a short-term security is deductible only to the extent that the interest expense exceeds the sum of the daily portions of acquisition discount.[54]

For taxable years ending after July 18, 1984, a transitional year election to accrue acquisition discount is available to taxpayers subject to mandatory accrual for all short-term securities held during the taxable year that includes July 18, 1984.[55] If the election is made, the accrual of discount is treated as a change in the taxpayer's accounting method, and the net adjustments to income required by the new rules are made over a five-year period, beginning with the year in which the election is made.[56]

For short-term government securities issued after July 18, 1984, a cash basis taxpayer can elect to include acquisition discount in income. Such an election applies to all short-term taxable securities acquired on or after the first day of the first year for which the election is made and continues in effect unless the IRS consents to a revocation.[57] Acquisition discount accrues ratably on a daily basis; the discount is divided by the number of days after the date the taxpayer acquires the security up to and including the date of maturity.[58] A taxpayer can elect, however, to use a constant interest rate (based on yield to maturity) for certain short-term securities and ratable accrual on other short-term securities.[59] As a practical matter, cash basis taxpayers may decide to elect to accrue acquisition discounts so they can currently deduct interest expense.

Gain or loss on the sale or redemption of a short-term security is

---

[52]I.R.C. § 1283(b)(1).

[53]I.R.C. § 1277(c).

[54]I.R.C. § 1282(a).

[55]DRA, *supra* note 38, at § 41(a) (codified at I.R.C. § 1282(b)(2)).

[56]DRA, *supra* note 38, at § 44(e)(2).

[57]I.R.C. § 1282(b).

[58]I.R.C. § 1283(b)(1).

[59]I.R.C. § 1283(b)(2).

generally treated as capital gain or loss for investors[60] and traders,[61] and ordinary income or loss to dealers,[62] hedgers,[63] and certain financial institutions.[64] For all taxpayers (including investors and traders) any OID recovered on a sale or redemption of a short-term security is treated as interest.[65]

(e) TAX-EXEMPT SECURITIES

Under IRS rulings issued prior to the DRA, OID on tax-exempt securities was apportioned among the original holder and subsequent holders of a security on a straight-line basis over the term of the security.[66] In many cases, the use of the straight-line method would result in artificially large portions of the OID of a security being attributed to its earlier bond periods. Further, because the holder of a tax-exempt security reduces the amount realized on disposition by the accrued (but tax-exempt) OID, the straight-line method could also result in the recognition of an artificial loss on disposition of the security for its market price.[67]

Such artificial losses are no longer available to taxpayers. For tax-exempt securities issued after September 3, 1982 and acquired after March 1, 1984, OID is accrued in the same manner as that required since 1982 for OID on taxable debt securities,[68] except that there is no di minimus exception. Thus, all discounts (including those which are less than .25 percent) are accounted for.[69] OID on tax-exempt securities

---

[60]See section 6.1.

[61]See section 6.2.

[62]See section 6.3.

[63]See section 6.4.

[64]See section 6.8.

[65]U.S. v. Midland-Ross Corp., 381 U.S. 54 (1965); Treas. Reg. § 1.1232-3A(b)(2) (1975); STAFF OF THE JOINT COMMITTEE ON TAXATION, 98TH CONG. 2D SESS., GENERAL EXPLANATION OF THE REVENUE PROVISIONS OF THE DEFICIT REDUCTION ACT OF 1984 103 (Joint Comm. Print 1984). The proposed Technical Corrections Act of 1985 makes this clear by treating any gain that represents OID as ordinary income. H.R. 1800, 99th Cong., 1st Sess. § 103(a) (1985).

[66]HOUSE CONFERENCE REPORT, DEFICIT REDUCTION ACT OF 1984, H.R. REP. NO. 861, 98th Cong., 2d Sess. 810, reprinted in 1984 U.S. CODE CONG. & AD. NEWS 1445, 1498; Rev. Rul. 73-112, 1973-1 C.B. 47.

[67]HOUSE WAYS AND MEANS COMMITTEE REPORT, DEFICIT REDUCTION ACT OF 1984, H.R. REP. NO. 432, 98th Cong., 2d Sess. 1178, reprinted in 1984 U.S. CODE CONG. & AD. NEWS 697, 851.

[68]I.R.C. § 1288(a).

[69]I.R.C. § 1288(b)(1).

is accrued under the "economic" or "constant" (compound) interest method, which reflects the actual market appreciation of these securities.[70]

§ 27.3 MARKET DISCOUNT BONDS

Generally, if a security is issued at a discount, the difference between the issue price and the redemption price is OID,[71] which is deemed to be additional interest income to the holder[72] and additional interest expense to the issuer. OID is allocated over the term of the security.[73] The prices of debt securities fluctuate as interest rates change and as the issuer's financial condition and credit ratings change. As a result, debt securities issued without OID can be acquired at a discount or a premium from the original issue price. A debt security purchased at a price that is less than its issue price has market discount.

Market discount is defined as the amount by which the stated redemption price of a security (i.e., a revised issue price in the case of a security with OID) exceeds the security's basis immediately after acquisition if it was issued at par.[74] It also includes the amount by which a security is purchased in the market for less than it was issued for, after its price is increased by the amount of OID accruing from issue until the date of purchase.[75] It does not apply to (1) short-term securities with fixed maturities not exceeding one year,[76] (2) tax-exempt securities,[77] (3) United States savings bonds,[78] (4) securities where the total market discount is less than .25 percent of the stated redemption price at maturity multiplied by the number of years until maturity,[79] and (5) certain installment bonds.[80]

Under pre-DRA law, a taxpayer who was an investor or trader and who purchased a security at a price below its issue price (i.e., a market discount bond) could treat the difference on sale or at maturity as a

---

[70]See H.R. REP. No. 432, *supra* note 67, at 1178-79.
[71]I.R.C. §§ 1278(a)(5), 1273(a)(1).
[72]I.R.C. § 1272(a)(1).
[73]I.R.C. § 163(e).
[74]I.R.C. § 1278(a)(2)(A).
[75]I.R.C. § 1278(a)(2).
[76]I.R.C. § 1278(a)(1)(B)(i).
[77]I.R.C. § 1278(a)(1)(B)(ii).
[78]I.R.C. § 1278(a)(1)(B)(iii); *see* section 2.1(a)(4); section 28.1(a)(2).
[79]I.R.C. § 1278(a)(2)(C).
[80]I.R.C. § 1278(a)(1)(B)(iv).

capital gain rather than as additional interest income.[81] This type of market discount arises whenever the value of a debt security declines after issuance (typically because of an increase in prevailing interest rates).[82]

From the standpoint of an owner of a debt security, market discount is indistinguishable from OID.[83] By making a financed purchase of a security with market discount, some taxpayers under pre-DRA law could effectively convert ordinary income (that would be offset by current interest deductions for interest incurred to carry the obligation) into capital gain (that is taxed on a deferred basis on the disposition of the security).[84] Two Code provisions now eliminate this opportunity for conversion for certain securities acquired with market discount. First, market discount is recharacterized as additional interest.[85] Second, interest incurred to purchase or carry a market discount bond is not deductible currently and must be deferred.[86] These rules are discussed in the remainder of this section.

(a) ACCRUED MARKET DISCOUNT

Gain on the disposition of market discount securities issued and acquired after July 18, 1984 must generally be recognized as interest income to the extent of the amount of market discount accrued by the taxpayer during the period he holds the security.[87] Accrued market discount for any security is an amount that bears the same ratio to the market discount on the security as the number of days during which the taxpayer held the security bears to the number of days from the date the taxpayer acquired the security until its maturity date.[88] At the election of the taxpayer, market discount can be computed using the constant (compound) interest method used to determine daily portions of OID accruing on debt securities issued after July 18, 1982.[89]

Market discount is not required to be included in income by a cash basis taxpayer until the security is sold or redeemed. For taxable years ending after July 18, 1984, however, a taxpayer can elect to include

[81] H.R. Rep. No. 432, *supra* note 67, at 1170.
[82] *Id.*
[83] *Id.*
[84] *Id.*
[85] I.R.C. § 1276(a)(3).
[86] I.R.C. § 1277.
[87] I.R.C. §§ 1276(a)(1), (3).
[88] I.R.C. § 1276(b)(1).
[89] I.R.C. § 1276(b)(2).

market discount as it accrues on certain securities. Once an election is made, it applies to all market discount securities (as defined to exclude short-term, tax-exempt, United States savings bonds, and certain installment securities) acquired by the taxpayer in the tax year of the election and in subsequent years unless he receives IRS approval to revoke the election.[90] Accrued market discount is generally treated as interest. Under this election, market discount is accrued on a straight-line basis, although the taxpayer can elect (irrevocably) to use a constant interest rate (i.e., the method used for OID on debt securities issued after July 1, 1982) for particular securities. If a taxpayer elects to accrue market discount on the straight-line basis, the discount is determined by dividing the total market discount by the number of days remaining after the acquisition until the date of maturity.[91] This method accrues market discount in equal daily installments during the period between acquisition and maturity.

Gain on the sale of a market discount security is generally treated as interest income to the extent of accrued but untaxed market discount up to the date of disposition.[92] If the taxpayer elects to include market discount in income currently, none of the gain upon disposition is treated as market discount.[93] Market discount on a convertible debt security is not recognized at the time of conversion but, instead, is carried over as an "attribute" of the stock acquired to assure that gain from the sale of the stock up to the accrued but untaxed market discount is treated as interest income.

(b) INTEREST DEFERRAL

A taxpayer's ability to currently deduct interest is limited for indebtedness incurred to purchase or carry securities with market discount. A taxpayer's net interest expense for debt securities acquired after July 18, 1984 is only deductible to the extent that the expense exceeds the amount of market discount allocable to the days during the taxable year on which the taxpayer held the securities.[94] For market discount bonds issued before July 18, 1984, any gain on the disposition of the securities is treated as interest income to the extent of any deferred interest ex-

---

[90]I.R.C. §§ 1278(b)(2), (3).
[91]I.R.C. § 1276(b).
[92]I.R.C. §§ 1276(a), (e).
[93]I.R.C. § 1278(b).
[94]I.R.C. § 1277(a).

pense.[95] To prevent the avoidance of this rule by financing debt securities through short sales,[96] the deduction of short sales expenses is also deferred where short sales of property are used to generate funds for the purchase of market discount bonds.[97] Interest expenses and other costs deferred as a result of this rule are allowed as a deduction for the taxable year in which the taxpayer disposes of the market discount securities,[98] or earlier at the taxpayer's election if and to the extent that the taxpayer has net interest income in the earlier year.

§ 27.4 PURCHASE PREMIUMS

A purchase premium is the amount a purchaser pays to acquire a debt security in excess of its face value. A purchaser is generally willing to buy a debt security at a premium if the security's interest rate or yield-to-maturity exceeds the current market interest rate. I.R.C. § 171 provides the rules on amortization of purchase premiums on debt securities. It does not apply to debt securities held during years before January 1, 1942, although it applies to the amount of the bond premium attributable to taxable years beginning after 1941. Premium attributable to periods prior to January 1, 1942 is treated as a capital loss at the time of the disposition of the securities. I.R.C. § 171 provides for the amortization of premiums on any interest bearing bond, debenture, note, certificate, or other evidence of indebtedness issued by any corporation, government, or political subdivision. It does not apply to any securities (1) that constitute stock in trade of the taxpayer,[99] (2) that would properly be included in the taxpayer's inventory if on hand at the end of the taxable year,[100] (3) held by the taxpayer primarily for sale to customers in the ordinary course of business,[101] and (4) held by dealers for purposes other than investment.[102] Amortization applies regardless of whether the security is in registered form or has interest coupons.[103]

---

[95]I.R.C. § 1277(d).
[96]See generally Chapter 16.
[97]H.R. Rep. No. 861, supra note 66, at 806.
[98]I.R.C. § 1277(b)(2)(A).
[99]I.R.C. § 171(d); Treas. Reg. § 1.171-4(a) (1957).
[100]I.R.C. § 171(d); Treas. Reg. § 1.171-4(a) (1957).
[101]I.R.C. § 171(d); Treas. Reg. § 1.171-4(a) (1957).
[102]Treas. Reg. § 1.171-4(c) (1957).
[103]Treas. Reg. § 1.171-4(a) (1957).

(a) IN GENERAL

(1) TAXABLE SECURITIES

Bond premiums paid on taxable and partially tax-exempt debt securities are deductible.[104] A taxpayer can elect to deduct the amount of the amortizable premium for the taxable year in computing taxable income.[105] If a taxpayer does not elect to amortize premiums, he reports a loss on redemption, either capital or ordinary depending on whether the security is a capital or ordinary asset in his hands.

If a taxpayer amortizes premiums, he must reduce the basis of the securities to account for the amount of the premium deducted each year.[106] Basis is adjusted to the extent of the amortizable bond premium attributable to the taxable year.[107]

A taxpayer who elects to amortize premiums and sells securities before maturity at a price above the amortized cost basis has a capital gain if he is not a dealer[108] or a financial institution.[109] If a taxpayer amortizes a security's premium from the date of acquisition, redemption at par should have no tax effect. If a taxpayer has not amortized all of the security's premium, however, its sale or redemption at face value results in a capital loss (for taxpayers who are neither dealers nor financial institutions).

Amortizable premium is an itemized deduction. As a result, a taxpayer cannot deduct amortizable premiums if he computes his taxes based on the optional tax tables[110] or if he elects the standard deduction.[111] A taxpayer who does not itemize but has elected to amortize bond premiums is nonetheless burdened with the reduction of his basis in the debt security to the extent that deductions for premium would have been allowed.[112]

Corporations, unlike other taxpayers, can only amortize bond premiums for fully taxable securities.[113] Taxpayers other than corporations, can elect to amortize premiums on partially tax-exempt securities as

---

[104]I.R.C. § 171(a)(1); Treas. Reg. §§ 1.171-1(b)(2), (3)(ii) (1957).

[105]Treas. Reg. § 1.171-1(b)(2) (1957).

[106]I.R.C. § 1016(a)(5); Treas. Reg. § 1.1016-5(b) (1980).

[107]I.R.C. §§ 171(a), 1016(a)(5); Treas. Reg. §§ 1.171-1(b)(2), (3) (1957).

[108]*See* section 6.3.

[109]*See* section 6.8.

[110]I.R.C. § 3.

[111]I.R.C. § 144 (repealed 1976).

[112]Treas. Reg. § 1.171-1(b)(5) (1957).

[113]Treas. Reg. § 1.171-3(a) (1957).

well.[114] Only the owners of common trust funds or foreign personal holding companies can authorize the election to amortize premiums.[115] Only the fiduciary of a trust or estate can elect to amortize premiums.[116]

An election to amortize the premium on any debt security applies to all debt securities held by the taxpayer at the beginning of the taxable year in which the election first applies, and it applies to all debt securities acquired in subsequent taxable years.[117] The IRS must consent to any revocation of the election.[118] The appropriate premium amounts must be deducted in the first taxable year for which the election applies and a taxpayer must attach a statement to his tax return showing the premium computation.[119] A taxpayer cannot subsequently decide to amortize premiums for prior years by filing an amended return or a refund claim.[120] Further, a taxpayer who did not amortize bond premiums in the year a security was acquired cannot report increased deductions in the remaining years to maturity. A taxpayer who originally did not elect to amortize premiums computes the applicable deduction by reducing the amount of the premium by the amount of premium that could have been taken in prior years and dividing that figure by the remaining years to maturity.[121]

Bond premium and the amortizable amount are determined using the method regularly employed by the taxpayer as long as the method is reasonable.[122] If the method is not reasonable, the bond premium and the amortizable amount are determined pursuant to Treasury regulations.[123] Under the regulations, the amortizable amount is an amount which bears the same ratio to the premium on the debt security as the number of months in the taxable year during which the security was held by the taxpayer bears to the number of months from the beginning of the taxable year (or, if the bond was acquired in the taxable year, from the date of acquisition) to the date of maturity or earlier call

---

[114]*Id.*

[115]I.R.C. § 171(c)(2). For the tax treatment of partially tax-exempt securities owned by such taxpayers, see Treas. Reg. § 1.171-3(c) (1957).

[116]I.R.C. § 171(c). For the tax treatment of partially tax-exempt securities owned by trusts or estates, see Treas. Reg. § 1.171-3(c) (1957).

[117]I.R.C. § 171(c)(2); Treas. Reg. § 1.171-3(a) (1957).

[118]I.R.C. § 171(c)(2); Treas. Reg. § 1.171-3(a) (1957).

[119]Treas. Reg. § 1.171-3(a) (1957).

[120]Barnhill v. Comm'r, 241 F.2d 496 (5th Cir. 1957).

[121]I.R.C. § 171(b)(1)(C); Treas. Reg. § 1.171-2(a)(4) (1968).

[122]I.R.C. § 171(b)(3)(A); Treas. Reg. § 1.171-2(f)(1) (1968).

[123]I.R.C. § 171(b)(3)(B); Treas. Reg. § 1.171-2(f) (1968).

date.[124] A security held for more than half of the days in one month is treated as if held for a full month.[125] Holding periods of fewer than half the days in one month are disregarded.[126] In Rev. Rul. 82-10,[127] the IRS approved the use of the yield-to-maturity method of amortizing bond premiums.[128]

Specific provisions regulate the tax treatment of amortizable premium on a debt security held by a decedent. For decedents who used cash basis accounting, interest earned on a debt security until the decedent's date of death is included in either the estate's or legatee's gross income.[129] The amount of amortizable bond premium attributable to the period prior to a decedent's death is not allowed as a deduction for the estate or legatee.[130] With partially tax-exempt bonds, the amount of the amortizable bond premium that a decedent can deduct cannot be used to reduce the estate's or the legatee's credit or deduction for interest for such period.[131] For decedents who used the accrual method of accounting, the interest earned on the securities during the period prior to the decedent's death is included in the decedent's income.[132] The deduction attributable to the amortizable bond premium is also taken into account in computing the decedent's gross income.[133]

(2) TAX-EXEMPT SECURITIES

(i) In General

A taxpayer who owns tax-exempt securities is required to amortize any premium he paid for the securities, although the amortized amount is not deductible.[134] A deduction for a premium paid to acquire tax-exempt securities would allow the taxpayer to reduce his income by an expense

---

[124]Treas. Reg. § 1.171-2(f)(2)(i) (1968).

[125]*Id.*

[126]*Id.*

[127]1982-1 C.B. 46.

[128]If enacted, the Tax Reform Act of 1985, H.R. 3838, would require constant interest amortization and would extend I.R.C. § 171 to obligations of individuals, such as auto buyers, whose receivables are pooled for purposes of creating asset-backed certificates. *See* section 1.1(e)(2).

[129]Treas. Reg. § 1.171-1(c)(1) (1957).

[130]*Id.*

[131]*Id.*

[132]Treas. Reg. § 1.171-1(c)(3) (1957).

[133]*Id.*

[134]I.R.C. §§ 171, 1016(a); Treas. Reg. § 1.171-1(b) (1957).

attributable to earning tax-exempt interest.[135] The premium paid, in effect, reduces the annual interest on tax-exempt securities because a portion of the interest received represents a partial return of premium.

The premium that must be amortized on a tax-exempt security is the amount by which the security's basis for determining loss (as adjusted to reflect a prior amortization) exceeds the face amount of the security at its maturity (or call date for callable securities).[136]

The amount of premium can be determined using any reasonable method, as long as it is used consistently in amortizing all tax-exempt securities owned by the taxpayer.[137] Any change in an amortization method must be approved by the IRS. The IRS has ruled that the "yield" method can be used for both taxable and tax-exempt securities.[138] In addition, Treasury regulations allow amortization where the taxpayer divides the number of months a security was held during the taxable year by the number of months from its acquisition to maturity, multiplied by the amount of premium.[139]

(ii) Dealers in Tax-Exempt Securities

Special provisions require the reduction of a taxpayer's "cost of goods sold" deduction by the amount of amortizable bond premiums to a dealer in "municipal bonds," defined to include all interest bearing tax-exempt securities issued by governments or political subdivisions.[140] For these purposes, a municipal security does not include any security where (1) the dealer sells or otherwise disposes of it within 30 days after its acquisition or the earliest maturity or call date is more than five years from the date the dealer acquired it, and (2) the amount realized from its sale (or the fair market value at the time of a disposition of which) exceeds its adjusted basis.[141]

In computing the gross income of a taxpayer subject to I.R.C. § 75 who uses inventories valued on any basis other than cost, the "cost of securities sold" is reduced by an amount equal to the amortizable bond premium that would be allowed as a deduction under I.R.C. § 171(a)(2). In the case of taxpayers subject to I.R.C. § 75 who compute their gross incomes without the use of inventories or with inventories valued at

---

[135]*See generally* section 7.3; section 28.2(b)(1).

[136]*See* section 27.4(c).

[137]Treas. Reg. § 1.171-2(f)(1) (1968).

[138]Rev. Rul. 82-10, 1982-1 C.B. 46.

[139]Treas. Reg. § 1.171-2(f)(2) (1968).

[140]I.R.C. § 75(b); Treas. Reg. § 1.75-1(a)(2) (1963).

[141]I.R.C. § 75(b)(1); Treas. Reg. § 1.75-1(a)(2) (1963).

cost, the adjusted basis of a municipal security is reduced by the amount of the adjustment required under I.R.C. § 1016(a) (5) for amortizable bond premiums.[142] The term "cost of securities sold" is the amount obtained by subtracting the value of the closing inventory of a taxable year from the sum of (1) the value of the opening inventory for such year, and (2) the cost of securities and other property purchased during the year that is included in the taxpayer's inventory if on hand at the close of the year.[143] The cost of securities sold is not reduced where the earliest call or maturity date is more than five years from the date the security is acquired and the security is owned by the taxpayer at the close of the taxable year.[144]

In the year a municipal security is sold or otherwise disposed of, the cost of securities sold for the year is reduced by the amounts provided by I.R.C. § 1016(a)(5),[145] without regard to the dealer's method of inventory valuation. If the dealer values his inventories at cost or does not use inventories, the adjusted basis of his municipal securities are not reduced until the taxable year in which the securities are sold or disposed of.[146]

Dealers are generally not required to amortize bond premiums.[147] However, because a dealer in tax-exempt securities may receive tax-free interest income, he may be more willing to pay a premium to acquire the securities. The adjustments required by I.R.C. § 75 were designed to eliminate the artificial loss and accompanying tax advantage that a dealer would otherwise receive by purchasing tax-exempt securities.

Example   27-1

Assume that a dealer must pay $1250 to acquire a bond that matures in five years and pays interest of $70 per year and $1000 at maturity. The premium is $250. If he holds the bond until maturity, he receives $350 in tax-exempt interest. Without the adjustments required by I.R.C. § 75, the dealer would have a loss of $250 on the disposition of the bond at maturity. This is an artificial loss because the bond actually provided $100 of revenue ($350 minus $250). To prevent an artificial loss, I.R.C. § 75 reduces the bond's cost basis.

---

[142]I.R.C. §§ 75(a)(1), (2).
[143]I.R.C. § 75(b); Treas. Reg. § 1.75-1(a)(3) (1963).
[144]Treas. Reg. § 1.75-1(b)(2) (1963).
[145]*Id.*
[146]I.R.C. § 75(a)(2); Treas. Reg. § 1.75-1(c) (1963).
[147]I.R.C. § 171(d).

Tax-exempt securities held for less than 30 days, or securities where the earliest call or maturity date is more than five years from the date of acquisition, that are sold or otherwise disposed of at a gain are not subject to the adjustments otherwise required by I.R.C. § 75.

(b) DETERMINATION OF AMORTIZABLE BOND PREMIUMS

In general, the bond premium of a security is the excess of the taxpayer's basis (for determining the loss on a sale or exchange) for the security over the amount payable at maturity.[148] A security is acquired on the date it was ordered under a firm commitment to buy (i.e., the trade date), and not the date it is delivered to the taxpayer (i.e., the settlement date).[149] Debt securities are considered to be acquired on the trade date even if the purchaser pays accrued interest through the settlement date.[150] The amount of premium amortizable during a taxable year is the amount of the premium attributable to that year.[151]

(c) CALLABLE SECURITIES

(1) TAXABLE SECURITIES

Callable securities are securities that an issuer can retire at a certain date or dates prior to the stated maturity date. To retire callable securities prior to the stated maturity date, the issuer usually must pay the owners an amount that exceeds face value. Amortizable premium on callable securities is often calculated differently from the premium on noncallable securities. Under some circumstances, the earlier call date is considered to be the maturity date for purposes of determining the amortization period.[152] The term "earlier call date" can have several meanings. It can be (1) the earliest call date specified in the security as a day certain, (2) the earliest interest payment date if the security is callable at such date, (3) the earliest date at which the security is callable at par, or (4) such other call date, prior to maturity, specified in the security as selected by the taxpayer.[153]

In the case of securities issued after January 22, 1951, acquired after

---

[148]*See* I.R.C. § 171(b)(1); Treas. Reg. § 1.171-2(a) (1968).

[149]Treas. Reg. § 1.171-2(a)(2)(i) (1968).

[150]Rev. Rul. 66-97, 1966-1 C.B. 190.

[151]I.R.C. § 171(b)(2); Treas. Reg. § 1.171-2(a)(6) (1968).

[152]Treas. Reg. § 1.171-2(b) (1968).

[153]*Id.*

January 22, 1954, and acquired before January 1, 1958, the earlier call date can be used to compute the amortizable bond premium only if the earlier call date is more than three years from the date the securities were originally issued. If the call date on such securities falls within three years of issue, the amortizable premium is determined by computing the difference between the security's basis and the amount payable at maturity.[154] In the case of callable securities acquired after December 31, 1957, the earlier call date is used to calculate the bond premium only if the excess of the security's basis over the amount payable on an earlier call date results in a smaller amortizable premium attributable to the period between the acquisition date and earlier call date than results by calculating the bond premium for that period using the excess of the security's basis over the amount payable at maturity.[155]

When a security has multiple call dates, the amount of the amortizable premium is initially calculated with reference to the earliest call date. If not called on that date, any remaining unamortized premium is amortized to a subsequent call date or maturity.[156]

If a callable security is redeemed prior to its maturity date, a compensating amortizing adjustment may be necessary in the year the bond is redeemed. The amount of the amortizable premium attributable to the tax year in which the security is called includes an amount equal to the excess of the security's adjusted basis, as of the beginning of that taxable year, over the amount received upon redemption of the security at an earlier call date.[157]

In cases where the taxpayer holding a callable security also has a "buy back agreement" or put option with the seller, the amount of the amortizable premium is nevertheless determined with reference to the call price.[158]

(2) TAX-EXEMPT SECURITIES

Special rules apply to tax-exempt callable securities. Where there is more than one call date, the premium must be amortized to the earliest call date.[159] If the security is not called at the earliest call date, the

---

[154]Treas. Reg. § 1.171-2(a)(2)(i) (1968).

[155]I.R.C. § 171(b)(1); Treas. Reg. § 1.171-2(a)(2)(i) (1968).

[156]Treas. Reg. § 1.171-2(b)(2) (1968).

[157]I.R.C. § 171(b)(2); Treas. Reg. § 1.171-2(a)(2)(iii) (1968).

[158]Industrial Research Prods., Inc. v. Comm'r, 40 T.C. 578, 588 (1963).

[159]Pacific Affiliate, Inc. v. Comm'r, 18 T.C. 1175, 1208 (1952), aff'd, 224 F.2d 578 (9th Cir. 1955), cert. denied, 350 U.S. 967 (1956).

premium is then amortized to the next call date or, if no other call date exists, to maturity.[160] The basis of the security is reduced accordingly.

Example   27-2

Assume that a taxpayer purchased two $1000 tax-exempt bonds on January 1, 1973 that mature in 20 years for $2200. The bonds are callable on January 1, 1977 for $2120. For the four-year period between January 1, 1973 and January 1, 1977, the taxpayer must reduce the basis of these bonds by $80 ($2200 minus $2120), the amount of the nondeductible, amortizable bond premium. If the bonds were not called on January 1, 1977, however, the remaining $120 premium would be amortized over the remaining 16 years to maturity. If there is no call date between the first call date and maturity, the remaining unamortized premium would be amortized on a straight-line basis to maturity.[161]

(d) CONVERTIBLE DEBT SECURITIES

Amortization of premium applies to convertible debt securities.[162] Under no circumstances, however, can any amount of the premium attributable to the owner's conversion privilege be amortized.[163] The value of a debt security's conversion feature is determined as of the date of the security's acquisition by subtracting the price that would have been paid for the security on the open market if it had not been convertible from the security's cost at acquisition. The determination of the assumed price for a nonconvertible security is a two step procedure. First, the yield on nonconvertible securities of a similar character is determined. Second, the price currently paid is ascertained by using standard bond tables to determine the current price of securities at the same yield that have the same classification and grade.[164]

If a security is converted before the full amount of the premium not attributable to the conversion feature is amortized, a taxpayer cannot deduct the unamortized premium in the year of conversion. Rather, the

---

[160]Rev. Rul. 60-17, 1960-1 C.B. 124. A premium paid on the call of a tax-exempt security before maturity is taxable as a capital gain (or ordinary income for dealers and certain financial institutions) not as tax-exempt interest. Rev. Rul. 72-587, 1972-2 C.B. 74; *see also* Rev. Rul. 74-172, 1974-1 C.B. 178; Bryant v. Comm'r, 2 T.C. 789 (1943); District Bond Co. v. Comm'r, 1 T.C. 837 (1943).

[161]Because there is only one call date in this example, the remaining premium of $120 is amortized at an annual rate of $7.50 over the next 16 years.

[162]For a discussion of convertible securities, see section 1.1(c) and section 28.3.

[163]National Can Corp. v. U.S., 687 F.2d 1107 (7th Cir. 1982); I.R.C. § 171(b); Treas. Reg. § 1.171-2(c)(1) (1968).

[164]Treas. Reg. § 1.171-2(c)(2) (1968).

portion of the premium remaining unamortized is treated as part of the cost basis of the new security received upon conversion of the old security. Thus, the basis of the new security is the same as that of the security relinquished.[165]

An issuing corporation cannot deduct a premium paid or incurred upon the repurchase of a convertible debt security into stock of (1) the issuing corporation or (2) a company in control of or controlled by the issuing corporation to the extent that the repurchase price of the debt security exceeds the adjusted issue price plus a normal call premium on nonconvertible securities.[166] The issuing corporation can claim a deduction, however, to the extent it can prove that the excess premium is attributable to the cost of borrowing and not the conversion feature.[167]

(e) AMORTIZATION OF CAPITALIZED EXPENSES

A taxpayer is permitted but is not required to amortize capitalized expenses, such as buying commissions, as a premium if he (1) regularly amortizes capitalized expenses and uses a reasonable method, (2) amortizes capitalized expenses and uses the method of amortization prescribed by Treasury regulations, or (3) uses a reasonable amortization method but does not amortize capitalized expenses.[168]

If there is a premium exclusive of capitalized expenses, there are two different methods available to capitalize expenses. First, a taxpayer who regularly amortizes capitalized expenses and uses a reasonable method of amortization must treat the capitalized expenses as part of the premium.[169] Second, if a taxpayer does not generally use an amortization method that treats capitalized expenses as part of the premium for purposes of amortization, the taxpayer can (but is not required to) treat the capitalized expenses as part of the premium.[170]

§ 27.5   ZERO COUPON SECURITIES

Zero coupon securities are debt securities payable without interest at a fixed maturity date.[171] They trade at very deep discount. The difference

---

[165]*See* Ades v. Comm'r, 38 T.C. 501, 512 (1962), *aff'd*, 316 F.2d 734 (2d Cir. 1963).

[166]I.R.C. § 249(a); Treas. Reg. § 1.249-1(a) (1973).

[167]I.R.C. § 249(a); Treas. Reg. § 1.249-1(b) (1973); *see* section 28.3(a).

[168]Treas. Reg. § 1.171-2(d)(1) (1968).

[169]Treas. Reg. § 1.171-2(d)(2)(i) (1968).

[170]Treas. Reg. § 1.171-2(d)(2)(iii) (1968).

[171]*See generally* section 2.2(e).

between the original discounted price and the par amounts represent a compounded annual yield at the original interest rate. There is no reinvestment risk because the original rate is locked in. In other words, the owner's yield is assured as long as the issuer meets its payment obligations when the zero matures.[172] For tax purposes, zeros issued after July 1, 1982 are considered to be OID securities so that OID is accrued in accordance with the OID rules.[173] This section looks first at taxable zeros and then at tax-exempt zeros. Because of the stripped bond rules, zeros are not attractive products for all taxpayers. They remain attractive, however, for tax-exempt entities (e.g., pension funds), certain foreign investors, and low bracket taxpayers. Zeros can also be attractive to fund a known future liability at a specified date with a guaranteed rate.

Of course, locking in an interest rate for a long time is only beneficial if the general level of interest rates remains constant or decreases. If interest rates increase, the market value of the securities declines to compensate for its low yield in relation to the market rate of interest.

(a) TAXABLE SECURITIES

Owners of taxable zeros report income on interest earned on a yearly basis. The Treasury issues STRIPS,[174] and some brokerage firms[175] and federal government agencies also issue taxable zeros.[176] In addition, there are certificate of deposit zeros that are insured by the FDIC and corporate zeros.

Example   27-3

A taxpayer buys a $1000 STRIPS security for $880. The taxpayer receives $1000 when the STRIPS security matures. The taxpayer is taxed each year on the interest as it accrues.

TEFRA[177] significantly altered the timing of interest deductions for issuers and the reporting of interest income for owners of zeros. For

---

[172]For a discussion of investment strategies using zeros, see section 2.2(e).

[173]*See generally* section 27.2.

[174]For a discussion of Treasury zeros, see section 2.2(e).

[175]Salomon Brothers issues CATS and Merrill Lynch issues TIGRs. (The brokerage firm detaches the interest coupons from the principal, deposits them with a trustee, and issues its own instruments.)

[176]For example, SLMA has offered zero coupon bonds aimed at foreign investors. *See* Monroe, *Sallie Mae Offers Zero-Coupon Bonds Aimed at European, Japanese Investors*, Wall St. J., Aug. 2, 1984, § 2, at 33, col. 2.

[177]Pub. L. 97-248, § 232, 96 Stat. 324, 499-501 (1982).

corporate debt securities issued after May 27, 1969 and before July 1, 1982, the owner was required to include in income the ratable monthly portion of OID multiplied by the sum of the complete months he held the security during the taxable year.[178]

(b) TAX-EXEMPT SECURITIES

Zero coupon municipal securities also pay no interest currently. Because one of the major attractions under current laws of tax-exempt securities is the receipt of tax-free interest,[179] zero coupon municipal securities are generally an attractive investment only if they sell at a very deep discount where the compounded return is very high.

Example 27-4

A taxpayer pays $5000 for a zero coupon municipal security that matures in seven years at $7000 to provide for future college expenses for his child. At maturity, the taxpayer receives $7000 tax-free (a 10 percent yield).

Prior to DRA, several tax strategies were used with zero coupon tax-exempt securities. One was to purchase a zero and hold it for less than the then current long-term capital gain holding period (which was one year at that time). The taxpayer would obtain a nontaxable short-term gain and a deductible short-term capital loss. The DRA changed this tax result for zero coupon securities issued after September 3, 1982 that are purchased after March 1, 1984,[180] thereby ending the practice of selling zero coupon municipal securities to generate so-called artificial tax losses.[181] The OID rules now apply to adjust the basis of zero coupon municipal securities.

Example 27-5

Assume that under pre-DRA law a taxpayer paid $5353 for zero coupon municipal securities with a compounded annual return of 10 percent redeemable for $100,000 in 30 years. Under pre-DRA law, if the taxpayer sold the securities before maturity, the taxpayer would report gain or loss on a straight-line basis over the 30 year period (i.e., $3155 per year).

---

[178] *See* section 27.2.
[179] *See generally* section 28.2(b)(1).
[180] DRA, *supra* note 38, § 44(f).
[181] *See* section 27.2(e).

If the taxpayer held the securities for less than the long-term capital gain holding period, the taxpayer's basis was $8508 ($5353 plus $3155).

Assume further that interest rates had not changed in this period. Because interest is determined on a compound basis, the market value of the securities was $5902. The taxpayer had a $549 tax-free gain ($5902 minus $5353) and a short-term capital loss of $2606 ($8508 basis minus $4902 sales price).[182]

§ 27.6   STRIPPED BONDS

Stripped bonds are debt securities issued with interest coupons[183] where the unmatured coupons are separated from ownership of the debt security.[184] In other words, the security is divided into two pieces: a right to receive principal and a right to receive interest. The principal portion of a stripped bond is economically equivalent to a zero coupon security because it no longer carries the right to receive periodic interest payments.[185] There are four separate ways that debt securities can be stripped. First, a debt security with the right to interest can be purchased. The coupons can be stripped and retained, while the principal portion is sold. Second, a debt security with the right to interest can be purchased, stripped, and the principal portion is retained while the coupon is sold. Third, a taxpayer can purchase already separated coupons. Fourth, a taxpayer can purchase the principal portion only (which is economically equivalent to zero coupon security).

(a)   STRIPPED BONDS PRIOR TO TEFRA

In 1982, the Treasury issued a release proposing certain legislative changes in the tax treatment of stripped bonds.[186] The Treasury proposed that sellers of stripped bonds be prohibited from claiming artificial losses and that purchasers of stripped bonds would have to treat the separated interest and principal portions as original issue discount securities, including amounts in income that reflect the increase in value of the debt

---

[182]Under post-DRA law, the OID rules apply to adjust the basis of the securities. *See* section 27.2(e).

[183]"Coupon" is defined broadly to include any right to receive interest on a security (whether or not evidenced by a coupon). I.R.C. § 1286(e)(5).

[184]I.R.C. § 1286(e)(2); *see also* S. REP. No. 494, 97th Cong., 2d Sess. 215 (1982).

[185]*See* section 27.5.

[186]Treasury Release No. R-822, TREASURY NEWS (June 9, 1982).

security for that year. This section discusses the tax positions taken for stripped bonds prior to enactment of TEFRA.

(1) TREATMENT OF THE SELLER

Under pre-TEFRA law (i.e., prior to July 1, 1982), a seller of a stripped bond who retained the right to receive the interest and sold the principal portion would take the position that all of his basis in the debt security was properly allocated to the principal portion.[187] The seller thus claimed so-called artificial losses to the extent of the difference between the amount for which he bought the debt security (with the right to receive interest) and the amount he received on the sale of the principal portion (without the right to receive interest).[188] Dealers[189] and certain financial institutions[190] would report an ordinary loss on the sale of a stripped bond, while investors[191] and traders[192] would report a capital loss.[193]

In addition, under pre-TEFRA law, the seller could accelerate income by selling only the right to receive the interest and retaining the principal portion.[194]

(2) TREATMENT OF THE PURCHASER

The purchaser of stripped coupons would allocate his tax basis among the coupons he purchased.[195] When a coupon was redeemed, the taxpayer would report ordinary income equal to the difference between the amount received for the coupon and his basis.[196] In the case of coupons disposed of prior to maturity, a taxpayer who was not a dealer or a financial institution would report capital gain for all of the gain

[187]S. Rep. No. 494, *supra* note 184, at 215.

[188]*Id.* at 216.

[189]*See* section 6.3.

[190]*See* section 6.8.

[191]*See* section 6.1.

[192]*See* section 6.2.

[193]S. Rep. No. 494, *supra* note 184, at 215.

[194]*See generally* Shafer v. U.S., 204 F. Supp. 473 (S.D. Ohio 1962), *aff'd per curiam*, 312 F.2d 747 (6th Cir.), *cert. denied*, 373 U.S. 933 (1963), where owners of Japanese government bonds on which interest payments had been suspended during World War II, but for which the Japanese government agreed to service after the war, were allowed under NYSE rules to strip the bonds and sell the coupons at a price that provided for the realization of accelerated income. The court held that the taxpayers received ordinary income, not capital gain, on the sale of the new and old coupons.

[195]S. Rep. No. 494, *supra* note 184, at 215.

[196]*Id.*

not attributable to accrued interest,[197] even though most or all of the increase in value may have been due to the passage of time.

(b) TAXATION OF STRIPPED BONDS

TEFRA made substantive changes to the taxation of stripped bonds by enacting I.R.C. § 1232B,[198] which the DRA[199] redesignated as I.R.C. § 1286 without any substantive changes.[200]

(1) TREATMENT OF THE SELLER

When a debt security is stripped, any interest accrued on that security prior to the time it is disposed of, not including any interest that had been previously included in the seller's gross income, must be included in taxable income.[201] This accrued interest increases the basis of the stripped bond.[202] Immediately before the disposition of either the stripped corpus or the coupons, the seller must allocate his basis between what he disposed of and what he retained in proportion to their respective fair market values on the date of disposition.[203] After a disposition, the seller must treat the retained portion of the security as an original issue discount bond having a purchase price equal to the cost basis allocated to it.[204] The seller is subject to the original issue discount periodic inclusion rules.[205]

Example 27-6

Assume a taxpayer sells for $578,435 the principal portion of a debt security on January 1st when there are four years until the security

---

[197]Treasury Release No. R-822, TREASURY NEWS (June 9, 1982).

[198]TEFRA, *supra* note 177, § 232.

[199]DRA, *supra* note 38, § 41(a).

[200]The only minor change in I.R.C. § 1286(a) is a provision that a stripped bond or coupon is treated as originally issued on the purchase date. Because a "purchase" is defined in I.R.C. § 1286 as any "acquisition," and the term "acquisition" presumably has a broader meaning than "purchase," a person who received a stripped bond as a gift after July 1, 1982, even though that debt security may have been purchased prior to July 1, 1982, most likely must comply with the requirements set forth in I.R.C. § 1286.

[201]I.R.C. § 1286(b)(1); I.R.C. § 1232B(b)(1) (1982), *repealed by* DRA, *supra* note 38, § 42(a)(1) (1984).

[202]I.R.C. § 1286(b)(2); I.R.C. § 1232B(b)(2) (1982), *repealed by* DRA, *supra* note 38, § 42(a)(1).

[203]I.R.C. § 1286(b)(3); I.R.C. § 1232B(b)(3) (1982), *repealed by* DRA, *supra* note 38, § 42(a)(1).

[204]I.R.C. § 1286(b)(4); I.R.C. § 1232B(b)(4) (1982), *repealed by* DRA, *supra* note 38, § 42(a)(1).

[205]S. REP. NO. 494, *supra* note 184, at 216; *see* section 27.2(a).

matures for $1 million. Assume that the taxpayer retains the eight sem-
iannual interest coupons each with a face amount of $100,000. The
taxpayer must allocate $578,435 of his basis to the principal and the
remaining $421,565 to the interest coupons. The taxpayer does not re-
alize any gain or loss on this sale. In addition, each coupon that the
taxpayer retains is allocated a portion of the remaining basis of $421,565.
Further, income accrues on each coupon as if each coupon were a separate security issued with OID.

(2) TREATMENT OF THE PURCHASER

The purchaser of the principal portion (without the right to receive
interest) of a debt security must treat it as an OID security subject to
the OID rules.[206] OID is equal to the stated redemption price at maturity
over the security's ratable share of the purchase price allocable to the
principal portion and coupon,[207] which is equal to the fair market value
of the principal portion and coupon of the security on the date of purchase.[208] For purchases after July 1, 1982, the term "purchase" is defined
broadly to include: "any acquisition of a debt instrument, where, the
basis of a debt instrument is not determined in whole or in part by
reference to the adjusted basis of such debt instrument in the hands of
the person from whom acquired."[209]

The purchaser of the interest portion of a stripped bond must report
as income under the OID rules the amount of the excess of the coupon's
face amount at maturity over its ratable share of the purchase price,[210]
which equals its fair market value on the date of purchase.[211] This OID
is included in income periodically between the date of purchase and
the maturity date of the coupon.

Example 27-7

Assume a taxpayer purchases stripped coupons that give him the right
to receive interest when each coupon matures. Each coupon is allocated
a portion of the basis that is allocated among the coupons and the
principal portion. (This basis is equal to the difference between the face

[206] I.R.C. § 1286(a); I.R.C. § 1232B(a) (1982), *repealed by* DRA, *supra* note 38, § 42(a)(1).

[207] I.R.C. § 1286(a); I.R.C. § 1232B(a) (1982), *repealed by* DRA, *supra* note 38, § 42(a)(1).

[208] S. REP. No. 494, *supra* note 184, at 216.

[209] I.R.C. §§ 1286(e)(6); 1272(d)(1).

[210] I.R.C. § 1286(a); I.R.C. § 1232B(a) (1982), *repealed by* DRA, *supra* note 38, § 42(a)(1).

[211] S. REP. No. 494, *supra* note 184, at 216.

amount of the debt security and the amount of basis allocated to the principal portion.) Income accrues from each coupon as if it were a separate security issued with original issue discount. If the face amount of the security equals $750,000 and the basis allocated to the principal equals $550,000, the remaining basis is $200,000. This $200,000 of remaining basis is allocated to the interest amounts each year according to the OID rules.

(3) TREATMENT OF THE ISSUER

The issuer of a stripped bond can deduct interest equal to the aggregate daily portion of the OID for the days in the taxable year.[212] The aggregate daily portion is calculated under I.R.C. § 1272(a). Because I.R.C. § 1286 treats stripped bonds as OID securities for purposes of I.R.C. § 1272(a) and not I.R.C. § 163(e), issuers may presumably still obtain interest deductions, notwithstanding the fact that the security may have been stripped.[213]

(4) TAX-EXEMPT SECURITIES

I.R.C. § 1286(d) provides special rules for tax-exempt securities. A seller who strips a tax-exempt security and disposes of either the principal portion or the coupon is deemed to purchase the portion he retains.[214] Because the seller is treated as having purchased an OID security, he must allocate his basis between the items disposed of and the items retained.[215] In addition, subsequent sales of the retained items are treated as if I.R.C. § 1232(c) of pre-TEFRA law was still in effect.[216] The accrued interest rules of I.R.C. § 1286(b)(1) do not apply to tax-exempt securities.[217]

Purchasers of stripped tax-exempt securities are not subject to the OID inclusion rules.[218] Also, if the purchaser disposes of the stripped tax-exempt security, I.R.C. § 1286(d)(3) applies I.R.C. § 1286(c) without regard to the date of purchase.[219]

Because any OID on tax-exempt securities is also tax-free, application

---

[212]I.R.C. § 163(e).

[213]I.R.C. §§ 163(e), 1286.

[214]I.R.C. § 1286(d)(2).

[215]S. Rep. No. 494, *supra* note 184, at 217.

[216]I.R.C. § 1286(d)(3).

[217]I.R.C. § 1286(d)(1).

[218]*Id.*

[219]I.R.C. § 1286(d)(3).

of the current rule for stripped bonds would allow purchasers and sellers of tax-exempt securities to increase their tax basis in the principal and interest portions.

Sellers are required, however, to allocate the cost of the securities between the principal and interest portions to assure that artificial losses are not available on the sale of the stripped bond. Finally, a purchaser of the stripped principal portion of a tax-exempt security and the seller of the interest portion have taxable gain on a subsequent sale or redemption of a stripped bond to the extent of the portion of the cost allocated to the detached interest portion.

(5) MORTGAGE POOLS

In general, the OID rules do not apply to obligations of an issuer who is not a corporation.[220] As a result, there is no requirement for the owner of a noncorporate debt security to accrue OID.[221] There is a different result, however, if a debt security becomes a stripped bond or stripped coupon. The definition of a bond in I.R.C. § 1286(e)(1) is broad enough to include a bond, debenture, note, or certificate or other evidence of indebtedness. For purposes of the stripped bond provisions, it does not matter who the issuer is.

The question raised with respect to mortgage pools is whether the packaging in a pool of residential mortgages (predominately debt obligations of individuals) and the sale of pass-through interests involves coupon stripping. A committee of the New York State Bar Association addressed this issue in a report in response to the Treasury's request for recommendations for regulations under the pre-DRA OID and stripped bond provisions.[222] The committee asserted that the pooling of mortgages for resale does not involve any form of coupon stripping "if the seller of the mortgages receives a servicing fee for services rendered but retains no other interest in the pool, or if the seller retains a pro rata interest in mortgage principal or interest."[223] If, on the other hand, "the seller retains disproportionate interests in mortgage principal and interest in order to adjust for the difference between the rate of interest on the mortgages and current market rates," the committee stated that the pooling involves coupon stripping.[224]

[220]I.R.C. § 1271(b).

[221]*See generally* section 27.2.

[222]New York State Bar Association Ad Hoc Committee on Original Issue Discount and Coupon Stripping, Report to Treasury, *reprinted in* 22 TAX NOTES 993 (1984).

[223]*Id* at 1023.

[224]*Id.*

§ 27.7 SECURITIES IN DEFAULT

Securities with interest payments in default, so-called flat bonds, are generally traded "flat," which means that they are traded at their full principal amount without any allocation between unpaid accrued interest and principal. The owner of such securities has the right to principal and any unpaid accrued interest without any additional or separate charges. The tax rules that apply to securities in default take into account the fact that accrued interest is likely to never be paid. Both cash and accrued basis taxpayers do not include interest as it "accrues" on securities in default while they own the securities until interest is paid or the securities are sold at a price in excess of their basis and a portion of the gain is attributable to interest.

Payments of interest that accrued prior to the date on which the taxpayer purchases the securities are treated as a recovery of cost (i.e., a return of capital)[225] that reduces the basis of the securities. The taxpayer is allowed to first recover his cost before reporting taxable income because it is not certain that the taxpayer will ever recover his investment.[226] Additional payments that relate to interest that accrued prior to purchase that exceed the taxpayer's cost are treated as capital gain.[227] These payments are not treated as interest.[228] As a result, the payment of interest accrued prior to acquisition of tax-exempt securities in default is first treated as a return of capital, with any excess treated as a capital gain—not as tax-exempt interest.[229]

Payments of interest accrued after the taxpayer purchases defaulted securities are treated as interest income when received by the taxpayer.[230] Such interest is taxable, irrespective of whether the amounts are paid by the issuer or a subsequent purchaser.[231]

---

[225]Treas. Reg. § 1.61-7(c) (1966).

[226]Hewitt v. Comm'r, 30 B.T.A. 962, 965 (1934).

[227]Rickaby v. Comm'r, 27 T.C. 886, 891 (1957), *acq.* 1960-2 C.B. 6; Rev. Rul. 60-284, 1960-2 C.B. 464.

[228]First Kentucky Co. v. Gray, 190 F. Supp. 824, 825 (W.D. Ky. 1960), *aff'd,* 309 F.2d 845 (6th Cir. 1962).

[229]R.O. Holton & Co. v. Comm'r, 44 B.T.A. 202, 206 (1941); Noll v. Comm'r, 43 B.T.A. 496, 502 (1941).

[230]Rev. Rul. 60-284, 1960-2 C.B. 464.

[231]Fisher v. Comm'r, 209 F.2d 513, 515 (6th Cir.), *cert. denied,* 347 U.S. 1014 (1954); Jaglom v. Comm'r, 303 F.2d 847, 849 (2d Cir. 1962), *aff'd* 36 T.C. 126 (1961); Tobey v. Comm'r, 26 T.C. 610, 618 (1956).

If securities in default are subsequently resold by the taxpayer at a flat price that exceeds the taxpayer's basis, any gain that represents interest that accrued while the taxpayer owned the securities is treated as ordinary income.[232] The portion of gain attributable to interest is determined on the basis of the ratio that the sales proceeds bears to the sum of the face amount of principal and all accrued but unpaid interest at the time of sale.[233]

If flat securities in default are sold short, it appears as if the payments made by the borrower to the short seller in lieu of interest are deductible as nonbusiness expenses if the requirements to deduct, rather than capitalize these amounts, are complied with.[234] If the owner recovers his securities before the payment of interest that accrued prior to purchase, the payment should generate short-term capital gain to the owner.

The redemption of securities in default raises the question of whether the payments are retirement proceeds, generally considered to be an exchange of the securities.[235] The case law is clear that the proceeds received on retirement of securities in default include any payments of accrued but unpaid interest which accrued prior to the taxpayer's purchases.[236]

§ 27.8   EXCHANGES OF DEBT SECURITIES

(a)   IN GENERAL

Without a specific statutory provision for tax-free status, exchanges of debt securities are taxable.[237] Exchanges of debt securities of the same issuer are taxable if there are any material changes in the terms of the

---

[232]*Jaglom*, 303 F.2d at 849; U.S. v. Langston, 308 F.2d 729, 731 (5th Cir. 1962).

[233]*Jaglom*, 303 F.2d at 850, where the court suggested, although it did not decide the issue, that if a sale occurs in anticipation of an imminent payment by the issuer, the fair market value of principal and interest would be more appropriate than face value. 303 F.2d at 850-51.

[234]*See generally* section 16.6.

[235]*See generally* section 27.8.

[236]*Tobey*, 26 T.C. at 618; *Hewitt*, 30 B.T.A. at 965 (1934); Chase v. Comm'r, 44 B.T.A. 39, 51, *nonacq.* 1941-1 C.B. 13, *aff'd per curiam sub nom.* Helvering v. Chase, 128 F.2d 740 (2d Cir. 1942); Adrian & James, Inc. v. Comm'r, 4 T.C. 708, 715 (1945), *acq.* 1945 C.B. 1.

[237]*See* I.R.C. § 1031(a)(2), which states that tax-free exchanges of property do not apply to bonds, notes, securities, or other evidences of indebtedness.

debt securities.[238] Exchanges of substantially identical securities with the issuer are viewed as debt refundings and are not taxable.[239] Where no physical exchange of securities takes place, a constructive exchange can result if there is a significant change in terms so that a new or materially different security is deemed to be issued.[240] It may also be possible that an "in-substance defeasance," whereby a corporation transfers assets to a trust that it has established for the sole purpose of making payments of principal and interest on its outstanding debt securities, can be a constructive exchange.[241]

(b) REORGANIZATIONS

Special Code provisions allow for tax-free exchanges of bonds in connection with reorganizations pursuant to I.R.C. §§ 354, 368, and 371. Because it is beyond the scope of this book to discuss tax-free corporate reorganizations in detail, it is sufficient to point out that the exchange of debt securities for other corporate bonds, securities, and stock may be tax-free if the exchange qualifies under one of the specific Code provisions.[242]

Special rules apply to Treasury securities and municipal securities. Treasury securities can be exchanged tax-free in accordance with the provisions of I.R.C. § 1037.[243] Municipal securities do not qualify for the corporate reorganization provisions of I.R.C. § 368(a)(1), which only applies to private corporations.[244]

---

[238]Mutual Loan & Sav. Co. v. Comm'r, 184 F.2d 161, 165 (5th Cir. 1950); Rev. Rul. 81-169, 1981-1 C.B. 429 (an exchange was taxable where there were differences in interest rates, maturity dates, and sinking fund provisions); LTR 7902002 (June 29, 1978) (an exchange of New York City Notes for Municipal Assistance Corporation Bonds, referred to as "Big MAC" bonds, was taxable because the securities were not viewed as substantially identical); Rev. Rul. 73-328, 1973-2 C.B. 296 (where an exchange of a note for corporate bonds was taxable).

[239]Rev. Rul. 56-435, 1956-2 C.B. 506, *as modified by* Rev. Rul. 81-169, 1981-1 C.B. 429.

[240]*See* Rev. Rul. 79-155, 1979-1 C.B. 153 (where I.R.C. § 354 was applied so that gain was not realized); Rev. Rul. 73-160, 1973-1 C.B. 365 (where the change in terms did not create a deemed exchange).

[241]*See* Rev. Rul. 85-42, 1985-14 I.R.B. 5.

[242]For an excellent discussion of reorganizations, see B. BITTKER & J. EUSTICE, FEDERAL INCOME TAXATION OF CORPORATIONS AND SHAREHOLDERS ch. 14 (4th ed. 1979) and R. WILLENS, TAXATION OF CORPORATE CAPITAL TRANSACTIONS: A GUIDE FOR CORPORATE, INVESTMENT BANKING, AND TAX ADVISERS ch. 8 (1984).

[243]*See* section 28.1(a)(4).

[244]*See* section 28.2(c); *see also* Emery v. Comm'r, 166 F.2d 27, 30-31 (2d Cir. 1948); Girard Trust Co. v. U.S., 166 F.2d 773, 775 (3d Cir. 1948).

§ 27.9 RETIREMENT, REDEMPTION, AND DISPOSITION OF DEBT SECURITIES

The retirement[245] of a taxable debt security is generally considered to be a taxable sale or exchange,[246] resulting in capital gain or loss except for OID,[247] market discount,[248] or for certain securities that are required to be in registered form.[249] If at the time of original issue there was an intention to call a debt security before maturity, any gain realized on a sale or exchange is treated as ordinary income up to the amount of the OID, reduced by the amount of OID previously included in the owner's income.[250] There are several exceptions to the requirement for ordinary income treatment. First, the provisions for ordinary income do not apply to tax-exempt securities.[251] Second, it does not apply to any owner who purchases a debt security at a premium.[252] Third, I.R.C. § 1271 does not apply to any obligations issued by natural persons or to any obligations issued before July 2, 1982 by noncorporate or non-governmental issuers.[253]

(a) ORIGINALLY ISSUED AT A DISCOUNT

Gain on the retirement or disposition of debt securities issued after 1954 at a discount of more than .25 percent held by an investor[254] is covered by separate provisions.[255] That portion of the gain representing OID in excess of this di minimus amount that has not been previously taxed is treated as ordinary income.[256] Excess gain, if any, is treated as capital

---

[245]The term "retirement" is read broadly to include redemptions, repurchases, and cancellations by the issuer. McClain v. Comm'r, 311 U.S. 527, 530 (1941); Estate of Monroe v. Comm'r, 45 B.T.A. 1060 (1941), *acq.* 1942-1 C.B. 12, *aff'd per curiam sub nom.* Pinnell v. Comm'r, 132 F.2d 126 (3d Cir. 1942); MacDougald v. Comm'r, 44 B.T.A. 1046 (1941).

[246]I.R.C. § 1271(a)(1).

[247]*See* section 27.2.

[248]*See* section 27.3.

[249]*See* section 27.11. In addition, debt securities issued prior to 1955 must either have interest coupons or be in registered form for a taxpayer to obtain capital gain treatment. I.R.C. § 1271(c)(1).

[250]I.R.C. § 1271(a)(2).

[251]I.R.C. § 1271(a)(2)(B).

[252]*Id.*

[253]I.R.C. § 1271(b).

[254]*See* section 6.1.

[255]I.R.C. §§ 1271(c)(2)(A), 1273(a)(3).

[256]Rev. Rul. 75-117, 1975-1 C.B. 273.

gain. To determine OID for convertible debt securities,[257] the issue price is not reduced by the value of the conversion feature.[258] For debt securities with detachable warrants,[259] a portion of the issue price is allocated to the warrants, based on the respective fair market values of the two components.[260] The fact that the warrants are not exercised does not affect the amount of OID, if any, determined at the time the debt securities were issued.[261]

(b) MARKET DISCOUNT BONDS

For debt securities issued before July 19, 1984, capital gain or loss results on the retirement or disposition of a debt security with market discount.[262] Gain is ordinary, up to the amount of interest expense allowed under I.R.C. § 1277(b)(1), if the debt security was purchased after July 18, 1984 and was directly financed.[263] Certain debt securities are exempt from the market discount rules if they are (1) short-term obligations,[264] (2) tax-exempt securities,[265] (3) United States savings bonds,[266] (4) certain installment obligations,[267] or (5) securities where the discount is less than .25 percent of the stated redemption price of a debt security at maturity multiplied by the number of complete years remaining to maturity of the security.[268]

§ 27.10 REPOS AND REVERSE REPOS

(a) IN GENERAL

Repos and reverse repos (collectively "repo transactions") generally are financing transactions where securities (typically government securi-

---

[257]See section 1.1(c).

[258]Treas. Reg. § 1.1232-3(b)(2), (1980); see also section 28.3(b)(2).

[259]See section 1.1(d).

[260]See Treas. Reg. § 1.1232-3(b)(2) (1980).

[261]Rev. Rul. 72-46, 1972-1 C.B. 50.

[262]I.R.C. § 1277(d). For a discussion of market discount bonds, see section 27.3.

[263]I.R.C. § 1277(d). For a discussion of the interest deferral provisions applicable to market discount bonds, see section 27.3(b).

[264]I.R.C. § 1278(a)(1)(B).

[265]Id.

[266]Id.

[267]Id.

[268]I.R.C. § 1278(a)(2)(C).

ties, municipals, and MBSs) are financed pursuant to an agreement between the parties to return substantially identical securities at the end of the loan term.[269] In a repo transaction, a taxpayer (referred to as the "seller-debtor") borrows money using securities he owns as collateral by "selling" the securities to the other party (referred to as the "buyer-creditor") while agreeing to repurchase equivalent securities from the buyer-creditor at a future date. In a reverse repo transaction (so named because the transaction is the reverse side of a repo), the buyer-creditor purchases securities from the seller-debtor and agrees to sell equivalent securities back to the seller-debtor at a future date.

Repo transactions can be overnight, for a longer specified period (term repos), or open. Open repos can generally be terminated by either side on one business day's notice. The buyer-creditor may or may not take physical possession of the securities and, depending on the terms of the agreement and the type of securities involved, may or may not reregister the securities in his name. Repo transactions are generally terminated in one of two ways. First, the securities can be returned to the seller-debtor at the same price as they were transferred to the buyer-creditor plus charges representing an agreed upon interest rate added to the principal at the maturity of the contract. Or, the securities can be returned to the seller-debtor at a predetermined price that is higher than the price at which they were transferred to the buyer-creditor.

On the date when a repo transaction is terminated, the money and securities equivalent to those securities first "sold" are returned to their original owner. The seller-debtor receives the same or equivalent securities back from the buyer-creditor, while the buyer-creditor receives his funds plus an additional amount back from the seller-debtor.

For REITs, repos do not qualify as real estate assets, cash or cash items (including receivables), or government securities under I.R.C. § 856(c)(5).[270] In addition, a REIT entering into repos is not considered to be holding property primarily for sale to customers in the ordinary course of business within the meaning of I.R.C. § 856(a)(4).[271] This characterization of repos can be a disadvantage to REITs because they are subject to varying tax consequences depending on whether 75 percent of their assets qualify as the types of assets mentioned above.[272]

The major tax questions with repo transactions are whether they qualify as a sale or a loan and whether the Straddle Rules apply. The

---

[269]For a discussion of repos, see section 2.2(c).

[270]Rev. Rul. 77-59, 1977-1 C.B. 196.

[271]*Id.*

[272]*See generally* I.R.C. §§ 851–855.

issue of whether the seller-debtor is the owner of the repoed security for tax purposes may arise independent of whether the interest rate on the repo is fixed or floating, or whether the repo is a term repo or an open repo. This section discusses the tax considerations for repo transactions involving both taxable and tax-exempt securities. For a discussion of possible application of the Straddle Rules to repos, see section 36.3(b).

(b) SALES OR FINANCING TRANSACTIONS

A repo transaction can be characterized as either a sale or a loan. In general, repos are treated as secured loans.[273] In certain circumstances, however, repo transactions are viewed as sales.[274]

(1) LOANS

When repos are treated as loans, neither gain nor loss is recognized by the seller-debtor on the initial transfer. The securities are "sold" as collateral to secure the loan. As with other financing transactions, repos may be subject to the OID rules for short-term obligations,[275] and to the market discount rules.[276] The seller-debtor cannot claim the accrual of OID on the repoed security as a gain qualified for capital treatment.

Further, it appears as if the security loan provisions of I.R.C. § 1058 may impose additional requirements on a repo to assure that the transaction qualifies as a loan.[277] I.R.C. § 1058(b)(3) requires, for securities lending transactions that fit within its terms, that the transfer of securities "not reduce the risk of loss or opportunity for gain of the transferor of the securities on the securities transferred." Proposed Treasury regulations provide that in order not to reduce a security lender's (i.e., the seller-debtor) risk of loss or increase his opportunity for gain, the agreement under which securities are borrowed must provide that the

---

[273]Rev. Rul. 74-27, 1974-1 C.B. 24 (a repo was a loan where the security subject to the repo was returnable on demand of the seller-creditor "on or before" a fixed date); Rev. Rul. 77-59, 1977-1 C.B. 196 (a repo was a loan where the securities subject to the repo agreement were transferred "generally overnight or not more than several days"); American Nat'l Bank of Austin v. U.S., 421 F.2d 442 (5th Cir.), *cert. denied*, 400 U.S. 819 (1970); First Nat'l Bank in Wichita v. Comm'r, 57 F.2d 7 (10th Cir.), *cert. denied*, 287 U.S. 636 (1932).

[274]Citizens Nat'l Bank of Waco v. U.S., 551 F.2d 832, 843 (Ct. Cl. 1977); American Nat'l Bank of Austin v. U.S., 573 F.2d 1205 (Ct. Cl. 1978).

[275]*See* section 27.2(d).

[276]*See* section 27.3.

[277]*See generally* Chapter 24.

lender can terminate the loan upon notice of not more than five business days.[278] If a seller-debtor has a term repo under which he cannot demand the return of the repoed securities until the term expires, the IRS may assert that I.R.C. § 1058 does not apply, so that gain or loss is recognized on the initial transfer of the repoed securities and again on reacquisition of the securities at the termination of the repo.[279] It is the author's view that a fixed rate term repo for less than the maturity of the security should be viewed as a loan. It does not protect a seller-debtor from risk of loss or preclude an opportunity for gain.

In a series of cases, banks who acquired tax-exempt securities in reverse repo transactions (i.e., as buyer-creditors) claimed that they were the owners of the securities and, therefore, entitled to tax-exempt interest during the period they held the securities. If repos are secured loans rather than sales, the interest is taxable to the buyer-creditor;[280] it remains tax-exempt, however, to the seller-debtor.[281]

It is unclear whether the seller-debtor in a repo transaction remains the owner for tax purposes of a repoed security when it is transferred by the buyer-creditor to a third party.[282] The transfer of the collateral by the buyer-creditor to a third party in a repo structured as a loan may be viewed the same as borrowing the securities as with margin accounts and short sales. In that case, the seller-debtor (i.e., the lender of the securities) receives ordinary income (not dividends or interest) in amounts equivalent to interest, dividends, and other distributions that the owner of the securities is entitled to receive during the period the securities have been transferred.[283] In addition, if the buyer-creditor transfers the collateral to a third party, the seller-debtor may not be able to accrue OID. The seller-debtor no longer owns the securities; instead he owns an obligation representing a claim against the buyer-creditor. Further, interest received by the seller-debtor on repos of tax-exempt securities is not tax-exempt interest to him.

---

[278]Prop. Treas. Reg. § 1.1058-1(b)(3) (1983).

[279]*See* section 24.3.

[280]*American Nat'l Bank of Austin*, 421 F.2d at 453; Union Planters Nat'l Bank of Memphis v. U.S., 426 F.2d 115, 118 (6th Cir.), *cert. denied*, 400 U.S. 827 (1970).

[281]Interest may be taxable to the seller-debtor, however, if the buyer-creditor subsequently transfers the securities to a third party.

[282]*See generally* Chapter 24.

[283]Rev. Rul. 80-135, 1980-1 C.B. 18; Rev. Rul. 60-177, 1960-1 C.B. 9; Prop. Treas. Reg. § 1.1058-1(d), (1983); *see generally* SENATE FINANCE COMMITTEE REPORT, INTERNAL REVENUE CODE OF 1954—NONMEMBER TELEPHONE COMPANIES—INCOME, S. REP. NO. 762, 95th Cong., 2d Sess. 3-9, 1978 U.S. CODE CONG. & AD. NEWS 1286, 1288-95.

(2) SALES

In those cases where a repo transaction is a sale, the buyer-creditor becomes the owner of and entitled to the income from tax-exempt securities acquired subject to repo agreements.[284] The seller-debtor cannot treat the interest he receives as tax-exempt. Of course, if the transaction is viewed as a sale, gain or loss is recognized on the transfer of the securities.

To determine whether the initial transfer of securities under a repo is a sale, various factors are relevant. A fixed rate term repo with a term up to maturity may be viewed as a sale for tax purposes at the time the repo is entered into. The seller-debtor may not be viewed as having any remaining risk of loss or opportunity for gain on the securities.[285] With a sale, the seller-debtor no longer has an economic interest in the securities, is not liable on any debt on which interest can be deducted, and is not entitled to accrue any interest or OID on the repoed securities.

In addition, a sale may occur if the seller-debtor cannot repurchase the securities unless he is requested to do so by the buyer-creditor.[286] Similarly, a sale may occur if the buyer-creditor has no right to resell the securities back to the seller-debtor unless he is so requested by the seller-debtor.[287] The IRS has taken the position in private letter rulings that sales of tax-exempt securities structured to protect buyer-creditors in the event of default are sales, not loans, and the buyer-creditors are the owners of the securities for tax purposes.[288] These "credit enhancers" provide for (1) guarantees of principal and interest in the event of default, which can be transferred to subsequent purchasers of the securities, (2) bank standby letters of credit to pay principal and interest in the event of default, (3) repurchase agreements in the event of default, and (4) participation arrangements to be at risk in the event of default.[289]

(c) ALTERNATIVE MINIMUM TAX

Interest deductions on repo transactions can result in the imposition of alternative minimum tax for noncorporate taxpayers.[290] Repo interest

---

[284]*Citizens Nat'l Bank of Waco*, 551 F.2d at 843 (Ct. Cl. 1977).

[285]*But see* I.R.C. § 1058; Prop. Treas. Reg. § 1.1058-1 (1983).

[286]*Id.* at 842.

[287]*American Nat'l Bank of Austin*, 421 F.2d at 453.

[288]LTR 8238052 (June 23, 1982); LTR 8108032 (Nov. 25, 1980).

[289]LTR 8238052 (June 23, 1982); LTR 8108032 (Nov. 25, 1980).

[290]For a discussion of the alternative minimum tax, see section 13.3(a)(2)(ii).

deductions can be viewed as excess itemized adjusted deductions for the taxable year. In *Wallach v. U.S.*,[291] the United States Court of Claims granted an IRS motion for summary judgment on the grounds that there was no genuine issue in the case, and that repo interest deductions that exceed 60 percent of the taxpayers' adjusted gross income are tax preference items. In 1978 and 1979, the taxpayers engaged in repo transactions, whereby they purchased Treasury securities, federal agency securities, and a bank certificate of deposit with a total purchase price of $12,760,000 from a securities dealer. They paid $229,000, borrowed the rest of the purchase price, and sold the securities back to the dealer, subject to their obligation to repurchase the securities at the same price. The "yield to maturity" on the securities was fixed and did not fluctuate, although the taxpayers' borrowing costs fluctuated depending on the cost of money. During both 1978 and 1979, the taxpayers' interest expense on the repo transaction exceeded their interest income (by $95,000 in 1978 and $322,000 in 1979). Their total repo interest expense for 1978 and 1979, when added to other deductions, caused their adjusted itemized deductions for each year to exceed 60 percent of their adjusted gross income for each year. The Court of Claims found, as a matter of law, that the excess deductions were tax preference items.[292]

(d) REPORTING REQUIREMENT

Because a repo transaction structured as a loan is a financing for tax purposes involving the payment of interest, the interest must be reported on Form 1099-INT, Statement for Recipients of Interest Income, if interest of $10 or more is paid.[293] For each unintentional failure to file such an information return, the penalty is $50 for each failure up to a maximum amount of $50,000 for any one year.[294] For intentional disregard of the filing requirement, however, the penalty is increased to not less than 10 percent of the aggregate unreported amounts and the $50,000 ceiling does not apply.[295] Although the interest income and expense in some repo transactions can net out to very little in the aggregate, the penalties for failure to file can be based on the gross amounts of the securities, which can obviously prove very costly.

---

[291]Eli Wallach and Ann (Jackson) Wallach v. U.S., 8 Ct. Cl. 631 (1985).

[292]*Id.*

[293]IR-83-92, 10 STAND FED. TAX REP. (CCH) ¶ 6630 (June 30, 1983).

[294]I.R.C. § 6652(a)(1) (applies to payments made before January 1, 1984); I.R.C. § 6652(a)(2) (applies to payments made after December 31, 1983).

[295]I.R.C. § 6652(a)(2) (applies to payments made before January 1, 1984); I.R.C. § 6652(a)(3) (applies to payments made after December 31, 1983).

§ 27.11   REGISTRATION REQUIREMENTS

(a) IN GENERAL

The IRS's concern with respect to securities issued in bearer form is that taxable interest income and gains on the sales of such securities may not be reported nor tax paid by the holder. TEFRA established a registration requirement for certain debt securities[296] and imposes penalties on issuers for issuing unregistered securities and on taxpayers for owning unregistered securities.[297] Registration allows the IRS to identify security owners (both past and present) and assures that transfers (by sale, gift, or inheritance) are properly reflected on the tax returns of transferors and transferees.

TEFRA originally provided a December 31, 1982 effective date for the Code amendments concerning registration requirements and a September 3, 1982 effective date for amendments to the Second Liberty Bond Act.[298] TCA '82 delayed the effective date until July 1, 1983 for debt securities that were not required to be in registered form prior to TEFRA.[299] The registration requirements do not apply to any debt security issued pursuant to the exercise of a warrant or convertible security issued before August 10, 1982 if the security was offered or sold outside of the United States without Securities Act registration.[300]

(b) REGISTRATION-REQUIRED SECURITIES

Registration is required for "registration-required obligations" defined in both I.R.C. §§ 163(f)(2) and 103(j)(2).[301] A registration-required obligation is defined in I.R.C. § 163(f)(2) to mean any security other than a security that:

1. Is issued by a natural person
2. Is not of a type offered to the public
3. Has a maturity (at issue) of not more than one year, or

---

[296]TEFRA, *supra* note 177, at § 310.

[297]*See* section 27.11(c).

[298]Second Liberty Bond Act, ch. 56, 40 Stat. 288 (1917), *amended by* TEFRA, *supra* note 177, § 310(d)(2); TEFRA, *supra* note 177, § 310(d)(1).

[299]TCA '82, Pub. L. 97-448, § 306(b)(2), 96 Stat. 2365, 2405-06 (1982).

[300]TEFRA, *supra* note 177, at § 310(d)(3).

[301]The same definition applies to the various Code provisions amended by TEFRA. Sometimes the Code language repeats the rules, while in other places a cross reference is provided.

4. Is described in I.R.C. § 163(f)(2)(b), which describes certain securities not subject to registration where there are arrangements reasonably designed to ensure that the securities will be sold (or resold in connection with the original issue) only to persons who are not United States persons

Although registration is not required for short-term debt securities (i.e., maturity at issue of not more than one year) and securities not offered to the public, the Treasury has authority to require registration of short-term and privately placed securities if the Treasury determines by regulation that the securities are "used frequently in evading federal taxes."[302] Any regulations expanding the registration requirements can have prospective effect only and can apply only to debt securities issued after the regulations are promulgated.[303]

A registration-required obligation must be "in registered form." This phrase can be viewed as requiring registration of both principal and interest elements. For purposes of registration-required obligations, however, registration can be in book entry form if the securities can be transferred in a manner consistent with Treasury regulations.[304] In addition, it is contemplated that the regulations will address the registration of securities held by nominees to assure proper identification of owners.[305]

(c) NONCOMPLIANCE WITH REGISTRATION REQUIREMENTS

The registration requirements for registration-required securities are contained in six separate Code sections and the Second Liberty Bond Act. Some of the provisions affect issuers, while others affect security owners. Both types of sanctions do not appear to apply to the same securities.

1. I.R.C. § 103(j) provides that registration-required tax-exempt securities must be issued in registered form for interest to be exempt from federal tax.[306]
2. I.R.C. § 163(f) prohibits an issuer from deducting interest paid on unregistered registration-required securities.

---

[302]I.R.C. § 163(f)(2)(C).

[303]*Id.*

[304]*See* I.R.C. §§ 103(j)(3)(A), 163(f)(3).

[305]I.R.C. § 103(j)(3)(B).

[306]*See* section 28.2(b)(1)(i)(b).

3. I.R.C. § 165(j) denies any loss on the sale, exchange, theft, loss, or other disposition of unregistered registration-required securities.

4. I.R.C. § 312(m) prohibits any reductions to a corporate issuer's earnings and profits for interest paid on unregistered registration-required securities.

5. I.R.C. § 1287 denies capital gain treatment on the disposition of unregistered registration-required securities.

6. I.R.C. § 4701 imposes an excise tax on issuers of unregistered registration-required securities equal to one percent of the principal amount multiplied by the number of calendar years (or portions thereof) from the date the securities are issued until their maturity.[307]

7. The Second Liberty Bond Act now requires registration of most long-term United States securities offered to the public.[308] Certain government securities held by non-United States persons are exempt from the registration requirements.

(d) EXCEPTIONS TO LOSS DENIAL AND ORDINARY INCOME TREATMENT

An owner of an unregistered security can deduct losses under I.R.C. § 165(j), or obtain capital gain on the sale of the securities under I.R.C. § 1287 in certain circumstances. The following discussion first lists the Code provisions and then lists proposed and temporary regulatory provisions that elaborate on the exemptions.

It is important to note that these exceptions only apply to a loss denial under § 165(j) and a capital gain denial under I.R.C. § 1287.[309] They do not affect § 163(f) (which denies interest deductions for interest paid) or I.R.C. § 103(j) (which denies tax-exempt status on interest earned on unregistered registration-required securities).[310]

The Code exemptions are as follows:

1. The securities are held in connection with a trade or business outside of the United States.[311]

2. The owner of the securities is a broker-dealer (registered under fed-

---

[307]I.R.C. § 4701(a).

[308]TEFRA, *supra* note 177, at § 310(a).

[309]I.R.C. § 165(j)(3).

[310]For a discussion of the controversy over the registration requirements for municipal securities, see section 28.2(b)(1)(i)(b).

[311]I.R.C. § 165(j)(3)(A).

eral or state law) who holds the securities for sale to customers in the ordinary course of business.[312]

3. The owner complies with reporting requirements with respect to ownership, transfer, and payment as the Treasury may require.[313]

4. The owner promptly surrenders the securities to the issuer for the issuance of new securities in registered form.[314]

Proposed and temporary Treasury regulations elaborate on the Code exemptions listed above and exempt the following persons from the loss denial and ordinary income rules:

1. Underwriters, brokers, dealers, or other persons who hold unregistered securities for a non-United States trade or business[315]

2. Broker-dealers who hold such unregistered securities for sale to customers if the securities are not delivered to any person in bearer form, except upon receipt of a certificate signed by the customer stating that the securities are not being acquired by a United States person, unless the person is otherwise exempt[316]

3. Financial institutions[317] that hold unregistered securities through an entity engaged in the business of holding such securities for members if it credits or debits members' accounts without physical delivery[318]

4. Any person who owns a registration-required security through a financial institution[319]

5. Any person who surrenders to the issuer or transfer agent an unregistered registration-required security within 30 days after acquisition to convert the security into registered form.[320]

---

[312]I.R.C. § 165(j)(3)(B).

[313]I.R.C. § 165(j)(3)(C).

[314]I.R.C. § 165(j)(3)(D).

[315]Temp. Treas. Reg. § 1.165-12T(c)(1) (1984).

[316]Id.

[317]Defined as any person or a 50 percent or more owner of the total voting power of stock entitled to vote for any person who (1) conducts a banking, financing, or similar business; (2) engages in the business as a broker or dealer in securities; (3) is an insurance company; (4) is a pension or profit sharing plan; (5) is an investment advisor; (6) is a regulated investment company; or (7) is a finance corporation where a substantial portion of its business is making loans, servicing debt obligations, acquiring accounts receivable notes, or acquiring installment obligations. Temp. Treas. Reg. § 1.165-12T(c)(1)(iv) (1984).

[318]Temp. Treas. Reg. § 1.165-12T(c)(2) (1984).

[319]Temp. Treas. Reg. § 1.165-12T(c)(3) (1984).

[320]Temp. Treas. Reg. § 1.165-12T(c)(4) (1984); Prop. Treas. Reg. § 1.1232-5(b)(4) (1983).

If any of the above exemptions are available, registration is not required and the loss denial and capital gain denial provisions do not apply.

(e) SECURITIES SOLD OUTSIDE OF THE UNITED STATES SUBSEQUENTLY ACQUIRED BY A UNITED STATES PERSON

Certain unregistered securities can be sold to non-United States persons if interest is payable outside the United States and the securities are properly legended.[321] If such unregistered securities are subsequently acquired by United States persons, this acquisition does not trigger the so-called issuer penalties and does not penalize the issuer, who can still deduct interest payments and reduce its earnings and profits for interest paid. The United States person acquiring the securities, however, is subject to two penalties denying a loss on the securities or a capital gain on sale. The United States person is denied a loss on the sale, exchange, theft, loss, or other disposition of the unregistered securities.[322] And, any gain from the sale or other disposition of the securities is taxed at ordinary income, not capital gain, rates.[323]

§ 27.12   WASH SALES

The wash sales rule applies to taxpayers who are not dealers in debt securities. For a discussion of the wash sales rule, see generally Chapter 17.

§ 27.13   SHORT SALES

The short sales rule may apply to debt securities that are capital assets in the hands of the taxpayer. For a discussion of the short sales rule, see generally Chapter 16.

§ 27.14   STRADDLE RULES

The Straddle Rules apply to offsetting positions in debt securities. For a discussion of the Straddle Rules, see generally Part 10.

[321]I.R.C. § 163(f)(2)(B); Second Liberty Bond Act § 28(b)(2), 31 U.S.C. 3121(g)(2) (1982).
[322]I.R.C. § 165(j).
[323]I.R.C. § 1287.

Twenty-eight

Specific Types of Debt Securities

This chapter addresses specific types of debt securities: governments (Treasury and federal agency securities), municipals, convertibles, and MBSs. The wash sales rule,[1] short sales rule,[2] and the Straddle Rules[3] apply to taxpayers holding debt securities unless specific exceptions are available.[4] For a discussion of the tax provisions that apply generally to debt securities, see Chapter 27.

§ 28.1 GOVERNMENT SECURITIES

(a) TREASURY SECURITIES

Treasury securities include both marketable securities (i.e., Treasury bills, notes, and bonds) and nonmarketable securities (e.g., savings bonds).[5] With some exceptions discussed in this section, Treasury securities are generally treated for federal income tax purposes in the same way as other debt securities. On the other hand, Treasury securities are exempt

---

[1] *See generally* Chapter 17.

[2] *See generally* Chapter 16.

[3] *See generally* Part 10.

[4] For example, the wash sales and short sales rules typically do not apply to dealers in the particular debt security.

[5] *See* section 2.1(a).

from all taxes imposed by state and local governments except for estate or inheritance taxes, franchise taxes, and other nonproperty taxes imposed on corporations.[6] Interest income earned on Treasury securities issued after 1941 is included in a taxpayer's gross income.[7]

Like other types of debt securities, Treasury securities are capital assets in the hands of investors[8] and traders.[9] They are ordinary income property in the hands of dealers,[10] hedgers,[11] commercial banks, mutual savings banks, savings and loans, and small business investment companies.[12]

Redemption of Treasury securities at maturity is generally taxable unless the securities are exchanged in a tax-free exchange that qualifies under I.R.C. § 1037 or I.R.C. § 454(c).[13] Tax provisions generally applicable to debt securities, including the rules on OID, market discount, premiums, and stripped bonds, are discussed in Chapter 27.

(1) TREASURY BILLS

(i) In General

Treasury bills are short-term obligations issued at a discount and payable without interest at a fixed maturity date not exceeding one year from the date of issue.[14] Income derived from Treasury bills is taxable for federal purposes.[15] The amount of discount at which Treasury bills are originally sold by the United States is considered to be interest and is subject to tax for federal tax purposes.[16] However, a cash basis taxpayer need not recognize interest or OID from a Treasury bill until it is sold or matures, whichever is earlier.[17]

---

[6]31 U.S.C. § 3124(a) (1982).

[7]Public Debt Act of 1941 § 4(a), 55 Stat. 7, 9 (1941). Treasury securities issued prior to 1941 are exempt from all federal taxes.

[8]*See* section 6.1.

[9]*See* section 6.2.

[10]*See* section 6.3.

[11]*See* section 6.4.

[12]*See* section 6.8.

[13]*See* section 28.1(a)(4).

[14]*See* section 2.1(a)(1).

[15]*See* section 2.1(a).

[16]*See* section 27.2(d).

[17]I.R.C. §§ 454(b), 1272(a)(2).

(ii)   Payment of Federal Taxes with Certain Treasury Bills

The Treasury has the authority to issue regulations to allow Treasury bills of any series to be accepted at maturity value, whether at or before maturity, to pay income taxes.[18] Although authorization and the procedure to tender Treasury bills at par is in place, the Treasury has not issued any such regulations. At this writing, Treasury bills are not available to pay taxes at par value prior to maturity.

(iii)   Capital Assets

Prior to enactment of ERTA,[19] Treasury bills were excluded from the definition of capital assets in I.R.C. § 1221.[20] Under pre-ERTA law, taxpayers who were not dealers,[21] hedgers,[22] or certain financial institutions[23] could seek to convert ordinary income into long-term capital gain through the use of Treasury bill futures contract spreads. Because Treasury bills were ordinary income assets, and the IRS had ruled in Rev. Rul. 78-414[24] that Treasury bill futures contracts were capital assets, taxpayers could establish Treasury bill futures contract spreads to attempt to generate capital gains and ordinary losses. Long Treasury bill futures contract positions that declined in value could be closed out by taking delivery of a Treasury bill and selling it to generate an ordinary loss. Appreciated positions were closed out by offset to generate capital gains.

Under current law, Treasury bills are capital assets unless they are held for sale by dealers, acquired as part of a hedging transaction, or held by certain financial institutions. Therefore, if an investor or trader closes out a long Treasury bill futures contract position by taking delivery and immediately resells the Treasury bills, the sale generates a capital gain or loss just as if he had closed out the position by offset.

---

[18]I.R.C. § 6312(a); 31 C.F.R. § 309.5(b) (1985).
[19]ERTA, Pub. L. 97-34, 95 Stat. 172 (1981).
[20]I.R.C. § 1221 (1976), amended by ERTA, *supra* note 19, § 505(a).
[21]*See* section 6.3.
[22]*See* section 6.4.
[23]*See* section 6.8.
[24]1978-2 C.B. 213.

(2)   SAVINGS BONDS

Savings bonds are nonnegotiable, nontransferable Treasury securities, which can be issued at a discount or pay interest semiannually.[25] The income tax treatment of interest earned on United States savings bonds is spelled out in the Treasury's offering for new bonds.[26] The federal tax treatment of interest income on savings bonds can be determined by looking at the Treasury Department Circular that offers the particular bond issue to the public. This section discusses savings bonds currently available to purchasers.

(i)   Series EE Savings Bonds

Series EE bonds (which replace Series E bonds) are zero coupon securities[27] issued at a discount.[28] Accrued interest is added to the issue price at stated intervals, although interest is payable only at redemption of the bonds as part of the redemption value.[29] The difference between the price paid for a Series EE bond and its redemption value is interest and is subject to all taxes imposed under the Code.[30] An owner of Series EE bonds can elect to defer federal tax on the interest income (the cash method), or pay it currently (the accrual method).[31] If a taxpayer elects to use the cash method, he can change the method to accrual without IRS consent.[32] Once a taxpayer elects the accrual method, however, he cannot change his method of reporting interest income to the cash method without first obtaining IRS approval.[33] The election applies to all savings bonds owned by the taxpayer at the beginning of the taxable year and to all savings bonds acquired thereafter.[34] The election does not bind anyone to whom the savings bonds are subsequently transferred.[35]

---

[25]*See* section 2.1(a)(4).

[26]The terms of the current Treasury offerings for Series EE and Series HH bonds are contained in Treasury Department Circular No. 3-80. 31 C.F.R. pt. 353 (1985).

[27]*See* section 2.2(e); *see also* section 27.5.

[28]*See* section 2.1(a)(4).

[29]31 C.F.R. § 353.30 (1985).

[30]31 C.F.R. § 351.8(a) (1985).

[31]31 C.F.R. § 351.8(b) (1985).

[32]I.R.C. § 454(a); 31 C.F.R. § 351.8(b)(3) (1985).

[33]I.R.C. § 454(a); 31 C.F.R. § 351.8(b)(3) (1985). The election cannot be made on an amended tax return. Rev. Rul. 55-655, 1955-2 C.B. 253.

[34]I.R.C. § 454(a). The taxpayer must include the actual increase in redemption value that occurs on the stated intervals in each year. Treas. Reg. § 1.454-1(a)(2) (1971).

[35]Treas. Reg. § 1.454-1(a) (1971).

(ii)   Series HH Savings Bonds

Series HH bonds (which replace Series H bonds) are current income bonds issued at par value.[36] Series HH bonds issued after October 31, 1982 can only be acquired in an exchange for Series E and EE bonds and United States Savings Notes.[37] Interest on Series HH bonds is paid semiannually, beginning six months from the issue date.[38] Interest on Series HH bonds ceases at maturity, or if the bond is redeemed before maturity, interest ceases as of the end of the preceding interest payment period.[39] The interest on the bonds is subject to all taxes imposed by the Code when the interest is paid (for cash method taxpayers) or accrues (for accrual method taxpayers).[40]

(iii)   Dispositions

Savings bonds can only be transferred under very limited circumstances.[41] The IRS has not viewed the transfer of Series E bonds to a grantor trust (where the transferor is treated as the trust's owner for tax purposes) as a disposition triggering tax on the accrued interest.[42] Some savings bonds (e.g., Series E and Series EE bonds) are issued at a discount and the owner can elect to accrue interest income currently or to defer taxation until retirement, redemption, or disposition.[43] Other savings bonds (e.g., Series HH bonds) are current income bonds issued at par paying interest semiannually. Taxpayers holding savings bonds issued at a discount can defer taxation on the interest income by using the cash method, which can be continued if zero coupon savings bonds are exchanged for other Treasury securities in a tax-free exchange under I.R.C. § 1037.[44]

Series EE savings bonds can be redeemed at any time after six months from issue at the current redemption value shown in Treasury Circular No. 1-80.[45] Series HH savings bonds can also be redeemed after six

---

[36]*See* section 2.1(a)(4).
[37]31 C.F.R. § 352.0 (1985).
[38]31 C.F.R. § 353.31(a) (1985).
[39]*Id.*
[40]31 C.F.R. § 352.10 (1985).
[41]*See* section 2.1(a)(4).
[42]Rev. Rul. 58-2, 1958-1 C.B. 236; LTR 7729003 (Apr. 19, 1977).
[43]I.R.C. § 454(a).
[44]*See* section 28.1(a)(4).
[45]31 C.F.R. § 353.35(b) (1985).

months, with those issued in a tax-free exchange paid at face amount and those issued for cash paid at the current redemption value shown in Treasury Circular No. 2-80.[46] If a Series HH bond is redeemed at less than face value, the difference represents an adjustment of interest.[47]

(3) PAYMENT OF ESTATE TAXES WITH CERTAIN TREASURY BONDS

Certain Treasury bonds can be redeemed at their face amount plus accrued interest, regardless of their redemption dates to pay estate taxes due on the death of the bond owner.[48] These bonds are referred to as "flower bonds" (perhaps because they "bloom" into full value when their owner dies or because flowers are suggestive of funerals). They have low interest rates and frequently sell at a substantial discount.[49] Flower bonds can be a potentially important estate planning device for an individual with a short life expectancy. Because of the low yield, an individual would not purchase flower bonds unless he thought his death was imminent and he wanted his estate to use the flower bonds to pay his estate taxes.[50] The Treasury has not been authorized to issue new flower bonds since 1971.[51] As a result, the outstanding flower bond issues decrease over time.

Flower bonds are redeemable at par by the representative of the estate or, if there is none, by those persons entitled to the estate. Flower bonds can be redeemed only to the extent of the net amount of the federal estate tax, after taking into account all allowable credits (including the credit for federal gift taxes paid).[52]

In determining a decedent's gross estate, flower bonds are valued at par rather than at their fair market value to the extent that they may be applied to pay federal estate taxes. Bonds that exceed the amount

---

[46] 31 C.F.R. § 353.35(c) (1985).

[47] Id.

[48] 31 C.F.R. § 306.28(a) (1985); Treas. Reg. § 20.6151-1(c) (1958); Rev. Rul. 69-489, 1969-2 C.B. 172; Rev. Proc. 69-18, 1969-2 C.B. 300.

[49] Certain Treasury bonds issued between 1953 and 1963 with interest rates between three percent and 4.25 percent and maturity dates in 1985, 1990, 1992 through 1995, and 1998 are redeemable at par to pay estate taxes. A current list of eligible flower bond issues can be obtained from any Federal Reserve bank or branch or from the Bureau of the Public Debt.

[50] The yield on a flower bond is less than that offered by a comparable Treasury issue with the same maturity date.

[51] I.R.C. § 6312 (1970), repealed by Pub. L. 92-5, § 4(a)(2), 85 Stat. 5 (1971) for Treasury securities issued after March 3, 1971. 31 U.S.C. § 3121(b)(2) (1983).

[52] Rev. Rul. 76-367, 1976-2 C.B. 259.

applied to pay the estate tax are valued at the mean between their highest and lowest quoted selling prices on the estate's valuation date.[53] Accrued interest to the date of death is taxed as part of the estate whether or not the bonds could have been used to pay estate taxes.[54] This reduces the overall tax benefit of acquiring flower bonds to the part that remains after paying the additional estate tax attributable to the discount from par.[55] Hence, greater benefits are available to taxpayers with lower marginal estate tax rates.

If an estate has excess flower bonds remaining after the representative of the estate pays estimated federal estate tax, a problem can result if any additional federal estate taxes become due after the representative sells the excess bonds at their fair market value. If the IRS subsequently assesses an estate tax deficiency, flower bonds sold at the market price are valued at their higher par value to the extent of any additional taxes. This can increase an estate's total federal estate tax.[56]

Careful planning is necessary prior to an individual's death if a redemption of flower bonds at par is contemplated.[57] Various conditions must be met for flower bonds to be redeemed at par. First, the bonds must have been owned by the decedent at the time of his death.[58] Second, bonds held in trust are redeemable at par (1) if the trust actually terminates in favor of the decedent's estate, (2) if the trustee is required to pay the decedent's estate tax, or (3) to the extent that the debts of the decedent's estate (including costs of administration, state inheritance taxes, and federal estate taxes) exceed the estate's assets, without taking the trust estate into account.[59] Third, bonds held in joint ownership are redeemable at par if (1) the bonds actually become the prop-

---

[53]Even if bonds are not actually used to pay estate taxes they must be valued at par to the extent they could have been so used. Bankers Trust Co. v. U.S., 284 F.2d 537, 538 (2d Cir. 1960).

[54]Rev. Rul. 69-489, 1969-2 C.B. 172.

[55]For example, a bond purchased for $900 that is redeemable to pay estate taxes at $1000 can generate a tax savings of $60 to an estate in the 40 percent bracket ($100 less the $40 increase in estate taxes caused by converting the $900 of cash into the $900 flower bond).

[56]Estate of Simmie v. Comm'r, 69 T.C. 890, 896 (1978), aff'd, 632 F.2d 93 (9th Cir. 1980), where the estate's representative sold what he believed to be excess flower bonds at the market price (which was less than par) after the estate tax return was filed and before an estate tax deficiency was assessed. The flower bonds sold at the market price were included in the estate at par value. But see Colorado Nat'l Bank v. U.S., 27 A.F.T.R. 2d (P-H) 1827, 1829 (D. Colo. 1971).

[57]For a discussion of various estate planning considerations in using flower bonds, see J. PRICE, CONTEMPORARY ESTATE PLANNING, TEXT AND PROBLEMS 768-71 (1983).

[58]31 C.F.R. § 306.28(b)(1) (1985).

[59]31 C.F.R. § 306.28(b)(1)(iii) (1985).

erty of the decedent's estate or (2) to the extent that the surviving joint owner is required to contribute toward payment of the federal estate tax.[60] Fourth, bonds held as community property are redeemable at par only to the extent of the decedent's one-half interest in the bonds.[61]

(4) TAX-FREE EXCHANGES

The exchange of Treasury securities is generally taxable, unless the provisions for tax-free exchanges of property under different Code provisions independently apply. However, the Treasury is authorized to issue regulations to provide for the tax-free surrender of certain Treasury securities issued under chapter 31 of title 31 of the United States Code in exchange for certain other Treasury securities issued under the same chapter.[62] An exchange not covered under I.R.C. § 1037 is taxable. In addition, any noncorporate cash basis taxpayers who retain Series E and EE savings bonds past maturity can elect to retain their investments in certain United States discount obligations without current tax.[63] The remainder of this section discusses tax-free exchanges under I.R.C. § 1037.

(i) General Rule

Exchanges are tax-free under I.R.C. § 1037 only if Treasury regulations specifically provide for tax-free status. The appropriate Treasury Department Circular can be used to ascertain whether an exchange of Treasury securities is tax-free.[64] Also, each offering circular announcing a new Treasury security states the specific terms for an exchange and whether the exchange is completely or partially tax-free. For example, the exchange of Series E and Series EE savings bonds for Series HH bonds on a tax-free basis was first offered to the public in 1982.[65] As a result, a taxpayer can exchange Series E or EE bonds for Series HH bonds with a continued deferral of untaxed interest until the new bonds are ultimately redeemed.[66]

---

[60] 31 C.F.R. § 306.28(b)(1)(i) (1985).
[61] 31 C.F.R. § 306.28(b)(1)(i)(A) n. 6 (1985).
[62] I.R.C. § 1037(a).
[63] I.R.C. § 454(c).
[64] Treas. Reg. § 1.1037-1(a) (1971).
[65] 31 C.F.R. pts. 351, 352 (1985); see section 28.1(a)(2).
[66] 31 C.F.R. §§ 351.8(c), 352.0 (1985); see section 2.1(a)(4); section 28.1(a)(2).

Example   28-1

Assume a taxpayer purchased a Series E bond for $800 and elects not to accrue the interest for tax purposes. The bond is redeemable at maturity for $1000 ($800 plus accrued interest). Rather than pay tax on the interest on redemption of the bond, the taxpayer elects to exchange the Series E bond for a $1000 Series HH bond. Pursuant to I.R.C. § 1037(a), the accrued interest is not recognized in the year of the exchange.[67]

An owner of Treasury securities who has not been reporting interest on the accrual basis can exchange those securities for new securities authorized for exchange by the Treasury until the taxable year in which the new securities reach final maturity or are otherwise disposed of.[68] Each new security issued in a tax-free exchange bears a legend showing how much of its issue price represents untaxed interest on the old securities that were exchanged.[69] Untaxed interest is taxable when the new securities mature, are redeemed, or are otherwise disposed of.

Example   28-2

Assume a taxpayer owns a $1000 Series E savings bond purchased for $750 with an issue date of May 1, 1948. The taxpayer surrenders the bond to the United States in exchange for a Series HH bond on March 15, 1985 when the Series E bond has a redemption value of $1304.80. If the taxpayer pays an additional $195.20 to the United States and obtains three $500 face amount Series HH bonds, none of the $554.80 gain ($1304.80 redemption value minus the $750 tax basis) is recognized at the time of the exchange.[70]

If a taxpayer receives any cash in an otherwise nontaxable exchange, gain is recognized up to the amount of cash received on the exchange.[71] Loss, however, is not recognized.[72]

---

[67]31 C.F.R. §§ 352.0, 352.7(g)(1) (1985).
[68]*See, e.g.,* 31 C.F.R. § 352.7(g)(1) (1985).
[69]*See, e.g.,* 31 C.F.R. § 352.7(g)(2) (1985).
[70]*See* Treas. Reg. § 1.1037-1(a), Example (1) (1971).
[71]I.R.C. § 1031(b).
[72]I.R.C. § 1031(c).

Example   28-3

In 1983, a taxpayer purchases a Treasury bond for $970 that was originally issued at its par value of $1000. In 1984, he surrenders the bond to the United States in an exchange authorized by the Treasury solely for a new Treasury bond with a fair market value of $950. The taxpayer's $20 loss on the exchange ($970 tax basis minus $950 redemption value) is not recognized at the time of the exchange.[73]

The basis of securities acquired in a completely nontaxable exchange is determined under I.R.C. § 1031.[74] The basis of the new securities is the cost of the old securities, increased by any gain recognized, and reduced by any cash received. Any premium paid by the owner on the exchange (i.e., cash paid other than for accrued interest on the new bonds) is added to the basis of the new securities.[75] For capital assets, the holding period of the new securities received in the exchange includes the holding period of the old securities.[76]

Example   28-4

Assume the facts are the same as in Example 28-3. The taxpayer's basis in the new bond, which has a market value of $950, is $970.[77] Assume that it is necessary for the taxpayer to pay an additional $10 to acquire the new bond. His basis in the new bond is now $980 to reflect his additional $10 cash payment.[78]

(ii)   Application of Original Issue Discount Rules

The OID[79] rules are generally applied to tax-free exchanges under I.R.C. § 1037 in accordance with the following provisions. If an exchange is tax-free under I.R.C. § 1037(a) and the new securities received in the exchange are disposed of or redeemed at a gain, ordinary income is realized in an amount equal to the OID on the old securities that, but for I.R.C. § 1037, would have been taxable as ordinary income at the

---

[73]See Treas. Reg. § 1.1037-1(a)(3), Example (2) (1971).

[74]Treas. Reg. § 1.1037-1(d) (1971).

[75]For a discussion of premiums, see section 27.4.

[76]Treas. Reg. § 1.1037-1(c) (1971); see section 27.8.

[77]See I.R.C. § 1031(d).

[78]Treas. Reg. § 1.1037-1(a)(3), Example (2) (1971).

[79]See section 27.2.

time of the exchange.[80] In other words, if a security that was originally issued at a discount is exchanged tax-free, a portion or all of the gain on the sale or exchange of the new security may be considered gain from the sale or exchange of property that is not a capital asset.[81]

In addition, different provisions apply to marketable and nonmarketable securities.[82] If a nonmarketable security issued at a discount is exchanged,[83] the amount that would have been ordinary income on the exchange of the old security cannot exceed the difference between the issue price and the stated redemption price of the old security at the time of the exchange.[84] The issue price of the new security received in the exchange is treated as the stated redemption price of the old security plus any consideration paid to the United States as part of the exchange.[85] If a marketable security issued at not less than par (e.g., a Treasury bond) is exchanged, the issue price of the new security received is treated as the issue price of the old security plus any consideration paid to the United States as part of the exchange.[86]

(b) FEDERAL AGENCY DEBT SECURITIES

Various federal agencies issue debt securities to help finance their operations.[87] Federal agency debt securities are generally taxed in the same way as Treasury securities.[88] Interest paid on debt securities issued by federal agencies is exempt from income taxation by state and local governments under 31 U.S.C. § 3124, but is not exempt from federal income taxes. This statute essentially codifies the Supreme Court's ruling in *McCulloch v. Maryland*,[89] which provides that all properties, functions, and instrumentalities of the federal government are exempt from state and local taxation.

In *Smith v. Davis*,[90] the Supreme Court established a four-part test

---

[80]Treas. Reg. § 1.1037-1(b) (1971).

[81]For a discussion of the rules used in computing OID on the disposition of debt securities, see section 27.2.

[82]*See* section 2.1(a).

[83]*E.g.*, I.R.C. § 454(c) (on Series E or Series EE bonds).

[84]I.R.C. § 1037(b)(1).

[85]I.R.C. § 1037(b)(1)(B); Treas. Reg. § 1.1037-1(b)(2)(ii) (1971).

[86]I.R.C. § 1037(b)(2); Treas. Reg. § 1.1037-1(b)(5) (1971).

[87]*See* section 2.1(b).

[88]For a discussion of taxation of debt securities, see generally Chapter 27.

[89]17 U.S. (4 Wheat.) 316 (1819).

[90]323 U.S. 111 (1944).

to determine whether a security is exempt from state and local taxation. Specifically, the Supreme Court noted that securities exempt from state and local tax "have been characterized by (1) written documents, (2) the bearing of interest, (3) a binding promise by the United States to pay specified sums at specified dates and (4) specific congressional authorization, which also pledged the faith and credit of the United States in support of the promise to pay."[91] This four-part test has been cited with approval in *Montgomery Ward Life Ins. Co. v. State, Department of Local Government Affairs*,[92] in which the court held that GNMA pass-through certificates were not exempt from state and local taxation.[93] Specifically, the court noted that GNMA pass-through certificates did not meet the four-pronged test in *Smith*. The obligation of the United States was not primary but rather was "a contingent and speculative obligation requiring default by the issuer before it arises."[94] The court indicated that "obligation[s] issued to secure money for a governmental purpose" come under the exemption from state and local taxation.[95] The Supreme Court has indicated, albeit in dicta, that debt securities issued by federal agencies and instrumentalities, even though not issued directly by the United States, qualify for the exemption from state and local taxation.[96]

§ 28.2   MUNICIPAL SECURITIES

Interest received on debt securities of a state, territory, or possession of the United States, or any political subdivision of the foregoing, or the District of Columbia, is excluded from gross income for federal tax purposes.[97] The securities of states and their political subdivisions, referred to as "municipal securities," constitute the most significant category of tax-exempt securities.[98] This section specifically addresses mu-

---

[91] 323 U.S. at 115.

[92] 89 Ill. App. 3d 292, 297, 301, 411 N.E.2d 973, 976, 980 (1980).

[93] For a discussion of GNMA pass-through certificates, see section 2.1(b)(2). *See also* section 28.4.

[94] *Montgomery Ward Life*, 89 Ill. App. 3d at 297, 411 N.E.2d at 977.

[95] 89 Ill. App. 3d at 298, 411 N.E.2d at 978.

[96] In *Memphis Bank & Trust Co. v. Garner*, 459 U.S. 392 (1983), the Supreme Court noted that the exemption established in the predecessor section to 31 U.S.C. § 3124 applies not only to Treasury securities but also to debt securities of instrumentalities of the United States. 459 U.S. at 394.

[97] I.R.C. § 103(a)(1).

[98] *See generally* Chapter 3.

nicipal securities used to finance or refinance government operations and public projects or activities, but it is important to note that the following discussion on the general tax principles of tax-exempt interest also applies to other types of tax-exempt securities. Despite the broad tax exemption contained in I.R.C. § 103(a)(1), interest on certain municipal securities (e.g., industrial development bonds, mortgage subsidy bonds, and arbitrage bonds) may not be exempt from tax. In addition, proposals are frequently introduced in Congress to repeal or limit applicability of the tax exemption for certain types of municipal securities.[99] The remainder of this section discusses tax considerations for various types of municipal securities and mentions general tax principles applicable to tax-exempt securities.

(a) TYPES OF MUNICIPAL SECURITIES

Municipal securities are defined in the Treasury regulations as "obligations issued by or on behalf of any State or local governmental unit by constituted authorities empowered to issue such obligations."[100] In addition, municipal securities include "[c]ertificates issued by a political subdivision for public improvements . . . which are evidence of special assessments against specific property . . . even though the obligations are satisfied out of special funds and not out of general funds or taxes."[101] Interest on special tax bills and special assessment bonds for municipal purposes may also be tax-exempt.[102] In short, the obligations must be incurred in the exercise of the borrowing power of a state or a political subdivision (e.g., counties, special districts, cities, and towns).[103]

(1) GENERAL OBLIGATION BONDS

General obligation bonds are secured by the issuing municipality's general taxing powers.[104] Some general obligation bonds are also secured

---

[99]See, e.g., 1985 Tax Reform, President's Tax Proposals to Congress for Fairness, Growth, and Simplicity, STAN. FED. TAX REP. (CCH) Rep. No. 25, Extra Ed., ch. 11 (May 29, 1985).

[100]Treas. Reg. § 1.103-1(b) (1972).

[101]Id.

[102]Bryant v. Comm'r, 111 F.2d 9, 12 (9th Cir. 1940); Avery v. Comm'r, 111 F.2d 19, 23 (9th Cir. 1940).

[103]See Rev. Rul. 69-171, 1969-1 C.B. 46 (where interest paid to a bank by a political subdivision on behalf of a student borrower was taxable); see also LTR 8142048 (July 21, 1981).

[104]See section 3.2(a).

by certain identified fees or charges, which provide an additional source of revenue to secure the bonds. Interest on general obligation bonds is tax-exempt.[105]

(2) REVENUE BONDS

Revenue bonds are usually issued by a municipality to finance or refinance a particular project. The municipality pledges the revenues generated by the project to meet interest and principal payment obligations, but it does not pledge its full taxing power in support of its payment obligations. Interest on revenue bonds is tax-exempt.[106]

(3) INDUSTRIAL DEVELOPMENT BONDS

IDBs are a type of revenue bond issued by a municipality for industrial or commercial purposes, where a major part of the project or facility is leased, owned, or used by a private business and the payment of principal or interest is secured at least in major part by the project, facility, or revenues of a nonexempt trade or business.[107] The attraction of IDB financing for a business is that the cost of borrowing the funds is lower than in the case of taxable bonds or loans from financial institutions.

Because of abuses in the types of facilities financed with IDBs, the tax exemption has been eliminated in many cases and restricted in others. In addition, proposals are frequently introduced in Congress to repeal or further limit the tax exemption available for certain IDBs, although it is not likely that currently outstanding IDBs will be affected by any legislation.[108] The remainder of this section briefly discusses the current tax treatment of IDBs.[109]

An IDB is a security that is issued nominally by a municipality, the payment of the principal or interest on which is secured, in whole or major part, by any interest in (1) property used in a trade or business of a nonexempt person, (2) payments with respect to such property, or (3) is derived from payments from the property or borrowed money used (or to be used) in a trade or business. In addition, a major portion of

---

[105]For a discussion of the justification for the tax exemption, see section 28.2(b)(1).

[106]For a discussion of the justification for the tax exemption, see section 28.2(b)(1).

[107]See section 23.4(b); see also Weinberg & Stock, Industrial Development Bonds: Overview in Light of the Tax Reform Act of 1984, 1 REAL ESTATE FINANCE L. J. 115 (1985).

[108]H.R. 1767, 2551, 3092, 3838, 99th Cong., 1st Sess. (1985); S. 981, 99th Cong., 1st Sess. (1981).

[109]It is likely, however, that IDBs will be modified by future legislation.

the proceeds from the issue are used in any trade or business of a non-exempt person and interest and principal payments may be secured by a lien or mortgage on the property used in a trade or business.[110] The phrase "major portion of the proceeds" is defined as more than 25 percent of the proceeds of an issue.[111] "Nonexempt persons" are any persons other than a governmental unit or an entity described in I.R.C. § 501(c)(3), which is exempt from tax under I.R.C. § 501(a).[112]

IDBs issued after December 31, 1982 must meet additional requirements to be tax-exempt.[113] First, a public hearing must be held after reasonable notice, prior to issuance of the bonds, and issuance must be approved after the hearing.[114] Second, an information report must be filed by the municipality shortly after the issuance of the bonds.[115] Third, the average maturity of the IDB cannot exceed 120 percent of the average economic life of the facilities to be financed.[116]

After TEFRA, IDBs cannot be issued to acquire property unless the first use of the property is after the acquisition financed by the IDB or the property is substantially rehabilitated.[117] Also, consumer loan bonds no longer qualify as IDBs.[118] Finally, there is now a prohibition on the issuance of IDBs where 25 percent or more of the proceeds are used to acquire land; and no part of the proceeds can be used directly or indirectly to acquire farm land.[119] (An exception is available for first-time farmers for land acquired for certain environmental purposes.)[120] The Code specifically provides that IDBs cannot be used to finance private airplanes, skyboxes or other luxury boxes, health club facilities, gambling facilities, or liquor stores.[121]

The Code now limits the aggregate amount of private activity bonds that a state can issue during any calendar year.[122] The current state limit is $150 multiplied by the greater of the state's population or $200

---

[110]I.R.C. § 103(b)(2); Treas. Reg. § 1.103-7(b)(1) (1983).

[111]Treas. Reg. § 1.103-7(b)(3)(iii) (1983).

[112]I.R.C. § 103(b)(3).

[113]TEFRA, Pub. L. 97-248, § 221, 96 Stat. 324, 477-78 (1982).

[114]I.R.C. § 103(k)(2); Temp. Treas. Reg. §§ 5f.103-2(c), (d) (1983).

[115]I.R.C. § 103(l)(2).

[116]I.R.C. § 103(b)(14).

[117]I.R.C. § 103(b)(17).

[118]I.R.C. § 103(o).

[119]I.R.C. § 103(b)(16)(A).

[120]I.R.C. §§ 103(b)(16)(B), (C).

[121]I.R.C. § 103(b)(18).

[122]I.R.C. § 103(n).

million.[123] Limitations are also imposed on the aggregate amount of bonds issued by state agencies[124] and other issuing authorities.[125] There is an aggregate limit on IDBs issued for the benefit of owners or principal users for facilities being financed.[126] The aggregate amount that can be issued for any beneficiary during the three-year test period is $40 million.[127]

The following discussion on the tax requirement of IDBs is intended to merely acquaint the reader with IDB financing. It is not intended to be a comprehensive analysis. Numerous statutory exceptions, special rules, and transitional provisions apply to IDBs.[128] In addition, temporary Treasury regulations have been issued to explain the limitations on the aggregate amounts of private activity bonds.[129] Even if a security meets the definition of an IDB under the general rule of I.R.C. § 103(b) and does not violate the TEFRA prohibitions, it is taxable unless it falls within one of the specific exemptions contained in I.R.C. § 103(b). These exemptions include exempt facility IDBs[130] and the small issue exemption.[131] The remainder of this section discusses these exemptions.

(i)   Exempt Facility IDBs

If an IDB is issued for the purpose of financing an exempt facility described in I.R.C. § 103(b)(4) and it meets all of the Code requirements, it qualifies for tax exemption under I.R.C. § 103(a). There is no limitation on the dollar amount available to finance exempt facilities. An IDB issue is exempt under the exempt facility exemption if substantially all of its proceeds are used to provide one of the following facilities:

1.   Certain projects for residential rental property[132]
2.   Sports facilities[133]
3.   Convention or trade show facilities[134]

[123]I.R.C. § 103(n)(4)(A).
[124]I.R.C. § 103(n)(2).
[125]I.R.C. § 103(n)(3).
[126]I.R.C. § 103(b)(15).
[127]I.R.C. § 103(b)(15)(A).
[128]See, e.g., DRA, Pub. L. 98-369, § 621, 98 Stat. 494, 915-18 (1984).
[129]See Temp. Treas. Reg. §§ 1.103(n)-1T, -6T (1984).
[130]I.R.C. § 103(b)(4).
[131]I.R.C. § 103(b)(6).
[132]I.R.C. § 103(b)(4)(A).
[133]I.R.C. § 103(b)(4)(B).
[134]I.R.C. § 103(b)(4)(C).

4. Airports, docks, wharves, mass commuting facilities, parking facilities, or storage or training facilities directly related to any of the foregoing[135]

5. Sewage or solid waste disposal facilities or facilities for furnishing electric energy or gas[136]

6. Air or water pollution control facilities[137]

7. Certain facilities to furnish water[138]

8. Certain hydroelectric and generating facilities[139]

9. Certain mass commuting vehicles[140]

10. Local district heating or cooling facilities[141]

I.R.C. § 103(b)(4) thus sets out a wide range of facilities eligible for tax-exempt financing.[142] If a particular IDB issue qualifies as an exempt facility project, interest is exempt from tax without regard to the dollar amount of the issue.[143]

(ii) Small Issue Exemption

Certain IDBs that qualify for the small issue exemption generate tax-exempt interest.[144] The $1 million small issue exemption is available to IDB issues with an aggregate authorized face amount of $1 million or less, if substantially all of the proceeds are used (1) for the acquisition, construction, reconstruction, or improvement of land (subject to the 25 percent TEFRA limit), or property of a character subject to an allowance for depreciation, or (2) to redeem all or part of a prior IDB issue that was used for such purposes.[145] The proceeds of a small issue exemption financing are not available to finance inventory or to provide working capital for a business.[146] The IRS has ruled that the simultaneous is-

---

[135]I.R.C. § 103(b)(4)(D).

[136]I.R.C. § 103(b)(4)(E).

[137]I.R.C. § 103(b)(4)(F).

[138]I.R.C. § 103(b)(4)(G).

[139]I.R.C. § 103(b)(4)(H).

[140]I.R.C. § 103(b)(4)(I).

[141]I.R.C. § 103(b)(4)(J).

[142]Recent legislative proposals reduce the list of exempt facilities. *See, e.g.,* STAFF OF THE JOINT COMMITTEE ON TAXATION, 99TH CONG., 1ST SESS., SUMMARY OF H.R. 3838 (TAX REFORM ACT OF 1985) 23–25 (Joint Comm. Print 1985).

[143]For the basic requirements of IDBs, see section 28.2(a)(3).

[144]I.R.C. § 103(b)(6)(A).

[145]*Id.*

[146]Treas. Reg. § 1.103-10(b)(1)(ii).

suance of several series of IDBs of $1 million may qualify for the small issue exemption if (1) the IDBs are not sold at substantially the same time, (2) the IDBs are not sold pursuant to a common plan of marketing, (3) the IDBs are not sold at substantially the same rate of interest, and (4) a common or pooled security is not used or available to pay debt service on the IDBs.[147]

A $10 million small issue limitation can be elected in certain cases for bonds issued after December 31, 1978.[148] Expenses of issuing bonds are capital expenditures that must be included in determining whether the $10 million limitation is met.[149] For the $10 million limitation, for three years before and three years after the date of issuance of the bonds, all capital expenditures relating to facilities in the same municipality and used by the same or a related user must be aggregated.[150] The proceeds of a $10 million issue must be used for the same purposes authorized for the $1 million exemption.

(4) MORTGAGE SUBSIDY BONDS

Mortgage subsidy bonds are securities issued by municipalities where a significant portion of the proceeds is used directly or indirectly to provide mortgages or other financing for owner-occupied residences.[151] Interest on mortgage subsidy bonds issued after April 24, 1979 is generally taxable unless the securities meet a comprehensive list of requirements as to the type of residence, its location, the aggregate amount of bonds, and arbitrage limits.[152] The remainder of this section discusses tax-exempt mortgage subsidy bonds: qualified mortgage bonds and qualified veterans' mortgage bonds.

Qualified mortgage bonds issued before 1988 as part of a qualified mortgage issue[153] are tax-exempt if the following conditions are met. First, all proceeds of the issue (except for issuance costs and a debt service reserve fund) must be used to finance owner-occupied residences.[154] Second, each residence (which must be located within the

---

[147]Rev. Rul. 81-216, 1981-2 C.B. 21 (revoking Rev. Rul. 74-380, 1974-2 C.B. 32; Rev. Rul. 77-55, 1977-1 C.B. 18; Rev. Rul. 78-159, 1978-1 C.B. 27).

[148]I.R.C. § 103(b)(6)(D).

[149]Rev. Rul. 77-234, 1977-2 C.B. 39.

[150]LTR 8406039 (Nov. 7, 1983); LTR 8347050 (Aug. 22, 1983); LTR 8347043 (Aug. 22, 1983); LTR 8347040 (Aug. 22, 1983); LTR 8345007 (Aug. 5, 1983); LTR 8234122 (May 27, 1982); G.C.M. 38597 (Dec. 30, 1980).

[151]I.R.C. § 103A(b)(1).

[152]See generally I.R.C. § 103A.

[153]I.R.C. § 103A(c)(1).

[154]I.R.C. § 103A(c)(2)(A)(i).

jurisdiction of the issuer) must be a single family residence that can reasonably be expected to become the principal residence of the mortgagor.[155] Third, at least 90 percent of the lendable proceeds must be used to finance residences of mortgagors who, within three years prior to the mortgage, had no present ownership interest in their principal residences.[156] Fourth, the purchase price for each residence must not exceed 110 percent of the average area purchase price for residences.[157] Fifth, the aggregate amount of bonds issued by the municipality during any calendar year must not exceed the statutory limitation.[158] Sixth, at least 20 percent of the issue proceeds must, with reasonable diligence, be made available to targeted areas.[159] Seventh, the bonds must not be arbitrage bonds.[160]

Qualified veterans' mortgage bonds are tax-exempt if substantially all of the proceeds are used to finance single family owner-occupied residences for veterans.[161] Qualified veterans' mortgage bonds issued after July 18, 1984 must meet additional requirements. First, each mortgagor must be a qualified veteran, defined as any veteran who served on active duty at some time before January 1, 1977 and who applies for financing before the later of January 1, 1985 or 30 years after he left active military service.[162] Second, the municipality's program for mortgages for veterans must have been in effect before June 22, 1984.[163] Third, the aggregate amount of bonds issued by the municipality as qualified veterans' mortgage bonds during the calendar year must not exceed the statutory limitation.[164] Fourth, both interest and principal repayment obligations for qualified veterans' mortgage bonds must be secured by the general obligation of the municipality.[165]

Qualified mortgage bonds and qualified veterans' mortgage bonds must comply with additional requirements to be tax-exempt. As a starting point, the securities must be issued in registered form.[166] In addition,

---

[155] I.R.C. § 103A(d).

[156] I.R.C. § 103A(e).

[157] I.R.C. § 103A(f)(1).

[158] I.R.C. § 103A(f)(2).

[159] I.R.C. § 103A(h)(1). Targeted area residences are defined in I.R.C. § 103A(k).

[160] I.R.C. § 103A(i); see section 28.2(b)(1)(i)(e).

[161] I.R.C. § 103A(c)(3).

[162] I.R.C. § 103A(o)(4).

[163] I.R.C. § 103A(o)(2).

[164] I.R.C. § 103A(o)(3).

[165] I.R.C. § 103A(c)(3)(B).

[166] I.R.C. § 103(j)(1). See the discussion of registration requirements at section 27.11 and section 28.2(b)(1)(i)(b).

for bonds issued after December 31, 1983, the municipality must file a statement with the Treasury containing (1) the name and address of the issuer; (2) the date of issue, amount of lendable proceeds, interest rate, term, and face amount of each obligation that is part of the issue; and (3) such other information as the Treasury requires.[167] Finally, the municipality must certify that the bond issue meets all of the requirements mentioned above and must also submit annual reports that include the policy statement adopted by it and a statement as to whether it has complied with its own policy statement.[168]

(b) GENERAL TAX PRINCIPLES

(1) INTEREST INCOME

(i) Federal Income Tax

Interest income earned on municipal securities is exempt from federal income tax,[169] which makes municipal securities attractive to taxpayers in a high marginal tax bracket. The tax exemption is based on the doctrine of reciprocal immunity of the United States Constitution, which provides that the states cannot interfere in operations of the federal government and the federal government cannot interfere in operations of state governments.[170] The Supreme Court's view was that taxing interest earned on municipal securities could impair a municipality's ability to finance its operations. Some commentators view the Sixteenth Amendment to the Constitution as removing the constitutional prohibition and placing in the political arena the issue of whether interest on municipal securities may be taxed by the federal government.[171]

If municipal securities are purchased when interest payments are in default, any amounts subsequently paid on the outstanding unpaid interest amount are treated as a return of capital, not as the payment of

---

[167]I.R.C. § 103A(j)(3)(A).

[168]I.R.C. §§ 103A(j)(4)(C), (5).

[169]I.R.C. § 103(a).

[170]Pollock v. Farmers' Loan & Trust Co., 157 U.S. 429, 586 (1895) (superseded by the Sixteenth Amendment as stated in U.S. v. Stillhammer, 706 F.2d 1072, 1077 (10th Cir. 1983), where the Supreme Court held that a federal tax on the interest on bonds of state and local institutions violated the reciprocal immunity doctrine).

[171]The Code has provided a tax exemption for municipal securities since 1913, so the issue of whether the tax exemption for municipal securities is required by the Constitution has not been tested. See section 27.11; section 28.2(b)(1)(i)(b).

tax-exempt interest.[172] The taxpayer's remaining cost basis is thereby reduced. For a discussion of flat bonds generally, see section 27.7.

Any OID on municipal securities is treated as interest, which means that discount is exempt from federal income taxes.[173] If municipal securities are sold before maturity, each holder of the security is entitled to apportion the amount of OID.[174] A premium received on a redemption of tax-exempt securities is not interest. Rather, it is taxable as an amount received in exchange for the securities. Gain on the sale of municipal securities, except to the extent attributable to accrued interest or OID, is also taxable income.[175]

The remainder of this section discusses current issues on the interest exemption from federal income tax.

(a) FEDERAL GUARANTEE

If municipal securities that are otherwise tax-exempt are directly or indirectly guaranteed by the United States government (or its instrumentalities or agencies), interest income on the securities is not exempt from tax.[176] This prohibition against federal guarantees generally applies to all municipal securities issued after December 31, 1983.[177] There are three different ways in which a security is viewed as federally guaranteed. First, an obligation is federally guaranteed if the payment of principal or interest is guaranteed in whole or in part by the United States government, any federal agency, or federal instrumentality.[178] Second, a security is federally guaranteed if a significant portion of the proceeds are used to make loans (where the payment of principal or interest is guaranteed by the United States, any federal agency, or federal instrumentality) or the proceeds are invested directly or indirectly in federally insured deposits or accounts.[179] Third, a security is federally guaranteed if the payment of principal or interest is indirectly guar-

---

[172]Clyde E. Pierce Corp. v. Comm'r, 120 F.2d 206, 208 (5th Cir. 1941); R.O. Holton & Co. v. Comm'r, 44 B.T.A. 202, 206 (1941); Treas. Reg. § 1.61-7(c) (1966).

[173]Rev. Rul. 73-112, 1973-1 C.B. 47.

[174]For a discussion of how OID is allocated for tax-exempt securities, see section 27.2(e).

[175]Willcuts v. Bunn, 282 U.S. 216, 224 (1931).

[176]I.R.C. § 103(h)(1).

[177]DRA, *supra* note 127, § 631(c)(1).

[178]I.R.C. § 103(h)(2)(A). Interest is also taxable if paid during any period in which payment is guaranteed in whole or in part under Title I of the New York City Loan Guarantee Act of 1978. I.R.C. § 103(f). In addition, interest on debt securities issued to develop geothermal energy is taxable if the repayment of principal or interest is guaranteed under Title V of the Department of Energy Act of 1978. Rev. Rul. 80-161, 1980-1 C.B. 21.

[179]I.R.C. § 103(h)(2)(B).

anteed by the United States government, any federal agency, or federal instrumentality.[180]

There are exceptions to the prohibition against federal guarantees. First, a security is not deemed to be federally guaranteed by reason of certain insurance programs, such as the insurance programs of FNMA, FHLMC, GNMA, SLMA, the Federal Housing Administration, or the Veteran's Administration (or the SBA for certain contracts for pollution control facilities).[181] Second, some securities generate tax-exempt interest even though they are federally insured (e.g., securities to finance residential rental property occupied by low or moderate income individuals,[182] qualified mortgage bonds,[183] and qualified veterans' mortgage bonds),[184] provided the proceeds are not invested in federally insured deposits or accounts. Other exceptions allow certain temporary investments, investments in Treasury obligations, and investments of a bona fide debt service fund.

In the past, certain municipal securities have been issued which were secured by certificates of deposit that are federally insured by either the FSLIC or the FDIC in amounts up to $100,000 per security holder. Municipal securities issued after April 14, 1983 (or issued pursuant to a binding contract in effect on or after March 4, 1983) are not tax-exempt if the proceeds of the issue are invested in federally insured deposits or accounts.[185]

At this writing, the issue of whether a standby letter of credit issued by a bank is federally guaranteed because of FDIC insurance is before the Supreme Court in *Philadelphia Gear Corp. v. Federal Deposit Insurance Corp.*[186] The Tenth Circuit Court of Appeals has held that standby letters of credit issued by a bank that subsequently becomes insolvent are "deposits" within the Federal Deposit Insurance Act and are, therefore, insured by the FDIC.[187] Bond counsel have been concerned that this decision may possibly be applied to taint the tax-exempt nature of municipal securities backed by bank standby letters of credit, because FDIC insurance is not specifically listed in I.R.C. § 103(h)(3)(A) as one of the insurance programs not deemed to be federal guarantees for

[180]I.R.C. § 103(h)(2)(C).

[181]I.R.C. § 103(h)(3)(A).

[182]I.R.C. § 103(b)(4)(A).

[183]I.R.C. § 103A(b)(2); *see* section 28.2(a)(4).

[184]I.R.C. § 103A(b)(2); *see* section 28.2(a)(4).

[185]I.R.C. § 103(h)(2).

[186]751 F.2d 1131 (10th Cir. 1984), *cert. granted*, 54 U.S.L.W. 3270 (U.S. Oct. 21, 1985) (No. 84-1972).

[187]751 F.2d at 1138.

purposes of I.R.C. § 103(h). The IRS has announced, however, that municipal securities issued prior to 120 days after the Supreme Court renders its decision in *Philadelphia Gear Corp.* that are guaranteed by letters of credit of banks with deposits insured by the FDIC are not treated as federally guaranteed obligations solely because of the letters of credit.[188]

(b) REGISTRATION REQUIREMENTS

The Code provides that municipal securities issued after December 31, 1982 must be issued in registered form for interest on them to be tax-exempt.[189] This provision, enacted as part of TEFRA,[190] provides certain exemptions for securities not issued to the public,[191] securities with a maturity of not more than one year after issuance,[192] and certain obligations intended to be sold to non-United States persons.[193] TEFRA originally provided a December 31, 1982 effective date for registration requirements.[194] TCA '82 delayed until July 1, 1983 the effective date for those tax-exempt securities that were not required to be in registered form on the day before TEFRA's enactment (i.e., September 2, 1982).[195]

An additional penalty is imposed on owners of nonregistered tax-exempt securities that are required to be in registered form. Any loss on the sale, exchange, theft, loss, or other disposition of nonregistered securities is not deductible if the security should be, but is not, in registered form.[196] In addition, gain on the disposition of securities required to be registered that would otherwise be tax-exempt (except that they are not issued in registered form) is taxed as ordinary income, not capital gain.[197]

The state of South Carolina filed a complaint in the Supreme Court against the Treasury on the grounds that registration requirements are unconstitutional. In *South Carolina v. Regan*,[198] the Supreme Court allowed South Carolina to file a complaint asserting that the doctrine of

---

[188]Internal Revenue News Release IR-85-32, 10 STAND. FED. TAX REP. (CCH) ¶ 6468 (Apr. 1, 1985); IR-85-42, 10 STAND. FED. TAX REP. (CCH) ¶ 6511 (Apr. 26, 1985); IR-85-113, 10 STAND. FED. TAX REP. (CCH) ¶ 6817 (Nov. 27, 1985).

[189]I.R.C. § 103(j).

[190]TEFRA, *supra* note 113, § 310(b)(1).

[191]I.R.C. § 103(j)(2).

[192]*Id.*

[193]*Id.*; Temp. Treas. Reg. § 1.163-5T(c) (1984).

[194]TEFRA, *supra* note 113, § 310(d)(1).

[195]TCA '82, Pub. L. 97-448, § 306(b)(2), 96 Stat. 2365, 2405-06 (1982).

[196]I.R.C. § 165(j)(1).

[197]I.R.C. § 1287. For a discussion of these penalty provisions, see section 27.11.

[198]465 U.S. 367, 382 (1984).

intragovernmental tax immunity precludes the federal government from imposing registration requirements on a municipality's otherwise tax-exempt bonds. A special master was appointed by the Court to develop a record sufficient for the Court to address the merits of the case.[199] At this writing, the Supreme Court has not ruled on the issue.

(c) ACQUISITION OF A PUT OPTION

Certain municipal securities have a put option feature, granting the owner the right to sell the securities back to the issuer at par prior to maturity.[200] If interest rates increase, a municipal securities owner may exercise the put option. The tax question is whether the put option affects the tax-exempt status of the interest. The IRS has ruled that a regulated investment company that purchases municipal securities with put options is the owner of the tax-exempt securities, despite the fact that the risk of loss on the security is shifted by simultaneously purchasing separate put options.[201] The IRS considered the following factors in reaching this decision. First, the taxpayer paid an arm's length price for the put options, which represented the parties' estimate of the value of the risk.[202] Second, the primary purpose for the taxpayer's acquisition of the put options was to increase liquidity, not to shift the risk of loss.[203] Third, the taxpayer would still benefit from any appreciation in the value of the tax-exempt securities. Fourth, the period during which the risk could be shifted was substantially less than the term of the municipal security.[204] Because of this last factor used in the IRS's analysis, it is not clear what effect, if any, a put option feature built into a municipal security that is conterminous with the term of the security would have on the tax-exempt status of the security. In 1983, without revoking this ruling, the IRS announced that it would not issue rulings "as to the true owner" of securities subject to put options.[205]

---

[199]*Id.* at 382.

[200]*See* section 3.3.

[201]Rev. Rul. 82-144, 1982-2 C.B. 34; LTR 8317017 (Jan. 21, 1983); LTR 8247025 (Aug. 18, 1982).

[202]Rev. Rul. 82-144, 1982-2 C.B. 34.

[203]*Id.*

[204]*Id.*

[205]Rev. Proc. 83-55, 1983-2 C.B. 572, *superseded by* Rev. Proc. 84-22, 1984-1 C.B. 449.

(d) INSURANCE

Municipal securities frequently are backed by insurance, an indemnity, or a guarantee (insuring the issuer's payment obligations), without subjecting the interest income to tax.[206] In the event of a default, the insurance company typically pays the owner of the securities any principal and interest that has not been paid by the issuer. The IRS has ruled that insuring municipal securities against a default in principal and interest does not affect the tax-exempt status of the interest paid on the securities.[207] In addition, if defaulted interest is eventually paid by the third party, the payment is not included in the gross income of the security owners.[208] Insurance proceeds representing defaulted interest on tax-exempt securities is exempt from gross income, irrespective of whether the insurance is paid for by the issuer, the underwriters, or the security owners.[209] Generally, if the securities are guaranteed by the federal government, the interest income on the securities is not tax-exempt.[210]

(e) ARBITRAGE BONDS

An arbitrage bond is a municipal security where all (or a major portion) of the proceeds of the issue are reasonably expected to be used directly or indirectly to acquire securities expected to produce a higher yield.[211] Prior to 1969, some municipalities would issue their own tax-exempt securities with the intention of investing a major portion of the proceeds in taxable debt securities with higher interest rates. As a result, the municipality's interest expense was less than the interest income it could earn on its investment in taxable debt securities. It would benefit from this interest rate spread between its arbitrage bonds and the taxable securities. Interest on arbitrage bonds issued after October 9, 1969

---

[206]*See* section 3.3.

[207]Rev. Rul. 76-78, 1976-1 C.B. 25; Rev. Rul. 72-134, 1972-1 C.B. 29, *amplified by* Rev. Rul. 72-575, 1972-2 C.B. 74, *amplified by* Rev. Rul. 76-78, 1976-1 C.B. 25; LTR 8347058 (Aug. 25, 1983); LTR 7801017 (Oct. 7, 1977), *modified by* LTR 7816004 (Jan. 17, 1978).

[208]Rev. Rul. 76-78, 1976-1 C.B. 25; Rev. Rul. 72-134, 1972-2 C.B. 29, *amplified by* Rev. Rul. 72-575, 1972-2 C.B. 74, *amplified by* Rev. Rul. 76-78, 1976-1 C.B. 25; LTR 8347058 (Aug. 25, 1983); LTR 7801017 (Oct. 7, 1977), *modified by* LTR 7816004 (Jan. 17, 1978).

[209]Unlike the line of rulings concerning tax-exempt interest, payments made by an insurance company or surety company to cover defaulted dividend payments may preclude application of the intercorporate dividends received deduction. *See* UNITED STATES STEEL CORPORATION, MONEY MARKET CUMULATIVE PREFERRED STOCK, SERIES S-A AND SERIES S-B, PROSPECTUS (Supp. Jan. 24, 1985).

[210]*See* section 28.2(b)(1)(i)(a).

[211]I.R.C. § 103(c)(2).

is taxable.[212] The arbitrage limits have been found to be violated by a municipality that entered into repos as a way of investing its funds.[213] The municipality (i.e., the seller-debtor) transferred its notes pursuant to a repo agreement to a securities dealer in exchange for cash, which the municipality invested in a local government investing pool at a "materially higher" yield.[214] The transaction violated the arbitrage yield limitations.

Recently, some municipalities have issued securities that intentionally do not comply with the arbitrage limitations and generate taxable interest income. As a result, the issuers can invest the proceeds of the issue at the highest rates available without regard to the so-called arbitrage restrictions. Taxable debt securities pay higher interest rates and thus have a higher interest cost to the municipalities. Nevertheless, because the municipalities are free to invest the funds at a higher rate than they otherwise could if they had to comply with the arbitrage restrictions, this may be a benefit to the issuer. For example, in December of 1985, Los Angeles County refinanced part of its capital requirements by selling taxable securities that did not meet the arbitrage restrictions.[215] In the same month, the Indiana Housing Authority also issued taxable securities.

The remainder of this section provides a brief overview of arbitrage bonds. A detailed discussion is beyond the scope of this book. The arbitrage regulations issued by the Treasury are complex and difficult to apply.[216] Somewhat different requirements apply to different kinds of municipal securities. For example, under TEFRA, IDBs are subject to requirements to rebate arbitrage profits to the federal government and to additional yield restrictions on the investment of bond proceeds.[217] Whether a security is an arbitrage bond depends on the issuer's reasonable expectations on the date of issue as to the amount and use of the proceeds.[218] The Treasury regulations contemplate that issuers can issue "no arbitrage certificates" to express their reasonable expectations

---

[212]I.R.C. § 103(c)(1). For a discussion of acceptable arbitrage transactions, see Buschman & Winterer, *Legal Arbitrage*, in 1 THE MUNICIPAL BOND HANDBOOK 204 (F. Fabozzi, S. Feldstein, I. Pollack & F. Zarb eds. 1983).

[213]Rev. Rul. 79-108, 1979-1 C.B. 75.

[214]*Id.*

[215]*See* Carlson, *Los Angeles County Discovers Benefits in Taxable Securities*, Wall St. J., Dec. 10, 1985, at 33, col. 1.

[216]The regulations were amended six times in a six-year period prior to adoption of final regulations.

[217]I.R.C. § 103(c)(6); Treas. Reg. § 1.103-15AT (1985).

[218]Treas. Reg. § 1.103-13(a)(2)(i) (1979).

that the bonds are tax-exempt.[219] Subsequent events do not affect a certification made in accordance with the issuer's reasonable expectations on the date of issue.[220] Certificates issued in bad faith, however, where a municipality reasonably expected to use all or a major portion of the proceeds to acquire higher yield securities, cannot be relied on and such bonds are arbitrage bonds.[221]

The IRS has taken the position in published rulings that certain outstanding municipal securities are taxable.[222] The IRS found that, after the securities had been issued, the issuers acted in a manner that violated the arbitrage rules. In fact, the investors had relied on "no arbitrage certifications" based on the reasonable expectations of the issuers at the time the securities were issued. In another published ruling where improper arbitrage actions of the issuer were found to have occurred at the time the securities were issued, the IRS found the securities to be taxable.[223] In addition, a municipality cannot rely on its no arbitrage certification if it was made in bad faith.[224] The major impact of these published rulings is that investors who acquire securities that they believe to be tax-exempt may subsequently find themselves taxed on interest earned on those securities due to certain actions taken by the issuer in violation of the arbitrage regulations.[225]

(ii)   Estate and Gift Taxes

Municipal securities are subject to estate and gift taxes.[226] The tax exemption provided in I.R.C. § 103(a) is limited to federal income tax on interest income. Estate tax[227] and gift tax[228] are viewed as excise taxes on the transfer of property, not as a tax on the property transferred. For

---

[219]Treas. Reg. § 1.103-13(a)(2)(ii)(B) (1979).

[220]Treas. Reg. § 1.103-13(a)(2)(ii)(F) (1979).

[221]Rev. Rul. 85-182, 1985-46 I.R.B. 4.

[222]See Rev. Rul. 80-91, 1980-1 C.B. 29; Rev. Rul. 80-92, 1980-1 C.B. 31; Rev. Rul. 85-182, 1985-46 I.R.B. 4.

[223]Rev. Rul. 80-328, 1980-2 C.B. 53.

[224]Rev. Rul. 85-182, 1985-46 I.R.B. 4.

[225]The IRS has announced it will consider entering into closing agreements with issuers who agree to give up their arbitrage profit to preserve the tax-exempt status of interest paid on their securities issued before April 30, 1982 or with respect to which a private ruling was sought before that date. Announcement of Rev. Rul. 82-101, 1982-1 C.B. 21, in the Internal Revenue Bulletin, IRS News Release I.R. 82-51, 10 STAND. FED. TAX REP. (CCH) ¶ 6488 (Apr. 30, 1982).

[226]Greiner v. Lewellyn, 258 U.S. 384 (1922); Knowlton v. Moore, 178 U.S. 41 (1900); *but see* Haffner v. U.S., 757 F.2d 920 (7th Cir. 1985).

[227]Treas. Reg. § 20.2033-1(a) (1963).

[228]Willcuts v. Bunn, 282 U.S. at 230; I.R.C. § 2511(a); Treas. Reg. § 25.2511-1(a) (1983).

estate tax purposes, a decedent's gross estate includes all property, real or personal, tangible or intangible, wherever situated.[229] In addition, a decedent's estate includes the value of all property to the extent of the decedent's interest in the property at the time of his death.[230] The same rationale applies to gifts.

(iii) Social Security Benefits

Gross income includes up to one-half of a taxpayer's social security and railroad retirement benefits received in any taxable year after 1983.[231] The amount included in gross income is the lesser of one-half of the benefit, plus modified adjusted gross income, minus the base amount.[232] Modified adjusted gross income includes tax-exempt interest received or accrued by the taxpayer during the taxable year.[233] This means that some recipients of social security and railroad retirement benefits who obtain tax-exempt interest income have a greater portion of their benefits subject to tax.

(iv) Original Issue Discount and Market Discount

The IRS has ruled that to the extent discount on municipal securities is OID, it is treated as tax-exempt interest.[234] Market discount, on the other hand, is not considered to be tax-exempt interest.[235] Prior to the DRA,[236] OID on tax-exempt securities was apportioned among the original holder and subsequent holders of a tax-exempt security on a straight-line basis over the term of the security.[237] In many cases, the straight-line method resulted in artificially large portions of a security's OID being attributed to its earlier periods, thereby increasing its owner's tax basis in the security. Furthermore, because the security owner reduces the amount realized on disposition by accrued (albeit tax-exempt)

---

[229]I.R.C. § 2031(1).

[230]I.R.C. § 2033.

[231]I.R.C. §§ 86(a), (d)(1).

[232]I.R.C. § 86(b)(1).

[233]I.R.C. § 86(b)(2).

[234]Rev. Rul. 73-112, 1973-1 C.B. 47.

[235]*Id.*

[236]DRA, *supra* note 128, § 41(a).

[237]Rev. Rul. 73-112, 1973-1 C.B. 47; *see also* HOUSE CONFERENCE REPORT, DEFICIT REDUCTION ACT OF 1984, H.R. REP. NO. 861, 98th Cong., 2d Sess. 810 (1984).

OID, the use of the straight-line method also frequently results in the recognition of a loss on a sale of the security at the market price.[238]

The DRA amended the Code to eliminate so-called artificial losses. OID on tax-exempt securities is now accrued in the same manner as is required for OID on debt securities issued by corporations and other entities.[239] This means that for tax-exempt securities issued after September 3, 1982 and acquired after March 1, 1984, OID is accrued under the economic or constant interest method (a compound interest method) to reflect the actual market appreciation of these securities.[240]

(2) STATE TAXATION

State, city, and other local taxes (collectively "state taxes") are beyond the scope of this book. Nevertheless, because state taxation frequently plays an important part in a taxpayer's decision to acquire municipal securities, this section mentions some state tax considerations. Typically, a decision to acquire a municipal security is based on the security's after-tax yield, which requires consideration of state as well as federal taxes. With state taxes currently deductible from gross income for federal tax purposes, the benefit of this deduction must also be factored in to determine the after-tax yield of a particular security.[241]

Interest income on municipal securities is not always subject to state taxes. There are basically three approaches to state taxation. First, some states do not tax municipal securities at all. Second, some states tax only nonlocal municipal securities. Third, other states tax all municipal securities. Furthermore, if a state taxes municipal securities, it can be in one of the three following forms: Some states impose a tax on interest, others impose a tax on personal property, while others tax gains on the sale of municipal securities. For a state-by-state discussion of state taxes, see the *State Tax Reporter (CCH)*.

---

[238]HOUSE WAYS AND MEANS COMMITTEE REPORT, DEFICIT REDUCTION ACT OF 1984, H.R. REP. NO. 432, 98th Cong., 2d Sess. 1178, *reprinted in* 1984 U.S. CODE CONG. & AD. NEWS 697, 851.

[239]I.R.C. § 1288(a).

[240]*See* H.R. REP. NO. 432, *supra* note 238, at 1178; section 27.2.

[241]Proposals before the Congress to reduce marginal tax rates and to repeal the deduction for state income taxes could affect the municipal security market. *See generally* Proctor & Rappaport, *Federal Tax Reform and the Regional Character of the Municipal Bond Market*, FRBNY Q. REV., Autumn 1985, at 6.

(3) SALES OF TAX-EXEMPT SECURITIES

Although interest income on municipal securities is exempt from federal income taxes, gains on the sale of such securities are taxable. The definition of gross income includes "gains derived from dealings in property,"[242] without any exemption for gains on sales of tax-exempt securities. Capital gain or loss results on the sale of municipal securities held as capital assets by investors[243] and traders.[244] Ordinary income results from the sale of municipal securities held by dealers,[245] hedgers,[246] and certain financial institutions.[247]

As with all types of property, gain or loss is computed by subtracting the adjusted basis of the property from the amount realized.[248] With tax-exempt securities, however, difficulties can result in determining the basis of the securities and the proceeds from their sale. For a discussion of premiums on tax-exempt securities, see section 27.4(a)(2). For a discussion of discounts and their effect on basis, see section 27.2(e) and section 27.3.

If a tax-exempt security is sold between interest payment dates for a specified price plus accrued interest, the accrued interest is treated as tax-exempt income and is neither part of the sales proceeds nor the cost basis of the security.[249] If the parties agree to allocate interest in a manner different from the accrual during their respective holding periods, the allocation adjusts the purchase price and does not affect the allocation of tax-exempt interest income.[250]

(4) INTEREST TO PURCHASE OR CARRY TAX-EXEMPT SECURITIES

A deduction is not available for interest on any indebtedness incurred or continued to purchase or carry tax-exempt securities.[251] For a discussion of the limitation on interest deductions, see section 7.3(b), section 8.3(b), and section 9.3(b).

---

[242]I.R.C. § 61(a)(3).

[243]*See* section 6.1.

[244]*See* section 6.2.

[245]*See* section 6.3.

[246]*See* section 6.4.

[247]*See* section 6.8.

[248]I.R.C. § 1001(a); *see generally* Chapter 14.

[249]Rev. Rul. 72-224, 1972-1 C.B. 30.

[250]Rev. Rul. 74-482, 1974-2 C.B. 267.

[251]I.R.C. § 265(2).

(c) DEFAULTED TAX-EXEMPT SECURITIES

In general, I.R.C. § 1001(a) provides for gain or loss on the disposition of property, including exchanges of securities that do not qualify as a tax-free reorganization under I.R.C. § 368(a)(1). Similarly, if changes in the terms of a security are so material as to amount virtually to the issuance of a new security, the transaction is taxable.[252] A municipality cannot exchange its securities in a transaction that qualifies as a Type E recapitalization under I.R.C. § 368(a)(1)[253] because the recapitalization provisions are only available to private corporations.[254] An exchange of defaulted municipal securities is generally taxable.[255]

If a municipal refunding is merely viewed as an extension of an outstanding loan agreement and not as an exchange, the IRS has ruled that there is no tax on the transaction.[256] A refunding that merely extends an outstanding loan agreement is not an exchange that gives rise to gain or loss. The transaction is taxable under I.R.C. § 1001 if the new securities have terms materially different from the old securities.[257]

(d) FLOW-THROUGH ENTITIES

(1) PARTNERSHIPS

A partner's adjusted basis in his partnership interest is increased by various items, including his distributive share of partnership income exempt from tax.[258] A basis adjustment is ordinarily made as of the end of the partnership's taxable year.[259] This increase in a partner's adjusted

---

[252]Rev. Rul. 73-160, 1973-1 C.B. 365.

[253]Emery v. Comm'r, 166 F.2d 27, 30 (2d Cir. 1948); Girard Trust Co. v. U.S., 166 F.2d 773, 775 (3d Cir. 1948).

[254]*Emery*, 166 F.2d at 30; *Girard Trust Co.*, 166 F.2d at 775.

[255]*See Emery*, 166 F.2d at 30; *Girard Trust Co.*, 166 F.2d at 775; Rev. Rul. 81-169, 1981-1 C.B. 429.

[256]Rev. Rul. 81-169, 1981-1 C.B. 429 (modifying Rev. Rul. 56-435, 1956-2 C.B. 506) (which removed the "implication that nontaxability is conditioned on the equality of fair market value rather than the fact that there are no material differences in the terms of the bonds").

[257]*See* Mutual Loan & Sav. Co. v. Comm'r, 184 F.2d 161, 164 (5th Cir. 1950) (where securities issued for defaulted municipal securities with a different date of issue and interest rate were held to be an extension or renewal of the original loan agreement); City Bank Farmers Trust Co. v. Hoey, 52 F. Supp. 665, 666 (S.D. N.Y. 1942), *aff'd per curiam*, 138 F.2d 1023 (2d Cir. 1943); West Missouri Power Co. v. Comm'r, 18 T.C. 105, 110 (1952); *see also* TAM 8451012 (Aug. 23, 1984); TAM 8052023 (Sept. 25, 1980) (revoking LTR 7948011 (Aug. 24, 1979)); LTR 7929061 (Apr. 19, 1979); TAM 7845001 (June 29, 1978).

[258]I.R.C. § 705(a).

[259]Treas. Reg. § 1.705-1(a)(1) (1956).

basis reflects his pro rata portion of the tax-exempt interest earned by the partnership. A basis adjustment assures that tax-exempt interest is not indirectly taxed if a partner disposes of his partnership interest or it is liquidated. Without such a basis adjustment, a tax would be imposed on the partner's share of the tax-exempt interest on a subsequent disposition or liquidation of his partnership interest or upon a distribution of cash in excess of basis.

(2) S CORPORATIONS

A stockholder's basis in his S corporation stock is increased by his pro rata share of the corporation's "items of income," defined to include tax-exempt income.[260] This basis adjustment, which reflects a stockholder's pro rata share of tax-exempt income, allows an S corporation to distribute tax-exempt interest to its stockholders without triggering capital gains tax because of a low stock basis.

(3) REGULATED INVESTMENT COMPANIES

The tax-exempt character of interest on municipal securities does not flow through to stockholders of C corporations. In addition, the earnings and profits of a C corporation are increased by tax-exempt interest income that the corporation receives.[261] Because dividends paid out of earnings and profits are taxable to the stockholders irrespective of the tax-exempt nature of the original source, a stockholder in a C corporation may incur an indirect tax on tax-exempt income. This indirect tax is avoided, however, on certain dividends paid by regulated investment companies.[262]

Prior to 1976, tax-exempt interest did not flow through from regulated investment companies that owned tax-exempt securities. Hence, there was no incentive for a regulated investment company to acquire tax-exempt securities. Although the interest on tax-exempt securities was not taxable to the company, tax-exempt interest increased the company's earnings and profits, resulting in taxation as ordinary dividends when distributed to its shareholders.[263] For taxable years beginning after 1975, regulated investment companies can pay exempt-interest

---

[260]I.R.C. § 1367(a)(1).

[261]Treas. Reg. § 1.312-6(b) (1955).

[262]*See* section 6.9.

[263]I.R.C. § 852(b) 1970, *amended by* Pub. L. 94-455, § 2137(c), 90 Stat. 1520, 1931 (1976).

dividends if at least 50 percent of the value of their total assets at the end of each quarter consists of tax-exempt securities.[264]

Exempt-interest dividends must meet certain conditions. First, they must be dividends (other than capital gain dividends) paid by a regulated investment company and designated as exempt-interest dividends in a written notice mailed to the company's shareholders not less than 45 days after the close of the taxable year.[265] Second, the aggregate amount designated as an exempt-interest dividend must be greater than the excess of the amount of tax-exempt interest over the amounts disallowed as deductions under I.R.C. §§ 265 and 171(a)(2).[266] Basically, I.R.C. § 265 prevents a regulated investment company from deducting the expenses allocable to tax-exempt portfolios.[267] It also prevents the shareholders from obtaining an interest deduction on indebtedness incurred by them to purchase or carry regulated investment company shares on which exempt-interest dividends are received during the taxable year.[268] Finally, a shareholder's loss on a sale or exchange of his shares in a regulated investment company is not allowed to the extent of exempt-interest dividends he has received, unless the shares have been held by him for at least 31 days.[269]

(e) INVESTMENTS BY FINANCIAL INSTITUTIONS IN TAX-EXEMPT SECURITIES

Banks and certain other financial institutions own municipal securities for various reasons, such as to lower their own taxes, in the course of underwriting or making a market in these securities, and to collateralize public deposits if required by state law. Historically, banks have been major participants in the municipal securities market.[270] Since 1981, banks have sharply reduced their purchases of municipal securities, which may be explained in large part by changes in the tax laws since

---

[264]I.R.C. § 852(b)(5).

[265]I.R.C. § 852(b)(5)(A).

[266]*Id.* For a discussion of I.R.C. § 265, see section 7.3, section 8.3, and section 9.3.

[267]I.R.C. § 265(3).

[268]I.R.C. § 265(4).

[269]I.R.C. § 852(b)(4)(B).

[270]*See* Proctor & Donahoo, *Commercial Bank Investment in Municipal Securities*, FRBNY Q. REV., Winter 1983–84, at 26.

ERTA in 1981.[271] Banks cannot deduct 20 percent of their interest expense incurred to purchase or carry tax-exempt securities. Other factors that may explain decreased bank investments include bank profitability, the level and volatility of interest rates, and credit risks.

Finally, certain financial institutions (defined to include commercial banks, mutual savings banks, savings and loan associations, cooperative banks, business development corporations, and small business investment corporations) realize ordinary income and loss on the sale or exchange of tax-exempt securities.[272]

§ 28.3 CONVERTIBLE DEBT SECURITIES

Convertible debt securities are typically "convertible" into the common stock of the issuing corporation.[273] The taxation of convertible debt securities is not governed by any single Code provision. Rather, one must look to various Code provisions, Treasury regulations, often conflicting judicial decisions, and IRS pronouncements to ascertain the appropriate tax treatment of convertible debt securities.[274]

This section discusses general tax principles applicable to convertible debt securities from the perspective of both corporate issuers[275] and owners of convertible debt securities.[276] This section also addresses mandatory convertible notes[277] issued by bank holding companies and adjustable rate convertible notes.[278]

---

[271]TEFRA amended the Code to deny a deduction for 15 percent of the interest expense incurred to purchase or carry tax-exempt securities acquired after December 31, 1982. I.R.C. § 291(a)(3) (1982), *amended by* DRA, *supra* note 128, § 68(a); *see* section 9.3(b)(3); *see also* Proctor & Donahoo, *Commercial Bank Investment in Municipal Securities, supra* note 270, at 31–32. The 15 percent nondeductible amount was increased to 20 percent by the DRA. I.R.C. § 291(a)(3).

[272]I.R.C. § 582(c)(1); *see* section 6.8.

[273]For a discussion of convertible securities, see section 1.1(c).

[274]*See generally* Fleischer & Cary, *The Taxation of Convertible Bonds and Stock*, 74 HARV. L. REV. 473 (1961); Panel Discussion, *Convertible Debentures and Strange Securities*, 28 N.Y.U. INST. ON FED. TAX'N 331 (1970); Thrower, *Conglomerates and Convertibles*, 1 TAX ADVISOR 4 (1970).

[275]*See* section 28.3(a).

[276]*See* section 28.3(b).

[277]*See* section 28.3(d).

[278]*See* section 28.3(c).

(a) TAX TREATMENT OF AN ISSUING CORPORATION

(1) ISSUANCE OF CONVERTIBLE DEBT SECURITIES

The major consideration when a corporation issues convertible debt securities is whether the securities are treated as debt obligations or equity interests. There have been many conflicting judicial decisions as to whether a security is a debt or an equity interest.[279] The classification of securities as debt or equity interests is important for the tax treatment of new security products with conversion features. Recharacterization of debt interests as equity interests can have significant, usually detrimental, tax consequences.[280]

I.R.C. § 385, enacted in 1969 to provide some guidance on debt and equity interests, lists some factors to consider as to whether a debtor-creditor relationship or a corporation-stockholder relationship exists. First, is there a written, unconditional promise to pay a fixed sum on demand or on a specified date and a fixed rate of interest, in return for an adequate consideration in money or money's worth?[281] Second, is the debt subordinated or does it have a preference over any indebtedness of the corporation?[282] Third, what is the corporation's ratio of debt to equity?[283] Fourth, is the security convertible into stock of the corporation?[284] Fifth, what is the relationship between the stockholders and the owners of the interest in question?[285] These factors are to be considered in light of all facts and circumstances.

If convertible debt securities are classified as equity rather than debt, (1) interest is not deductible, (2) issue premium or discount does not arise, (3) retirement premiums and discounts are tested for capital gain or ordinary income under the stock redemption rules, (4) installment reporting is not available under I.R.C. § 453, (5) the securities cannot be issued in Type B or Type C reorganizations under I.R.C. § 368(a)(1) (because the securities do not qualify as voting stock), and (6) conversion

---

[279]See generally B. BITTKER & J. EUSTICE, FEDERAL INCOME TAXATION OF CORPORATIONS AND SHAREHOLDERS ¶¶ 4.03–4.05, at 4-8 to 4-16 (4th ed. 1979).

[280]See section 28.3(c); section 28.3(d).

[281]I.R.C. § 385(b)(1).

[282]I.R.C. § 385(b)(2).

[283]I.R.C. § 385(b)(3). In LTR 8523009 (Feb. 25, 1985), the IRS ruled that convertible debt securities issued in a leveraged buyout qualified as debt even though the issuer had an enormous amount of debt compared to equity.

[284]I.R.C. § 385(b)(4).

[285]I.R.C. § 385(b)(5).

into other stock might be tax-free.[286] For convertible debt securities that are treated as debt, the issuing corporation treats the securities in the same way as other debt obligations, and the corporation services the debt according to its terms.[287]

In addition, I.R.C. § 385(a) specifically authorizes the Treasury to issue debt-equity regulations. At this writing, after several attempts to issue such regulations, all proposed and final regulations have been withdrawn.[288] The only available guidelines as to whether a security is a debt instrument or an equity interest are those listed in I.R.C. § 385(b), IRS rulings, and sometimes conflicting judicial decisions.

If debt securities are issued at their face value, the corporation realizes no gain or loss.[289] Expenses incurred by the corporation to issue the debt securities are treated as capital expenditures, recoverable over the term of the securities in the same manner as discount is recoverable.[290]

(2) ORIGINAL ISSUE DISCOUNT

OID is the excess that a corporation must pay on the retirement of its debt securities over the amount of consideration it receives from purchasers on issuance of the securities.[291] OID is basically a cost of borrowing money, which is deductible by the corporation ratably over the life of the debt.[292] For corporate debt securities issued at a discount, the net amount of the discount is treated as an additional cost of borrowing and is deductible by the corporation ratably over the life of the debt securities.[293]

No part of the issue price of convertible debt securities is deemed to be attributable to the conversion feature. The issue price of a convertible debt security is deemed to include any amount paid for the conversion

---

[286]B. BITTKER & J. EUSTICE, *supra* note 279, ¶ 4.06.6, at 4-23.

[287]For a discussion of debt securities, see generally Chapter 27.

[288]The effective date of the final Treasury regulations, issued on December 31, 1980, was continually delayed until the regulations were formally withdrawn by the Treasury on August 5, 1983.

[289]Treas. Reg. § 1.61-12(c)(1) (1980).

[290]Helvering v. Union Pac. R.R. Co., 293 U.S. 282, 287 (1934); Denver & Rio Grande W.R.R. Co. v. Comm'r, 32 T.C. 43, 51–52 (1959), *aff'd on other grounds*, 279 F.2d 368 (10th Cir. 1960); Leach Corp. v. Comm'r, 30 T.C. 563, 579 (1958); Rev. Rul. 59-387, 1959-2 C.B. 56.

[291]For a discussion of OID, see section 27.2.

[292]Temp. Treas. Reg. § 1.1232 (1980); Treas. Reg. §§ 1.163-3(a)(1), 4(a)(1) (1973).

[293]Treas. Reg. § 1.163-3(a)(1) (1973) (for corporate debt securities issued on or before May 27, 1969); Treas. Reg. § 1.163-4(a)(1) (1973) (for corporate debt securities issued after May 27, 1969); *see also* Treas. Reg. § 1.1232 (1980); *see* section 27.2.

factor.[294] Therefore, a convertible debt security sold at par is not issued at a discount regardless of the value of the conversion feature, because the issue price and the maturity amount of the debt security are equal. A conversion feature does not affect OID calculations.[295]

(3) PREMIUMS

(i) In General

If debt securities are issued at a premium, the net amount of the premium (excluding any portion attributable to a conversion premium)[296] is treated as corporate income to be prorated or amortized over the life of the debt securities.[297] This also applies to convertible debt securities issued at a premium.[298] The amount of the premium is not reduced by any amount attributable to the conversion feature.[299]

(ii) Conversion Features

The portion of the purchase price of convertible debt securities that is attributable to a conversion feature is not treated as a premium.[300] The value of a conversion feature on a debt security is determined as of the date the security is acquired by subtracting the market price for the security if it had not been convertible from the purchase price of the convertible security.[301] Determining the assumed price for a nonconvertible security is a two-step procedure. First, a taxpayer must determine the yield on nonconvertible debt securities with a similar character. Second, the price currently paid on such a security (at the specified

---

[294]Treas. Reg. § 1.1232-3(b)(2)(i) (1980).

[295]Chock Full O'Nuts Corp. v. U.S., 453 F.2d 300, 305 (2d Cir. 1971); *accord* Hunt Foods & Industries, Inc. v. Comm'r, 57 T.C. 633, 638 (1972), *aff'd per curiam*, 496 F.2d 532 (9th Cir. 1974); AMF, Inc. v. U.S., 476 F.2d 1351, 1353 (Ct. Cl. 1973), *cert. denied*, 417 U.S. 930 (1974); *see* Note, *Original Issue Discount Does Not Occur When a Corporation Issues Convertible Bonds at Par—Chock Full O'Nuts Corp. v. United States, 453 F.2d 300 (2d Cir. 1971)*, 39 BROOKLYN L. REV. 1305 (1973).

[296]*See* section 28.3(a)(3)(ii).

[297]Treas. Reg. § 1.61-12(c)(2) (1980). For a general discussion of premiums, see section 27.4.

[298]Treas. Reg. § 1.61-12(c)(6) (1980).

[299]*See* section 28.3(a)(3)(ii).

[300]National Can Corp. v. U.S., 687 F.2d 1107, 1112 (7th Cir. 1982); I.R.C. § 171(b); *see* Treas. Reg. § 1.171-2(c)(1) (1968).

[301]*See* Crawford, *Amortization of Conversion Feature Discount: What is the Proper Treatment*, 32 J. TAX'N 102 (1970).

yield, classification, and grade) is determined using standard bond tables.[302] Once the value of the conversion feature is determined, it is subtracted from the issue price to determine the amount of premium, if any, relating to the debt element of the security.

(iii) Unamortized Premiums on Conversion

If a debt security is converted before the full amount of the premium not attributable to the conversion feature is included in the income of the corporate issuer, the unamortized premium is not taxable to the issuer at conversion. Rather, the unamortized premium is treated as additional proceeds from the sale of stock.[303]

(4) EXERCISE OF CONVERSION RIGHTS

Prior to DRA amendments, gain or loss was not recognized by the issuing corporation on the exchange of its convertible debt securities for its stock. The stock was considered to be a form of payment for the debt securities. It was not viewed as a discharge of indebtedness, irrespective of whether the par value or the market value of the stock was different from the face amount of the debt securities.[304]

The DRA revoked this so-called debt-equity exception in all cases except where the issuer is in bankruptcy or is insolvent.[305] Cancellation income results for transfers after July 18, 1984 in tax years ending after such date to the extent that the adjusted issue price of the debt securities exceeds the value of the stock issued on the retirement.[306]

(5) ACCRUED INTEREST ON CONVERSIONS

A corporate issuer on the accrual basis can deduct interest that accrues on convertible securities as the interest accrues.[307] In addition, accrued interest is generally deductible, even if payment is deferred under the terms of the securities until after the final payment of principal and interest on other securities issued by the corporation.[308]

[302]Treas. Reg. § 1.171-2(c)(2) (1968).

[303]I.R.C. § 171(b)(1).

[304]Comm'r v. Motor Mart Trust, 156 F.2d 122, 127 (1st Cir. 1946).

[305]DRA, *supra* note 128, § 59.

[306]I.R.C. § 108(e)(10).

[307]I.R.C. § 163(a); Hummel-Ross Fibre Corp. v. Comm'r, 40 B.T.A. 821 (1939); Shamrock Oil & Gas Co. v. Comm'r, 42 B.T.A. 1016 (1940); Central Electric & Tele. Co. v. Comm'r, 47 B.T.A. 434 (1942).

[308]Natco Corp. v. U.S., 240 F.2d 398 (3d Cir. 1956).

If the provision in the debt security as to the proper treatment for accrued interest is ambiguous, so that it is not clear whether interest is forfeited or paid through the issuance of stock, the corporation may be denied an interest deduction. In *Columbia Gas System, Inc. v. U.S.*,[309] a corporate taxpayer issued convertible debt securities. The securities provide for interest payable semiannually and a provision that relieved the issuer of any interest that was accrued but was unpaid at the date of conversion. The clause provided that "there shall be no adjustment in respect of interest or dividends on the conversion of any Debenture or Debentures."[310] The court found the clause unclear as to whether a discharge of accrued interest or a payment was intended, construed the ambiguity against its drafter, and denied the corporation an interest deduction.[311]

If the terms of a debt security provide that an owner forfeits his right to accrued interest on conversion, the corporate issuer cannot deduct the accrued interest from the period after the last interest date to the date of the conversion.[312] Similarly, the corporate issuer, at the end of its taxable year, cannot deduct interest that has accrued between payment dates because the payment obligation does not become fixed until the interest payment is actually due.[313]

In addition, a corporate issuer cannot deduct interest payments made to its parent corporation upon the conversion of the issuer's convertible debt securities into the common stock of its parent.[314] The Tax Court held that the owners of the convertible debt securities have alternative rights to demand either payment from the corporate issuer or shares of common stock from the issuer's parent. When one right is exercised by the security owner, the alternate obligation is discharged.[315] A debt security owner's election to convert it to common stock extinguishes the corporate issuer's obligations to accrue interest.[316]

---

[309]473 F.2d 1246, 1247 (2d Cir. 1973).

[310]*Id.* at 1246.

[311]*Id.* at 1249; *see Comment, Tax Treatment of Accrued Interest on Convertible Bonds—A Dilemma for Corporate Taxpayers*, 15 WM. & MARY L. REV. 192 (1973); *see also* Bethlehem Steel Corp. v. U.S., 434 F.2d 1357 (Ct. Cl. 1970); Tandy Corp. v. U.S., 79-1 U.S. Tax Cas. (CCH) ¶ 9160 (N.D. Tex. 1979), *aff'd*, 626 F.2d 1186 (5th Cir. 1980).

[312]Rev. Rul. 74-127, 1974-1 C.B. 47; Rev. Rul. 68-170, 1968-1 C.B. 71, *clarified by* Rev. Rul. 74-127, 1974-1 C.B. 47.

[313]Scott Paper Co. v. Comm'r, 74 T.C. 137, 165-66 (1980); Rev. Rul. 74-127, 1974-1 C.B. 47.

[314]Husky Oil Co. v. Comm'r, 83 T.C. 717, 735 (1984).

[315]*Id.* at 735.

[316]*Id.*

(6) REPURCHASE BY THE ISSUER

A corporate issuer's deduction for a retirement premium is limited to a normal call premium on nonconvertible debt securities. A corporate issuer cannot deduct any premium[317] paid or incurred after April 22, 1969 to repurchase a security convertible into stock of the issuer or a company in control of or controlled by the issuing corporation[318] to the extent that the repurchase price of such a security exceeds the adjusted issue price plus a normal call premium on securities that are not convertible.[319]

A normal call premium is defined as an amount equal to a normal call premium on a nonconvertible debt security that is comparable to the convertible debt security.[320] It is a call premium specified in dollars under the debt security's terms.[321] As a result, if a specified call premium is constant over the entire term of the debt security, the normal call premium is the amount specified.[322] If, on the other hand, the specified call premium varies during the period a comparable nonconvertible debt security is callable (or if it is not callable over its entire term), the normal call premium is the amount specified for the period during the term of such comparable nonconvertible debt security, which corresponds to the period during which the convertible debt security was repurchased.[323] In addition, a call premium of a convertible debt security specified in dollars is treated as a normal call premium on a nonconvertible debt security if the call premium at the time of repurchase does not exceed an amount equal to one year's interest payable on the security, increased by the amount of deductible discount.[324]

A corporate issuer can deduct a redemption premium in excess of a normal call premium on convertible debt securities to the extent it can prove that the excess premium is attributable to the cost of borrowing funds and not to the conversion feature.[325] The portion of a repurchase premium that is attributable to the conversion feature is the amount by which the selling price of the convertible debt security increased

---

[317]See section 27.4.

[318]Control means the ownership of stock possessing at least 80 percent of the total combined voting power of all classes of stock entitled to vote and at least 80 percent of the total number of the shares of all classes of stock. I.R.C. §§ 249(b)(2), 368(c)(1).

[319]I.R.C. § 249(a); Treas. Reg. §§ 1.249-1(a), (c) (1973).

[320]Treas. Reg. § 1.249-1(d)(1) (1973).

[321]Id.

[322]Id.

[323]Id.

[324]Treas. Reg. § 1.249-1(d)(2) (1973).

[325]I.R.C. § 249(a); Treas. Reg. § 1.249-1(e)(1) (1973).

between the date it was issued and the date it was repurchased due to a general decline in yields on comparable nonconvertible securities.[326]

(b) TAX TREATMENT OF A CONVERTIBLE DEBT SECURITY OWNER

(1) ACQUISITION OF CONVERTIBLE DEBT SECURITIES

A taxpayer can acquire a convertible debt security in either a taxable or nontaxable transaction. In a taxable transaction, the taxpayer's basis in the security is his cost basis,[327] which is subject to various adjustments.[328] In a nontaxable transaction, the taxpayer's basis is either a carry-over basis (for transactions other than certain acquisitions from decedents) or a stepped-up basis (for certain acquisitions from decedents).[329] A taxpayer obtains a new holding period for securities acquired in a taxable transaction and a tacked holding period for securities acquired in a nontaxable transaction.[330] As with other types of debt securities, convertible debt securities are capital assets in the hands of investors[331] and traders,[332] and are ordinary assets in the hands of dealers,[333] hedgers,[334] and certain financial institutions.[335]

(2) ORIGINAL ISSUE DISCOUNT

The tax treatment of OID has changed several times in recent years. As a result, the owner of a convertible debt security includes OID in income in accordance with the rules in place for debt securities issued at the time when the securities were issued without adjustment for the portion of the issue price allocable to the conversion feature.[336] The sum of the daily portion of OID determined for each day during the tax year in which a convertible debt security is owned is included in the owner's

---

[326]Treas. Reg. § 1.249-1(e)(2) (1973).

[327]*See* section 14.2.

[328]*See, e.g.,* section 27.2(b).

[329]*See* section 14.3.

[330]*See generally* Chapter 15.

[331]*See* section 6.1.

[332]*See* section 6.2.

[333]*See* section 6.3.

[334]*See* section 6.4.

[335]*See* section 6.8.

[336]For a discussion of OID generally, see section 27.2.

income for debt securities issued after July 1, 1982.[337] For convertible debt securities issued after May 27, 1969 and before July 2, 1982, the owner must include in income his ratable monthly portion of OID multiplied by the number of complete months and fractions thereof during which he has held the convertible debt security.[338] For convertible debt securities issued before May 28, 1969, a taxpayer is not required to report OID until the year the convertible debt security is sold, exchanged, or redeemed.[339]

If a taxpayer acquires a convertible debt security for cash, the OID rules can be relatively simple. The issues concerning OID become more complicated in situations where a security is acquired as part of a package offering[340] or is acquired in a tax-free exchange where the property exchanged is worth less than the convertible debt security.[341] Finally, the conversion feature of convertible debt securities does not create OID even if both parties acknowledge that the securities would have been sold for less than face value if they had not been issued with conversion privileges.[342]

In a recent offering, the Tenax Co. took the position that its debt securities that are convertible into the stock of its parent, the Timken Co., gives rise to OID in an amount equal to the portion of the issue price allocable to the conversion feature.[343] The issuer took this position notwithstanding the decision in *National Can Corp. v. U.S.*,[344] based on Rev. Rul. 69-265,[345] in which the IRS ruled in the context of a reorganization that a conversion feature is an item of property separate and distinct from the debt security to which it relates.[346] The rationale for the creation of OID in the Tenax-Timken offering was that unlike *Na-*

---

[337] I.R.C. § 1272(a)(1); see section 27.2.

[338] I.R.C. § 1272(b)(1); *see* section 27.2(b).

[339] I.R.C. § 1271(c)(2)(A); *see* section 27.2(c).

[340] For a discussion of package offerings of convertible debt securities, see Burns & Levitt, *Package Offerings of Convertible Debentures*, 19 TUL. TAX INST. 307-35 (1970).

[341] For a discussion of OID generally, see Paine & Westheimer, *Original Issue Discount Regulations Revised But Remain Controversial*, 35 J. TAX'N 282-5 (1971); Sheffield, *Debt Issued For Traded and Nontraded Property*, 62 TAXES 1022 (1984); Lee, *The Tax Reform Act and Convertible Debt Securities*, 44 ST. JOHNS L. REV. 1081 (special ed. 1970).

[342] National Can Corp. v. U.S., 687 F.2d 1107, 1111-12 (7th Cir. 1982).

[343] *Tenax Offering May Open Door to Big Savings on Convertibles*, CORP. FINANCING WEEK, Sept. 16, 1985, at 1.

[344] 687 F.2d at 1107.

[345] 1969-1 C.B. 109.

[346] The purchasers of the convertible debt securities of the Tenax Co. were mostly tax-exempt entities that do not pay tax on OID income as it accrues.

tional Can Corp., where the subsidiary was obligated to honor the conversion, Timken, the parent corporation, is not so obligated.

(3) PREMIUMS

The fact that a debt security is convertible into stock does not, in itself, deny the security owner a deduction under I.R.C. § 171 for a premium paid.[347] If the owner of the security has control over whether to convert the security, the security is within the scope of I.R.C. § 171.[348] The amount of the premium, however, must be reduced by the portion of the issue price attributable to the conversion feature.[349] The value of the conversion feature is ascertained as of the time of acquisition by reference to an assumed price for the same security without a conversion feature.[350]

If a convertible debt security is converted when a portion of the premium remains unamortized, the security owner cannot deduct the unamortized premium remaining at conversion. Rather, the unamortized premium is treated as part of the cost basis of the new security acquired. The basis of the new security is the same as that of the debt security that preceded it.[351]

(4) CHANGE IN CONVERSION RATIOS OR CONVERSION PRICES

It is possible for a change in the conversion ratio or the conversion price of convertible debt securities to be treated as a deemed distribution, which is taxable to those security owners who are deemed to have received the distribution under I.R.C. § 305(b)(2).[352] In general, a stock dividend (or a series of distributions) is taxable if it results in the receipt of cash or other property by some stockholders and an increase in the proportionate interests of other stockholders in the assets or earnings and profits of the corporation.[353] Any disproportion in the deemed distribution, no matter how minor, can trigger taxability under I.R.C. § 305(b)(2). The Senate Finance Committee had provided for a de min-

---

[347]Treas. Reg. § 1.171-2(c)(1) (1968).

[348]*Id.*

[349]I.R.C. § 171(b); Treas. Reg. § 1.171-2(c)(1) (1968).

[350]Treas. Reg. § 1.171-2(c)(2) (1968); *see* section 28.3(a)(3)(ii).

[351]*See* Ades v. Comm'r, 38 T.C. 501, 512 (1962), *aff'd per curiam*, 316 F.2d 734 (2d Cir. 1963).

[352]For a discussion of dividends generally, see Chapter 22.

[353]I.R.C. § 305(b)(2); *see* section 22.2(b)(2).

imis exception in the Tax Reform Act of 1969,[354] but it was rejected by the Conference Committee.[355]

A change in a conversion ratio or redemption price is treated as a distribution for any stockholder whose proportionate interest in either the earnings and profits or assets of the corporation is increased.[356] To determine whether any stockholder's proportionate interest has been increased, the outstanding stock of the distributing corporation is deemed to include securities convertible into such stock, regardless of whether the securities are convertible during the taxable year.[357] This creates a serious obstacle to paying stock dividends when convertible securities are outstanding—unless the convertible securities provide for a "full adjustment" in the conversion ratio or conversion price to reflect all stock dividends.[358] The "presence of convertible debentures functions as a 'spoiler' for other equity shareholders . . . the payment of interest on the debentures apparently will trigger taxability for stock dividends paid to common stockholders."[359]

The IRS has ruled in Rev. Rul. 75-513[360] that an increase in the conversion ratio of convertible debt securities is a deemed distribution to the debt security owners, where the conversion ratio is adjusted each year to reflect the differential between the interest rate of the securities and the yield that could have been obtained by investing in the corporation's stock on the date the debt securities were issued. In Rev. Rul. 75-513, the corporation paid a cash dividend to its stockholders and adjusted the conversion ratio of the debt securities to entitle the debt security owners to acquire additional shares. The IRS ruled that the distribution was a deemed taxable distribution to the debt holders to which I.R.C. § 301 applies by reason of I.R.C. §§ 305(b)(2) and 305(c).[361] The adjustment of the conversion ratio resulted in a cash dividend to the stockholders and an increase in the interest of the debt securities owners. The distribution was found to be disproportionate.

[354]SENATE FINANCE COMMITTEE REPORT, TAX REFORM ACT OF 1969, S. REP. NO. 552, 91st Cong., 1st Sess. 154, *reprinted in* 1969 U.S. CODE CONG. & AD. NEWS 2027, 2186.

[355]HOUSE CONFERENCE REPORT, TAX REFORM ACT OF 1969, H.R. REP. NO. 782, 91st Cong., 1st Sess. 309-10, *reprinted in* 1969 U.S. CODE CONG. & AD. NEWS 2392, 2424.

[356]I.R.C. § 305(c).

[357]Treas. Reg. § 1.305-3(b)(5) (1974).

[358]Treas. Reg. § 1.305-3(d)(1)(i) (1974).

[359]B. BITTKER & J. EUSTICE, *supra* note 279, ¶ 7.62.10, at 7-94 to 7-95.

[360]1975-2 C.B. 114.

[361]*Id.*

(5) CONVERSION INTO COMMON STOCK

Gain or loss is generally not recognized when a taxpayer exchanges a convertible debt security for stock of the corporation that issued the debt security.[362] A taxpayer's basis in the stock received in the conversion is the same as his basis in the convertible debt security.[363] Gain or loss is recognized only when the stock is subsequently disposed of.[364] The exchange is regarded as a transformation of the security rather than a disposition.[365] Additionally, the conversion right must be contained in the debt security.[366]

There are situations, however, where the Code specifically requires the recognition of gain on an exchange of debt securities for stock. One such situation is on the disposition of installment obligations under I.R.C. § 453.[367] Further, conversion of convertible debt securities of one corporation into common stock of another corporation can also be taxable.[368] No gain or loss was recognized on conversion into a parent's stock where, pursuant to a Type A reorganization, the acquiring corporation and its parent were liable for convertible securities acquired in the merger, the securities were convertible into the parent's stock, and the securities' interest rate and maturity date would change.[369] Because the convertible debt securities are issued by one corporation and the stock is issued by a separate and distinct corporation, the nonrecognition provisions of the Code do not apply to such a conversion.[370] As a result, gain or loss is recognized to the extent of the difference between the fair market value of the common stock received on con-

---

[362]Rev. Rul. 72-265, 1972-1 C.B. 222 (which superseded and restated G.C.M. 18436, 1937-1 C.B. 101, under the 1954 Code and regulations).

[363]*Id.*

[364]For a discussion of the holding period of stock acquired by conversion of a convertible security, see section 15.3(a)(3).

[365]*See* Fleisher & Cary, *The Taxation of Convertible Bonds and Stock*, 74 HARV. L. REV. 473, 478 (1961).

[366]Rose v. Trust Co. of Georgia, 77 F.2d 355, 356 (5th Cir. 1935); G.C.M. 18436, 1937-1 C.B. 101, *superseded by* Rev. Rul. 72-265, 1972-1 C.B. 222.

[367]Rev. Rul. 72-264, 1972-1 C.B. 131 (where the IRS ruled that deferred installment proceeds evidenced by convertible debt securities were taxable when the taxpayer subsequently disposed of the securities).

[368]International Tel. & Tel. Corp. v. Comm'r, 77 T.C. 60, 78 *supp. op.*, 77 T.C. 1367 (1981), *aff'd per curiam*, 704 F.2d 252 (2d Cir. 1983); Rev. Rul. 69-135, 1969-1 C.B. 198, *distinguished by* Rev. Rul. 79-155, 1979-1 C.B. 153; *see also* Eisenberg, *IRS Position on Right to Convert into Another Corporation's Stock is Confusing*, 33 J. TAX'N 25 (1970).

[369]Rev. Rul. 79-155, 1979-1 C.B. 153.

[370]Rev. Rul. 69-135, 1969-1 C.B. 198, *distinguished by* Rev. Rul. 79-155, 1979-1 C.B. 153.

version and the cost or other basis of the debt securities converted into stock.[371]

(c) ADJUSTABLE RATE CONVERTIBLE NOTES

The IRS ruled in Rev. Rul. 83-98[372] that ACRNs are equity interests, rather than debt obligations, of the corporate issuer. Under most eventualities ACRNs will be converted into common stock.[373] Moreover, it is to the advantage of the issuing corporation to force conversion so as not to pay additional cash to ACRN owners. ACRNs usually do not represent a promise to pay a certain sum because of the high probability of conversion.[374] As a result, "interest" payments are not deductible as interest by the issuer and are taxed as dividends to the ACRN owners. Corporate ACRN owners can qualify for the intercorporate dividends received deduction.[375]

ACRNs, initially offered in 1982, were structured to comply with the requirements for hybrid debt instruments under the final Treasury regulations issued pursuant to I.R.C. § 385(a). These regulations were subsequently withdrawn by the Treasury.[376] ACRNs typically are convertible into stock, callable after a few years for a principal amount that is low in relation to the value of the common stock into which they are convertible, and "interest" payments on ACRNs are unreasonably low when compared to other debt instruments issued at the same time. Further, the future annual yield on ACRNs is based on the level of dividends paid on the corporation's common stock.

In LTR 8523009,[377] the IRS ruled that convertible debt issued in a leveraged buy out qualified as debt even though the amount of debt was substantially in excess of the equity. The private ruling addressed Rev. Rul. 83-98 and appears to have narrowed the "high probability of conversion" test stated in the ruling. The IRS stated that to the extent the newly acquired assets of the issuers were purchased at fair market value, there would not be sufficient economic incentive to convert the debt securities into the stock of the issuer.[378] On the other hand, to the extent the assets were acquired for less than fair market value, there would

---

[371]*Id.*

[372]1983-2 C.B. 40.

[373]*Id.* ACRNs are also referred to as "floating rate convertible notes" or "FRCNs."

[374]*Id.*

[375]*See* section 22.9.

[376]For a discussion of the debt-equity regulations, see section 28.3(a)(1).

[377](Feb. 25, 1985).

[378]LTR 8523009 (Feb. 25, 1985).

be an incentive to convert the debt securities into the issuer's stock, which would reflect the higher value of the newly acquired assets.[379]

(d) MANDATORY CONVERTIBLE NOTES

Since 1982, banks have issued nearly $10 billion of mandatory convertible notes, which are securities issued by some domestic bank holding companies to meet capital requirements imposed by the FRB and the Comptroller of the Currency.[380] The IRS ruled in Rev. Rul. 85-119[381] that mandatory convertible notes are debt interests for tax purposes. Under Rev. Rul. 85-119, the periodic payments made to noteholders are deductible as interest by the bank holding company that issues the notes. Mandatory convertible notes generally provide that the rights of the noteholders are subordinated to the bank's general creditors. In addition, at maturity (or call) the notes can be exchanged for equity interests in the bank holding company, although they are generally expected to be redeemed for cash.

The IRS limited Rev. Rul. 85-119 to the mandatory convertible notes it considered in the ruling. Although explicitly limited to its facts, Rev. Rul. 85-119 is very significant; it provides usable guidelines for bank holding companies that want to expand their regulatory capital without issuing equity interests. On the facts, the IRS found the notes, designated as debt by the parties, created a debtor-creditor relationship.[382] Some of the factors considered by the IRS in the ruling include the following. First, the mandatory convertible notes were issued for cash at 100 percent of their face amount in a public offering and were not held in proportion to the bank holding company's stock. Second, the notes could not be called for 12 years and were freely transferable. Third, the noteholders could neither vote nor participate in the management of the bank holding company. Fourth, the notes bore a market rate of interest payable irrespective of earnings. Fifth, the noteholders could sue to compel payment of any amounts in default. Sixth, the bank holding company was not thinly capitalized and its debt-to-equity ratio was within industry standards.

---

[379] *Id.*

[380] In 1982, the FRB and the Comptroller of the Currency issued capital adequacy guidelines for assessing the capital of banks and bank holding companies. Mandatory convertible notes are deemed to be primary capital. *See generally* Saunders, *Lord, Make Me Chaste, but Not Just Yet,* FORBES, Sept. 9, 1985, at 56; *Fed Seeks Comments on Perpetual Debt,* BANKING EXPANSION REP., Nov. 18, 1985, at 15; *Too Much Preferred Stock is a No-No,* BANKING EXPANSION REP., Dec. 16, 1985, at 2. *See also* 50 Fed. Reg. 46739 (Nov. 13, 1985).

[381] 1985-30 I.R.B. 21.

[382] *Id.* (citing Rev. Rul. 68-54, 1968-1 C.B. 69 and Rev. Rul. 73-122, 1973-1 C.B. 66, both of which were distinguished by Rev. Rul. 83–98, 1983-2 C.B. 40).

§ 28.4   MORTGAGE-BACKED SECURITIES

(a) IN GENERAL

Tax treatment is a major factor in structuring offerings for MBSs. A traditional tax concern for MBSs has been to avoid corporate tax at the level where the mortgages are "pooled." Mortgage pools are quite popular because pooling assures that MBS owners do not have any direct responsibility for collecting payments from mortgages in the pool. A common form of mortgage pool is a grantor trust in which the participants are issued pass-through certificates.[383] Income is taxed only to the MBS owners, not to the trust. A recent development in the MBS area has been the formation of corporations that issue debt securities, referred to as "pay-through bonds," collateralized by mortgages. The pay-through bond structure was introduced in 1983 by FHLMC to provide one vehicle with different payment priorities for MBS owners.[384] The concern with using a grantor trust is that the existence of multiple classes of MBS certificate owners could reclassify the trust as an association taxable as a corporation.[385] With pay-through bonds, tax at the corporate level is minimized because deductions are available for the interest paid to the owners of the debt securities. A popular type of pay-through bond is a CMO, which is a series of bonds issued by a corporation in various classes with different payment priorities and payment schedules.[386]

The remainder of this section discusses tax considerations for the structure of MBS offerings and major tax considerations for MBS owners.

---

[383] I.R.C. §§ 671–679.

[384] *See* section 2.1(b)(4).

[385] *See* section 28.4(b)(2). A legislative proposal would amend the grantor trust provisions to permit a trust with multiple classes of ownership interests to be classified as a grantor trust in certain circumstances. *See* S. 1978, 99th Cong., 1st Sess. (1985). On March 21, 1986, the Treasury issued final regulations, effective on April 29, 1985, on the tax classification of trusts with multiple classes of ownership. The regulations provide that investment trusts with multiple classes of ownership are associations taxable as corporations. Treas. Reg. § 301.7701-4 (1986). The regulations provide that "trust classification may be appropriate for a multiple class trust if the trust is formed to serve the traditional custodial purposes of a fixed investment trust and the existence of multiple classes of beneficial interests is incidental to such purposes." T.D. 8080, 10 STAND. FED. TAX REP. (CCH) ¶ 6817 (Mar. 21, 1986).

[386] For a discussion of CMOs issued by FHLMC, see section 2.1(b)(4); *see also* section 1.1(e)(3).

(b) MBS STRUCTURES

(1) PASS-THROUGH CERTIFICATES

Pass-through certificates are generally issued by a trust that holds and services a fixed mortgage pool. Each certificate represents a pro rata interest in each mortgage making up the pool. Mortgage payments received by the trust are distributed (i.e., passed through) to the MBS certificate owners minus all fees and expenses incurred to service the mortgages and administer the pool (including expenses, if any, for guarantees or pool insurance).[387] Because the fees attributable to servicing mortgages are usually fixed in advance, MBS certificate owners are assured a fixed rate of interest on the principal balance of their certificates.

To avoid taxation at the pool level, the grantor trust structure is used for pass-through certificates.[388] The trust is generally ignored for tax purposes, so the certificate owners, rather than the trust, are subject to tax. Such pools are structured to avoid classification as an association taxable as a corporation. For tax purposes, the term "corporation" includes unincorporated "associations" that have corporate characteristics.[389] Although an entity may be a trust (or a partnership) for local law purposes, it can, under certain circumstances be deemed an association and treated as a corporation for tax purposes. An investment trust, such as a trust holding a mortgage pool, is treated as an association if there is a power under the trust agreement to vary the investment of the certificate holders.[390] Therefore, mortgage pools organized as trusts permit the trustee to exercise only ministerial powers and to vary the contents of the pool only by disposing of mortgages in default.

The enabling documents for the trust must provide that the trustee has no power to vary the investments in the mortgage pool. In fact, various trust provisions allow a minimal level of activity on the part of the trustee. Minor activities on the part of trustees have been approved by the IRS in published rulings. For example, the IRS has ruled that a trust that holds mortgages and makes quarterly distributions to the certificate owners can reinvest the monthly payments it receives on the mortgages in the pool in high quality obligations under certain circumstances. The obligations must mature prior to the next trust distribution

---

[387]*See generally* Treas. Reg. § 1.671-3(a) (1969).

[388]*See generally* I.R.C. §§ 671-679.

[389]I.R.C. § 7701(a)(3).

[390]Comm'r v. North American Board Trust, 122 F.2d 545, 546 (2d Cir.), *cert. denied*, 314 U.S. 701 (1941); Treas. Reg. § 301.7701-4(c) (1986).

date, and they must be held to maturity.[391] In addition, the IRS has allowed a trustee two years to accept new mortgages in exchange for mortgages initially included in the trust which did not conform to representations and warranties, without subjecting the trust to taxation as a corporation.[392] (It is unclear whether an exchange period that extends beyond two years might change the tax result.)[393]

A mortgage pool structured as a trust is treated as a grantor trust if the grantor holds "the beneficial enjoyment of the corpus or the income therefrom" and has a power to dispose of the corpus without the approval or consent of any adverse party.[394] The equitable ownership in each separate mortgage is transferred on a pro rata basis to the MBS certificate owners who own an undivided interest in the pool. The certificate owners compute their tax liability by including in income all items of income, deductions, and credits attributable to their pro rata interests.[395] Certificate owners (whether on the cash or accrual method of accounting) report income at the time the mortgage payments are received by the trust, even if distributions are not made to them at that time. The trustee is viewed simply as an agent acting on behalf of the certificate holders. This tax result has been confirmed in numerous revenue rulings addressing pass-through certificates guaranteed by GNMA, FNMA, and FHLMC, and private pools with private mortgage insurance.[396]

(2)   PAY-THROUGH BONDS

Pay-through bonds, including CMOs, are debt securities issued by a corporation subject to corporate tax. Interest payments made to the bond owners are deductible by the corporation in determining its taxable income, which means that the corporation's taxable income is based on the difference between the yields on the mortgage (income) and the payment obligations of the CMOs (deductible by the corporation as interest expense). Typically, the corporation uses the proceeds from

---

[391]Rev. Rul. 75-192, 1975-1 C.B. 384.

[392]Rev. Rul. 71-399, 1971-2 C.B. 433.

[393]For a discussion of mortgage pools taxable as trusts, see Peaslee, *Federal Income Tax Treatment of Mortgage-Backed Securities*, in HANDBOOK OF MORTGAGE-BACKED SECURITIES 569, 571-75 (F. Fabozzi ed. 1985).

[394]I.R.C. § 674(a).

[395]Treas. Reg. § 1.671-3(a) (1969).

[396]*See generally* Rev. Rul. 84-10, 1984-1 C.B. 155; Rev. Rul. 81-204, 1981-2 C.B. 157; Rev. Rul. 81-203, 1981-2 C.B. 137; Rev. Rul. 80-96, 1980-1 C.B. 317; Rev. Rul. 77-349, 1977-2 C.B. 20; Rev. Rul. 74-300, 1974-1 C.B. 169; Rev. Rul. 74-221, 1974-1 C.B. 365; Rev. Rul. 74-169, 1974-1 C.B. 147; Rev. Rul. 72-376, 1972-2 C.B. 647; Rev. Rul. 71-399, 1971-2 C.B. 433; Rev. Rul. 70-545, 1970-2 C.B. 7; Rev. Rul. 70-544, 1970-2 C.B. 6; Rev. Rul. 61-175, 1961-2 C.B. 128.

the sale of its CMOs to acquire mortgages (and perhaps pass-through certificates representing ownership in mortgage pools) to collateralize the CMOs.

The introduction of CMOs by FHLMC in 1983[397] revolutionized the pay-through bond market. CMO pass-through bonds were developed to provide investors with a way to hold mortgages in different ownership interests. CMOs are an attractive concept, especially in light of Treasury regulations that generally define fixed investment trusts to preclude trust tax status for trusts with more than one class of ownership except in limited circumstances.[398]

(3) REAL ESTATE INVESTMENT TRUSTS

REITs can be used to pool mortgages directly or to hold MBSs issued by others in the form of pass-through certificates or pay-through bonds. REITs must have more than 100 shareholders and satisfy various income tests based on the types of income earned by the entity.[399] Although REITs can be formed as either trusts or corporations, they are taxable as corporations. Unlike regular corporations, however, REITs are allowed deductions in computing taxable income for qualified dividends paid to their shareholders.[400] REITs are not widely used for pooling mortgages. There are structural limitations on REITs. In fact, at the time of this writing, there has not been a public offering of MBSs using REITs.

To deduct dividends paid to its shareholders, REITs must hold most of their assets in the form of real property and real property loans.[401] MBS pass-through certificates qualify as "real estate assets"[402] and the interest income on MBS pass-through certificates also qualifies as "interest on obligations secured by mortgages on real property or on interests in real property."[403] On the other hand, pay-through bonds do not qualify as real estate assets. As a result, REITs are more likely to

---

[397]For a discussion of FHLMC/CMOs, see section 2.1(b)(4).

[398]Treas. Reg. § 301.7701-4(c)(1) (1986) (effective for interests issued after April 27, 1984); see Peaslee, *Federal Income Tax Treatment of Mortgage-Backed Securities, supra* note 393, at 575-78; Taylor, *Debt/Equity and Other Tax Distinctions: How Far Can We Go?*, 62 TAXES 858, 850-52 (1984).

[399]*See generally* I.R.C. §§ 851–859.

[400]*See* section 22.6.

[401]I.R.C. § 856(c)(5).

[402]I.R.C. § 856(c)(5)(A).

[403]I.R.C. § 856(c)(3)(B); *see* Rev. Rul. 74-300, 1974-1 C.B. 169; Rev. Rul. 70-544, 1970-2 C.B. 6; Rev. Rul. 70-545, 1970-2 C.B. 7.

acquire MBS pass-through certificates than pay-through bonds. Investments in pay-through bonds could adversely affect a REIT's tax treatment. A second problem encountered in using REITs to pool mortgages is that REITs must distribute at least 95 percent of their taxable income to their shareholders as dividends.[404] This distribution requirement can further limit the usefulness of REITs to pool mortgages.

(4) LEGISLATIVE PROPOSALS

Recently, legislative proposals have been made to change the tax treatment of mortgage-related and other asset-backed securities.[405] In 1983, a legislative proposal was introduced in Congress to create a new type of pass-through entity, referred to as a "TIM." If authorized by Congress, a TIM would be available to pool mortgages, while providing flow-through benefits similar to those available to REITs and regulated investment companies.[406] Although at this writing there is no legislative proposal for TIMs pending before Congress, it is quite possible that the TIM concept might be considered at a future date. In the original TIM proposal, it was proposed that TIMs could acquire pass-through securities guaranteed by GNMA, FNMA, and FHLMC.[407] The Treasury viewed a TIM's ability to hold government guaranteed MBSs as abusive. In 1984 the Treasury distributed an alternative TIM proposal that would have prohibited GNMA, FNMA, and FHLMC from issuing TIMs.[408] Because it is likely that any new TIM proposals will be different from the original and alternative TIM proposals, a detailed discussion of these proposals is not appropriate at this writing.[409]

In late 1985, two legislative proposals were introduced in Congress to change the tax treatment of mortgage-backed securities. One proposal

---

[404]I.R.C. § 857(a)(1).

[405]*See generally* JOINT COMMITTEE ON TAXATION, DESCRIPTION OF BILLS RELATING TO THE TAX TREATMENT OF MORTGAGE RELATED SECURITIES (S. 1959 AND S. 1978) AND ENVIRONMENTAL ZONES (S. 1859) (JCS-3-86) Jan. 30, 1986, *reprinted in* DAILY TAX REP. (BNA) No. 21, at J-1 (Jan. 31, 1986) [hereinafter referred to as "Joint Committee Description of Bills on Mortgage Related Securities"].

[406]S. 1822, 98th Cong., 1st Sess. (1983).

[407]*Id.*

[408]21 TAX NOTES 629 (1983).

[409]For a discussion of the 1983 TIM proposal, see Liles, *Mortgage-Backed Securities—Current Status and Recent Proposals*, 25 TAX MGMT. (BNA) Memorandum 123, 126-28 (1984). For a discussion of the Treasury's alternative TIM proposal, see K. LORE, MORTGAGE-BACKED SECURITIES, DEVELOPMENT AND TRENDS IN THE SECONDARY MORTGAGE MARKET, ch. 6, at 10–28 (Clark Boardman, Securities Law Series, 1985).

provides rules under which an entity that holds mortgages on real estate can issue interests that entitle holders to receive specified cash flows generated by the mortgages without characterizing the entity as an association taxable as a corporation.[410] These interests would be known as "collateralized mortgage securities" or "CMSs," which could be issued (1) by a corporation, trust, or partnership; (2) in the form of an ownership interest or debt obligation; and (3) with different classes of maturities.[411] Another proposal would amend the grantor trust provisions to permit a trust with multiple classes of interests to be treated as a grantor trust in certain circumstances.[412] It would allow multiple classes of interests for trusts that hold financial instruments (including most debt obligations, accounts receivable, and lease receivables) that are identified when the trust interests are issued and cannot be substituted for other financial instruments except in very limited circumstances.[413]

(c) TAXATION OF MBS PASS-THROUGH CERTIFICATE OWNERS

(1) GENERAL TAX PRINCIPLES

MBS pass-through certificates, typically ownership interests in trusts, represent undivided ownership interests in each mortgage making up the pool.[414] This can be significant for thrift institutions (because they must own real estate mortgages to qualify for a special bad debt reserve deduction)[415] and REITs (because they must own real estate interests to deduct dividends paid to their shareholders).[416] Certificate owners compute their tax liability by including all items of income, deductions, and credits attributable to their pro rata interests in the pool in income (irrespective of whether on the cash or accrual method of accounting) at the time the mortgage payments are received by the trust,[417] even if the distributions are not made to the certificate owners at that time.

---

[410]S. 1959, 99th Cong., 1st Sess. (1985).

[411]For a description of CMSs, see generally Joint Committee Description of Bills on Mortgage Related Securities, *supra* note 405.

[412]S. 1978, *supra* note 385.

[413]For a description of the amendments proposed by S. 1978, see generally Joint Committee Description of Bills on Mortgage Related Securities, *supra* note 405.

[414]*See* section 28.4(b)(1); *see also* 1.1(e)(2).

[415]I.R.C. § 593(b)(1).

[416]I.R.C. § 856(c)(3).

[417]Treas. Reg. § 1.671-3(a) (1969).

The trustee is simply viewed as an agent of the certificate holders. A pass-through certificate owner, as the beneficial owner of each mortgage, should calculate income or loss on each mortgage separately. As a practical matter, however, allocation is usually not necessary because the tax results are the same if the mortgages are viewed separately or in the aggregate.

Each payment a certificate holder receives includes interest, principal, and payments for various charges and fees. Repayment of principal is a tax-free return of capital.[418] Interest and fees received are taxable as ordinary income. Fees paid to service the mortgage, custodian fees, and other fees are deductible expenses. In addition, a certificate owner's gain or loss on the sale of a certificate is based on the difference between the certificate's tax basis and the net proceeds on the sale.[419] Investors[420] and traders[421] may obtain capital gain or loss, reduced by any gain attributable to interest or discount income, which is taxable at ordinary income rates. Dealers,[422] hedgers,[423] and certain financial institutions[424] obtain ordinary income.

Taxation of MBS pass-through certificates purchased at discounts[425] or premiums[426] can be very confusing. As a result, it is necessary to consider separately the tax treatment of pass-through certificates purchased at the principal amount, a premium, and at a discount to determine the appropriate tax treatment for an owner of an MBS pass-through certificate. The remainder of this section discusses some of these major issues.

(2) PURCHASES AT THE PRINCIPAL AMOUNT

The taxation of MBS pass-through certificates purchased at their principal amounts is relatively straightforward. The only interest element is the stated interest amount. Principal payments are a tax-free return of capital. If a certificate is sold for an amount different from the amount of the principal balance outstanding at the time of sale, gain or loss

---

[418]Rev. Rul. 84-10, 1984-1 C.B. 155; Rev. Rul. 70-545, 1970-2 C.B. 7.

[419]See generally Chapter 14.

[420]See section 6.1.

[421]See section 6.2.

[422]See section 6.3.

[423]See section 6.4.

[424]See section 6.8.

[425]See section 28.4(c)(4).

[426]See section 28.4(c)(3).

results on the sale. Capital gain or loss (long-term or short-term depending on the owner's holding period) is available to investors[427] and traders.[428] Ordinary income is available to dealers,[429] hedgers,[430] and certain financial institutions.[431]

(3) PURCHASES AT A PREMIUM

It is unlikely that an owner of a pass-through certificate will purchase it at a premium.[432] Rev. Rul. 84-10[433] provides that certificate owners can amortize their proportionate shares of premium to the extent allowed by I.R.C. § 171. Premiums on residential mortgages generally cannot be amortized because I.R.C. § 171 does not apply to obligations of individuals.[434] This means that only premiums on those mortgages that are issued by corporations can be amortized. All premiums paid on the purchase of a residential mortgage or pass-through certificate evidencing such a mortgage must be allocated among the principal payments in proportion to the principal amounts.[435] The premium paid is then deductible as an ordinary loss as the principal payments to which the premium amounts are allocated are made (for cash method taxpayers) or accrued (for accrual method taxpayers).[436]

(4) PURCHASES AT A DISCOUNT

The treatment of pass-through certificates purchased at a discount depends on whether the discount is OID[437] or market discount.[438] OID is included in the certificate owner's income as the discount accrues,[439] while market discount is included in income only when the principal

---

[427]*See* section 6.1.

[428]*See* section 6.2.

[429]*See* section 6.3.

[430]*See* section 6.4.

[431]*See* section 6.8.

[432]Premiums are uncommon. Purchasers are typically unwilling to purchase MBSs at a premium because the certificates offer either limited or no call protection.

[433]1984-1 C.B. 155.

[434]I.R.C. § 171(d). For a general discussion of premiums, see section 27.4.

[435]Peaslee, *Federal Income Tax Treatment of Mortgage-Backed Securities, supra* note 393, at 612–13.

[436]*Id.* at 613.

[437]*See* section 27.2.

[438]*See* section 27.3.

[439]I.R.C. § 1272.

payments are received (for cash method taxpayers) or accrued (for accrual method taxpayers) or when the certificate is sold.[440] It is not likely that an MBS pass-through certificate has OID, unless the stripped bond rules apply[441] or interest payments on the underlying mortgages increase over time.[442]

Most MBS pass-through certificates represent interests in residential mortgage obligations of individuals. Because the rules that require the inclusion in income of OID on obligations of individuals (i.e., natural persons) apply to mortgages closed after March 1, 1984,[443] one must first determine when a mortgage obligation is incurred. As a rule of thumb, gain from a sale of an MBS pass-through certificate issued after July 18, 1984 is ordinary income to the extent of the market discount that accrued during the period the seller owned the security.[444] To further confuse the issue, the way in which discount is allocated among principal payments depends on whether the certificate is subject to the DRA provisions.

Gain realized on the sale of a pass-through certificate that represents OID or market discount not previously included in income is treated as ordinary income if the mortgage is an obligation of an individual.[445] Therefore, any gain on amortized or prepaid principal is treated as ordinary income, irrespective of the certificate owner's holding period.[446] Treating amortized or prepaid principal as ordinary income can be a substantial tax disadvantage to an owner of a pass-through certificate.[447] Once the certificate is sold, gain or loss on the remaining principal balance, if any, is treated as a capital gain or loss (long-term or short-term depending on the owner's holding period).

[440]See I.R.C. §§ 1276–1278.

[441]See section 27.6.

[442]For an excellent discussion of the application of the OID, market discount, and stripped bond rules to pass-through certificates, see Peaslee, *Federal Income Taxation of Mortgage-Backed Securities*, supra note 393, at 582–612.

[443]DRA supra note 128, § 41(a) (codified at I.R.C. § 1272(a)(2)(D)).

[444]I.R.C. § 1276(a)(1).

[445]I.R.C. § 1271(a)(1) does not apply to natural persons. I.R.C. § 1271(b)(1).

[446]See Peaslee, *Federal Income Tax Treatment of Mortgage-Backed Securities*, supra note 393, at 591.

[447]This may explain, in part, why tax-exempt entities invest in pass-through certificates while many taxable entities and individuals do not invest in pass-through certificates.

(5) SPECIAL CONSIDERATIONS FOR GRADUATED PAYMENT MORTGAGES

GPMs are different from traditional mortgages because the monthly mortgage payments on a GPM are not all equal.[448] GPM payments are smaller in the early years and increase during the life of the mortgage. Owners of GPM certificates on the accrual method must pay taxes on the entire amount of interest that would be paid if the GPM were a traditional mortgage, even though less interest is received on the GPM mortgage. The interest short fall is treated as a deferred item, and any mortgage prepayments are used to reduce any deferred interest outstanding.[449]

(d) TAXATION OF MBS PAY-THROUGH BOND OWNERS

(1) GENERAL TAX PRINCIPLES

Pay-through bonds are the debt obligations of corporate issuers,[450] which means that the owner of a pay-through bond simply owns a debt security.[451] A pay-through bond owner does not own an interest in the mortgages used to collateralize the loan.[452] In addition, pay-through bond owners are taxed on those payments they receive from the corporation (for cash method taxpayers) or as they accrue (for accrual method taxpayers), not on the payments the corporation is entitled to receive on the mortgages. Interest paid on the bonds is taxable as ordinary income. Gain or loss recognized on the sale of pass-through bonds is equal to the difference between the owner's tax basis in the bonds and the net proceeds from their sale. Investors and traders incur capital gain or loss[453] to the extent there is any gain not attributable to interest

---

[448]*See* section 2.1(b)(2).

[449]*See* Senft, *Pass-Through Securities,* in Handbook of Fixed Income Securities 469, 503 (F. Fabozzi & I. Pollack eds. 1983).

[450]*See* section 28.4(b)(2).

[451]*See generally* Chapter 27.

[452]This is a disadvantage to thrift institutions and REITs because they are subject to varying tax consequences depending on whether their assets are characterized as mortgages and real estate investments.

[453]*See* section 6.1; section 6.2.

or discount income, while dealers,[454] hedgers,[455] and certain financial institutions[456] report ordinary income or loss.

It is necessary to separately consider the tax treatment of pay-through bonds purchased at their principal amount, purchased at a premium, and purchased at a discount to determine the appropriate tax treatment for an owner of a pay-through bond. The remainder of this section highlights these issues.

(2) PURCHASE AT THE PRINCIPAL AMOUNT

Taxation of pay-through bonds purchased at their principal amount is relatively straightforward. The only interest element is the stated interest amount. A bond holder recognizes gain or loss on the sale of the bond if it is sold for an amount different from the principal amount. Capital gain or loss (long-term or short-term depending on the owner's holding period) is available to investors[457] and traders,[458] while ordinary income is available to dealers,[459] hedgers,[460] and certain financial institutions.[461]

(3) PURCHASE AT A PREMIUM

If a pay-through bond is purchased at a premium, the owner can elect to amortize the premium as an offset to interest income.[462] The owner of such a corporate obligation can use any method of amortizing bond premium which is regularly employed by him as long as the method is reasonable.[463] This can be an advantage over pass-through certificates, because premiums on pass-through certificates cannot usually be amortized.[464] In all other cases, bond premium is amortized under the straight-line method.[465]

[454]*See* section 6.3.

[455]*See* section 6.4.

[456]*See* section 6.8.

[457]*See* section 6.1.

[458]*See* section 6.2.

[459]*See* section 6.3.

[460]*See* section 6.4.

[461]*See* section 6.8.

[462]I.R.C. § 171.

[463]I.R.C. § 171(b)(3); Treas. Reg. § 1.172-2(f)(1) (1968).

[464]*See* section 28.4(c)(3).

[465]*See* Treas. Reg. § 1.171-2(f) (1968). For a discussion of premiums generally, see section 27.4.

(4) PURCHASE AT A DISCOUNT

Taxation of pay-through bonds purchased at a discount depends on whether the bonds have OID[466] or market discount.[467] In general, OID is included in the bond owner's income as the discount accrues,[468] while market discount is included in income only when the principal payments are received (for cash basis taxpayers) or accrue (for accrual method taxpayers), or when the bonds are sold.[469] Because the mortgages used as collateral for pay-through bonds frequently are purchased at a discount, pay-through bonds themselves frequently are issued at a discount.[470] A bond owner who purchases a pay-through bond with OID must include in his income the portion of the OID that accrues in each year he owns the bond.[471]

---

[466]*See* section 27.2.

[467]*See* section 27.3.

[468]I.R.C. § 1272(a)(1). The rules requiring the current inclusion in income of OID have applied to corporate debt securities since 1969.

[469]*See* I.R.C. §§ 1276-1278.

[470]Peaslee, *Federal Income Tax Treatment of Mortgage-Backed Securities, supra* note 393, 584-85.

[471]I.R.C. § 1272(a)(1). For an excellent discussion of how the rules on OID, market discount, and stripped bonds apply to pay-through bonds, see Peaslee, *Federal Income Tax Treatment of Mortgage-Backed Securities, supra* note 393, at 582–612.

Twenty-nine

Options on Debt Securities

Options on physical debt securities commenced trading on option exchanges in 1982.[1] (The various types of options on debt securities are discussed in section 5.2(a)(2).) In addition, options on futures contracts on debt securities (e.g., Treasury bonds) trade on commodity exchanges.[2] Options on futures contracts are discussed generally in Chapter 31.

§ 29.1 PRE-DRA TRANSACTIONS

Prior to the DRA amendments to section 1256,[3] options on debt securities (whether listed or unlisted options) were not eligible for section 1256 treatment. As a result, the same tax rules that apply to equity options were applied to options on debt securities established prior to the DRA amendments. For a discussion of the tax treatment of equity call options, see section 26.3(b). For a discussion of equity put options, see section 26.3(c).

Offsetting positions on debt options established after the enactment of ERTA and prior to the DRA's extension of section 1256 treatment to additional products (including exchange-traded options on debt secu-

---

[1] *See* section 5.1.
[2] *See* section 5.2(b).
[3] DRA, Pub. L. 98-369, 98 Stat. 494 (1984).

rities) were subject to the Straddle Rules.[4] This is because options on debt securities qualify as both personal property[5] and positions in personal property,[6] subject to the Straddle Rules.

§ 29.2   POST-DRA TRANSACTIONS

The tax treatment of debt option positions established after enactment of the DRA[7] depends on whether the options are listed for trading on an exchange. Listed option positions on debt securities (i.e., options on debt securities traded on commodity exchanges, national security exchanges, and other markets designated by the Treasury)[8] established generally after July 18, 1984[9] are nonequity options[10] subject to section 1256 treatment.[11] For a discussion of the DRA transitional rules, see section 32.5. For a discussion of nonequity options, see section 32.3. For a discussion of section 1256 treatment, see generally Part Nine.

Unlisted debt security options are taxed in the same manner as unlisted equity options (i.e., options on stock and narrow based stock indexes), that is, in accordance with the provisions of I.R.C. § 1234.[12] For a discussion of equity call options, see section 26.3(b). For a discussion of equity put options, see section 26.3(c).

---

[4]*See generally* Part Ten.

[5]*See* section 36.2.

[6]*See* section 36.3; section 36.4(b); and section 36.4(c).

[7]DRA, *supra* note 3. For a discussion of DRA transitional rules, see section 32.5.

[8]I.R.C. §§ 1256(g)(5), (7).

[9]The date of enactment of the DRA.

[10]I.R.C. § 1256(g)(3).

[11]I.R.C. § 1256(b)(3).

[12]*See* section 26.3.

Part Eight

Taxation of Physical Commodities and Options on Commodities

Thirty

Physical Commodities

The acquisition, maintenance, and sale of physical commodities in cash transactions embodies many of the tax rules that apply to all commodity transactions.[1] Therefore, the discussion of cash transactions in this chapter introduces many of the tax rules that apply to all types of commodity positions. There are three ways that a taxpayer can acquire, maintain, and sell physical commodities in cash transactions. First, a taxpayer can simply purchase a physical commodity for immediate or deferred delivery, paying the entire purchase price with his own funds (outright purchase). The taxpayer can accept immediate delivery or agree to buy the commodity for future delivery, taking delivery at a later date. Theoretically, the taxpayer can obtain an unlimited economic profit or a total loss of his investment if he subsequently sells the commodity at the prevailing market price.

Second, a taxpayer can finance all or a portion of the purchase price (financed purchase). The tax question is whether the interest expense is deductible. The taxpayer is not protected from the risk that the commodity will decline in value; he has the potential for unlimited economic profit or a total loss of his investment.

Third, a taxpayer can establish an offsetting position, subject to the Straddle Rules.[2] This reduces his risk of loss in owning a commodity. He can sell the commodity for a fixed price at a future date, or establish an options position. By entering into an offsetting position the taxpayer locks in the sales price, thereby reducing the risk of market price fluctuations and profit potential. In addition, he can finance his purchase.

---

[1]For a discussion of the cash market for commodities, see section 4.2(a).
[2]*See generally* Part Ten.

§ 30.1   OUTRIGHT PURCHASES OF COMMODITIES

A taxpayer can acquire a physical commodity in the cash or spot market by purchasing it outright, for immediate or deferred delivery, paying cash on delivery for the entire purchase price.[3] The taxpayer can purchase the commodity for future delivery by (1) entering into a long futures contract position, (2) privately negotiating a forward contract, (3) establishing a short put options position, or (4) establishing a long call options position. The taxpayer closes out the position by taking delivery of the underlying commodity. He does not own the commodity until he actually acquires it. Commissions and fees to purchase the commodity are part of its cost and are added to its basis.[4]

(a)   ACQUISITION PURSUANT TO A LONG FUTURES CONTRACT POSITION

A taxpayer can acquire a commodity by taking delivery of it pursuant to a long futures contract position. To establish the initial futures contract position (i.e., an opening transaction), the taxpayer purchases a standardized futures contract traded on a commodity exchange, the only open term being the price at which the underlying commodity is to be purchased.[5] The taxpayer holds the long futures contract position until the delivery month, taking delivery when the contract matures at the agreed purchase price.[6] If a taxpayer wants to close out his long position without accepting delivery, he can enter into a short futures contract position to sell the same amount of the same underlying commodity for delivery in the same month as the long position (i.e., a closing transaction).

For those commodities for which options on futures contracts are traded, a taxpayer can enter into a long call options position, exercise the option, and receive the underlying futures contract.[7] The taxpayer can hold the futures contract until it matures, taking delivery pursuant to the futures contract position. A taxpayer may also enter into a short put options position, whereby the holder of the long position can, at the holder's option, sell the underlying property (either the commodity or a futures contract) to the taxpayer.[8] With a short put position, however,

[3] See section 4.2(a).

[4] Comm'r v. Covington, 120 F.2d 768, 770 (5th Cir. 1941), cert. denied, 315 U.S. 822 (1942); see section 7.1(c)(1); section 8.1(d); section 9.1(b).

[5] See section 4.2(b).

[6] See section 33.6(a).

[7] For a discussion of call options, see section 5.4(a).

[8] For a discussion of put options, see section 5.4(b).

the taxpayer will never receive the underlying property unless the holder of the long position decides to exercise it.

A taxpayer can hold the futures contract until it matures and take delivery in the delivery month pursuant to the contract's terms. The underlying property is a capital asset in the hands of investors[9] and traders[10] and is ordinary income property in the hands of hedgers[11] and dealers.[12] At delivery, the futures contract is valued (i.e., marked-to-market) and gain or loss is recognized for tax purposes (just as if it had been closed out by offset).[13] If a taxpayer takes delivery under a futures contract position that is part of a straddle consisting of two or more futures contract positions, any futures contracts open on the delivery date are treated as if sold for their fair market value on the delivery date.[14] This allows the taxpayer to treat the remaining futures contract positions as if terminated and acquired on that date. Moreover, the taxpayer can make a section 1256(d) identified mixed straddle election on the date of delivery.[15]

The holding period of property acquired by taking delivery pursuant to a long futures contract position that is subject to section 1256 treatment begins to run on the date of delivery.[16] (Prior to amendment by TCA '82, the holding period of a long futures contract was added to that of the property received under the long futures contract.)[17] Thus, the holding period of property acquired pursuant to a futures contract subject to section 1256 treatment does not include the period for which the futures contract was held.[18] On the other hand, the holding period for a commodity acquired pursuant to a non-section 1256 futures contract position includes the period during which the long position was held.[19] This tacked on holding period applies, for example, to futures contracts

---

[9]*See* section 6.1.

[10]*See* section 6.2.

[11]*See* section 6.4.

[12]*See* section 6.3.

[13]*See* section 33.6.

[14]I.R.C. § 1256(c)(2); *see* section 33.6.

[15]*See* HOUSE WAYS AND MEANS COMMITTEE REPORT, TECHNICAL CORRECTIONS BILL OF 1982, H.R. REP. NO. 794, 97th Cong., 2d Sess. 24 (1982); SENATE FINANCE COMMITTEE REPORT, TECHNICAL CORRECTIONS ACT OF 1982, S. REP. NO. 592, 97th Cong., 2d Sess. 26, *reprinted in* 1982 U.S. CODE CONG. & AD. NEWS 4149, 4173; *see also* section 45.2.

[16]I.R.C. § 1223(8).

[17]I.R.C. § 1223(8) (1976), *amended by* TCA '82, Pub. L. No. 97-448, § 105(c)(4), 96 Stat. 2365, 2385 (1982).

[18]*See* section 15.3(b).

[19]I.R.C. § 1223(8); *see* section 15.3(b).

traded on foreign exchanges. It also applies to futures contracts that are part of an identified section 1256(d) mixed straddle where there is a mixed straddle election in effect.[20]

(b) ACQUISITION PURSUANT TO A LONG FORWARD CONTRACT POSITION

A taxpayer can acquire a commodity by entering into a forward contract position to acquire it in the future.[21] The owner of a long forward contract position does not own the underlying property for tax purposes. Forward contracts cannot generally be terminated prior to delivery unless both parties agree. If a forward contract is assignable or can be offset, the holder of the long position can dispose of his forward contract position prior to its maturity, taking his profit or loss at that point.

In addition, the holder of a long forward contract position who wants to profit from a rise in the market price of the underlying commodity (or to stop his losses in a declining market prior to maturity of the forward contract) can sell short an equivalent amount of the underlying commodity. The short sale could be closed using the commodity acquired pursuant to the long forward contract. For application of the Straddle Rules, see Part Ten.

(c) ACQUISITION PURSUANT TO A LONG CALL OPTIONS POSITION

A taxpayer can establish a long call options position, whereby he pays the short position (i.e., the writer or grantor) a premium for granting him the option to purchase the underlying commodity at the option's strike price.[22] Options are traded on certain futures contracts (futures options), which means there is an exchange market for trading in certain options for which the underlying property is a futures contract.[23] If a taxpayer decides not to exercise the option, it expires worthless and he has lost the amount of the premium he paid for the option; he does not obtain the underlying property.[24]

---

[20]*See* section 45.2.
[21]For a discussion of forward contracts, see section 4.2(a) and section 4.3(b).
[22]*See* section 5.1.
[23]*See* section 4.2(b).
[24]*See* section 5.4(a).

(d) ACQUISITION PURSUANT TO A SHORT PUT OPTIONS POSITION

A taxpayer can write a put option (short position), whereby he receives a premium for granting the holder of the option (long position) the option to sell the underlying property to the taxpayer at the option's strike price.[25] Certain futures options are traded where the property underlying the option is a futures contract on the physical commodity.[26] By establishing a short put position, the taxpayer may never obtain the underlying property. If the long position does not exercise the option, the option expires worthless, although the taxpayer can keep the premium income he received from the long position.

(e) SALE OF A COMMODITY

In an outright cash purchase, irrespective of whether the commodity is acquired immediately or delivery is deferred, a taxpayer can realize an unlimited economic profit on the sale of the commodity if the price of the commodity rises, or a total economic loss if the price of the commodity declines in value. If the taxpayer reduces his risk of loss by entering into an offsetting position (to sell the commodity he now owns at a specified date in the future), his profit potential is also minimized.[27]

For investors and traders, the sale of a physical commodity generates capital gain or loss,[28] long-term or short-term, depending on the taxpayer's holding period.[29] For a commodity acquired pursuant to a long section 1256 futures contract position, the holding period does not begin to run until the taxpayer actually acquires the commodity.[30] In addition, closing out a futures contract position by taking delivery of the underlying commodity is a taxable event subject to special rules.[31] On the other hand, if delivery is made under a long non-section 1256 futures contract (e.g., futures contracts traded on foreign exchanges), the hold-

---

[25]*See* section 5.4(b).

[26]*See* section 4.2(b).

[27]The tax consequences of holding offsetting positions are discussed in Part Ten.

[28]*See generally* Part Three.

[29]I.R.C. § 1222.

[30]I.R.C. § 1223(8).

[31]I.R.C. § 1256(c); *see* section 33.6.

ing period includes the period during which the long futures contract was held.[32] Losses are deferred on offsetting positions.[33]

Dealers and hedgers receive ordinary income or loss on their sales of physical commodities in the ordinary course of business.[34] Of course, dealers and hedgers can purchase commodities for investment purposes, where sales generate capital gain or loss treatment.[35] If a dealer or hedger holds an offsetting position, losses are deferred unless the transaction qualifies for the statutory hedging exemption.[36]

§ 30.2   FINANCED PURCHASES OF COMMODITIES

A taxpayer can finance his purchase of a physical commodity, subject to his obligation to repay the funds he borrows. The taxpayer can purchase the commodity for immediate or deferred delivery.[37] Theoretically, the taxpayer can obtain unlimited profits or a total loss of his investment; he is not protected against any risk of loss on a decline in the market value of the commodity.

With a financed purchase, a taxpayer incurs interest expenses that might not be deductible. First, if the commodity is an investment asset, the amount of interest currently deductible is subject to the statutory limitation on investment interest established under I.R.C. § 163(d).[38] The investment interest limitation applies to investors and may apply to traders as well. To avoid the investment interest limitation, however, a taxpayer may be able to assert that his investment activity is a "trade or business" and that the investment interest limitation does not apply. By successfully showing that he is in business, however, he runs the risk that his commodities will need to be inventoried or the IRS may attempt to assert that the commodities are ordinary income property, not capital assets.[39] Second, a current deduction for interest expense is not available if the taxpayer holds an offsetting position in the com-

---

[32]I.R.C. § 1223(8); *see* section 15.3(b).

[33]*See generally* Part Ten.

[34]*See generally* Part Four.

[35]*See generally* Part Three.

[36]*See generally* Chapter 21.

[37]The techniques for purchasing a commodity for deferred delivery are discussed in section 30.1.

[38]For a discussion of the investment interest limitations, see section 7.2(e), section 8.2(e), and section 9.2.

[39]*See generally* Part Two.

modity (e.g., a futures contract, forward contract, or options position). Interest on offsetting positions must be capitalized.[40]

§ 30.3 PURCHASES OF COMMODITIES WITH OFFSETTING POSITIONS

To reduce the risks of economic loss on owning a physical commodity, a taxpayer can sell a futures contract position, enter into a privately negotiated forward contract, or establish a short call option or a long put options position. The taxpayer holds offsetting positions. The short position (or long put option) reduces the risks of holding the long physical commodity position. The remainder of this section merely highlights some of the tax issues for offsetting positions. Offsetting positions are discussed in detail in Part Ten.

By entering into an offsetting position, a taxpayer can lock in the price at which he can sell the commodity. Both his risks on holding the commodity and his gain potential are limited. Because it is possible for the spot market to operate differently from the futures, options, and forward markets, there is some risk of loss and some possibility for profit even with offsetting positions. Interest expense while holding offsetting positions is not deductible and must be added to the commodity's basis.[41]

Offsetting positions are generally subject to the Straddle Rules,[42] which defers losses on closing out one position while there is an unrecognized gain inherent in an open straddle position.[43] Interest and carrying charges must be capitalized.[44] If a taxpayer holds a short futures contract position (or short call option or long put option) in a section 1256 contract[45] while holding a physical commodity, the futures contract and nonequity options positions are subject to section 1256 treatment, unless the taxpayer elects to treat the position as an identified section 1256(d) mixed straddle[46] or the taxpayer places the positions in a mixed straddle account.[47] The modified wash sales rule[48] and the

---

[40]*See generally* Chapter 43.

[41]I.R.C. § 263(g)(1). For a discussion of cash and carry transactions, see section 4.3(d) and section 43.1.

[42]*See generally* Part Ten.

[43]*See generally* Chapter 37.

[44]I.R.C. § 263(g)(1); *see* section 43.2.

[45]I.R.C. § 1256(b); *see generally* Part Nine.

[46]I.R.C. § 1256(d)(4); *see* section 45.2.

[47]*See* section 45.4.

[48]*See* section 42.3.

modified short sales rule[49] may also apply. Qualified hedging trans-actions[50] are exempt from the Straddle Rules, section 1256 treatment, and the requirement to capitalize interest and carrying charges.

§ 30.4 CASH AND CARRY TRANSACTIONS

Cash and carry transactions involve an outright purchase of a com-modity in the cash market and the sale of a futures contract or forward contract for the same commodity.[51] The tax treatment of cash and carry transactions changed dramatically with ERTA,[52] which requires capi-talization of interest and carrying charges on offsetting positions.[53] Prior to ERTA, taxpayers who held a physical commodity (long position) and a futures contract or forward contract to sell the commodity in the future (short position) were able to deduct their expenses while limiting their risk of loss.

§ 30.5 LEVERAGE TRANSACTIONS

Leverage transactions are contracts for the purchase of commodities, usually precious metals, on a deferred delivery basis.[54] Leverage con-tracts are taxed in the same manner as non-section 1256 forward con-tracts.[55] In addition, if a taxpayer holds offsetting positions, the Straddle Rules apply.[56]

§ 30.6 EXCHANGE OF FUTURES FOR PHYSICALS

EFP transactions involve transfers of futures contracts not executed on a commodity exchange floor by open and competitive outcry.[57] The taxation of EFP transactions varies, depending on the particular trans-actions. EFPs typically are entered into by commercial firms to hedge

---

[49]*See* section 42.4.
[50]*See generally* Chapter 21.
[51]*See* section 4.3(d); section 43.1.
[52]ERTA, Pub. L. 97-34, § 502, 95 Stat. 172, 327 (1981).
[53]I.R.C. § 263(g)(1); *see* section 43.2.
[54]*See* section 4.3(e).
[55]For a discussion of forward contracts, see section 4.3(c) and section 30.1(b).
[56]*See generally* Part Ten.
[57]*See* section 4.3(f).

against cash market risks. Such EFP transactions may qualify for the hedging exemption.[58] Basically, there are two types of EFP transactions. In the first, both parties initially own opposite futures positions. In the second, only one party initially owns a futures contract position.

If both parties initially hold opposite futures contract positions, the EFP transaction results in the transfer of a physical commodity and the termination of the futures contract obligations of both parties. One side sells the futures contract and the other purchases the physical commodity. When the futures contract position terminates, this is a taxable transaction.[59] Gain or loss is computed at 60/40 rates for futures contracts that qualify for section 1256 treatment,[60] and at ordinary income rates for hedging and ordinary income transactions.[61] If only one of the parties to the EFP transaction initially owns a futures contract position, that position is transferred to the other party who assumes all obligations associated with the transferred futures contract position. The party transferring the futures contract is taxed on the transfer, at 60/40 rates for capital transactions,[62] and ordinary income rates for hedging transactions[63] and other ordinary income transactions.[64]

There is a possibility for price manipulation because EFP transactions are not executed at competitive prices in the futures market. Even though pricing does not reflect the commodity's price in the futures market for that day, the EFP price may nevertheless reflect the prevailing price for the commodity in a different, yet legitimate, market. If the IRS finds a pattern of trading EFPs outside the price range established in the futures market or a comparable commodity market, it may seek to adjust the price of an EFP to the closing price for the futures contract for that day.

---

[58]See generally Chapter 21.
[59]See section 33.5; section 33.6.
[60]See generally Part Nine.
[61]See section 21.3(c).
[62]See generally Part Nine.
[63]See generally Chapter 21.
[64]See section 21.3(c).

Thirty-one

Options on Commodities

§ 31.1 IN GENERAL

The types of options on physical commodities (referred to as "cash options") and options on futures contracts (referred to as "futures options") are discussed generally in Chapter Five. (Cash options and futures options are collectively referred to as "commodity options.") Certain options on commodities are listed options,[1] which means that they are traded on commodity exchanges designated as contract markets by the CFTC, or other markets designated by the Treasury.[2] Futures options must be traded on commodity exchanges. Therefore, futures options qualify as listed options. Those cash options traded on exchanges or markets designated by the Treasury are listed options, while those cash options that are not so traded are unlisted options.[3] For a discussion of stock options, see generally Chapter 26. For a discussion of options on debt securities, see generally Chapter 29.

The tax treatment of cash options and futures options depends on whether the options are listed for trading on an exchange. All listed option positions established after October 31, 1983 are nonequity options subject to section 1256 treatment.[4] Unlisted cash options are taxed

---

[1]*See* section 26.1(a).

[2]I.R.C. §§ 1256(g)(5), (7).

[3]*See* section 32.3(a).

[4]I.R.C. § 1256(a)(1), as amended by DRA, Pub. L. 98-369, 98 Stat. 494 (1984); *see* section 31.3(b).

in the same way as unlisted equity options, that is, in accordance with the provisions of I.R.C. § 1234.[5]

§ 31.2   OPTIONS ON PHYSICAL COMMODITIES

(a)   UNLISTED CASH OPTIONS

The tax treatment of unlisted cash options follows the tax treatment of equity options (i.e., options on stock and narrow based stock indexes). For a discussion of the taxation of equity call options, see section 26.3(b). For a discussion of equity put options, see section 26.3(c).

(b)   LISTED CASH OPTIONS

Cash options listed for trading on an exchange[6] are now nonequity options subject to section 1256 treatment. For a discussion of nonequity options, see section 32.3. For a discussion of section 1256 treatment, see generally Part Nine.

§ 31.3   OPTIONS ON FUTURES CONTRACTS

(a)   FUTURES OPTION POSITIONS BEFORE NOVEMBER 1, 1983

When ERTA[7] established section 1256 treatment for RFCs in 1981, futures options were banned from trading on commodity exchanges.[8] This may explain, in part, why ERTA made no mention of the tax treatment of futures options. The result is that when futures options commenced trading in 1981,[9] the tax consequences were not clearly established in the Code. This uncertainty was resolved for futures options established after October 31, 1983. The DRA provides that such options are nonequity options subject to section 1256 treatment.[10]

Because the DRA amendments to I.R.C. § 1256 only apply to option

---

[5]*See generally* section 26.3.

[6]47 Fed. Reg. 56996 (Dec. 22, 1982).

[7]ERTA, Pub. L. 97-34, 95 Stat. 172 (1981).

[8]*See* section 5.2(b).

[9]46 Fed. Reg. 54500 (Nov. 3, 1981).

[10]DRA, *supra* note 4.

positions established after October 31, 1983, however, taxpayers have taken conflicting reporting positions with respect to futures option positions established prior to November 1, 1983. Some taxpayers have taken the position that such futures options were section 1256 contracts,[11] while other taxpayers have taken the position that such futures options were not eligible for section 1256 treatment.[12] For a discussion of the conflicting reporting positions for futures options, see section 32.3(c).

(b) FUTURES OPTION POSITIONS AFTER OCTOBER 31, 1983

All futures option positions established after October 31, 1983 are non-equity options subject to section 1256 treatment. For a discussion of nonequity options, see section 32.3. For a discussion of section 1256 treatment, see generally Part Nine.

[11]*See* section 32.3(c)(1).
[12]*See* section 32.3(c)(2).

Part Nine

Taxation of Section 1256 Contracts

This Part Nine discusses the special tax regime applied to section 1256 contracts. Section 1256 treatment was originally provided for regulated futures contracts, was later extended to foreign currency contracts,[1] and was most recently expanded to cover nonequity options and dealer equity options.[2]

In general, gains and losses from section 1256 contracts are subject to both the Mark-to-Market Rule and the 60/40 Rule, collectively referred to as "section 1256 treatment." Section 1256 treatment does not apply to qualified hedging transactions,[3] identified section 1256(d) mixed straddles (where a mixed straddle election has been made), or mixed straddle accounts.[4] In addition, 60/40 treatment does not apply to section 1256 transactions entered into by dealers in the underlying property.[5]

The Mark-to-Market Rule provides that open section 1256 contracts are treated as if closed and unrecognized gains and losses are taken into account for tax purposes at the end of the tax year. In other words, each section 1256 contract held at the close of a taxable year is treated as if it were sold for its fair market value on the last business day of that taxable year, and all gains and losses are tallied up at year-end for

---

[1] TCA '82, Pub. L. 97-448, § 105(c)(5)(B), 96 Stat. 2365, 2386 (1982).

[2] DRA, Pub. L. 98-369, § 102(a)(2), 98 Stat. 494, 620 (1984).

[3] *See generally* Chapter 21.

[4] *See generally* Chapter 45.

[5] *See* section 33.2(a).

computing taxable income. Such year-end reporting prevents the deferral of income previously attempted under prior law using straddle transactions.[6]

Under the 60/40 Rule, section 1256 contracts are taxed as 60 percent long-term and 40 percent short-term capital gain or loss, irrespective of the length of time the taxpayer held such positions.

Example

To illustrate how the Mark-to-Market and 60/40 Rules work, assume that a noncorporate taxpayer has $100 of gain from section 1256 contracts on open as well as closed positions. The 60/40 Rule automatically characterizes the gain as $60 of long-term and $40 of short-term capital gain. Because 60 percent of the long-term capital gain is excluded from tax under current law,[7] only $24 (60 percent of the $60 long-term capital gain portion) is taxable. The entire $40 short-term capital gain portion is taxable. Hence, a total of $64 ($24 plus $40) of the $100 gain from section 1256 contracts is reported as income. Assuming the taxpayer is in the 50 percent tax bracket (the now current maximum rate), the tax due on $64 is $32. Therefore, the current maximum tax on $100 of section 1256 contract gain is $32, yielding a maximum tax rate of 32 percent.

This Part Nine discusses section 1256 contracts and summarizes the rules generally affecting them.

[6]*See* section 35.1; section 35.2.
[7]I.R.C. § 1202(a); *see* section 13.3(a)(2)(i).

Thirty-two

Statutory Definitions

Section 1256 contracts consist of regulated futures contracts, foreign currency contracts, nonequity options, and dealer equity options.[1] A discussion of each of these section 1256 contracts follows.

§ 32.1 REGULATED FUTURES CONTRACTS

RFCs, which were first subject to section 1256 treatment in 1981, formed the original basis for the entire tax system embodied in section 1256. In fact, the justification for imposing section 1256 treatment, with a year-end mark-to-market, on futures contracts was based on the special way they are traded and how they are subject to a daily mark-to-market system. The value of futures contracts is recalculated each day based on the closing or settlement price for that particular contract on that day.[2] Despite this initial justification, the scope of section 1256 treatment has been liberalized since 1981 to include types of property within its scope that are not subject to a mark-to-market system like futures contracts. Because mark-to-market amounts are added to or subtracted from the value of a futures contract, taxing unrealized gains and losses made some sense for futures contracts under an expanded view of the doctrine of constructive receipt.[3]

[1]I.R.C. § 1256(b).
[2]See section 4.4(b)(1).
[3]See section 33.1(a).

An RFC must meet two requirements. First, the contract must require that amounts to be deposited or allowed to be withdrawn follow a system of marking-to-market.[4] Second, the contract must be traded on or made subject to the rules of a qualified board or exchange,[5] defined as a national securities exchange registered with the SEC, a domestic board of trade designated as a contract market by the CFTC, or any other market determined by the Treasury to have rules adequate to carry out the purposes of I.R.C. § 1256.[6]

The RFC definition originally contained two additional requirements. One has been eliminated completely and the other has been liberalized. First, the contract itself had to require delivery of personal property.[7] This requirement was eliminated in 1982[8] and retroactively applied back to ERTA's date of enactment in 1981.[9] Second, the contract had to be traded on a domestic commodity exchange registered with the CFTC (or another market authorized by the Treasury).[10] This requirement was eliminated in 1984 for positions entered into after July 18, 1984 at the same time that the concept of a qualified board or exchange was introduced into the Code.[11] Now, RFCs can be traded on national securities exchanges, as well as commodity exchanges, without the need for prior Treasury approval.

(a) CASH SETTLEMENT CONTRACTS

When I.R.C. § 1256 was enacted in 1981, the definition of RFCs was broad enough to cover all futures contracts traded on domestic commodity exchanges. In 1981, all futures contracts called for the delivery of personal property. Subsequently, however, trading commenced in futures contracts that settled in cash (referred to as "cash settlement contracts") rather than by the delivery of a physical commodity. Under the RFC definition, it was unclear whether cash settlement contracts (e.g., futures contracts on stock indexes and Eurodollar futures con-

---

[4]I.R.C. § 1256(g)(1)(A). For a discussion of how futures contracts are marked-to-market, see section 4.4(b).

[5]I.R.C. § 1256(g)(1)(B).

[6]I.R.C. § 1256(g)(7); *see* section 32.1(b).

[7]I.R.C. § 1256(b)(1) (Supp. V 1981), *amended by* TCA '82, Pub. L. 97-448, § 105(c)(5)(A), 96 Stat. 2365, 2385 (1982).

[8]TCA '82, *supra* note 7, § 105(c)(5)(A).

[9]*Id.* § 105(c)(5)(D)(ii)(I).

[10]I.R.C. § 1256(b)(3) (1981), *amended by* TCA '82, *supra* note 7, § 105(c)(5)(A).

[11]DRA, Pub. L. No. 98-369, § 102(a)(3), 98 Stat. 494, 620 (1984); *see* section 32.1(b).

tracts) qualified for section 1256 treatment. In fact, the only reference to cash in ERTA's legislative history indicated that U.S. currency was not personal property.[12] To eliminate this uncertainty, TCA '82 retroactively eliminated the requirement for delivery of personal property.[13] Cash settlement contracts, which call for payment of trading profits or losses by a cash payment (rather than by delivery of personal property) and which are traded on domestic commodity exchanges (now expanded to qualified boards or exchanges), were retroactively made eligible for section 1256 treatment.[14]

(b) QUALIFIED BOARDS OR EXCHANGES

Originally, RFCs needed to be traded on domestic commodity exchanges or in other markets determined by the Treasury to have rules adequate to carry out the purposes of I.R.C. § 1256.[15] The Treasury has designated markets other than CFTC registered markets as markets adequate to carry out the purposes of section 1256. In 1984, the IRS ruled that an exchange seeking a ruling had rules adequate to carry out the purposes of I.R.C. § 1256 and that its contracts qualified for section 1256 treatment.[16] The exchange maintains a system of marking its contracts to the settlement price. Each clearing member calculates the mark-to-market payments and collects the deficits or reimburses the excess amounts for each account it carries on a daily basis. In turn, the clearing organization affiliated with the exchange pays out any profit or demands payment of any loss incurred by settling its members' accounts on a daily basis.[17] In 1986, a foreign exchange was found to be a qualified board or exchange.[18]

Under current law, RFCs can be traded on a qualified board or exchange (defined to include securities exchanges as well as commodity exchanges).[18] As a result, RFCs entered into after June 18, 1984 technically can be traded on national securities exchanges registered with the SEC without prior designation of the market by the Treasury.

---

[12]STAFF OF THE JOINT COMMITTEE ON TAXATION, 97TH CONG., 1ST SESS., GENERAL EXPLANATION OF THE ECONOMIC RECOVERY TAX ACT OF 1981 289 (Joint Comm. Print 1981) [hereinafter referred to as "General Explanation of ERTA"].

[13]TCA '82 *supra* note 7, §§ 105(c)(5)(A), 105(c)(5)(D)(ii)(I).

[14]*Id.* § 105(c)(5)(D)(ii)(I).

[15]I.R.C. § 1256(g)(7)(B) (1981), *amended by* TCA '82, *supra* note 7, § 105(c)(5)(A).

[16]LTR 8437122 (June 18, 1984).

[17]*Id.*

[18]In Rev. Rul. 86-7, 1986-4 I.R.B. 6, the IRS ruled that the Mercantile Division of the Montreal Exchange is a qualified board or exchange.

§ 32.2   FOREIGN CURRENCY CONTRACTS

Gains and losses on forward contracts[19] generally are not eligible for section 1256 treatment. Rather, forward contracts are personal property of the type subject to the Straddle Rules.[20] There is an exception, however, for foreign currency contracts, defined to cover forward contracts on certain foreign currencies traded through the interbank markets.[21] Foreign currency contracts, made subject to section 1256 treatment in 1982[22] (when such treatment was only available to RFCs), are afforded section 1256 treatment even though these contracts are not subject to a mark-to-market system.[23] This expansion was the first departure from the original rationale of section 1256 treatment.

To qualify for section 1256 treatment, a foreign currency contract must meet three requirements. First, the contract must require delivery of a foreign currency of a type in which either regulated futures contracts are traded or the contract's settlement value depends on such a currency.[24] In other words, the contract must either require the delivery of a foreign currency that is also deliverable under a futures contract traded on a qualified board or exchange or have its settlement depend on the value of such a currency. The DRA expands this provision to include cash settlement forward contracts.[25]

Second, the forward contract must be traded in the interbank market,[26] which is an informal market among certain commercial banks established for trading foreign currencies. Contracts traded in the interbank market generally include contracts between a commercial bank and another person and contracts entered into with an FCM or other similar market participants.[27]

Third, the contract must be "entered into at arm's length at a price determined by reference to the price in the interbank market."[28] A price is determined by reference to the interbank market if it is a price that

---

[19]*See* section 4.2(a); section 4.3(b).

[20]*See generally* Part Ten.

[21]I.R.C. § 1256(g)(2)(A).

[22]TCA '82, *supra* note 7, at § 105(c)(5) (codified at I.R.C. § 1256(b)).

[23]SENATE FINANCE COMMITTEE REPORT, TECHNICAL CORRECTIONS ACT OF 1982, S. REP. NO. 592, 97th Cong., 2d Sess. 26, *reprinted in* 1982 U.S. CODE CONG. & AD. NEWS 4149, 4172.

[24]I.R.C. § 1256(g)(2)(A)(i).

[25]DRA, *supra* note 11, at § 102(a)(3) (codified at I.R.C. § 1256(g)(2)(A)(i)).

[26]I.R.C. § 1256(g)(2)(A)(ii).

[27]HOUSE CONFERENCE REPORT, TECHNICAL CORRECTION ACT OF 1982, H.R. REP. NO. 986, 97th Cong., 2d Sess. 25, *reprinted in* 1982 U.S. CODE CONG. & AD. NEWS 4203, 4213.

[28]I.R.C. § 1256(g)(2)(A)(iii).

would be obtainable from a bank that is a substantial participant in the interbank market.[29] Certain adjustments are allowed for differences attributable to contract variations customary in the interbank market, including provisions relating to commissions, the amount of currency under the contract, and the credit worthiness of the parties.[30] The Treasury has broad authority to issue regulations to carry out the purpose of granting section 1256 treatment to foreign currency contracts.[31] The legislative history of TCA '82 assumes that the IRS will publish periodic rulings or statements to provide guidance as to whether a price is determined by reference to the interbank market and specify a type of contract (or identify specific contracts) excluded from the definition of foreign currency contracts.[32]

If the parties to a foreign currency contract are changed, the original contract is deemed to terminate and a new contract is created. Thus, a foreign currency contract that originally qualifies for section 1256 treatment can lose section 1256 status if the new party does not meet all of the statutory requirements, and the new contract must independently qualify as a foreign currency contract.[33]

§ 32.3 NONEQUITY OPTIONS

Nonequity options receive section 1256 treatment for positions established after July 18, 1984;[34] special transitional year elections for different effective dates were provided by the DRA.[35] The definition of a nonequity option is somewhat circular, defined by reference to other terms also created by the DRA: listed options, equity options, and qualified boards or exchanges. A nonequity option is defined as any listed option that is not an equity option.[36] Hence, listed options and equity options also must be defined in order to define a nonequity option. A listed option is any option (other than a right to acquire stock from an issuer) that is traded on or subject to the rules of a qualified board or

---

[29]H.R. No. 986, *supra* note 27, at 25.
[30]*Id.*
[31]I.R.C. § 1256(g)(2)(B).
[32]H.R. REP. No. 986, *supra* note 27, at 25.
[33]*Id.*
[34]DRA, *supra* note 11, § 102(a)(2) (codified at I.R.C. § 1256(b)(3)).
[35]*See* section 32.5.
[36]I.R.C. § 1256(g)(3); *see* section 32.4; section 26.3.

exchange.[37] An equity option is any option to buy or sell stock or any option the value of which is determined directly or indirectly by reference to stock, a group of stocks, or a stock index.[38] However, an equity option does not include any option on any group of stocks or stock indexes if either (1) the CFTC has designated the exchange where it is traded as a contract market for the option, or (2) the Treasury has determined that the option meets the requirements for such a designation.[39]

After reviewing the relevant definitions, it appears that a nonequity option is any option—whether traded on securities exchanges or commodity exchanges—on commodities, commodity futures contracts, debt instruments, foreign currency, and broad based stock indexes. Even if an option's value is determined by reference to stocks or stock indexes, it is a nonequity option if futures contracts are or could be traded on such contracts. Nonequity options do not include options on stock, small groups of stocks, or narrow based stock indexes.

(a) TREASURY DESIGNATION

Several stock index options that are traded on securities exchanges have not been, but could be, designated for trading by the CFTC.[40] These options only qualify for section 1256 treatment after the Treasury determines such contracts could be designated, if a designation was requested, for trading on an exchange regulated by the CFTC.[41] It is possible that Treasury designations might have prospective effect only, raising questions about the tax treatment of these contracts prior to designation.[42]

(b) FUTURES OPTION POSITIONS AFTER OCTOBER 31, 1983

The DRA applies section 1256 treatment to options on futures contract positions established after October 31, 1983, ending the uncertainty over

---

[37]I.R.C. § 1256(g)(5).

[38]I.R.C. § 1256(g)(6)(A).

[39]I.R.C. § 1256(g)(6)(B).

[40]HOUSE CONFERENCE REPORT, DEFICIT REDUCTION ACT OF 1984, H.R. REP. NO. 861, 98th Cong., 2d Sess. 909 (1984).

[41]I.R.C. §§ 1256(b)(3), (g)(6)(B). In LTR 8526035 (Apr. 1, 1985), the Treasury adopted the joint guidelines promulgated by the CFTC and the SEC for determining whether an index is a nonequity option as defined by I.R.C. § 1256(g)(3); SEA Release No. 20578, Jan. 18, 1984, 49 Fed. Reg. 2884 (1984). *See*, e.g., Rev. Rul. 86-8, 1986-4 I.R.B. 6.

[42]H.R. REP. NO. 861, *supra* note 40, at 909.

the tax treatment of such options. Futures options were banned from trading in 1978, which may explain why ERTA (which enacted section 1256) made no special reference to the tax problems raised by commodity options. In late 1981, however, the CFTC approved a pilot program for exchange-traded futures options and trading commenced on various domestic commodity exchanges. Because futures options appeared to be subject to both the option rules under I.R.C. § 1234 and the rules for RFCs under I.R.C. § 1256, the tax treatment of futures options was not clear under the law in effect at that time. Although a request for a revenue ruling on the tax treatment of options on futures was submitted to the Treasury in early 1982, a revenue ruling was never issued. Legislative action was necessary to resolve the issue of whether futures options were subject to 60/40 treatment. Because the DRA provisions are only effective for futures option positions established after October 31, 1983, the tax treatment for futures options entered into prior to that date remains unsettled.

(c) FUTURES OPTION POSITIONS BEFORE NOVEMBER 1, 1983

Because the DRA provides that futures option positions established after October 31, 1983 are section 1256 contracts, the question of how futures options entered into before November 1, 1983 are taxed remains open. Some taxpayers may take the position that futures options entered into before November 1, 1983 are eligible for section 1256 treatment, while other taxpayers may take the position that such futures options are governed by the option rules contained in I.R.C. § 1234. Under these circumstances, contradictory reporting positions are inevitable. The commodity exchanges have advanced the position that futures options prior to the DRA amendments are eligible for 60/40 treatment. The securities exchanges have advanced the position that futures options are not eligible for 60/40 treatment but, rather, are taxed as capital assets (for traders and investors) and as ordinary income property (for dealers and hedgers). The remainder of this section summarizes the conflicting tax positions for futures options entered into before November 1, 1983.

(1) POSITION THAT FUTURES OPTIONS ARE ELIGIBLE FOR 60/40 TREATMENT

On May 13, 1982, the CSC filed a ruling request with the Treasury concerning the tax treatment of futures options on sugar futures contracts to be traded on that exchange.[43] In addition, the CBT has endorsed the views of the commodity exchanges in a brochure published jointly by the CBT, CSE, and COMEX.[44] The principal rulings that the CSC requested were that (1) a short futures option is an RFC, and (2) gain or loss on the lapse or closing of a long futures option is taxable under the 60/40 Rule but not the Mark-to-Market Rule.[45]

(i)   Short Futures Options as Regulated Futures Contracts

The commodity exchanges claimed that a short futures option met the definition of an RFC for two reasons. First, the amount required to be deposited by the grantor of a futures option and the amount that may be withdrawn by such grantor depend on a system of marking-to-market. Second, the futures options are traded on markets that are designated as contract markets by the CFTC.

In the view of the commodity exchanges, there was no inconsistency under pre-DRA law between the statutory provisions of I.R.C. § 1256, which governs RFCs, and the provisions of I.R.C. § 1234, which governs the tax treatment of options. I.R.C. § 1234(b) (which clearly applies to futures options) provides that a grantor's gain or loss from any closing transaction with respect to, and gain from the lapse of, an option is treated as gain or loss from the sale or exchange of a capital asset held for not more than one year. The commodity exchanges argued that because I.R.C. § 1256 applied to RFCs held by the taxpayer as capital assets (and provided that gains and losses are subject to the 60/40 Rule irrespective of the actual holding period of the RFC), it followed that even though an option was deemed to have been held for less than the long-term holding period under I.R.C. § 1234(b), gain or loss from its disposition was 60/40 gain or loss by application of I.R.C. § 1256. Moreover, the commodity exchanges argued that even if a conflict did exist between the provisions of I.R.C. §§ 1256 and 1234(b), the conflict should be resolved in favor of I.R.C. § 1256 because that section was enacted after I.R.C. § 1234(b).

Although both I.R.C. §§ 1234(b) and 1256 appeared to be applicable to short futures options, their provisions were incompatible under pre-DRA law. I.R.C. § 1256 provides that gain or loss from the disposition

---

[43]Letter from Donald Schapiro of Barrett Smith Schapiro Simon & Armstrong to Assistant Commissioner (Technical), IRS (May 13, 1982).

[44]CBT, CSC & COMEX, TAX CONSEQUENCES OF FUTURES OPTIONS TRADING (1982).

[45]*See* section 33.1; section 33.2.

of an RFC is treated as 60 percent long-term and 40 percent short-term capital gain or loss without regard to the actual holding period. I.R.C. § 1234(b) provided that gain or loss from the disposition of an option was treated as 100 percent short-term capital gain or loss without regard to the actual holding period. If a short futures option was both an RFC and a short option, then the Code provided for two completely inconsistent methods of taxation for the same product and the determination of what treatment was dominant did, in fact, require legislative action.

(ii)   Long Futures Options as Subject to the 60/40 Rule

The commodity exchanges conceded that long futures options did not meet the statutory definition of an RFC because the holder of a futures option was not subject to a mark-to-market system governing deposits and withdrawals. Nevertheless, the commodity exchanges pointed out that under I.R.C. § 1234(a) the "character" of gain or loss attributable to the lapse, sale, or exchange of an option to buy or sell property was the same as the "character" that the underlying property would have in the hands of the taxpayer. It was their view that I.R.C. § 1256(a)(3) directed that any gain or loss with respect to an RFC "be treated" as part long-term and part short-term. Therefore, under this interpretation, because the underlying property of a futures option is an RFC, gain or loss from the sale or exchange of the futures option should be subject to the 60/40 Rule.

As used in I.R.C. § 1234(a), the term "character" refers only to the capital or ordinary aspect of the underlying property and not to the holding period. Indeed, it would be impossible to determine the holding period that such property "would have in the hands of the taxpayer if acquired by him" as I.R.C. § 1234(a) requires. The determination of whether capital gain or loss with respect to an option is long-term or short-term is made by reference to the period of time for which the taxpayer held the option.[46] If the holding period of the option were determined by reference to the holding period of the underlying property (presumably the current owner's holding period in the case of a long call or the taxpayer's holding period in the case of a short put), then the disposition of a one-day old option on property held by its current owner for over one year would generate long-term capital gain or long-term capital loss for the holder.

The commodity exchanges advanced the argument that, in enacting I.R.C. § 1256, Congress intended to create a new category of assets. These

---

[46]Treas. Reg. § 1.1234-1(a)(1) (1979).

assets, section 1256 assets, are neither capital nor ordinary but simply are taxed as if they were capital assets, 60 percent of which were held for over a year and 40 percent for less than a year. This interpretation would have allowed long futures options to be taxed as RFCs because I.R.C. § 1234(a) provides that long options have the same character (in this case section 1256 asset status) as the underlying property. However, the legislative history of ERTA makes clear that RFCs are capital assets and that the rules in I.R.C. § 1256 are simply intended to provide a holding period assumption:

> Any capital gain or capital loss on a regulated futures contract which is marked-to-market is treated as if 40% of the gain or loss is short-term capital gain or loss, and as if 60% of the gain is long-term capital gain or loss . . . . Regulated futures contracts continue to constitute capital assets in all cases in which they would have constituted capital assets under prior law. Treatment of gains and losses as partially short-term and partially long-term is not intended to affect the character of such contracts as capital assets.[47]

In summary, the tax rules urged by the commodity exchanges would apply the following tax treatment to futures option transactions of traders or investors prior to November 1, 1983. First, all gain or loss taken into account by holders or grantors of futures options would be subject to the 60/40 Rule. Second, writers (grantors) of futures options who were required to provide and who were entitled to receive daily mark-to-market payments would recognize gain or loss on termination of their obligations under the option and on positions open at the end of the tax year under the Mark-to-Market Rule. Third, holders of futures options, who were not subject to a mark-to-market system, were not subject to the Mark-to-Market Rule; long futures options were not RFCs. No gain or loss would be recognized by holders of futures options on their exercise and acquisition of the underlying RFCs. The premium paid for the option would be treated as an adjustment when gain or loss on the RFC was recognized (thereby increasing loss or decreasing gain). Gain or loss would be taken into account by holders of futures options on lapse of the options or on their termination by offset. Of course, commodity dealers who use futures options for hedging transactions would receive ordinary income or loss treatment.

---

[47]General Explanation of ERTA, *supra* note 12, at 297.

(2) POSITION THAT FUTURES OPTIONS ARE INELIGIBLE FOR 60/40 TAX TREATMENT

On August 19, 1982 the AMEX, CBOE, and PHLX submitted a memorandum to the Treasury urging rejection of the positions advanced by the commodity exchanges.[48] The securities exchanges argued that, as a matter of policy, futures options should not be entitled to more favorable tax treatment than options on debt securities and physical commodities traded on domestic securities exchanges. Moreover, the securities exchanges argued that the tax treatment of futures options proposed by the commodity exchanges was not authorized under existing law.

According to this view of pre-DRA law, a long futures option was not an RFC because it was not a contract with respect to which the amount required to be deposited and the amount which could be withdrawn did not depend on a system of marking-to-market. Because futures options were not entitled to RFC treatment, their taxation was governed by the rules in I.R.C. § 1234. The securities exchanges took issue with the commodity exchanges' position that the "character" of gain or loss for an option holder was determined by reference to the "character" of the gain or loss on the underlying property, that is, 60/40 treatment. Rather, the securities exchanges asserted that the "character" of the underlying property, as the term is used in I.R.C. § 1234(a), refers to its status as a capital or ordinary asset and that the character of property does not encompass the special tax rate provided in I.R.C. § 1256.

Furthermore, the securities exchanges argued that under I.R.C. § 1234 the exercise of an option was not a taxable event in itself. Rather, that the gain or loss that inures to the holder or writer during the option period was recognized when the underlying property was sold. This argument, if accepted, would have opened a substantial opportunity for tax avoidance. If a futures option holder could choose how his gain or loss was to be taxed, he could have structured his transactions to convert short-term capital gain into 60 percent long-term capital gain and 40 percent short-term capital gain. This opportunity could have been maximized by using straddles in futures options that, when closed out by offset and exercise, would generate short-term capital loss and gain subject to the 60/40 Rule. The Straddle Rules would not affect such straddles in futures options because the option holder would not be

---

[48]Letter from Robert A. Rudnick of Cadwalader, Wickersham & Taft to John E. Chapoton, Assistant Secretary of the Treasury (Aug. 19, 1982).

recognizing losses while deferring unrealized gain in offsetting positions. Rather, the holder simply would choose to recognize the gains under section 1256 and the losses as short-term capital loss.

To avoid the conversion possibility inherent in this position, the securities exchanges argued that Congress intended to limit section 1256 treatment to gain or loss with "respect to" RFCs. Thus, they asserted that if a futures option was exercised, the gain or loss from the option element had to be "segregated" from any gain or loss attributable to the RFC. The segregated amount had to either be recognized upon the exercise of the option or suspended until the RFC gain or loss was recognized.[49]

In summary, the tax rules proposed by the securities exchanges apply the following tax treatment to futures options entered into by investors or traders prior to November 1, 1983.[50] First, holders of futures options recognized capital gain or loss, long-term or short-term, depending on their holding period in the option, on the lapse or offset of the futures options. The 60/40 Rule did not apply to option holders and the option was treated as a separate asset. On exercise of a futures option, gain or loss was calculated and was recognized at such time or segregated and suspended for future recognition. If recognized when exercised, gain or loss was either short-term or long-term depending on the holding period of the option. If segregated and suspended, the gain or loss was long-term or short-term depending on the period for which the RFC and any property delivered pursuant to the RFC were held. Second, grantors of futures options recognized short-term capital gain or short-term capital loss on lapse or closing of futures options. On an assignment of the option, gain or loss was calculated and either recognized at that time or segregated and suspended for later recognition.

§ 32.4   DEALER EQUITY OPTIONS

Dealer equity options established after July 18, 1984 are subject to section 1256 treatment.[51] To qualify as dealer equity options, the options must meet four requirements. First, all dealer equity options must be

---

[49]There was no precedent in the law for this "segregation" concept and, therefore, this part of the securities exchanges' argument was, in effect, a proposal for new legislation to deal with the conversion problem.

[50]The proposals do not affect the tax treatment of hedgers and dealers who would receive ordinary gain or loss treatment on their futures option transactions.

[51]DRA, *supra* note 11, at § 102(a)(2) (codified at I.R.C. § 1256(b)(4)).

held by an options dealer, defined as any person registered with an appropriate national securities exchange as a market maker or specialist in listed options.[52] This definition of an options dealer can be expanded with Treasury approval to include any person who performs similar functions to the extent appropriate to carry out the purposes of I.R.C. § 1256.[53] Indeed, under this authority, the definition of an options dealer can include those dealers who trade options in the over-the-counter market and in certain foreign markets.

Second, the option must be a listed option that is also (1) an equity option,[54] (2) traded on or subject to the rules of a qualified board or exchange,[55] and (3) either an option on stock or an option that has its value is determined (directly or indirectly) by reference to stock, a group of stocks, or a stock index.[56]

Third, a dealer equity option must be purchased or granted by an options dealer in the normal course of his trade or business.[57] It is not clear from the Code or legislative history whether any sort of identification might be required of an options dealer to demonstrate that his trading is in the normal course of business or what the tax treatment might be if he cannot meet this requirement.

Fourth, a dealer equity option must be listed on the qualified board or exchange on which the options dealer is "registered."[58] It is not clear from the code or legislative history what type of registration is contemplated by this requirement.

Granting option dealers capital gain and loss treatment under the 60/40 Rule is a radical departure from prior law as viewed by such taxpayers. Under prior law, option dealers viewed themselves as dealers for tax purposes and reported their transactions in options and the stock underlying such options as ordinary income and loss. Now, however, if option dealers are not dealers in the underlying property, they receive section 1256 treatment on their dealer equity options, notwithstanding the fact that they continue to view themselves as dealers for all other purposes. The House Conference Report of the DRA states that the treatment of option dealers as obtaining capital gain or loss changes the

---

[52]I.R.C. § 1256(g)(8)(A); *see* section 6.2(b); section 6.3(d).

[53]I.R.C. § 1256(g)(8)(B).

[54]I.R.C. § 1256(g)(4).

[55]I.R.C. § 1256(g)(5).

[56]I.R.C. § 1256(g)(6)(A).

[57]I.R.C. § 1256(g)(4)(B).

[58]I.R.C. § 1256(g)(4)(C).

claimed tax treatment of option dealers except to the extent that an option is acquired to hedge property that would generate ordinary loss.[59] The Conference Committee amendments require that loss on hedge property be ordinary loss.[60] Option dealers need not treat their dealer equity options as investment assets in any respect and need not comply with the identification requirements otherwise imposed on securities dealers for investment assets under I.R.C. § 1236.[61]

Finally, limited partners and limited entrepreneurs, including stockholders in S corporations who do not actively participate in the management of the business, are prohibited from reporting gains and losses from dealer equity options allocated to them as 60 percent long-term and 40 percent short-term capital gain or loss. Rather, any gain or loss with respect to dealer equity options allocable to limited partners or limited entrepreneurs is marked-to-market and taxed as short-term capital gain or loss.[62]

§ 32.5   DRA TRANSITIONAL YEAR ELECTIONS FOR SECTION 1256 OPTIONS

The Straddle Rules apply to nonequity options and dealer equity options established after December 31, 1983.[63] The extension of section 1256 treatment applies to positions established after July 18, 1984. The DRA provides a transitional rule for nonequity options and dealer equity options held during a taxpayer's taxable year in which the DRA was enacted. Under the DRA provisions, a taxpayer can elect section 1256 treatment either for (1) all of the positions held by him on July 18, 1984 ("date of enactment election") or (2) all of the positions held by him during the full taxable year in which July 18, 1984 was included ("full year election").[64] Under the date of enactment election, a taxpayer applies section 1256 treatment to all positions held on that date. The Straddle Rules, but not section 1256 treatment, apply to all positions acquired after December 31, 1983 and disposed of before July 18, 1984. If a taxpayer makes a full year election to have section 1256 treatment

---

[59]See H.R. REP. No. 861, *supra* note 40, at 909.

[60]See id.

[61]Id. at 909.

[62]I.R.C. § 1256(f)(4); *see* section 33.2(c).

[63]DRA, *supra* note 11, § 101(e)(1).

[64]Id. § 102(g).

apply to all positions at any time during the transitional year, all non-equity options (and equity options held by an options dealer at any time during the transitional year) are marked-to-market on the last business day of such year.[65] Thus, a taxpayer using a calendar year can elect section 1256 treatment for the entire 1984 year.

If a flow-through entity (including a partnership, trust, or S corporation) held a position made subject to section 1256 during the period or date covered by the election, only the flow-through entity can make an election with respect to such contracts.[66] For example, if a partnership held nonequity options or dealer equity options on July 18, 1984, only the partnership—not the partners—can elect to treat those options as section 1256 contracts.[67] However, a taxpayer who is a partner in a partnership can make an election with respect to contracts held by him outside the partnership, without regard to whether the partnership also makes such an election.[68]

If a taxpayer makes the full year election or has an interest in a flow-through entity that has made the full year election, he can elect to pay part or all of the deferrable tax in two or more (but not more than five) equal installments.[69] This election is made at the same time and with the same tax return as the full year election.[70] If a taxpayer elects to defer the payment of tax, the first installment must be paid on or before the due date for filing the return for the taxable year which includes July 18, 1984, with the succeeding installment to be paid on or before the date that is one year after the last date prescribed for payment of the preceding installment.[71]

The deferrable tax amount is defined as the excess of (1) the tax applying the amendments made by the DRA to all section 1256 contracts held by the taxpayer during the transitional year, over (2) the tax computed by applying the DRA amendments to all section 1256 contracts held during the transitional year.[72] Stock options that are section 1256 contracts and stock positions held as part of option straddles that were held as ordinary assets on the last day of the preceding taxable year are treated as having been acquired for their market value in the preceding

[65]*Id.* § 102(h)(1)(B)(ii)(II).

[66]Temp. Treas. Reg. § 1.1256(h)-2T(d) (1986).

[67]*Id.*

[68]*Id.*

[69]Temp. Treas. Reg. § 1.1256(h)-3T(a) (1985).

[70]*See* Temp. Treas. Reg. § 1.1256(h)-3T(c) (1985).

[71]Temp. Treas. Reg. § 1.1256(h)-3T(d) (1985).

[72]Temp. Treas. Reg. § 1.1256(h)-3T(b)(1) (1985).

tax year.[73] The deferrable tax definition restricts the benefit of the five-year pay-in provision to those option dealers who treated their stock and option positions as inventory prior to the DRA. The definition allows option dealers to pay in installments the tax relating to unrecognized gains in both stock and options "pushed" into the transitional year from prior years. Option dealers electing the full year election also are entitled to elect to pay the portion of the tax liability attributable to the unrealized appreciation of their stock and stock option positions for years prior to the transitional year in two to five equal annual installments, with interest.[74] The five-year pay-in is limited to unrealized appreciation in stock and stock option positions that would have generated ordinary income if the positions had been disposed of on the last day of the preceding year. Elections must be made on IRS Form 6781 by the due date of the income tax return (taking valid extensions into account) for the transitional year.[75]

To obtain the benefits of the multi-year pay-in, option dealers with interests in flow-through entities (such as partners in partnerships) who make the full year election must also make an individual election to pay the deferrable tax in installments.[76] This requirement creates an unexpected problem for taxpayers with a different taxable year than that of their flow-through entities. For example, a partner with a September 30th fiscal year-end, who participates in a calendar year partnership receives a distribution of the income resulting from the full year election in a taxable year that does not include July 18, 1984. Since the election only allows a taxpayer to defer the payment of taxes relating to years including July 18, 1984, it appears that such a taxpayer cannot qualify for the five-installment pay-in election.

---

[73]Temp. Treas. Reg. § 1.1256(h)-3T(b)(2)(ii) (1985).

[74]DRA, *supra* note 11, § 102(h)(1)(A); Temp. Treas. Reg. § 1.1256(h)-3T(a) (1985).

[75]Temp. Treas. Reg. § 1.1256(h)-3T(c) (1985).

[76]Temp. Treas. Reg. § 1.1256(h)-3T(a) (1985).

Thirty-three

General Tax Rules for Section 1256 Contracts

S ection 1256 contracts are subject to two unique tax rules: the Mark-to-Market Rule and the 60/40 Rule, collectively referred to as "section 1256 treatment." The Mark-to-Market Rule applies to all section 1256 contracts, while the 60/40 Rule applies only to section 1256 contracts that are capital assets in the hands of the taxpayer. The Mark-to-Market Rule eliminates the tax advantage previously available for straddle transactions, which were used under prior law to defer the payment of tax by currently reporting losses while deferring unrecognized gains on offsetting positions.[1] General tax rules for section 1256 contracts are discussed in this chapter.

§ 33.1 MARK-TO-MARKET RULE

Under the Mark-to-Market Rule, a section 1256 contract open at the end of a taxable year is marked-to-market; that is, it is treated as if it were sold for its fair market value on the last business day of the taxable year.[2] Additionally, when a taxpayer terminates a section 1256 contract position during the year (by offset or otherwise), the contract is marked-to-market. In other words, mark-to-market is required if a taxpayer (1)

---

[1]*See* section 35.1.
[2]I.R.C. § 1256(a)(1).

offsets a section 1256 position, (2) makes or takes delivery under a section 1256 contract, (3) exercises or is exercised on a section 1256 option position, (4) makes or is the recipient of an assignment under a section 1256 option, or (5) has a position closed by lapse or otherwise.[3]

The fair market value of a section 1256 contract is its settlement price, determined by the qualified board or exchange where the contract is traded on the last business day of the taxable year or on the day during the tax year when the contract is terminated.[4] The Mark-to-Market Rule applies to all section 1256 contracts unless the contracts are (1) part of a qualified hedging transaction,[5] (2) part of an identified section 1256(d) mixed straddle for which a mixed straddle election has been made,[6] or (3) has been included in a mixed straddle account.[7] The Mark-to-Market Rule also applies even if nonrecognition of gain or loss might result from the application of other Code sections.[8]

(a) CONSTRUCTIVE RECEIPT DOCTRINE

The Mark-to-Market Rule applies an expanded constructive receipt concept to unrecognized section 1256 contract gains at year-end and expands the doctrine to cover the recognition of losses.[9] It was first applied to futures contracts on the grounds that such contracts were subject to a unique mark-to-market system that could justify such treatment.[10] The Mark-to-Market Rule, however, applies the concept of constructive receipt of cash under a daily cash settlement system (used to adjust futures contract prices to the market price)[11] to all section 1256 contracts (including contracts not subject to a daily mark-to-market settlement

---

[3]I.R.C. § 1256(c)(1).

[4]I.R.C. § 1256(c)(3). *See* STAFF OF THE JOINT COMMITTEE ON TAXATION, 97TH CONG., 1ST SESS., GENERAL EXPLANATION OF THE ECONOMIC RECOVERY TAX ACT OF 1981 296-97 (Joint Comm. Print 1981) [hereinafter referred to as "General Explanation of ERTA"].

[5]I.R.C. § 1256(e); *see generally* Chapter 21.

[6]I.R.C. § 1256(d)(1); *see* section 45.2.

[7]I.R.C. § 1092(b)(2)(B); *see* section 45.4.

[8]General Explanation of ERTA, *supra* note 4, at 297.

[9]*Id.* at 296.

[10]*See id.* at 296 (where the Joint Committee refers to the mark-to-market system as margin adjustments); *see also* section 4.4(b).

[11]*See* section 4.4(b). The CBTCC Bylaws provide, for example, that open futures contract positions are marked to the settlement price of the day, on each day the positions remain open, payments are made to bring the positions to the settlement price of that day, and "after such payments have been made, the buyer shall be deemed to have bought and the seller shall be deemed to have sold such commodity to the Clearing Corporation at the settlement price of such day." CBTCC Bylaw 503.

process). It treats funds subtracted from or added to a taxpayer's section 1256 contract account as taxable gains and losses on the last day of the tax year. Hence, the Mark-to-Market Rule effectively eliminates the use of section 1256 contract straddle transactions to defer the payment of tax. With the application of section 1256 treatment to contracts not subject to daily cash settlement—first to foreign currency contracts and later to nonequity options and dealer equity options—the doctrine of constructive receipt was extended well beyond its original expansion for futures contracts. In fact, section 1256 treatment now applies to contracts for which the constructive receipt doctrine cannot be used to justify section 1256 treatment.

(b) SUBSEQUENT GAIN OR LOSS

Because the Mark-to-Market Rule requires taxes to be paid on unrecognized as well as recognized section 1256 contract gains, taxpayers pay tax on gain that, in fact, may never be realized. If a taxpayer continues to hold a section 1256 contract that was marked-to-market at the end of a taxable year, any gain or loss subsequently realized on the section 1256 contract is adjusted to reflect any gain or loss taken into account in the preceding year.[12] As a result, the Mark-to-Market Rule can distort a taxpayer's income, causing substantial economic hardship.

Example   33-1

Assume that on the last business day of the taxable year a taxpayer holds a section 1256 contract position with an unrealized gain of $100. Under the Mark-to-Market Rule, the gain is included in the taxpayer's income for the year. In addition, the taxpayer's basis in the contract in the second year is increased by $100 to reflect the tax reported in the first year. Further, suppose that at the beginning of the second year the market moves against the taxpayer's position, so that the section 1256 contract declines in value by $150. The taxpayer then closes out the section 1256 contract in the second year with an actual loss on the position of $50. Irrespective of this actual loss, the taxpayer reports a $100 gain in the first year and a $150 loss in the second year (because the contract's tax basis was adjusted in the second year to reflect the tax paid in the first year). This basis adjustment may be small comfort, given that the taxpayer is out-of-pocket the amount of his tax liability for 12 months on the $100 gain reported as income in the first year.

---

[12]I.R.C. § 1256(a)(2).

To ameliorate some of the harsh effects of the Mark-to-Market Rule in certain situations, special provisions exempt qualified hedging transactions[13] and identified section 1256(d) mixed straddles (composed of section 1256 contracts and non-section 1256 positions in personal property) from the Mark-to-Market rule.[14]

§ 33.2   60/40 RULE

Under the 60/40 Rule, section 1256 contracts that are capital assets in the hands of the taxpayer are taxed as 60 percent long-term and 40 percent short-term capital gains and losses.[15] 60/40 treatment applies to all positions, whether short or long, without regard to the length of time the taxpayer holds the contracts.[16] Hence, the capital gain holding period requirement is eliminated for those section 1256 contracts subject to section 1256 treatment.[17] With the highest individual income tax rate now at 50 percent, the maximum tax rate on section 1256 contracts taxed under the 60/40 Rule is 32 percent.[18]

(a)   DEALERS IN THE UNDERLYING PROPERTY

Dealers in the underlying property obtain ordinary income treatment on both the underlying property for which they are dealers and on their section 1256 contract transactions to the extent the section 1256 contracts are held for purposes of hedging the underlying property.[19] Section 1256 contracts not held as a hedge under the statutory hedging exemption are subject to the Mark-to-Market Rule and the 60/40 Rule (unless the asset is an ordinary income asset). Dealers holding section 1256 contracts to hedge their dealer positions in the underlying property are subject to the loss deferral rule of I.R.C. § 1092 and the requirement

[13]I.R.C. § 1256(e); *see generally* Chapter 21.

[14]I.R.C. § 1256(d)(1); *see generally* Chapter 45.

[15]I.R.C. § 1256(a)(3).

[16]*See id.*

[17]For exceptions to section 1256 treatment, see section 34.1 and section 34.2. For the special rules that apply to mixed straddle accounts, see section 45.4.

[18]Under the current 60 percent exclusion for noncorporate taxpayers for long-term capital gains under I.R.C. § 1202, 60 percent of the long-term portion is excluded from taxable income, so only 40 percent of the long-term capital gain amount is taxable. Because the entire short-term capital gain portion is taxable, this means that on $100 of section 1256 gain, a total of $64 ($24 plus $40), rather than $100, is taxable. For a taxpayer in the 50 percent tax bracket, the tax due is $32, or a tax rate of 32 percent.

[19]*See* section 6.3; section 6.4.

to capitalize interest and carrying charges under I.R.C. § 263(g), unless they meet the statutory hedging exemption.[20]

The 60/40 Rule does not apply to section 1256 contracts that are ordinary assets.[21] Section 1256 contracts that are ordinary income property in the taxpayer's hands continue to generate ordinary income or loss.[22] Such contracts open at year-end are marked-to-market at ordinary income rates.[23] Section 1256 contracts identified as section 1256(d) mixed straddles[24] or as part of qualified hedging transactions[25] are not marked-to-market at year-end.[26]

The Corn Products doctrine[27] is codified to provide that capital asset treatment is not available to any section 1256 contract to the extent that the contract is held to hedge other property and any loss with respect to the property is an ordinary loss.[28] The fact that a taxpayer actively deals or trades in section 1256 contracts is not taken into account to determine whether gain or loss on the underlying property is ordinary.[29] Legislative history of the DRA explains that the reference to the hedging exemption in I.R.C. § 1256(f)(3)(B) is not intended to limit the scope of the hedging exemption under present law.[30] In other words, a section 1256 contract may hedge property to be acquired or obligations to be incurred to the extent those results are obtained under the hedging exemption of I.R.C. § 1256(e).[31]

(b) COMMODITY DEALERS AND OPTION DEALERS

Taxpayers eligible for designation as commodity dealers under I.R.C. § 1402(i)(2)(B) or option dealers under I.R.C. § 1256(g)(8) are granted special tax treatment in a number of areas. (The criteria to determine whether a taxpayer is eligible for either designation is discussed in section 6.2(b), section 6.2(c), section 6.3(d), and section 6.3(e).) I.R.C. § 1256(f)(3) makes it clear that professional commodity and option deal-

---

[20]*See generally* Chapter 21.

[21]I.R.C. § 1256(f)(2).

[22]General Explanation of ERTA, *supra* note 4, at 297.

[23]*Id.*

[24]*See* section 45.2.

[25]*See generally* Chapter 21.

[26]I.R.C. §§ 1256(d)(1), (e)(1).

[27]350 U.S. 46 (1955).

[28]I.R.C. § 1256(f)(3)(B).

[29]I.R.C. § 1256(f)(3)(C).

[30]HOUSE CONFERENCE REPORT, DEFICIT REDUCTION ACT OF 1984, H.R. REP. NO. 861, 98th Cong. 2d Sess. 909 (1984).

[31]*Id.*

ers (i.e., traders) generate capital gains and losses on section 1256 contract transactions. Because gain and loss from section 1256 contracts is treated as from the sale or exchange of a capital asset,[32] option dealers (who claimed ordinary income treatment prior to the DRA and viewed themselves as securities dealers who traded options and underlying securities) and professional commodity traders now report capital gain and loss on section 1256 contracts, except to the extent that the position is a hedge against ordinary income property.[33]

Under pre-DRA law, a dealer in options was deemed to be a dealer in the underlying property simply because he was a dealer in the options overlaying the property.[34] This rule was reversed by the DRA; the Code now provides that in determining whether gain or loss is ordinary income or loss, "the fact that the taxpayer is actively engaged in dealing in or trading section 1256 contracts related to such property shall not be taken into account."[35] An options dealer does not report ordinary income or loss with respect to his transactions in property underlying the options he trades unless under general tax rules he is a dealer in the underlying property.[36]

DRA changes the treatment of option market makers by providing that market makers, defined as "option dealers," are treated as buying and selling capital assets unless the option positions are acquired as a hedge against ordinary income property.[37] Accordingly, a market maker no longer reports ordinary income or loss on transactions in options, stock, or securities unless he is also a dealer, independent of his options business, in the underlying stock or securities.[38] Under current law, option dealers generally receive 60/40 treatment under section 1256 for their option transactions and capital gain or loss on their transactions in the underlying property (unless they qualify as dealers in the underlying property).

Section 1256 treatment is not available to property underlying section 1256 positions.[39] This means that gain or loss on the underlying property is recognized only upon a sale or exchange of that property, not on a

---

[32] I.R.C. § 1256(f)(3)(A).

[33] HOUSE WAYS AND MEANS COMMITTEE REPORT, DEFICIT REDUCTION ACT OF 1984, H.R. REP. NO. 432, Pt. II, 98th Cong., 2d Sess. 1270, *reprinted in* 1984 U.S. CODE CONG. & AD. NEWS 697, 932.

[34] I.R.C. § 1234(a)(1); *see also* H.R. REP. NO. 861, *supra* note 30, at 915.

[35] I.R.C. § 1256(f)(3)(C).

[36] H.R. REP. NO. 432, *supra* note 33, at 1270.

[37] *Id.*

[38] *Id.*

[39] Section 1256 treatment applies only to section 1256 contracts as defined in I.R.C. § 1256(b).

mark-to-market basis. Furthermore, market makers who are not dealers in the underlying securities no longer are treated as trading ordinary income assets.[40] Any gain or loss from the sale or exchange of stock or securities underlying the options in which they trade is capital gain or loss, irrespective of whether the option positions are held for investment or in the course of making a market in options.[41] Under the combination of the modified short sales and wash sales rules incorporated in I.R.C. § 1092(b), the Treasury has issued regulations, discussed generally in Chapter 42, that may preclude long-term capital gain treatment for stock or securities positions used to balance option positions established in the course of making a market.

(c) DEALER EQUITY OPTIONS UNAVAILABLE TO LIMITED PARTNERS AND LIMITED ENTREPRENEURS

Limited partners and limited entrepreneurs of partnerships, S corporations, and other entities that qualify as option dealers cannot report their allocable gain or loss from dealer equity options as 60/40 gains or losses.[42] Rather, all such gains and losses are treated as short-term capital gains and losses for such taxpayers.[43] This limitation on 60/40 treatment precludes the flow-through of 60/40 gains and losses from dealer equity options to passive investors and those members of professional option firms who do not actively participate in the entity's management.[44] This section discusses the impact of this limitation on the tax treatment of such taxpayers and the possible impact of option dealer partnerships on general partners.

(1) UNINTENDED TAX RESULT

Because of the way the exclusion for 60/40 gains or losses for limited partners and limited entrepreneurs is structured, it is possible that a dealer trading firm could generate 60/40 gains on section 1256 contracts while generating losses on dealer equity options, which flow through to its limited partners and limited entrepreneurs as short-term capital loss. The short-term capital loss could then be used to offset the short-term

---

[40]*Compare* I.R.C. § 1234(a)(1) *with* I.R.C. § 1256(f)(3)(C) (which was first introduced by the DRA, Pub. L. 98-369, § 102(b), 98 Stat. 494, 621-22).

[41]I.R.C. § 1256(f)(3)(C); *see* section 6.2(b); section 6.3(d).

[42]I.R.C. § 1256(f)(4).

[43]*Id.*

[44]For a discussion of limited entrepreneurs, see section 21.4(c).

capital gain portion of other section 1256 contracts. As a result, it is possible that limited partners and limited entrepreneurs could receive an unintended tax benefit by being able to shelter their short-term capital gains.

(2) GENERAL PARTNERS AS LIMITED ENTREPRENEURS

Certain general partners of option dealer partnerships might be viewed as limited entrepreneurs, recharacterizing their allocable share of gains and losses on dealer equity options as short-term capital gain or loss. Because the term "limited entrepreneur"[45] (introduced into the Code in 1976 to deny farm losses for certain entities with passive investors) is a vague concept, it is unclear whether the limited entrepreneur designation can be applied to certain general partners.

Treasury regulations proposed under I.R.C. § 464 state that a limited entrepreneur is someone with an interest other than as a limited partner who does not actively participate in the management of the enterprise.[46] The standard for when a taxpayer is a limited entrepreneur is not clear. To avoid limited entrepreneur status, I.R.C. § 464(e) might require active participation in the "enterprise," while I.R.C. § 1256(e) might require active participation in the "entity." Literal application of the proposed Treasury regulation to general partners may require a general partner to actively participate in both the enterprise, as required in I.R.C. § 464(e), and the entity, as required in I.R.C. § 1256(e) (which incorporates I.R.C. § 464(e) by reference). It is unclear which, if either, requirement must be complied with to assure a general partner is not viewed as a limited entrepreneur. It is the author's view that neither requirement is appropriate and that the exclusion from 60/40 treatment should only apply to general partners who have both limited their risks and do not participate in the business.

In addition, it is not clear what activities are required of a general partner to assure he is not a limited entrepreneur. Although all partners might actively participate in a partnership's business, some partners may trade only equity options while others may trade other products, if they trade at all. Are all partners sufficiently involved in the business to avoid classification as limited entrepreneurs to obtain 60/40 treatment on the firm's dealer equity options? What if some partners are active in the general management and operation of the partnership, while others are involved in the trading activities? Are those partners

[45]I.R.C. § 464(e)(2).
[46]Prop. Treas. Reg. § 1.464-2(a)(3) (1983).

who are involved in general firm management viewed as limited entre-preneurs? Or, what if the partnership agreement delegates certain man-agement rights to a management committee or a managing partner? Are those partners not active in the management viewed as limited entrepreneurs?

The answers to these questions are not clear, although it seems appropriate to assert that the exclusion from 60/40 treatment should apply only to general partners who, much like limited partners, have entered into agreements to limit their risk of loss from the business and who do not participate in the management of the partnership. If the at risk rule under I.R.C. § 465(b)(4) is examined to provide guidance as to when a general partner has limited his risk, the partner would be protected against loss through nonrecourse financing, guarantees, stop loss agreements, or similar arrangements.

§ 33.3   STRADDLES MADE UP EXCLUSIVELY OF SECTION 1256 CONTRACTS

If all positions in a straddle consist of section 1256 contracts, the Straddle Rules do not apply and the positions are subject to section 1256 treatment.[47] In addition, the requirement to capitalize interest and carrying charges is not applied.[48] According to the legislative history of ERTA, Treasury regulations (yet to be promulgated) will define the manner in which such straddle positions in section 1256 contracts are to be matched.[49] This exemption is consistent with the policy behind the Straddle Rules because there is no opportunity to defer income. All offsetting positions comprising a straddle made up exclusively of section 1256 contracts are subject to section 1256 treatment, which means that recognized and unrecognized gains and losses are reported for tax purposes at year-end.[50]

In addition, straddles made up exclusively of section 1256 contracts can be designated as identified straddles,[51] which means that the positions of the identified straddle cannot be paired up with any other position not part of the identified straddle that otherwise offsets an identified straddle position. Under pre-DRA law, it was unclear whether

---

[47]I.R.C. §§ 1092(d)(5)(A), 1256(a)(4); *see* section 44.7.

[48]I.R.C. §§ 263(g)(1), 1256(a)(4).

[49]SENATE FINANCE COMMITTEE REPORT, ECONOMIC RECOVERY TAX ACT OF 1981, S. REP. NO. 144, 97th Cong., 1st Sess. 147-48, *reprinted in* 1981 U.S. CODE CONG. & AD. NEWS 105, 247.

[50]I.R.C. § 1256(a).

[51]*See* section 44.1.

straddles made up exclusively of RFCs could qualify as identified strad-dles. The statutory language of I.R.C. § 1256(a)(4), when enacted by ERTA, provided that if all positions making up a straddle were RFCs, the provisions of I.R.C. § 1092 did not apply.[52] However, because the identified straddle provisions are found in I.R.C. § 1092(a)(2), it ap-peared under pre-DRA law as if the identified straddle provisions were unavailable to RFC straddles.[53] It also appeared inequitable to permit positions of an RFC straddle (where the positions were identified in accordance with the identified straddle provisions) to be matched up with other positions outside of the straddle.[54] DRA resolved this issue by providing that I.R.C. § 1256(a)(4) does not preclude an identified straddle election for a straddle that consists exclusively of section 1256 contracts.[55] The risk of having a section 1256 contract position paired up with another position not part of the identified section 1256 straddle is no longer present.

§ 33.4   LOSS CARRY-BACK RULES FOR SECTION 1256 CONTRACT LOSSES

Special loss carry-back rules are available for section 1256 contract losses. Taxpayers can use section 1256 losses incurred in one year to reduce income generated on such contracts in a prior tax year, providing a form of income averaging generally not available to other taxpayers.[56] ERTA introduced a three-year carry-back rule for losses from section 1256 contracts subject to the Mark-to-Market Rule ("loss carry-back election").[57] This carry-back rule is quite complicated, applying only after netting section 1256 contracts with unrelated capital gains and

---

[52]ERTA, Pub. L. 97-34, § 503(a), 95 Stat. 172, 328 (1981).

[53]*See* STAFF OF THE JOINT COMMITTEE ON TAXATION, 98TH CONG., 2D SESS., GENERAL EXPLANATION OF THE REVENUE PROVISIONS OF THE DEFICIT REDUCTION ACT OF 1984 311 (Joint Comm. Print 1981).

[54]*Id.*

[55]I.R.C. § 1092(d)(5)(B).

[56]Prior to ERTA, taxpayers other than corporations were not allowed to carry-back capital losses. Although individual taxpayers with significant increases in income can qualify for income averaging (a gain carry-back provision), taxpayers with significant decreases in income are not eligible for income averaging. *See* I.R.C. §§ 1301-1305. The inability to carry-back capital losses was a significant tax disadvantage to commodity traders in light of the volatility of the commodity markets. General Explanation of ERTA, *supra* note 4, at 305. Commodity traders could not use trading losses from one year to offset trading gains in prior years; losses could only be carried forward under general tax rules.

[57]I.R.C. § 1212(c).

losses, which results in a net capital loss that could otherwise be carried forward under I.R.C. § 1212(b). If a taxpayer other than a corporation, estate, or trust makes a loss carry-back election, "net section 1256 contract losses" recognized under the Mark-to-Market Rule can be carried back to each of the three preceding years and applied against net section 1256 contract gain recognized under the Mark-to-Market Rule during such periods.[58]

Net section 1256 contract loss is defined as the lesser of (1) the net capital loss for the taxable year from section 1256 contracts, or (2) the sum of net short-term capital loss and net long-term capital loss for the taxable year.[59] Net section 1256 contract gain is defined as the lesser of (1) the capital gain net income for the taxable year from section 1256 contracts, or (2) the net capital gain income for the taxable year.[60]

The loss carry-back election is available after netting capital losses from section 1256 contracts under the Mark-to-Market Rule with capital gains from other sources if two requirements are met. First, a net capital loss must exist for the year.[61] Second, the net capital loss must be a capital loss that could be carried forward under the provisions of I.R.C. § 1212(b).[62] Losses on stock underlying options are capital losses for all taxpayers except for hedgers and dealers in the stock underlying the options.[63] For option dealers eligible for 60/40 treatment on their dealer equity option positions,[64] stock positions established after the effective date of DRA (giving effect to their transitional year elections) generate capital gain or loss,[65] and the loss carry-back election can be used (for post-DRA years) to reduce stock gains.

Losses carried back are treated as if 60 percent of the losses were long-term and 40 percent were short-term capital loss.[66] Carry-back losses cannot be used to increase or produce a net operating loss for the taxable year.[67] In addition, such losses are carried back to the earliest of the three preceding taxable years in which there is a net section 1256

---

[58] Id.

[59] I.R.C. § 1212(c)(4).

[60] I.R.C. § 1212(c)(5).

[61] I.R.C. § 1212(c)(4)(A).

[62] I.R.C. § 1212(c)(4)(B).

[63] I.R.C. § 1221.

[64] I.R.C. §§ 1256(a)(3), (b)(4).

[65] DRA, *supra* note 40, § 102(f)(1).

[66] I.R.C. § 1212(c)(1).

[67] I.R.C. § 1212(c)(3).

contract gain.[68] Any portion of the loss not absorbed in the earliest of the three preceding years may then be carried forward to the next taxable year and, if any loss remains, to the next (most recent) taxable year.[69] Any net section 1256 contract loss carried forward from the first carry-back year is again recharacterized as 60 percent long-term and 40 percent short-term capital loss.[70]

Example 33-2

Assume that in 1986, a taxpayer has net section 1256 contract losses of $100,000 and has $50,000 in long-term capital gain from other sources. The section 1256 contract loss is characterized as $60,000 long-term and $40,000 short-term capital loss.[71] The net section 1256 contract losses are applied against the $50,000 long-term capital gain, thereby leaving a net section 1256 contract loss of $50,000 for 1986.

Assume that the taxpayer does not make the loss carry-back election. In this case, the remaining loss of $50,000 from section 1256 contracts can be carried forward to 1987.[72] Because the $100,000 of section 1256 contract loss is treated under the 60/40 Rule as 60 percent long-term ($60,000) and 40 percent short-term ($40,000) capital loss, $10,000 is treated as long-term capital loss ($60,000 minus $50,000 from the long-term capital gain from other sources) and $40,000 as short-term capital loss.

On the other hand, assume that the taxpayer decides to make the loss carry-back election. Net losses from section 1256 contracts are carried back three years. Net losses are carried back first (in this example) to 1983, but only to the extent of $50,000, which is the net section contract loss which could have been carried forward to 1987. However, the amount carried back to 1983 is recharacterized under the 60/40 rule and is treated as 60 percent long-term and 40 percent short-term capital loss, rather than $10,000 long-term and $50,000 short-term capital loss as in the previous example where the taxpayer did not make the loss carry-back election. Hence, in 1983, the $50,000 carry-back loss yields $30,000 of long-term and $20,000 of short-term capital loss.

[68] I.R.C. § 1212(c)(2).
[69] *Id.*
[70] I.R.C. § 1212(c)(6)(A).
[71] I.R.C. § 1256(a)(3).
[72] I.R.C. § 1212(b).

Assume further that in 1983 the taxpayer had net section 1256 contract gains of $20,000.[73] This $20,000 of section 1256 gains is composed of $12,000 long-term and $8,000 short-term capital gain. When the section 1256 contract loss to be carried back under the loss carry-back election is carried back to 1983, there remains $30,000 in unused 1986 section 1256 contract losses ($50,000 minus $20,000) which then can be carried forward to 1984. This $30,000 once again is recharacterized as 60/40 loss and, therefore, is recharacterized as $18,000 long-term (60 percent of $30,000) and $12,000 short-term capital loss (40 percent of $30,000), which can be used to offset any section 1256 contract gain in 1984. Remaining loss, if any, can be carried forward to 1985. If, after application to the relevant carry-back periods, any section 1256 contract losses remain, these losses can be carried forward to years after 1986 to offset capital gains incurred in those years.

§ 33.5 TERMINATION OF SECTION 1256 CONTRACTS PRIOR TO DELIVERY OR EXERCISE DATE

To terminate rights and obligations under a section 1256 contract prior to its delivery or exercise, the taxpayer must enter into a closing transaction, that is, the acquisition of a long position to liquidate a short position or a short position to liquidate a long position. A closing transaction for a futures contract covers the same number of units of the same underlying commodity for delivery in the same month. With respect to an option, a closing transaction covers the same quantity and strike price as the option position previously established.[74] Gain or loss on a closing transaction is the difference between the price of the opening transaction and the price of the closing transaction. When the opening transaction is a long position, the trade is profitable if the closing transaction's contract price is greater than the opening transaction's contract price. When the opening transaction is a short position, the trade is profitable if the contract price of the opening transaction is greater than the contract price for the closing transaction.

If a taxpayer transfers his rights in a section 1256 contract, the transfer is treated as a termination.[75] Gains and losses are taken into account at the transfer as if the section 1256 contract was terminated by offset

---

[73]The only section 1256 contracts traded in 1983 were RFCs and certain foreign currency contracts.

[74]For a discussion of closing transactions, see section 4.3(c).

[75]I.R.C. § 1256(c)(1).

or delivery.[76] Thus, transfers made to and from partnerships and other flow-through entities are viewed as terminations.[77] Presumably, transfers of all other sorts, even those not permitted under the rules of a domestic commodity exchange, are also treated as terminations.

A termination or transfer segregates any 60/40 gain or loss inherent in an open section 1256 contract from any gain or loss subsequently realized by the taxpayer. In general, the rules of section 1256 apply if the taxpayer terminates (or transfers) his obligations or rights with respect to a section 1256 contract by offset, making or taking delivery, exercise or being exercised, assignment or being assigned, lapse, or otherwise.[78] Gain or loss is determined on the basis of the contract's fair market value at the time of termination (or transfer), which is usually the actual price received or paid.[79] Any gain or loss at termination (or transfer) is treated as 60 percent long-term and 40 percent short-term capital gain or loss under the 60/40 Rule.[80]

Example   33-3

Assume a taxpayer entered into a futures contract position to purchase wheat for delivery in June at $3.50 per bushel (long position). Two months later, when June wheat is trading for $4.00 per bushel, the taxpayer decides to liquidate his long position. Under the rules of all domestic commodity exchanges, the taxpayer cannot privately negotiate with a third party to sell his rights to purchase the wheat nor can he negotiate with the clearing organization to release him from his rights and obligations under his long futures contract position. Instead, the taxpayer must enter into a closing transaction by entering into a short position to sell June wheat at $4.00 per bushel. As a result, the taxpayer's long and short positions are netted and closed out by the clearing organization affiliated with the domestic commodity exchange on which the futures contract is traded. The taxpayer receives a gain of $.50 per bushel (minus commissions). The contracts are extinguished, that is,

---

[76]This rule does not apply to the transfer of contracts of third party taxpayers between FCMs. HOUSE WAYS AND MEANS COMMITTEE REPORT, TECHNICAL CORRECTIONS ACT OF 1982, H.R. REP. NO. 794, 97th Cong., 2d Sess. 24, n.4 (1982); SENATE FINANCE COMMITTEE REPORT, TECHNICAL CORRECTIONS ACT OF 1982, S. REP. NO. 592, 97th Cong., 2d Sess. 27, n.4, *reprinted in* 1982 U.S. CODE CONG. & AD. NEWS 4149, 4173.

[77]H.R. REP. NO. 794, *supra* 76, at 24; S. REP. NO. 592, *supra* note 76, at 27.

[78]I.R.C. § 1256(c)(1).

[79]S. REP. NO. 144, *supra* note 49, at 158.

[80]I.R.C. § 1256(c)(1).

they are no longer open, and the taxpayer has no remaining rights or obligations with respect to either the long or short position.

Example 33-4

Assume that when XYZ foreign currency is trading for $.45 per unit, a taxpayer purchases, for a $1000 premium, one July 50 call option granting him the option, at any time before the July expiration date, to purchase 100,000 units of XYZ currency at $.50 per unit. If the taxpayer wants to close out the option position when the currency is trading for $.55 per unit, he enters into an offsetting short position by selling one July 50 call option on XYZ currency. At the sale, the taxpayer has a profit equal to the price at which he sold his option minus the $1000 he paid for the option and any transaction costs.

Example 33-5

Assume two option dealers, as defined in I.R.C. § 1256(g)(8)(A), enter into a partnership to trade section 1256 option contracts. Notwithstanding the rules of all domestic securities and commodity exchanges, which prohibit the private transfer of positions off the exchange floors, the two option dealers agree to contribute their open section 1256 contracts to the capital of their newly formed partnership. This transfer is treated as a termination. All gain or loss on section 1256 contracts is marked-to-market at their fair market value at the time of contribution to the partnership's capital. Gain or loss is 60 percent long-term and 40 percent short-term.

§ 33.6 MAKING OR TAKING DELIVERY AND EXERCISING OR BEING EXERCISED ON SECTION 1256 POSITIONS

(a) DELIVERY UNDER FUTURES CONTRACTS

Delivery occurs pursuant to a futures contract when the taxpayer holding a long (or short) futures contract position has the obligation during the delivery month to take (or make) delivery of the underlying property or cash. The short position is obligated to deliver the property or cash to the long position. The property acquired upon delivery is a capital asset for investors and traders and ordinary income property for hedgers and dealers.[81]

---

[81]*See generally* Part Two.

If the holder of a long futures contract position takes delivery under the futures contract, the futures contract is valued, that is, marked-to-market, on the delivery date.[82] Gain or loss is recognized on the long futures contract position just as if it had been closed out by offset.[83] Under the 60/40 Rule, the character of that gain or loss for capital assets is 60 percent long-term and 40 percent short-term. The tax basis of the property acquired pursuant to a long futures contract position, that is, the contract price, is increased or decreased to reflect any gain or loss recognized upon termination of the futures contract.[84] Delivery segregates any gain or loss inherent in the section 1256 contract from the gain or loss on the underlying property.

Example   33-6

Assume that the taxpayer holds a long futures contract position to acquire wheat for $3.50 per bushel and holds the position until its delivery date, when wheat is selling at $4.50 per bushel. The taxpayer has a $1.00 per bushel gain inherent in his position. The taxpayer takes delivery of the wheat pursuant to his futures contract position, which has a value equal to the settlement price of the contract on the date of delivery. Therefore, if the value of June wheat is $4.50 per bushel at the time of delivery, the taxpayer recognizes a $1.00 per bushel gain at 60/40 rates on the date of delivery ($4.50 minus $3.50). The taxpayer's tax basis for the wheat acquired is $4.50 per bushel ($3.50 per bushel paid under the futures contract position plus $1.00 of gain recognized at delivery under the futures contract position).

(b) EXERCISE OF OPTION POSITIONS

The holder of an unprofitable option generally does not exercise the position and simply lets it expire worthless. The holder of a profitable long option position (put or call) who wants to close out the position can either exercise the option or enter into a closing transaction by selling the option itself at a profit.[85] With a call option, the taxpayer can exercise the option, take delivery of the underlying property, and

---

[82]See General Explanation of ERTA, *supra* note 4, at 297–98.

[83]I.R.C. § 1256(c)(1).

[84]The provision to tack on the holding period under I.R.C. § 1223(8) does not apply to a commodity acquired pursuant to a futures contract that is taxed under section 1256. *See* section 15.3(b).

[85]See section 5.1.

sell it for a profit.[86] In the case of a put option, the holder of the long position can buy the underlying property (if he does not already own it), and after exercising the option can deliver it to the short position.[87] If the holder of a long position exercises a call option, he thereby agrees to buy the property underlying the option from the short position at the option price. For a put option, the holder of a long position who exercises the option thereby agrees to sell the underlying property to the short position at the option price.

(c) DELIVERY OR EXERCISE OF PART OF A STRADDLE

There is a special rule for situations when a taxpayer takes delivery or exercises any section 1256 contracts that are part of a straddle consisting of two or more section 1256 contracts. At delivery or exercise, each of the remaining section 1256 contracts is treated as if terminated and sold for its fair market value on the day the taxpayer takes delivery of the underlying property.[88] This allows the taxpayer to treat the remaining section 1256 positions as if terminated on the date of delivery and as if new positions are acquired on that date. Therefore, the taxpayer can make a section 1256(d) identified mixed straddle election on the date of delivery, even though the short position was previously acquired.[89]

Example   33-7

Assume a taxpayer holds a silver straddle consisting of long and short futures contract positions. Assume further that the taxpayer takes delivery of the physical silver under the long futures contract. On the delivery date, both positions are treated as sold for their fair market value on that date.[90] For section 1256 positions that are capital assets, gain or loss is 60/40 gain or loss. The holding period of the long futures contract position is not tacked onto the period of time the taxpayer

---

[86]By exercising the option and selling the underlying property, the call holder loses whatever time value remains in the option. In addition, transaction costs are generally higher when buying and selling the property underlying an option rather than simply entering into a closing transaction.

[87]Purchasing the underlying property to deliver upon exercise of the option is generally more costly than simply entering into a closing transaction.

[88]I.R.C. § 1256(c)(2).

[89]S. Rep. No. 592, *supra* note 76, at 27; *see* section 45.2.

[90]I.R.C. § 1256(c)(3).

holds the physical silver to determine the holding period for the physical silver.[91]

Example   33-8

Assume a taxpayer holds a straddle position consisting of a July 40 long call position on ABC stock and an ABC September 40 short call position. The taxpayer holds a straddle as defined in I.R.C. § 1092(c)(1). Assume that the long position increases in value and the short position incurs a loss. The taxpayer decides to exercise his rights under the long position prior to its expiration to take delivery of the ABC stock at the strike price (exercise price) of $40 per share. His securities broker provides a notice of exercise to OCC, thereby obligating the taxpayer to pay the aggregate exercise price for the underlying security on the exercise settlement date, regardless of the market price of ABC stock on that date.[92]

---

[91]*See* section 15.3(b).

[92]The taxpayer, as an exercising holder of a put option (long position), is contractually obligated to deliver the specified number of units of the underlying property on the exercise settlement date. *See* section 5.4(b).

Thirty-four

Exceptions to Section 1256 Treatment

The Code provides exceptions to the application of the Mark-to-Market Rule and the 60/40 Rule for certain mixed straddles and hedging transactions. These exceptions are mentioned in this chapter.

§ 34.1 MIXED STRADDLES

Mixed straddles, that is, straddles composed partially of section 1256 contracts and partially of other positions,[1] are exempt from section 1256 treatment if the taxpayer makes one of several elections. For a discussion of the scope and application of the various mixed straddle elections, see generally Chapter 45.

§ 34.2 HEDGING TRANSACTIONS

Hedging transactions that qualify under I.R.C. § 1256(e) are exempt from section 1256 treatment. As a result, such transactions are not marked-to-market and are not eligible for 60/40 treatment. Qualified hedging transactions are taxed at ordinary income rates when the position is closed and not under the Mark-to-Market Rule. For a discussion of the scope and application of the hedging exemption, see generally Chapter 21. For a discussion of hedgers generally, see section 6.4.

[1] I.R.C. § 1256(d)(4).

Part Ten

Tax Consequences of Holding Offsetting Positions (Straddles)

Positions making up a straddle are referred to as "offsetting positions." Several tax rules, which vary depending upon the type of property making up the straddle, apply to straddle transactions. This Part Ten addresses the rules applicable to positions in personal property, defined to include any personal property, including certain positions in stock, of a type that is actively traded.[1] This Part Ten does not deal with the situation where all of the positions making up a straddle consist of section 1256 contracts, as that term is defined in I.R.C. § 1256(b). Such a straddle is not subject to the rules discussed in this section.[2] Rather, section 1256 straddles are subject to section 1256 treatment.[3]

ERTA introduced the tax regime now in place for offsetting positions.[4] This regime originally applied to commodities and securities other than corporate stock.[5] It was expanded by the DRA to include exchange-traded stock options ("listed options") and certain stock positions.[6] I.R.C. § 1092, entitled "straddles," embodies the loss deferral rule, which re-

---

[1]I.R.C. § 1092(d)(1).

[2]I.R.C. §§ 1092(d)(5)(A), 1256(a)(4).

[3]*See generally* Part Nine.

[4]ERTA, Pub. L. 97-34, §§ 501-509, 95 Stat. 172, 323-35 (1981).

[5]I.R.C. § 1092(d)(2) (1982), *amended by* DRA, Pub. L. 98-369, § 101(a)(1), 98 Stat. 494, 616 (1984).

[6]DRA, *supra* note 5, § 101(a)(1).

quires deferral of a loss on one position up to the unrecognized gain inherent in an offsetting position.[7] It also includes the modified wash sales rule that prevents a deduction for the disposition of a position at a loss if the taxpayer has an unrecognized gain in a successor position.[8] The holding period for a position is suspended under the modified short sales rule during the period a taxpayer holds offsetting positions and positions that are successor positions to the initial offsetting position.[9] In addition, a taxpayer must capitalize interest and carrying charges allocable to personal property that are part of a straddle.[10] All of these rules—the loss deferral rule, the modified wash sales rule, the modified short sales rule, and the requirement to capitalize interest and carrying charges—are referred to collectively as the Straddle Rules. A taxpayer who does not hold offsetting positions can deduct losses and expenses incurred with respect to personal property, subject to limitations imposed under other tax principles without regard to the Straddle Rules.[11]

The separate rules that comprise the Straddle Rules are summarized below as a brief introduction to the chapters contained in this Part Ten. The key concept underlying the loss deferral rule is that losses incurred with respect to a position in personal property are not deductible if the taxpayer holds an offsetting position in the personal property with an inherent unrecognized gain.[12] If the loss deferral rule applies, a taxpayer must defer the losses realized on any position in personal property while he holds the offsetting position.[13]

The Treasury has broad authority to issue regulations to cover offsetting positions that are similar to the wash sales rule in effect for stocks and securities and the short sales rule in effect for the short sales of capital assets.[14] This regulatory authority, expanded by the DRA, required the Treasury to issue regulations on mixed straddles not later than January 18, 1985.[15] Although these regulations were issued, many additional issues remain unresolved and need to be addressed.

The modified wash sales rule prevents a taxpayer from disposing of the loss position of a straddle to obtain a loss deduction while replacing

[7]I.R.C. § 1092(a)(1)(B).

[8]Temporary Treasury regulations provide guidance on coordination of the loss deferral rule and modified wash sales rule.

[9]Temp. Treas. Reg. § 1.1092(b)-2T(a)(1) (1986).

[10]I.R.C. § 263(g).

[11]*See, e.g.,* section 30.1.

[12]I.R.C. § 1092(a)(1)(A).

[13]I.R.C. § 1092(a)(1)(B).

[14]I.R.C. § 1092(b).

[15]DRA, *supra* note 5, § 103(b).

the loss position with a substantially identical position 30 days before or after the disposition.[16] When a taxpayer holds a position that offsets a loss position, any loss incurred on disposing of the loss position cannot be recognized if he replaces it within 30 days with a substantially identical position.[17] Without such a rule, a taxpayer could report a tax loss for positions not covered by the loss deferral rule and protect the unrecognized gain in the open position by remaining in a balanced position.[18] Temporary Treasury regulations expand the loss deferral rule and the modified wash sales rule to what they characterize as "successor positions."[19]

The modified short sales rule suspends the holding period for property that is part of a straddle until the offsetting positions (and successor positions) are disposed of by the taxpayer.[20] It supplements the loss deferral rule by preventing the use of offsetting positions to extend, without risk of loss, the holding period of positions in personal property.[21]

The final Straddle Rule, contained in I.R.C. § 263(g), provides that a taxpayer must capitalize "interest and carrying charges" allocable to personal property that is part of a straddle. Interest and carrying charges that must be capitalized while holding offsetting positions include (1) interest expense incurred to purchase or carry property; (2) expenses incurred to store, insure, or transport personal property; and (3) amounts paid or incurred in connection with personal property used in a short sale.[22]

The consequences of holding offsetting positions in personal property, as well as the scope and application of the Straddle Rules, are discussed in this Part Ten.

---

[16]I.R.C. § 1091(a).
[17]*Id.*
[18]*See* section 42.3.
[19]Temp. Treas. Reg. § 1.1092(b)-1T(a) (1986).
[20]Temp. Treas. Reg. § 1.1092(b)-2T(a)(1) (1986).
[21]*See* section 42.4.
[22]*See* section 43.2.

Thirty-five

Background on Pre-ERTA Rules

§ 35.1 EXPLANATION OF STRADDLE TRANSACTIONS

The taxation of spreads, referred to as "straddles" for tax purposes, was totally changed in 1981 by the enactment of ERTA and the imposition of the Straddle Rules.[1] Nevertheless, spread positions are still established for economic purposes to obtain a profit as a legitimate trading strategy.[2]

From an economic perspective, a taxpayer's gain or loss on a pre-ERTA straddle transaction may have been small in comparison to the tax deferral available—or at least asserted.[3] Transaction costs and margin requirements on futures contracts are low when one looks at the value of the underlying commodity. The amount of margin required to enter into a straddle transaction is based on the price spread between the long and short positions.[4] This is much smaller in absolute value than the margin requirements to establish separate futures contract positions. Furthermore, since the unrealized gain in a profitable position of a straddle approximately equals the unrealized loss in the losing position of the straddle, the taxpayer generally does not need to deposit additional margin or mark-to-market payments to maintain the losing position. Accordingly, significant leverage is available and a taxpayer

---

[1]For a discussion of the Straddle Rules, see generally Part Ten.

[2]*See* section 4.3(c).

[3]*See* section 35.2.

[4]For a discussion of futures margin and mark-to-market payments, see section 4.4(b).

can lose (or make) a substantial amount of money by opening a futures contract position with a small deposit.

In its simplest form, a taxpayer establishes a straddle by entering into a futures contract obligating him to purchase a fixed amount of a commodity for delivery in a future month (long position) and a futures contract obligating him to sell the same quantity of the identical commodity for delivery, usually in a different month (short positions).[5]

To establish a straddle, a taxpayer may, for example, enter into a long futures contract position to purchase wheat for delivery in September and a short futures contract position to sell wheat for delivery in December. Because the long and short positions call for delivery in different calendar months, the positions do not cancel out one another and are not offset (as in the case of a closing transaction) by the clearing organization affiliated with the commodity exchange on which the wheat futures contracts are traded.[6] As the market price moves up or down, there is a gain in one position and a loss in the other. Under pre-ERTA rules, a taxpayer might have decided to wait until there had been sufficient market movement before closing out the losing position ("lift" the losing "leg" of the straddle) in the current tax year, hoping to generate a deductible tax loss. After recognizing the loss for tax purposes, the taxpayer might have immediately reestablished a straddle in the current tax year (to protect the "naked" leg of the straddle and "lock in" his gain) by purchasing or selling a new futures contract position for a different delivery month on the same side of the market (either long or short) as the position that had been closed out at a loss (referred to by the IRS as a "switch transaction"). In the next tax year, the taxpayer would liquidate all of the positions in the new straddle (lift both "legs" of the straddle) and recognize a taxable gain approximately equal to the loss reported in the first tax year.

A common type of tax motivated straddle is a butterfly straddle, referred to as such because the transaction resembles a butterfly's wings when diagrammed. Basically, a butterfly straddle consists of at least two spreads established as mirror images of each other with the same intermediate delivery date, and involving the purchase and sale of non-offsetting futures contract positions. For example, a butterfly straddle could consist of a long position in a near delivery date (e.g., January), a similar long position in a distant delivery date (e.g., November), and two short positions with a delivery date in between the long and short

---

[5]Straddles in options and cash commodities can also be established if a taxpayer acquires long and short positions.

[6]Futures positions for delivery in different calendar months are not viewed as substantially identical property for short sales purposes. *See* section 16.4(e).

positions (e.g., June).[7] Of course, the positions could be entered into in the reverse order so that the butterfly straddle consists of one near and one distant short position and two long positions with delivery dates in between the delivery dates for the short positions.[8]

Because the two spreads making up the butterfly mirror each other, a butterfly straddle provides some protection against a change in the price of the underlying commodity, irrespective of whether the market price moves up or down. In addition, each of the positions of the two separate spreads making up the butterfly provides protection against a change in the price of the positions making up the other spread. Some taxpayers would establish butterfly straddles that mirrored each other in order to further reduce the risk of price changes in the underlying commodity.

Example 35-1

Assume that a taxpayer purchases one December Treasury bond contract at 75 (long position), sells two March Treasury bond contracts at 74 16/32 (short position), and buys one June Treasury bond contract at 74 4/32 (long position). Assume further that the taxpayer closes out these positions with the following results. The one short December contract is closed out at 71, the two long March contracts are closed out at 70 28/32, and the one short June contract is closed out at 70 28/32. The taxpayer loses $4000 on the December contract, makes $7250 on the March position, and loses $3250 on the June position. The net profit or loss to the taxpayer was zero.

This butterfly is made up of two separate spread trades. In this example the taxpayer is long one December–March Treasury bond spread (i.e., long one December Treasury bond futures contract, short one March Treasury bond futures contract) and short one March–June Treasury bond spread (short one March Treasury bond futures contract, long one June Treasury bond futures contract).

In outright long or short positions, gains and losses occur from changes in absolute price levels. In spread positions, gains and losses result only from changes in the relative prices of the spread positions, not from absolute price changes. In butterfly positions, gains or losses result from changes in the relative prices of the two spreads. In this example, even though the price of the December contract fell four points and the De-

---

[7]This transaction is referred to as "selling a butterfly."
[8]This transaction is referred to as "buying a butterfly."

cember–March spread went from 16/32 to 4/32, the net value of the position did not change at all.

Example   35-2

A taxpayer enters into a futures contract to buy gold at $320 for delivery in February (i.e., a long position with a near delivery date), buys a gold futures contract at $390 for delivery in October (i.e., a long position with a distant delivery date), and sells two gold futures contracts at $367 for delivery in June (i.e., two short positions with identical intermediate delivery dates).[9] The taxpayer now holds a butterfly straddle consisting of two separate spreads—one spread consists of a long February position and a short June position, while the other spread consists of a long October position and a short June position. Assume that the price of gold increases so that the short positions decline in value and the long positions increase in value. Assume further that the price of gold on December 20th stands at $370, $397, and $420 for February, June, and October delivery, respectively. Prior to ERTA, a taxpayer who wished to generate tax losses would close out the short positions for delivery in June on December 20th by buying two June gold contracts at $397, thereby generating a $6000 realized loss. To lock in the appreciation inherent in the February and October long contracts, the taxpayer would either replace the June position by selling two June contracts at $397 (i.e., a switch) or would "sell around" the June delivery date by selling one April gold contract trading at $385 and an August contract trading at $409.

At the end of the day on December 20th, the taxpayer would have two balanced straddles (i.e., short April against long February and short August against long October), which effectively locks in a $6000 gain. He would also have a $6000 short-term capital loss to use against capital gains from other transactions. In the next tax year, the taxpayer would liquidate all of the remaining positions in the new straddle (lift the "legs" of the spread) and recognize a taxable gain approximately equal to the loss incurred in the first tax year.[10]

Spread transactions using futures contract positions thus were used under pre-ERTA law to "push" a taxpayer's income forward into the

[9]Gold futures contracts traded on the COMEX are traded for delivery in February, April, June, August, October, and December.

[10]For an example of the economic and tax consequences of holding a butterfly straddle, see *Commodity Tax Straddles Hearing Before the Subcomm. on Taxation and Debt Management and the Subcomm. on Energy and Agricultural Taxation of the Senate Comm. on Finance*, 97th Cong., 1st Sess. 33-35 (1981).

subsequent tax year. Furthermore, if the loss in the first year was on the short position, the loss would be short-term capital loss because gain or loss on closing a short position is short-term.[11] When the gain recognized in the second year was on the long side and the long position had been held for more than six months (half as long as the then current holding period to receive long-term capital gain for other capital assets), the taxpayer would have converted short-term capital gain into long-term capital gain.[12] If the loss was on the long position, it would be short-term or long-term capital loss, depending on whether the long position had been held for more than six months.[13] Certain other tax straddle transactions (such as spreads using actual Treasury bills and Treasury bill futures contracts) were also used to convert ordinary income into short-term capital gain, and taxpayers would enter into futures contract spreads to convert the short-term capital gain generated on the initial spread transactions into long-term capital gain.[14]

§ 35.2 TAX RULES IN EFFECT FOR PRE-ERTA TRANSACTIONS

Prior to ERTA, public attention focused on the taxation of commodity transactions because a number of gaps in the Code allowed taxpayers to receive—or at least to attempt to claim—certain tax advantages using commodity and government security transactions. Congress was concerned with the growing perception that "it was possible—indeed, perhaps legitimate—to pay no tax at ordinary income rates."[15] Revelations about the substantial tax revenues lost by the use of futures contract straddles (and other commodity-related transactions) ultimately resulted in enactment of ERTA's commodity provisions.[16] In addition, Congress believed that the revenue loss to the government might grow

[11]See I.R.C. § 1233(b) (1976).

[12]I.R.C. § 1222(3) (1976). Futures contracts had a more than six month holding period to obtain long-term capital gain.

[13]I.R.C. § 1222(2), (4).

[14]See section 35.2.

[15]STAFF OF THE JOINT COMMITTEE ON TAXATION, 97TH CONG., 1ST SESS., GENERAL EXPLANATION OF ECONOMIC RECOVERY TAX ACT OF 1981 282 (Joint Comm. Print 1981) [hereinafter referred to as "General Explanation of ERTA"]; FINANCE COMMITTEE REPORT, ECONOMIC RECOVERY TAX ACT OF 1981, S. REP. No. 144, 97th Cong., 1st Sess. 146, reprinted in 1981 U.S. CODE CONG. & AD. NEWS 105, 246.

[16]The General Explanation of ERTA stated that enactment of the tax straddle provisions would increase fiscal year budget receipts by an estimated $37 million in 1981, $623 million in 1982, $327 million in 1983, and $273 million in 1984. General Explanation of ERTA, supra note 15, at 315.

substantially and that widespread tax sheltering activities were threatening to disrupt the commodity markets.[17] Congress was prepared to change the law even though it acknowledged that the "commodity futures markets play an important role in the economy" and that the "efficiency of these markets be preserved and the liquidity of these markets maintained."[18]

To understand the tax framework for commodity transactions, it is useful to consider the tax rules in effect prior to ERTA—many of which continue to apply in certain circumstances. Before ERTA, gains and losses from commodity transactions were generally treated in the same manner as all other gains and losses from the sale of capital assets. This was the case for traders and investors alike.[19] The exceptions to capital asset treatment were for dealers in physical commodities, who derived ordinary income with respect to their inventory transactions,[20] and hedgers, who received ordinary income treatment with respect to their hedging transactions.[21] As capital assets, physical commodities were subject to the customary holding period of more than one year to qualify for long-term capital gain or loss treatment. Commodity futures contracts were allowed a shortened holding period of more than six months to receive long-term capital treatment.[22] Physical commodities and futures contracts held for less than their respective long-term holding periods generated short-term capital gain or loss.[23]

Neither the wash sales rule of I.R.C. § 1091 (disallowing losses on the disposition of stocks and securities if a taxpayer acquires substantially identical property within 30 days before or after the disposition),[24] nor the short sales rule of I.R.C. § 1233 (preventing conversion of short-term capital gain to long-term capital gain or long-term capital loss to short-term capital loss)[25] applies to futures contracts with different delivery months. In addition, the IRS ruled in 1971 that the wash sales rule of

---

[17]See id. at 282-83; S. Rep. No. 144, supra note 15, at 146-47.

[18]General Explanation of ERTA, supra note 15, at 283; S. Rep. No. 144, supra note 15, 146.

[19]See section 6.1; section 6.2.

[20]See section 6.3.

[21]See section 6.4.

[22]I.R.C. § 1222 (1977), amended by DRA, Pub. L. 98-369, § 1001(a), 98 Stat. 494, 1011 (1984). The DRA reduced to six months the long-term holding period for assets acquired after June 22, 1984 and before January 1, 1988.

[23]These general tax rules continue to be applicable, subject to the modifications discussed in the remainder of Part Ten.

[24]See generally Chapter 17.

[25]See generally Chapter 16.

I.R.C. § 1091 did not apply to futures contracts.[26] This was confirmed in *Smith v. Comm'r*,[27] when the Tax Court held that neither the statutory wash sales rule of I.R.C. § 1091 nor a nonstatutory wash sales rule applies to straddles of futures contracts. Furthermore, prior judicial decisions had supported the view that the sale of one futures contract position in a straddle is a closed and completed transaction, even though the taxpayer simultaneously purchases a similar futures contract position with a different delivery date.[28]

The IRS attack on pre-ERTA commodity straddle transactions has been widespread. The first published attempt by the IRS to disallow losses claimed by taxpayers arising from straddle losses was in 1977 with Rev. Rul. 77-185.[29] The first court case to address the deductibility of straddle losses under pre-ERTA law was *Smith v. Comm'r*.[30] Since the *Smith* decision, a legislative solution was enacted as section 108 of the DRA ("Section 108"), which basically limits the arguments that the IRS can advance to deny straddle losses to the issue of whether the taxpayer had a profit motive sufficient to allow a loss deduction. At this writing, several cases have been decided interpreting the scope of Section 108.

The remainder of this chapter discusses Rev. Rul. 77-185, Section 108, and recent judicial decisions of pre-ERTA straddles. Because stock options and certain stock positions are subject to the Straddle Rules but are not afforded the protection of Section 108, many of the issues that are no longer relevant for commodity transactions covered by Section 108 remain important for taxpayers who entered into pre-DRA option and stock spread positions.[31]

(a) REVENUE RULING 77-185

In Rev. Rul. 77-185,[32] the IRS denied a deduction for certain straddle losses in silver futures contracts and out-of-pocket expenses on the grounds that the taxpayer had no reasonable expectation of deriving an economic profit from the transactions.[33] Although not relying on any specific Code

[26]Rev. Rul. 71-568, 1971-2 C.B. 312.

[27]78 T.C. 350, 385-86, 388 (1982).

[28]*See* Valley Waste Mills v. Page, 115 F.2d 466, 468 (5th Cir. 1940), *cert. denied*, 312 U.S. 68 (1941); Harriss v. Comm'r, 143 F.2d 279, 282 (2d Cir. 1944).

[29]1977-1 C.B. 48; *see* section 35.2(a).

[30]78 T.C. at 350.

[31]For a discussion of pre-DRA option and stock spread transactions, see section 26.2.

[32]1977-1 C.B. 48, *amplified by* Rev. Rul. 78-414, 1978-2 C.B. 213.

[33]The IRS ruled in Rev. Rul. 78-414, 1978-2 C.B. 213, that the positions it advanced in Rev. Rul. 77-185, 1977-1 C.B. 48, apply to straddle transactions in Treasury bills.

provisions, the IRS ruled that straddle transactions were shams without economic substances and were not completed and closed out until the year in which the last straddle position was closed out. The IRS's rationale for not allowing a short-term capital loss on closing out the losing position of the straddle in the first year was that a taxpayer who reestablished a similar position with a different delivery date had not really changed his position in a true economic sense. The IRS further ruled that a lack of profit motive precluded a deduction for out-of-pocket expenses incurred to close out the straddle in the second year.[34] Rev. Rul. 77-185, which has been the subject of both controversy and litigation, ignored court cases that supported the view that the sale of one futures contract position in a straddle was a closed and completed transaction even though a similar futures contract position with a different delivery date was simultaneously purchased.[35]

(b) SMITH V. COMM'R

In *Smith v. Comm'r*,[36] which was the first case to address the issue of the deductibility of pre-ERTA commodity straddle losses, the Tax Court accepted the legitimacy of commodity straddle transactions. However, under the particular facts before it, the Tax Court denied the straddle losses, because the straddles were not entered into for profit within the meaning of I.R.C. § 165(c)(2). Because of the need to establish a lack of profit motive on a case by case basis (motive being a matter of subjective expectation), the *Smith* victory was somewhat hollow for the government. The Tax Court found that the four elements necessary to recognize capital losses under I.R.C. § 165 were present in a commodity straddle. First, property was acquired by the taxpayer. Second, a closed and completed transaction, fixed by identifiable events, occurred in the taxable year in which the taxpayer claimed the capital loss. Third, the taxpayer had a tax basis in the property. And fourth, the amount realized by the closing transaction was ascertainable. Therefore, the elements necessary to claim a capital loss were present in closing one leg of a commodity straddle position.[37]

In analyzing commodity straddles generally, the Tax Court held that

---

[34]*See* I.R.C. § 165(c).
[35]*E.g.s.*, Valley Waste Mills v. Page, 115 F.2d at 468; Harriss v. Comm'r, 143 F.2d at 282.
[36]78 T.C. at 350.
[37]*Id.* at 371-83.

the transactions were neither shams nor devoid of economic substance.[38] The Tax Court based its determination, in part, on the fact that futures contracts are binding on the parties to the contracts under the rules of the applicable commodity exchange and impose substantial rights and obligations with respect to the underlying commodities on the parties to the contracts.[39] In addition, the Tax Court held that a futures contract straddle could not be treated as a single indivisible unit for tax purposes.[40] In so holding, the court concluded that the separate long and short positions must be treated as independent positions and, as such, disposition of either position of the straddle constitutes a closed and completed transaction. As a matter of law, the wash sales rule of I.R.C. § 1091 was held inapplicable to futures contracts.[41] Moreover, neither a nonstatutory wash sales rule nor the step transaction doctrine could be applied to disallow losses arising from futures contract straddle transactions.[42]

With respect to profit motive, the Tax Court held that as long as a taxpayer had a nontax profit motive for his commodity futures transactions, he was entitled to recognize losses even if there was a strong tax avoidance purpose for the transactions.[43] A taxpayer with a profit motive could recognize a loss under I.R.C. § 165. He must only have had a bona fide expectation of a profit and his expectation need not be reasonable.[44]

The Tax Court only addressed the taxation of the commodity futures transactions occurring in the first taxable year of the straddle and did not consider whether the gain recognized in the second taxable year on closing the straddle was taxable in that year. Therefore, in an attempt to force the Tax Court to modify its decision, the IRS filed a motion for reconsideration of *Smith*, advising the Tax Court that unless the court changed its decision, the IRS "intend[ed] . . . to follow the logical consequences of the . . . opinion and seek the disallowance of the tax straddle losses, coupled with the recognition of tax straddle gains."[45] Such a

---

[38]The Tax Court did not accept the market values assigned to the straddle positions because the values were assigned to the positions after the trade was executed. Hence, the Tax Court readjusted the amount of losses to reflect the settlement prices for the positions on the days the positions were closed out. *Id.* at 384, n.26.

[39]*Id.* at 385.

[40]*Id.* at 376.

[41]*See generally* Chapter 17.

[42]78 T.C. at 388.

[43]*Id.* at 391. *But see* Fox v. Comm'r, 82 T.C. 1001 (1984).

[44]*Id.*

[45]IRS Motion for Reconsideration, ¶ 6(c), Smith v. Comm'r, 78 T.C. 350 (1982).

result—if supported by the courts—would have placed a taxpayer in the worst possible position: Straddle losses would be denied in the first taxable year and straddle gains would be recognized in the second taxable year. The IRS further stated that it intended to continue to litigate straddle cases based on the analysis of Rev. Rul. 77-185, where "[l]osses and gains are netted at the termination of the tax straddle [with] the losses essentially cancel[ing] out the gains."[46] On April 8, 1982, the Tax Court denied the IRS motion, thus rejecting by implication the IRS interpretation of *Smith*, but leaving open the possible disallowances of straddle losses in one year without requiring offset of those losses with gains generated in subsequent years.[47]

(c) LEGISLATIVE SOLUTION FOR CERTAIN STRADDLES

The IRS has continued to challenge deductions for pre-ERTA straddle losses after *Smith*.[48] At this writing, many of these cases are still being litigated. A major reason the IRS continues its attack appears to be that Congress, in enacting the commodity provisions of ERTA, failed to take a position on whether Rev. Rul. 77-185 was a correct interpretation of pre-ERTA law.[49] The Tax Court in *Smith* specifically stated its belief that ERTA did not affect the case before it and that Congress did not intend to influence the resolution of the issues in that case.[50] In 1982, however, Senators Dole, Moynihan, Percy, and Dixon acknowledged that "there were straddles that appeared to have been legitimate for tax

---

[46]*Id.*

[47]This argument has been precluded by Section 108 for positions subject to its coverage. *See* section 35.2(c).

[48]78 T.C. at 350.

[49]*See* General Explanation of ERTA, *supra* note 15, at 279, 281-83; SENATE CONFERENCE REPORT, ECONOMIC RECOVERY TAX ACT OF 1981, S. REP. NO. 176, 97th Cong., 1st Sess. 258 (1981); S. REP. NO. 144, *supra* note 15, at 145-47.

[50]Throughout the consideration of [ERTA], constant reference was made to the fact that the Internal Revenue Service disputed the tax benefits claimed by pre-1981 tax straddles. . . . Tax benefits from pre-1981 tax straddles were referred to only as "allegedly available" in the Senate Finance Committee Report. . . . In committee prints prepared by the Joint Committee on Taxation to explain the proposed Senate and House of Representatives versions of the new tax straddle legislation, specific references were made to the instant cases, both by name and Tax Court docket number. . . . Rarely can a court be as certain as we are here that the provisions of a new law were not to affect the case before it.
78 T.C. at 394-95 (citations omitted).

purposes" and urged adoption of Treasury regulations that did not penalize taxpayers who "rolled" income.[51]

The commodities industry sought a legislative solution to the audit issues raised by the IRS. As a result, the DRA contains a provision located at Section 108[52] that, in effect, codifies the Tax Court's decision in *Smith*, thereby limiting the ability of the IRS to challenge straddle losses predating the effective date of ERTA for certain straddles other than straddles in stock or stock options.[53] Section 108 is intended to provide "certainty" as to the tax treatment of commodity straddles entered into by taxpayers prior to the effective date of ERTA.[54]

Under Section 108, the IRS cannot advance the arguments it advanced in Rev. Rul. 77-185,[55] Rev. Rul. 78-414,[56] or *Smith*[57] to deny straddle losses. Rather, the IRS can attempt to deny pre-ERTA straddle losses if and only if the taxpayer did not have a profit motive for entering into the transaction. Under Section 108, losses incurred through the disposition of pre-ERTA straddle positions can generally be deducted in the year the loss positions were disposed of if the straddle was entered into for profit.[58] The Conference Committee Report of DRA states that the profit motive requirement is satisfied "if there is a reasonable prospect of any profit from the transaction."[59]

---

[51]*See* Letter from Senator Bob Dole to Roscoe Egger, Jr., Director of the IRS (June 23, 1982); Letter from Senator Daniel Patrick Moynihan to Roscoe Egger, Jr., Director of the IRS (Apr. 29, 1982); Letter from Senators Charles H. Percy and Alan J. Dixon to Roscoe Egger, Jr., Director of the IRS (Mar. 15, 1982). It is interesting to note that both Senator Moynihan and Senator Dole were actively involved in the enactment of the commodity provisions of ERTA.

[52]The Tax Reform Act of 1985, H.R. 3838, 99th Cong., 1st Sess. § 1508(d) (1985), passed by the House of Representatives in December of 1985 (the "House Bill"), includes a proposed amendment to Section 108. The provision in the House Bill is characterized as a technical correction to the DRA. As a result, if the House Bill dies in the Congress, the amnesty provision (along with other so-called technical corrections) could be carved out as separate legislation, standing a greater chance of enactment in 1986. The House Bill would make an essentially technical amendment to Section 108. *See infra* note 70.

[53]DRA, Pub. L. 98-369, § 108, 98 Stat. 494, 630-31 (1984).

[54]The effective date generally is June 23, 1981. However, for those taxpayers who elected retroactive treatment back to the beginning of 1981, the effective date is January 1, 1981. ERTA, Pub. L. 97-34, § 509(a)(1), 95 Stat. 172, 333-34 (1981).

[55]1977-1 C.B. 48.

[56]1978-2 C.B. 213.

[57]78 T.C. at 350.

[58]For a discussion of the profit motive standard, see section 35.2(d) and section 35.2(e).

[59]HOUSE CONFERENCE REPORT, DEFICIT REDUCTION ACT OF 1984, H.R. REP. No. 861, 98th Cong., 2d Sess. 917 (1984).

In *Fox v. Comm'r*,[60] the Tax Court disallowed the taxpayer's straddle losses from Treasury bill option straddles because a profit motive was not the taxpayer's *primary* motive for entering into the transaction. If applied to pre-ERTA straddle transactions, a primary motive standard could be difficult to satisfy. Although it is not free from doubt, Section 108 and the accompanying legislative history appear to make the *Fox* standard inapplicable to pre-ERTA commodity straddles.[61]

Section 108 also provides that if a straddle was not entered into for profit, the loss cannot be deducted in the year the loss position was disposed of, although the loss can be used to offset the gain realized on closing the straddle.[62] Thus, the taxpayer ultimately can net the losses against the gains from a straddle not entered into for profit, with the loss deferred until the gain is recognized.[63]

A rebuttable presumption of profit motive for pre-ERTA straddles is available if the taxpayer was (1) a commodities dealer, defined as a person actively engaged in trading futures contracts and who is registered with a commodity exchange, or (2) any other person regularly engaged in investing in futures contracts.[64] Taxpayers eligible for the presumption are collectively referred to as "professional traders." To qualify for the presumption of profit motive available to professional traders, a pre-ERTA straddle must meet two requirements. First, there must be a reasonable possibility of profit.[65] A significant factor in determining profit motive is the amount of the transaction costs.[66] Second, the professional trader who entered into the pre-ERTA straddle cannot be a syndicate, defined as any partnership or S corporation where more than 35 percent of the losses were allocated to limited partners or stockholders who did not actively participate in the management of the business.[67] If either of these requirements is not met, the presumption of profit motive is not available to even a professional trader. For professional traders eligible for the presumption, Section 108 shifts the burden

---

[60]82 T.C. at 1023.

[61]*See* section 35.2(d). The *Fox* standard, however, appears to continue to apply to straddles in stock options and stock positions specifically not covered by Section 108. *See* section 26.2.

[62]DRA, *supra* note 53, § 108(c).

[63]Section 108 thereby prevents the IRS from successfully making the assertion made in its motion for reconsideration in *Smith*, that straddle losses can be denied while straddle gains in a subsequent tax year are recognized. *See* section 35.2(b). *See supra* text accompanying note 45.

[64]DRA, *supra* note 53, § 108(b).

[65]H.R. REP. No. 861, *supra* note 59, at 917.

[66]*Id.*

[67]DRA, *supra* note 53, § 108(h).

to the IRS of proving a lack of profit motive. Other taxpayers for whom the profit motive presumption does not apply must prove they entered into pre-ERTA straddle transactions for profit.

At this writing, the IRS has continued to challenge the deductibility of losses from pre-ERTA straddles for the open audits and docketed court cases, including some cases against professional traders eligible for the profit motive presumption. Also, exchange-traded stock options were excluded from application of Section 108. Therefore, Section 108 does not affect the IRS's authority to seek to disallow—subject, of course, to judicial review—straddle losses involving stock options.

(d) MILLER V. COMM'R

On May 13, 1985, the Tax Court issued the first decision interpreting Section 108.[68] In *Miller v. Comm'r*,[69] the Tax Court held that the taxpayer's commodity straddle losses were deductible pursuant to the provisions of Section 108. The court made clear that in the absence of Section 108, however, it would have denied the deductions because the taxpayer lacked the otherwise necessary profit motive.[70]

In the *Miller* case, the taxpayer opened a commodity trading account in 1974 and traded commodities through 1983. During the period 1975 through 1983, the taxpayer entered into 158 commodity futures trades for his own account. Of these transactions, 114 were outright positions and 44 were straddles. Of the 44 straddles, only four gold futures contract transactions involved switches, defined by the court as closing out the loss leg to realize a tax loss and reestablishing a similar position in a different delivery month. Three of these switches were challenged by the IRS and were at issue in the case.

The taxpayer's switches, unlike his other trades, were done in consultation with his broker's "Tax Straddle Department." The court noted

---

[68]*See* section 35.2(c).

[69]84 T.C. 827, 846 (1985).

[70]The *Miller* case was decided by the full Tax Court, 10 judges voting with the majority and eight judges dissenting. The Tax Court's decision in *Miller* can be appealed by the government to the Tenth Circuit Court of Appeals and, thereafter, to the United States Supreme Court.

The House Bill (H.R. 3838, *supra* note 52, § 1508(d)) would reverse *Miller* and make clear that by enacting Section 108, Congress did not intend to change the standard for a profit motive sufficient to justify a tax deduction; that is, the Bill would make clear that (at least for customers) the standard in *Fox*, not that in *Miller*, is the law.

The proposed House Bill amendments to Section 108 do not change the scope of the section. Nevertheless, the difference between the "primarily for profit" and the "reasonable expectation of any profit" standards could be significant.

that these trades were contrary to the taxpayer's customary trading practices. Hence, but for Section 108, the losses would have been denied under the prior commodity straddles cases—*Smith v. Comm'r*[71] and *Fox v. Comm'r*[72]—because the transactions were not entered into primarily to make a profit. According to the Conference Committee Report, however, Section 108 allows the deduction of losses "if there is a reasonable prospect of any profit from the transaction."[73] Therefore, the court was asked to decide whether, in transactions governed by Section 108, the taxpayer must establish that his straddle was entered into primarily for profit (applying the *Smith* and *Fox* standard) or whether he can prevail if he can show merely a reasonable prospect of any profit from the transaction.

The IRS attempted to disallow the taxpayer's deductions on two principal grounds. First, under the temporary Treasury regulations issued shortly after enactment of Section 108—which reflected the *Smith* and *Fox* "primarily for profit" standard—the taxpayer lacked the requisite profit motive. Second, the taxpayer's straddles did not have economic substance.[74] Under the temporary Treasury regulations, a pre-ERTA transaction was considered to have been entered into for profit only if it satisfied the requirements of I.R.C. § 165(c)(2).[75] In *Fox*, the Tax Court held that I.R.C. § 165(c)(2) is not satisfied unless the *primary* motive behind the transaction is to realize an economic profit.[76] The Tax Court in *Miller* held that Section 108 does not require satisfaction of the I.R.C. § 165(c)(2) standard and that the temporary Treasury regulations are invalid insofar as they require the taxpayer to establish anything beyond "a reasonable prospect of any profit" from the transaction.[77] With respect to the IRS's "economic substance" argument, the court simply concluded that Section 108 precluded such arguments.[78]

Given the court's interpretation of Section 108, the only issue remaining in *Miller* was whether the taxpayer actually had a reasonable prospect of any profit from the switches. The Tax Court found that, although relatively remote, there was indeed a possibility that the taxpayer's gold straddles, even as modified by the switches, could have

[71] 78 T.C. at 350.
[72] 82 T.C. at 1001.
[73] H.R. REP. NO. 861, *supra* note 59, at 917.
[74] *See* Temp. Treas. Reg. § 1.165-13T (1984).
[75] Temp. Treas. Reg. § 1.165-13T (A-2) (1984).
[76] 82 T.C. at 1021.
[77] 84 T.C. at 842.
[78] *Id.* at 845.

resulted in an economic profit and that, as a result, it was bound by the intent of Congress, as reflected in Section 108 and the Conference Committee Report, to decide the case in favor of the taxpayer.[79]

The court in *Miller* did not make clear whether it viewed the taxpayer as a professional trader entitled to the presumption of profit motivation. There are two possible explanations for this. First, it may be that the court found that both the taxpayer and the government had offered sufficient evidence to establish their positions and, thus, each had met any burden of proof that the presumption (or its absence) would have assigned to either position. Second, some dissenting judges found that the majority opinion rendered the presumption useless. Practically all taxpayers who entered into pre-ERTA straddles—whether they are professional traders or not—can establish the minimal profit motive standard required by the majority's opinion.[80] Whatever the reason for the lack of attention paid by the court to the taxpayer's possible status as a professional trader, it is clear that the presumption of profit motive in Section 108 may turn out to be less important in the resolution of straddle cases than many commentators had previously assumed.

Obviously, for pre-ERTA commodity straddle cases, the *Miller* decision is enormously important. Indeed, taxpayers under audit or with pending litigation involving straddle deductions taken before 1982 should take great comfort from *Miller*.[81] Particular attention should be focused on the following open issues. First, Section 108 does not apply to straddles involving stock options. Therefore, *Miller* does not affect the IRS's ability to disallow stock option losses that do not satisfy the requirements in *Smith* and *Fox*. Indeed, the *Fox* case has been reaffirmed for non-Section 108 cases by the *Miller* decision, and the "primarily for profit" test appears to be the standard that must be met in non-Section 108 situations. Second, just how far Section 108 extends beyond futures contracts is unclear. For example, does Section 108 apply to forward contracts, options on government securities, or government securities themselves? The *Miller* decision does not provide any guidance with respect to these issues. Third, the IRS can succeed in challenging loss deductions for pre-ERTA commodity straddles if the taxpayer did not have any profit motive. There must be some prospect for an economic gain over the cash investment and transaction costs if the deductions are to stand up. Fourth, the significance of the professional trader's

---

[79]*Id.* at 846.

[80]*Id.* at 855 (Simpson, J., dissenting).

[81]The IRS has announced it will appeal the court's decision in *Miller*.

presumption is unclear after *Miller*. Whoever has the burden of proof, the taxpayer, as a practical matter, will have to show that there was at least some possibility of profit from the transaction. Fifth, to survive an IRS challenge, pre-ERTA straddles subject to Section 108 must have been properly established by the taxpayer and cannot be shams, fakes, or fictitious trades. In addition, all transactions must be properly priced. Section 108 will not be applied if the transactions did not take place as reported.

(e) SUBSEQUENT DECISIONS

The Tax Court ruled in two recent memoranda decisions, *Landreth v. Comm'r*[82] and *Kurtz v. Comm'r*,[83] that pre-ERTA straddle losses are allowable under Section 108. In *Landreth*, the taxpayer entered into a commodity straddle program to defer taxes on his capital gains from the sale of a sawmill business. The taxpayer's straddle trades in Treasury bill and gold futures were executed between December 1978 and March 1979 and resulted in economic losses. Judge Scott found that the taxpayer's motive in entering into the straddle transactions was to generate tax losses and the preference for an economic profit was "merely incidental."[84] Nevertheless, Judge Scott, finding that the holding in *Miller*[85] controlled the case, ruled that the taxpayer could deduct his losses because each of his straddles had a reasonable (though small) prospect for some profit at the time it was acquired.[86]

In *Kurtz v. Comm'r*,[87] pre-ERTA commodity straddle losses from gold and silver futures contracts were held to be deductible even though the Tax Court found that the transactions were primarily tax motivated. Judge Whitaker acknowledged that the taxpayers "had a genuine interest, hope, and perhaps expectation, of substantial profits from their straddle investments."[88] Nevertheless, Judge Whitaker found that the taxpayers would not "have undertaken this course of investment activity, over a preordained 6-month period and totally in reliance upon the advice of others, if they had not been convinced that it would result in

---

[82] 1985 Tax Ct. Mem. Dec. (P-H) ¶ 85,413 (Aug. 12, 1985).

[83] 1985 Tax Ct. Mem. Dec. (P-H) ¶ 85,410 (Aug. 12, 1985).

[84] 1985 Tax Ct. Mem. Dec. (P-H) ¶ 85,413, at 1843.

[85] 84 T.C. at 827.

[86] 1985 Tax Ct. Mem. Dec. (P-H) ¶ 85,413, at 1844.

[87] 1985 Tax Ct. Mem. Dec. (P-H) ¶ 85,410.

[88] *Id.* at 1812-13.

substantial tax savings at little cost."[89] Although the "tax objective was predominate,"[90] application of Section 108 and the *Miller* decision[91] control to allow deductions for pre-ERTA straddle losses.

These decisions reaffirm the Tax Court's position that as long as a taxpayer can show that pre-ERTA commodity straddles had a reasonable prospect of generating *any* profit, the losses reported from the disposition of any part of the straddle will be allowed to stand.[92]

In *Perlin v. Comm'r*,[93] The Tax Court held that a commodity trader's futures transactions were not shams for tax purposes and that they satisfied the "entered into for profit" requirement of Section 108. The IRS alleged that portions of the taxpayer's straddles were prearranged trades effected in a noncompetitive manner and disallowed the resulting tax losses. The Tax Court dismissed the IRS's allegations and found that all of the taxpayer's trades had been effected by open outcry in accordance with the rules of the CBT (notwithstanding the testimony of some members of the exchange who claimed that the taxpayer had not traded in the pit on the dates in question).

In *Perlin*, the IRS also contended that the taxpayer's straddles were invalid pursuant to provisions in the temporary Treasury regulations promulgated under Section 108. (The temporary regulations provide that, for the commodity tax amnesty to apply, a professional trader's futures transactions have to be in property that is the subject of his regular trading activity.) For example, the temporary Treasury regulations specify that a commodity dealer who regularly trades only in agricultural futures will not qualify for the profit motive presumption for a silver futures straddle transaction. The Tax Court found that the taxpayer's trading activity was broad enough to include the straddles challenged by the IRS. But, the Tax Court did state that the temporary Treasury regulations did not reflect the wording of the statute approved by Congress. Nevertheless, the Tax Court found it unnecessary to invalidate that portion of the temporary regulations.

The IRS also charged that the taxpayer's straddles had no possibility of a profit as a result of the transaction costs that the taxpayer incurred. The Tax Court, upon examination of the actual transaction costs in-

---

[89]*Id.* at 1813.

[90]*Id.*

[91]84 T.C. at 827.

[92]The IRS has decided not to acquiesce to the *Miller* holding and will appeal the Tax Court's decision. Therefore, the final outcome of pending cases and audits that have pre-ERTA tax straddles as their principal contested issue may not be decided for some time.

[93]86 T.C. ___, No. 25 (Mar. 19, 1986).

volved, disagreed with this contention and found that a possibility of a profit existed despite these transaction costs.

The IRS also contended that the taxpayer's straddles had tax results that were disproportionate to their economic consequences. The temporary Treasury regulations provide that the extent to which straddle transactions have tax results that are disproportionate to their economic consequences is a factor in determining whether they were entered into with a profit motive. The Tax Court ruled that this provision of the temporary Treasury regulations is invalid and refused to apply the disproportionate results test in determining whether the taxpayer's straddles were profit motivated.

As their final assault, the IRS alleged that the taxpayer's straddles were shams because he utilized special instructions to prevent the CBTCC's computer from offsetting positions acquired during the same day. As a result of the special instructions, the computer used FIFO when calculating the effects of each trade. The Tax Court noted that, under the CFTC's regulations, a trader is permitted to specifically identify the position that he wishes to close out and it is only if no such identification is made that the clearing organization will offset the positions on a FIFO basis. The court held that the taxpayer's use of the special instructions was consistent with the requirements of these regulations and was perfectly valid for tax purposes.

Thirty-six

Straddle Definitions

The starting point for any inquiry on the applicability of the Straddle Rules is with the statutory definitions of certain key terms. Basically, the Straddle Rules apply to positions in personal property if the taxpayer holds a position in personal property that offsets the position from which the loss (or expense) arose. Hence, the statutory definitions are crucial to ascertain whether the Straddle Rules apply to a taxpayer's position.

§ 36.1   STRADDLE

A straddle consists of "offsetting positions with respect to personal property."[1] Simply stated, a taxpayer holds a straddle when he holds two or more positions in personal property if holding one position reduces his risk of loss from holding the other position. In fact, if one position protects the other, this is enough to establish a straddle even if the other position is not protected in the same manner.

Example   36-1

Assume that a taxpayer owns gold bullion and he enters into a futures contract position to sell the same amount of gold bullion at a future date. The taxpayer has substantially reduced his risk of loss in holding gold bullion (long position) because he simultaneously holds a position to sell gold bullion in the future (short position). The taxpayer holds

---

[1]I.R.C. § 1092(c)(1).

offsetting positions with respect to gold bullion and has thus entered into a straddle.

_____

Example   36-2

_____

Assume a taxpayer enters into a long futures contract position to buy gold bullion and enters into a forward contract to sell gold coins (short position). The taxpayer has reduced his risk of loss in holding the gold bullion and in agreeing to sell the coins because he holds the other position, even though the property is not of the same kind (i.e., gold bullion and gold coins) and the interests in gold are not the same types of positions (i.e., a futures contract and forward contract). The positions are deemed to be offsetting and the taxpayer holds a straddle.

_____

§ 36.2   PERSONAL PROPERTY

Personal property is defined as any personal property of a type that is actively traded.[2] Because real estate is not actively traded, it is excluded, by definition, from the term "personal property."

(a)   ACTIVELY TRADED

To be subject to the Straddle Rules, personal property must be actively traded. The Code provides no guidance as to when property is actively traded. In addition, the legislative history of ERTA provides only minimal guidance, stating that "[i]n order to be treated as actively traded, property need not be traded on an exchange or in a recognized market."[3] Hence, the definition of personal property is broader than the types of property traded on an exchange or in a recognized market and may include items not generally thought of as actively traded property. Treasury regulations are needed to clarify which property is actively traded. The temporary regulations issued at the time of publication provide no such clarification.

Interests in personal property, such as futures contracts, forward contracts, and options are positions in personal property as well as personal property if they are actively traded.[4]

[2]I.R.C. § 1092(d)(1).
[3]STAFF OF THE JOINT COMMITTEE ON TAXATION, 97TH CONG., 1ST SESS., GENERAL EXPLANATION OF THE ECONOMIC RECOVERY TAX ACT OF 1981 289 (Joint Comm. Print 1981) [hereinafter referred to as "General Explanation of ERTA"].
[4]_Id._

Example   36-3

A debt security that entitles its holder to cash at a future date (e.g., a Treasury bill, note, or bond traded in a recognized market) also constitutes personal property if the debt security, itself, is actively traded.

Example   36-4

Index options and futures contracts that settle in cash are personal property because these products are traded on a securities or commodity exchange.

Example   36-5

An agreement to sell the assets of a business for future delivery is neither personal property nor a position in personal property; the agreement is not actively traded and the assets sold under the agreement are not actively traded.

(b)   UNITED STATES CURRENCY

Although the statutory definition of personal property does not address this point, United States currency is not viewed as personal property. The only reference to currency in ERTA's legislative history indicates that United States currency does not fall into this category. Personal property, as defined, only includes "property or interests in property that may result in gain or loss on their disposition."[5] There is no gain or loss on the disposition of United States currency.

(c)   CERTAIN STOCK POSITIONS

(1)   IN GENERAL

Prior to January 1, 1984, personal property did not include stock within its scope.[6] This was changed by the DRA, which repeals the blanket exemption for corporate stock from the definition of personal property for stock positions established after December 31, 1983.[7] Certain stock

---

[5]*Id.*
[6]I.R.C. § 1092(d)(1) (1982).
[7]DRA, Pub. L. No. 98-369, § 101(b)(1), 98 Stat. 494, 618 (1984).

positions are now personal property.[8] First, stock is defined as personal property if the stock is part of a straddle where at least one of the offsetting positions in the straddle is (1) an option with respect to such stock (or substantially identical stock or securities), or (2) Treasury regulations view it as a position with respect to substantially similar or related property (other than stock).[9] Hence, corporate stock is personal property if it is held in a straddle with an option on the same stock or substantially identical stock or securities (such as convertible debt instruments). In addition, stock is personal property if the stock is part of a straddle where the offsetting position is stock in a corporation formed or availed of to take positions which offset positions taken by any stockholder of the corporation ("offsetting position stock").[10] The term personal property does not include stock if all of the positions in the straddle consist of stock positions or the short sale of stock.[11]

(2) STOCK OFFSETTING OPTIONS OR SUBSTANTIALLY SIMILAR OR RELATED PROPERTY

Turning first to the situation where a stock position offsets options or substantially similar or related property, the Straddle Rules apply to certain options, futures contracts, and stock indexes. In addition, the position is a mixed straddle and is subject to all of the mixed straddle elections.[12] Options and futures contracts are traded on securities and commodity exchanges on stock indexes (e.g., the Standard & Poor's 100 and 500 indexes, the Major Market Index, Market Value Index, the New York Stock Exchange Composite, Value Line Composite, Airline Index, Computer Index, Technology Index, Oil Index, Gold/Silver Stock Index, and PSE Technology Index). A taxpayer might create a straddle if he holds a "basket" of stocks (short or long) and enters into an opposite stock index option or stock index futures contract position (collectively

---

[8]I.R.C. § 1092(d)(3).

[9]I.R.C. § 1092(d)(3)(B)(i).

[10]I.R.C. § 1092(d)(3)(B)(ii); DRA, *supra* note 7, § 101(e)(2) makes this provision applicable for positions taken by a stockholder on or after May 23, 1983, in taxable years ending after such date.

[11]The proposed Technical Corrections Act of 1985 makes it clear that the exception for stock in I.R.C. § 1092(d)(3)(A) is limited to stock and does not apply to interest in stock. JOINT COMMITTEE ON TAXATION, 99TH CONG., 1ST SESS., DESCRIPTION OF AMENDMENTS BY CHAIRMAN ROSTENKOWSKI AND MR. DUNCAN TO H.R. 1800 (THE TECHNICAL CORRECTIONS ACT OF 1985) AND H.R. 2160 (TECHNICAL CHANGES TO THE RETIREMENT EQUITY ACT OF 1984) (Joint Comm. Print 1985). Other rules can apply to limit losses on stock. *See generally* Chapter 16; section 17.3(f).

[12]*See generally* Chapter 45.

referred to as "index contract positions") where some of the stock making up the index contract also make up his stock position. The risk of loss of holding the stock position may be substantially diminished by holding the opposite index contract position. The DRA Conference Committee Report provides examples of straddles consisting of stock and substantially similar or related property. First, offsetting positions of stock and a convertible debt security of the same corporation, where the price movements of the two positions are related, are a straddle.[13] Second, a straddle includes a short position in a stock index RFC (or option on the RFC or stock index, itself) and stock in a regulated investment company whose principal holdings mimic the performance of the stocks included in the stock index.[14] Third, holding an index and a portfolio of stocks whose performance mimics the performance of an index is a straddle.[15] The Conference Committee makes the point, however, that stock offset by another position (other than an option) in substantially related stock might reduce a corporate taxpayer's holding period for the intercorporate dividends received deduction,[16] but is not a straddle.[17]

Extension of the Straddle Rules to stock offset by positions in substantially similar or related property raises potential problems. A taxpayer might own a portfolio of various stocks and enters into an S & P 500 futures contract or option or an S & P 100 option contract. If the taxpayer's stock portfolio consists of less than all of the 500 or 100 stocks underlying the index contract positions, at what point is the risk of loss of holding a particular stock position viewed as substantially diminished by holding the index contract position? Or, what if a taxpayer constructs a portfolio of stocks the value of which correlates to some degree to the value of an index contract? Or, what if an index contract is based on a specific industry and one company makes up a major portion of the market share for the industry, and the taxpayer holds stock in the company whose stock value is included in and makes up a major portion of the price in the index? In this last situation, it is likely that the taxpayer holds a straddle. These questions and many other gray areas need to be addressed in the Treasury regulations.

Portfolios of stocks (long or short) are traded against opposite stock

---

[13]HOUSE CONFERENCE REPORT, DEFICIT REDUCTION ACT OF 1984, H.R. REP. NO. 861, 98th Cong., 2d Sess. 908 (1984).

[14]*Id.*

[15]*Id.*

[16]*Id.; see* section 22.9; section 15.7.

[17]H.R. REP. NO. 861, *supra* note 13, at 908.

index positions (short or long). A relatively new trading strategy, referred to as "program trading," arbitrages stocks against stock indexes if the value of those stocks reflected in the price of a stock index future is "out of line."[18] The following discussion, based on two articles from *The New York Times* on August 30, 1985,[19] demonstrates how program trading uses stock positions to offset what may qualify for tax purposes as offsetting positions of substantially identical property. Positions so established are subject to the Straddle Rules and are mixed straddles subject to the mixed straddle rules.[20] Program trading typically is conducted by institutional investors and other professionals who buy or sell shares in 100 or more large companies that they view as a surrogate for the broader S & P 500 index. (Although there are several types of stock index futures, the S & P 500 futures index is the most commonly used; it offers the greatest liquidity.) By buying a stock index future, an investor or trader expects that the market will rise above its current level prior to the date when the contract expires. When the difference in price between the actual level of the current S & P 500 index and the level of a futures contract is out of line, investors or traders lock in a profit by buying futures in one market and selling stocks in another, or vice versa.

Example 36-6

A taxpayer buys an S & P futures contract and sells stocks included in the index in the stock market with an equal value to the settlement value of the futures contract. At current futures margin rates, the taxpayer margins his S & P futures contract position for $3000. The taxpayer holds property substantially identical to the stock position. The short and long positions are offsetting positions subject to the Straddle Rules. In addition, the taxpayer holds a mixed straddle.[21]

(3) TREASURY REGULATIONS

For positions entered into after January 1, 1984, the DRA directs the Treasury to promulgate regulations to identify which stock positions

---

[18]*See* section 6.7.

[19]*See* Sterngold, *Those Strange Market Turns*, N.Y. Times, Aug. 30, 1985, at D1, col. 3; *What Catches the Arbitrageur's Eye*, N.Y. Times, Aug. 30, 1985 at D4, col. 4.

[20]*See generally* Chapter 45.

[21]*Id.*

are to be viewed as offset by index contract positions.[22] At this writing, the only Treasury regulations that mention positions that offset stock are temporary regulations in the area of mixed straddle accounts.[23] At this writing, no regulations specifically identify those index contract positions that are viewed as offsetting corporate stock. In fact, objective and workable standards will be difficult to develop.

The temporary Treasury regulations provide an example of a taxpayer holding stock in three corporations and options on a broad based stock index futures contract. The values of the corporate stocks are included in the index.[24] The example assumes that a reasonable person, on the basis of all of the facts and circumstances, would expect the stock in these corporations to be offsetting positions with respect to the options on the broad based stock index future.[25] It is unlikely, however, that stock in three corporations could offset a broad based stock index. The example seems more appropriate as an illustration of a narrow based index than a broad based index.

(4) OFFSETTING POSITION STOCK

The Straddle Rules also are applied to offsetting position stock, defined as any stock in a corporation "formed or availed of" to take positions opposite to positions taken by the stockholders of the corporation.[26] This provision defers losses from trading in personal property by a stockholder to the extent of any unrecognized gain in the stock of the corporation. The phrase "availed of" might not require any kind of intentional or purposeful matching of offsetting positions.[27] As a result, stock might be treated as offsetting position stock without any intentional matching of positions.

What about the situation where a corporation may have been "formed or availed of" to take positions that offset positions of its stockholders? Do the Straddle Rules make the stock of the corporation the relevant position or are the corporation's positions in personal property the relevant positions? When should stock be treated as a position? If the test looks only to the intention of forming or utilizing the corporation, the Straddle Rules might be circumvented. Or, should the definition of

[22] DRA, *supra* note 7, § 103(c).

[23] Temp. Treas. Reg. § 1.1092(b)-4T(b) (1985).

[24] Temp. Treas. Reg. § 1.1092(b)-4T(b)(3), Example (1985).

[25] *Id.*

[26] I.R.C. § 1092(d)(3)(B)(ii).

[27] *See* Garrett v. U.S., 479 F.2d 598, 602 (5th Cir. 1973).

offsetting position stock look to objective criteria, such as the assets of the corporation and the extent to which the corporation has other characteristics that avoid the Straddle Rules?

(d) EXAMPLES

To be subject to the Straddle Rules, the products in question must fall within the definition of personal property. Some assets that qualify as personal property and others that do not include the following:

- Actively traded physical commodities (e.g., corn, wheat, or silver) are personal property.
- Foreign currency that is freely convertible into other currencies and that is actively traded is personal property. It is not necessary for futures contracts to be traded on the currency for the currency to be viewed as personal property.
- Corporate stock positions offset by other stock positions are not personal property.
- Corporate stock offset by an option on the same stock or substantially identical stock or securities (such as convertible debt instruments) is personal property.
- A portfolio of corporate stock offset by a stock index (futures contract or option) is personal property if the value of the stocks correlate to a significant degree to the value of the index.
- Real property is not personal property.
- Actively traded options to purchase or sell commodities, stock, or other securities are personal property.
- Government securities are personal property.
- Actively traded debt securities are personal property.
- An option, futures contract, or forward contract is personal property if it is actively traded.
- A futures contract or option that does not require delivery of personal property or shares of stock but calls for cash settlement is personal property if the contract is actively traded.

§ 36.3 POSITIONS

The Straddle Rules apply to offsetting positions, so it becomes necessary to ascertain what a position is. A position is defined as "an interest (including a futures contract or forward contract or option) in personal property."[28] There is no requirement that there be active trading in the position; the only requirement is that it be an interest in personal property. Positions in personal property can offset other positions even if they are not in the same underlying property or are not the same types of interests in property.[29]

(a) DEFINITION

A position consists of an interest in property, including a futures contract, forward contract, or option contract. This definition, however, does not provide sufficient guidance for many of the complex issues that arise when a taxpayer has interests in property. Some examples of positions, which may or may not meet the definition of personal property, include the following:

- An owner of a physical commodity that is actively traded, such as, gold or silver bullion, holds a position.
- A party to either a long or short futures contract or exchange-traded options contract holds a position.
- An owner of foreign currency of a type that is convertible into other currencies holds a position.
- An owner of United States currency does not hold a position, because he does not hold personal property or an interest in personal property.
- A party to a contract to buy or sell a physical commodity of a type that is actively traded (e.g., gold or silver bullion) holds a position, irrespective of whether the contract is actively traded. The contract, itself, is an interest in personal property, and if the contract is actively traded it also is personal property; on the other hand, if the contract is not actively traded, it is not personal property.
- A party to a forward contract to buy or sell a physical commodity that is actively traded (e.g., corn, wheat, or soybeans) holds a position, irrespective of whether the contract, itself, is actively traded. If the contract is actively traded, the contract is both a position and personal property.

---

[28]I.R.C. § 1092(d)(2).
[29]I.R.C. § 1092(c)(2)(A).

(b) REPURCHASE AGREEMENTS (AND REVERSE REPURCHASE AGREEMENTS)

It is not settled whether a transaction structured as a repo or a reverse repo is a position subject to the Straddle Rules.[30] The remainder of this section discusses tax issues concerning application of the Straddle Rules to repo transactions.

(1) DEFINITION

Repos and reverse repos generally are financing transactions where securities are financed pursuant to the terms of an agreement. One party is viewed as the borrower and the other party is viewed as the lender. In a repo transaction, a taxpayer who owns securities borrows funds and uses his securities as collateral. He obtains cash by "selling" the securities to the other party and agrees to repurchase equivalent securities from the other party at a future date. In a reverse repo transaction (so named because the transaction is the reverse side of a repo), the taxpayer purchases securities from the other party and agrees to sell equivalent securities to the other party at a future date. In both repo and reverse repo transactions, the initial seller is referred to as the "seller-debtor," while the initial buyer is referred to as the "buyer-creditor."

On the date when the repo or reverse repo transaction is terminated, the money (plus an interest factor to reflect the use of the money) and securities equivalent to those securities first "sold" are returned to their original owners. The seller-debtor receives the same or equivalent securities back from the buyer-creditor, while the buyer-creditor receives his funds (plus an interest factor) back from the seller-debtor.

Example 36-7

A taxpayer purchases Treasury bills in one year that mature in the following taxable year. The taxpayer (in this case the seller-debtor) enters into an agreement to sell the Treasury bills to a buyer-creditor and to buy them back at a later date. When looked at from the side of the seller-debtor, this is a repo transaction. It is a reverse repo when looked at from the side of the buyer-creditor. The repurchase price is the original cash received plus an additional amount reflecting interest on the financing.

---

[30]For a discussion of repos, see section 2.2(c) and section 27.10.

(2) TAX ANALYSIS

If a repo or a reverse repo transaction is treated as a position, it might be subject to the Straddle Rules. In addition, any interest expense incurred on the transaction (except for hedging transactions eligible for the statutory hedging exemption) would need to be capitalized under the provisions of I.R.C. § 263(g).[31]

(i) Repos as Financing Transactions

For tax purposes, a repo transaction generally is treated as a secured loan. The seller-debtor gives the securities to the buyer-creditor as collateral to secure the seller-debtor's obligations under the loan.[32] It is the author's view that the seller-debtor's side of the repo transaction is not a position. Borrowing United States currency does not meet the definition of a position under I.R.C. § 1092(d)(2), because United States currency is not personal property.[33] Hence the seller-debtor does not have an interest in personal property as defined in I.R.C. § 1092(d)(1).[34] In addition, the buyer-creditor simply lends money to the seller-debtor, taking the securities as collateral for the loan. The buyer-creditor holds the seller-debtor's obligation to repay the borrowed funds. The obligation to repay borrowed funds could be viewed as personal property in the hands of the creditor. The buyer-creditor's side of the transaction should not be a position if, as typically is the case, either the seller-debtor's obligation to repay the borrowed funds is not actively traded or the property is not personal property (i.e., it is not of a type which is actively traded). A borrowing creates a property interest in the buyer-creditor with the right to receive payment under the debt. It does not create a property interest in the seller-debtor who is obligated to repay borrowed funds:

> [D]ebts . . . are not property of the debtors in any sense; they are obligations of the debtors, and only possess value in the hands of the creditors. With [creditors] they are property . . . . To call debts property of the debtors is simply to misuse terms. All the property there can be in the nature

---

[31]*See generally* Chapter 43.

[32]American National Bank of Austin v. U.S., 421 F.2d 442, 452 (5th Cir.), *cert. denied*, 400 U.S. 819 (1970); *see* Rev. Rul. 79-108, 1979-1 C.B. 75; Rev. Rul. 77-59, 1977-1 C.B. 196; Rev. Rul. 74-27, 1974-1 C.B. 24; *cf.* Rev. Rul. 82-144, 1982-2 C.B. 34 (the taxpayer was not holding the position as security on a loan or for the benefit of the seller).

[33]General Explanation of ERTA, *supra* note 3, at 289; *see also* section 36.2(b).

[34]General Explanation of ERTA, *supra* note 3, at 289.

of things in debts of corporations, belongs to the creditors, to whom they are payable.[35]

Thus, an obligation on the side of the buyer-creditor, who has a right to receive repayment of the debt in the transaction, should not be a position if the seller-debtor's obligation to repay the borrowed funds is not actively traded.

(ii) Repos as Sales Transactions

If a repo transaction goes beyond borrowings of the types typically found in financing transactions, it is possible that a repo transaction is a position. Officials at the Treasury have indicated that it is the Treasury's view that repos are positions subject to the Straddle Rules.[36] Deferral and conversion opportunities, present in certain types of repo transactions, have raised concern at the Treasury. Treasury regulations addressing repos have not been promulgated to date, but the Treasury has announced that the applicability of the Straddle Rules to repo transactions is an issue that the Treasury regulations, when issued, will address.[37]

It is the author's understanding that the IRS has taken the position that repo transactions may, under certain circumstances, be the economic equivalent of a forward contract. In certain circumstances, repo transactions have been held to be sales.[38] This has been supported by the IRS's view of repos as purchases and sales and is the position of some other commentators. One commentator has stated that "a repo of fixed term with a fixed interest rate can be the economic equivalent of a long forward contract to purchase the shirt-tail security on termination of the repo, and might be treated as such under the tax law."[39] The view that repos might be forward contracts may be limited to those transactions where the securities are bought and "sold" at the same time and "there has been a reduction of the repo borrower's 'risk of loss

---

[35]Case of State Tax on Foreign-Held Bonds, 82 U.S. 300, 320 (1872).

[36]*See* Address by John E. Chapoton, Assistant Secretary of the Treasury for Tax Policy, National Conference on Domestic and International Uses of Options and Futures, in New York City (Sept. 26, 1983), *reprinted in* 21 TAX NOTES 347 (1983).

[37]*Id.*

[38]Citizens Nat'l Bank of Waco v. U.S., 551 F.2d 832 (Ct. Cl. (1977)).

[39]Schapiro, *Sheltering the Revenue From Shelters: A Legislative Proposal Involving the Minimum Tax and Accounting Provisions*, 22 TAX NOTES 811, 820 n. 40 (1984).

or opportunity for gain.' "[40] In addition, the repo borrower appears to lose the ownership of the securities under I.R.C. § 1058 (security loan agreements) and the Treasury regulations proposed thereunder.[41]

(iii) Short-Term Obligations and Market Discount Obligations

For obligations acquired after July 18, 1984, the DRA may make the question of whether a repo transaction is a position less important with respect to certain taxpayers for short-term obligations, including Treasury bills, and market discount obligations.[42] The DRA changed the rules for short-term obligations and contains two provisions designed to eliminate the opportunity for conversion of market discount obligations: The first recharacterizes market discount as additional interest and the second defers deductions for interest incurred to carry a market discount bond.

Under pre-DRA law, if a Treasury bill was used in a repo transaction, it was believed that the seller-borrower could defer interest accrual until the Treasury bill matured or was sold.[43] Short-term government obligations payable without interest and due in one year or less were exempted from the general rule requiring the periodic inclusion of OID.[44] A similar exemption from the OID rules was available for nongovernmental short-term obligations held by cash basis taxpayers.[45] Interest on indebtedness incurred to purchase or carry obligations eligible for these exemptions had been deductible from unrelated income.

Also under pre-DRA law, if a market discount security was used in a repo transaction, the seller-borrower claimed the accrual of market discount as capital gain. A taxpayer purchasing an obligation at a price below its issue price treated the difference upon the sale or at maturity as capital gain rather than additional interest income.[46] Under pre-DRA law, a taxpayer could convert ordinary income into capital gain by entering into a repo if the value of the obligation declined after its issuance (typically because of an increase in prevailing interest rates).

[40]*Id.*

[41]*See generally* Chapter 24; section 27.10.

[42]*See* section 27.2(d); section 27.3(b).

[43]See I.R.C. § 454(b); H.R. Rep. No. 861, *supra* note 13, at 806.

[44]H.R. Rep. No. 861, *supra* note 13, at 807; *see* section 27.2.

[45]H.R. Rep. No. 861, *supra* note 13, at 807.

[46]*See id.* at 805; *see also* section 27.3.

(3) SUMMARY IF STRADDLE RULES APPLY

In conclusion, if repos and reverse repos are positions (i.e., interests in personal property that are actively traded), they are subject to the Straddle Rules unless the transactions qualified for the hedging exemption.[47] Under the Straddle Rules, losses (if any) with respect to the repo transactions are deferred to the extent of unrecognized gains until all of the positions are closed out.[48] Moreover, interest and carrying charges are capitalized and cannot be currently deducted.[49] The inability to deduct interest expense is the major problem.

§ 36.4   OFFSETTING POSITIONS

Losses realized on a position in personal property cannot be recognized for tax purposes to the extent that the taxpayer has unrecognized gains in offsetting positions.[50] In other words, once a taxpayer holds positions in personal property, losses on closing out any of those positions cannot be deducted to the extent that there is unrecognized gain in any positions that reduce the risk of holding the position closed out at a loss. Determining which positions offset other positions is critical to ascertain whether losses are currently deductible.

(a) IN GENERAL

When a taxpayer has a substantial diminution of risk of loss from holding any position in personal property by reason of holding one or more other positions in personal property (whether or not of the same kind), he holds offsetting positions.[51] Where one or more positions offset only a portion of one or more other positions, the positions are treated as offsetting only to the extent of the portion that is balanced.[52] Positions can be offsetting even if they are not in the same underlying property or are not the same types of interests in property.[53] The Code provides rebuttable presumptions for determining when offsetting positions exist

---

[47]*See generally* Chapter 21.
[48]I.R.C. § 1092(a)(1).
[49]I.R.C. § 263(g)(1).
[50]I.R.C. § 1092(a)(1)(A).
[51]I.R.C. § 1092(c)(2)(A).
[52]General Explanation of ERTA, *supra* note 3, at 288.
[53]*Id.*

and explicitly authorizes the Treasury to establish additional presumptions by regulations,[54] which have not yet been issued. Positions are presumed to be offsetting if:

1. The positions are in the same personal property or the property and a contract for such property (e.g., gold and a short gold futures contract), provided that the value of one position increases when the value of the other position decreases.

2. The positions are in the same personal property or any altered form of the property (e.g., soybeans and a short soybean oil futures contract), provided that the value of one position increases when the value of the other position decreases.

3. The positions are in debt securities with similar maturities if the value of the positions ordinarily move inversely to each other (e.g., holding a long Treasury bill position and a short Treasury note position with scheduled maturities in sufficiently close proximity to each other such that a change in the value of one will correspond substantially to a change in the value of the other).

4. The positions are sold or marketed as offsetting, irrespective of whether the positions ordinarily change in value inversely.

5. The aggregate margin requirements for maintaining the positions are lower than the sum of the margin requirements for each position if held separately, irrespective of whether the positions ordinarily change in value inversely.

6. Other factors (including subjective or objective tests) as may be defined in future Treasury regulations indicate that the positions are offsetting.

Any of these presumptions can be rebutted (by either the taxpayer or the government) by demonstrating that there is no substantial diminution of risk of loss from holding the positions presumed to be offsetting.[55] Neither the Code nor the legislative history provide guidance regarding the extent to which risk of loss in holding positions must be diminished to be deemed substantially reduced. The only references in the legislative history indicate that mere diversification of assets usually does not substantially diminish the risk of loss, and a taxpayer generally is not considered to be holding offsetting positions if he holds no short

[54]I.R.C. § 1092(c)(3).
[55]I.R.C. § 1092(c)(3)(B).

positions.[56] Thus, a taxpayer holding a portfolio of government securities does not hold offsetting positions if he holds no short positions in the same or similar securities.[57] In addition, if a taxpayer holds short positions, the positions should only be treated as offsetting other positions to the extent that the positions are balanced.[58] As of this writing, Treasury regulations have not been issued on the question of what constitutes a substantial diminution of risk of loss. It is not likely that clarifying regulations will be issued.

Loss is deferred to the extent of unrecognized gain in an offsetting position. The deferred loss is the amount of gain the taxpayer would recognize if the gain position was sold or otherwise transferred at its fair market value on the last business day of the taxable year. For a section 1256 contract subject to the loss deferral rule,[59] fair market value is determined by the final settlement price established by the securities or commodity exchange on which the contract is traded on the final trading day of the year.[60] The applicable settlement price for other personal property normally is considered as its fair market value.[61]

Even if a taxpayer enters into an offsetting position in the ordinary course of his business, the Straddle Rules apply unless the transaction qualifies as a hedging transaction.[62] If a taxpayer enters into offsetting positions using investment assets, the hedging exemption does not apply and the transactions are subject to the Straddle Rules.

(b) OPTION POSITIONS

Options are subject to the Straddle Rules if a taxpayer substantially reduces his risk of loss in holding one or more positions in personal property by reason of holding an option in personal property. The hard question in most situations is: Does holding an options position substantially reduce the risk of holding another position? Or, is the options

---

[56]General Explanation of ERTA, *supra* note 3, at 288; SENATE FINANCE COMMITTEE REPORT, ECONOMIC RECOVERY TAX ACT OF 1981, S. REP. No. 144, 97th Cong., 1st Sess. 150, *reprinted in* 1981 U.S. CODE CONG. & AD. NEWS 105, 249.

[57]General Explanation of ERTA, *supra* note 3, at 288.

[58]*Id.*

[59]I.R.C. § 1092(d)(5)(A); *see generally* Chapter 45.

[60]General Explanation of ERTA, *supra* note 3, at 285.

[61]*Id.* at 285-86.

[62]I.R.C. § 1092(e); *see generally* Chapter 21.

position capable of being protected by another position? This section addresses options as offsetting positions subject to the Straddle Rules.[63] This section does not, however, address straddles consisting entirely of options that are section 1256 contracts, because such options are subject to section 1256 treatment and are exempt from the Straddle Rules.[64]

Actively traded options are personal property.[65] Furthermore, if the options are on property that is actively traded, they are positions in personal property.[66] In either of these situations, offsetting positions involving options are subject to the Straddle Rules.[67] Options subject to the Straddle Rules include options (whether traded on securities exchanges, commodity exchanges, or in the over-the-counter market) on physical commodities, futures contracts, foreign currencies, stock, other securities, stock groups, and stock indexes. Any of these option positions can substantially reduce the risk of holding another position.

The Straddle Rules now apply to most option spreads. Nevertheless, there are some gray areas. For instance, the Straddle Rules should not apply to the purchase of a put option (long position) and a purchase of a call option (long position) on the same underlying property. Holding both positions of a "long option straddle" does not reduce the risk of holding either position. In other words, a taxpayer's risk of loss in holding one position is not reduced by holding the other position. As the long call option goes up in value, the long put option declines in value and vice versa, but the two positions increase or decrease in value independently of each other. On the other hand, the Straddle Rules are likely to apply to a sale of a put (short position) and a sale of a call (short position). Unlike the situation where the taxpayer purchased both option positions, the premium income from one position serves to offset the loss from holding the other position. The Straddle Rules certainly will apply to conversion and reverse conversion transactions. Determining when an option substantially reduces the risk of holding another position or when the option position is protected by another position is difficult.

---

[63]For a discussion of the tax treatment of options that are not subject to the Straddle Rules, see section 32.3 and section 32.4.

[64]I.R.C. §§ 1092(d)(5)(A), 1256(a)(4); *see generally* Part Nine.

[65]*See* I.R.C. § 1092(d)(1); *see also* General Explanation of ERTA, *supra* note 3, at 289.

[66]I.R.C. § 1092(d)(2); *see also* General Explanation of ERTA, *supra* note 3, at 289.

[67]*See* I.R.C. § 1092(a)(1)(A); *see also* General Explanation of ERTA, *supra* note 3, at 287–88.

Example 36-8

A taxpayer holds offsetting option positions when he holds long and short call option contracts for the same underlying stock. Ownership of the long contract protects the taxpayer from risk of loss on owning the short contract. Risk of loss on the short contract is reduced by the taxpayer's holding of the long contract. The long option is capable of protecting the short position and it also is capable of being protected by the short position. The short option also has the same characteristic—it is capable of protecting the long position and it is also capable of being protected by the long position.

With respect to an option writer (short position), the risk of loss on the potentially offsetting position is reduced only to the extent of the premium received on writing the option. The short position may not protect the long, but the long position does protect the short, or vice versa, and this is enough to have offsetting positions. Whether the option writer holds offsetting positions may depend upon the relationship between the market value and volatility of the underlying property and the premium the option writer received to write the option. An option writer (short position) transfers to the option holder (long position) a profit opportunity in return for a measure of protection against loss. The greater the profit opportunity transferred to the holder, presumably the higher the premium and hence the greater the protection provided to the writer.

Example 36-9

A taxpayer holding a share of stock with a market value of $50 sells an option to buy the stock at $60 for a $2 premium. The taxpayer has reduced the risk of loss on his long position by $2 or four percent. If the same taxpayer had sold an option to buy the stock at $50 for, say, $8, he would have reduced his risk of loss by $8 or 16 percent.

At a minimum, an option holder should be viewed as holding offsetting positions based on the relationship between the market value and volatility of the underlying property and the sum of the strike price plus the premium paid for the option. Just because a taxpayer holds an option to buy property does not mean he has substantially reduced the risk of carrying a short position in that property. Nevertheless, the positions may be viewed as offsetting.

Example 36-10

A taxpayer agrees to sell silver at $50 (short position) and purchases a call option to buy silver at $60 (long position), paying a $2 premium. If the market price of the silver drops below $48, the taxpayer makes money. If the market price goes up, the taxpayer can lose up to $12 before his option gives him any protection from loss. All the taxpayer did by buying the call option position was provide insurance against the price of silver going above $62. There has been a substantial risk reduction and this may be an offsetting position.

In addition, an option that is out-of-the-money is capable of protecting another position, but may not be capable of being protected itself.[68] If the taxpayer holds both a long and a short put option or a long and a short call option at the same exercise price, regardless of whether the exercise price is in-the-money, the long and short options are offsetting positions; that is, they protect each other. Further, the writer of a put or call that is out-of-the-money has a position that is capable of being protected but is not generally capable of protecting another position. This can still be a straddle. On the other hand, in-the-money options are like bilateral contracts and thus are capable of being protected, as well as providing protection for another position. In Rev. Rul. 80-238,[69] the IRS ruled for purposes of the intercorporate dividends received deduction that a taxpayer does not reduce his holding period under I.R.C. § 246(c)(1)(A) by writing a call option, but noted that in-the-money call options were explicitly excluded from this holding.[70] For purposes of the dividends received deduction, the issue is whether the long stock position is protected; the issue of protection of a put or call position is irrelevant.

(c) DEBT SECURITIES

Debt security positions are presumed to be offsetting if they have similar maturities and the value of the positions ordinarily move inversely to each other.[71] To determine whether debt security positions are offset-

---

[68]For a discussion of in-the-money, out-of-the-money, and at-the-money options, see section 5.1.

[69]1980-2 C.B. 96.

[70]*See* section 22.9; section 15.7.

[71]I.R.C. § 1092(c)(3)(A).

ting, one first must examine whether the positions are in personal property as defined in the Code. This is because the Straddle Rules only apply to offsetting positions in personal property. Next, one should determine whether the debt securities are of similar maturities and have values that move inversely to each other. An open issue is whether the debt securities must be from the same issuer to be viewed as offsetting positions.

Debt securities are subject to the Straddle Rules if the securities themselves or the positions in the securities (options, futures, forward contracts, or other interests) are actively traded. To qualify as personal property, the positions or the property underlying the positions must be actively traded.[72]

Example 36-11

Assume a taxpayer owns Treasury bills in the principal amount of $100,000 that mature in March (long position) and he agrees to sell Treasury notes in the same principal amount that also mature in March (short position). The taxpayer holds offsetting positions. The debt securities are from the same issuer, that is, the Treasury. Furthermore, the debt securities are actively traded and fall within the definition of personal property. And, since the maturities of the two Treasury securities are in the same calendar month, there is no question but that the scheduled maturities are sufficiently close to each other to assume that a change in the value of one position corresponds inversely to a change in the value of the other position. It is expected that as the value of the long Treasury bill position increases, the value of the short Treasury note position decreases and vice versa.

Offsetting positions might not be as obvious as in the previous example. Currently, there are no guidelines to determine whether two positions are offsetting. It is not clear when debt securities are of a similar maturity and presumptively offsetting. To date, neither case law nor Treasury regulations provide any guidance.[73] It appears that the length of time until a debt security matures should indicate how close the maturity dates of "offsetting" securities positions (long and short) need to be to substantially diminish the risk of loss in holding opposite positions.

---

[72]I.R.C. § 1092(d)(1).

[73]For a discussion of substantially identical bonds for wash sales purposes, see section 17.9(g).

Example 36-12

If a debt security matures in 24 months, it might offset another debt security position that matures in 18 months. On the other hand, if a debt security matures in six years, it should not offset another debt security that matures in 12 years, because holding one position would not substantially reduce the risk of loss in holding the other position.

In addition, certain debt securities might not need to be of the same issuer to be offsetting. With securities of different issuers possibly offsetting each other, complicated problems in comparing debt instruments must be addressed. It is one thing to view a Treasury security (i.e., a Treasury bill, note, or bond) as possibly offsetting a federal agency security guaranteed by the federal government (e.g., a GNMA security). It is another thing to view the debt instrument of one corporation as offsetting the debt instrument of another unrelated corporation. When should debt securities be treated as offsetting? Must the issuers have the same credit worthiness? What other factors should be considered for debt security positions of different issuers to be viewed as offsetting? Treasury regulations, when issued, should provide some guidance.

A taxpayer with a portfolio of debt securities who does not hold any short positions in the same or similar securities does not hold offsetting positions. (The legislative history of ERTA makes it clear that a taxpayer generally does not hold offsetting positions if he holds no short positions.)[74] Mere diversification of assets does not substantially diminish the risk of loss in holding positions.[75] Finally, if a taxpayer holds both short and long positions, the positions are viewed as offsetting only to the extent that the positions are balanced.[76] Therefore, where positions are not balanced, only part of the loss from a single position might be subject to the Straddle Rules.

Example 36-13

A taxpayer holds a short position in one debt security in the principal amount of $1000 and a long position in the same security (i.e., same issuer, maturity date, and interest rate) in the principal amount of $100,000. The positions offset each other to the extent of $1000. Loss,

---

[74]General Explanation of ERTA, *supra* note 3, at 288.
[75]*Id.*; S. Rep. No. 144, *supra* note 58, at 150.
[76]*Id.*

if any, incurred on the remaining $99,000 worth of the principal amount of the long position should not be subject to the Straddle Rules.

The Treasury is authorized to issue regulations prescribing the method for determining the portion of a position that is taken into account as offsetting.[77]

§ 36.5 UNRECOGNIZED GAIN

Losses incurred on closing a position in personal property are currently deductible only to the extent that the losses exceed unrecognized gain on an offsetting position acquired before the loss was realized.[78] The concept of unrecognized gain, therefore, is important to ascertain whether losses incurred in one taxable year are deductible in that year or must be deferred until the offsetting position is closed out.

Unrecognized gain is the amount of gain that would be taken into account if a position were sold at its fair market value on the last business day of the taxable year.[79] Under the cash method of accounting, gains from the sale of property generally are not recognized until the sale proceeds are actually or constructively received, while losses are recognized as of the contract date. Furthermore, unrecognized gain includes the amount of gain that has been realized on the sale or exchange of a position even if that gain has not been recognized.[80] The distinction between realized gain and recognized gain is that under tax accounting rules, realization refers to actual gain, while recognition addresses the year when gain is taken into account for tax purposes.[81] The difference between recognized and unrecognized gain is that unrecognized gain is generally not reported for tax purposes until some further event occurs.

Inclusion of "unrealized gain" in the definition of "unrecognized gain" prevents deferral of gains to the subsequent year and deduction of losses in the current year. The Straddle Rules originally provided for losses to be deferred on closing out the losing position of a straddle only to the extent that there were unrealized gains. Deferring losses only to the extent of unrealized gains, however, was perceived as a loophole available to a cash basis taxpayer who sold property in one tax year and

---

[77]I.R.C. § 1092(c)(2)(B); General Explanation of ERTA, *supra* note 3, at 288.

[78]I.R.C. § 1092(a)(1)(A).

[79]I.R.C. § 1092(a)(3)(A)(i).

[80]I.R.C. § 1092(a)(3)(A)(ii).

[81]*See* section 12.3; section 12.4.

received the sales proceeds in the next tax year. Such a cash basis taxpayer was not subject to the loss deferral rule as originally enacted, because he had no unrealized gains in the first year. A cash basis transaction locked in the gain to be received at a future time not subject to the occurrence of any further legal event. However, such a taxpayer did have unrecognized gain insofar as he had a right to receive proceeds in the subsequent year. Hence, to close this loophole, the word "unrecognized" was substituted for "unrealized."[82] The continued deferral for a cash basis taxpayer who realized—but did not recognize—gain was thereby eliminated.

---

[82]TCA '82, Pub. L. No. 97-448, § 105(a)(1), 96 Stat. 2365, 2384 (1982); SENATE FINANCE COMMITTEE REPORT, TECHNICAL CORRECTIONS ACT OF 1982, S. Rep. No. 592, 97th Cong., 2d Sess. 25, *reprinted in* 1982 U.S. CODE CONG. & AD. NEWS 4149, 4171.

Thirty-seven

Limitation on Recognition of Straddle Losses While Holding an Offsetting Position

The concept of the loss deferral rule—that a taxpayer cannot deduct losses while holding an offsetting position—is taken one step further with the modified wash sales rule.[1] These rules apply to straddles consisting of non-section 1256 positions and to certain mixed straddles. They do not apply to straddles consisting solely of section 1256 positions.[2] This chapter first discusses the limitations on recognition of straddle losses provided by the loss deferral rule. Then it discusses the attempt made by the temporary Treasury regulations to coordinate the loss deferral rule with the modified wash sales rule.

§ 37.1 LOSS DEFERRAL RULE

The Code provides that losses on closing out a position in personal property are postponed and cannot be recognized for tax purposes to

---

[1]*See* section 42.3.

[2]I.R.C. § 1256(a)(4); *see* section 44.7.

the extent that there is an unrecognized gain inherent in offsetting positions in personal property.[3] In other words, losses are currently deductible only to the extent that they exceed unrecognized gains in an offsetting position acquired before the loss position was closed out.

The Code provides rebuttable presumptions to determine when a taxpayer holds offsetting positions and explicitly authorizes the Treasury to establish additional presumptions by regulation.[4] It is assumed that one dollar of unrecognized gain in a position that remains open at the end of any taxable year will defer at most only one dollar of recognized loss in an offsetting position closed out during the same year.[5]

The amount of loss deferred is the amount of gain a taxpayer would recognize if the gain position were sold (or otherwise disposed of) at its fair market value on the last business day of the taxable year.[6] Fair market value for a section 1256 contract that is subject to the loss deferral rule[7] and remains open at the end of the year is determined by the final settlement price for that contract on its last trading day of the year.[8] The settlement price for personal property not traded on an exchange normally is considered to be its fair market value.[9]

Example   37-1

___

On December 1st, a taxpayer enters into offsetting long and short positions in physical gold that are not subject to section 1256 treatment. On December 10th, the taxpayer disposes of the short position at an $11 loss, at which time there is $5 of unrealized gain in the offsetting long position. At year-end there is still $5 of unrecognized gain in the offsetting long position. Under these circumstances, $5 of the $11 loss is disallowed for the taxable year because there is $5 of unrecognized gain in the offsetting long position; the remaining $6 of loss, however, is taken into account in the first taxable year.[10]

___

[3] I.R.C. § 1092(a)(1)(A).

[4] I.R.C. § 1092(c)(3)(A); *see* section 36.4.

[5] *See* STAFF OF THE JOINT COMMITTEE ON TAXATION, 97TH CONG., 1ST SESS., GENERAL EXPLANATION OF ECONOMIC RECOVERY TAX ACT OF 1981 284 (Joint Comm. Print. 1981) [hereinafter referred to as "General Explanation of ERTA"].

[6] *Id.* at 285.

[7] I.R.C. § 1092(d)(5)(A). *See generally* Chapter 45.

[8] General Explanation of ERTA, *supra* note 5, at 285.

[9] *See id.* at 285-86.

[10] Temp. Treas. Reg. § 1.1092(b)-1T(g), Example (1) (1986).

§ 37.2 COORDINATION OF LOSS DEFERRAL AND MODIFIED WASH SALES RULES

This section provides a brief summary of the coordination between the loss deferral and the modified wash sales rules. Coordination between these rules is discussed in detail in section 42.2, which also provides illustrative examples.

If a taxpayer disposes of less than all of the positions of a straddle, any loss is disallowed to the extent there is unrecognized gain in (1) a successor position, (2) positions that are offsetting with respect to the loss position, and (3) positions that are offsetting with respect to the successor position.[11] The terms "straddle" and "offsetting position" are defined in I.R.C. § 1092. Basically, a taxpayer holds a straddle if he holds offsetting positions.[12] This means that a taxpayer holds a straddle if there is a substantial diminution of risk of loss in holding any position with respect to personal property by reason of holding one or more other positions with respect to such property (whether or not of the same kind).[13]

A successor position is defined in the temporary Treasury regulations as any position that offsets (at any time) a second position in either of two situations: (1) the second position offsets a loss position that was disposed of by the taxpayer, and (2) the successor position is entered into during a period commencing 30 days prior to and ending 30 days after the disposition of the loss position.[14] A successor position is one that is on the same side of the market as the loss position.

The successor position rule is a hybrid of the wash sales rule and the loss deferral rule. Basically, Temp. Treas. Reg. § 1.1092(b)-1T incorporates the loss deferral rule in its scope by providing that a loss can be taken into account only to the extent it exceeds year-end unrecognized gain in offsetting positions or successor positions. The concept of loss deferral is applied to not only offsetting positions but to successor po-

---

[11] Temp. Treas. Reg. § 1.1092(b)-1T(a) (1986).

[12] I.R.C. § 1092(c)(1).

[13] I.R.C. § 1092(c)(2)(A).

[14] Temp. Treas. Reg. § 1.1092(b)-5T(n) (1986). When the temporary regulations were initially released in January, 1985, the definition of a successor position was substantially broader than the current definition. A successor position was defined to include any position offsetting a successor position that was entered into within 30 days after the loss position was no longer part of the straddle. This meant that loss could be deferred because of unrecognized gains in positions that were never part of the original straddle. The author believes that the first definition of a successor position was beyond the intent of Congress in enacting I.R.C. § 1092(b). The current definition of a successor position is more appropriate.

sitions as well. The modified wash sales rule is embodied in the definition of a successor position.

Any loss that is disallowed by operation of the loss deferral rule of I.R.C. § 1092 is treated as sustained in the succeeding taxable year (subject to operation once again of the loss deferral rule).[15] For stock or securities that are part of a straddle, any disallowed loss is subject to further application of Temp. Treas. Reg. § 1.1092(b)-1T(a)(1) and to the limitations of Temp. Treas. Reg. § 1.1092-(b)-1T(a) (2).[16] However, a loss for stock or securities positions disallowed in one year under the rule set out in Temp. Treas. Reg. § 1.1092(b)-1T(a) (1) is not allowed in the succeeding taxable year unless two conditions are met. First, substantially identical stock or securities (the acquisition of which caused the loss to be disallowed in the first year) must be disposed of during the second year, and two, neither Temp. Treas. Reg. § 1.1092(b)-1T(a) (1) nor Temp. Treas. Reg. § 1.1092(b)-1T(a) (2) can apply in the second year to disallow the loss.[17] If the disposition of a loss position would (except for application of the loss deferral rule) result in a capital loss, the loss allowed in the carry-over year is also treated as a capital loss.[18] Conversely, a disallowed ordinary loss is carried over to the succeeding taxable year as an ordinary loss.[19] If the disposition of a section 1256 contract position at a loss would (but for application of these deferral rules) result in 60 percent long-term and 40 percent short-term capital loss, the carried-over loss is treated as 60/40 loss, irrespective of whether any gain or loss on any successor position would be treated as 100 percent long-term or short-term capital gain or loss.[20]

---

[15]Temp. Treas. Reg. § 1.1092(b)-1T(b) (1986).

[16]Temp. Treas. Reg. § 1.1092(b)-1T(b) (1986).

[17]Id.

[18]Temp. Treas. Reg. § 1.1092(b)-1T(c)(1) (1986).

[19]Id.

[20]Temp. Treas. Reg. § 1.1092(b)-1T(c)(2) (1986).

Thirty-eight

Losses Carried Forward

Losses that are not deductible in one taxable year ("deferred losses") can be carried forward to the succeeding taxable year.[1] Once carried forward, deferred losses are treated as incurred in the succeeding taxable year and are again subject to the loss deferral rule.[2] This procedure may require a continued deferral of the loss until the position offsetting it is closed out.[3] In addition, the character of the deferred loss (i.e., capital or ordinary) is determined at the time the loss is realized, rather than at the time the loss is allowed as a deduction to the taxpayer.[4] If the disposition of a loss position would result in 60 percent long-term capital loss and 40 percent short-term capital loss, the loss allowed on disposition is treated as 60/40 loss, irrespective of whether any gain or loss with respect to a successor position would be treated as 100 percent long-term or 100 percent short-term capital gain or loss.[5] Carrying deferred losses forward creates complex problems in determining when such losses are deductible.

Example 38-1

Assume that in 1986 a taxpayer enters into a forward contract position to sell gold (short position) and purchases gold bullion (long position). The taxpayer holds offsetting positions in personal property. If before

[1] I.R.C. § 1092(a)(1)(B).

[2] Temp. Treas. Reg. § 1.1092(b)-1T(b) (1986). If a stock or securities position is part of a straddle, loss on one position is disallowed under Temp. Treas. Reg. § 1.1092(b)- 1T(a)(1) until the substantially identical stock or securities position is also disposed of. *Id.*

[3] *See* I.R.C. § 1092(a)(1)(B).

[4] Temp. Treas. Reg. § 1.1092(b)-1T(c)(1)(1985).

[5] Temp. Treas. Reg. § 1.1092(b)-1T(c)(2)(1986).

the end of the year the taxpayer closes out the short forward contract position at a $10 loss, that loss is deductible only to the extent it exceeds any appreciation in the gold bullion he still holds at the end of the year. If at the end of 1986 the gold bullion position has an unrecognized gain of $6, only $4 of the $10 loss is deductible in 1986. The $6 deferred loss is carried forward into 1987 as a capital loss (long-term or short-term depending upon the taxpayer's holding period).[6] In addition, the holding period regulations may apply.[7]

Deferred loss is carried forward until there is no offsetting gain inherent in a position acquired before the loss position was closed out.[8] In fact, gain may arise before an offset is recognized or after an offsetting position is disposed of. This is a technical glitch in the code that provides curious results.

Example   38-2

Assume that throughout 1987 the taxpayer in Example 38-1 maintained the long gold bullion position that he acquired prior to closing out the short forward contract position at a loss. The $6 deferred loss carried forward from 1986 cannot be recognized in 1987 because the offsetting gain inherent in the gold bullion position has not been recognized. Even if the amount of the unrecognized gain in the gold bullion declines below $6, the entire loss must be deferred because there continues to be offsetting gain in a position (i.e., the gold bullion position) that was acquired before the loss position (i.e., the short forward contract position) was closed out. If the taxpayer disposes of the gold bullion in 1988, he can recognize the $6 deferred loss in that year, notwithstanding any other long gold positions held at the end of 1988 if these other positions were established after the original short position was closed out in 1986.[9]

[6] ERTA provides that a taxpayer's straddle losses are deferred to the extent the taxpayer had unrealized gains in offsetting positions. If a taxpayer realizes a loss on closing out one or more positions, the amount of loss he can deduct is the excess of the loss over the unrealized gain (if any) in the positions that offset the loss position and which are acquired before disposing of the loss position. STAFF OF THE JOINT COMMITTEE ON TAXATION, 97TH CONG., 1ST SESS., GENERAL EXPLANATION OF THE ECONOMIC RECOVERY TAX ACT OF 1981 283-84 (Joint. Comm. Print 1981) [hereinafter referred to as "General Explanation of ERTA"]; FINANCE COMMITTEE REPORT, ECONOMIC RECOVERY TAX ACT OF 1981, S. REP. NO. 144, 97th Cong., 1st Sess. 147, reprinted in 1981 U.S. CODE CONG. & AD. NEWS 105, 247.

[7] Temp. Treas. Reg. §§ 1.1092(b)-2T(a), (b)(1986).

[8] General Explanation of ERTA, supra note 5, at 284; S. REP. NO. 144, supra note 5, at 147. It should be noted that the legislative history refers to "unrealized," not "unrecognized," gains. The concept was changed by the TCA '82 (Pub. L. No. 97-448, § 105(a)(1)(A), 96 Stat. 2365, 2384) to close a "loophole" discussed in section 36.5.

[9] General Explanation of ERTA, supra note 5, at 284; S. REP. NO. 144, supra note 5, at 147.

Thirty-nine

Attribution Rules

§ 39.1 GENERAL RULES

In determining whether a taxpayer holds offsetting positions subject to the Straddle Rules, positions held by certain related parties are deemed to be held by the taxpayer.[1] Attribution is applied before determining whether two or more positions are offsetting.[2]

There are two general attribution rules. First, positions held by a taxpayer's spouse or a corporation that files a consolidated return with a corporate taxpayer[3] are treated as if held by the taxpayer.[4] This limits the persons subject to attribution to those parties (such as the taxpayer's spouse)[5] whose income can be reported on the same tax return.[6] Hence, positions established by a taxpayer's wholly owned corporation are generally not attributed to the taxpayer unless a consolidated return is filed with the taxpayer. Attribution results, however, if the stock is viewed as offsetting position stock.[7]

Another attribution rule provides that positions held by a flow-through entity in which the taxpayer has an interest, such as a trust, partnership,

[1] I.R.C. § 1092(d)(4).
[2] I.R.C. § 1092(d)(4)(A).
[3] I.R.C. § 1501.
[4] I.R.C. § 1092(d)(4).
[5] I.R.C. § 1092(d)(4)(B).
[6] *See* Staff of the Joint Committee on Taxation, 97th Cong., 1st Sess., General Explanation of the Economic Recovery Tax Act of 1981 290 (Joint Comm. Print 1981); Finance Committee Report, Economic Recovery Tax Act of 1981, S. Rep. No. 144, 97th Cong., 1st Sess. 151, *reprinted in* 1981 U.S. Code Cong. & Ad. News 105, 250.
[7] For a discussion of offsetting position stock, see section 36.2(c)(4).

or S corporation, are treated as if the positions were held by the taxpayer as beneficiary, grantor, partner, or stockholder if part (or all) of the gain or loss from the positions held by the flow-through entity would be taken into account in determining the taxpayer's own offsetting positions.[8] Treasury regulations, not yet promulgated, may identify circumstances where positions held by flow-through entities will not be attributed to a taxpayer.[9]

§ 39.2 STATUTORY ELECTIONS

A number of questions must be addressed to determine how statutory elections can be made when the attribution rules are applied to a particular taxpayer. At what levels can elections be made? Assuming the proper election or specific identification requirements are met, can positions held, for example, by a taxpayer and his spouse become part of an identified section 1256(d) straddle, an identified section 1092(b) straddle, or a mixed straddle? Can one corporation in a consolidated group make a hedging exemption election for another corporate member of the consolidated group? It is unclear under the statutory provisions and the legislative history of both ERTA and the DRA whether a taxpayer can make a valid election for another party whose positions are attributed to him. Regulatory guidance is necessary.

The only information concerning elections provided to date is contained in an IRS announcement on elections under ERTA's transitional rules for positions held by partnerships[10] and temporary regulations under the DRA.[11] The IRS announced that elections made under ERTA's transitional rules[12] were to be made at the partnership level.[13] In addition, partners in partnerships that made one election could make an additional separate election with respect to individually held positions either to pay their tax in installments or make no election at all.[14] The same provisions should apply to DRA elections because there have been no changes to the attribution rules by the DRA.[15]

---

[8]I.R.C. § 1092(d)(4)(C).

[9]*Id.*

[10]IRS News Release No. IR-82-13, 10 STAND. FED. TAX REP. (CCH) ¶ 6330 (Jan. 22, 1982).

[11]Temp. Treas. Reg. § 1.1092(b)-4T(f) (1985).

[12]*See* ERTA, Pub. L. 97-34, §§ 508(c), 509, 95 Stat. 172 (1981) (concerning the effective date for application of the Straddle Rules and section 1256 treatment).

[13]IRS News Release No. IR-82-13, *supra* note 10, at 71,420.

[14]*Id.*

[15]*See* DRA, Pub. L. 98-369, § 101(b)(2), 98 Stat. 494, 618-19 (1984).

§ 39.3   SECTION 1256 CONTRACTS

What is the scope of the attribution rules for section 1256 contract positions subject to the Mark-to-Market Rule?[16] One of the attribution rules provides that positions held by a partnership are treated as if such positions are held by its partners.[17] This rule leaves important issues open. Suppose a partner dies or sells his partnership interest so that he ceases to be a partner in the partnership. Is there a deemed disposition of the partner's proportionate share of the section 1256 contracts held by the partnership? Such a deemed disposition would treat the former partner as having realized gain or loss on his proportionate share of the partnership's section 1256 contracts at the date he died or disposed of his partnership interest. It is not clear at what date section 1256 contracts held by a partnership are to be marked-to-market and reported on the partners' tax returns.

§ 39.4   MIXED STRADDLES

Various elections are provided for establishing mixed straddle accounts and specifically identifying section 1092(b)(2) identified mixed straddles. For a discussion of the elections, see generally Chapter 45. The temporary Treasury regulations provide that the term "related person or flow-through entity," as used in the regulations, is defined in I.R.C. §§ 1092(d)(4)(B), (C).[18] Although the attribution rules apply to identify those positions that are part of a straddle, it is not clear whether the attribution rules are available for making elections with respect to positions attributed to the taxpayer.

---

[16]For a discussion of the Mark-to-Market Rule, see section 33.1.
[17]*See* I.R.C. § 1092(d)(4)(C).
[18]Temp. Treas. Reg. § 1.1092(b)-5T(j) (1986); *see* section 39.1.

Forty

Disclosure of Unrecognized Gain

§ 40.1 GENERALLY REQUIRED

To verify that a loss is deductible, a taxpayer must, with some exceptions, disclose on his tax return all unrecognized gains in positions in personal property, regardless of whether the positions are part of a straddle.[1] Obviously, this reporting requirement enables the IRS to determine which returns to select for audit and to identify possible offsetting positions by comparing positions closed at a loss with gain positions open at year-end.

The Treasury is authorized to issue regulations prescribing the time, manner, and form for a taxpayer to disclose unrecognized gain and the amount of unrecognized gain in open positions.[2] At the date of this writing, the only required reporting rules for use by taxpayers to disclose unrecognized gains are set out in IRS Form 6781.[3] Part III of Form 6781 generally requires reporting of each position for which there is unrecognized gain (whether or not part of a straddle) if the position is held by the taxpayer at the end of the tax year.

---

[1] I.R.C. § 1092(a)(3)(B).

[2] I.R.C. § 1092(a)(3)(B)(i).

[3] IRS Form 6781, Gains and Losses from Section 1256 Contracts and Straddles, Pt. III.

§ 40.2 EXCEPTIONS

There are five statutory exceptions to the disclosure requirements.[4] First, reporting is not required for unrecognized gains that are part of an identified straddle.[5] Second, reporting is not required for inventory items.[6] Third, disclosure is not required for positions that are part of hedging transactions.[7] Fourth, reporting is not required for depreciable property or real property used in the taxpayer's trade or business.[8] And fifth, reporting is not required where the taxpayer incurred no loss during the taxable year on any position (including section 1256 contracts), or where the only loss is in a position described in the three previous exceptions.[9] If a taxpayer carries a deferred loss forward from a prior year to the current tax year, the taxpayer must report his unrecognized gain positions.[10]

Another exception to disclosure, which is discussed in the Joint Committee Report on ERTA, states that taxpayers who have incurred losses from the disposition of long positions and who have neither disposed of nor held any short positions during the taxable year, "generally would not hold offsetting positions and would not be expected to report unrealized gain."[11] Although there is no statutory basis for this rule, it is sensible and excludes from reporting obligations those taxpayers with portfolios of appreciated property who have not engaged in any short transactions during the year.

§ 40.3 EXAMPLES

Example 40-1

Assume a gold dealer holds gold bullion in his inventory (long position) and enters into a forward contract to sell gold in the future (short position). Clearly, the dealer holds offsetting positions. Assume further

---

[4]I.R.C. §§ 1092(a)(3)(B)(ii)(I)-(III).

[5]I.R.C. § 1092(a)(3)(B)(ii)(I); *see* section 44.1.

[6]I.R.C. § 1092(a)(3)(B)(ii)(II).

[7]*Id.; see generally* Chapter 21.

[8]I.R.C. § 1092(a)(3)(B)(ii)(II).

[9]I.R.C. § 1092(a)(3)(B)(ii)(III).

[10]Staff of the Joint Committee on Taxation, 97th Cong., 1st Sess., General Explanation of the Economic Recovery Tax Act of 1981 286 (Joint Comm. Print 1981).

[11]*Id.*

that the dealer fails to comply with the requirements to qualify the straddle as a hedging transaction[12] so that the positions are subject to the Straddle Rules.[13] Also, assume that before the end of the year the dealer disposes of the short forward contract position at a loss, and at the end of the year he has gain in the long gold position.

Finally, assume that the dealer maintains the appreciated gold position. Under these assumptions, the dealer need not report his unrecognized gain, because the gain is on inventory property that is exempt from the disclosure requirements.[14] However, because the dealer did not comply with the requirements of the hedging exemption,[15] the loss deferral rule still applies to preclude him from recognizing, to the extent of the unrecognized gain inherent in the gold inventory, his loss on closing out the short forward contract position.

Example 40-2

Assume that the price of gold fell drastically prior to the end of the year. Based on the assumption of the previous example, the dealer's short forward contract has unrecognized gain, while the gold inventory has an inherent unrecognized loss. If the dealer sells the gold inventory at a loss and the only losses sustained by the dealer are on inventory positions in that taxable year, the dealer does not need to report the unrecognized gain on the short forward contract.[16] Provided the dealer does not have other types of losses that need to be reported for the year, unrealized gains need not be reported.

In conclusion, because the transaction does not qualify for the hedging exemption, the loss deferral rule precludes recognition of loss on the sale of the gold to the extent of the unrecognized gain inherent in the short forward contract position.[17]

---

[12]*See generally* Chapter 21.

[13]*See generally* Part Ten.

[14]I.R.C. § 1092(a)(3)(B)(ii)(II).

[15]*See* I.R.C. §§ 1092(e), 1256(e).

[16]I.R.C. § 1092(a)(3)(B)(ii)(II).

[17]I.R.C. § 1092(a)(1)(A).

Forty-one

Penalties

§ 41.1 PENALTIES FOR FAILURE TO DISCLOSE UNRECOGNIZED GAIN

A taxpayer who fails to report, without reasonable cause, all unrecognized gains required to be reported under I.R.C. § 1092(a)(3)(B) is subject to a penalty if he (1) held an offsetting gain position during the taxable year, and (2) has a tax deficiency attributable (in whole or in part) to the denial of the loss deduction.[1] Failure to report unrecognized gains is treated as negligent or intentional disregard of the rules and regulations, without an intent to defraud.[2]

The penalty for failure to disclose unrecognized gain is equal to five percent of the amount of the underpayment.[3] In addition, a penalty equal to 50 percent of the interest payable on the deficiency is also imposed.[4] This penalty is computed for the period commencing on the date the tax return was due (determined without regard to any extensions) and ending on the date the tax is assessed or paid, whichever occurs first.[5] It is imposed for failure to report unrecognized gains, irrespective of whether the taxpayer holds offsetting positions. Hence, a taxpayer is subject to a penalty if he did not report the gain, even if he obtained an opinion of counsel that the gain position did not offset a loss position. Although a taxpayer can rely on an opinion of counsel

[1] I.R.C. § 6653(f).
[2] Id.
[3] I.R.C. § 6653(a)(1).
[4] I.R.C. § 6653(a)(2).
[5] I.R.C. § 6653(a)(2)(B).

that he holds no offsetting gain position to claim a loss deduction, he still must disclose all unrealized gain positions and indicate that none of the disclosed gain positions offset the loss position.[6]

Example 41-1

Assume a taxpayer with unrecognized gain positions open at year-end obtains a legal opinion that these positions did not offset any positions for which he reported loss during the tax year for positions in personal property. Assume further that the taxpayer does not report any of his unrecognized year-end gain positions on his tax return. The taxpayer is subject to the penalty because he did not disclose his unrecognized gain positions.[7] The taxpayer must disclose all of his unrecognized gain positions[8] and, further, must indicate that none of the gain positions he disclosed are considered offsetting positions.[9]

Because Treasury regulations have not yet been issued providing exemptions from the reporting requirements, it is possible that the penalty provisions would not apply to a failure to fully report all positions with unrecognized gain.

§ 41.2   INCREASED INTEREST RATE

The DRA increases the interest rate applied to underpayments of tax if the underpayment is attributable to tax motivated transactions and if the underpayment exceeds $1000.[10] Generally, interest is imposed on any amount not paid on or before the last date prescribed for payment without regard to any extension of time for payment.[11] The annual rate of interest (on amounts not paid by the last date prescribed for payment) is established on a semiannual basis by the Treasury and is equal to

[6]STAFF OF THE JOINT COMMITTEE ON TAXATION, 97TH CONG., 1ST SESS., GENERAL EXPLANATION OF THE ECONOMIC RECOVERY TAX ACT OF 1981 291 (Joint Comm. Print 1981) [hereinafter referred to as "General Explanation of ERTA"]; SENATE FINANCE COMMITTEE REPORT, ECONOMIC RECOVERY TAX ACT OF 1981, S. REP. NO. 144, 97th Cong., 1st Sess. 152, *reprinted in* 1981 U.S. CODE CONG. & AD. NEWS 105, 251.

[7]I.R.C. § 6653(f).

[8]I.R.C. § 1092(a)(3)(B)(i).

[9]General Explanation of ERTA, *supra* note 6, at 291.

[10]I.R.C. § 6621(d) (originally enacted as DRA, Pub. L. 98-369, § 144(a), 98 Stat. 494, 682-83 (1984)).

[11]I.R.C. § 6601(a).

the adjusted prime rate charged by banks for the six-month period ending on September 30th and March 31st of any calendar year.[12] Any adjusted rate of interest established for the six-month period ending September 30th becomes effective January 1st of the succeeding year, whereas an adjusted rate of interest established for the six-month period ending March 31st becomes effective on July 1st of the same year.[13]

In the event an underpayment of tax is substantial and attributable to a tax motivated transaction, the annual rate of interest is 120 percent of the rate established for each six-month period ending September 30th and March 31st.[14] An underpayment of tax is considered substantial if the underpayment for any taxable year exceeds $1000.[15] A substantial underpayment of tax is attributable to a tax motivated transaction if, among other things, the underpayment arises from any straddle.[16] For purposes of this section, a straddle is defined as offsetting positions with respect to personal property,[17] without regard to either the special rules contained in I.R.C. § 1092(d)[18] or the hedging exemption contained in I.R.C. § 1092(e).[19]

Any underpayment of tax in excess of $1000 that is attributable to a straddle bears interest at a rate equal to 120 percent of the rate established by the Treasury. The 120 percent rate applies to interest accruing after December 31, 1984.[20]

For purposes of determining whether a substantial underpayment is attributable to a straddle or other tax motivated transaction, the tax liability is calculated as if all items of income, gain, loss, deduction, or credit had been reported properly on the income tax return of the taxpayer. The difference between the tax liability based on this computation and the tax liability computed without taking into account any adjustments to items attributable to tax motivated transactions equals the amount of the tax motivated underpayment.[21]

---

[12]I.R.C. § 6621(d)(1).

[13]I.R.C. § 6621(b).

[14]I.R.C. § 6621(d)(1).

[15]I.R.C. § 6621(d)(2).

[16]I.R.C. § 6621(d)(3)(A).

[17]I.R.C. §§ 1092(c), 6621(d)(3)(A); *see generally* Chapter 36.

[18]I.R.C. § 1092(d) provides various definitions and special rules for application of the Straddle Rules.

[19]*See generally* Chapter 21.

[20]DRA, *supra* note 10, § 144(c).

[21]Temp. Treas. Reg. § 301.6621-2T, Question 5 (1984).

Forty-two

Modified Wash Sales and Short Sales Rules

The Treasury has broad authority to issue regulations to establish modified wash sale and modified short sale rules to apply to strad-dles.[1] This regulatory authority, originally granted by ERTA, was ex-panded by the DRA. Temporary regulations were issued in early 1985[2] and amended in early 1986.[3] ERTA called for regulations imposing rules for straddle transactions that were to be "similar" to the wash sales rule applicable for stock and securities[4] and the short sales rule already established for substantially identical property.[5] The DRA expanded the Treasury's authority to issue regulations "with respect to gain or loss on positions which are part of a straddle as may be appropriate" to carry out the purposes of the Straddle Rules and "to apply the princi-ples" of the wash sales and short sales rules to straddle transactions.[6] The DRA's grant of regulatory authority is substantially broader than the original authority to issue rules "similar" to the wash sale and short sale rules. There are exceptions to application of these rules. Hedging transactions that qualify for the hedging exemption are exempt from all of the Straddle Rules, including the modified wash sales and modified

---

[1] I.R.C. § 1092(b)(1).
[2] Temp. Treas. Reg. §§ 1.1092(b)-1T to 1.1092(b)-5T (1986).
[3] T.D. 8070 1986-12 I.R.B. 6.
[4] I.R.C. §§ 1091(a), (d).
[5] I.R.C. §§ 1092(b)(1), 1233(b), 1233(d); ERTA, § 501(a), 95 Stat. 172, 324 (1981).
[6] I.R.C. § 1092(b)(1).

short sales rules.[7] In addition, these rules do not apply to loss positions included in a mixed straddle account, or to losses on positions in a straddle that only consists of section 1256 contracts.[8]

§ 42.1 COORDINATION WITH THE WASH SALES AND SHORT SALES RULES

The modified wash sales and short sales rules apply, unless a specific exemption is available, to positions that are part of a straddle. In many cases the wash sales rule of I.R.C. § 1091 or the short sales rule of I.R.C. § 1233 may also apply. The short sales rule of I.R.C. § 1233[9] explicitly provides that "property" subject to the short sales rule does not include any position to which the modified short sales rule applies.[10] As a result, the scope of the short sales rule of I.R.C. § 1233 can now be read narrowly and may, in fact, be limited to short sales of stock.[11] On the other hand, when the Straddle Rules were extended in 1984 to stock options and certain stock positions,[12] it was unclear whether the wash sales rule of I.R.C. § 1091, the modified wash sales rule, or both rules applied to stock or securities positions that were part of a straddle. Because some transactions clearly fall within the statutory language of both rules, the coordination of these rules had to be addressed in Treasury regulations or clarifying legislation. On January 14, 1986, the Treasury amended the temporary regulations, issued in 1985 under I.R.C. § 1092(b) to "coordinate" the application of the wash sales rule, modified wash sales rule, and the loss deferral rule for stock and securities positions that are part of a straddle. The amended temporary regulations, which apply retroactively to dispositions of loss positions on or after January 24, 1985,[13] provide that I.R.C. § 1092(b) applies in lieu of I.R.C. § 1091 to defer losses incurred from the disposition of stock and securities positions in a straddle.[14] After January 24, 1985, the wash sales rule contained in I.R.C. § 1091 applies only to stock or securities positions that

---

[7]*See generally* Chapter 21. *See also* Temp. Treas. Reg. § 1.1092(b)-1T(d)(1)(i) (1986).

[8]Temp. Treas. Reg. § 1.1092(b)-1T(d) (1986).

[9]*See generally* Chapter 16.

[10]I.R.C. § 1233(e)(2).

[11]*See* section 16.1.

[12]*See* section 36.2(c).

[13]T.D. 8070, 1986-12 I.R.B. 6.

[14]Temp. Treas. Reg. § 1.1092(b)-1T(e) (1986).

are not part of a straddle (e.g., outright stock positions and the short sale of stock).[15]

§ 42.2 COORDINATION WITH THE LOSS DEFERRAL RULE

The temporary Treasury regulations, as amended, generally provide that if a taxpayer disposes of less than all of the positions of a straddle, any loss on the disposition of the loss position is not deductible to the extent there is unrecognized gain as of the close of the taxable year in one or more of the following positions: (1) successor positions, (2) offsetting positions to loss positions, and (3) offsetting positions to any successor positions.[16] Any loss that is not deductible because of this general rule is carried over and is treated as sustained in the succeeding taxable year.[17]

A special rule is applied first to losses from the disposition of stock or securities positions that are part of a straddle before the general rule mentioned above is applied. Any loss on the disposition of stock or securities is not taken into account if, within a period beginning 30 days before the date of disposition and ending 30 days after such date, the taxpayer has acquired (by purchase or in a taxable exchange) substantially identical stock or securities or entered into a contract or option to acquire such securities.[18] The term "substantially identical" has the same meaning as it has when it is used in I.R.C. § 1091(a).[19] The term "securities" has the same meaning as it has in I.R.C. § 1236(c).[20] If any loss on the disposition of stock or securities remains deductible after application of this special rule,[21] the general rule[22] applies and may further defer a deduction for the remaining losses.

---

[15]For a discussion of application of the Straddle Rules to certain stock positions, see section 36.2.

[16]Temp. Treas. Reg. § 1.1092(b)-1T(a)(2) (1986). The provisions of Temp. Treas. Reg. § 1.1092(b)-1T do not apply to losses sustained on (1) positions that are part of a hedging transaction, (2) positions included in a mixed straddle account (as defined in Temp. Treas. Reg. § 1.1092(b)-4T), or (3) positions that are part of a straddle consisting only of section 1256 contracts. Temp. Treas. Reg. § 1.1092(b)-1T(d) (1986).

[17]Temp. Treas. Reg. § 1.1092(b)-1T(b) (1986).

[18]Temp. Treas. Reg. § 1.1092(b)-1T(a)(1) (1986). This rule does not apply to losses sustained by a dealer in securities if the losses are sustained in transactions made in the ordinary course of business. Temp. Treas. Reg. § 1.1092(b)-1T(d)(2) (1986).

[19]Temp. Treas. Reg. § 1.1092(b)-5T(p) (1986). See also section 17.9.

[20]Temp. Treas. Reg. § 1.1092(b)-5T(q) (1986). See also section 17.6(a).

[21]Temp. Treas. Reg. § 1.1092(b)-1T(a)(1) (1986).

[22]Temp. Treas. Reg. § 1.1092(b)-1T(a)(2) (1986).

The term "successor position" is defined in the temporary Treasury regulations as any position that is or was at any time offsetting to a second position if (1) the second position was offsetting to a loss position disposed of, and (2) the position is entered into during a period commencing 30 days before and ending 30 days after the disposition of the loss position.[23] In short, a successor position is one that is on the same side of the market as the loss position.

The successor position rule is a hybrid of the wash sales rule and the loss deferral rule. Basically, Temp. Treas. Reg. § 1.1092(b)-1T incorporates the loss deferral rule by providing that a loss can be taken into account only to the extent it exceeds year-end unrecognized gain in offsetting positions or successor positions. The concept of loss deferral is applied to not only offsetting positions but to successor positions as well. The modified wash sales rule is embodied in the definition of a successor position.

Any loss disallowed by the modified wash sales rule is carried forward and treated as if sustained in the succeeding taxable year (when it will again be subject to these deferral rules). For stock or securities that are part of a straddle, any disallowed loss is subject to further application of Temp. Treas. Reg. § 1.1092(b)-1T(a)(1) and to the limitations of Temp. Treas. Reg. § 1.1092(b)-1T(a)(2).[24] However, a loss for stock or securities positions disallowed in one year under the rule set out in Temp. Treas. Reg. § 1092(b)-1T(a)(1) is not allowed in the succeeding taxable year unless (1) substantially identical stock or securities (the acquisition of which caused the loss to be disallowed in the first year) are disposed of during the second year, and (2) neither Temp. Treas. Reg. § 1092(b)-1T(a)(1) nor Temp. Treas. Reg. § 1092(b)-1T(a)(2) apply in the second year to disallow the loss.[25]

If capital loss is deferred in this manner, the loss allowed in the subsequent taxable year is also treated as a capital loss.[26] In all other cases, the loss is an ordinary loss.[27] If the disposition of a section 1256 contract position at a loss would (but for application of these deferral rules) result in 60 percent long-term and 40 percent short-term capital loss, the carried-over loss is treated as 60 percent long-term and 40 percent short-term capital loss, irrespective of whether any gain or loss

---

[23]Temp. Treas. Reg. § 1.1092(b)-5T(n) (1986).

[24]Temp. Treas. Reg. § 1.1092(b)-1T(b) (1986).

[25]Id.

[26]Temp. Treas. Reg. § 1.1092(b)-1T(c)(1) (1986).

[27]Id.

on any successor positions would be treated as 100 percent long-term or short-term capital gain or loss.[28]

Example 42-1

On December 1st, a taxpayer enters into offsetting long and short positions. On December 10th he disposes of the short position at an $11 loss, when the long position has a $5 unrealized gain. At the end of the year the long position still has a $5 unrecognized gain inherent in it. As a result, $5 of the $11 loss is not deductible in 1985 because there is $5 of unrecognized gain in the offsetting long position.[29]

Example 42-2

Assume the facts are the same as in Example 42-1, except that at year-end there is $11 of unrecognized gain in the offsetting long position. In this example, the entire $11 loss is not deductible in the taxable year in which it is incurred because of the $11 unrecognized gain in the long position.[30]

Example 42-3

On November 1st, a taxpayer enters into offsetting long and short positions. On November 10th, he disposes of the long position at a $10 loss. On November 11th, he enters into a new long position that is a successor position to the long position disposed of, and that is not substantially identical to the long position disposed of. Assume further that both the original short position and the successor long position are open at year-end, and there is $10 of unrecognized gain in the successor long position and no unrecognized gain in the offsetting short position. The entire $10 loss is not deductible for the taxable year because there is $10 of unrecognized gain inherent in the successor long position.[31]

Example 42-4

Assume the facts are the same as in Example 42-3, except that at year-end there is $4 of unrecognized gain in the successor long position and $6 of unrecognized gain in the short position. The entire $10 loss on the

[28]Temp. Treas. Reg. § 1.1092(b)-1T(c)(2) (1986).
[29]Temp. Treas. Reg. § 1.1092(b)-1T(g), Example (1) (1986).
[30]Temp. Treas. Reg. § 1.1092(b)-1T(g), Example (2) (1986).
[31]Temp. Treas. Reg. § 1.1092(b)-1T(g), Example (4) (1986).

original long position is not deductible for this year because there is a total of $10 of unrecognized gain in both the successor long position and the short position.[32]

Example 42-5

Assume the facts are the same as in Example 42-3, except that at year-end there is $8 of unrecognized gain in the successor long position and $8 of unrecognized loss in the short position. Only $8 of the total $10 realized loss on the original long position is disallowed for the taxable year because of the $8 of unrecognized gain in the successor long position.[33] The remaining $2 loss is deductible.

Example 42-6

On November 1st, a taxpayer enters into offsetting long and short positions. By November 10th the market has moved so that there is $20 of unrecognized gain in the long position, and the taxpayer disposes of the short position at a $20 loss. By November 15th, the value of the long position has declined, thereby eliminating all unrealized gain in the position. On November 15th, the taxpayer establishes a second short position that is a successor position which offsets the long position. The successor position is not substantially identical to the short position disposed of on November 10th. Assume further that at year-end there is no unrecognized gain in the offsetting long position or the successor short position. The entire $20 loss incurred on the disposition of the original short position is allowed for the year because there is no unrecognized gain in the successor short position or the offsetting long position.[34]

§ 42.3 MODIFIED WASH SALES RULE

In general, the modified wash sales rule prevents a taxpayer from disposing of a loss position in a straddle to obtain the benefit of a loss deduction when he immediately replaces the loss position with a substantially identical position or a successor position. Although the Code

---

[32]Temp. Treas. Reg. § 1.1092(b)-1T(g), Example (5) (1986).
[33]*Id.*
[34]Temp. Treas. Reg. § 1.1092(b)-1T(g), Example (10) (1986).

does not establish a priority between the modified wash sales rule and the loss deferral rule, the legislative history of ERTA provides that when the modified wash sales rule applies, it disallows losses prior to application of the loss deferral rule.[35] Under this analysis, the modified wash sales rule should prevent a taxpayer with offsetting positions from disposing of the loss position and recognizing a loss while he remains in a balanced position by virtue of his unrecognized gain position. Far reaching attribution rules are used to apply the modified wash sales rule.[36]

The statutory mandate to the Treasury to issue regulations left many open questions on the scope and application of the modified wash sales rule. Some, but not all, of these questions have been resolved by the temporary Treasury regulations. Because positions can be opened and closed in rapid succession throughout the year, a mechanism to trace positions subject to the modified wash sales rule is necessary.

---

[35]The legislative history of ERTA assumes that the replacement position of a straddle subject to the modified wash sales rule has a tax basis equal to its cost plus the amount of loss not deductible after the application of the modified wash sales rule. STAFF OF THE JOINT COMMITTEE ON TAXATION, 97TH CONG., 1ST SESS., GENERAL EXPLANATION OF ECONOMIC RECOVERY TAX ACT OF 1981 286-87 (Joint Comm. Print 1981) [hereinafter referred to as "General Explanation of ERTA"]; SENATE FINANCE COMMITTEE REPORT, ECONOMIC RECOVERY TAX ACT OF 1981, S. REP. NO. 144, 97th Cong., 1st Sess. 149, *reprinted in* 1981 U.S. CODE CONG. & AD. NEWS 105, 244. For example, if a position in a straddle was acquired at a cost of $100, was sold for $50, and was replaced with a new position that cost $60, the $50 loss (not allowed under the modified wash sales rule) is added to the basis of the replacement position. In this example, the replacement position has a tax basis of $110 ($60 purchase price plus $50 of denied loss).

By analogy to the wash sales rule of I.R.C. § 1091, which disallows losses if a taxpayer acquires a substantially identical security 30 days before or 30 days after the sale (i.e., a 61-day prohibited period), it was assumed after enactment of ERTA that the modified wash sales rule would substitute the concept of "offsetting positions" for the apparently broader concept of "substantially identical property." General Explanation of ERTA at 287; S. REP. NO. 144 at 149. It was also assumed after enactment of ERTA that Treasury regulations would provide that a deduction be denied for a loss incurred on closing out a position in a straddle that subsequently is replaced with another position (whether or not substantially identical) that offsets the remaining position (or positions) in the same straddle. *See* General Explanation of ERTA at 286; S. REP. NO. 144 at 149. In other words, it was assumed that a loss position and the position that replaces it would be subject to the modified wash sales rule if any other position offsets both positions. It was also assumed that a loss allowed under the modified wash sales rule could be deferred by subsequent application of the loss deferral rule. General Explanation of ERTA at 286; S. REP. NO. 144 at 149. This is because the loss deferral rule applies irrespective of whether the taxpayer replaces a loss position, thereby applying to more transactions than those covered by the modified wash sales rule.

[36]I.R.C. § 1092(d)(4). *See generally* Chapter 39.

§ 42.4 MODIFIED SHORT SALES RULE

(a) APPLICATION

The modified short sales rule substitutes the concept of offsetting positions for substantially identical property contained in the original short sales rule of I.R.C. § 1233.[37] Presumably, this prevents a taxpayer from either converting short-term capital gain into long-term capital gain or long-term capital loss into short-term capital loss.

It was thought that the modified short sales rule prevented the use of offsetting positions to extend, without risk of loss, the holding period of positions in personal property. Therefore, the modified short sales rule applies to offsetting positions so that the holding period for property that is part of a straddle is suspended and does not begin to run again until the offsetting position is disposed of by the taxpayer. While offsetting positions remain open, no position in the straddle should increase its holding period. Presumably, for investors[38] and traders[39] any gain from the disposition of the short position is short-term capital gain and the holding period of the long position begins on the earlier of the date on which the short position is disposed of or the date on which the long position is disposed of.[40] In addition, any loss on one position of a straddle is long-term capital loss if, at the time the straddle was established, the other position was held for the long-term holding period.[41] Attribution rules are used in applying the modified short sales rule.[42]

The temporary Treasury regulations provide that the holding period of any position that is part of a straddle does not begin until the date

---

[37]The General Explanation of ERTA provides some suggestions on the scope of the modified short sales rule. For example, it indicates that a short futures contract is equivalent to the short sale of a long futures contract for the same commodity or of the short sale of the commodity itself. General Explanation of ERTA, *supra* note 35, at 287; S. REP. NO. 144, *supra* note 35, at 149. Additionally, the General Explanation of ERTA assumes that regulations will provide rules to suspend the commencement of the holding period for any positions that are part of a straddle subject to the Straddle Rules. General Explanation of ERTA, *supra* note 35, at 287; S. REP. NO. 144, *supra* note 35, at 149. This means that the modified short sales rule terminates the holding period of a long position in a straddle unless the long-term holding period requirement already was satisfied with respect to that position. General Explanation of ERTA, *supra* note 35, at 287; S. REP. NO. 144, *supra* note 35, at 149.

[38]*See* section 6.1.

[39]*See* section 6.2.

[40]I.R.C. § 1233(b).

[41]I.R.C. § 1233(d).

[42]I.R.C. § 1092(d)(4); *see also* Chapter 39.

the straddle is terminated—that is, the date the taxpayer no longer holds (either directly or indirectly through a related person or flow-through entity) an offsetting position with respect to that position.[43] This rule does not apply to a position held by a taxpayer for the long-term capital gain holding period (or longer) before a straddle that includes such position is established.[44] Similarly, loss incurred on the disposition of one or more positions of a straddle is treated as a long-term capital loss if (1) on the date the taxpayer entered into the loss position the taxpayer held directly or indirectly one or more offsetting positions with respect to the loss position, and (2) one or more positions in the straddle constitute capital assets that have been held for the long-term holding period on the day the loss position was acquired.[45]

There is an exception (often referred to as the "killer rule") to the holding period rule for positions that do not qualify for section 1256 treatment but are part of a mixed straddle. Losses from the disposition of one or more loss positions that are part of a mixed straddle and that are non-section 1256 positions are treated as 60 percent long-term and 40 percent short-term capital losses if (1) gain or loss from the disposition of one or more of the section 1256 contracts in the mixed straddle would be considered gain or loss from the sale or exchange of a capital asset, (2) the disposition of no position in the straddle (other than a section 1256 contract) would result in long-term capital gain or loss, and (3) a valid election relating to either straddle-by-straddle identification or mixed straddle accounts has *not* been made by the taxpayer.[46]

Example   42-7

On October 1, 1984, a taxpayer acquires gold. On January 1, 1985, the taxpayer enters into an offsetting forward contract position to sell gold (short position). On April 1, 1985, the taxpayer disposes of the short gold forward contract at no gain or loss. On April 10, 1985, he sells the gold for a profit. Because the gold has not been held for more than six months before the offsetting short position was entered into, the holding period for the gold begins no earlier than the time the straddle is terminated. Thus, the holding period of the original gold purchased on October 1, 1984 and sold on October 10, 1985 begins on April 1, 1985,

---

[43]Temp. Treas. Reg. § 1.1092(b)-2T(a)(1) (1986).
[44]Temp. Treas. Reg. § 1.1092(b)-2T(a)(2) (1986).
[45]Temp. Treas. Reg. § 1.1092(b)-2T(b)(1) (1986).
[46]Temp. Treas. Reg. § 1.1092(b)-2T(b)(2) (1986).

the date the straddle was terminated. Consequently, gain recognized with respect to the gold is short-term capital gain.[47]

Example 42-8

On January 1, 1985, the taxpayer enters into a forward contract to buy gold (long position) and on August 4, 1985, enters into an offsetting short forward contract to sell gold (short position). On September 1, 1985, the taxpayer disposes of the short position at a loss. Because an offsetting long position had been held by the taxpayer for more than six months prior to the acquisition of the offsetting short position, the loss with respect to the closing of the short position is treated as a long-term capital loss.[48]

Example 42-9

On March 1, 1985, the taxpayer enters into a long forward contract and on July 17, 1985, the taxpayer enters into an offsetting short gold futures contract. He does not make any election with respect to mixed straddles. On August 10, 1985, the taxpayer disposes of the long gold forward contract at a loss. Because the forward contract was part of a mixed straddle, and the disposition of none of the positions in the straddle (other than the futures contract) would give rise to a long-term capital loss, the loss recognized on the termination of the gold forward contract is treated as 40 percent short-term and 60 percent long-term capital loss.[49]

Example 42-10

Assume that the facts are the same as in Example 42-9 above, except that on August 11, 1985, the taxpayer disposes of the short gold futures contract at a gain. Under these circumstances, the gain is still treated as 60 percent long-term and 40 percent short-term capital gain because the holding period rules of the regulations are not applicable to section 1256 contracts.[50]

---

[47] Temp. Treas. Reg. § 1.1092(b)-2T(f), Example (1) (1986).
[48] Temp. Treas. Reg. § 1.1092(b)-2T(f), Example (4) (1986).
[49] Temp. Treas. Reg. § 1.1092(b)-2T(f), Example (5) (1986).
[50] Temp. Treas. Reg. § 1.1092(b)-2T(f), Example (6) (1986).

The implications of the rules presented in Examples 42-9 and 42-10 set forth above (these examples were taken from the temporary Treasury regulations) can be astounding for an active trader of section 1256 contracts and offsetting non-section 1256 property. For example, an options dealer who routinely trades both stock options and the underlying stock can have a large number of his stock losses recharacterized as 60/40 losses, thereby offsetting the 60/40 treatment derived from his stock option gains. A commodity futures trader who actively trades the underlying property could also lose the benefit of the blended tax rate generated by the 60/40 Rule for his futures contract gains.

Example 42-11

Throughout 1985, the taxpayer, an active options dealer, enters into thousands of mixed straddle transactions involving stock options and the underlying stock. The taxpayer did not hold any position for more than six months, did make the straddle-by-straddle identification, and did not elect a mixed straddle account. These transactions, prior to the application of the rules in the temporary Treasury regulations, resulted in 60/40 gains and losses from the options and short-term capital gains and losses from the stock. The results of the mixed straddles are presented below in gross totals for each item traded:

Corporation Name	Gross Stock Gains	Gross Stock Losses	Gross Option Gains	Gross Option Losses
XYZ	$ 50,000	$ 40,000	$ 50,000	$ 50,000
ABC	40,000	40,000	40,000	35,000
ZZZ	40,000	25,000	40,000	40,000
Total	$130,000	$105,000	$130,000	$125,000

The taxpayer's net options gain from these transactions (generally qualifying for 60/40 treatment) is $5000 and his net stock gain is $25,000 for an overall economic gain of $30,000. He also actively traded AAA options during 1985 (although he did not acquire or sell any AAA stock) deriving a net gain, generally qualifying for 60/40 treatment, of $100,000. All gains and losses are recognized at year-end. Under these circumstances, the taxpayer's gross stock losses are recharacterized as 60/40 losses because they resulted from mixed straddles in which no positions were held for the long-term holding period. The resulting tax computation is as follows:

60/40 RESULTS

Net Option Gains Qualifying for 60/40 Treatment	100,000
Gross Option Losses from Mixed Straddles	(125,000)
Gross Option Gains from Mixed Straddles	130,000
Recharacterized Stock Losses from Mixed Straddles	(105,000)
Net 60/40 Gains Qualifying for Blended Tax Rate	-0-

SHORT-TERM CAPITAL RESULTS

Gross Stock Gains	130,000
Net Short-Term Capital Gain Taxable at 50 Percent Rate	130,000

The taxpayer could have protected the 60/40 treatment of his net option gains by making either a straddle-by-straddle identification[51] or a mixed straddle account election.[52]

A special rule applies to positions held by regulated investment companies[53] that, in order to qualify as such for tax purposes, must derive less than 30 percent of their gross incomes from the disposition of securities held for less than three months.[54] The rule of Temp. Treas. Reg. § 1.1092(b)-2T(a), which provides that holding periods do not begin

---

[51]*See* section 45.3.
[52]*See* section 45.4.
[53]*See* section 6.9.
[54]I.R.C. § 851(b)(3).

until the date the taxpayer no longer holds an offsetting position, is not applied for purposes of determining whether a regulated investment company qualifies for the statutory definition.[55] If the short sales rule of I.R.C. § 1233(b) would have applied to the positions held by a regulated investment company, these rules continue to apply.[56] Similarly, the effect of daily marking-to-market provided under I.R.C. § 1.1092(b)-4T(c) is disregarded for purposes of the statutory definition of a regulated investment company.[57]

The provisions of the temporary Treasury regulations apply to positions in a straddle established after June 23, 1981, in taxable years ending after such date,[58] and to positions in a mixed straddle established on or after January 1, 1984.[59] These provisions do not apply to positions that (1) constitute part of a hedging transaction, (2) are included in a straddle consisting only of section 1256 contracts, or (3) are included in a mixed straddle account.[60]

(b) MIXED STRADDLES

Significant questions as to the scope of the modified short sales rule are raised where one, but not all, of the positions of a straddle is a section 1256 contract subject to the Mark-to-Market Rule and the 60/40 Rule.[61] Before the DRA, it had been argued that the purpose of the modified short sales rule was to prevent taxpayers from generating long-term capital gain from the sale of personal property (or to require that they report a short-term capital loss on the sale of loss positions) if they hold other positions that protect them from the risk of loss. The legislative history of ERTA explaining the intended scope of the modified short sales rule envisioned only the suspension or elimination of the holding period with respect to property that is part of a straddle. The problem was that 60/40 treatment from the section 1256 elements does not depend upon a holding period computation and thus it was unclear whether 60/40 treatment was compromised by holding offsetting non-section

---

[55]Temp. Treas. Reg. § 1.1092(b)-2T(d) (1986).

[56]*Id.*

[57]*Id.*

[58]Temp. Treas. Reg. § 1.1092(b)-2T(e)(1) (1986).

[59]Temp. Treas. Reg. § 1.1092(b)-2T(e)(2) (1986).

[60]Temp. Treas. Reg. § 1.1092(b)-2T(c) (1986).

[61]*See generally* Part Nine.

1256 positions.[62] However, the expansion under the DRA of the Treasury's authority to regulate offsetting positions to carry out the purposes of the Straddle Rules and the principles of the short sales rule makes it possible for the Treasury to prevent conversions by limiting the availability of 60/40 treatment on mixed straddles. The same analysis should apply to prevent conversion of long-term capital loss into short-term capital loss using straddles.

In addition, the DRA grants the Treasury authority to issue regulations for mixed straddles to apply in lieu of the modified short sales rule if so elected by a taxpayer.[63] For an analysis of these elective rules to adopt straddle-to-straddle netting or mixed straddle accounts, see generally Chapter 45.

[62]Upon review of ERTA's legislative history, it was argued that if a taxpayer holds a position with a long-term capital loss but sells another offsetting position that would generate short-term capital loss, the loss on the sale is converted to long-term capital loss. What would happen, however, if the offsetting position was a section 1256 contract eligible for 60/40 treatment? Loss on the position that is not a section 1256 contract might be treated as 60 percent long-term and 40 percent short-term loss. If this analysis were correct, a section 1256 contract subject to section 1256 treatment could shorten the holding period of another position (although the holding period of the section 1256 contract, itself, is immaterial). On the other hand, it was also argued that as a position in a straddle, a section 1256 contract might cause 60 percent of the capital loss of the position that is not a section 1256 contract to be converted from short-term to long-term capital loss. The character of gain as 60 percent long-term and 40 percent short-term capital gain for the section 1256 contract itself, however, would not have been affected.

[63]I.R.C. § 1092(b)(2) (originally enacted as DRA, § 103(a), Pub. L. 98-369, 98 Stat. 494, 627).

Forty-three

Capitalization of Straddle Interest and Carrying Charges

Deductions are not allowed for interest and carrying charges that are allocable to personal property which is part of a straddle that does not consist solely of section 1256 positions.[1] As a result, the loss deferral rule and the modified wash sales and short sales rules also apply to "cash and carry transactions" and other straddle positions entered into after June 23, 1981.[2]

Under current law, when a taxpayer enters into a cash and carry transaction where not all of the positions are section 1256 contracts, the transaction is a mixed straddle subject to the mixed straddle rules.[3] Of course, because the capitalization requirements only apply to straddle transactions, they do not apply to property that is not part of a straddle or to hedging transactions.[4] This chapter first discusses pre-ERTA cash and carry transactions and then discusses the current requirements to capitalize interest and carrying charges.

---

[1] I.R.C. § 263(g)(1). The capitalization requirement applies to positions of a straddle consisting of non-section 1256 positions and does not apply to a straddle consisting solely of section 1256 positions. I.R.C. § 1256(a)(4).

[2] See generally Part Ten. For a discussion of cash and carry transactions, see section 4.3(d).

[3] See generally Chapter 45.

[4] See generally Chapter 21.

§ 43.1 PRE-ERTA TRANSACTIONS

Under the law in effect prior to ERTA, taxpayers established cash and carry transactions in an attempt to convert ordinary income into long-term capital gain.[5] A taxpayer holds a cash and carry straddle if he acquires a physical commodity and enters into a short position to sell the commodity at a future date, preferably in excess of the long-term capital gain holding period.[6] In addition, if a taxpayer enters into long and short futures contract positions, subsequently takes delivery of the underlying property under the long position, and continues to maintain his short position, this is referred to as a "full carry straddle." Cash and carry straddles and full carry straddles are referred to collectively as "cash and carry straddles." This section discusses the law in effect prior to ERTA, which helps put the current law into perspective.[7]

Cash and carry straddles were used under pre-ERTA law to defer payment of tax and to convert ordinary income into long-term capital gain.[8] Carrying charges, such as storage, transportation, insurance, and interest expense incurred (or continued) to purchase or carry a commodity held for investment, were deductible under pre-ERTA law by investors as section 212 expenses (paid or incurred for the management, conservation, or maintenance of property held for the production of income) and by traders and dealers as ordinary business expenses.[9] Under pre-ERTA law, a taxpayer would deduct the interest and carrying charges associated with holding (referred to as carrying) the physical commodity, and to minimize his risk, the taxpayer would establish an offsetting short position.[10] In addition, the taxpayer typically financed

---

[5]Staff of the Joint Committee on Taxation, 97th Cong., 1st Sess., General Explanation of the Economic Recovery Tax Act of 1981 292 (Joint Comm. Print 1981) [hereinafter referred to as "General Explanation of ERTA"]; House Ways and Means Committee Report, Tax Incentive Act of 1981, H.R. Rep. No. 201, 97th Cong., 1st Sess. 203 (1981); Senate Finance Committee Report, Economic Recovery Tax Act of 1981, S. Rep. No. 144, 97th Cong., 1st Sess. 153, reprinted in 1981 U.S. Code Cong. & Ad. News 105, 252.

[6]Id.

[7]For a discussion of current law, see section 43.2.

[8]General Explanation of ERTA, supra note 5, at 292; H.R. Rep. No. 201, supra note 5, at 203; S. Rep. No. 144, supra note 5, at 153.

[9]Id.

[10]See id. Under pre-ERTA law, closing a short position by delivering the property held by the taxpayer (long position) was not a short sale and would generate long-term capital gain if the property had been held for more than one year, the long-term capital gain holding period then in effect for the period immediately prior to ERTA. I.R.C. § 1233(e) (Supp. IV 1980). See generally Chapter 16.

the purchase with borrowed funds and deducted the interest expense, subject to the investment interest limitations.[11] Assuming the commodity was a capital asset in the hands of the taxpayer (investor or trader), the taxpayer attempted to convert ordinary income into long-term capital gain.

Cash and carry transactions were frequently utilized with commodities in which the price differential between the delivery months for the futures contracts was primarily a function of the cost of interest and other carrying charges, and the contract price for the futures contract was "approximately equal to the total payment for the physical commodity plus interest and carrying charges."[12] The commodity also had to be able to be stored and held for the time period necessary to obtain long-term capital gain and, if desired, used to satisfy delivery obligations under the short position.

The underlying property had to be a capital asset in the hands of the taxpayer in order to obtain long-term capital gain.[13] An investor not otherwise required to inventory property would deduct interest and carrying charges under I.R.C. § 212(2) as ordinary and necessary expenses for the management, conservation, or maintenance of property held for the production of income.[14] Traders who are not required to inventory property would deduct interest and carrying charges under I.R.C. § 162 (a) as trade or business expenses.[15] In *Higgins v. U.S.*,[16] the Court of Claims allowed a taxpayer who was neither a commodities trader nor dealer to deduct storage and insurance expenses. The court found that storage and insurance expenses were properly classified as ordinary and necessary rather than capital items, and were not part of either the purchase or sale of the commodity.[17] Rather, such expenses were incurred after the time the purchase was completed and prior to the time the sales transaction began.[18]

---

[11]I.R.C. § 163(d) (Supp. IV 1980); *see* section 7.2(e); section 8.2(e).

[12]General Explanation of ERTA, *supra* note 5, at 292; H.R. REP. NO. 201, *supra* note 5, at 203; S. REP. NO. 144, *supra* note 5, at 153.

[13]*See generally* Part Three.

[14]*See* section 7.1.

[15]*See* section 8.1.

[16]75 F. Supp. 252 (Ct. Cl. 1948).

[17]*Id.* at 255.

[18]*Id.*

Example 43-1

Assume that in 1979, prior to ERTA's enactment, a taxpayer owns 100,000 ounces of gold for which he paid $350 per ounce and sells 100 short gold futures contracts (the amount of gold underlying each futures contract is 100 ounces per contract) for $375 per ounce, thereby agreeing to sell all of his gold at the futures contract price in the future. The short position calls for delivery at a date in excess of the long-term capital gain holding period. The taxpayer locks in a "profitable" sales price for his gold, and his position is essentially riskless (he owns the physical gold and holds a short gold futures contract position). Historically, the difference between the gold's purchase price and the sales price of the futures contract position was a function of carrying the gold until the delivery date. The taxpayer has established a cash and carry straddle. When the gold was held for the long-term holding period, the gold could be delivered to satisfy the taxpayer's obligation under the short position, thereby obtaining long-term capital gain in 1980. On the other hand, if the price of gold increased, the taxpayer could sell it in the cash market for long-term capital gain, while closing the short futures contract position at a short-term capital loss.[19] In 1979 and 1980, investment income was taxed at rates of up to 70 percent. With the requisite profit motive, a taxpayer could attempt to defer investment income from 1979 to 1980 and convert it into long-term capital gain taxable at maximum rates of up to 28 percent.[20] For a discussion of investment interest limitations, see section 7.2(e).

Example 43-2

In June of 1979 a taxpayer established a long position to acquire silver for delivery in October of 1979 and a short position to sell silver for delivery in July of 1980. If the taxpayer took delivery of the silver under his long position in October 1979 and continued to hold the short position, he had established a full carry straddle. Holding the property for a full year from the date the long futures position was acquired resulted in long-term capital gain. The holding period for the long futures contract position was tacked onto the holding period of the prop-

---

[19]*See* section 4.2(a); section 4.3(d).

[20]*See* General Explanation of ERTA, *supra* note 5, at 292-93; H.R. Rep. No. 201, *supra* note 5, at 203-04; S. Rep. No. 144, *supra* note 5, at 153-54.

erty acquired under it.[21] Full carry straddles generated less carrying charges than other cash and carry transactions. The tacked holding period for the long futures contract position allowed the taxpayer to add the period that the futures contract position was held to his holding period for the underlying property. The actual property did not need to be "carried" for a full year.

To provide the hoped for tax benefits under pre-ERTA law, taxpayers (who claimed capital gain treatment on the underlying property) had to be careful not to execute sufficient transactions so as to be required to maintain an inventory for tax purposes. Inventories are necessary at the beginning and end of each taxable year to clearly reflect income in those situations where the production, purchase, or sale of property is an income-producing factor.[22] If a taxpayer takes delivery of property underlying futures contracts and sells the property on a regular basis, he might be required to inventory the underlying property, which might include interest and other carrying charges.[23] The IRS takes the position that the need for inventories is not confined to a taxpayer who technically qualifies either as a dealer or manufacturer, and the purchase or sale of commodities can be an income-producing factor for taxpayers engaged in cash and carry transactions.[24]

An economic consideration for cash and carry transactions where the taxpayer holds the underlying property (long position) is the possibility that the long position increases in value, necessitating a margin call on the short futures contract position (the short position declines in value as the long position increases in value). Although documents of title or warehouse receipts for the underlying property probably can be used instead of cash for initial margin deposits, additional maintenance and mark-to-market payments must be made in cash.[25]

The first court cases, decided in 1984, directly addressing cash and carry transactions under pre-ERTA law were found to be without profit

----

[21]I.R.C. § 1223(8). A tacked on holding period still is available under current law for property acquired pursuant to a futures contract that is not subject to section 1256 treatment. *See* section 15.3(b).

[22]Treas. Reg. § 1.471-1 (1958).

[23]*See* Rev. Rul. 74-226, 1974-1 C.B. 119.

[24]*Id.*

[25]*See* section 4.4(b).

motive. In *Julien v. Comm'r*[26] and *Hirai v. Comm'r*,[27] the Tax Court denied interest deductions because the taxpayers did not prove that the transactions actually took place, the taxpayers had no profit motive, and they did not establish an economic purpose for the transactions. These cases should not control in situations where taxpayers can show that actual transactions were entered into for economic purposes to obtain profit. In both *Julien* and *Hirai*, the taxpayers entered into cash and carry silver transactions marketed by a London brokerage firm as a way to convert ordinary income into long-term capital gain; the taxpayers acquired silver and entered into forward contracts to sell the silver in the future. The promotional materials included in the sales package provided by the broker discussed only contemplated tax results and did not refer to any profit potential. "Loans" to finance the purchase of the silver were obtained by a London finance company that would be repaid only out of the proceeds of the sale of silver.[28] The loans were without recourse against the taxpayers.[29]

In denying all of the interest deductions, the court discussed those circumstances in which interest on pre-ERTA cash and carry transactions is deductible. As a starting point, taxpayers defending pre-ERTA transactions must prove the transactions were bona fide. It also appears that transactions entered into in the domestic commodity markets might be more supportable than offshore transactions of the type addressed in *Julien* and *Hirai*. Domestic transactions may be less suspicious, and the taxpayers may be better able to provide third party evidence that the transactions actually took place.[30] In *Julien* the Tax Court stated "that the paucity of proven facts from overseas" fully justifies IRS skepticism "that an investment prospectus, cancelled checks, and confirmation statements issued in connection with an investment in futures contracts with a foreign investment firm are insufficient to substantiate the existence of transactions entitling the taxpayer to a loss deduction.[31]

The sole issue before the court in *Hirai* was the deductibility of interest expenses to finance silver while holding an offsetting short position to deliver silver in the future. The Tax Court, in a memorandum decision, analyzed I.R.C. § 163, which provides a deduction for "interest

---

[26]82 T.C. 492 (1984).

[27]48 T.C.M. (CCH) 1134 (1984).

[28]*Julien*, 82 T.C. (CCH) at 497; *Hirai*, 48 T.C.M. (CCH) at 1138.

[29]*Julien*, 82 T.C. (CCH) at 507; *Hirai*, 48 T.C.M. (CCH) at 1142.

[30]*But see* Brown v. Comm'r, 85 T.C.—, No. 57, Tax Ct. Rep. Dec. (P-H) ¶85.57 (Dec. 18, 1985) (where a U.S. government securities market was held to be a sham).

[31]*Julien*, 82 T.C. at 501-02; *see* Rev. Rul. 80-324, 1980-2 C.B. 340.

paid or accrued within the taxable year on indebtedness."[32] For purposes of I.R.C. § 163, the term "interest" denotes "that which is paid for the use of borrowed funds or compensation for the use or forbearance of money."[33] The "indebtedness" on which such a payment is made must be an "existing, unconditional, and legally enforcible [sic] obligation."[34] In determining whether a payment constitutes interest on indebtedness, economic realities govern over the form in which a transaction is cast.[35] The taxpayer must prove that the cash and carry transactions served some purpose beyond generating an interest deduction.[36]

In light of the *Julien* and *Hirai* cases, taxpayers seeking to support the deductibility of interest on pre-ERTA cash and carry transactions would need to demonstrate the following: (1) the transactions were not prearranged at the outset so that there was no risk to the taxpayer and the broker;[37] (2) the commodity was actually purchased and the offsetting short sales position established;[38] (3) the taxpayer had the potential for making money as a result of various market forces and some risk of losing money;[39] (4) there was some economic purpose (such as the procurement of a profit) to support the acquisition of the commodity and to support the interest deduction;[40] and (5) the interest payments actually were made.[41] Although *Hirai* was decided after the DRA was enacted, it did not mention whether Section 108[42] might apply to limit the IRS's positions to the profit motive test. It is possible that the court did not feel it was necessary to address this issue because it concluded that no transactions took place.[43]

---

[32]*Hirai*, 48 T.C.M. (CCH) at 1141.

[33]*Id.* (citing Old Colony R. Co. v. Comm'r, 284 U.S. 552, 560 (1932) and Deputy v. Du Pont, 308 U.S. 488, 498 (1940)).

[34]*Id.* (citing Kovtun v. Comm'r, 54 T.C. 331, 338 (1970), *aff'd per curiam*, 448 F.2d 1268 (9th Cir. 1971), *cert. denied*, 405 U.S. 1016 (1972); Titcher v. Comm'r, 57 T.C. 315, 322 (1971)).

[35]*See* Knetsch v. U.S., 364 U.S. 361, 365-66 (1960); Goldstein v. Comm'r, 364 F.2d 734, 740 (2d Cir. 1966).

[36]*See Hirai*, 48 T.C.M. (CCH) at 1142; Welch v. Helvering, 290 U.S. 111, 115 (1933).

[37]*See Julien*, 82 T.C. at 505-06.

[38]*See id.* at 506.

[39]*Id.* at 508.

[40]*Hirai*, 48 T.C.M. (CCH) at 1143.

[41]*Id.* at 1143-44.

[42]DRA, Pub. L. 98-369, § 108, 98 Stat. 494, 630-31 (1984).

[43]*See* section 35.2(c).

§ 43.2   CAPITALIZATION REQUIREMENTS

Congress believed that the use of cash and carry straddle transactions executed with deductible interest and carrying charges was "a serious tax-avoidance problem threatening substantial revenue losses."[44] To discourage these transactions, Congress enacted I.R.C. § 263(g) as part of ERTA, which requires the capitalization of "certain otherwise deductible expenditures for personal property if the property is held as part or all of an offsetting position belonging to a straddle."[45]

Cash and carry transactions continue to be established irrespective of potential tax detriments to seek a profit. In fact, the ERTA requirement to capitalize interest and carrying charges has not stopped cash and carry and full carry transactions from being executed. These transactions continue to be used as a form of arbitrage by market participants and not by taxpayers simply seeking tax deductions. An example of a typical cash and carry transaction follows.

Example   43-3

Assume that on September 15th cash soybeans are trading at $6.00 per bushel. In addition, interest rates are at 12 percent. Other carrying charges total $.05 per bushel per month. November futures are trading at $6.22 per bushel. The cost of borrowing $6.00 per bushel for two months is approximately $.12 per bushel. Therefore, the total cost to buy cash soybeans and carry them to delivery under the futures contract in November is $6.22 ($6.00 + $.12 + $.10 = $6.22). This provides an effective ceiling on November soybean futures prices, because if they traded at a price higher than $6.22 it would be profitable to buy cash soybeans and deliver them pursuant to the November futures contract. The market participants would continue to do this arbitrage trade until the guaranteed profit was gone.[46]

The November futures market, trading at $6.22, is said to be at full carry. Traders buy the cash position and sell the futures position at full carry, because they are locking in, under the worst case, a break even transaction. If nothing happens, or if the futures price increases more than the cash position, they deliver their soybeans pursuant to the No-

---

[44]General Explanation of ERTA, *supra* note 5, at 292; H.R. REP. No. 201, *supra* note 5, at 203; S. REP. No. 144, *supra* note 5, at 153.

[45]General Explanation of ERTA, *supra* note 5, at 293; H.R. REP. No. 201, *supra* note 5, at 204; S. REP. No. 144, *supra* note 5, at 154.

[46]*See generally* section 6.7.

vember futures contract. If, on the other hand, futures happen to decline or increase less than the cash market, they unwind the trade (sell the cash soybeans and buy back the November futures) at a profit.

(a) IN GENERAL

In general, a taxpayer cannot deduct "interest and carrying charges" allocable to personal property that is part of a straddle.[47] Interest and carrying charges include the amount of interest incurred or continued to purchase or carry personal property; all amounts paid or incurred to store, insure, or transport personal property; and any amounts paid or incurred in connection with personal property used in a short sale.[48] The types of nondeductible expenses have increased since ERTA. First, the definition of interest and carrying charges was expanded to include, for property acquired and positions established after September 22, 1982, all charges for the temporary use of a commodity in a short sale.[49] When it became clear that this definition was not broad enough, "interest" was redefined by the DRA to include "any amount paid or incurred in connection with personal property used in a short sale."[50] Interest and carrying charges are capitalized and added to the basis of the property, thereby reducing the gain or increasing the loss upon its disposition. Without a rule requiring capitalization of interest and carrying charges, a taxpayer could otherwise generate deductions against ordinary income. And, assuming the taxpayer is not a dealer in the property, the taxpayer could obtain long-term capital gain on the sale of the property.[51]

If a taxpayer holds a short position, this position could be used to require capitalization of interest and carrying charges on any offsetting long position with which it could be paired, regardless of whether the long position is the position with which the short contract is paired for purposes of terminating the holding period under the modified short sales rule.[52] In other words, it is possible for a short position to terminate the holding period of another short position while also being paired

---

[47]I.R.C. § 263(g)(1). The capitalization requirement does not apply to a straddle consisting solely of section 1256 positions. I.R.C. § 1256(a)(4).

[48]I.R.C. § 263(g)(2); *see generally* Chapter 16.

[49]TCA '82, Pub. L. 97-448, § 105(b), 96 Stat. 2365, 2385 (1982).

[50]DRA, *supra* note 42, § 102(e)(7).

[51]*See* section 43.1.

[52]*See* section 42.4.

with a long position to require capitalization of interest and carrying charges.

Example   43-4

Assume that in June of 1985 a taxpayer enters into a short futures contract position to deliver silver in February of 1986 at $10 per ounce and simultaneously purchases silver ingots (long position) for $9 per ounce. The taxpayer incurs interest and carrying charges of $1 per ounce to hold the silver ingots from June through December 31, 1985 and an additional $.50 per ounce from January through February 1986. Assume further that the market price of the taxpayer's positions does not change during 1985, so under section 1256 there is no mark-to-market gain or loss on the short futures contract position held at the end of December 1985. The taxpayer must capitalize the entire $1 per ounce interest and carrying charges in 1985, as well as the $.50 per ounce charge incurred in 1986. The $1.50 per ounce of interest and carrying charges is added to the basis of the silver ingots, irrespective of whether the silver is used to satisfy the short futures contract position or is sold in the cash market.

Example   43-5

In February of 1986, a taxpayer buys gold bullion at $400 per ounce and enters into a short gold futures contract position to deliver gold 16 months later for $475 per ounce. The taxpayer holds a mixed straddle, but a mixed straddle identification under section 1256(d) is not made and the taxpayer does not have a mixed straddle account for gold. To purchase and carry the gold bullion, the taxpayer incurs expenses of $30.

Assume further that at the end of 1986 the price of gold increases so that there is a $30 unrealized gain on the gold bullion and a $40 loss on the futures contract position. The $40 loss (60 percent long-term capital loss and 40 percent short-term capital loss under section 1256) is deferred under the loss deferral rule.[53] The $30 paid to purchase and carry the gold bullion is added to its basis, thereby eliminating the $30 unrealized gain on the gold bullion position.[54]

[53]I.R.C. § 1092(a)(1).
[54]I.R.C. § 263(g)(1).

(b) STRADDLE INCOME

Interest and carrying charges that are capitalized and added to the basis of property are reduced to the extent that a straddle position generates certain income from interest, discount income, and dividends.[55] Amounts which must be capitalized are reduced by the sum of the following: (1) interest income (including OID)[56] includable in gross income earned on the property;[57] (2) any amounts of acquisition discount or market discount with respect to such property;[58] and (3) the excess of any dividends includible in gross income with respect to such property minus, for corporate stockholders, the amount of the intercorporate dividends received deduction.[59] Therefore, interest and carrying charges are currently deductible only to the extent that a straddle position generates interest and dividend income of the three types previously outlined. The DRA added items (2) and (3)[60] for property acquired and positions established after July 18, 1984 in tax years ending after that date.[61]

A lender of securities used in a short sale receives compensation from the borrower to replace interest, dividends, and other compensating amounts on loaned property.[62] The lender can also incur interest and other carrying costs for the loaned securities. Current law does not provide for the inclusion of compensating payments to the lender of securities in those taxable amounts that reduce interest and other costs required to be capitalized under I.R.C. § 263(g).[63]

---

[55]I.R.C. § 263(g)(2)(B).

[56]I.R.C. §§ 1271–1275; *see generally* Chapter 23; *see also* section 27.2.

[57]I.R.C. § 263(g)(2)(B)(i).

[58]I.R.C. § 263(g)(2)(B)(ii); *see* section 27.2; section 27.3.

[59]I.R.C. § 263(g)(2)(B)(iii); *see* section 22.9.

[60]DRA, *supra* note 42, § 102(e)(7).

[61]*Id.* § 102(f)(1).

[62]*See generally* Chapter 24.

[63]The Technical Corrections Act of 1985 (H.R. 1800) as introduced by the House Ways and Means Committee on March 28, 1985 would include such compensating payments in those amounts that reduce interest and other carrying charges. STAFF OF THE JOINT COMMITTEE ON TAXATION, 99TH CONG., 1ST SESS., DESCRIPTION OF THE PROVISIONS OF THE TECHNICAL CORRECTIONS ACT OF 1985 25 (Joint Comm. Print 1985).

Example 43-6

To speculate on interest rate movements, a taxpayer purchases a call option (long position), sells stock short (short position), and sells a put option (short position), all in XYZ Corporation. The taxpayer incurs interest expense on the call position and income from the short stock position (consisting of the short stock rebate received, less any payments made in lieu of dividends). The income received from the short stock position is not interest as currently defined in I.R.C. § 263(g)(2) and, therefore, cannot reduce the amount of interest and carrying charges that otherwise must be capitalized.[64]

(c) SHORT SALES

For positions established after September 22, 1982, charges for the temporary use of personal property in a short sale must be capitalized.[65] The capitalization requirement was extended in 1982, once Congress determined that a taxpayer could, for example, sell a borrowed government security short and buy another similar security to obtain long-term capital gain.[66] A taxpayer would pay the owner of a borrowed security (e.g., a Treasury bond) a charge equal to interest due on the bond, but since this charge was not "interest," it was not subject to I.R.C. § 263(g) and was deducted from ordinary income.[67] I.R.C. § 263(g), therefore, was modified to require capitalization of such interest equivalent charges.[68]

The DRA further amended I.R.C. § 263(g) to make it clear that "interest" that must be capitalized "includes any amount paid or incurred in connection with personal property used in a short sale."[69] This applies after July 18, 1984 to any amount paid or incurred in a short sale.[70]

One final point is that I.R.C. § 263(g) applies to short sales only after

----

[64]The result of this example would be different if the Technical Corrections Act of 1985 is enacted in the form proposed by H.R. 1800. *See* H.R. 1800, 99th Cong., 1st Sess. § 108(b) (1985).

[65]TCA '82, *supra* note 49, § 105(b); SENATE FINANCE COMMITTEE REPORT, TECHNICAL CORRECTIONS ACT OF 1982, S. REP. NO. 592, 97th Cong., 2d Sess. 28, *reprinted in* 1982 U.S. CODE CONG. & AD. NEWS 4149, 4174.

[66]*Tax Report*, Wall St. J., Oct. 13, 1982, at 1, col. 5.

[67]*Id.*

[68]TCA '82, *supra* note 49, § 105(b).

[69]I.R.C. § 263(g)(2).

[70]DRA, *supra* note 42, § 102(f)(1).

the application of I.R.C. § 263(h), which denies certain deductions for certain payments incurred in connection with short sales.[71]

(d) MIXED STRADDLE ACCOUNTS

If individual straddles are identified by a taxpayer, it is possible to identify the expenses incurred in holding offsetting positions and the amount of income received from the straddle. On its face, I.R.C. § 263(g) apparently assumes that all positions of the straddle can be identified and that interest income and interest expense with respect to such positions can be identified. However, this assumption is not correct in many cases. If a taxpayer establishes a mixed straddle account for mixed straddle positions, individual straddles are not identified.[72] In providing the election for a mixed straddle account, Congress recognized that identifying individual straddle transactions is difficult (and perhaps impossible) for certain taxpayers.[73] If a taxpayer maintains a mixed straddle account, the capitalization requirement is applied to the account rather than to individual straddles held, but not otherwise identified, within the account.[74]

The temporary Treasury regulations originally issued on January 18, 1985 (and as subsequently amended) provide some guidance on whether interest expense attributable to the account should be netted against all gains in the account or only netted against that portion of the gain generated from debt financed assets.[75] The temporary Treasury regulations apply I.R.C. § 263(g) to a mixed straddle account as if the account contains only one straddle.[76] The gross expenses and income of the mixed straddle account are netted on an annual basis, and any excess expense from the mixed straddle account is capitalized to prevent excess expense from reducing ordinary income unrelated to the account positions.[77] The temporary Treasury regulations further provide that no deduction is allowed for interest and carrying charges that are "properly allocable" to a mixed straddle account.[78] Interest and carrying charges

---

[71]I.R.C. § 263(g)(4)(A); *see* section 43.2(e); section 16.6(e).

[72]I.R.C. § 1092(b)(2)(A)(i); *see* section 45.4.

[73]HOUSE CONFERENCE REPORT, DEFICIT REDUCTION ACT OF 1984, H.R. REP. NO. 861, 98th Cong., 2d Sess. 913 (1984).

[74]Temp. Treas. Reg. § 1.1092(b)-4T(c)(3) (1985).

[75]Temp. Treas. Reg. § 1.1092(b)-4T(c)(3)(i), T.D. 8008, 1985-9 I.R.B. 10, *amended by* T.D. 8058, 1985-46 I.R.B. 30; *see* section 45.4(d).

[76]*See* Temp. Treas. Reg. § 1.1092(b)-4T(c)(3) (1985).

[77]*Id.*

[78]*Id.*

properly allocable to a mixed straddle account are defined as the excess of (1) the sum of (a) interest (including short sale expenses) on debt incurred to purchase or carry any position in the account, and (b) all amounts paid or incurred to insure, store, transport, etc., personal property with respect to a position in the account; *over* (2) the sum of (a) interest includible in gross income with respect to all positions in the account, (b) ordinary income from the holding, retirement, or sale of debt securities in the account, and (c) dividends received with respect to positions in the account, net of certain dividend deductions.[79] Any nondeductible interest and carrying charges are capitalized by treating such charges as an adjustment to the annual mixed straddle account net gain or loss and are allocated on a pro rata basis between net short-term and long-term capital gain or loss.[80]

Example   43-7

Assume that a taxpayer has a mixed straddle account for ABC stock and options. During the taxable year he incurs $40 of net interest expense properly allocable to positions in the ABC mixed straddle account. Under these circumstances, the $40 of net interest expense is not deductible but is allocated to the annual net gain or loss of the ABC mixed straddle account. The $40 of interest expense reduces proportionately the long-term and short-term elements of the ABC capital gain or increases proportionately the long-term and short-term elements of the ABC capital loss.

(e)   APPLICATION AFTER CERTAIN PROVISIONS

Other Code provisions take priority over application of the capitalization requirement established in I.R.C. § 263(g).[81] In the case of any short sale, I.R.C. § 263(g) applies after application of I.R.C. § 263(h), which denies deductions for payments made in lieu of dividends on short sales of stock.[82] For securities subject either to the market discount rules under I.R.C. § 1277 for the deferral of net direct interest on indebtedness with respect to market discount bonds or the rules under I.R.C. § 1282 with respect to deferral of interest on indebtedness with respect to short-

---

[79]*Id.*

[80]*Id.*

[81]I.R.C. § 263(g)(4).

[82]I.R.C. § 263(g)(4)(A); *see* section 16.6(e).

term obligations, the provisions of I.R.C. § 263(g) apply after application of these other provisions.[83]

(f) HEDGING TRANSACTIONS

When Congress enacted ERTA it recognized that certain legitimate business transactions that result only in ordinary income or loss lacked sufficient tax avoidance potential to be covered by I.R.C. § 263(g).[84] Hedging transactions that qualify for the statutory hedging exemption are exempt from the capitalization requirements.[85] This means that interest and carrying charges incurred to purchase and carry positions qualifying for the statutory hedging exemption can be deducted currently and need not be added to the basis of the property. If the hedging exemption is not properly elected, however, capitalization is required in otherwise exempt ordinary income dealer transactions.[86]

Example   43-8

The taxpayer, a dealer in securities, is a general partnership. It borrows money and incurs expenses to finance its inventory and ordinary income trading accounts. The taxpayer qualifies as a hedger for those positions entered into to hedge its inventory and ordinary income trading account positions. All transactions qualify as hedges. Interest and other carrying charges incurred by the taxpayer are deductible.[87]

Example   43-9

A farmer borrows money and incurs other expenses to finance, store, and transport his corn and wheat crops. The farmer does not hedge his corn crop and does not enter into any short positions (e.g., options, futures, or forward contracts) for the sale of corn. The farmer holds no offsetting positions with respect to his corn. Under these circumstances, the farmer can currently deduct his interest and carrying charges incurred on his corn crop. The expenses are not attributable to a position

---

[83]I.R.C. § 263(g)(4)(B); *see* section 27.2(d); section 27.3.

[84]General Explanation of ERTA, *supra* note 5, at 293; H.R. REP. No. 201, *supra* note 5, at 204; S. REP. No. 144, *supra* note 5, at 154.

[85]I.R.C. § 263(g)(3); *see generally* Chapter 21.

[86]*See* section 21.8.

[87]*See* General Explanation of ERTA, *supra* note 5, at 293; H.R. REP. No. 201, *supra* note 5, at 204; S. REP. No. 144, *supra* note 5, at 154.

that is part of a straddle as is required for capitalization under I.R.C. § 263(g).

Assume, on the other hand, that with respect to the wheat crop the farmer enters into short futures contracts to sell his wheat crop for delivery after it is harvested. The farmer holds a straddle. As long as the transactions are properly identified as hedge transactions, the farmer can currently deduct his costs.[88] If the transactions do not meet the statutory hedging exemption, however, capitalization is required.

---

[88] *See* I.R.C. § 263(g)(3).

Forty-four

Exceptions to Application of the Straddle Rules

Certain transactions are exempt from the Straddle Rules—identified straddles, hedging transactions, qualified covered calls, certain stock positions, and straddles made up exclusively of section 1256 contracts. In addition, certain exchange-traded stock options established prior to July 18, 1984 are exempt from the Straddle Rules. This section discusses transactions exempt from the Straddle Rules.

§ 44.1 IDENTIFIED STRADDLES

(a) REQUIREMENTS

Identified straddles are exempt from the Straddle Rules, and are subject to special rules[1] if the positions qualify for and are properly designated as identified straddles. To qualify as an identified straddle, offsetting positions must meet four conditions. First, the straddle must be clearly identified as an identified straddle on the taxpayer's records before the close of the day on which the straddle is acquired (or an earlier time if required by Treasury regulations).[2] Second, all of the original positions

---

[1]I.R.C. § 1092(a)(2)(A).
[2]I.R.C. § 1092(a)(2)(B)(i).

in the straddle must be acquired on the same day.[3] Third, either (1) all of the positions in the straddle must be disposed of on the same day during the taxable year, or (2) none of the positions are disposed of as of the close of the taxable year.[4] Fourth, the straddle must not be part of a larger straddle (e.g., a butterfly, box, conversion, or reverse conversion).[5]

Identified straddles must be clearly identified on the taxpayer's records as an identified straddle before the close of the day on which the straddle is acquired or at an earlier time if required by Treasury regulations. To date, such regulations have not been issued and guidance is needed as to how a taxpayer must comply with this identification requirement. Of course, where the taxpayer's own records are used to designate identified straddles, the problem of verification can arise on audit. Presumably, the taxpayer would need to demonstrate that the records were kept in a manner contemplated by I.R.C. § 1092(a)(2)(B)(i).

The advantage to making an identified straddle designation is that a taxpayer can segregate his identified straddle transactions from his non-straddle transactions. Identified straddle positions are not treated as offsetting any positions that are not identified as part of the identified straddle.[6] Therefore, positions that are part of an identified straddle will not (1) affect the holding periods, by application of the modified short sales rule, of other positions not part of the identified straddle; (2) defer the recognition of losses by application of the modified wash sales rule; or (3) cause either the deferral of losses or the capitalization of interest and carrying charges as to positions that are not part of the identified straddle. Any loss sustained with respect to an identified straddle position, however, is treated as sustained not earlier than the day on which all of the positions making up the identified straddle are disposed of.[7]

Example 44-1

Assume a taxpayer acquires gold bullion (long position), enters into a forward contract to sell gold (short position) on the same day, and properly designates the straddle as an identified straddle. Assume further that the taxpayer subsequently acquires additional gold positions that could be viewed as offsetting and at year-end he continues to hold the identified straddle. Because the taxpayer properly identified the

[3] I.R.C. § 1092(a)(2)(B)(ii).
[4] I.R.C. §§ 1092(a)(2)(B)(ii)(I), (II).
[5] I.R.C. § 1092(a)(2)(B)(iii).
[6] I.R.C. § 1092(c)(2)(C).
[7] I.R.C. § 1092(a)(2)(A)(ii).

original positions as an identified straddle and both positions remained open at year-end, those positions do not offset any of the other gold positions held by the taxpayer.

(b) SUBSEQUENT TRANSACTIONS

Because all of the positions in an identified straddle must be acquired on the same day, a straddle ceases to be an identified straddle if a successor or substitute position is acquired to replace an original straddle position. In addition, it appears that no loss can be claimed on any positions that were once part of an identified straddle until all of the remaining positions are disposed of. This results even if a loss is disallowed because of the application of the modified wash sales rule.[8] If a taxpayer disposes of a position at a loss and the loss is disallowed under the modified wash sales rule (because the original position is replaced), other losses sustained on positions not part of the identified straddle may be disallowed because of unrealized gain on positions making up the identified straddle.[9]

An identified straddle no longer qualifies as an identified straddle in a subsequent tax year if, after having been kept open through the end of the tax year in which it was created, one of the straddle positions is closed out in the subsequent tax year before the other identified straddle positions are also closed out.[10] Neither the Code nor the legislative history of ERTA indicate directly whether the identified straddle designation applies in such a situation to the first year or not. One possible reading is that since none of the positions were disposed of as of the close of the first taxable year, the straddle qualifies as an identified straddle in the first tax year but not in the second year.

Finally, although a taxpayer generally must disclose unrecognized gains on his tax return, identified straddles need not be disclosed.[11] In addition, if a taxpayer initially designates offsetting positions as an identified straddle in the first year, and the straddle no longer qualifies in a subsequent year, the taxpayer must disclose any unrecognized gains on the open positions.[12]

---

[8]See generally Chapter 42.

[9]STAFF OF THE JOINT COMMITTEE ON TAXATION, 97TH CONG., 1ST SESS., GENERAL EXPLANATION OF THE ECONOMIC RECOVERY TAX ACT OF 1981 284 (Joint Comm. Print 1981) [hereinafter referred to as "General Explanation of ERTA"].

[10]Id.

[11]See id. at 286; see generally Chapter 40; section 41.1.

[12]See General Explanation of ERTA, supra note 9, at 286.

§ 44.2   HEDGING TRANSACTIONS

Hedging transactions that qualify for the statutory hedging exemption are exempt from the Straddle Rules and from section 1256 treatment. Hence, qualified hedging transactions are exempt from the loss deferral rule,[13] modified wash sales rule,[14] modified short sales rule,[15] requirement to capitalize interest and carrying charges,[16] the Mark-to-Market Rule,[17] and the 60/40 Rule.[18] For a detailed discussion of the hedging exemption, see generally Chapter 21. Although a taxpayer generally must disclose unrecognized gains on his tax returns, hedging transactions need not be disclosed.[19]

If a transaction does not comply with the specific requirements of I.R.C. § 1256(e)(2)—but is subject to ordinary treatment under the Corn Products[20] doctrine—the transaction nevertheless generates ordinary income or loss while remaining subject to the Straddle Rules and section 1256 treatment. In other words, the gains and losses from a Corn Products hedge transaction are always ordinary, rather than capital.

§ 44.3   QUALIFIED COVERED CALLS

Taxpayers frequently write (sell) covered call options to enhance the return on their investment in the stocks and securities underlying the options. A covered call has been described as a call option "that is written with respect to stock that is held by the taxpayer (or acquired by the taxpayer in connection with the granting of the option)."[21] In addition, writing (selling) a covered call option "does not substantially reduce a taxpayer's risk of loss with respect to holding the underlying long stock position unless the option is deep-in-the-money."[22]

---

[13]*See* section 37.1.

[14]*See* section 42.3.

[15]*See* section 42.4.

[16]*See* section 43.2.

[17]*See* section 33.1.

[18]*See* section 33.2.

[19]*See generally* Chapter 40; section 41.1.

[20]350 U.S. 46 (1955).

[21]REPORT OF THE COMMITTEE ON WAYS AND MEANS, DEFICIT REDUCTION ACT OF 1984, H.R. REP. NO. 432, Pt. II, 98 Cong., 2d Sess. 1268, *reprinted in* 1984 U.S. CODE CONG. & AD. NEWS 697, 930.

[22]*Id.* at 1268.

(a) SCOPE OF EXEMPTION

Taxpayers entering into qualified covered call transactions established after December 31, 1983 are not required to postpone the deduction of losses on call option positions even if there is unrecognized gain in the underlying corporate stock.[23] The qualified covered call exemption is limited to the disposition of qualified covered call options written on corporate stock and is not available for options on other securities, stock indexes, or foreign currencies.[24] This means that if all of the positions making up a straddle consist of qualified covered call options and underlying corporate stock, and the straddle is not part of a larger straddle (e.g., a conversion or reverse conversion transaction, a butterfly, or box), the positions are not subject to the Straddle Rules.[25]

(b) DEFINITION

A taxpayer holds a qualified covered call option if five conditions are met at the time the option is written. First, the option has more than 30 days before its expiration.[26] Second, it is traded on a national securities exchange.[27] Third, it is not deep-in-the-money.[28] Fourth, it is not granted by an options dealer in the course of his dealer activity.[29] And fifth, gain or loss with respect to the option is capital gain or loss.[30]

Whether an option is deep-in-the-money is determined by reference to the strike price of the option and, generally, the closing stock price on the last day the stock was traded before the option was written. A deep-in-the-money option is defined as an option having a strike price lower than the lowest qualified bench mark,[31] which generally means the highest available strike price below the applicable stock price.[32] Applicable stock price is defined as either (1) the closing price of the stock on the most recent day the stock was traded before the option was sold or (2) the opening price of the stock on the day on which the option

---

[23]I.R.C. § 1092(c)(4)(A).
[24]I.R.C. § 1092(c)(4)(B).
[25]I.R.C. § 1092(c)(4)(A).
[26]I.R.C. § 1092(c)(4)(B)(ii).
[27]I.R.C. § 1092(c)(4)(B)(i).
[28]I.R.C. § 1092(c)(4)(B)(iii).
[29]I.R.C. § 1092(c)(4)(B)(iv).
[30]I.R.C. § 1092(c)(4)(B)(v).
[31]I.R.C. § 1092(c)(4)(C).
[32]I.R.C. § 1092(c)(4)(D)(i).

was granted if this price exceeds the price under clause (1) by 110 percent.[33] Under current securities exchange rules, the lowest qualified bench mark for stock trading below $25 is $2.50 in-the-money, between $25 and $200 is $5 in-the-money, and for stock trading above $200 is $10 in-the-money.[34]

Example 44-2

Assume a stock is trading at $48 per share and has call options over-laying it that are trading with strike prices of $30, $35, $40, $45, $50, and $55. Because the qualified covered call exemption does not apply if the option's strike price is more than one bench mark below the stock's closing price, options with a strike price of $30, $35, and $40 are deep-in-the-money and, hence, are not eligible for the exemption. Options with a strike price of $45, $50, and $55 are not deep-in-the-money and are eligible for the exemption.

(c) LIMITATIONS ON EXEMPTION

There are three exceptions to the general rule for determining the lowest qualified bench mark. First, in the case of an option that is granted more than 90 days before its date of expiration and has a strike price in excess of $50, the lowest qualified bench mark is the second highest available strike price below the applicable stock price.[35] Second, if the applicable stock price is $25 or less and the highest available strike price below the stock price is less than 85 percent of the stock price, the lowest qualified bench mark is 85 percent of the stock price.[36] Third, if the applicable stock price is $150 or less and the highest available strike price below the stock price is less than the stock price reduced by $10, the lowest qualified bench mark is equal to the stock price minus $10.[37]

Example 44-3

Assume that a stock trading at $48 per share has call options overlaying it with strike prices of $30, $35, $40, $45, $50, and $55. Assume further that the stock price increases to $53 per share. Options written when

---

[33]I.R.C. § 1092(c)(4)(G).
[34]CBOE Rule 5.5, Interpretation .01 (Apr. 10, 1985).
[35]I.R.C. § 1092(c)(4)(D)(ii).
[36]I.R.C. § 1092(c)(4)(D)(iii).
[37]I.R.C. § 1092(c)(4)(D)(iv).

the stock was trading at $48 more than 90 days before expiration with strike prices of $45, $50, or $55 are not deep-in-the-money.

Other conditions must be met for a qualified covered call to be exempt from the Straddle Rules. First, the loss deferral rule applies to a loss realized on the call option if the underlying stock is sold in a subsequent tax year within 30 days after the call option position is closed out.[38] In determining whether a taxpayer held the stock for 30 days after closing the call option, the rules of I.R.C. § 246(c), which address the holding period of stock for purposes of the intercorporate dividends received deduction, are applied.[39]

Second, a qualified covered call option that was in-the-money when written and was established after June 30, 1984 is subject to the modified short sales rule that (1) suspends, but does not eliminate, the holding period in the underlying stock,[40] and (2) treats any loss on the option position as a long-term loss if the underlying stock had a long-term holding period at the time the loss on the call option was realized.[41] The DRA Conference Report provides that these rules apply in lieu of the modified short sales rule of I.R.C. § 1092(b)(1).[42]

The Treasury has broad authority to issue such regulations necessary or appropriate to carry out the qualified covered call exemption from the Straddle Rules.[43] The regulations can include modifications to the statutory provisions, if appropriate, to take into account changes in the practices of national securities exchanges (e.g., modification of designated strike price intervals) or to prevent the use of option transactions for tax avoidance purposes.[44]

§ 44.4   MARRIED PUT TRANSACTIONS

It is unclear whether the married put exception provided in the short sales rule[45] is available as an exemption from the Straddle Rules.[46]

[38] I.R.C. § 1092(c)(4)(E).

[39] *Id.; see* section 22.9; section 15.7.

[40] I.R.C. § 1092(f)(2).

[41] I.R.C. § 1092(f)(1).

[42] HOUSE CONFERENCE REPORT, DEFICIT REDUCTION ACT OF 1984, H.R. REP. NO. 861, 98th Cong., 2d Sess. 908 (1984). *See generally* Chapter 42.

[43] I.R.C. § 1092(c)(4)(H).

[44] *Id.*

[45] I.R.C. § 1233(c).

[46] *See* section 16.4(d).

Married put transactions were not addressed in the Code or the legislative history in enacting the Straddle Rules. Nevertheless, married put options might be exempt from the Straddle Rules. Nothing in the legislative history of the DRA indicates that Congress intended to repeal the married put exception contained in I.R.C. § 1233(c) when it extended the scope of the Straddle Rules to publicly traded options.

For a put to be deemed "married" to stock for purposes of the short sales rule, the put option must be acquired on the same day as the stock and the stock must be identified on the put holder's records as the stock to be delivered upon exercise of the put. Furthermore, it may be possible that the married put criteria can be met only by delivering the married stock or by allowing the put to expire. If the put expires, the cost of the put is added to the stock's basis. Treasury regulations or clarifying legislation is needed to resolve the issue.[47] The better view at present appears to be to allow the married put exception to continue to exist for put option positions. Accordingly, a married put transaction should be able to provide a taxpayer with some downside protection, upside potential, and the accrual of the holding period for long-term capital gain purposes.

§ 44.5   CERTAIN STOCK POSITIONS

Certain stock positions remain exempt from the Straddle Rules. Prior to enactment of the DRA, stock was explicitly excluded from the definition of personal property, thereby excluding stock entirely from the application of the Straddle Rules. Personal property was defined as "any personal property (other than stock) of a type which is actively traded."[48] This exemption was narrowed significantly by a DRA amendment that brought actively traded stock into the definition of personal property.[49] There are exceptions to this general rule.[50] First, the definition of personal property does not include stock positions unless the stock is part of a straddle where at least one of the offsetting positions is either (1) an option on the same stock (or substantially identical stock or securities), or (2) characterized by Treasury regulations as a position with

[47]Treasury regulations could incorporate the married put exception and confirm that the short sales rule of Temp. Treas. Reg. § 1.1092(b)-2T does not apply to qualified married puts.

[48]I.R.C. § 1092(d)(1), prior to amendment by DRA, Pub. L. 98-369, §101(b)(1), 98 Stat. 494, 618 (1984).

[49]*See* section 36.2(c).

[50]I.R.C. § 1092(d)(3)(B).

respect to property other than stock that is substantially similar or related property.[51] In addition, stock is personal property if it is part of a straddle where the offsetting position is stock in a corporation "formed or availed of" to take positions which offset positions established by any stockholder ("offsetting position stock").[52] In other words, the Straddle Rules apply to straddles where at least one of the positions is a stock position, unless the positions offsetting the stock are other stock positions or the short sale of stock. Hence, a short sale against the box is not subject to the Straddle Rules, although it may be subject to the wash sales rule or the short sales rules.[53]

The Treasury has broad regulatory authority to issue regulations to identify which stock positions are offset by property other than actual stock that is substantially similar or related to the stock.[54] The regulations, when promulgated, will not apply to mixed straddles where all of the positions were established prior to January 1, 1984.[55]

§ 44.6 SHORT-TERM STOCK OPTION POSITIONS ESTABLISHED PRIOR TO JULY 18, 1984

Prior to July 18, 1984, positions in exchange-traded stock options with a maximum exercise period less than the then current holding period to obtain long-term capital gain ("short-term stock options") were exempt from the Straddle Rules. An exemption was available because a short-term stock option was excluded from the definition of a "position."[56] Because all stock options traded on domestic securities exchanges before July 18, 1984 had an exercise period of less than the then applicable long-term capital gain holding period (i.e., more than one year), all such stock options were exempt from the Straddle Rules.

This exemption, originally granted in 1981, was provided for short-term stock options on the belief that the use of straddle transactions to defer taxes prevalent in the commodity markets was not occurring in exchange-traded stock options. The Treasury expressed concern at commodity straddle hearings held in 1981 that the abuses in the commodity

[51]I.R.C. § 1092(d)(3)(B)(i).
[52]I.R.C. § 1092(d)(3)(B)(ii).
[53]*See* section 17.3(f); *see generally* Chapter 16.
[54]I.R.C. § 1092(d)(3)(B)(i)(II).
[55]DRA, *supra* note 48, § 103(c).
[56]I.R.C. § 1092(d)(2)(B) (1982).

markets might be shifted to the stock option markets if exchange-traded stock options were exempt from the legislation.[57] In addition, several legislative proposals, since ERTA was enacted in 1981, would have completely eliminated the exclusion for stock options in I.R.C. § 1092.[58] It was not until enactment of the DRA in 1984 that the short-term stock options exemption from the Straddle Rules was eliminated.

Despite the exemption for short-term stock options entered into prior to July 18, 1984, the pre-DRA use of short-term stock option straddles to defer the payment of tax on capital gains (for investors and traders) or ordinary income (for dealers and hedgers) may be subject to IRS attack. Transactions may be challenged if there was no profit motive and under the rationale of Rev. Rul. 77-185.[59] In addition, it is important to note that for dealers in those stocks underlying short-term stock options, the hedging exemption may be available, under certain circumstances, to exempt their stock option transactions from the Straddle Rules.[60]

§ 44.7   STRADDLES MADE UP EXCLUSIVELY OF SECTION 1256 CONTRACTS

If all positions in a straddle consist of section 1256 contracts, the Straddle Rules do not apply[61] and the positions are subject to section 1256 treatment. In addition, the requirement to capitalize interest and carrying charges is not applied.[62] According to the legislative history of ERTA, Treasury regulations (yet to be promulgated) will define the manner in which such straddle positions in section 1256 contracts are to be matched.[63] This exemption is consistent with the policy behind the Straddle Rules because there is no opportunity to defer income. All offsetting positions comprising a straddle are subject to section 1256 treatment, which means that recognized and unrecognized gains and losses are reported for tax purposes at year-end.

---

[57]*Commodity Tax Straddles: Hearing on S. 626 before the Subcomm. on Taxation and Debt Management and the Subcomm. on Energy and Agricultural Taxation of the Senate Comm. on Finance*, 97th Cong., 1st Sess. 48-66 (1981).

[58]*See e.g.*, S. 2062, 98th Cong., 1st Sess. § 105 (1983).

[59]1977-1 C.B. 48; *see* section 35.2.

[60]*See generally* Chapter 21.

[61]I.R.C. §§ 1092(d)(5)(A), 1256(a)(4).

[62]I.R.C. § 263(g).

[63]Senate Finance Committee Report, Economic Recovery Tax Act of 1981, S. Rep. No. 144, 97th Cong., 1st Sess. 148, *reprinted in* 1981 U.S. Code Cong. & Ad. News 105, 248.

Forty-five

Mixed Straddles

A mixed straddle is composed partially of section 1256 contracts and partially of other positions.[1] Since the enactment of ERTA, the concern with mixed straddles has been the disparity in 60/40 treatment for section 1256 contracts and short-term capital gain or loss for non-section 1256 positions. This disparity provided taxpayers with an incentive to convert short-term capital gain into 60/40 gain by mixed straddles that offered the opportunity to accomplish this conversion. Basically, a mixed straddle (or a series of increasingly larger mixed straddles) could have been used to generate short-term loss in the non-section 1256 property with an offsetting 60/40 gain. The short-term loss could eliminate either unrelated short-term gain (leaving the taxpayer only with 60/40 gain) or the 40 percent short-term gain element (leaving the taxpayer only long-term capital gain). Without a preventive rule, mixed straddles could have been used to convert all short-term capital gain into 60/40 gain and, ultimately, into long-term capital gain.

Example 45-1

Assume there are no rules in place to prevent the conversion of short-term capital gain into 60/40 gain or long-term capital loss into 60/40 loss. A taxpayer with an unrelated short-term gain of $100 for the tax year sells a section 1256 contract and buys the underlying property (which is not a section 1256 position). The taxpayer holds a mixed straddle. If the price of the underlying property falls, producing a $100 loss, the taxpayer could close out both positions—claiming a $100 60/40

[1]I.R.C. § 1256(d)(4)(A).

gain on the section 1256 contract and a short-term loss of $100 on the non-section 1256 position. The short-term capital loss would be deductible against the unrelated short-term capital gain, leaving only a $100 60/40 gain for the year. On the other hand, if the value of the underlying property increased by $100, the taxpayer would incur a $100 short-term gain on the underlying property and a $100 60/40 loss on the section 1256 position. This result would be detrimental to a taxpayer with long-term capital gain for the year; the $100 short-term gain and the $100 60/40 loss would convert $40 of the long-term gain into short-term gain. A short-term gain and a 60/40 loss, however, might not pose a problem for those taxpayers who enter into additional mixed straddles in larger sizes to generate gains on the section 1256 positions, thereby converting short-term capital gain into 60/40 gain. Of course, long-term losses could be converted to 60/40 losses in the same manner.

Although Congress recognized the possibility of conversion using mixed straddles in 1981, the possibility was not precluded by ERTA. Rather, ERTA authorized a mixed straddle election under I.R.C. § 1256(d) that allows taxpayers to forego application of section 1256 treatment for futures contracts and certain foreign currency contracts that are part of a section 1256(d) identified mixed straddle.[2]

It was possible with unidentified mixed straddles to convert short-term gain into 60/40 gain and long-term loss into 60/40 loss. Although some commentators speculated that the modified short sales rule, once promulgated by the Treasury, would convert long-term capital loss into 60/40 loss, the first indication of the Treasury's position was an internal memorandum of the IRS. The memorandum asserted that 60/40 treatment should not be available for the section 1256 contracts part of an unidentified mixed straddle.[3] This position was not supported at that time by the language of the Code. The problem has since been addressed by the DRA amendments to the Code.

If a taxpayer made no election, the section 1256 contract positions

---

[2]*See* I.R.C. § 1256(d).

[3]Because section 1092 provides that in the case of an unidentified mixed straddle the provisions of section 1092 shall apply to any regulated futures contract, both the short sale, as well as wash sale, rules are to be applied to each futures contract and thus the 60/40 rule of section 1256(a)(3) is not to apply. If the 60/40 rule were to apply there would be a chance for a taxpayer to convert a short-term gain into a long-term gain and a long-term loss into a short-term loss. Consequently, the reason section 1233(b) and (d) were enacted are applicable here and it logically follows that section 1233 needs to and therefore should apply in the case of the regulated futures contract portion of an unidentified mixed straddle.

G.C.M. 39151 (June 17, 1983) (footnote omitted); *see* LTR 8348033 (Aug. 30, 1983).

that were part of the mixed straddle were subject to both the Mark-to-Market Rule, and the 60/40 Rule while the non-section 1256 positions were not subject to such treatment. Gain or loss on the section 1256 contract positions were taxed at year-end, although no such rule applied to the unrealized gain or loss in the non-section 1256 positions. Further, taxpayers would report 60/40 gain or loss with respect to the section 1256 positions and (depending on the taxpayer's holding period) 100 percent short-term or long-term capital gain or loss on the non-section 1256 positions. It was quite possible that taxpayers who failed to make a mixed straddle election would be subject to the modified short sales rule.[4] This would convert a short-term capital loss to a 60/40 loss when offset by a 60/40 gain in a mixed straddle. Without Treasury regulations, however, taxpayers used mixed straddles—subject to the possibility of denial on audit—to convert short-term gains into 60/40 gains.

In extending section 1256 treatment to dealer equity options,[5] Congress extended such treatment to products that are frequently traded in combination with underlying property not eligible for section 1256 treatment, that is, stock. As a result, the mixed straddle issue finally had to be addressed to prevent rampant conversion of short-term gain and long-term loss into 60/40 gain and loss. The DRA thus continued the one-time section 1256(d) mixed straddle election established by ERTA, but added an anticonversion rule and two additional elections for netting straddle gains or losses.[6] The new rules are intended to prevent the conversion of short-term capital gain into long-term capital gain while taking into consideration the administrative burdens imposed upon taxpayers who enter into a large volume of mixed straddle transactions.[7]

The DRA provides two netting rules for taxpayers holding mixed straddles. Taxpayers can elect to either (1) offset gains against losses by separately identifying each mixed straddle,[8] or (2) establish a "mixed straddle account" for each class of activities in which trading gains and losses would be recognized and offset on a periodic basis.[9] Under either of these elections, 60/40 treatment is available only for the net gain or loss from the straddle transactions attributable to section 1256 contracts. Under the rules applicable to a mixed straddle account election,

---

[4]*See* section 42.4.

[5]*See* section 32.4.

[6]I.R.C. § 1092(b)(2)(A).

[7]*See* STAFF OF THE JOINT COMMITTEE ON TAXATION, 98TH CONG., 2D SESS., GENERAL EXPLANATION OF THE REVENUE PROVISIONS OF THE DEFICIT REDUCTION ACT OF 1984 316-17 (Comm. Print 1984).

[8]*See* section 45.3.

[9]*See* section 45.4.

not more than 50 percent of any net gain derived from any positions in the account (whether or not qualified for section 1256 treatment) can be treated as long-term capital gain, and not more than 40 percent of any net loss can be treated as short-term capital loss.[10]

The DRA required the Treasury to issue regulations governing these new mixed straddle netting provisions within six months after the date the DRA was enacted (i.e., by January 18, 1985).[11] On January 18, 1985, the Treasury met the deadline and issued temporary regulations addressing the election for straddle-by-straddle identification and mixed straddle accounts. These temporary Treasury regulations affect all taxpayers who trade section 1256 contracts in combination or simultaneously with offsetting positions in non-section 1256 contracts (whether or not any coordination of these positions is intended by the taxpayer).

The netting rules authorized by the DRA are in lieu of having the modified short sales rule apply to a taxpayer's mixed straddle positions.[12] The modified short sales rule provides that losses on the disposition of one or more positions that are part of a mixed straddle and are non-section 1256 positions are treated as 60 percent long-term and 40 percent short-term capital loss, unless the taxpayer elects to either (1) offset gains or losses from positions that are part of a mixed straddle by separately identifying the positions of each straddle for which offset treatment is elected, or (2) establish a mixed straddle account for determining gains or losses from all positions in a designated class of activities.[13] If a taxpayer fails to elect either of these rules—or fails to apply them properly—the Treasury can apply the modified short sales rule to the mixed straddle.[14] This means that a loss on a non-section 1256 contract can be converted to 60/40 loss, without any corresponding conversion of section 1256 contract losses to short-term capital losses. This one-way conversion (sometimes referred to as the "killer rule") can have a punitive effect on a taxpayer with a loss on a section 1256 contract position and long-term capital gain from other sources (such as the long-term element of section 1256 contract gains).[15] For a taxpayer with a substantial volume of mixed straddles, the killer rule could eliminate

---

[10]Temp. Treas. Reg. § 1.1092(b)-4T(c)(4) (1985).

[11]DRA, Pub. L. 98-369, § 103(b), 98 Stat. 494, 628 (1984).

[12]Temp. Treas. Reg. § 1.1092(b)-2T(b)(2)(iii) (1986).

[13]*Id.*

[14]*See id.*

[15]*See* HOUSE CONFERENCE REPORT, DEFICIT REDUCTION ACT OF 1984, H.R. REP. NO. 861, 98th Cong., 2d Sess. 912 (1984).

the possible tax benefit of 60/40 treatment altogether. Even without a mixed straddle account election or a specific identification election, the killer rule does not apply to positions that (1) are part of a hedging transaction,[16] or (2) are a part of a straddle consisting solely of section 1256 contracts.[17]

§ 45.1 SUMMARY OF CHOICES AVAILABLE WHEN HOLDING A MIXED STRADDLE

A taxpayer who holds mixed straddles essentially has five choices. First, the taxpayer can do nothing, in which case the killer rule applies to convert any short-term loss from a non-section 1256 position in a mixed straddle to 60/40 loss.[18] Short-term gains offset by 60/40 losses are left unchanged. The killer rule "converts" only one way, in the government's favor, and it is a "killer" to any taxpayer with a substantial volume of mixed straddles.[19] The mixed straddle is subject to the Straddle Rules, including the requirement to capitalize interest and carrying charges,[20] and the modified wash sales and short sales rules.[21] Second, the taxpayer can make the one-time identified section 1256(d) mixed straddle election under section 1256(d) and identify each separate straddle that makes up a mixed straddle.[22] In this case, the section 1256 contracts of an identified mixed straddle are excluded from section 1256 treatment but remain subject to the Straddle Rules. Mixed straddle positions not so identified are subject to the modified wash sales and short sales rules.[23] Third, a taxpayer can identify straddles as section 1092(b)(2) mixed straddles, netting gains and losses in accordance with the Treasury regulations.[24] In this case, the taxpayer is subject to straddle-by-straddle netting of gains and losses in lieu of the application of the modified wash sales and short sales rules.[25] Fourth, if the straddle otherwise

---

[16]Temp. Treas. Reg. § 1.1092(b)-2T(c)(1)(i) (1986); *see generally* Chapter 21.

[17]Temp. Treas. Reg. § 1.1092(b)-2T(c)(1)(ii) (1986); *see* section 44.7; section 33.3.

[18]*See* Temp. Treas. Reg. § 1.1092(b)-2T(b)(2) (1986).

[19]It can be avoided by making the separate section 1092(b)(2) straddle-by-straddle identification election or the mixed straddle account election.

[20]*See* section 43.2.

[21]*See generally* Chapter 42.

[22]*See* section 45.2.

[23]*See generally* Chapter 42.

[24]*See* section 45.3.

[25]*See generally* Chapter 42.

qualifies as an identified straddle under I.R.C. § 1092 (where all of the positions are acquired on the same day),[26] the taxpayer can designate the straddle as a mixed straddle and further identify the straddle as an identified straddle. In this case, the section 1256 positions are not subject to section 1256 treatment and the straddle is not subject to the loss deferral rule of I.R.C. § 1092. The straddle, however, remains subject to the identified straddle, modified wash sales, and modified short sales rules. Interest and carrying charges incurred to carry identified straddles are required to be capitalized.[27] And finally, the taxpayer with a large number of transactions can establish a mixed straddle account maintained in accordance with the Treasury regulations.[28]

§ 45.2   IDENTIFIED SECTION 1256(d) MIXED STRADDLES

A taxpayer can elect to identify mixed straddle positions on a straddle-by-straddle basis under I.R.C. § 1256(d), referred to as "identified section 1256(d) mixed straddles." If such an election is in effect and the straddle was properly identified, the section 1256 positions are excluded from section 1256 treatment.[29] This election is not attractive for most taxpayers because section 1256 contracts receive short-term (rather than 60/40 treatment) and are still subject to the Straddle Rules.[30]

(a)   ONE-TIME MIXED STRADDLE ELECTION

To remove identified section 1256(d) mixed straddles from section 1256 treatment, a taxpayer must make a one-time, mixed straddle election.[31] Once made, this election can be revoked only with the consent of the Treasury.[32] Thereafter, the section 1256 positions are subject to all of the Straddle Rules[33] and long-term capital gain treatment is only available if the section 1256 positions were not part of a straddle for a period in excess of the long-term capital gain holding period.[34]

---

[26]*See* section 44.1.
[27]*See* section 43.2.
[28]*See* section 45.4.
[29]I.R.C. § 1256(d)(1).
[30]*See generally* Part Ten.
[31]I.R.C. § 1256(d)(1).
[32]I.R.C. § 1256(d)(3).
[33]*See generally* Part Ten.
[34]*See* Temp. Treas. Reg. § 1.1092(b)-2T(a) (1986).

(b) LIMITED SCOPE OF ELECTION

The section 1256(d) mixed straddle election is quite restrictive. It is not available to a taxpayer who has "legged into" a mixed straddle after first acquiring the section 1256 position.[35] In addition, taxpayers who cannot identify all of their mixed straddle transactions run the risk of having their characterizations challenged on audit and having the killer rule applied to certain transactions.[36] Also, those taxpayers who enter into thousands of mixed straddle transactions might find it impossible to comply with the identification requirements necessary to identify mixed straddles.

A taxpayer cannot elect to bring any positions in personal property within the Mark-to-Market and the 60/40 Rules. Only section 1256 contract positions are eligible for section 1256 treatment.

One final point is that an identified section 1256(d) mixed straddle may also qualify as an identified straddle if the identified straddle provisions are complied with.[37]

(c) MIXED STRADDLES CREATED BY TAKING DELIVERY UNDER OR EXERCISING A LONG SECTION 1256 CONTRACT

There is an exception to the requirement that an identified section 1256(d) mixed straddle election must be made before the close of the day on which the first section 1256 contract forming the straddle is acquired. The exception is provided for mixed straddles created by taking delivery under (or exercising) a long section 1256 contract.[38] This special rule allows the taxpayer (1) to make a section 1256(d) mixed straddle election on the date of delivery or exercise and (2) treat the remaining section 1256 contract positions as if they were terminated and new section 1256 contract positions were acquired on that date.[39] If a taxpayer (1) takes delivery of property under a section 1256 position, or (2) exercises a section 1256 contract position that is part of a straddle that includes section 1256 contracts, each of the remaining section 1256 contracts is treated as if terminated and sold for its fair market value on the day the taxpayer takes delivery under (or exercises) the long section 1256 contract.[40]

[35]I.R.C. § 1256(d)(4)(B).

[36]For a discussion of the killer rule, see section 45.1.

[37]*See* section 44.1.

[38]I.R.C. § 1256(c)(2).

[39]Senate Finance Committee Report, Technical Corrections Act of 1982, S. Rep. No. 592, 97th Cong., 2d Sess. 27, *reprinted in* 1982 U.S. Code Cong. & Ad. News 4149, 4173.

[40]I.R.C. § 1256(c)(2).

Example 45-2

Assume a taxpayer holds a straddle position in silver consisting of long and short section 1256 contracts and takes delivery of the silver under the long position. The section 1256 contract positions are treated as if sold for their fair market value on the delivery date.[41] On the day the taxpayer takes delivery of the silver, the taxpayer can make an identified section 1256(d) mixed straddle election for the new straddle consisting of the actual silver (long position) and the short section 1256 contract position.

§ 45.3 STRADDLE-BY-STRADDLE NETTING

A taxpayer can elect to identify individual mixed straddles when they are established and have them treated under separate netting rules provided in Treasury regulations.[42] Such straddles are referred to as "section 1092(b)(2) identified mixed straddles" because this method is authorized in I.R.C. § 1092(b)(2). If elected, it prevents application of the killer rule to the positions held in the identified section 1092(b)(2) mixed straddles. A taxpayer identifies each 1092(b)(2) identified mixed straddle when the straddle is established. The offsetting gains and losses from the straddle positions are netted together, with the excess of section 1256 gain or loss over non-section 1256 gain or loss treated as 60/40 gain or loss. The utility of this election for active investors and traders depends largely on their ability to comply with the complex rules for matching up straddle positions. One obvious advantage of the netting provision is that it allows taxpayers to make mixed straddle identifications in situations where the straddles are legged into, unlike the identified section 1256(d) mixed straddle election.

A taxpayer's determination of what constitutes a mixed straddle generally will be accepted by the IRS if the taxpayer adopts a reasonable and consistently applied method of identifying straddle positions and the method clearly reflects income.[43] The taxpayer's identification need not be accepted if the circumstances indicate that the taxpayer did not properly identify the straddles pursuant to such a method.[44]

---

[41] Id.

[42] I.R.C. § 1092(b)(2)(A)(i).

[43] H.R. REP. No. 861, *supra* note 15, at 912.

[44] Id.

(a) CLEAR IDENTIFICATION

After making a section 1092(b)(2) identified mixed straddle election, a taxpayer must clearly identify each position that is part of the mixed straddle on a "reasonable and consistently applied economic basis" before the "close of the day" on which the straddle is established.[45] For a taxpayer who is an individual, the "close of the day" is midnight (local time) in the location of the taxpayer's principal residence. For all other taxpayers, the "close of the day" is midnight (local time) in the location of the taxpayer's principal place of business.[46] If the taxpayer disposes of part of the mixed straddle before the close of the day on which the straddle was established, identification must be made at or before the time the taxpayer disposes of the position. Identification and calculation of gain or loss on "day trades" is unclear. Only the person or entity that directly holds all of the positions of a straddle can make this election.[47] The regulations do not provide any guidance for determining what is a reasonable and consistently applied economic basis for identification.

A taxpayer is presumed to have timely identified a section 1092(b)(2) mixed straddle only if he receives "independent verification" of the identification.[48] Under temporary Treasury regulations, the following procedures constitute independent verification:

(1) SEPARATE ACCOUNTS

Independent verification includes placement of one or more positions of a section 1092(b)(2) identified mixed straddle in a separate account designated as a "section 1092(b)(2) identified mixed straddle account" that is maintained by a broker, FCM, or similar person by whom notations are made identifying all positions of the identified mixed straddle and stating the date the straddle was established.[49]

(2) CONFIRMATIONS

Independent verification includes written confirmation from a broker, FCM or similar person. It also includes a written confirmation from the

---

[45]Temp. Treas. Reg. § 1.1092(b)-3T(d)(1) (1985).
[46]Id.
[47]Id.
[48]Temp. Treas. Reg. § 1.1092(b)-3T(d)(2) (1985).
[49]Temp. Treas. Reg. § 1.1092(b)-3T(d)(4)(i) (1985).

party from which one or more of the positions of the section 1092(b)(2) identified mixed straddle are acquired. Confirmation must state the date the straddle is established and identify the other positions of the straddle.[50]

(3) OTHER METHODS

Independent verification includes such other methods of independent verification as the Commissioner of the IRS approves in his discretion.[51]

The presumption that a taxpayer timely identified a mixed straddle by independent verification can be rebutted by clear and convincing evidence to the contrary.[52] If the presumption does not apply, the burden is on the taxpayer to establish that he made a timely identification by the time specified. In the absence of independent verification, the taxpayer must prove that timely identification was made and must present evidence other than his own testimony, unless he shows good cause for failure to produce additional evidence.[53]

Notwithstanding the identification rules and required time periods, a taxpayer can identify mixed straddles that were established before February 25, 1985 as section 1092(b)(2) identified mixed straddles if he adopts a "reasonable and consistent economic basis" for identifying the positions of such straddles.[54]

(b) SUMMARY OF RULES TO NET GAINS AND LOSSES

The DRA authorizes the promulgation of Treasury regulations to establish how a taxpayer can offset gains and losses that are part of a section 1092(b)(2) identified mixed straddle on a straddle-by-straddle basis.[55] Under this netting rule, the gain or loss on the section 1256 contract positions are netted with the gain or loss on the non-section 1256 contract positions for the purpose of testing whether gain or loss on a closed position should be given 60/40 treatment or short-term treatment. If gain or loss is attributable to section 1256 contract positions, the resulting amount is a 60/40 gain or loss.[56] If gain or loss is attributable

---

[50]Temp. Treas. Reg. § 1.1092(b)-3T(d)(4)(ii) (1985).

[51]Temp. Treas. Reg. § 1.1092(b)-3T(d)(4)(iii) (1985).

[52]Temp. Treas. Reg. § 1.1092(b)-3T(d)(2) (1985).

[53]Temp. Treas. Reg. § 1.1092(b)-3T(d)(3) (1985).

[54]Temp. Treas. Reg. § 1.1092(b)-3T(d)(5) (1985).

[55]I.R.C. § 1092(b)(2)(A)(i).

[56]Temp. Treas. Reg. § 1.1092(b)-3T (1985).

to positions that are non-section 1256 contracts, the resulting amount is a short-term capital gain or loss.[57]

Six rules in the Conference Report of the DRA identify those situations to be addressed in regulations where one position of a mixed straddle is acquired before another and where one position is disposed of before the other position.[58] These situations have been addressed by the temporary Treasury regulations.

First, any pre-straddle gain or loss with respect to a position of a straddle is recognized at the time the straddle is established. The character is either 60/40 gain or loss or short-term or long-term capital gain or loss, as the case may be.[59]

Second, if a taxpayer disposes of the section 1256 position at a loss and retains the non-section 1256 position, the loss is recharacterized as a short-term capital loss to the extent of the offsetting gain, and the positions are subject to the Straddle Rules. Any excess loss is treated as a 60/40 loss.[60]

Third, if a taxpayer disposes of the section 1256 position at a gain and retains the non-section 1256 position, the gain is recharacterized as a short-term capital gain to the extent of the offsetting loss. Any excess gain is treated as 60/40 gain.[61]

Fourth, if a taxpayer disposes of the non-section 1256 position and retains the section 1256 position, the gain or loss on the two positions is realized and netted at the time the non-section 1256 position is disposed of by the taxpayer.[62]

Fifth, the holding period for the non-section 1256 position is eliminated.[63]

Sixth, for mixed straddles held at the end of the tax year, gain or loss on the non-section 1256 contract is not recognized. Any gain on the section 1256 contract is recognized as short-term capital gain to the extent of the offsetting loss, and any loss on the section 1256 contract is treated as short-term capital loss to the extent of offsetting non-section 1256 gain and is subject to the Straddle Rules. Excess gain or loss, if any, is treated as 60/40 gain or loss.[64]

---

[57]*Id.*

[58]H.R. Rep. No. 861, *supra* note 15, at 912-13.

[59]Temp. Treas. Reg. § 1.1092(b)-3T(b)(6) (1985).

[60]Temp. Treas. Reg. § 1.1092(b)-3T(b)(4) (1985).

[61]*Id.*

[62]Temp. Treas. Reg. § 1.1092(b)-3T(b)(3) (1985).

[63]Temp. Treas. Reg. § 1.1092(b)-3T(b)(7) (1985).

[64]Temp. Treas. Reg. §§ 1.1092(b)-3T(b)(3), (4), (7) (1985).

(c) ACCRUED GAIN AND LOSS ON ESTABLISHING STRADDLES

If one or more positions of a section 1092(b)(2) identified mixed straddle were held by the taxpayer on the day prior to the day the straddle was established, such position or positions must be marked to the market as of the last business day before the day the straddle is established.[65] An adjustment (through an adjustment to basis or otherwise) will be made to any subsequent gain or loss realized (or deemed realized) with respect to such position or positions. Accordingly, gain or loss in a non-section 1256 position offset by a section 1256 contract position is realized when the section 1256 contract position is realized.[66]

Example 45-3

On January 1, 1985, a taxpayer establishes a non-section 1256 position. As of the close of the day on July 9, 1985, there is $500 of unrealized long-term capital gain in the non-section 1256 position. On July 10, 1985, the taxpayer enters into an offsetting section 1256 contract and makes a valid election to treat the straddle as a section 1092(b)(2) identified mixed straddle by designating it to an account marked "section 1092(b)(2) identified mixed straddles." Under these circumstances, on July 9, 1985, the taxpayer recognizes $500 of long-term capital gain on the non-section 1256 position.[67]

(d) SAME DAY DISPOSITION OF ALL POSITIONS

If all positions of a section 1092(b)(2) identified mixed straddle are disposed of on the same day, section 1256 gains and losses are netted and non-section 1256 gains and losses are netted.[68] First, net section 1256 contract gain or loss is determined by netting all section 1256 gains and losses. Second, non-section 1256 gain or loss is determined by netting all non-section 1256 gains or losses. Third, the net section 1256 gain or loss is offset against the net non-section 1256 gain or loss to determine the net straddle gain or loss. And fourth, the net straddle gain or loss is short-term if the non-section 1256 gain or loss is greater than the section 1256 gain or loss. The net straddle gain or loss is 60/40 if the

[65]Temp. Treas. Reg. § 1.1092(b)-3T(b)(6) (1985).
[66]*Id.*
[67]Temp. Treas. Reg. § 1.1092(b)-3T(b)(6), Example (1) (1985).
[68]Temp. Treas. Reg. § 1.1092(b)-3T(b)(2) (1985).

section 1256 contract gain or loss is greater than the non-section 1256 gain or loss. If both the section 1256 and non-section 1256 legs of the straddle result in either gain or loss, gain or loss derived from section 1256 contracts is given 60/40 treatment and non-section 1256 gain or loss is treated as short-term.

Example   45-4

On April 1, 1985, a taxpayer enters into a non-section 1256 position and an offsetting section 1256 position and makes a valid election to treat the straddle as a section 1092(b)(2) identified mixed straddle. On April 10, 1985, the taxpayer disposes of the non-section 1256 position at a $600 loss and the section 1256 contract at a $600 gain. Under these circumstances, the $600 loss on the non-section 1256 position is offset against the $600 gain on the section 1256 contract, and the net gain or loss from the straddle is zero.[69]

(e) NON-SECTION 1256 POSITIONS DISPOSED OF FIRST

If all of the non-section 1256 positions of a section 1092(b)(2) identified mixed straddle are disposed of on the same day, the gain and loss realized from the non-section 1256 positions disposed of are netted.[70] Second, the net section 1256 gain or loss is determined by netting section 1256 gains and losses for all positions disposed of during the day and all of the positions that have not been disposed of (i.e., the section 1256 gain or loss includes realized and unrealized gains and losses). Third, the net section 1256 gain or loss and the net non-section 1256 gain or loss is offset to determine the net straddle gain or loss. Fourth, the net gain or loss from the straddle attributable to the non-section 1256 position is recognized and treated as short-term capital gain or loss. Only the net amount is realized; the part of the non-section 1256 gain or loss offset by section 1256 gain or loss is eliminated. Net gain or loss from the straddle attributable to section 1256 contracts is realized and treated as 60 percent long-term and 40 percent short-term capital gain or loss. And fifth, any gain or loss subsequently realized on the remaining section 1256 contracts is adjusted (through an adjustment to basis or otherwise) to take into account the extent to which gain or loss was used to offset the gain or loss of the previously disposed of non-section 1256 or the section 1256 contracts.

[69]Temp. Treas. Reg. § 1.1092(b)-3T(b)(2), Example (1) (1985).
[70]Temp. Treas. Reg. § 1.1092(b)-3T(b)(3) (1985).

Example   45-5

On July 20th, a taxpayer enters into a section 1256 contract and an offsetting non-section 1256 position, and makes a valid election to treat the straddle as a section 1092(b)(2) identified mixed straddle. On July 27th, the taxpayer disposes of the non-section 1256 position at a $1500 loss, at which time there is $1500 of unrealized gain in the section 1256 contract. The taxpayer holds the section 1256 contract at year-end at which time there is $1800 of gain. Under these circumstances, on July 27th, the taxpayer offsets the $1500 loss of a non-section 1256 position against the $1500 gain of the section 1256 contract and realizes no gain or loss. On December 31st, the taxpayer realizes a $300 gain on the section 1256 contract when the position is marked-to-market. The $300 gain is equal to $1800 of gain minus a $1500 adjustment for unrealized gain offset against the loss realized in a non-section 1256 position on July 27th. The gain is treated as 60/40 gain.[71]

(f)   SECTION 1256 POSITIONS DISPOSED OF FIRST

If all of the section 1256 contracts of a section 1092(b)(2) identified mixed straddle are disposed of on the same day before all of the offsetting non-section 1256 positions are disposed of, the gain or loss realized is netted.[72] Realized and unrealized gain or loss with respect to the non-section 1256 positions of the straddle are netted on that day by marking-to-market the non-section 1256 position of the straddle. Net gain or loss from section 1256 contracts then will be treated as short-term capital gain or loss to the extent of the net gain or loss from the non-section 1256 positions. Net gain or loss on the section 1256 contracts in excess of the net gain or loss on the non-section 1256 positions of the straddle are treated as 60 percent long-term and 40 percent short-term capital gain or loss. When the remaining non-section 1256 positions are disposed of, the gain or loss is realized and treated as short-term to the extent that the gain or loss is attributable to the period when the non-section 1256 contract positions were part of the straddle. The treatment of the remaining gain or loss depends upon the holding period of the non-section 1256 position.

---

[71]Temp. Treas. Reg. § 1.1092(b)-3T(b)(3), Example (1) (1985).
[72]Temp. Treas. Reg. § 1.1092(b)-3T(b)(4) (1985).

Example   45-6

On July 20, 1987, a taxpayer enters into a straddle with a section 1256 position and an offsetting non-section 1256 position. The taxpayer makes a valid election to treat this straddle as an identified section 1092(b)(2) mixed straddle. On July 27, 1987, the taxpayer disposes of the section 1256 position at a $1400 loss, at which time there is $1500 of unrealized gain in the non-section 1256 contract. Under these circumstances, on July 27, 1987, the taxpayer treats the $1400 loss on the section 1256 position as a short-term capital loss.

(g) PARTIAL DISPOSITION OF STRADDLE POSITIONS

Where one or more, but not all, of the positions of a section 1092(b)(2) identified mixed straddle are disposed of on the same date, gain or loss from each of the non-section 1256 positions disposed of on that date are netted and the gain and loss from each of the section 1256 contracts that are disposed of on that date also are netted.[73] First, net gain or loss from the non-section 1256 positions that are disposed of is netted. Second, the gain or loss from the section 1256 positions disposed of is netted. Third, the net gain or loss from non-section 1256 positions disposed of is offset against the net section 1256 gain or loss from section 1256 positions disposed of. Fourth, if net gain or loss from the dispositions is attributable to non-section 1256 positions, the realized and unrealized gains and losses from all section 1256 contracts in the straddle are netted. The net non-section 1256 gain or loss from non-section 1256 positions disposed of then will be offset against the net section 1256 gain or loss from positions retained as well as disposed of. Net gain or loss that is attributable to non-section 1256 positions are recognized and treated as short-term capital gain or loss. Net gain or loss attributable to realized gain or loss with respect to section 1256 contracts is recognized and treated as 60/40 gain or loss.

Fifth, if net gain or loss from dispositions is attributable to section 1256 contracts that are disposed of, realized and unrealized gain or loss with respect to the non-section 1256 positions of the straddle are netted by marking-to-market the entire non-section 1256 leg of the straddle. Realized net gain or loss from section 1256 contracts actually disposed of are then treated as short-term to the extent of the net gain or loss from the non-section 1256 positions to determine the net gain or loss

[73]Temp. Treas. Reg. § 1.1092(b)-3T(b)(5) (1985).

from the straddle. If gain or loss on the section 1256 contracts exceeds the net gain or loss from the non-section 1256 positions of the straddle, the excess is treated as 60/40 gain or loss. Net gain or loss attributable to the non-section 1256 positions is treated as short-term capital gain or loss.

Sixth, if the net gain or loss from the section 1256 and the non-section 1256 contract positions disposed of are either both gains or losses, the net section 1256 gain or loss is treated as described in point five. The net non-section 1256 gain or loss is treated as described in point four. The gain or loss later realized on the remaining straddle positions must be adjusted so that any gain or loss previously used for offset purposes are not used for that purpose again.

Example 45-7

On July 15, 1985, a taxpayer enters into a straddle consisting of four non-section 1256 positions and four section 1256 contracts and designates it as a section 1092(b)(2) identified mixed straddle. On July 20, 1985, the taxpayer disposes of one non-section 1256 position at a gain of $800 and one section 1256 contract at a loss of $300. On the same day there is $400 of unrealized net loss on the section 1256 contracts retained by the taxpayer and $100 of unrealized net loss on his non-section 1256 positions. Under these circumstances, the loss of $300 on the section 1256 contract disposed of is offset against the gain of $800 on the non-section 1256 position that is disposed of. The net gain of $500 is attributable to the non-section 1256 position. Therefore, the net mark-to-market loss of $700 on the section 1256 contracts is offset against the net gain of $800 attributable to the disposed of non-section 1256 position. The net gain of $100 is treated as short-term capital gain because it is attributable to the disposed of non-section 1256 position. Gain or loss subsequently realized on the section 1256 contracts will be adjusted to take into account the unrealized loss of $400 that was offset against the $800 gain attributable to the disposed of non-section 1256 position.[74]

Assume the facts are the same as in the previous situation, except that the section 1256 contract was disposed of at a $500 gain. Under these circumstances, there is a $500 gain attributable to the disposed of section 1256 contract and a gain of $800 attributable to the non-section 1256 position. Therefore, the realized and unrealized gains and losses on the section 1256 contracts are netted, resulting in a net gain

[74]Temp. Treas. Reg. § 1.1092(b)-3T(b)(5), Example (1) (1985).

of $100 ($500 minus $400). The section 1256 net gain does not offset the gain on the disposed of non-section 1256 position. Therefore, the gain of $800 on the disposed of non-section 1256 position is treated as a short-term capital gain because there is no net loss on the section 1256 contracts. In addition, the realized and unrealized gains and losses in the non-section 1256 positions are netted, resulting in a non-section 1256 net gain of $700 ($800 minus $100). Because there is no net loss on the non-section 1256 positions, the $500 gain realized on the section 1256 contract is treated as 60/40 gain.[75]

(h) LOSS DEFERRAL AND HOLDING PERIOD RULES

Any loss realized under the rules for section 1092(b) identified mixed straddles can be recognized at year-end only if there is no unrecognized gain in (1) any position offsetting to the loss position, (2) any successor position, or (3) any position that offsets a successor position.[76] A successor position is a position that is or was at any time offsetting to a second position offsetting to any loss position disposed of, and the position is entered into during a period commencing 30 days before and ending 30 days after the disposition of the loss position.[77]

Gain or loss on a non-section 1256 position that is part of a section 1092(b)(2) identified mixed straddle and that is held after all section 1256 contracts in the straddle are disposed of will be treated as short-term capital gain or loss to the extent the gain or loss is attributable to the period when the positions were part of the mixed straddle.[78]

These rules apply to loss positions disposed of on or after January 24, 1985. Losses from positions disposed of before that date in straddles established after December 31, 1983 can be recognized only if there is no unrecognized gain in an offsetting position at the end of the year. Disallowed losses are treated as occurring in the next taxable year unless there is unrecognized gain inherent in an offsetting position.

Example   45-8

Assume a taxpayer enters into a section 1092(b)(2) identified mixed straddle on December 1, 1985. On December 31, 1985, the last day of the taxpayer's tax year, the taxpayer disposes of the section 1256 con-

---

[75]Temp. Treas. Reg. § 1.1092(b)-3T(b)(5), Example (3) (1985).
[76]Temp. Treas. Reg. § 1.1092(b)-3T(c) (1985).
[77]Temp. Treas. Reg. § 1.1092(b)-5T(n) (1986).
[78]Temp. Treas. Reg. § 1.1092(b)-3T(b)(7) (1985).

tract leg of the straddle at a $1000 loss. On the same day, there is $1000 of unrecognized gain in the non-section 1256 position. Under these circumstances, the $1000 loss is disallowed in 1985. On July 15, 1986, the taxpayer disposes of the non-section 1256 position at a $1500 gain, $500 of which is attributable to the post-straddle period. Under these circumstances, $1000 of the gain on the non-section 1256 positions is treated as short-term capital gain, because that amount of the gain is attributable to the period when the position was part of a section 1092(b)(2) identified mixed straddle. The remaining $500 of the gain is long-term capital gain. The disallowed loss of $1000 from 1985 will be allowed as a short-term capital loss in 1986.[79]

§ 45.4   MIXED STRADDLE ACCOUNTS

The DRA introduced the concept of a mixed straddle account as a new method for netting gains and losses with respect to mixed straddles.[80] The need for mixed straddle accounts was suggested by option dealers[81] (as well as other taxpayers) who engage in frequent transactions in section 1256 contracts and the non-section 1256 property underlying such contracts. The purpose of a mixed straddle account is to accommodate taxpayers with such a large volume of transactions that identification of specific mixed straddles is impractical.[82] Mixed straddle accounts provide simplification because taxpayers can avoid the daily identification of straddles and the application of the loss deferral and netting rules.

To reduce the possibilities of conversion of short-term capital gain into 60/40 gain within a mixed straddle account, a compromise solution was reached. Not more than 50 percent of the annual net gain derived from any positions in a mixed straddle account (whether or not qualified for section 1256 treatment) can be treated as long-term capital gain, and not more than 40 percent of the annual net loss from positions in a mixed straddle account can be treated as short-term capital loss.[83]

A taxpayer can establish mixed straddle accounts in which both section 1256 and non-section 1256 property are traded. Within the account, the positions are marked-to-market daily. (An adjustment to the account

[79]Temp. Treas. Reg. § 1.1092(b)-3T(b)(7), Example (1985).

[80]DRA, *supra* note 11, § 103(a) (codified at I.R.C. § 1092(b)).

[81]*See* section 6.2(b); section 6.3(c); section 6.3(d).

[82]H.R. REP. NO. 861, *supra* note 15, at 913.

[83]Temp. Treas. Reg. § 1.1092(b)-4T(c)(4) (1985).

through a basis adjustment or otherwise is made to prevent double counting of gains or losses realized on previous days.)[84]

An account gain or loss for each day is computed by (1) netting section 1256 gains and losses, (2) netting non-section 1256 gains and losses, and (3) offsetting the net section 1256 gain or loss against the net non-section 1256 gain or loss, with the excess treated as 60/40 (if from section 1256 contracts) or as short-term (if from non-section 1256 positions).[85]

The gains and losses from each day are then combined on an annual basis and adjusted for the capitalization of net interest and expenses under I.R.C. § 263(g).[86] If the aggregate net gain for the year from all accounts is greater than 50 percent long-term, the excess over 50 percent is converted to short-term. Similarly, if over 40 percent of a net loss for the year from all accounts is short-term, the excess is recharacterized as long-term.[87]

A taxpayer can elect to establish one or more mixed straddle accounts for determining gains and losses from all positions in a designated class of activities.[88]

The temporary Treasury regulations explain how to make the election and provide rules for determining gains and losses from positions in a mixed straddle account. A taxpayer can "designate as a class of activities the types of positions that a reasonable person, on the basis of all facts and circumstances, would ordinarily expect to be offsetting positions."[89] A separate mixed straddle account is required for each designated class of activities. A class of activities for option positions, for example, is on a symbol by symbol basis.[90]

Gains and losses from positions that are offsetting with respect to positions in more than one straddle account must be allocated among the accounts under a "reasonable and consistent method that clearly reflects income."[91]

A taxpayer's mixed straddle account must include all positions of a type ordinarily considered offsetting and cannot include non-offsetting positions. The temporary Treasury regulations give the IRS broad au-

---

[84] Temp. Treas. Reg. § 1.1092(b)-4T(c)(1) (1985).
[85] *Id.*
[86] Temp. Treas. Reg. §§ 1.1092(b)-4T(c)(2), (3) (1985).
[87] I.R.C. § 1092(b)(2)(B); Temp. Treas. Reg. § 1.1092(b)-4T(c)(4) (1985).
[88] Temp. Treas. Reg. § 1.1092(b)-4T(a) (1985).
[89] Temp. Treas. Reg. § 1.1092(b)-4T(b)(2) (1985).
[90] Temp. Treas. Reg. § 1.1092(b)-4T(b)(1) (1985).
[91] Temp. Treas. Reg. § 1.1092(b)-4T(b)(3) (1985).

thority to remove or include positions in the account if the taxpayer's designations are considered improper.[92]

The taxpayer's gain or loss from positions in his mixed straddle accounts is determined by applying the following operating rules.

(a) ACCOUNT CONTENTS

A taxpayer can elect on a yearly basis to establish one or more mixed straddle accounts for all positions held as capital assets in a designated class of activities where gains and losses are determined in accordance with the rules established in Treasury regulations.[93] A mixed straddle account is established as of the first day of the taxable year for which the election is made.[94] In addition, a separate mixed straddle account must be established for each separate designated class of activities.[95] A taxpayer can designate as a class of activities those positions that "a reasonable person, on the basis of all the facts and circumstances, would ordinarily expect to be offsetting positions."[96]

Example 45-9

Assume a taxpayer, who is an options dealer,[97] trades dealer equity options[98] on XYZ Corporation stock, stock in XYZ Corporation, dealer equity options on ABC Corporation stock, and stock in ABC Corporation. If the taxpayer makes a mixed straddle account election for all positions, he must designate two accounts—one for XYZ Corporation stock and options and the other for ABC Corporation stock and options—and he must maintain two separate mixed straddle accounts. The taxpayer can elect to trade one symbol in a mixed straddle account and the other symbol as an identified mixed straddle. ABC and XYZ cannot be traded in the same account.[99]

Certain positions that would be expected to offset more than one mixed straddle account are required to be allocated among all such

[92]Temp. Treas. Reg. § 1.1092(b)-4T(b)(4) (1985).
[93]*See* section 45.4(g).
[94]Temp. Treas. Reg. § 1.1092(b)-4T(a) (1985).
[95]Temp. Treas. Reg. § 1.1092(b)-4T(b)(1) (1985).
[96]Temp. Treas. Reg. § 1.1092(b)-4T(b)(2) (1985).
[97]*See* section 6.2(b); section 6.3(d).
[98]*See* section 32.4.
[99]Temp. Treas. Reg. § 1.1092(b)-4T(b)(2), Example (1985).

accounts under a "reasonable and consistent method that clearly reflects income."[100] Index options that offset the positions in more than one account must be allocated among the accounts on a reasonable basis.[101] The regulations do not explain when an index position should be considered offsetting to positions in the underlying accounts.[102]

If a taxpayer makes a mixed straddle account designation to include positions in an account that the IRS determines a reasonable person would not expect to be offsetting, the IRS can amend the class of activities designated by the taxpayer and either (1) remove the positions from the account that are not within the amended designated class of activities, or (2) establish two or more mixed straddle accounts.[103] On the other hand, if the IRS determines that positions not included in an account should be included in the account, the IRS can amend the class of activities designated by the taxpayer to (1) include the positions within the account, or (2) to exclude from the account those types of positions that offset positions that are not included in the account.[104] In other words, the IRS has broad discretion to move positions into a mixed straddle account, move positions from one account to another, or to remove positions from accounts altogether. However, the taxpayer's own designation will be respected if a reasonable person would have designated the positions in the same manner that the taxpayer did.[105]

(b) DAILY MARK-TO-MARKET

The temporary Treasury regulations provide that all mixed straddle account positions, whether or not composed of section 1256 contracts, are marked-to-market at the close of each business day.[106] A daily non-section 1256 net gain or loss is determined for each account by netting all non-section 1256 gains and losses from positions disposed of during the day or marked-to-market at the close of the day. A daily section 1256 contract net gain or loss is determined for each account in the same manner.

The net non-section 1256 gain or loss is offset against net section 1256

---

[100]Temp. Treas. Reg. § 1.1092(b)-4T(b)(3) (1985).

[101]Temp. Treas. Reg. § 1.1092(b)-4T(b)(3), Example (1985).

[102]See section 36.2(c).

[103]Temp. Treas. Reg. § 1.1092(b)-4T(b)(4)(i) (1985).

[104]Temp. Treas. Reg. § 1.1092(b)-4T(b)(4)(ii) (1985).

[105]See Temp. Treas. Reg. §§ 1.1092(b)-4T(b)(4)(i), (ii) (1985).

[106]Temp. Treas. Reg. § 1.1092(b)-4T(c)(1) (1985).

gain or loss to determine the daily account net gain or loss for each account.[107] The net gain or loss is treated as 60/40 gain or loss if the section 1256 gain exceeds the non-section 1256 loss or the section 1256 loss exceeds the non-section 1256 gain.[108]

Similarly, the net gain or loss is short-term if the non-section 1256 gain exceeds the section 1256 loss or the non-section 1256 loss exceeds the section 1256 gain.[109] If both the section 1256 and non-section 1256 contracts result in net gains or net losses, the non-section 1256 gain or loss is short-term and the section 1256 gain or loss is 60 percent long-term and 40 percent short-term.[110]

(c) ANNUAL ACCOUNT NET GAIN OR LOSS

An annual account net gain or loss is determined for each mixed straddle account on the last business day of the taxable year by netting all of the daily mark-to-market results for that year.[111] This annual netting is done under the regular capital gain and loss netting rules. To accomplish this, 60/40 gains and losses are separated into their long-term and short-term components. Long-term gains and losses are then netted. In addition, short-term gains and losses are netted to arrive at net short-term and long-term results for each account. Long-term gains or losses in each account are then offset against short-term gains or losses.

No more than 50 percent of total annual account net gain for the taxable year is treated as long-term capital gain.[112] Any long-term gain in excess of the 50 percent limit is treated as short-term capital gain.[113] In addition, no more than 40 percent of total annual account net loss for the taxable year is treated as short-term capital loss, and any short-term loss in excess of the 40 percent limit is treated as long-term capital loss.[114]

[107] Id.
[108] Id.
[109] Id.
[110] Id.
[111] Temp. Treas. Reg. § 1.1092(b)-4T(c)(2) (1985).
[112] I.R.C. § 1092(b)(2)(B)(i); Temp. Treas. Reg. § 1.1092(b)-4T(c)(4) (1985).
[113] Temp. Treas. Reg. § 1.1092(b)-4T(c)(4) (1985).
[114] I.R.C. § 1092(b)(2)(B)(ii); Temp. Treas. Reg. § 1.1092(b)-4T(c)(4) (1985).

Example 45-10

The taxpayer, an options market maker who specializes in ABC and XYZ options and stock, elects to establish mixed straddle accounts for each of his two specialty symbols. The taxpayer's stock option trading qualifies for 60/40 treatment, while his stock transactions generally are given short-term capital gain or loss treatment. For simplicity, only four consecutive trading days are illustrated. They are intended to represent the entire 1986 trading year. The rules illustrated here are equally applicable to a futures trader who trades the underlying commodity and elects to use a mixed straddle account. Short-term capital gain and loss are referred to in this example as "STCG" and "STCL," respectively.

ABC MIXED STRADDLE ACCOUNT

	Non-Section 1256 Stock	Section 1256 Options	Daily Net	Character
December 28	(150)	(50)	(200)	(150) STCL
				(50) 60/40
December 29	160	(100)	60	60 STCG
December 30	(150)	300	150	150 60/40
December 31	50	150	200	50 STCG
				150 60/40

XYZ MIXED STRADDLE ACCOUNT

	Non-Section 1256 Stock	Section 1256 Options	Daily Net	Character
December 28	(100)	150	50	50 60/40
December 29	100	(50)	50	50 STCG
December 30	(50)	(50)	(100)	(50) STCL
				(50) 60/40
December 31	(100)	50	(50)	(50) STCL

ANNUAL ABC ACCOUNT GAIN OR LOSS

60/40	Short-Term	Long-Term
(50)	(20)	(30)
150	60	90
150	60	90
—	(150)	—
—	60	—
—	50	—
Total	60	150

Under these circumstances, because no more than 50 percent of the net gain from a mixed straddle account can be treated as long-term capital gain, only 105 of the 210 net gain from the ABC account will be characterized as long-term and 105 will be characterized as short-term.

ANNUAL XYZ ACCOUNT GAIN OR LOSS

60/40	Short-Term	Long-Term
(50)	(20)	(30)
50	20	30
—	(50)	—
—	50	—
—	(50)	—
Total	(50)	0

Under these circumstances, no more than 40 percent of a mixed straddle account net loss can be treated as a short-term capital loss, and as a result, 20 of the 50 net loss will be treated as short-term capital loss and 30 as long-term capital loss. The taxpayer's net results for the trading year will be as follows:

TAXPAYER TOTALS

Short-Term	Long-Term
105	105
(20)	(30)
85	75

The taxpayer's net long-term gain of 75 will be subject to a tax rate not to exceed 20 percent, while his short-term gain of 85 could be taxed at a rate up to 50 percent.

(d) CAPITALIZATION OF INTEREST AND CARRYING CHARGES

The Treasury is responsible for establishing rules to capitalize interest and carrying charges for mixed straddle accounts to the extent such charges exceed income on such positions.[115] The purpose of capitalizing excess straddle expenses (after netting the expenses and income of a straddle) is to prevent conversion of unrelated ordinary income into long-term capital gain. The income and expense items include interest, carrying charges, dividends, payments in lieu of dividends, and short stock rebates. To prevent this conversion, I.R.C. § 263(g) requires excess straddle expenses to be capitalized rather than deducted as ordinary expense deductions. This means that no expense attributable to a straddle can be used to reduce ordinary income that is unrelated to the straddle.[116]

On its face, I.R.C. § 263(g) assumes that all positions of the straddle can be identified and that the interest income and interest expenses with respect to such positions can also be identified. In providing the election for a mixed straddle account, however, Congress recognized that identifying individual straddle transactions would be difficult (and perhaps impossible) for certain taxpayers.[117] If a taxpayer maintains a mixed straddle account, he may be required to capitalize interest and carrying charges allocable to the account, rather than to individual straddles held, but not otherwise identified, within the account.[118]

The regulations provide that no deduction is allowed for interest and carrying charges that are "properly allocable" to a mixed straddle account.[119] Interest and carrying charges "properly allocable" to a mixed straddle account are defined as the excess of (1) the sum of (a) interest (including short sale expenses) on debt incurred to purchase or carry any position in the account, and (b) all amounts paid or incurred to insure, store, transport, etc., personal property with respect to a position

---

[115]I.R.C. § 1092(b)(1).

[116]*See* section 43.2.

[117]H.R. Rep. No. 861, *supra* note 15, at 913.

[118]*See* Temp. Treas. Reg. § 1.1092(b)-4T(c)(3) (1985).

[119]*Id.*

in the account; over (2) the sum of (a) interest includible in gross income with respect to all positions in the account, (b) ordinary income from the holding, retirement, or sale of debt securities in the account; and (c) dividends received with respect to positions in the account, net of certain dividends received deductions.[120]

The temporary Treasury regulations do provide some guidance as to whether the interest expense attributable to the account should be netted against all gains in the account or only against that portion generated from assets that are debt financed. The temporary Treasury regulations apply I.R.C. § 263(g) to a mixed straddle account as if the account contains one straddle.[121]

First, income and expense items are allocated to each account pursuant to a reasonable method. Second, income and expense items are netted for the year within each account. Third, net expense is capitalized by reducing the annual account net gain or increasing the annual account net loss. Fourth, any interest and carrying charges disallowed under this rule are capitalized; that is, they are treated as an adjustment to the annual account net gain or loss and are allocated pro rata between net short-term and long-term capital gain or loss.[122]

Example 45-11

Assume the same facts as in Example No. 45-10 except that the taxpayer also incurred $40 of net interest expense properly allocable to positions in the ABC mixed straddle account. Under these circumstances, the $40 of net interest expense is not deductible but must be allocated to the annual results of the ABC mixed straddle account. The $40 of interest expense reduces proportionately the long-term and short-term elements of the ABC capital gain. Therefore, $11.42 (60/210 times $40) of the interest expense reduces the taxpayer's ABC short-term capital gain and $28.58 (150/210 times $40) reduces the taxpayer's ABC long-term capital gain.

(e) TOTAL ANNUAL ACCOUNT NET GAIN OR LOSS

The results of all mixed straddle accounts for the year are netted to yield the total annual account net gain or loss.[123] Thus, for the year, the

---

[120]*Id.*

[121]*Id.*

[122]*Id.*

[123]Temp. Treas. Reg. § 1.1092(b)-4T(c)(2) (1985).

taxpayer has a single result from trading in all mixed straddle accounts of (1) long-term gain or loss, (2) short-term gain or loss, (3) a combination of long-term and short-term gains, or (4) a combination of long-term and short-term losses.

(f) ACCOUNT CAP

The annual total from all mixed straddle accounts for each year cannot exceed 50 percent long-term gain or 40 percent short-term loss.[124] Thus, if the total of all accounts is a gain, then the long-term portion is limited to 50 percent. If the total of all accounts is a loss, the short-term portion is limited to 40 percent.

(g) YEARLY MIXED STRADDLE ELECTIONS

The temporary Treasury regulations issued on January 18, 1985 provided that section 1092(b)(2) identified straddles or mixed straddle accounts, once made, were effective for all subsequent tax years unless the IRS consented to their revocation.[125] The revised temporary regulations issued October 11, 1985 provide, however, that an election is effective only for the taxable year for which it is made.[126]

The election must be made by the due date (without regard to extensions) of the taxpayer's income tax return for the immediately preceding taxable year.[127] This means that individual taxpayers on a calendar year must make their elections by April 15th of the year in which the elections are to be effective. Similarly, corporate taxpayers on the calendar year must make their elections by March 15th of the year for which the election is to be effective.

In conclusion, taxpayers now have until the date their tax return is due for the preceding taxable year (without extensions) to consider whether they should choose the mixed straddle account election or the straddle-by-straddle identification election to comply with the regulations, taking into account their trading practices for the year and the nature of their accounting records. Elections after that date must be approved by the IRS.[128] Many taxpayers have found that they prefer the straddle-

---

[124]Temp. Treas. Reg. § 1.1092(b)-4T(c)(4) (1985).

[125]Temp. Treas. Reg. § 1.1092(b)-4T(f)(3), T.D. 8008, 1985-9 I.R.B. 10.

[126]Temp. Treas. Reg. § 1.1092(b)-4T(f)(4) (1985); *see* IRS Announcement 85-112, 1985-33 I.R.B. 26.

[127]Temp. Treas. Reg. § 1.1092(b)-4T(f)(1) (1985).

[128]*Id.*

by-straddle identification method, if they could track mixed straddles using their accounting systems on a day-by-day basis. However, many of these same taxpayers discovered that their accounting records as they existed for 1984 did not allow them to make the tax computations required by the straddle-by-straddle method and, as a result, they preferred the mixed straddle account for 1984 only. The amended temporary Treasury regulations issued October 17, 1985 make it clear that taxpayers can use the mixed straddle account for purposes of convenience in filing their 1984 tax returns but may thereafter elect straddle-by-straddle identification.[129] The temporary regulations extended the date for making the election generally until December 31, 1985.[130]

If a taxpayer begins trading or investing in positions in a new class of activities during a taxable year, the election for the new class of activities must be made by the taxpayer by the latter of the due date of the taxpayer's income tax return for the immediately preceding taxable year (without any extensions) or 60 days after the first mixed straddle in the new class of activities is entered into.[131] In addition, if on or after the date the taxpayer made a mixed straddle account election he begins trading positions that were not specified in the original election but are includible in a mixed straddle account, the taxpayer must make an amended election by the latter of the due date of his income tax return for the immediately preceding taxable year (without any extensions) or 60 days after the acquisition of the first of the positions.[132] An election made after the specified time is permitted only if the taxpayer had reasonable cause for failing to make a timely election.[133]

Example   45-12

A calendar year taxpayer holds only a few positions in one class of activities prior to April 15th of a taxable year. He greatly increases his trading activity in this type of position after April 15th. The IRS can conclude that the taxpayer had reasonable cause for failing to make a timely election and allow him to make a mixed straddle account election for that year.[134]

---

[129]Announcement 85-112, *supra* note 126, also provided that taxpayers who already filed their 1985 returns without making a mixed straddle account election could make the election by filing an amended return on or before October 15, 1985.

[130]Temp. Treas. Reg. § 1.1092(b)-4T(f)(3) (1985).

[131]Temp. Treas. Reg. § 1.1092(b)-4T(f)(1) (1985).

[132]*Id.*

[133]*Id.*

[134]*Id.*

(h) MANNER FOR MAKING ELECTION

A taxpayer must make a mixed straddle election on IRS Form 6781 in the manner prescribed therein by attaching the form to his income tax return for the immediately preceding taxable year (or his request for an automatic extension).[135] The taxpayer also must attach a statement to Form 6781 designating the class of activities for which a mixed straddle account election is established. The designation must provide sufficient detail so that the IRS can determine, on the basis of the designation, whether specific positions are includable in the mixed straddle account.[136] If a taxpayer establishes more than one mixed straddle account, the IRS must be able to determine that specific positions are placed in the appropriate account.[137] An election applies to all positions held in the designated class of activities during the taxable year.

Amended elections and elections made for new classes of activities in which the taxpayer begins trading during a taxable year are to be made on Form 6781. The election must be made by the latter of the due date of the taxpayer's return for the preceding taxable year (without extensions) or 60 days after the first of the positions is acquired.[138] The activity designation statement must be attached.

An election to establish a mixed straddle account, including any amendments to the election, is effective only for the taxable year for which the election is made. Once made, the election for that year can only be revoked during the taxable year with the consent of the IRS. One item that must be provided with the application for consent to revoke a mixed straddle account is a statement that the taxpayer's volume or nature of trading activities has changed substantially, and that his activities no longer warrant the use of a mixed straddle account.[139]

(i) TRANSITIONAL ELECTIONS

Special transitional rules apply to mixed straddle accounts. First, the mixed straddle account rules can be applied retroactively by a calendar year taxpayer to all positions established after December 31, 1983 and before January 1, 1985.[140] In general, all positions held on December

---

[135]Temp. Treas. Reg. § 1.1092(b)-4T(f)(2)(i) (1985).
[136]*Id.*
[137]*Id.*
[138]Temp. Treas. Reg. § 1.1092-4T(f)(2)(ii) (1985).
[139]Temp. Treas. Reg. § 1.1092(b)-4T(f)(2)(ii) (1985).
[140]Temp. Treas. Reg. § 1.1092(b)-4T(f)(3) (1985).

31, 1983 that are brought into a mixed straddle account on January 1, 1984 are marked-to-market on December 31, 1983. The resulting gains and losses are included in 1984 and are subject to the 60/40 Rule. Although the regulations are not clear, the Treasury apparently intends that the pre-1984 gains and losses not be included in the account computations. Account positions held at the end of 1984 are marked-to-market on December 31, 1984. These mark-to-market gains and losses are combined with the gains and losses from account positions disposed of in 1984 and are netted and offset as if the entire 1984 period was a single day. After December 31, 1984, the daily marking rules apply to each account.

Second, because section 1256 treatment applies retroactively to 1984, the regulations permit the account rules to be applied to 1984 on a simplified basis.[141] The regulations are not entirely clear on the treatment of the pre-1984 gain or loss on the positions that are included in an account. It appears as if the intention under the regulations was to leave the pre-1984 gain or loss outside the account. Therefore, gain or loss remaining unrecognized at the end of 1983 is recognized in 1984 and is subject to section 1256 treatment. Thus, the section 1256 gain or loss is treated as 60/40 and the non-section 1256 gain or loss is treated as short-term. The cross-netting rules do not apply. All account positions are marked-to-market at the end of 1984. The 1984 gains and losses for each account are combined as if the entire period was one day.

Third, there is a special transitional rule for mixed straddle accounts. An election to establish a mixed straddle account for any taxable year that includes July 17, 1984 and any taxable year that ends before September 1, 1986 (or in the case of a corporation October 1, 1986) must be made by the latter of December 31, 1985 or the due date for the taxpayer's 1984 tax return (without extensions) if the due date is after December 31, 1985.[142] The election is made by attaching both Form 6781 and the required statement to the taxpayer's income tax return, amended return, or other form filed on or before the deadline date. The statement must designate with specificity the class of activities for which the account is established.[143]

---

[141]*Compare* Temp. Treas. Reg. § 1.1092(b)-4T(f)(3) (1985) *with* Temp. Treas. Reg. §§ 1.1092(b)-4T(f)(1), (2) (1985).

[142]Temp. Treas. Reg. § 1.1092(b)-4T(f)(3) (1985).

[143]*See* section 45.4(h).

Example 45-13

The tax return for a fiscal year taxpayer with a taxable year that ended September 30, 1985 is due (without regard to extensions) on January 15, 1986. The mixed straddle election must be made on or before January 15, 1986 with the taxpayer's tax return or his request for an automatic extension.[144]

Example 45-14

A calendar year taxpayer who filed his 1984 income tax return before October 15, 1985 without making a mixed straddle account election for either 1984 or 1985 (or both years) can make the mixed straddle account election for either or both of the years with an amended return filed on or before December 31, 1985.[145]

A mixed straddle account elected on an amended return is effective for all positions in the designated class of activities even if the taxpayer elected straddle-by-straddle netting.[146] For taxable years beginning in 1984 and 1985, the election is effective for the entire year. For taxable years beginning in 1983, the election is effective for those days of the year after December 31, 1983 for which a DRA carry-back election is made.[147]

§ 45.5 METHODS OF IDENTIFYING AND NETTING MIXED STRADDLES ARE NOT MUTUALLY EXCLUSIVE

Nothing in the Code or temporary Treasury regulations prevents a taxpayer from using any or all of the methods of identifying and netting mixed straddles if the designations are proper and taxpayers only make one election for any straddle. Taxpayers need not use mixed straddle accounts if they can comply with the mixed straddle rules. Taxpayers can elect to use mixed straddle accounts for certain transactions and section 1092(b)(2) identified straddles for other positions.

---

[144]Temp. Treas. Reg. § 1.1092(b)-4T(f)(3) (1985).
[145]*Id.*
[146]*See* section 45.3.
[147]*See* section 32.5.

For example, it is quite common for taxpayers to trade in only some of the property underlying their section 1256 contracts. In addition, the volume of trading in the underlying property often varies at different times, depending upon the taxpayer's trading strategy and market conditions. The temporary Treasury regulations provide that once a mixed straddle account is established it can only be terminated with IRS consent.[148]

Of course, given the broad discretion granted to the IRS to move positions to and from accounts, any accounting system which allows the taxpayer to pick and choose the location of positions to achieve favorable tax treatment runs the risk of being challenged by the IRS.

§ 45.6 LIMITATIONS ON WHO CAN MAKE SECTION 1092(b)(2) ELECTIONS

The temporary Treasury regulations provide requirements as to how a taxpayer can identify section 1092(b)(2) identified mixed straddles and establish mixed straddle accounts.

Turning first to identification of section 1092(b)(2) identified mixed straddles, the temporary regulations provide that only the person or entity that *directly* holds *all* positions of a straddle can make the identification.[149] This requirement of direct ownership of all positions is too narrow, because it does not apply to all positions that should be eligible for identification as section 1092(b)(2) identified straddles. For purposes of defining a straddle, a taxpayer is treated as holding any position held by a related person.[150] Related persons are defined to include a taxpayer's spouse, another corporation which files a consolidated return with the taxpayer, and certain flow-through entities (e.g., trusts, partnerships, and S corporations). However, if only taxpayers directly holding all straddle positions can make section 1092(b)(2) identified mixed straddle elections, then those taxpayers subject to aggregation of their positions under I.R.C. § 1092(d)(4) with positions held by related persons cannot make a section 1092(b)(2) identified straddle elections with respect to those straddles which are deemed to be held by them under I.R.C. § 1092(d)(4). Related persons cannot jointly make a section 1092(b)(2) election under the temporary regulations.

Because corporations filing consolidated returns within I.R.C. § 1502 are "related persons" under I.R.C. § 1092(d)(4), the section 1092(b)(2)

---

[148]Temp. Treas. Reg. § 1.1092(b)-4T(f)(4) (1985).
[149]Temp. Treas. Reg. § 1.1092(b)-3T(d)(1) (1985).
[150]I.R.C. § 1092(d)(4)(A); *see generally* Chapter 39.

identified straddle election should be available to the members of a consolidated group (or any group to which the rules of I.R.C. § 1092(d)(4) apply) even if different members of the group hold the positions making up the straddle. However, a joint election is unavailable under a literal reading of the temporary regulations. Hence, the scope of the temporary regulations is too limited to cover all of the transactions for which the section 1092(b)(2) identified mixed straddle election should be available.

A less restrictive standard from the one for identified straddles appears to apply to taxpayers who establish mixed straddle accounts. The temporary Treasury regulations do not specifically address the issue of whether the person or entity directly holding all of the positions must make the mixed straddle account election. Rather, the temporary regulations provide that the election must be made by the "taxpayer."[151] If the taxpayer who must make a mixed straddle account election is not required to directly hold all of the positions of a straddle, a more liberal standard than the one established for section 1092(b)(2) identified straddles is available to him.

Different standards for electing section 1092(b)(2) identified straddles and mixed straddle accounts are not appropriate, despite the Treasury's broad authority to promulgate regulations under I.R.C. § 1092(b)(2). In fact, it should be possible to assert that both section 1092(b)(2) identified straddles and mixed straddle account elections should be available to any taxpayer for positions which are attributed to him under I.R.C. § 1092(d)(4).

§ 45.7 SUMMARY OF EFFECTIVE DATES

The temporary Treasury regulations provide various effective dates that are summarized in this section. Application of the loss deferral rule under Temp. Treas. Reg. § 1.1092(b)-1T applies to loss positions on or after January 24, 1985. The holding period rule contained in Temp. Treas. Reg. § 1.1092(b)-2T applies to positions of straddles, except for straddles made up exclusively of section 1256 positions, established after June 23, 1981 in taxable years ending after that date. The killer rule contained in Temp. Treas. Reg. § 1.1092(b)-2T(b)(2) applies to mixed straddle positions established after January 1, 1984. In addition, the straddle-by-straddle nettings rule under Temp. Treas. Reg. § 1.1092(b)-3T applies to positions established after January 1, 1984. Finally, the mixed straddle account rules under Temp. Treas. Reg. § 1.1092(b)-4T apply to positions held on or after January 1, 1984.

---

[151]Temp. Treas. Reg. § 1.1092(b)-4T(f)(2)(i) (1985).

Part Eleven

Treatment of Gain or Loss on Terminations of Certain Contract Rights and Obligations

If a taxpayer's rights or obligations with respect to personal property are terminated by cancellation, lapse, expiration, or any other termination and the personal property is a capital asset in the hands of the taxpayer,[1] gain or loss is treated as from the sale of a capital asset.

---

[1] I.R.C. § 1234A.

Forty-six

Terminations of Contract Rights and Obligations

§ 46.1 PRE-ERTA CANCELLATION TRANSACTIONS

Under the law in effect prior to ERTA, a taxpayer with a profit motive could seek to create ordinary losses on certain dispositions of capital assets which, if sold at a gain, would produce capital gain. Some of the more typical of these transactions involved cancellations of forward contracts for government securities or foreign currency.[1]

One of the most common methods of closing out a forward contract is to enter into an offsetting contract, which requires the consent of both parties. Thus, if a taxpayer enters into a long (short) forward contract and he wants to terminate his obligations, he can enter into an offsetting short (long) contract with the same party, assuming the other party consents. The obligations of the two contracts offset each other and neither party is obligated to go through the formality of taking or making delivery. The taxpayer's gain or loss is determined by the difference in the price of the underlying property for each contract.

A forward contract is an executory contract. General principles of contract law allow the rights and obligations of a party to an executory contract to be assigned to a third party if the terms of the contract so permit. Further, since the rights in a forward contract can constitute capital assets, it appears that such an assignment would constitute the

[1]For a discussion of forward contracts, see generally section 4.3(b).

sale or exchange of a capital asset and, therefore, give rise to capital gain or loss. The IRS has taken this position with regard to the assignment of a long futures contract.[2] If a taxpayer holds a long contract for more than the long-term holding period (more than one year for transactions immediately prior to ERTA), he obtains long-term gain whether he assigns the contract or purchases an offsetting short contract. There is no possibility for manipulation of the holding period rules. An entirely different situation occurs when a taxpayer assigns a short contract. If the taxpayer subsequently closed the short contract by offsetting it with a substantially identical long contract, he recognizes short-term capital gain regardless of the length of time he held the short contract before acquiring the long contract.

Under pre-ERTA law, to obtain ordinary, rather than capital, loss treatment, a disposition of a capital asset could be structured as a lapse or cancellation. Such a disposition was not considered a sale or exchange. In addition, a straddle could be established to minimize the taxpayer's risk. The taxpayer could seek to generate ordinary loss on the "cancellation" (by payment of an amount in settlement of his obligation to the other party to the contract), and a corresponding long-term capital gain on the sale or assignment of the contract. Closing out the two positions in different manners would generate a different tax result.

Example 46-1

Under the law in effect prior to ERTA, a taxpayer entered into short and long forward contracts to buy and sell German marks. The taxpayer held a straddle. If the price of German marks declined, the taxpayer could sell or assign his short contract to a bank or other financial institution for a capital gain (equal to the excess of the forward contract price over the market price) and cancel his long contract for a capital loss (by payment of an amount in settlement of his obligation to the other party of the contract). The taxpayer would report the sales proceeds as capital gain but treat the amount paid to terminate his obligation to buy as an ordinary loss.[3]

[2]*See* Rev. Rul. 78-414, 1978-2 C.B. 213.
[3]*See* JOINT COMMITTEE ON TAXATION, 97TH CONG., 1ST SESS., GENERAL EXPLANATION OF THE ECONOMIC RECOVERY TAX ACT OF 1981 313-14 (Joint Comm. Print 1981) [hereinafter referred to as "General Explanation of ERTA"]; HOUSE WAYS AND MEANS COMMITTEE REPORT, TAX INCENTIVE BILL OF 1981, H.R. REP. NO. 201, 97th Cong., 1st Sess. 213 (1981); SENATE FINANCE COMMITTEE REPORT, ECONOMIC RECOVERY TAX ACT OF 1981, S. REP. NO. 144, 97th Cong., 1st Sess. 171, *reprinted in* 1981 U.S. CODE CONG. & AD. NEWS 105, 267.

Several cases hold that when a contract is cancelled, the mutual rights and obligations of the parties simply "disappear," and there is no sale or exchange of any assets.[4] Accordingly, taxpayers took the position under pre-ERTA law that cancellation of a forward contract generated ordinary income or loss. In *The Hoover Co. v. Comm'r*,[5] the taxpayer, seeking ordinary loss on forward contract transactions, asserted that it had cancelled some of its contracts. The Tax Court found as a question of fact, however, that the contracts had been offset rather than cancelled, noting in a footnote the potential applicability of ordinary income treatment upon the cancellation of a forward contract.[6] Taxpayers claimed ordinary loss treatment on the grounds that a release from their obligations under the forward contracts was not a sale or exchange and no property rights were transferred. The legal theory was that the mere relinquishment of simple contract rights does not constitute a sale or exchange and gives rise to ordinary income or loss.[7]

In *Foote v. Comm'r*,[8] the Tax Court held that an agreement to terminate tenure rights entered into by a college professor did not constitute a sale or exchange. The Tax Court stated that the agreement "simply terminated petitioner's rights; his tenure did not pass to the University, but was extinguished."[9] The agreement released the University of its obligations. Rights were not transferred but merely came to an end and vanished. Citing other cases, the Tax Court stated that there was no sale or exchange upon execution of the agreement.[10]

At this writing, no cases have been decided as to the character of loss on the termination of certain forward contract rights and obligations of the type viewed as "abusive" by Congress and changed by I.R.C. § 1234A. It is possible that Section 108 of the DRA[11] should apply to forward contract cancellations to limit IRS arguments to the amount of loss, the character of loss (ordinary or capital), and whether the

[4]Comm'r v. Starr Bros., Inc. 204 F.2d 673, 674 (2d Cir. 1953); General Artists Corp. v. Comm'r, 205 F.2d 360 (2d Cir.), *cert. denied*, 346 U.S. 866 (1953).

[5]72 T.C. 206, 228 (1979).

[6]*Id.* at 249 n.7.

[7]*Id.* at 248.

[8]81 T.C. 930, 936 (1983).

[9]*Id.*

[10]*See* Billy Rose's Diamond Horseshoe, Inc. v. United States, 448 F.2d 549 (2d Cir. 1971); United States Freight Co. v. U.S., 422 F.2d 887 (Ct. Cl. 1970); Comm'r v. Pittston Co., 252 F.2d 344 (2d Cir. 1958), *cert. denied*, 357 U.S. 919 (1958); *Starr Bros., Inc.*, 204 F.2d 673; Leh v. Comm'r, 27 T.C. 892 (1957), *aff'd*, 260 F.2d 489 (9th Cir. 1958); *see also* Rev. Rul. 56-531, 1956-2 C.B. 983, *clarified by* Rev. Rul. 72-85, 1972-1 C.B. 234; Rev. Rul. 75-527, 1975-2 C.B. 30.

[11]DRA, Pub. L. 98-369, § 108, 98 Stat. 494, 630-31 (1984); *see* section 35.2(c).

taxpayer had the requisite profit motive.[12] In addition, when Congress enacted I.R.C. § 1234A, it viewed this provision as a change in the sale or exchange rule under I.R.C. § 1222 to prevent tax avoidance transactions.[13] Prior law may have supported the tax treatment claimed on certain forward contract cancellation transactions entered into with a profit motive.

Two cases involving the cancellation of losing forward contract positions have been decided by the Tax Court. The issue of the character of the loss on the cancellations was not addressed in either case because the Tax Court found that both forward contract markets were shams. In *Forseth v. Comm'r*,[14] the taxpayers entered into forward contract straddle transactions in gold and platinum futures contracts, which were executed in London between November 1980 and July 1981. The taxpayer reported ordinary losses on cancellation of the forward contract positions. The Tax Court found that the taxpayers' purported losses were factual shams for the following reasons. First, the reported losses achieved a high degree of correlation to the taxpayers' tax needs, offsetting 55 percent to 94 percent of their adjusted gross incomes.[15] Second, the predicted losses contained in promotional material were remarkably close to the actual losses reported.[16] Third, throughout the period of years during which the accounts were open, no margin calls or additional deposits were made even though the forward contracts were not subject to any limits on price movements and there was no limit on losses that might be sustained.[17] Fourth, some trading occurred in accounts before margin was deposited.[18] Fifth, the taxpayers reported gains roughly equal to the difference between their reported losses less the margin deposits.[19] Sixth, no evidence existed that the broker was "laying off" its positions with dealers to reduce risk.[20] And seventh, there was apparent manipulation of trading records.[21]

---

[12]*See* section 35.2(c).

[13]*See* General Explanation of ERTA, *supra* note 3, at 313; H.R. REP. NO. 201, *supra* note 3, at 212; S. REP. NO. 144, *supra* note 3, at 170.

[14]85 T.C. 127 (1985).

[15]*Id.* at 151.

[16]*Id.* at 152-53.

[17]*Id.* at 157.

[18]*Id.* at 154-55.

[19]*Id.* at 158-59.

[20]*Id.* at 161-63.

[21]*Id.* at 163-64.

In *Brown v. Comm'r*,[22] the taxpayers entered into forward contract straddle transactions in GNMA securities and FHLMC securities with a United States government securities dealer. The taxpayers received offering memoranda predicting that a minimum margin deposit of $10,000 would generate ordinary losses on the cancellation of the contracts of $100,000. The Tax Court held that the program existed solely to provide tax benefits and denied the taxpayers' deductions.[23] The court based its decision on the following facts that it believed to be relevant. First, the taxpayers did not prove that the prices for the contracts were determined by the open market.[24] Second, the government securities firm did not follow industry standards of the securities industry.[25] Third, the court found that cancellations in the securities industry generally were used only to correct errors.[26]

In both *Forseth* and *Brown* the taxpayers were assessed penalties for underpayment of tax liability.[27] In *Brown*, however, the Tax Court initially imposed damages under I.R.C. § 6673 in the amount of $5000 against each taxpayer for filing Tax Court petitions primarily for the purpose of delaying the payment of tax.[28] The court found that the taxpayers were sufficiently sophisticated in business and tax matters to have known, and actually did know, at the time the disputed transactions were entered into that such transactions were shams.[29] The court used its opinion in *Brown* to serve notice to other taxpayers that it will have no reluctance in assessing this penalty against taxpayers who file Tax Court petitions or maintain positions based on transactions that they knew or reasonably should have known to be factual shams.[30]

---

[22]85 T.C. —, No. 22 (Aug. 26, 1985), 1985 TAX CT. REP. (CCH) DEC. 42,340, at 3461, *withdrawn and reissued at* 85 T.C. —, No. 57 (Dec. 18, 1985).

[23]*Id.*

[24]*Id.*

[25]*Id.*

[26]*Id.*

[27]I.R.C. § 6653(a).

[28]The initial decision assessing a penalty under I.R.C. § 6673 was withdrawn and when the decision was reissued, the penalty assessment under I.R.C. § 6673 was removed.

[29]*Brown*, 85 T.C. —, No. 57 at —.

[30]*Id.*

§ 46.2 CAPITAL GAIN OR LOSS ON TERMINATIONS

The tax result sought by some taxpayers on pre-ERTA cancellation transactions was viewed as inappropriate by Congress. As a result, I.R.C. § 1234A was enacted as part of ERTA so that gains and losses from economically equivalent transactions are taxed the same way.[31] Congress considered ordinary income treatment inappropriate if a transaction was economically equivalent to a sale or exchange of the contract.[32]

The definition of capital gains and losses requires that there be a sale or exchange of a capital asset.[33] ERTA expanded capital treatment to include the cancellation, lapse, expiration, or other termination of personal property (as defined in I.R.C. § 1092(d)(1)) which is (or would be on acquisition) a capital asset in the hands of the taxpayer.[34] ERTA also extended capital treatment to include a section 1256 contract that is not (or acquisition of which would not be) personal property if the contract is a capital asset in the hands of the taxpayer.[35]

Despite the statement in I.R.C. § 1234A that its provisions cover section 1256 contracts, the rules of domestic commodity and securities exchanges provide that contracts traded on the exchanges can only be terminated by offset or by making or taking delivery of the underlying property. Therefore, exchange rules prohibit termination of section 1256 contracts by cancellation, lapse, or expiration. Nevertheless, I.R.C. § 1234A includes such contracts to assure that taxpayers do not seek to manipulate the termination of section 1256 contracts to obtain ordinary losses.

All personal property of a type that is actively traded is subject to I.R.C. § 1234A. As a result, I.R.C. § 1234A also includes stock as covered under I.R.C. § 1092(d)(3)(B) that is or would be a capital asset in the hands of the taxpayer. This provision applies generally to property acquired and positions established after June 23, 1981.

The scope of I.R.C. § 1234A was amended by the DRA to exclude from its application the retirement of any debt instrument (whether or not through a trust or other participation agreement, such as a mortgage pass-through certificate).[36] The General Explanation of the DRA, prepared by the Joint Committee, states that I.R.C. § 1234A was not in-

---

[31] For a discussion of pre-ERTA cancellation transactions, see section 46.1.

[32] *See* General Explanation of ERTA, *supra* note 3, at 313; H.R. REP. No. 201, *supra* note 3, at 212; S. REP. No. 144, *supra* note 3, at 170–71.

[33] *See* I.R.C. § 1222.

[34] I.R.C. § 1234A(1).

[35] I.R.C. § 1234A(2).

[36] DRA, *supra* note 11, at § 102(e)(9); HOUSE CONFERENCE REPORT, DEFICIT REDUCTION ACT OF 1984, H. REP. No. 861, 98th Cong., 2d Sess. 911 (1984); *see also* 28.4.

tended to change the longstanding as ordinary income tax treatment of market discount on residential mortgage investments and other obligations of natural persons. Therefore, the DRA amendment clarifies that ordinary income is also obtained when the holder's interest is an indirect one, such as an interest in a fixed investment trust.[37] The DRA amendment is applied retroactively and is effective as if it had been included as part of ERTA.[38]

---

[37]See JOINT COMMITTEE ON TAXATION, 98TH CONG., 2D SESS., GENERAL EXPLANATION OF THE REVENUE PROVISIONS OF THE DEFICIT REDUCTION ACT OF 1984 316 (Joint Comm. Print 1984); see also 28.4(b)(1).

[38]DRA, supra note 11, at § 102(f)(4).

Appendix

TAX TREATMENT OF ACTIVELY TRADED SECURITIES, COMMODITIES, AND OPTIONS

Product Information		Current Law				Effective Date (13)	Pre-DRA Law			
		Investors and Traders		Option Dealers/ Market Makers	Hedgers/ Dealers in Underlying Property		Investors and Traders		Option Dealers/ Market Makers	Hedgers/ Dealers in Underlying Property
Product	Market Where Product Is Traded	Long Position	Short Position				Long Position	Short Position		
Options										
Stock Options (1)	AMEX, CBOE, PHLX, PSE	(A)(2)	(B)(2)(3)	(C)(4)(5)	(F)	7/18/84	(A)(7)	(B)(7)	(F)	(F)
Index Options (Securities Options)										
Airline	AMEX	(A)(9)	(B)(9)	(C)(5)	(F)	7/18/84	(A)(10)(11)	(B)(10)(11)	(F)	(F)
AMEX Market Value	AMEX	(C)(5)(8)	(C)(5)(8)	(C)(4)(5)	(D)	7/18/84	(A)(10)(11)	(B)(10)(11)	(F)	(F)
Computer Technology	AMEX	(A)(9)	(B)(9)	(C)(4)(5)	(F)	7/18/84	(A)(10)(11)	(B)(10)(11)	(F)	(F)
Gold/Silver	PHLX	(C)(5)(8)	(C)(5)(8)	(C)(5)	(D)	7/18/84	(A)(10)(11)	(B)(10)(11)	(F)	(F)
Major Market	AMEX	(C)(5)(8)	(C)(5)(8)	(C)(5)	(D)	7/18/84	(A)(10)(11)	(B)(10)(11)	(F)	(F)
NASDAQ 100 (15)	NASDAQ System	(A)(9)	(B)(9)	(C)(4)(5)	(F)	7/18/84	(A)(10)(11)	(B)(10)(11)	(F)	(F)
National O-T-C	AMEX	(C)(5)(8)	(C)(5)(8)	(C)(5)	(D)	7/18/84	(A)(10)(11)	(B)(10)(11)	(F)	(F)
NYSE Composite	NYSE	(C)(5)(8)	(C)(5)(8)	(C)(5)	(D)	7/18/84	(A)(10)(11)	(B)(10)(11)	(F)	(F)
NYSE Composite Double	NYSE	(C)(5)(8)	(C)(5)(8)	(C)(5)	(D)	7/18/84	(A)(10)(11)	(B)(10)(11)	(F)	(F)
Oil	AMEX	(A)(9)	(B)(9)	(C)(4)(5)	(F)	7/18/84	(A)(10)(11)	(B)(10)(11)	(F)	(F)
S&P 100, 500	CBOE	(C)(5)(8)	(C)(5)(8)	(C)(5)	(D)	7/18/84	(A)(10)(11)	(B)(10)(11)	(F)	(F)
Technology	PSE	(C)(5)(8)	(C)(5)(8)	(C)(5)	(D)	7/18/84	(A)(10)(11)	(B)(10)(11)	(F)	(F)

Transportation	AMEX	(A)(9)	(B)(9)	(C)(4)(5)	(F)	7/18/84	(A)(10)(11)	(B)(10)(11)	(F)	(F)
Value Line	PHLX	(C)(5)(8)	(C)(5)(8)	(C)(5)	(D)	7/18/84	(A)(10)(11)	(B)(10)(11)	(F)	(F)
Options on Government Securities										
Treasury Bills	AMEX, CBOE	(C)(5)	(C)(5)	(C)(5)	(D)	7/18/84	(A)(11)	(B)(11)	(F)(11)	(F)(11)
Treasury Notes	AMEX, CBOE	(C)(5)	(C)(5)	(C)(5)	(D)	7/18/84	(A)(11)	(B)(11)	(F)(11)	(F)(11)
Treasury Bonds	CBOE	(C)(5)	(C)(5)	(C)(5)	(D)	7/18/84	(A)(11)	(B)(11)	(F)(11)	(F)(11)
Options on Futures Contracts										
Corn	CBT	(C)(5)	(C)(5)	(C)(5)	(D)	10/31/83	(E)(11)	(E)(11)	(F)(11)	(F)(11)
Cotton	NYCE	(C)(5)	(C)(5)	(C)(5)	(D)	10/31/83	(E)(11)	(E)(11)	(F)(11)	(F)(11)
Eurodollars, Marks, Pounds, Swiss Francs	CME	(C)(5)	(C)(5)	(C)(5)	(D)	10/31/83	(E)(11)	(E)(11)	(F)(11)	(F)(11)
Gold (33.2 & 100 ounces)	COMEX, MidAm	(C)(5)	(C)(5)	(C)(5)	(D)	10/31/83	(E)(11)	(E)(11)	(F)(11)	(F)(11)
Live Cattle & Hogs	CME	(C)(5)	(C)(5)	(C)(5)	(D)	10/31/83	(E)(11)	(E)(11)	(F)(11)	(F)(11)
NYSE Composite Index	NYFE	(C)(5)	(C)(5)	(C)(5)	(D)	10/31/83	(E)(11)	(E)(11)	(F)(11)	(F)(11)
Silver (100 & 500 ounces)	COMEX, CBT	(C)(5)	(C)(5)	(C)(5)	(D)	10/31/83	(E)(11)	(E)(11)	(F)(11)	(F)(11)
Soybeans (1000 & 5000 bu.)	CBT, MidAm	(C)(5)	(C)(5)	(C)(5)	(D)	10/31/83	(E)(11)	(E)(11)	(F)(11)	(F)(11)
S&P 500	COMEX	(C)(5)	(C)(5)	(C)(5)	(D)	10/31/83	(E)(11)	(E)(11)	(F)(11)	(F)(11)
Sugar	CSC	(C)(5)	(C)(5)	(C)(5)	(D)	10/31/83	(E)(11)	(E)(11)	(F)(11)	(F)(11)
Treasury Bonds	CBT	(C)(5)	(C)(5)	(C)(5)	(D)	10/31/83	(E)(11)	(E)(11)	(F)(11)	(F)(11)
Treasury Notes	CBT	(C)(5)	(C)(5)	(C)(5)	(D)	10/31/83	(E)(11)	(E)(11)	(F)(11)	(F)(11)
Value Line Index	KCBT	(C)(5)	(C)(5)	(C)(5)	(D)	10/31/83	(E)(11)	(E)(11)	(F)(11)	(F)(11)
Wheat (Spring, Hard & Soft Winter)	KCBT, MGE, MidAm	(C)(5)	(C)(5)	(C)(5)	(D)	10/31/83	(E)(11)	(E)(11)	(F)(11)	(F)(11)

TAX TREATMENT OF ACTIVELY TRADED SECURITIES, COMMODITIES, AND OPTIONS (CONTINUED)

| Product Information | | Current Law | | | | Effective Date (13) | Pre-DRA Law | | | |
| Product | Market Where Product Is Traded | Investors and Traders | | Option Dealers/ Market Makers | Hedgers/ Dealers in Underlying Property | | Investors and Traders | | Option Dealers/ Market Makers | Hedgers/ Dealers in Underlying Property |
		Long Position	Short Position				Long Position	Short Position		
Foreign Currency Options										
Canadian Dollars, French Francs, Marks, Pounds, Swiss Francs, Yen	CBOE, PHLX	(C)(5)	(C)(5)	(C)(5)	(D)	7/18/84	(A)(11)	(B)(11)	(F)(11)	(F)(11)
Options on Commodities										
Gold	ACC	(C)(5)	(C)(5)	(C)(5)	(D)	7/18/84	(A)(11)	(B)(11)	(F)(11)	(F)(11)
Commodities (RFCs)										
Agricultural	CBT, NYCE, KCBT, MGE, CSC, MidAm	(C)(5)	(C)(5)	N/A	(D)	6/23/81	(C)	(C)	N/A	(D)
Metals & Petroleum	CMX, NYME, CBT, INTEX(14)	(C)(5)	(C)(5)	N/A	(D)	6/23/81	(C)	(C)	N/A	(D)
Livestock & Meat	CME	(C)(5)	(C)(5)	N/A	(D)	6/23/81	(C)	(C)	N/A	(D)
Wood	CME	(C)(5)	(C)(5)	N/A	(D)	6/23/81	(C)	(C)	N/A	(D)
Financial	CBT, CME, NYFE, KCBT, INTEX(14)	(C)(5)	(C)(5)	N/A	(D)	6/23/81	(C)	(C)	N/A	(D)

Securities

Stock

National
Securities
Exchanges
Registered
with the SEC

(G)	(G)(12)	(G)(6)	(F)	7/18/84	(G)	(G)(12)	(F)	(F)

NOTES ACCOMPANYING TAX TREATMENT OF ACTIVELY TRADED SECURITIES, COMMODITIES, AND OPTIONS

(A) I.R.C. § 1234(a) provides that for capital assets, capital gain or loss treatment, long-term or short-term depending on the taxpayer's holding period, results when the position is closed.

(B) I.R.C. § 1234(b) provides short-term capital gain or loss when the position is closed.

(C) I.R.C. § 1256 provides section 1256 treatment (i.e., positions are marked-to-market as 60% long-term and 40% short-term capital gain or loss), except for option dealers who also are dealers in the underlying property.

(D) I.R.C. § 1256(e) provides that qualified hedging transactions are exempt from section 1256 treatment and the Straddle Rules. If transactions qualify for I.R.C. § 1256(e) treatment, ordinary income or loss results when the transactions are closed. If a transaction does not qualify for the statutory hedging exemption but includes a section 1256 contract, the contract is marked-to-market at ordinary income rates.

(E) The character of gain or loss derived from options on futures prior to November 1, 1983 is uncertain. Some authorities believed that long positions automatically qualified for 60/40 treatment because I.R.C. § 1234(a) borrows the "character of the underlying property" (the question is whether that means 60/40 treatment or merely capital versus ordinary). On the other hand, I.R.C. § 1234(b) may have required that all gains and losses from short positions be reported as short-term capital gains and losses.

(F) Ordinary income or loss results when the position is closed.

(G) Capital gain or loss treatment results when the property is sold.

(1) Stock options are options to purchase or sell equity securities. See I.R.C. § 1256(g)(6)(A) for definition of "equity options."

(2) Offsetting positions are subject to the Straddle Rules. I.R.C. § 1092(a)(1)(A).

(3) Qualified covered calls are exempt from the Straddle Rules. I.R.C. § 1092(c)(4).

(4) Gain or loss on dealer equity options that are allocable to limited partners are marked-to-market, not eligible for 60/40 treatment, and generate short-term capital gain or loss. I.R.C. § 1256(f)(4).

(5) Trading in the underlying property creates a mixed straddle. I.R.C. § 1256(d)(4).

(6) An options dealer recognizes ordinary income or loss if he is also a dealer in the underlying stock.

NOTES (CONTINUED)

(7) Prior to DRA, short-term stock options were not "positions" subject to the Straddle Rules. DRA, Pub. L. 98-369, § 101(a)(1), 98 Stat. 494, 616.

(8) It appears that the S&P 100, S&P 500, NYSE Composite, PSE Technology, NYSE Double, Value Line, National O-T-C, Major Market, and AMEX Market Value indexes are nonequity options as defined in I.R.C. § 1256(g)(3) and should qualify as broad based index options. In LTR 8526035 (Apr. 1, 1985), the Treasury adopted the joint guidelines promulgated by the CFTC and the SEC for determining whether an index is a nonequity option as defined by I.R.C. § 1256(g)(3). Securities Exchange Act Release No. 20578, Jan. 18, 1984, 49 Fed. Reg. 2884 (1984), Rev. Rul. 86-8, 1986-4 I.R.B. 6. The legislative history of the DRA notes that the Treasury must approve section 1256 treatment for certain options to qualify as nonequity options. It is possible that Treasury designations might have prospective effect only, raising questions about the tax treatment of certain option contracts traded prior to such designation. CONFERENCE REPORT, DEFICIT REDUCTION ACT OF 1984, H. R. REP. NO. 461, 98th Cong. 2d Sess. 909 (1984).

(9) These index options appear to be equity options that are not eligible for 60/40 treatment unless held by options dealers.

(10) Ordinary income or loss treatment may be accorded certain transactions because it was uncertain whether I.R.C. § 1234 applied to cash settlement options, such as index options, that may not be options on "property." DRA amended I.R.C. § 1234 to add subsection (c) "Treatment of Options on Section 1256 Contracts and Cash Settlement Options." DRA, supra note 7, § 105(a).

(11) Pre-DRA transactions were subject to the Straddle Rules after enactment of ERTA unless the hedging exemption was applicable. ERTA Pub. L. 97-448, § 501, 95 Stat. 172, 323-35.

(12) The short sales rule of I.R.C. § 1233 applies to adjust the holding period.

(13) The DRA amendments to I.R.C. § 1256 provide that the 60/40 Rule can apply, at the taxpayer's election, to positions held on July 18, 1984 or to positions held at any time during the taxpayer's year that includes the date of enactment. DRA, supra note 7, § 102(g). ERTA provided that the 60/40 Rule can apply, at the taxpayer's election, to positions held on June 23, 1981 or to positions held at any time during the taxpayer's year that includes the date of enactment. ERTA, supra note 11, § 503(a).

(14) INTEX, which offers gold and freight futures contracts, was designated a qualified board or exchange for purposes of I.R.C. § 1256 in Rev. Rul. 85-72, 1985-1 C.B. 286.

(15) Because the NASDAQ 100 option is not traded on a qualified board or exchange, it does not meet the definition of a listed option under I.R.C. § 1256(g)(5). At the date of this writing, the NASD is considering applying to the Treasury for a ruling to qualify their trading system as a qualified board or exchange under I.R.C. § 1256(g)(7).

Table of Cases

(References are to book sections.)

(References are to book sections.)

(References are to book sections.)

(References are to book sections.)

(References are to book sections.)

(References are to book sections.)

(References are to book sections.)

(References are to book sections.)

(References are to book sections.)

(References are to book sections.)

(References are to book sections.)

(References are to book sections.)

(References are to book sections.)

Table of Internal Revenue Code Sections

(References are to book sections.)

(References are to book sections.)

(References are to book sections.)

I.R.C.

163(e) .... 27.2(a), 27.3, 27.6(b)(3)
163(f) ....27.11(d)
163(f)(2) ....27.11(b)
163(f)(2)(b) ....27.11(b)
163(f)(2)(B) ....27.11(e)
163(f)(2)(C) ....27.11(b)
163(f)(3) ....27.11(b)
165 .... 35.2(b)
165(a) ....10.1, 11.2(a)(2)
165(c) .... 35.2(a)
165(c)(2) ....35.2(b), 35.2(d)
165(g) .... 25.3(d)
165(g)(1) ....15.1(c)
165(j) .....27.11(c), 27.11(d), 27.11(e)
165(j)(1) .... 28.2(b)(1)(i)(b)
165(j)(3) ....27.11(d)
165(j)(3)(A) ....27.11(d)
165(j)(3)(B) ....27.11(d)
165(j)(3)(C) ....27.11(d)
165(j)(3)(D) ....27.11(d)
171 ......27.4, 27.4(a)(1), 27.4(a)(2)(i),
     28.3(b)(3), 28.4(c)(3), 28.4(d)(3)
171(a) ....7.4, 8.4, 27.4(a)(1)
171(a)(1) ....27.4(a)(1)
171(a)(2) ..... 27.4(a)(2)(ii), 28.2(d)(3)
171(b) .... 28.3(a)(3)(ii), 28.3(b)(3)
171(b)(1) ....27.4(b), 27.4(c)(1),
                 28.3(a)(3)(iii)
171(b)(1)(C) ....27.4(a)(1)
171(b)(2) ....27.4(b), 27.4(c)(1)
171(b)(3) ....28.4(d)(3)
171(b)(3)(A) ....27.4(a)(1)
171(b)(3)(B) ....27.4(a)(1)
171(c) ....27.4(a)(1)
171(c)(2) ....27.4(a)(1)
171(d) ...27.4, 27.4(a)(2)(ii), 28.4(c)(3)
171(e) ....9.4(b)
212 ....7.1, 7.1(a), 7.1(c), 7.1(c)(1),
     7.1(c)(2), 7.1(c)(3), 7.1(c)(5),
     7.1(c)(8), 7.1(c)(9), 8.1(b),
     16.6(a), 16.6(e)(1)
212(1) ....7.1(a)
212(2) ....7.1(a), 43.1
212(3) ....7.1(a)
233 .... 15.7
243 ....15.7, 22.9(a)
243(a) .... 22.7(c), 25.6(c)

I.R.C.

243(a)(1) .... 22.9(a)
243(a)(2) .... 22.9(a)
243(a)(3) .... 22.9(a)
243(b) ....22.9(c)
243(b)(1) .... 22.9(a)
243(b)(1)(B)(i) .... 22.9(a)
243(b)(1)(B)(ii) .... 22.9(a)
243(b)(1)(C) .... 22.9(a)
243(b)(2) .... 22.9(a)
243(b)(5) .... 22.9(a)
243(c)(1) .... 22.9(a)
244 .... 22.9(a)
246 .... 22.9(a)
246(a)(2)(B) ....22.9(d), 25.5(b)
246(b) .... 22.9(a)
246(c) .... 17.9(f), 22.5, 44.3(c)
246(c)(1)(A) ... 15.7, 22.9(b), 22.9(b)(1)
246(c)(1)(B) ....22.9(b)(2)
246(c)(2) ....15.7, 22.9(b)
246(c)(3) ....17.9(f)
246(c)(3)(A) 15.7
246(c)(3)(B) 15.7
246(c)(3)(C) 15.7
246(c)(4) 14.6, 15.7
246(c)(4)(C) .... 25.3(b)(ii)
246A(a) ....22.9(c)
246A(b) ....22.9(c)
246A(c)(2) ....22.9(c)
246A(c)(3) ....22.9(c)
246A(c)(4) ....22.9(c)
246A(d)(1) ....22.9(c)
246A(e) ....22.9(c)
246A(f) ....22.9(c)
247 .... 22.4
247(a) 22.4
247(b)(1) 22.4
249(a) ....27.4(d), 28.3(a)(6)
263 ....8.1(c)
263(g) ......7.7, 8.2(f), 8.7, 9.10, 10.1,
     16.6(e)(5), 33.2(a), Part Ten,
     36.3(b)(2), 43.2, 43.2(b), 43.2(c),
     43.2(d), 43.2(e), 43.2(f), 44.7,
                   45.4, 45.4(d)
263(g)(1) ......7.2(f), 30.3, 30.4, 33.3,
             36.3(b)(3), 43, 43.2(a)
263(g)(2) ....43.2(a), 43.2(c)
263(g)(2)(B) ....43.2(b)

(References are to book sections.)

(References are to book sections.)

(References are to book sections.)

(References are to book sections.)

(References are to book sections.)

(References are to book sections.)

(References are to book sections.)

(References are to book sections.)

(References are to book sections.)

Table of Treasury Pronouncements

TREASURY REGULATIONS
(References are to book sections.)

TREASURY REGULATIONS *(Continued)*

(References are to book sections.)

TREASURY REGULATIONS (Continued)
(References are to book sections.)

TREASURY REGULATIONS *(Continued)*

(References are to book sections.)

TEMPORARY TREASURY REGULATIONS

(References are to book sections.)

TEMPORARY TREASURY REGULATIONS (Continued)
(References are to book sections.)

PROPOSED TREASURY REGULATIONS (Continued)
(References are to book sections.)

Prop. Treas. Reg.		Prop. Treas. Reg.	
35a.9999-2(A-15)	27.2(a)	1.1058(e)(2)	24.3
301.6621-2T, Question 5	41.2	1.1058-1(f)	24.2(g)
1.385-10(b)	25.3(b)(2)(i)	1.1223-2(a)	15.8, 24.2(d)
1.464-2(a)(3)	21.4(b), 33.2(c)(2)	1.1223-2(b)(1)	15.8, 24.3
1.1058-1	27.10(b)(2)	1.1223-2(b)(2)	15.8, 24.3
1.1058-1(a)	24.2(a)	1.1232-5(b)(4)	27.11(d)
1.1058-1(b)	24.2(b), 24.3	1.1613A-3(f)	25.9(a)
1.1058-1(b)(3)	24.2(b), 27.10(b)(1)	1.7872-5	7.2(c)(2)
1.1058-1(c)(1)	24.2(c)	1.7872-5(b)(13)	7.2(c)(2)
1.1058-1(c)(2)	24.2(c)	301.7701-4(c)(4)	1.1(e)(2)
1.1058-1(d)	16.6(a), 22.9(b)(3), 24.2(e), 27.10(b)(1)		

REVENUE RULINGS
(References are to book sections.)

Rev. Rul.		Rev. Rul.	
53-45, 1953-1 C.B. 178	22.7(g)	58-211, 1958-1 C.B. 529	17.9(g), 17.9(h)
55-68, 1955-1 C.B. 372	15.3(c)(2)		
55-76, 1955-1 C.B. 239	23.4(a)	58-234, 1958-1 C.B. 265	26.3(b)(2)(iii)
55-355, 1955-1 C.B. 418	18.2(d)		
55-655, 1955-2 C.B. 253	28.1(a)(2)(i)	58-234, 1958-1 C.B. 279	26.3(b)(1)(i), 26.3(b)(1)(iii),
56-153, 1956-1 C.B. 166	22.7(c)		26.3(b)(2)(i), 26.3(b)(2)(ii),
56-179, 1956-1 C.B. 187	25.3(c)(2)		26.3(c)(1)(iv), 26.3(c)(2)(i),
56-406, 1956-2 C.B. 523	17.6(a), 17.9(b)		26.3(c)(2)(ii), 26.3(c)(2)(iv)
56-431, 1956-2 C.B. 171	22.7(d)	58-384, 1958-2 C.B. 410	16.4(c), 16.10, 17.9(f)
56-435, 1956-2 C.B. 506	27.8(a), 28.2(c)	59-44, 1959-1 C.B. 205	17.9(h)
56-452, 1956-2 C.B. 525	17.8(c)	59-242, 1959-2 C.B. 125	16.4(c)
56-510, 1956-2 C.B. 168	22.8, 25.5(a)(1)	59-373, 1959-2 C.B. 37	23.4(a)
		59-387, 1959-2 C.B. 56	28.3(a)(1)
56-531, 1956-2 C.B. 983	46.1	59-418, 1959-2 C.B. 184	17.3(e)
56-602, 1956-2 C.B. 527	17.3(b)	60-17, 1960-1 C.B. 124	27.4(c)(2)
56-653, 1956-2 C.B. 185	18.2(c)	60-24, 1960-1 C.B. 171	6.4(b), 21.3(c)
57-29, 1957-1 C.B. 519	15.2(a)(6), 25.3(d)	60-177, 1960-1 C.B. 9	22.9(b)(3), 24.2(e), 24.4, 27.10(b)(1)
57-151, 1957-1 C.B. 64	23.4(a)		
58-2, 1958-1 C.B. 236	28.1(a)(2)(iii)	60-195, 1960-1 C.B. 300	17.9(h)
58-40, 1958-1 C.B. 275	6.4	60-284, 1960-2 C.B. 464	27.7
58-210, 1958-1 C.B. 523	17.9(h)	60-321, 1960-2 C.B. 166	6.3(b)

REVENUE RULINGS *(Continued)*
(References are to book sections.)

Rev. Rul.	Rev. Rul.
60-331, 1960-2 C.B. 189 ....22.7(c)	70-269, 1970-1 C.B. 82 ......25.4(b)(3)
61-97, 1961-1 C.B. 394 ......18.2(a)(2)	70-291, 1970-1 C.B. 168 ....14.4(a),
61-145, 1961-2 C.B. 21 .... 23.4(a)	14.4(g)
61-175, 1961-2 C.B. 128 ....25.9(a),	70-344, 1970-2 C.B. 50 ....12.5(d),
28.4(b)(1)	15.2(a)(2)(ii), 15.2(a)(5)
61-181, 1961-2 C.B. 21 .... 23.4(a)	70-521, 1970-2 C.B. 72 .....22.2(a)(7),
62-21, 1962-1 C.B. 37 ....7.1(c)(7)	26.3(e)(1)(ii)
62-42, 1962-1 C.B. 133 ....16.6(d),	70-544, 1970-2 C.B. 6 ....25.9(a),
16.6(e)(1)	28.4(b)(1), 28.4(b)(3)
62-58, 1962-1 C.B. 158 .... 25.6(b)	70-545, 1970-2 C.B. 7 ....25.9(a),
62-140, 1962-2 C.B. 181 .....15.3(a)(3)	28.4(b)(1), 28.4(b)(3),
62-153, 1962-2 C.B. 186 .... 15.3(a)(3),	28.4(c)(1)
16.2(c), 17.9(e)	70-598, 1970-2 C.B. 188 ....15.1(b),
63-27, 1963-1 C.B. 57 ....7.3(a)	15.2(a)(5)
63-65, 1963-1 C.B. 142 .... 16.2(a)	70-627, 1970-2 C.B. 159 ......7.1(c)(8)
63-225, 1963-2 C.B. 339 ..26.3(e)(1)(ii)	70-647, 1970-2 C.B. 38 ....7.2(b)
64-160, 1964-1 C.B. 306 ....9.7(c)	71-15, 1971-1 C.B. 149 ....9.7(c)
64-236, 1964-2 C.B. 64 ....7.1(c)(4)	71-21, 1971-1 C.B. 221 ....18.2(e),
65-291, 1965-2 C.B. 290 .... 25.6(b)	20.2(c)
66-7, 1966-1 C.B. 188 .... 15.1(b)	71-30, 1971-1 C.B. 226 ...6.3(b), 9.7(f)
66-97, 1966-1 C.B. 190 ....15.1(a),	71-316, 1971-2 C.B. 311 ......17.3(b),
15.2(a)(5), 27.4(b)	17.7, 17.8
67-419, 1967-2 C.B. 265 ....9.7(c)	71-399, 1971-2 C.B. 433 ......25.9(a),
67-436, 1967-2 C.B. 266 .....18.2(a)(2)	28.4(b)(1)
68-54, 1968-1 C.B. 69 .... 28.3(d)	71-520, 1971-2 C.B. 311 .... 17.8(a)
68-126, 1968-1 C.B. 194 ......12.5(a),	71-521, 1971-2 C.B. 313 ....
22.7(a)	............26.3(b)(1)(i), 26.3(c)(1)(iv)
68-151, 1968-1 C.B. 363 .. 26.3(b)(1)(i)	71-568, 1971-2 C.B. 312 ....17.6(b)(1),
68-170, 1968-1 C.B. 71 ......28.3(a)(5)	35.2
68-601, 1968-2 C.B. 124 .... 17.9(a)	71-594, 1971-2 C.B. 91 .... 23.4(a)
69-15, 1969-1 C.B. 95 ....22.2(b)(3)	72-46, 1972-1 C.B. 50 .... 27.9(a)
69-135, 1969-1 C.B. 198 .... 25.3(c)(5),	72-71, 1972-1 C.B. 99 ......15.2(c)(2),
25.3(c)(8), 28.3(b)(5)	15.4(a)
69-142, 1969-1 C.B. 107 .....25.4(b)(3)	72-85, 1972-1 C.B. 234 ....46.1
69-171, 1969-1 C.B. 46 .... 28.2(a)	72-134, 1972-1 C.B. 29 ....
69-202, 1969-1 C.B. 95 .... 15.4(a)	.... 28.2(b)(1)(i)(d)
69-265, 1969-1 C.B. 109 .... 25.3(c)(5),	72-179, 1972-1 C.B. 57 ....6.4(b),
25.3(c)(8), 28.3(b)(2)	6.4(c)(1), 10.1, 16.11, 21.3(c)
69-416, 1969-2 C.B. 159 ....9.7(c)	72-198, 1972-1 C.B. 233 ....
69-489, 1969-2 C.B. 172 .....28.1(a)(3)	...26.3(b)(2)(i), 26.3(c)(2)(i), 26.3(e)(2)
69-574, 1969-2 C.B. 130 ....25.9(c)	72-224, 1972-1 C.B. 30 .....28.2(b)(3)
70-6, 1970-1 C.B. 172 ....15.3(c)(4)	72-264, 1972-1 C.B. 131 .....28.3(b)(5)
70-41, 1970-1 C.B. 77 ....25.4(b)(3)	72-265, 1972-1 C.B. 222 .... 25.3(c)(2),
70-221, 1970-1 C.B. 33 ....7.2(b)	28.3(b)(5)
70-231, 1970-1 C.B. 171 ....17.3(e)	72-359, 1972-2 C.B. 478 .....15.3(c)(5)

REVENUE RULINGS *(Continued)*
(References are to book sections.)

Rev. Rul.	Rev. Rul.
72-376, 1972-2 C.B. 647 ....25.9(a), 28.4(b)(1)	74-300, 1974-1 C.B. 169 ....25.9(a), 28.4(b)(1), 28.4(b)(3)
72-381, 1972-2 C.B. 233 .... 12.5(b)	74-380, 1974-2 C.B. 32 ...28.2(a)(3)(ii)
72-415, 1972-2 C.B. 463 ....18.2(a)(1)(iii)	74-384, 1974-2 C.B. 152 ......7.1(c)(1)
72-478, 1972-2 C.B. 288 .... 16.2(a)	74-482, 1974-2 C.B. 267 .....28.2(b)(3)
72-521, 1972-2 C.B. 178 ....16.6(b), 16.6(c), 16.6(e)(1)	74-530, 1974-2 C.B. 188 .... 25.9(a)
72-522, 1972-2 C.B. 215 ....25.4(b)(3)	74-562, 1974-2 C.B. 28 ....22.7(c)
72-575, 1972-2 C.B. 74 .... 28.2(b)(1)(i)(d)	75-13, 1975-1 C.B. 67 .... 6.4
72-587, 1972-2 C.B. 74 ......27.4(c)(2)	75-39, 1975-1 C.B. 272 .... 27.2(a)
73-13, 1973-1 C.B. 42 ....7.1(c)(2)	75-117, 1975-1 C.B. 273 .... 27.9(a)
73-27, 1973-1 C.B. 46 ....7.3(a)	75-192, 1975-1 C.B. 384 ....25.9(a), 28.4(b)(1)
73-31, 1973-1 C.B. 217 ....18.2(e), 20.2(c)	75-236, 1975-1 C.B. 106 ....25.3(a), 25.3(b)(1)
73-37, 1973-1 C.B. 374 ....18.2(e), 20.2(c)	75-337, 1975-2 C.B. 124 .....25.4(b)(1)
73-112, 1973-1 C.B. 47 ....27.2(e), 28.2(b)(1)(i), 28.2(b)(1)(iv)	75-360, 1975-2 C.B. 110 .....25.4(b)(3)
	75-513, 1975-2 C.B. 114 .....28.3(b)(4)
73-122, 1973-1 C.B. 66 .... 28.3(d)	75-523, 1975-2 C.B. 257 ....7.1(c)
73-160, 1973-1 C.B. 365 ....27.8(a), 28.2(c)	75-527, 1975-2 C.B. 30 .... 46.1
	75-548, 1975-2 C.B. 331 .....15.2(a)(5)
73-328, 1973-2 C.B. 296 .... 27.8(a)	76-53, 1976-1 C.B. 87 ....18.2(f)
73-329, 1973-2 C.B. 302 .... 17.8(b)	76-78, 1976-1 C.B. 25 . 28.2(b)(1)(i)(d)
73-403, 1973-2 C.B. 308 ....9.7(a)	76-299, 1976-2 C.B. 211 .... 22.5
73-524, 1973-2 C.B. 307 ....14.3(b), 16.2(c)	76-346, 1976-2 C.B. 247 .... 17.9(h)
	76-367, 1976-2 C.B. 259 ....25.3(a), 28.1(a)(3)
73-563, 1973-2 C.B. 24 .... 23.4(a)	76-387, 1976-2 C.B. 96 .... 25.3(a)
74-4, 1974-1 C.B. 51 .... 17.4	77-40, 1977-1 C.B. 248 ...26.3(b)(2)(i), 26.3(e)(2)
74-27, 1974-1 C.B. 24 .... 27.10(b), 36.3(b)(2)(i)	77-55, 1977-1 C.B. 18 ....28.2(a)(3)(ii)
	77-59, 1977-1 C.B. 196 ....27.10(a), 27.10(b), 36.3(b)(2)(i)
74-127, 1974-1 C.B. 47 ......28.3(a)(5)	77-108, 1977-1 C.B. 86 .... 25.3(b)(2)(iii), 25.3(b)(4)
74-169, 1974-1 C.B. 147 ....25.9(a), 28.4(b)(1)	77-137, 1977-1 C.B. 178 .....25.8(a)(3)
74-172, 1974-1 C.B. 178 .....27.4(c)(2)	77-185, 1977-1 C.B. 48 ..26.2(b), 35.2, 35.2(a), 35.2(b), 35.2(c), 44.6
74-197, 1974-1 C.B. 143 ....25.9(c)	77-201, 1977-1 C.B. 250 .... 17.9(a)
74-218, 1974-1 C.B. 202 .....17.6(b)(2)	77-234, 1977-2 C.B. 39 ...28.2(a)(3)(ii)
74-221, 1974-1 C.B. 365 .... 25.9(a) 28.4(b)(1)	77-238, 1977-2 C.B. 115 .....25.3(c)(2)
74-223, 1974-1 C.B. 23 .... 20.1(b)	77-349, 1977-2 C.B. 20 ....25.9(a), 28.4(b)(1)
74-226, 1974-1 C.B. 119 ....7.2(e), 8.1(e), 20.1(b), 43.1	77-415, 1977-2 C.B. 311 .....25.3(c)(4)
74-227, 1974-1 C.B. 119 ......20.1(b), 20.2(a), 20.2(b)	78-5, 1978-1 C.B. 263 .... 15.2(b)
	78-73, 1978-1 C.B. 265 ......26.3(e)(2)

REVENUE RULINGS *(Continued)*
(References are to book sections.)

REVENUE PROCEDURES
(References are to book sections.)

REVENUE PROCEDURES (Continued)
(References are to book sections.)

Rev. Proc.	Rev. Proc.
72-13, 1972-1 C.B. 735 .... 25.8(b)	80-55, 1980-2 C.B. 849 ...... 7.3(b)(4),
72-18, 1972-1 C.B. 740 ..... 7.3(b)(4),	9.3(b)(1), 9.3(b)(3)
8.3(b), 9.3(b)(1), 9.3(b)(2)	81-16, 1981-1 C.B. 688 ...... 7.3(b)(4),
74-8, 1974-1 C.B. 419 .... 7.3(b)(4),	9.3(b)(1), 9.3(b)(3)
9.3(b)(1)	83-11, 1983-1 C.B. 674 .... 25.9(a)
74-17, 1974-1 C.B. 438 .... 25.8(b)	83-55, 1983-2 C.B. 572 ....
74-37, 1977-2 C.B. 568	..........................28.2(b)(1)(i)(c)
...25.3(b)(2)(iii), 25.4(b)(2), 25.4(b)(3)	84-22, 1984-1 C.B. 449 ....
79-14, 1979-1 C.B. 496 ..25.3(b)(2)(iii)	..........................28.2(b)(1)(i)(c)

GENERAL COUNSEL'S MEMORANDA
(References are to book sections.)

G.C.M.	G.C.M.
17322, XV-2 C.B. 151 .... 6.4(b),	38178 (Nov. 27, 1979) .... 6.4(c),
21.3(c)	6.4(d), 21.3(c)
18436, 1937-1 C.B. 101 ... 25.3(c)(2),	38597 (Dec. 30, 1980) ..28.2(a)(3)(ii)
28.3(b)(5)	39036 (Sept. 22, 1983) .... 17.9(b)
28274 (June 14, 1954) .... 17.9(b)	39151 (June 17, 1983) 45
37332 (Nov. 25, 1977) ....17.9(e),	
17.9(f)	

INCOME TAX UNIT RULINGS
(References are to book sections.)

I.T.	I.T.
1353, I-1 C.B. 150 ....17.3(e)	3858, 1947-2 C.B. 71 ....17.9(e)
3721, 1945 C.B. 164 .... 15.2(a)(6),	3985, 1949-2 C.B. 51 .... 15.1(a)
25.3(d)	

INTERNAL REVENUE NEWS RELEASES
(References are to book sections.)

I.R.	I.R.
IR-81-42, 10 STAND. FED. TAX REP.	IR-82-13, 10 STAND. FED. TAX REP.
(CCH) ¶ 6552 (Apr. 9, 1981)	(CCH) ¶ 6330 (Jan. 22, 1982) 39.2
............................9.3(b)(3)	

INTERNAL REVENUE NEWS RELEASES
(References are to book sections.)

I.R.	I.R.
IR-82-51, 10 STAND. FED. TAX REP. (CCH) ¶ 6488 (Apr. 30, 1982) ....28.2(b)(1)(i)(e)	IR-85-42, 10 STAND. FED. TAX REP. (CCH) ¶ 6511 (Apr. 26, 1985) ....28.2(b)(1)(i)(a)
IR-83-92, 10 STAND. FED. TAX REP. (CCH) ¶ 6630 (June 30, 1983) ....27.10(d)	IR-85-113, 10 STAND. FED. TAX REP. (CCH) ¶ 6817 (Nov. 27, 1985) ....28.2(b)(1)(i)(a)
IR-85-32, 10 STAND. FED. TAX REP. (CCH) ¶ 6468 (Apr. 1, 1985) ....28.2(b)(1)(i)(a)	

TREASURY DECISIONS
(References are to book sections.)

T.D.	T.D.
7747, 1981-1 C.B. 141 .... 25.3(b)(2)(i)	8070, 1986-12 I.R.B. 6 ...... 17.2, 42., 42.1
7920, 1983-2 C.B. 69 ..... 25.3(b)(2)(i)	
8008, 1985-9 I.R.B. 10 ....43.2(d), 45.4(g)	8080, 10 STAND. FED. TAX REP. (CCH) ¶ 6817 (Mar. 21, 1986) ....
8058, 1985-46 I.R.B. 30 .... 43.2(d)	.... 28.4(a)

PRIVATE LETTER RULINGS *(Continued)*
(References are to book sections.)

LTR	LTR
7729003 (Apr. 19, 1977) ....28.1(a)(2)(iii)	8223015 (Feb. 26, 1982) .... 25.9(a)
7801017 (Oct. 7, 1977) .... 28.2(b)(1)(i)(d)	8234122 (May 27, 1982) ....28.2(a)(3)(ii)
7816004 (Jan. 17, 1978) .... 28.2(b)(1)(i)(d)	8238052 (June 23, 1982) .. 27.10(b)(2)
7902002 (June 29, 1978) ...... 27.8(a)	8247025 (Aug. 18, 1982) ....28.2(b)(1)(i)(c)
7929061 (Apr. 19, 1979) ....28.2(c)	8317017 (Jan. 21, 1983) ....28.2(b)(1)(i)(c)
7948011 (Aug. 24, 1979) ....28.2(c)	8331065 (May 2, 1983) .... 25.9(a)
8037096 (June 20, 1980) ...... 25.3(a)	8345007 (Aug. 5, 1983) ...28.2(a)(3)(ii)
8108032 (Nov. 25, 1980) .... 27.10(b)(2)	8347040 (Aug. 22, 1983) ....28.2(a)(3)(ii)
8111056 (Dec. 16, 1980) ....22.2(a)(3)	8347043 (Aug. 22, 1983) ....28.2(a)(3)(ii)
8113068 (Dec. 31, 1980) ...... 25.9(a)	
8142048 (July 21, 1981) .... 28.2(a)	8347050 (Aug. 22, 1983) ....28.2(a)(3)(ii)
8210065 (Dec. 10, 1981) ...... 25.3(a)	

PRIVATE LETTER RULINGS *(Continued)*
(References are to book sections.)

LTR	LTR
8347058 (Aug. 25, 1983) .... 28.2(b)(1)(i)(d)	8526035 (Apr. 1, 1985) .... 32.3(a)
8348033 (Aug. 30, 1983) 45	8527041 (Apr. 8, 1985) .. 4.3(a), 4.3(b)
8406039 (Nov. 7, 1983) ..28.2(a)(3)(ii)	8529095 (Apr. 25, 1985) .. 25.3(b)(2)(i)
8411017 (Dec. 7, 1983) .... 25.9(a)	8535010 (May 28, 1985) ......22.7(c), 22.9(b)(2)
8435054 (May 29, 1984) ....6.4(d), 21.3(c)	8610016 (Nov. 29, 1985) ....15.8, 25.3(b)(2)
8437122 (June 18, 1984) ...... 32.1(b)	7101131330A (Jan. 13, 1971) ..20.2(c)
8503016 (Oct. 9, 1984) ....22.7(c). 22.9(b)(2)	7107230380A (July 23, 1971) ...9.7(e)
8519038 (Feb. 12, 1985) .... 22.7(d)	
8523009 (Feb. 25, 1985) ....25.2, 25.3(c)(6), 28.3(a)(1), 28.3(c)	

TECHNICAL ADVICE MEMORANDA
(References are to book sections.)

TAM	TAM
7845001 (June 29, 1978) ....28.2(c)	8451012 (Aug. 23, 1984) ....28.2(c)
8052023 (Sept. 25, 1980) ......28.2(c)	8538001 (June 6, 1985) ....22.9(b)(3), 24.4
8131008 (April 4, 1981) ....9.7(f)	
8141035 (June 30, 1981) ....6.3(c)	

Legislative History Table

INTERNAL REVENUE BILL OF 1921
(References are to book sections.)

HOUSE WAYS AND MEANS COMMITTEE REPORT, INTERNAL REVENUE BILL OF 1921, H.R. REP. NO. 350, 67th Cong., 1st Sess. 11 (1921)	17.1
SENATE FINANCE COMMITTEE REPORT, INTERNAL REVENUE BILL OF 1921, S. REP. NO. 275, 67th Cong., 1st Sess. 14 (1921)	17.1

REVENUE ACT OF 1950
(References are to book sections.)

HOUSE WAYS AND MEANS COMMITTEE REPORT, REVENUE ACT OF 1950, H.R. REP. NO. 2319, 81st Cong., 2d Sess. 96 (1950)	17.9(b)
SENATE FINANCE COMMITTEE REPORT, REVENUE ACT OF 1950, S. REP. NO. 2375, 81st Cong., 2d Sess. 44, *reprinted in* 1950 U.S. CODE CONG. & AD. NEWS 3053	16, 16.4(b), 17.9(d)

INTERNAL REVENUE CODE OF 1954
(References are to book sections.)

HOUSE WAYS AND MEANS COMMITTEE REPORT, INTERNAL REVENUE CODE OF 1954, H.R. REP. NO. 1337, 83rd Cong., 2d Sess. A278, *reprinted in* 1954 U.S. CODE CONG. & AD. NEWS 4019	26.3(b)(1)

TAX REFORM ACT OF 1969
(References are to book sections.)

HOUSE CONFERENCE REPORT, TAX REFORM ACT OF 1969,   22.2(b), 28.3(b)(4)
    H. R. REP. NO. 782, 91st Cong., 1st Sess. 309 *reprinted*
    in 1969 U.S. CODE CONG. & AD. NEWS 2392

SENATE FINANCE COMMITTEE REPORT, TAX REFORM ACT   28.3(b)(4)
    OF 1969, S. REP. NO. 552, 91st Cong., 1st Sess. 154,
    reprinted in 1969 U.S. CODE CONG. & AD. NEWS 2027

TAX REFORM ACT OF 1976
(References are to book sections.)

HOUSE WAYS AND MEANS COMMITTEE REPORT, TAX RE-   21.4(b)
    FORM ACT OF 1976, H. R. REP. NO. 658, 94th Cong., 2d
    Sess. 107, *reprinted in* 1976 U.S. CODE CONG. & AD.
    NEWS 2897

HOUSE WAYS AND MEANS COMMITTEE REPORT, TAX   6.3(c)
    TREATMENT OF GRANTOR OF CERTAIN OPTIONS, H.R.
    REP. NO. 1192, 94TH CONG., 2D SESS. 10 (1976), *re-
    printed in* 1976-3 C.B. (Vol. 3) 19

SENATE FINANCE COMMITTEE REPORT, TAX REFORM ACT   26.2(b),
    OF 1976, S. REP. NO. 938, 94th Cong., 2d Sess. 45,   26.3(e)(2)
    reprinted in 1976 U.S. CODE CONG. & AD. NEWS 3439

REVENUE ACT OF 1978
(References are to book sections.)

HOUSE WAYS AND MEANS COMMITTEE REPORT, REVENUE   25.7, 26.2(b)
    ACT OF 1978, H. R. REP. NO. 1445, 95th Cong., 2d Sess.
    67, *reprinted in* 1978 U.S. CODE CONG. & AD. NEWS
    7046

HOUSE CONFERENCE REPORT, REVENUE ACT OF 1978,   26.2(b)
    H.R. REP. NO. 1800, 95th Cong., 2d Sess. 219, *re-
    printed in* 1978 U.S. CODE CONG. & AD. NEWS 7198

ECONOMIC RECOVERY TAX ACT OF 1981
(References are to book sections.)

HOUSE WAYS AND MEANS COMMITTEE REPORT, TAX IN-   21.3(d), 43.1,
    CENTIVE ACT OF 1981, H.R. REP. NO. 201, 97th Cong.,   43.2, 43.2(f),
    1st Sess. 200 (1981)   46.1, 46.2

SENATE FINANCE COMMITTEE REPORT, ECONOMIC   10.1, 21.2,
RECOVERY TAX ACT OF 1981, S. REP. NO. 144, 97th Cong.,   21.3(d), 21.5,

1st Sess. 146, *reprinted in* 1981 U.S. CODE CONG. & AD. NEWS 105	33.3, 33.6(c), 35.2, 35.2(c), 36.4(a), 36.4(c), 38, 39.1, 41.1, 42.3, 42.4, 43.1, 43.2, 43.2(f), 44.7, 46.1, 46.2
SENATE CONFERENCE REPORT, ECONOMIC RECOVERY TAX ACT OF 1981, S. REP. NO. 176, 97th Cong., 1st Sess. 258 (1981)	35.2(c)
STAFF OF THE JOINT COMMITTEE ON TAXATION, 97TH CONG, 1ST SESS., GENERAL EXPLANATION OF ECONOMIC RECOVERY TAX ACT OF 1981 279 (Joint Comm. Print 1981)	6.4, 6.4(d), 21.5, 21.6, 32.1(a), 32.3(c)(1)(ii), 33.1, 33.2(c), 33.6(a), 35.2, 35.2(c), 36.2, 36.2(a), 36.3(b)(2)(i), 36.4(a), 36.4(b), 36.4(c), 37.1, 38, 39.1, 40.1, 40.2, 41.1, 42.3, 42.4, 43.1, 43.2, 43.2(f), 44.1(b), 46.1, 46.2
STAFF OF THE JOINT COMMITTEE ON TAXATION, 97TH CONG., 2D SESS., GENERAL EXPLANATION OF THE ECONOMIC RECOVERY TAX ACT OF 1981 300 (Joint Comm. Print 1981)	21.2, 21.3(c), 21.3(d), 21.4(b), 21.4(d), 21.7

TAX EQUITY AND FISCAL RESPONSIBILITY ACT OF 1982
(References are to book sections.)

SENATE FINANCE COMMITTEE REPORT, TAX EQUITY AND FISCAL RESPONSIBILITY ACT OF 1982, S. REP. NO. 494, 97th Cong., 2d Sess. 215 (1982), *reprinted in* 1982 U.S. CODE CONG. & AD. NEWS 781	27.6, 27.6(a)(1), 27.6(a)(2), 27.6(b), 27.6(b)(1), 27.6(b)(2), 27.6(b)(4), 27.11(a), 27.11(b), 27.11(c), 28.2(b)(1)(i)(b), 28.2(e)

TECHNICAL CORRECTIONS ACT OF 1982
(References are to book sections.)

House Ways and Means Committee Report, Technical Corrections Act of 1982, H.R. Rep. No. 794, 97th Cong., 2d Sess. 23 (1982)	21.4(b), 30.1(a), 33.5
Senate Finance Committee Report, Technical Corrections Act of 1982, S. Rep. No. 592, 97th Cong., 2d Sess. 26, *reprinted in* 1982 U.S. Code Cong. & Ad. News 4149	21.4(b), 30.1(a), 32.2, 33.5, 33.6(c), 36.5, 43.2(c), 45.2(c)
House Conference Report, Technical Corrections Act of 1982, H.R. Rep. No. 986, 97th Cong., 2d Sess. 25, *reprinted in* 1982 U.S. Code Cong. & Ad. News 4203	32.2

DEFICIT REDUCTION ACT OF 1984
(References are to book sections.)

House Ways and Means Committee Report, Deficit Reduction Act of 1984, H.R. Rep. No. 432, 98th Cong., 2d Sess. 1178, *reprinted in* 1984 U.S. Code Cong. & Ad. News 697	25.7, 27.2(e), 27.3, 28.2(b)(1)(iv), 33.2(b), 44.3
House Conference Report, Deficit Reduction Act of 1984, H.R. Rep. No. 861, 98th Cong., 2d Sess. 807-1012, *reprinted in* 1984 U.S. Code Cong. & Ad. News 1445	6.3(c), 7.2(c)(2), 17.5(b), 21.3(d), 21.5, 22.9(c), 27.2(e), 27.3(b), 28.2(b)(1)(iv), 32.3(a), 32.4, 33.2(a), 33.2(b), 35.2(c), 35.2(d), 36.2(c)(2), 36.3(b)(2)(iii), 43.2(d), 44.3(c), 45, 45.3(b), 45.4(b), 46.2
Staff of The Joint Committee on Taxation, 98th Cong., 1st Sess., Background on Tax Shelters, in *Abusive Tax Shelters: Hearing Before the Subcomm. on Oversight of the Internal Revenue Service of the Senate Comm. on Finance*, 98th Cong., 1st Sess. (1983)	26.2(a)

STAFF OF THE JOINT COMMITTEE ON TAXATION, 98TH CONG., 2D SESS., GENERAL EXPLANATION OF THE REVENUE PROVISIONS OF THE DEFICIT REDUCTION ACT OF 1984 103 (Joint Comm. Print 1984)	6.3(c), 6.3(e), 14.6, 15.6, 15.7, 21.4(c), 21.5, 22.1(c), 22.1(f)(2), 22.5, 22.9, 22.9(b), 22.9(b)(1), 22.9(c), 22.9(d), 25.5(b), 27.2(d), 29.1, 29.2, 33.3, 45, 46.2
STAFF OF SENATE COMM. ON FINANCE, 98TH CONG., 2D SESS., PRELIMINARY REPORT ON THE REFORM AND SIMPLIFICATION OF THE INCOME TAXATION OF CORPORATIONS (Comm. Print 1983)	25.9(d)

TECHNICAL CORRECTIONS ACT OF 1985
(References are to book sections.)

STAFF OF THE JOINT COMMITTEE ON TAXATION, 99TH CONG., 1ST SESS., DESCRIPTION OF THE PROVISIONS OF THE TECHNICAL CORRECTIONS ACT OF 1985 25 (Joint Comm. Print 1985)	43.2(b)
STAFF OF THE JOINT COMMITTEE ON TAXATION, 99TH CONG., 1ST SESS., DESCRIPTION OF AMENDMENTS BY CHAIRMAN ROSTENKOWSKI AND MR. DUNCAN TO H.R. 1800 (THE TECHNICAL CORRECTIONS ACT OF 1985) AND H.R. 2160 (TECHNICAL CHANGES TO THE RETIREMENT EQUITY ACT OF 1984) (Joint Comm. Print 1985)	36.2(c)(1)

TAX REFORM ACT OF 1985
(References are to book sections.)

1985 *Tax Reform, President's Tax Proposals to the Congress for Fairness, Growth, and Simplicity*, STAND. FED. TAX REP. (CCH) Rep. No. 25, Extra Ed., ch. 11 (May 29, 1985)	3.1
STAFF OF THE JOINT COMMITTEE ON TAXATION 99TH CONG., 1st SESS., SUMMARY OF H.R. 3838 (TAX REFORM ACT OF 1985) 23 (Joint Comm. Print 1985)	25.9(d), 28.2(a)(3)(i), 35.2(d)

REGULATION OF GOVERNMENT SECURITIES
(References are to book sections.)

Failure of Bevill, Bresler & Shulman, A New Jersey Government Securities Dealer: Hearings Before a Subcomm. of the House Comm. on Government Operations, 99th Cong., 1st Sess. 162 (1985) (statement of E. Gerald Corrigan, President, FRBNY)	2
HOUSE COMMITTEE ON ENERGY AND COMMERCE, GOVERNMENT SECURITIES ACT OF 1985, H.R. REP. NO. 258, 99th Cong. 1st Sess. 13 (1985)	2.1(a)(1)
REGULATION OF THE GOVERNMENT SECURITIES MARKET, REPORT BY THE SECURITIES AND EXCHANGE COMMISSION TO THE SUBCOMMITTEE ON TELECOMMUNICATIONS, CONSUMER PROTECTION AND FINANCE OF THE COMMITTEE ON ENERGY AND COMMERCE OF THE U.S. HOUSE OF REPRESENTATIVES (June 20, 1985)	2
REPORT OF THE JOINT TREASURY-SEC-FEDERAL RESERVE STUDY OF THE GOVERNMENT-RELATED SECURITIES MARKETS, 96TH, CONG., 2D SESS. (Comm. Print 1980)	2.2(b)

SPECIAL REPORTS AND STUDIES
(References are to book sections.)

JOINT COMMITTEE ON TAXATION, DESCRIPTION OF BILLS RELATING TO THE TAX TREATMENT OF MORTGAGE RELATED SECURITIES (S. 1959 AND S. 1978) AND ENVIRONMENTAL ZONES (S. 1859) (JCS-3-86) Jan. 30, 1986, *reprinted in* DAILY TAX REP. (BNA) No. 21, at J-1 (Jan. 31, 1986)	28.4(b)(4)
REPORT OF THE SPECIAL STUDY OF THE OPTIONS MARKETS TO THE SECURITIES AND EXCHANGE COMMISSION, 96TH CONG., 1ST SESS. 73 (Comm. Print 1978)	5.1, 5.4(e)(1), 5.4(e)(3), 6.3(c)
REPORT OF THE SPECIAL STUDY OF THE SECURITIES MARKETS OF THE SECURITIES AND EXCHANGE COMMISSION, H.R. DOC. NO. 95, Pt. 2, 88th Cong., 1st Sess. 47 (1963)	1.2, 1.2(a), 6.2(a), 6.3(b)
SENATE COMMITTEE ON AGRICULTURE AND FORESTRY REPORT, TRADING IN ONION FUTURES—PROHIBITION, S. REP. NO. 1631, 85th Cong. 2d Sess., *reprinted in* 1958 U.S. CODE CONG. & AD. NEWS 4210	4.1
SENATE FINANCE COMMITTEE REPORT, INTERNAL REVENUE CODE OF 1954, NONMEMBER TELEPHONE COMPANIES—INCOME, S. REP. NO. 762, 95th Cong., 2d Sess. *reprinted in* 1978 U.S. CODE CONG. & AD. NEWS 1286	24.1, 27.10(b)(1)

Index

(References are to book sections.)

E

Q

ABOUT THE AUTHOR

ANDREA S. KRAMER is a partner in the Chicago law firm of
Coffield Ungaretti Harris & Slavin. She is a graduate of the
University of Illinois (B.A., summa cum laude) and of North-
western University School of Law (J.D., cum laude). Ms. Kramer is a member of the Illinois Bar and a member of the United
States Tax Court. She is a member of the Tax Committee (Division on Partnerships, Real Estate, and other Tax Sheltered
Investments) and the Commodities Law Committee of the Chicago Bar Association. She is also a member of the Section of
Taxation (Committee on Partnerships) and the Section of Corporation, Banking, and Business Law (Commodities Regulation Committee) of the American Bar Association. Ms. Kramer
has published numerous articles on the taxation of commodities, options, and financial products. In addition, she has participated in continuing legal education programs in the areas
of taxation and commodities law. Her national legal practice
is primarily in the areas of taxation and general business rep-
resentation of security, commodity, option, and government
security firms. Ms. Kramer is recognized as a leading commentator on the taxation of financial products.